Global Perspectives on Legal Capacity Reform

This edited collection is the result of the Voices of Individuals: Collectively Exploring Self-determination (VOICES) project based at the Centre for Disability Law and Policy, National University of Ireland Galway. Focusing on the exercise of legal capacity under Article 12 of the UN Convention on the Rights of Persons with Disabilities, the stories of people with disabilities are combined with responses from scholars, activists and practitioners, addressing four key areas: criminal responsibility, contracts, consent to sex, and consent to medical treatment. Sustainable law and policy reforms are set out based on the storytellers' experiences, promoting a recognition of legal capacity and supported decision-making. The perspectives are from across a wide range of disciplines (including law, sociology, nursing, and history) and 13 countries.

The volume is a valuable resource for researchers, academics and legislators, judges or policy makers in the area of legal capacity and disability. It is envisaged that the book will be particularly useful for those engaged in legal capacity law reform processes worldwide and that this grounded work will be of great interest to legislators and policy makers who must frame new laws on supported decision making in compliance with the UNCRPD.

Eilionóir Flynn is a Senior Lecturer at the School of Law and Director of the Centre for Disability Law and Policy, National University of Ireland Galway. She is the Principal Investigator of the VOICES project, funded by a European Research Council Starting Grant. She holds a Ph.D. and B.C.L. from University College Cork. Her current research interests are in the areas of legal capacity, disability advocacy, access to justice, and the intersectionality of gender, disability and ageing.

Anna Arstein-Kerslake is a Senior Lecturer in the Melbourne Law School, University of Melbourne and the Academic Co-ordinator of the Disability Research Initiative (DRI). She has developed and co-ordinates the Disability Human Rights Clinic (DHRC) at Melbourne Law School. She holds a Ph.D. in Law from the National University of Ireland, Galway (NUIG), a J.D. from the City University of New York (CUNY) School of Law and a B.A. in Sociology from San Diego State University (SDSU).

Clíona de Bhailís is a Research Assistant at the Centre for Disability Law and Policy, National University of Ireland Galway working on the VOICES project. She graduated with first class honours from the LL.M. in Public Law in NUI Galway in 2013 and wrote a minor thesis in the area of legal capacity and access to justice for people with disabilities.

María Laura Serra is a Research Associate/Postdoctoral Researcher at the Centre for Disability Law and Policy, National University of Ireland, Galway. She holds a Ph.D. in Human Rights from Charles III University of Madrid (Spain), a Master's degree in Advanced Studies in Human Rights from the same university and a Law degree from the National University of Mar del Plata (Argentina).

Routledge Research in Human Rights Law

Available titles in this series include:

The Right to Religious Freedom in International Law
Between group rights and individual rights
Anat Scolnicov

The Right to Development in International Law
The Case of Pakistan
Khurshid Iqbal

Global Health and Human Rights
Legal and Philosophical Perspectives
John Harrington and Maria Stuttaford

Human Rights, Constitutional law and Belonging
The Right to Equal Belonging in Democratic Society
Elena Drymiotou

Dignity, Degrading Treatment and Torture in Human Rights Law
The Ends of Article 3 of the European Convention on Human Rights
Elaine Webster

The Right to Housing in Law and Society
Nico Moons

Human Rights and America's War on Terror
Edited by Satvinder Juss

Beyond Human Rights and the War on Terror
Edited by Satvinder Juss

Global Perspectives on Legal Capacity Reform
Our Voices, Our Stories
Edited by Eilionóir Flynn, Anna Arstein-Kerslake, Clíona de Bhailís and María Laura Serra

For more information about this series, please visit: www.routledge.com/Routledge-Research-in-Human-Rights-Law/book-series/HUMRIGHTSLAW

Global Perspectives on Legal Capacity Reform

Our Voices, Our Stories

Edited by
Eilionóir Flynn, Anna Arstein-Kerslake, Clíona de Bhailís and María Laura Serra

Routledge
Taylor & Francis Group
LONDON AND NEW YORK

First published 2019 by Routledge

2 Park Square, Milton Park, Abingdon, Oxfordshire OX14 4RN
52 Vanderbilt Avenue, New York, NY 10017

Routledge is an imprint of the Taylor & Francis Group, an informa business

First issued in paperback 2019

British Library Cataloguing-in-Publication Data
A catalogue record for this book is available from the British Library

Library of Congress Cataloguing-in-Publication Data
Names: Flynn, Eilionoìir, 1986– editor. | Arstein-Kerslake, Anna, editor. | Bhailiìs, Cliìona de, editor. | Serra, Mariìa Laura, editor.
Title: Global perspectives on legal capacity reform: our voices, our stories / edited by Eilionoìir Flynn, Anna Arstein-Kerslake, Cliìona de Bhailiìs, And Mariìa Laura Serra.
Description: Abingdon, Oxon [UK]; New York, NY: Cambridge University Press, 2018. |
Series: Routledge Research in Human Rights Law |
Includes bibliographical references and index.
Identifiers: LCCN 2018008076 | ISBN 9781138298910 (hbk) | ISBN 9781351579711 (web pdf) | ISBN 9781351579704 (epub) | ISBN 9781351579698 (mobipocket)
Subjects: LCSH: Capacity and disability. | People with disabilities—Legal status, laws, etc. | Mental health laws. | Informed consent (Medical law) | Convention on the Rights of Persons with Disabilities and Optional Protocol (2007 March 30) | Law reform.
Classification: LCC K634 .G56 2018 | DDC 346.01/3—dc23
LC record available at https://lccn.loc.gov/2018008076

ISBN: 978-1-138-29891-0 (hbk)
ISBN: 978-0-367-47370-9 (pbk)

Typeset in Galliard
by codeMantra

For Rusi Stanev, whose fierce pursuit of justice and freedom reminds us to sustain hope, in the face of seemingly insurmountable obstacles.

Contents

Foreword

Dr Michael Bach

The VOICES project and this ground-breaking book are based on a simple yet profound idea. If people are to have power over their own lives then their voices must matter.

Our voices tell others about who we are, our history, the futures we intend, what we hope for. One of our most basic needs is that others listen to us, make sense of what we want and give value to what we say. In some ways we are private beings; yet, if we are to act in the world, we must also become public beings. Our voices make that exchange with others possible. But if the public spaces of meaning refuse our voice, as *our* voice, then we are diminished as persons, deprived of citizenship, made alien in some ways to ourselves, and certainly to others. The world over, we are seeing where that leads.

Countless people living with experience of disability share in what it feels like to be silenced and rejected. Many never have opportunity to speak in the first place, their gestures to the world left hanging, as if in mid-air. Without public space for their intentions and choices to matter, they are bereft of power over their own lives.

In its making and publication, *Global Perspectives on Legal Capacity Reform: Our Voices, Our Stories* speaks back to this violence. It shows how we can universally design and transform the public square so that even the most tentative gestures of voice can be heard and come to matter. It is an inspiring and remarkable guide to making inclusive and radically democratic public spaces possible. With a multitude of voices from all corners of the globe, this book levels the playing field for what it means to have a voice – some seem fragile at first; others boldly declare; some quietly remember or painfully recount; some deeply inquire; another's speaking out is interrupted, fragments gathered from an author now passed. Together, the chapters in this book break new ground for ways of speaking, listening and writing ourselves into the world.

What is remarkable about this text, these many texts, is how they enable the voices of often excluded 'storytellers' to be heard. These aren't solo performances. Life never is. No story resides in a singular account by an author defining their world and journey solely in their own terms. Instead, we are first invited into storytellers' personal worlds. Then, and always with utmost care, respondents write gently into the space to show how these voices touch deeply – both themselves and the world as we know it. Thereby, reflections alter our perspective, disrupt what still normalises and excludes, and weave social and political possibilities anew.

With *Global Perspectives on Legal Capacity Reform: Our Voices, Our Stories*, this collective of authors leave us both a legacy and a challenge. The legacy is their living evidence that storytelling for social change, millennia in the making, can take root in places many never imagine possible. The challenge back to us is: reach out and generously support voices not yet heard. Theirs is an appeal to grow this work of interpreting and translating, of scribing and *a*scribing, of making public meaning with those so often silenced and disregarded.

Artfully, poetically and brilliantly, they show not only that it's possible, but how to make it happen.

About the project

The VOICES project was created to respond to a serious gap in the literature and in law reform efforts concerning the right to legal capacity for persons with disabilities. The overarching objective of the VOICES project is to make visible the lived experience of persons with disabilities in the exercise and denial of their right to legal capacity and to use this experience as a starting point for legal, social and political reform. It has sought to achieve this in three key ways. First, the project has developed narratives on the exercise, restriction and/or denial of legal capacity. Second, it has applied the concepts of universal legal capacity, and support to exercise legal capacity to previously unexamined areas of law (including criminal responsibility, contract law, consent to medical treatment and intimate relationships). Finally, it has constructed critical legal and social policy responses to the lived realities of people with disabilities in these previously unexamined areas of law.

The work of the VOICES project has been underpinned by a set of core values, which are shared by all participants, including the authors in this edited collection.

1. We believe that everyone has an equal right to enjoy legal capacity

This project is committed to the principles set out under Article 12 of the UN Convention on the Rights of Persons with Disabilities (CRPD) that people with disabilities enjoy legal capacity on an equal basis with others. The enjoyment of legal capacity should not be based on a person's perceived decision-making ability.

2. We believe that people with disabilities should be supported in exercising their legal capacity

Based on Article 12(3) of the CRPD, we believe that all forms of substituted decision-making which discriminate against persons with disabilities should be abolished in favour of systems that support people with disabilities to exercise their legal capacity.

3. We believe in respecting other people's voices and opinions

Listening to and learning from the personal experiences of people is at the core of our work. Therefore, we ask all participants to not make statements which dismiss the lived experience of an individual or suggest that it is less valuable than other kinds of evidence. All participants will be given an opportunity to speak during the workshops, and no one individual or group will be allowed to dominate the space. We will also ensure that the workshops are a safe space in which people feel comfortable sharing their stories and that personal information or experiences shared by the participants will remain confidential.

4. We believe in empowering people to drive change

We believe that stories of people's lived experiences can be powerful forces in driving change. However, we ask that in speaking about their lived experience, participants agree to only speak about their own individual experiences, rather than to tell the stories of others they know.

Acknowledgements

As editors we wish to acknowledge the incredible privilege it has been to be entrusted with the stories which have emerged through this project. At the beginning of this project, we could never have imagined how many dreamers, thinkers, doers and troublemakers would join us on our journey to make visible the experiences of people with disabilities in the exercise and denial of their legal capacity. It has been our immense pleasure to get to know the storytellers and respondents who have contributed chapters to this edited collection over the last three years.

This book and the VOICES project as a whole could not have been completed without the help, support and guidance of so many people. In particular, we are indebted to all those who supported the stories to emerge at each of the VOICES conferences and workshops, and all the pair meetings that happened in between these events. Key among these are all the support persons and interpreters who created the space in which the storytellers' voices could be heard and understood. We also know that this edited collection would not exist without the vital input of creative writing facilitators at our workshops and the mentors who supported the pairs to develop their chapters throughout the project.

At each of the VOICES events, we benefited from the expertise of a wide range of speakers – from disability rights scholars and activists to researchers in feminist theory, philosophy, contract and criminal law. Your collective wisdom has been invaluable in shaping our thinking about legal and social change. Our profound thanks also go to all of the artists (including the dancers, choreographers, poets, theatre-makers, writers, sculptors, illustrators and visual artists) who participated in each of the VOICES events. Your work has powerfully demonstrated that there should be no single way to tell a story.

The members of the Advisory Board and Steering Group of the VOICES project have guided us every step of the way in this project. They have informed our values throughout this research, reached out to storytellers and respondents who would otherwise never have heard of this project, read and provided feedback on draft chapters and encouraged us to look beyond the completion of this edited collection to all the challenges and opportunities that lie ahead. We appreciate all their support and look forward to continued collaborations.

A phenomenal amount of behind-the-scenes work has been needed to keep the VOICES ship afloat. This monumental task has been gamely undertaken by the powerhouse of past and present staff and students at the Centre for Disability Law and Policy in the National University of Ireland, Galway. Our colleagues have gone above and beyond the call of duty to make sure every single storyteller, respondent, speaker and artist made it to each of our events, had a good experience in Galway and safely made it home again. We could never have completed this work without their invaluable support.

Notes on contributors

Paul Alford works with the advocacy team in Inclusion Ireland. He has been in this current role for the past 11 years and has worked on numerous projects with the organisation.

Fiona Anderson is currently studying for an LLM in International and Comparative Disability Law and Policy at the Centre for Disability Law and Policy, NUI Galway. She has experience of researching, writing and speaking on mental health disorders and is working on a minor dissertation centred on medical and mental health issues. Fiona will share her experiences of consent to medical and mental health treatments and the consequences arising from mismanaged therapies.

Anna Arstein-Kerslake is a lecturer in the Melbourne Law School, University of Melbourne and the Academic Co-ordinator of the Disability Research Initiative (DRI). She has developed and co-ordinates the Disability Human Rights Clinic (DHRC) at Melbourne Law School. She holds a PhD in Law from the National University of Ireland, Galway (NUIG), a JD from the City University of New York (CUNY) School of Law and a BA in Sociology from San Diego State University (SDSU).

Michelle Browning is a doctoral student at the Living with Disability Research Centre, La Trobe University in Melbourne, Australia. Her doctoral research is exploring the practice of supported decision-making in British Columbia, Canada in the context of legal mechanisms such as representation agreements and microboards. Over the last three years, Michelle has consulted with guardianship offices in Victoria and New South Wales, Australia to explore how the support paradigm can be realised in these jurisdictions through changes to practice and law reform. She has been involved in the development of three trials of supported decision-making in Australia and is passionate about the ongoing development of supported decision-making practice.

Bo Chen is currently a PhD student at the Centre for Disability Law and Policy, NUI Galway. He is also working with a NGO advocating for law reforms in adult guardianship law and mental health law in mainland China.

Nicholas Clarke is an autism awareness advocate campaigning for fairer treatment and better understanding towards autistic individuals that find themselves involved in the British Justice System. Nick has a specific interest in equal access for autistic individuals that are unfortunate enough to find themselves in police custody, courts and prisons.

Clíona de Bhailís is a Research Assistant at the Centre for Disability Law and Policy, National University of Ireland, Galway working on the VOICES project. She graduated with first class honours from the LLM in Public Law in NUI Galway in 2013 and wrote a minor thesis in the area of legal capacity and access to justice for people with disabilities.

Amita Dhanda is Professor of Law at the National Academy of Legal Studies and Research, Hyderabad. She also heads the Centre for Disability Studies at the University. She has a substantive interest in the field of public law and human rights with special reference to disability rights. Professor Dhanda's doctoral thesis, critically appraising the laws relating to the mentally ill, was a pioneering effort at evaluating the human rights conformity of mental health laws in the country. The thesis was later brought out as a book entitled 'Legal Order and Mental Disorder'. Dr Dhanda has been closely involved in the law reform work in her own country to formulate disability rights laws especially legal capacity and support regimes which are in conformity with the Convention on the Rights of Persons with Disabilities.

Eilionóir Flynn is Senior Lecturer at the School of Law and Director of the Centre for Disability Law and Policy, National University of Ireland, Galway. Her interest in disability law stemmed from a broader interest in social justice and a recognition of the invisibility of people with disabilities at the time in broader human rights discourse. Her current passions in this field include assisted and supported decision-making, rights-enforcement mechanisms and access to justice.

Gábor Gombos is a world renowned independent disability rights defender. His work and activism over the past two-decades has ranged from grassroots peer support by users and survivors of psychiatry, through national, international, regional and non-governmental organisations, up to the United Nations. His work in the field of disability and mental health rights has been recognised by the Order of Merit of the Republic of Hungary (2009). Mr Gombos is an adjunct professor at NALSAR Law University in Hyderabad, India and at the Centre for Disability Law and Policy, NUI Galway. Until the end of 2012, Gábor served as a Member of the UN Committee on the Rights of Persons with Disabilities, a body of independent experts, which monitors the implementation of the Disability Convention.

Piers Gooding has a research background in law, history and cultural studies. His research focuses on mental health law and policy, legal capacity, access to justice and the CRPD. Dr Gooding is a Postdoctoral Research Fellow at the Melbourne Social Equity Institute and the University of Melbourne Law School. He has previously held research posts at the Centre for Disability Law and Policy, NUI Galway, and the Centre for the Advancement of Mental Health Law, Monash University Law School.

Ronnie Harris is from Dublin and works in the New Life Centre and the Sudocrem factory. He lives with his fiancée, Denise, and enjoys music and bowling. He won three medals for Ireland in the Special Olympics in China.

Claire Hendrick was born and raised in Beaumount and has lived in Dublin her whole life. Claire has an intellectual disability and, when she was 23, her mother died. Claire inherited her mother's home and as a result her solicitor applied to make her a Ward of Court. In 2010, she was made a Ward of Court and she didn't know what was happening until it was too late. Being a Ward of Court meant that Claire wasn't allowed to make any decisions for herself and decisions about where she lived, going to the doctor, relationships and her money were made for her. All Claire wanted was to buy her own home and have the security, but this proved impossible while she was a Ward of Court. In 2012, Claire successfully applied to be released from being a Ward of Court and, with the support of her family, bought her own home on Valentine's Day 2013.

Chloe Hocking is a PhD student at the University of Nottingham, School of Law. She is funded by the ESRC. Chloe's research explores the experiences of autistic individuals who are arrested and detained in police custody as suspects. The research aims to learn more about the difficulties autistic individuals may experience throughout the custody process and as a result of the custody setting and what support could be put in place. Chloe is also interested in the Police and Criminal Evidence Act 1984 and wider disability legislation such as the Equality Act 2010 and the UNCRPD.

Moira Jenkins is an academic lawyer teaching social care students at Cork Institute of Technology. She is a doctoral candidate in law at NUI Galway researching independent advocacy from the perspective of older Irish citizens. She practised as a barrister in Victoria, Australia before lecturing in constitutional law and legal skills and analysis at University College Cork. She was admitted as a solicitor in the Supreme Court of England and Wales. She has worked as a community and residential care-based advocate. Her research interests include advocacy as a right to access justice, the participation/agency rights of people in situations of vulnerability and the future role of social care professionals in integrated care. She has worked in community, carnival and theatre arts in London, Melbourne and Cork and her Masters in Theatre thesis was on the staging of oral story-telling traditions.

Maths Jesperson was born in 1954. Since 1988, he has worked as a regional officer of RSMH (the Swedish National Organisation for Social and Mental Health). He was a founding member of ENUSP (the European Network of

Users and Survivors of Psychiatry) in 1991. He was the initiator, the leader and later a board member of PO-Skåne, a professional service with a personal ombudsman for people with severe psychosocial disabilities. In 2006, he represented PO-Skåne at a seminar in the UN headquarters in New York.

Dermot Lowndes is a member of the National Platform of Self Advocates and serves as Deputy Leader on the board of Inclusion Ireland. Dermot was also a panellist during the press launch of the 'Right to Love' Bill by Senator Katherine Zappone.

Maria Mahony is a self-advocate from Dublin. She was Secretary of the National Platform of Self Advocates. She competed in gymnastics for Ireland in the Special Olympics and brought home five medals. Maria has also graduated from a hairdressing course.

Donna McNamara is currently a PhD candidate and Assistant Lecturer at Dublin City University. Her research considers the rights of suspects with disabilities in the pre-trial criminal justice system. Donna graduated with a BCL (Law and Society) degree from Dublin City University in 2013 and achieved an LLM (first class honours) from University College Cork in 2014. In 2016, Donna was appointed Visiting Research Fellow at the Burton Blatt Institute, Syracuse University, New York.

Nell Munro is an Assistant Professor of Law at the University of Nottingham. She obtained an LLB with first class honours from Queen Mary University of London in 2004. She received her MA in Socio-legal and Criminological Research Methods with distinction from the University of Nottingham in 2005. She was awarded a PhD by the University of Nottingham in 2008. Nell has also worked as a mental health advocacy worker, a care worker in residential care for people with learning disabilities and as a helpline worker for the National Autistic Society all of which have played a part in shaping her current research interests.

Roxanne Mykitiuk is a Professor at Osgoode Hall Law School, York University where she teaches in the areas of Disability Law, Health Law, Bioethics and Family Law. She is the Director of the Disability Law Intensive clinical programme. From 1990 to 1992 she was Senior Legal Researcher for the Canadian Royal Commission on New Reproductive Technologies. From 2002 to 2006 she was a member of the Ontario, Advisory Committee on Genetics and from 2005 to 2008, she was a member of the Ethics Committee of the Society of Obstetricians and Gynecologists of Canada. In 2009, Professor Mykitiuk was scholar in residence at the Law Commission of Ontario working on the Disability and Law Project. She is currently on the Board of Directors of ARCH Disability Law Clinic. Professor Mykitiuk was the Chair of York University's Senate between 2013 and 2015. Professor Mykitiuk is an active, engaged and collaborative researcher. She is the author or co-author of numerous articles, book chapters and books investigating the legal, ethical and social implications of new reproductive technologies and the new genetics and the legal construction and regulation of embodiment and disability. More recently, her research has begun to create and investigate arts-based methods – digital stories and drama-based narratives – a means of challenging and re-representing experiences, images and conceptions of disability and normalcy.

Jana Offergeld currently works for Professor Theresia Degener at the Bochum Centre for Disability Studies (BODYS) on the project AKTIF. BODYS conducts human rights-based, participative and intersectional research and Disability Studies in research and teaching. In her PhD studies, Jana interviews persons with disabilities on their experiences with legal guardianship and organises capacity-building workshops on legal capacity and supported decision-making in cooperation with Mensch zuerst e.V. (People First Germany). Jana holds a degree in Education Sciences/Social Pedagogy and obtained an International Diploma in Mental Health Law and Human Rights from the Indian Law Society. She is a member of Mental Health Worldwide and sits on the editorial board of the *Journal on Disability and International Development*.

Emer O'Shea has supported people within a variety of marginalised groups to achieve personalised goals, empowerment and social inclusion over the past 14 years in both a professional and voluntary capacity. She holds an honours degree in Social Care, a certificate in Adult and Community Education and is also training as a mediator. Alongside her current role as a Rehabilitation Assistant, Emer is also involved in the medication management system for the organisation in which she is currently employed and promoting a person-centred human rights approach through the training of staff and the review of relevant policies and documents. This interest in achieving an equal, inclusive society is what led Emer to join the VOICES Project.

Marieta Petrova is a self-advocate and Chairperson of the National Self-Advocacy Platform in Bulgaria. She was a part of the Next Steps Program run by the Bulgarian Association of People with Intellectual Disabilities (BAPID) and the Bulgarian Center for Not-for-Profit Law (BCNL).

Joy Rehema is a 25 year-old self-advocate from Kenya Association of the Intellectually Handicapped. She is also a member of Jiwakilishe Self-advocacy Group which consists of self-advocates and support persons aimed at creating awareness of intellectual disability in Kenya and giving a voice to self-advocates as well as economically empowering them to be self-reliant with support. In the self-advocacy group, she was recently elected treasurer.

Sarah Richardson trained as a Learning Disability Nurse qualifying in 1995 after working for five years in inpatient and community-based services. Following this, she worked in Thailand doing voluntary work with a French

NGO running nurse training programmes for refugees from Burma living on the Thai/Burma border. She then enrolled on a Master's degree in the Theory and Practice of Human Rights with the University of Essex Human Rights Centre which led to her working for the United Nations Economic and Social Commission for Asia and the Pacific based in Bangkok. While there she edited a manual on rights-based approaches to disability collated from examples of best practice from member countries. After returning to the UK, she decided to train as a teacher, teaching Health and Social Care before joining the University of East Anglia in 2012 where she was appointed Course Director for the BSc Learning Disability Nursing programme. She joined the University of Suffolk in June 2016.

Helen Rochford-Brennan is from Tubbercurry in County Sligo, Ireland. Helen spent many years working in the tourism and disability sectors and has also devoted tireless years to community activism, working at board level in several organisations. In July 2012, Helen was diagnosed with early-onset Alzheimer's disease. She is Chair of the Irish Dementia Working Group, which is resourced by The Alzheimer Society of Ireland. Helen has used her time with the Irish Dementia Working Group to raise awareness of dementia and raise the profile of human rights for people with dementia. Helen is also Chair of the European Working Group of People with Dementia.

Cath Roper held one of four pioneering staff-consumer consultant positions in mental health services in Victoria between 1995 and 1999 and later became the first consumer academic in Australia, at the Centre for Psychiatric Nursing, University of Melbourne. She has a teaching background and holds a Master's in Social Health from the University of Melbourne. Cath had annual involuntary admissions to mental health services over a 13-year period and these experiences continue to drive her research, teaching, training and policy work particularly around exposing the human rights breaches caused by mental health laws. Cath believes that madness and distress are meaningful experiences and she has a particular interest in all forms of consumer scholarship.

María Laura Serra is a Research Associate/Postdoctoral Researcher at the Centre for Disability Law and Policy, National University of Ireland Galway. She holds a PhD in Human Rights from the Charles III University of Madrid (Spain), a Master's degree in Advanced Studies in Human Rights from the same university and a Law degree from the National University of Mar del Plata (Argentina).

Lavanya Seshasayee is a mental health activist, self-advocate, women's activist, creative writer cum exceptionally revolutionary and creative thinker on women's rights with a PhD specialising in gender and mental health issues. Lavanya has been involved in the Indian recovery movement for women who are psychosocially challenged and has an intense interest in capturing their narratives through creative fiction. Lavanya is an ardent supporter of the feminist cause, who believes in reaching out to meet the needs of the disabled and psychosocially challenged women all around the world. She has established the 'The Global Women's Recovery Movement'. People from all over the world are welcome to contribute their ideas to this movement that seeks to improve and change realities for women who are psychosocially challenged. The way they choose to deal with these psychosocial challenges in the context of societal reformation and personal reformation, will change their destiny and this is what the movement will teach them to do via a very unique mental health user perspective-based support system. She believes anybody with a disability can do things that they wish to via this unique support system.

Rusi Stanev was born in 1956. He was the plaintiff in the landmark European Court of Human Rights (ECtHR) case *Stanev v. Bulgaria*. In 2000 Rusi was placed under partial guardianship and in 2002 he was sent to a social care institution by his guardian. He was not able to legally challenge either of these measures in the domestic courts and so took the case to the ECtHR in 2006. The case focused on lack of access to justice as well as the substantive issues of deprivation of liberty. He was successful in the ECtHR but sadly, he died in March 2017 while still under guardianship in Bulgaria.

Jan Strnad is from the Czech Republic. He obtained a Master's degree in law and legal science from the Faculty of Law at Charles University in Prague in 2013. He works as a lawyer in Quip, an NGO that mainly supports people with learning difficulties. He is involved in direct legal support of people, consultancy, advocacy and litigation, especially in the field of legal capacity and related topics. He also acts as a Lecturer in training programmes for social service providers, public administration and support persons.

Reshma Valliappan, also known as Val Resh, is the founder-director of The Red Door, a community led initiative that uses creativity and holistic approaches in and around mental health work and recovery. She describes herself as an alien come to earth to spread love through madness, however, since humans do not understand multiplicity she sells the same through her label: paranoid schizophrenia. Reshma is the protagonist of an award-winning documentary 'A Drop of Sunshine' by film-maker Aparna Sanyal for having found holistic ways to live without medications for schizophrenia. She is the author of her memoir *Fallen, Standing; My Life As a Schizophrenist* published by Women Unlimited/Kali for Women, is a part-time honorarium professor teaching an elective course on 'Exploring mental health through creativity', and has several other published academic and non-academic publications. She is also a painter, who is attempting to make a living through a recently established merchandise business, as well as a mime artist who runs workshops and performances at local theatre groups. She is also a known speaker at many platforms including TEDx, educational institutions, women's groups and a long list of others. Reshma also acts as an independent consultant to several other organisations and groups working in the areas of disability, mental health and sexuality while also being a mentor, consultant and co-conspirator to local and international groups working with creativity and mental health.

Reshma is a member of WNUSP and TCI Asia while currently focusing on the implementation of Articles 19 and 25 of UNCRPD through her new initiative under The Red Door called Merchants of Madness which is based on a research thesis she published as a play. She has survived and lived through Reye's Syndrome as a child, schizophrenia and a meningioma causing epilepsy and sleep disorders. There might be other things Reshma does which perhaps no one really knows about including Reshma herself.

Sheila Wildeman is an Associate Professor at the Schulich School of Law, Dalhousie University (Nova Scotia, Canada). Her research and writing has addressed conflicts of values such as between experts and subjects of capacity assessment, and the global politics of legal capacity. Sheila's current work aims at bridging emerging models of supported decision-making with a structural analysis of distributive injustice and state duties to advance social and economic rights.

Aylin Yumerova obtained a Master's in Legal Studies at the Faculty of Law of St Kliment Ohridski University in Sofía. She speaks fluent French and Turkish. Since July 2013, Aylin has worked at the Bulgarian Center for Not-for-Profit Law (BCNL) Foundation. She provides legal consultations relating to the legal framework of NGOs and also provides legal and technical assistance on drafting of documents for registration of non-profit legal entities. She works in the field of abolishing guardianship and the adoption of the new concept of assisted decision-making in the Bulgarian legislation.

1 Theoretical framework for the VOICES Project

Clíona de Bhailís

The right to equal recognition before the law is a key concept in international human rights law. The belief that people with disabilities have a right to legal capacity on an equal basis with others, founded on Article 12 of the UN Convention on the Rights of Persons with Disabilities (CRPD), is at the core of the VOICES project's values and overall ethos. The right to legal capacity encompasses both the ability to be the holder of rights (including legal standing) and the ability to be an actor in law (legal agency). On a fundamental level, this can be categorised as the right to make decisions which have legal consequences and to have those decisions respected by the law.

The project recognises that there are other approaches to legal capacity and has addressed some of the critiques of the approach in Article 12 and General Comment No. 1 elsewhere.[1] However, the project is founded on the CRPD as a treaty developed with the direct input of people with lived experience under the motto of 'Nothing about us, without us' and on the Committee on the Rights of Persons with Disabilities' (the Committee's) interpretation of its content as the only international body with jurisdiction to interpret the CRPD.

Article 12 CRPD and General Comment No. 1

At the outset it is important to clarify a number of key conditions regarding the application of Article 12 CRPD. The Convention adopts a broad definition of disability under Article 1. Therefore, the Convention, Article 12 and the subsequent General Comment, applies to all people with disabilities and does not distinguish based on impairment or condition. While Article 12 broadly states the right to legal capacity for people with disabilities on an equal basis with others, the General Comment, described as a roadmap for legal capacity law reform (Arstein-Kerlsake and Flynn, 2016), provides further detail on the key terms and clearly sets out States' obligations.

Perhaps the most important statement under Article 12 and General Comment No. 1, and therefore the basis for understanding the framework, is that a person cannot be denied their right to legal capacity based on an assessment of mental capacity, and that instead people should supported to exercise their legal capacity (CRPD Committee, 2014). Legal capacity is a universal attribute inherent in all human beings and means that a person is both a holder of rights and an actor in law (CRPD Committee, 2014). In contrast, mental capacity is a person's decision-making ability which many will recognise can be affected by a number of factors at any given time. Many people with disabilities, particularly people with cognitive or psychosocial disabilities, are denied their legal capacity based on their mental capacity. This process is often based on either the status, outcome or functional tests[2] and the result is that an individual is placed under a substituted decision-making regime, such as guardianship, and a third party is appointed to make some or all decisions on their behalf and in their "best interests" (CRPD Committee, 2014, para. 27). It is in response to this ongoing issue, and to the lack of understanding observed in the initial reports from States Parties, that the Committee clearly outlines States' obligations under Article 12.

The General Comment calls for an overhaul of all existing laws concerning legal capacity and identifies three core obligations that States Parties must fulfil – 1. to abolish substituted decision-making regimes, 2. to make mechanisms available to support persons with disabilities to exercise their legal capacity and 3. to create safeguards for the exercise of legal capacity which are based on respect for the rights, will and preferences of the individual.

The first element of this is expanding Article 12 paragraph 3 to clarify that States must stop denying legal capacity and instead provide support to exercise legal capacity. Support to exercise legal capacity is the support a person receives when they are making a decision which has legal consequences and must respect the rights, will and preferences of the person (CRPD Committee, 2014). However, there is no exhaustive definition of support, recognising that each individual will have their own preferences and needs in this regard. Instead, the General Comment provides examples of both formal and informal arrangements which can be used to fulfil this right, including peer support, advocacy, recognition of non-traditional communication methods and universal design or accessibility accommodations. The lived experience of support described in later chapters of this volume also provides examples of the diverse nature of support and how people must be given the opportunity to choose what works best for them based on the decision they need to make. The Committee also note that people should be free to not use support. Therefore, supported decision making cannot be imposed on the person against her will nor can it only be provided based on assessments of mental capacity.

The second element of States' obligations outlined in the General Comment is the requirement to abolish all substituted decision-making regimes. As noted above, examples of substituted decision making include plenary or partial guardianship. Substituted decision making was defined in the General Comment as when:

1 a person has her legal capacity removed, even for a single decision, and
2 where a substituted decision maker is appointed by a third party against the person's will and
3 where decisions made by this appointee are supposed to be based on the person's "best interests". (Committee on the Rights of Persons with Disabilities, 2014, para. 27; 2018).

States are only obliged to abolish substituted decision-making regimes that meet the definition above. Therefore as argued by members of the project team elsewhere, some situations which may come within the common understanding of substituted decision making may not be covered by the definition (Arstein-Kerslake and Flynn, 2016). For example, where someone is appointed to discover, or make a best interpretation of the will and preferences of a coma patient, or where a person chooses to delegate decision-making powers to those they trust in certain areas of their lives, under a power of attorney or similar mechanisms, these do not constitute human rights violations and do not need to be abolished.

Finally, States Parties have an obligation to create safeguards to ensure people can exercise their legal capacity. Safeguards should be designed to ensure that the individual's will and preferences are respected and that they protect the individual from abuse (CRPD Committee, 2014). The safeguards must be proportional and tailored to the person's circumstances[3] and as with all aspects of Article 12, must be applied to persons with disabilities on an equal basis with others. This marks a shift from the paternalistic safeguards of the past and prevents persons with disabilities having their legal capacity restricted to safeguard their interests. It states that the 'best interests' principle does not comply with Article 12 (CRPD Committee, 2014, para. 36) and therefore, that many existing safeguards are no longer appropriate.[4] Examples of safeguards which comply with Article 12 include methods to verify a support person's identity or methods for third parties to challenge a support person if they believe they are not acting on the person's will and preferences.

Unanswered questions

Following the adoption of the CRPD, and particularly the publication of General Comment No. 1, much of the literature and commentary focused on what legal capacity meant in general or abstract terms, who should or could exercise this right and on how supported decision making and substituted decision making should be defined. As a result, there was a significant gap in the literature regarding how States should apply the right to legal capacity in key areas. To address this gap, the project examined three foundational questions which were as follows:

1. What constitutes an exercise of legal agency from an individual?
2. What are the justifiable limits on individual agency which can be imposed by the State and apply to everyone, regardless of disability or decision-making ability?
3. How can we ascertain whether an individual is giving free and informed consent (necessary to make an action legally binding), without engaging in a functional assessment of that person's mental capacity?

Below we summarise the concepts developed and the reasoning behind the questions addressed in an effort to provide a background for readers of the responses in later chapters. However, those interested in detailed accounts of the concepts discussed should refer to the project's special issue of the International Journal of Law in Context (Degener, 2017).

1. What constitutes an exercise of legal agency from an individual?

Legal agency is one element encompassed in the overarching right to legal capacity. Also known as the ability to be an actor in law, it is distinct from legal standing or the ability to be the holder of rights. Historically, legal agency has been denied to individuals (for example, women, slaves etc.) based on varying factors and even the most recent scholarship in the area links agency and cognitive capacity (Nussbaum, 2006; Brammer, 2012). As outlined above, Article 12 rejects any links between legal capacity, and by extension legal agency, and cognitive ability. However, neither Article 12 in itself, General Comment No. 1, nor the Committee in any of its reports define legal agency. What constitutes legal agency is fundamental to the understanding of how to operationalise Article 12 in practice as we must determine what exactly is an exercise of legal agency in order to know which decisions are protected under Article 12 and as a result when States are obliged to provide support (Arstein-Kerslake and Flynn, 2017).

Therefore, based on our understanding of the drafters' of Article 12 intentions and the application of the concept of legal agency in domestic legal systems we have developed the following definition – 'an action or inaction that the individual intended and which has legal consequences; or creates, modifies, or extinguishes a legal relationship' (Arstein-Kerslake and Flynn, 2017, p. 25). We believe that everyone is capable of forming some level of intention including those with significant or complex disabilities and that some level of intention is necessary to exercise legal agency. While a full exploration of the concept of intention is beyond the scope of this chapter, we argue that that intention is an expression of inner will and preferences and that there should not be a requirement that the individual demonstrate a certain level of "understanding" or "mental capacity" to prove intention. That is a person can intend an action without understanding the nature or consequences of her action or inaction. An example of this is when a person signs a contract without understanding the terms. The individual intended to sign the document and enter into the agreement but did not understand the consequences of not meeting the obligations for example. We view her signing of the contract as an exercise of legal agency.

Based on our proposed definition of legal agency, a wide range decisions now come within the scope of legal agency, and therefore, must be recognised as part of exercising legal capacity which is protected by Article 12. As a result, individuals are also entitled to support for these decisions. This is particularly relevant when people with disabilities make decisions in the informal sphere, for example making day-to-day decisions within a service environment or the family. These decisions do not typically have legal consequences but may be when the most damaging decision-making denials occur. For example where people with disabilities are prevented from making decisions in their daily lives in relation to meals, clothing, or schedules, this will not usually come within the definition of creating, modifying, or extinguishing a legal relationship. However, in some cases, people with disabilities may have to assert their legal agency (for example by initiating legal action) to have their decision respected.

A clear example of this is individuals living in an institutional setting.[5] Policies govern the day-to-day schedules in these settings and individuals are deprived of the opportunity to make decisions about some of the most basic aspects of their life including for example getting up, washing, and meals. Take for example a man who had lived with his parents until they died and then decided to move into a group home to get the daily support he felt he needed. He had developed his own routines in life such as staying up late to watch a movie on television on a Friday evening, attending religious services on a Sunday and working part time in a local grocery shop. When he moved into the group home he had to adhere to a strict bedtime routine and they could not provide support for him to attend church on a Sunday or drive him to work due to a shortage of staff. He complained but nothing changed and so he began to refuse food and stated that he would eat again when he was allowed to go to work, attend church and choose his own bedtime. In our view, his refusal to eat is an exercise of legal agency and he is therefore entitled to protection under Article 12 CRPD. Leaving the fact that some of his wishes may not be practical aside for this purpose, this example highlights how someone who lives in an institutional setting may need to assert their legal agency to have their decisions respected.

2. What are the justifiable limits on individual agency which can be imposed by the State and apply to everyone, regardless of disability or decision-making ability?

The level of state intervention that should be allowed into the private lives of individuals is an age-old question. The extent to which States may intervene in the private lives of individuals in emergency situations or where there is a perception of risk is often one of the first questions States pose when faced with reforming their legislation to comply with Article 12 of the CRPD. People with disabilities experience a disproportionately higher level of state intervention in their private lives than people without disabilities and the denial of legal capacity is one of the most serious forms of intervention faced. With all this in mind, we endeavoured to provide a disability neutral basis for state intervention which recognises an individual's legal capacity and respects her will and preferences.

On this basis, we defined state intervention as "an intervention that is taken by the state or an agent of the state, which constitutes an interference with personal autonomy and may have the purpose or effect of denying the legal capacity of an individual" (Flynn and Arstein-Kerslake, 2017, p. 40). We propose that the State should be allowed to intervene in the private lives of all individuals (with or without disabilities) in the event of a risk of imminent and serious harm to the individual's life, health or safety and argue for the abolition of all disability specific forms of state intervention. We recognise that other commentators[6] have also addressed this issue and set the threshold for intervention at a different level however, we felt that 'risk of imminent and serious harm to the individual's life, health or safety' was the appropriate standard to ensure adequate State support in grievous situations while maintaining a disability neutral approach.

Our approach has led to criticism from some commentators who state that facially neutral provisions for state intervention will still amount to disability discrimination in practice and that this practice will in fact be more perilous because it will not be as readily apparent.[7] While we accept that any facially neutral provision has the potential to have a discriminate in practice, we believe that this a risk that we must be prepared to take in order to achieve a disability neutral, pragmatic standard for state intervention. We also acknowledge that our proposal is entrenched in a theoretical space and would need further refinement if it were to be applied in reality in legislation. It is also important to note that this concept was developed from the basis that is not the only intervention the State should be responsible for. This is a measure of last resort and crisis services, peer support and other less invasive supports should also be provided. This should replace, not supplement, existing discriminatory provisions such as guardianship and adult protection laws.

3. How can we ascertain whether an individual is giving free and informed consent (necessary to make an action legally binding), without engaging in a functional assessment of that person's mental capacity?

The concept of consent interacts with many other aspects of both civil and criminal law. It has a wide range of legal consequences not least of which is that the absence of consent can turn a lawful interaction into an assault. In all of its current manifestations, consent includes some element of mental capacity testing. Therefore, the solution to our third question required a reformulation of consent to place it on a disability neutral footing by removing this discriminatory testing. To achieve this, we engaged with feminist literature and human rights standards and advocated for a "freedom to negotiate" model. We applied this model, used previously in the area of consent to sex (Anderson, 2004), to the areas of consent to sex and consent to medical treatment for people with cognitive disabilities.[8] These areas were chosen due to the often State -sanctioned methods in which people with disabilities have their ability to consent either denied, restricted or ignored on a regular basis.

Under our proposed framework we present three essential elements for consent – recognition of legal capacity, freedom to negotiate, and finally, information, respect for will and preferences and voluntariness (Brosnan and Flynn, 2017). In the third and final element – information, respect for will and preferences and voluntariness – all three must be present as a cluster and this will be explained further below. In keeping with the overall project ethos, for valid consent a person must be recognised as a person before the law with full legal capacity. In practice this excludes any frameworks for consent which require cognitive testing of an individual's mental capacity. Critically, this in our view does not mean that a person gave informed consent in situations where a person misunderstood the information or was misled in some way. It simply removes a discriminatory test and ensures that any examination of whether consent was free and informed starts from a position of equality before the law. The second element is that an individual is free to negotiate their consent or refusal. In our view, this includes that it must be an active agreement, that there is a positive obligation on the person who wishes to act upon another's body to initiate this negotiation and that communication occurs in an accessible way in a form both parties understand. The third element or cluster ensures that an individual has all the relevant information and that it is present in an accessible way. It also highlights the need for consent to be free from coercion and undue influence and in keeping with a person's will and preferences.

Final hurdle: applying theory to project practice

The project team attempted to provide answers to these questions to give storytellers and respondents a starting point for reflecting on their experiences in their pair chapters. However, agreement with that position was not a pre-requisite for inclusion in this edited collection and pairs were encouraged to build on, disregard or critique our position as appropriate. What was critical to the process was that each individual agreed with the core values of the project as set out in the About the Project section and there will be a more detailed account of the project's methodology in the next chapter.

Notes

1 See de Bhailís and Flynn (2017).
2 For a more detail on the status, outcome and functional tests see Dhanda (2006–2007, p. 431).
3 For a more detailed discussion of this requirement see Holness (2014).
4 The 'best interests' principle still applies to children.
5 The following example is an abridged version of the case study which appears in Arstein-Kerslake and Flynn, 2017 at p. 29.
6 See for example Bach and Kerzner (2010) who advocate for a threshold of "serious adverse effects".
7 See for example Minkowitz (2017).
8 For a more detailed discussion of our freedom to negotiate model and consent to treatment in mental health context see Chapter 19 of this volume.

Bibliography

Anderson, M. (2004). Negotiating sex. *Southern California Law Review*, 78, pp. 1401–1438.

Arstein-Kerslake, A., and Flynn, E. (2016). The General Comment on Article 12 of the Convention on the Rights of Persons with Disabilities: A roadmap for equality before the law. *The International Journal of Human Rights*, *20*(4), pp. 471–490.

Arstein-Kerslake, A. and Flynn, E. (2017). The right to legal agency: Domination, disability and the protections of Article 12 of the Convention on the Rights of Persons with Disabilities. *International Journal of Law in Context*, 13(1), pp. 22–38.

Bach, M., and Kerzner, L. (2010). *A New Paradigm for Protecting Autonomy and the Right to Legal Capacity' Ontario: Law Commission of Ontario*. [online] Available at: https://www.lco-cdo.org/wp-content/uploads/2010/11/disabilities-commissioned-paper-bach-kerzner.pdf [Accessed 25 Jan. 2018].

Brammer, A. (2012). Inside the Court of Protection. *Journal of Adult Protection*, 14(6), pp. 297–301.

Brosnan, L., and Flynn, E. (2017). Freedom to negotiate: A proposal extricating 'capacity' from 'consent'. *International Journal of Law in Context*, 13(1), pp. 58–76.

Committee on the Rights of Persons with Disabilities. (2014). General Comment No. 1. Article 12: Equal Recognition Before the Law, UN Doc. No. CRPD/C/GC/1.

Committee on the Rights of Persons with Disabilities. (2018). General Comment No. 1. Corrigendum, UN Doc. No. CRPD/C/GC/1/Corr.1

de Bhailís, C., and Flynn, E. (2017). Recognising legal capacity: Commentary and analysis of Article 12 CRPD. *International Journal of Law in Context*, 13(1), pp. 6–21.

Degener, T. ed. (2017). Legal Capacity and Human Rights. *International Journal of Law in Context*, 13(1).

Dhanda, A. (2006–2007). Legal Capacity in the Disability Rights Convention: Stranglehold of the Past or Lodestar of the Future? *Syracuse Journal of International Law and Commerce,* 34, pp. 429–462.

Flynn, E., and Arstein-Kerslake, A. (2017). State intervention in the lives of people with disabilities: The case for a disability-neutral framework. *International Journal of Law in Context*, 13(1), pp. 39–57.

Holness, W. (2014). Equal recognition and legal capacity for persons with disabilities: Incorporating the principle of proportionality. *South African Journal on Human Rights*, 30, pp. 313–344.

Minkowitz, T. (2017) CRPD and Transformative Equality. *International Journal of Law in Context*, 13(1), pp. 77–86.

Nussbaum, M. (2006). *Frontiers of Justice: Disability, Nationality, Species Membership*. Cambridge, United States: The Belknap Press of Harvard University.

2 Project methodology and background

Eilionóir Flynn

The overarching objective of the VOICES project is to make visible the lived experience of disabled people in the exercise and denial of their right to legal capacity and to use this experience as a starting point for legal, social and political reform. The project was born out of our frustration as researchers at the parallel silos in which legal capacity discourse and law reform efforts operated. In our experience, policy-makers were not meaningfully involving people with lived experience in processes to reform guardianship laws and other forms of substituted decision-making; and most of the new thinking on legal capacity and support being developed by activists in the field was not being reflected in academic literature on the subject. We sought to bridge this gap by developing a project which would generate new knowledge from lived experience and demonstrate to law-makers why and how systems needed to change to recognise the legal capacity of persons with disabilities on an equal basis with others.

As described in the About the Project chapter, the project has two key components – a theoretical framework and narratives and responses on the exercise and denial of legal capacity. This book represents the outcome of the second component of the project, and the majority of this chapter will describe the methodologies employed to develop these narratives and responses. However, prior to this discussion it is worth setting out in brief how the project's theoretical framework was developed.

The purpose of the project's theoretical framework (as discussed in further detail in Chapter 1) was to provide answers to previously unexplored questions in the literature on legal capacity, which would provide context and a starting point for the development of responses to narratives emerging from the project. Primary responsibility for the development of the theoretical framework lay with the VOICES project team, and the team members co-authored four peer-reviewed articles setting out our position on the issues of legal agency, state intervention and capacity to consent along with an overview of existing literature in the field. However, these articles were developed in a highly collaborative manner.

Workshops to develop ideas for each topic were organised by the VOICES team at an early stage of drafting the articles with key informants drawn from the project's Advisory Group and Steering Committee, and invited experts from outside the field of disability and legal capacity who could provide fresh perspectives on how these concepts might be developed in a universal manner. Draft articles finalised following these workshops were circulated for comment to the entire Advisory Group and Steering Committee[1] and further revised prior to submission for peer review as part of the journal editing process. The project team did not implement all the changes suggested by members of the Advisory Group and Steering Committee – and instead provided a space for members who wished to do so to write critical reflective pieces which would be published alongside the team's articles. As a result, the final articles which form the theoretical framework for the project, published in a special issue of the International Journal of Law in Context, represent a wide range of views on how the values of the VOICES project should be understood in the development of law reform in the field of legal capacity.

Once the theoretical framework had been developed, the focus of the VOICES project team shifted to the recruitment of participants to develop narratives and critical responses related to the exercise and denial of legal capacity.

In advance of the recruitment process, the project team selected four different aspects of law related to legal capacity on which narratives and responses would be sought – criminal responsibility, contract law, consent to medical treatment and consent to sex. These themes were chosen in advance by the project team as they represented underexplored areas in the literature on legal capacity – and ones where lived experience was seldom used as a basis for reform. However, applicants who wished to participate in the development of narratives and responses were not asked to select a topic as part of the initial application process – in order to encourage as wide a range of applications as possible, and to ensure that the project remained open to including new areas of law where experiences of exercising or being denied legal capacity might emerge.

The project's approach to developing narratives and responses was to recruit storytellers (those with lived experience who wanted to write a narrative piece) and respondents (individuals from a range of personal and professional backgrounds, including people with lived experience, who would respond to the narratives developed). The idea was to form pairs of storytellers and respondents, and that each pair would produce a narrative and an accompanying response piece that related to one of the areas of law on which the project was focused.

A number of recruitment strategies were undertaken from January 2016 to attract applicants for both storyteller and respondent roles to the project. The project team and members of the Advisory Board and Steering Group circulated the call for applications through personal and professional networks of contacts. Individuals active in the field were identified and sent specific invitations. The project team also travelled to meet with key groups of self-advocates and researchers to explain the process and encourage individuals to apply. Application forms were made available in plain English and easy-to-read formats to ensure accessibility, and applicants were asked to self-select into either a storyteller or a respondent role, as many of those interested would have met the criteria for either role. Finally, the project team developed a draft set of ground rules for participants which were circulated with the application forms to give participants an understanding of how the project would maintain a safe space for stories to be told and shared. These ground rules were discussed and amended as needed at each of the subsequent workshops throughout the VOICES project.

A workshop method was chosen for this aspect of the project because it provided a safe space for participants to share personal narratives and to critically reflect on these experiences. Each workshop included a closed session for invited participants only and a public day where the participants made conference-style presentations on their work. During the closed sessions, creative writing facilitators worked to assist storytellers in developing their narratives. The workshop format also enabled us to involve a wide range of artists, who demonstrated different ways in which stories could be told – through dance, visual art, poetry and theatre. Finally, the workshops, in their open sessions, provided the opportunity to engage with those who had previously not been involved in discussions on legal capacity reform at national and international levels – including students, frontline staff in health and social care, family members and self-advocates. Speakers were invited to these events to provide a mix of perspectives – as each workshop included speakers with previous knowledge of the CRPD and those who were new to or unfamiliar with disability-rights research and activism (including feminist, philosophical and critical legal perspectives). This wide range of perspectives aimed to mainstream legal capacity discourse in other research domains beyond the fields of disability and human rights.

The original project proposal had aimed to form eight pairs – two for each of the four thematic areas. However, the project team received so many high-quality applications that we decided to invite 18 storytellers and 18 respondents to the first workshop in April 2016. The high number of applications can also indicate that this is an innovative way of conducting research, since applicants were eager to have the opportunity to tell their stories and respond to the stories of others – in many cases, because these opportunities had never been made available before. We chose these applicants based on previously agreed selection criteria. For example, storyteller applicants must have lived experience to be eligible to participate and this experience must relate to legal capacity. Many potential applicants had lived experience of disability and some experience of discrimination but as far as we could tell, this experience did not relate specifically to the exercise or denial of legal capacity, so these applicants were not ultimately selected. For the respondents, it was essential that they shared a commitment to the rights enshrined in the CRPD, could demonstrate that they would be able to work one-to-one with a storyteller, and had some basic knowledge about how the right to legal capacity could be applied in practice.

The selection process also aimed to ensure some degree of gender balance (although far more women than men applied), a wide range of experiences of disability, and a mix of representation from the Global North and Global South. Ultimately, participants from 11 countries: Australia, Bulgaria, Canada, China, Czech Republic, Germany, India, Ireland, Kenya, Sweden, and the United Kingdom, have been included in this final edited collection. The geographic diversity of the pairs in the VOICES project is one of the greatest strengths of the project, but also presents significant challenges – as the legal, political, social and cultural contexts in which legal capacity may be exercised differ significantly between countries. It was important to us to represent this diversity in the project, in part because some of the most exciting developments in legal capacity reform have occurred in the Global South, while significant challenges to achieving similar reforms persist in the Global North. While the working language of the project was English, we provided interpreters where required to ensure that all storytellers could participate equally. Participants were also given the option to bring a support person where required to enable their full participation in each workshop, and where a person needed support but could not identify or bring their own supporter, volunteer supporters were recruited and briefed on the project values by the project team.

We also sought to include among the participants a range of personal and professional expertise. This included a mix of different experiences of disability/impairment, and different disciplinary backgrounds. We found it important to include storytellers who also had experience of advocacy and activism, or research, and respondents who might also have personal/lived experience of disability or denials of legal capacity. It was particularly important for the project that the pairs were diverse and we were conscious of the potential for actual and perceived power imbalances if all the pairs were viewed as being comprised of a disabled storyteller and non-disabled respondent. Finally, we sought to include among the storytellers those whose stories were already well known, such as Rusi Stanev, who had taken a famous case before the European Court of Human Rights, as well as those who had never previously told their story in a public forum. It was important to us to include this combination of known and unknown stories in the project as we believe this helps to highlight the extent of legal capacity denials and the creativity among people with lived experience and their allies in developing forms of support to exercise legal capacity.

Following the selection of participants for the April 2016 workshop, the project team deliberated on possible pairings. We created a photobook of storytellers and respondents which included the person's country, languages spoken, experience, and a seven-word autobiography. Participants were invited to tell us when they received the photobook if there was anyone they were particularly interested in meeting and working with. Each individual storyteller was introduced to all possible respondents at the beginning of the private day of the April workshop through an ice-breaker exercise and throughout the day each storyteller worked with four different respondents selected by the project team (facilitating participants' individual preferences). At the end of this workshop, participants were asked to give the project team their top three preferences for pairing. Of the 16 pairs ultimately formed following this workshop, only two storytellers were matched with respondents who were not in their initial list of top three preferences. In forming the pairs, the project team took account of participants' values, styles of working and expectations from the project, as well as practical considerations such as the geographical distance between pairs and participants' abilities to use communications technology, or experience in working with someone who communicated differently.

Following the pairing process, the project team circulated guidelines for working together to all pairs and asked each pair to submit a plan outlining how they would work together to produce their chapter for the VOICES edited collection. We offered pairs the option of a mentor to support their work (especially for respondents where their storyteller's experience was a subject they had not written extensively about previously, or where respondents were unfamiliar with the storyteller's cultural and legal context) and in general drew mentors from the project's Advisory Board and Steering Group. All the pairs chose a specific thematic workshop based on the area of law which was most relevant to the storyteller's experience, and the pairs developed story and response presentations, delivered to the public at each of these events.

Thematic workshops were held between September 2016 and September 2017. Following their specific thematic workshop, pairs were asked to develop their first draft of their contribution to the book within six months, to allow for staged feedback from the project team, and where desired, from the pair's mentor and/or other members of the Advisory Board and Steering Group. Each pair also had ongoing support from a member of the project team, which included regular email updates and reminders of upcoming deadlines, facilitating pair communication through setting up Skype sessions and/or conference calls, transcription of storytellers' narratives, comments on draft chapters and suggestions of relevant literature which could be included, and support to develop the technical aspect of presentations (using images, sounds, recordings, etc.) as well as practicing for the public presentations at each workshop.

Of the 16 pairs selected, 14 have produced chapters in this edited volume. The project adopted a policy in the guidance developed for pairs, which set out that if storytellers chose to leave, the respondents would not be able to continue in the project; but that if a respondent wanted to leave, alternative arrangements would be made if the storyteller wished to continue with the project. While one of the storytellers, Rusi Stanev, died during the course of the project, he had already produced some written material for his chapter, and his respondent Sheila Wildeman, in discussion with Rusi's supporter Aneta Genova, decided to continue their work and produce a chapter in his memory which appears at the end of this edited collection. Two further storytellers chose to leave the project for personal reasons and were not replaced. There were also changes to the original respondents paired with storytellers due to a range of personal and professional commitments. These changes were accommodated by sourcing replacements or adding additional respondents as agreed with storytellers.

The pairs faced a number of challenges during the course of the project and various strategies to mitigate these were pursued by the project team. For some pairs, the geographical distance between storyteller and respondent (and resulting differences in time zones) posed a practical problem in setting regular pair meetings. This challenge arose because in the pairing process, we made a conscious decision to respect the preferences of participants for who they wanted to be paired with – even if that led to challenges with technology and pair communication. Most participants expressed a desire to have more time to work together face to face and some participants found it very difficult to use communication technology to meet virtually on a regular basis. Support and privacy needed to facilitate Skype/phone meetings were lacking for some storytellers and the project team made trips to visit various storytellers to enable regular communication with their respondents. Project funding was also used for certain pairs to enable face-to-face meetings to happen in between the workshops in Galway. Differences in language and the need to understand the storyteller's context (including relevant laws, cultural beliefs and practices) also posed a challenge – and the use of interpreters, mentors and supporters with local knowledge was key to addressing this.

Further challenges emerged during the writing process, as some respondents were transcribing narratives told to them by storytellers, while other storytellers were writing their own narratives directly. Respondents engaged in this work were conscious of the need to capture the authenticity of storyteller's voices. In other cases, respondents felt the storyteller's narrative should stand alone and that they had nothing to add. Power imbalances were discussed throughout the project, as all pairs were sensitive to the fact that only one person, the storyteller, was disclosing personal experience in their written contribution and that this could lead to an imbalance of power between the storyteller and respondent. A further challenge for respondents was the fact that many of the storytellers' experiences could be perceived to conflict with how certain rights were framed in the CRPD – particularly where storytellers reported positive experiences in segregated disability services.

For the VOICES project team, there were several challenges in the process of editing this collection. Our goal is to respect the authentic storyteller voice, and we debated whether and how to edit grammar and syntax in storyteller narratives and the potential for this kind of editing to interfere with the individual's natural storytelling style. Several respondents sought guidance from the project team on how to frame arguments about the application of the CRPD to the storytellers' experience, and we were conscious of the risk of over-influencing respondents with our interpretations of Convention rights. Finally, a constant challenge throughout this project was the potential for third parties to be identified in the chapters, especially since the storytellers are writing under their own names. We discussed this issue at length with the pairs and tried to find a balance in order to protect the authors and project team against defamation charges, while giving individuals the freedom to tell their stories the way they wanted.

Following the publication of this edited collection, there are some ongoing challenges which remain to be addressed in the VOICES project. These include meeting the expectations of the storytellers and respondents about the impact of the project and follow-up actions – including providing support for pairs who want to continue their work after the project officially ends, and/or to reflect on, and publish material about their working processes in more detail. Following the publication of this book, we are also committed to producing more detailed explorations of our methodology, as well as a practical 'how-to' guide which can be used by others interested in learning from our processes or engaging in similar research. There is clearly need to continue this work to make sure the stories shared in this volume have an impact on processes of change. It is vital that those who hold decision-making power to implement legal capacity reform listen to those with lived experience and act to bring about their visions for change. As a project team, we are committed to sustaining our efforts to achieve legal capacity reform and maximising the impact of the stories and responses presented here.

The challenges we identify with our approach in this project have been described so that others can build on and expand research and advocacy in the field of legal capacity reform that is rooted in the lived experience of persons with disabilities. The issues that were not addressed within this project provide opportunities for further exploration in other research – including an extension of this approach to participants with higher support needs, those working in languages other than English, and the representation of stories and responses in formats other than the texts and images which appear in this book. Our intention is that the VOICES project represents the beginning of a broader conversation, not just about how to change law, policy and practice on legal capacity but also about how to do research in this field that is valuable and respects the integrity of those with lived experience of legal capacity denials.

Note

1 These groups are comprised of international experts with both professional and personal experience in the area of legal capacity. The Advisory Board was formed of experts with more than 20 years' experience to give insight on the overall direction of the project, whereas the Steering Group in general included more emerging scholars and activists who could be more actively involved in the ongoing running of the project.

Part 1

Criminal responsibility – diversion and the insanity defence

3 Introduction to criminal responsibility

Anna Arstein-Kerslake

Equal recognition before the law is not a simple concept. Equality itself is a complex concept and an attempt to guarantee equality before the law adds an infinite number of complexities – many of which can be seen throughout this book. One of the particularly difficult challenges is that equal recognition before the law requires that a person be equal in both rights and responsibilities. In other words, in order to be recognised before the law on an equal basis with others, an individual must be recognised as a rights holder on an equal basis with others – but also, she or he must be recognised as having equal responsibility for upholding the law. Without both being recognised as holding equal rights and responsibilities before the law, an individual is not truly equal. However, with responsibility comes burden.

As part of the social contract, we implicitly agree to live within social structures and to be bound by the laws of those structures. One of the greatest burdens of our social structures is the criminal law. It is no secret that the burden of the criminal law has historically been significantly heavier for marginalised groups. For example, 'paupers' and those of lower feudal classes were prosecuted at a higher rate than those of noble background in medieval Europe.[1] In modern society, ethnic minorities and other marginalised groups often continue to experience overrepresentation in criminal justice systems. For example, African Americans in the United States represent 34% of the prison population and are incarcerated at more than five times the rate of white people.[2] Similarly, people with disability are overrepresented in criminal justice systems around the world.[3] This is evidence that our criminal justice systems may be acting, not as deterrence from breaking the law, but as a kind of social control that is laden with prejudice and is constructed in such a way that those in power are often exempt from its trappings.

Keeping in mind that prejudice appears to continue to dominate criminal justice systems, and that those in positions of power and privilege are often exempted from the burden of such systems, it may seem counterintuitive to demand that an already marginalised group – people with disability – carry the burden of criminal culpability on the same basis as others. It is particularly counterintuitive when such a demand is made in the name of equality itself. There is a distinct possibility that recognising people with disability as possessing equal criminal culpability as those without disability will result in more people with disability in the existing prison system and may result in more people with disability facing the death penalty, in countries where that is still in force. However, the current unequal criminal culpability laws create extensive damage, both in the disability related stigma they perpetuate throughout the social consciousness and also in the actual practical results of finding of lack of culpability on the basis of disability.

When people are excused from criminal responsibility on the basis of disability they are often left more disadvantaged than if they were to have been held fully responsible for the crime (Minkowitz, 2014). For example, when people are found unfit to plead or successfully use the insanity defence, they can often be detained for longer and sometimes, indefinitely (Arstein-Keslake et al., 2017). In addition, the mere existence of such laws, perpetuates stigma related to disability and the concept that people with disability cannot be held responsible for their actions on an equal basis with others – in other words, people with disability cannot be trusted as decision-makers on an equal basis with others. This stigma and misperception creeps into multiple layers of society. In furthers the notion that people with disability can't be trusted as decision-makers in other areas of life – voting, marriage, signing contracts, deciding where to live, and others.

The two pieces of work in this part describe the legal and social implications of denying decision-making to people with disability in the criminal justice context. Gabor Gombos and Amita Dhanda explore the black letter law and legal theory on the topic. They conclude that the criminal justice system is in need of reform to ensure equality for people with disability. Nicholas Clarke poignantly describes the lived experience of being a person with disability who is engaging with the criminal justice system and is not respected as a decision-maker. Chloe Hocking and Nell Munro discuss the social and legal implications of Nicholas' story and the disempowerment and further marginalisation that is caused by denying decision-making rights.

Notes

1 For example, see Wright (1893); Steinert (1986); Fitzgerald, McLennan, and Pawson (2003); and Adler (1989).
2 Statistics from 'Prison Inmates at Midyear 2009 – Statistical Tables' (NCJ 230113). U.S. Bureau of Justice Statistics; and 'Criminal Justice Fact Sheet'. National Association for the Advancement of Colored People, NAACP. For a discussion, see Bonilla-Silva (2017).
3 For a discussion, see Davis (2014).

Bibliography

Adler, J.S. (1989). A historical analysis of the law of vagrancy. *Criminology*, 27(2), pp. 209–229.

Arstein-Kerslake, A. et al. (2017). Human Rights and Unfitness to Plead: The Demands of the Convention on the Rights of Persons with Disabilities. *Human Rights Law Review*, 17(3), pp. 399–419.

Bonilla-Silva, E. (2017). *Racism without racists: Color-blind racism and the persistence of racial inequality in America*. Lanham, MD: Rowman & Littlefield.

Davis, A.Y. (2014). *Disability incarcerated: Imprisonment and disability in the United States and Canada*. New York: Springer.

Fitzgerald, M., McLennan, G. and Pawson, J. eds. (2003). *Crime and society: Readings in history and theory*. Routledge.

Minkowitz, T. (2014). Rethinking criminal responsibility from a critical disability perspective: The abolition of insanity/incapacity acquittals and unfitness to plead, and beyond. *Griffith Law Review*, 23(3), pp. 434–466.

Steinert, H. (1986). Beyond crime and punishment. *Contemporary Crises*, 10(1), pp. 21–38.

Wright, C.D. (1893). The relation of economic conditions to the causes of crime: 'The destruction of the poor is their poverty.' – Proverbs x. 15. *The ANNALS of the American Academy of Political and Social Science*, 3(6), pp. 96–116.

4 Going to pot: Nick's journey through the criminal justice system

Nicholas Clarke, Nell Munro and Chloe Hocking

Nick: Red mist hovered above my head while going through a meltdown period after enduring five months of verbal, physical and emotional abuse at the previous two hostels[1] after terminating my contract for breach of peace due to my disruptive mood swings. Hostel three felt like I had stepped into the gateway of hell! I kicked and cracked a reinforced wire mesh fire exit door panel due to anger and frustration as the red mist turned into a sea of blood! Three support workers tried pinning me down onto the floor. My comfort zone turned to a red circle of danger, defending myself against their intimidating approach. Adrenaline kicked in as I resisted being taken down, pinching and scratching their arms, causing superficial cuts and bruises for invading my personal space.

The circle of red turned to amber once the support staff stepped out of the circle to call the police. The circle of amber tuned to green when I was left alone, calming down without the presence of the support workers in the room. Two police officers arrested me for charges of criminal damage and Actual Bodily Harm (ABH).[2] The custody suite was like stepping into hell with no natural daylight, apart from the artificial fluorescent lighting illuminating the custody desk, like a Devil's cauldron fuelled by the fires of hell, surrounded by dark shadows of evil.

After reporting to the Custody Sergeant, I was escorted by the two arresting officers into the furnace my accommodation for two nights. I was cocooned into a small tight space with no natural daylight, surrounded by concrete walls with one single fluorescent circular light on the ceiling staring down at me like an evil eye. A big blue metal door was my focus point hoping that it would suddenly miraculously open so I could make a quick exit, away from the cocoon that was pressing against my head, that was raising my anxiety and stress levels. There was no escape, trapped in a negative dark environment.

***

Nell and Chloe: The events that Nick recounts here are the climax of a period of disruption in his life. Nick had experienced months of abuse. This abuse had taken place in three hostels where he had been accommodated after moving out of his parents' house following an episode of severe depression during which he was diagnosed with autism. In this same period, Nick's father had been diagnosed with terminal cancer. That he should later be convicted on grounds of criminal damage and ABH as a result of the distress he felt in response to these events seems unjust.

Acknowledging that in most cases individuals will be responsible for their criminal behaviour, it does not seem fair that Nick was held morally culpable for this behaviour. Nick's arrest seems wholly disproportionate to the situation at hand. He and his family had been repeatedly trying to access help and support which was never provided; his actions were the result of a heightened emotional state attributable to this failure. Whilst Nick's actions can be technically classified as 'criminal', alternatives to criminal punishment would have been available. Civil penalties could have been pursued for the damage to property within Nick's home. In 2018, another option would be calling on specialist diversion and liaison services which support disabled people within the Criminal Justice System (CJS) and could help someone in Nick's situation access the services he and his family desired.

***

Nick: A Force Medical Examiner[3] (FME) assessed me after I disclosed to the Custody Sergeant that I was self-harming with mental health issues. The FME said I was fit to carry on being detained and interviewed. A duty solicitor attended the recorded interview with an Appropriate Adult[4] (AA) present. Because of my autism, I was advised by the solicitor to give a no comment interview. I wanted to give my interpretation of the emotional abuse and physical threats I had to endure from the staff by being open and honest.

It was a brief stress release being taken into police custody in the hope that I would finally get the professional help and support that my family and I had been desperately asking for since I was first moved to a hostel in January 2005. My nightmare situation increased when I found out that the staff were pressing charges against me.

On Friday 13 May 2005 at Birmingham Criminal Court, my solicitor advised me to plead guilty to charges of criminal damage and ABH during my pre-sentencing. I was remanded for three weeks at in Winson Green Prison in Birmingham. There were no family in the public gallery for much needed moral support due to miscommunication between my social worker and family. They only knew about my fate once I was in prison. I was convicted on Friday 3 June 2005, paying compensation, damages and prosecution fees totalling £355.00 even though my actions at the time were non-intentional.

I felt threatened by the hostel staff's restraining techniques and going into self-defence mode out of sheer desperation I lashed out, not realising that the consequences of my actions would lead to a life-long criminal record and psychological barrier when applying for jobs supporting vulnerable adults and young people – negatively labelled throughout my life with a conviction haunting my Enhanced DBS Certificate[5] until my hundredth birthday.

***

Chloe: Police custody was wholly unsuited to Nick's needs. It was small; it was bright, triggering his sensory sensitives and creating additional stress. This combined with the lack of appropriate support ultimately prevented Nick from effectively exercising his rights in police custody. Although Nick was supported by an AA (Appropriate Adult) during his police interview it is unclear that this was an effective way of supporting Nick to make decisions during the custody process. Without knowledge of Nick's specific communication and sensory needs, an inexperienced new person could simply intensify the stress Nick felt in custody rather than reduce it. They might not have recognised the signs that Nick was in distress or that he might not have understood something.

In addition, no support was provided at court to help Nick exercise his legal capacity. Like most individuals would reasonably have been expected to do in his position, Nick chose to act according to the advice of his solicitor and plead guilty. However, he was not given enough information by his solicitor to help him understand that doing this would create long-term barriers in his life.

By failing to provide Nick with appropriate accommodations, he was effectively prevented from accessing the CJS on an equal basis with others. In the absence of suitable support, Nick made decisions on the basis that it would be the quickest way to get out of the police station; he could not cope with the stresses of being in police custody and just wanted to escape. He did not realise that by making these decisions greater consequences would follow as nobody took steps to explain this. If Nick had been supported more appropriately, he would have been in a better position to participate in these processes effectively; demonstrating the importance of having not just general support, but support *tailored* to his specific needs.

***

Nick: I would like to introduce you to the king of petrol cylinder lawnmowers: the Qualcast Suffolk Punch 35DL with its distinctive green colour blending in with the green green grass. The sound of the engine combined with the smell of the exhaust fumes and the scent of freshly mown grass is my ideal sensory sensation heaven.

A cylinder lawnmower has a roller that leaves a dark and light strip when mowing up and down that looks stunning to the eye. No matter what the ground conditions were like, I had to mow the lawn once a week on a Saturday morning, even if the grass had not grown much during week and it was pouring with rain, I would still cut the lawn. It was regimental ritual routine for me to go through, getting agitated if I went away on a summer holiday leaving the grass to grow long.

Since early childhood, I have been fascinated by petrol cylinder lawnmowers. I have another fascination, the British car registration number plate system. In March 2004, I purchased a brand new Seat Cordoba 1.9 TDI SE after being put under immense pressure from a pushy salesman on the internet. I was very disappointed that the registration plate was not right, to a point that I could no longer sleep. This triggered my breakdown. Mowing the lawn was one of the few activities I still enjoyed doing.

April 2004: I wanted to start up my Qualcast Suffolk Punch 35DL, the engine did not kick in. I did a standard routine check that I have done in the past to get it working without success. My parents told me they would go to the local lawnmower repair shop to get my pride and joy back into full working order. Instead of getting it repaired they came back with a brand new Qualcast Classic Petrol 35s cylinder lawnmower.

I felt very sad that they got rid of my Qualcast Suffolk Punch 35DL without consulting me first. I did my best not to show my disappointment, as I did not want to hurt their feelings after spending £400. However, I could not hide my disappointment telling them that they should have got the Qualcast Suffolk Punch 35DL repaired. My parents could see from my facial expression and reaction that I was upset and unhappy and had made the wrong decision for me.

I could not cope and manage with the sudden changes in my life, with the wrong car registration playing on my mind. The purchasing of the Qualcast Classic Petrol 35s felt like a punch in the face for me, deepening my depression even more. My parents meant well, thinking that they made the right decision for me by surprising me with a brand new Qualcast Classic Petrol 35s, thinking it would cheer me up after the disappointment with the purchase of the brand new Seat Cordoba 1.9 TDI SE. Unfortunately, it had the reverse effect. I could no longer mow the back-garden lawn after the sad loss of my pride and joy.

***

Nell and Chloe: We loved this bittersweet story by Nick the very first time he shared it. It captures the absurdity of defining Nick's autism spectrum condition (ASC) as an impairment. Nick's ASC makes him conscientious, highly aware of other people's feelings and profoundly anxious if he cannot complete a task to exacting standards. These are strengths. When the routine, which is fundamental to Nick's well-being, is disturbed, he needs support, and throughout Nick's life his large extended family including his parents and seven siblings have been on hand to provide this.

The story Nick describes here illustrates the particular needs he may have had in police custody; ones that were not met through the support provided to him. Being arrested was a huge disruption to Nick's life, at a time when he was already finding it difficult to manage what was happening around him. He was not unable to make decisions; what he needed was extra support to help him make those decisions. In police custody, Nick needed to be supported by people who were familiar with those needs, or who had an understanding of when he might need additional support and what support would help him at a specific point in the CJS.

***

Nick: My anxiety and stress levels felt like a pressure cooker building up to boiling point. As the steam builds up, my anxiety rises. Once it reaches boiling point and full pressure, the cooker gives out a loud whistle as the steam comes through the vent pipe hitting the pressure regulator making a loud whistle and hissing sounds like a demented snake. The threat of eviction from my family home into a hostel setting fuelled my already fragile state of mind into total mayhem. The demented hissing snake was controlling my mind and body in order to cope and manage with the sudden changes to my daily routine.

This is how I was feeling, fuelled by sleep deprivation with no desire or motivation to get out of bed during the day. My usual high personal hygiene standards fell apart, not brushing my teeth or showering and wearing the same clothes for several weeks. I started whining like a siren during the night, feeling emotional and tearful. My brain felt scrambled as the demented hissing sounds reached boiling point, causing anger and loss of control with unpredictable aggressive rages like a bull in a china shop.

While I was having breakfast the doorbell rang, it was my social worker with a police officer telling me that I had 20 minutes to pack my personal belongings to a hostel across the road for adults with mental health needs. I was being kicked out of my family home in an abrupt manner, stoking my fragile state into an even deeper depression. The eviction from my family home happened during the same week when my father got diagnosed with a terminal form of acute myeloid leukaemia by a cancer specialist in January 2005.

My mother could not cope and manage my mood swings and unpredictable rages fuelled by a combination of antidepressants and anti-psychotics that my consultant psychiatrist wrongly prescribed to me. This was a massive shock and a bitter pill to swallow. Looking after a terminally ill husband and mentally unwell son was a challenge for the whole family. My already fragile state of mind was spiralling into a deep dark tunnel that I could not get out of. I was alone and petrified after an abrupt and unexpected eviction from familiar surroundings and home comforts.

I could not settle down and relax at the hostel. Seeing my parents' house from the landing window deepened my already fragile state of mind as the dreaded demented snake took over my mind triggering an aggressive outburst; smashing up the hostel flowerpots in the front garden, rudely disturbing Bill and Ben the Flower Pot Men, characters from the classic British children's BBC TV programme, popping out of their pot before I had a chance to show them the rear end of my right foot as they ran away for safety seeing their homes going to pot. The warden called the police who swiftly took me away to the station before I had a chance to catch up with Bill and Ben to give them a smashing time.

I was released a few hours later, returning to the hostel threatening me with an eviction notice if I misbehaved again. Early morning, there was an almighty bang. The door flew open. Before I knew what was happening, I felt a sharp blow and pain at the top of my right cheek bone. I had been physically assaulted by a resident, with the hostel manager standing with her hands on her hips watching me being punched, before making a quick exit. It was my 7am alarm wake-up call for refusing to get up to go into work.

The incident of physical abuse was a massive shock during a stressful period in my life, knowing that my father was going to die soon. My pressure cooker meltdown started building up pressure once again, with unpredictable mood swings – smashing up my bedroom furniture, throwing hand cream across the wall and carpet due to frustration for not being allowed back to the home that I could see every day from the landing window. I moved all my furniture out of my bedroom onto the landing throwing my TV down the staircase due to anger and frustration for not being allowed back home.

I hid a kitchen knife under my mattress for self-harming by cutting myself to help release the anger and tension that had bottled up inside me slashing into my right thigh so no one could see that I had cut myself. Seeing the blood oozing out of my leg made me feel better, thinking that I was getting the bad toxins out of my body and a stress release.

***

Nell and Chloe: Nick did not decide to leave his home. This decision was made for him by social workers concerned about his parents. They had no legal authority to compel him to move into the hostel without consent. The arrangements for a supported housing placement such as this would have been planned after an assessment made under the National Health Service and Community Care Act 1990 (now repealed) and funded by the local authority. Nick should have signed a licence agreement with the hostel for the placement to be funded which he did not do. The social services department were not using a legal power to make a substitute decision based on what they thought was in Nick's best interests. Instead, Nick and his family experienced soft coercion or leverage; manoeuvred into accepting inappropriate services because more suitable services were not offered.

The decision to place Nick in the hostel was a decision made about Nick. Even though the decision to provide care to Nick was a decision to deliver care for a disabled person, it is not clear whose interests were really being taken into account. Although Nick's parents agreed that Nick needed to move out of the house, they were uncomfortable that he continued to live so close by and that he was under strict instructions not to see them. Nick clearly felt compelled to agree with the arrangements the social worker had made. This is understandable, since the police were asked to escort him to his new address.

Nick and his family felt as if they had no control over where Nick was accommodated. Yet Nick had strong views on the kind of care he wanted. Nick's sisters, in particular his older sister Bernadette, had tried to help him express how he was feeling and get support from people who knew about autism. Bernadette wrote many letters on Nick's behalf to the social services department describing how the hostel Nick was placed in was not an appropriate setting for him. She also contacted autism charities to research autism specialist services which might be able to help. The following excerpt comes from notes made by his sister Bernadette when trying to help Nick explain how he was feeling:

> I feel rebellious because I am completely out of my routine.
> Scared I will not be like I used to be.
> I do not like myself.
> I hurt my cat and my Mum and then feel sorry. I do not know why I hurt them.[6]

Nick was able to communicate with his sister Bernadette that his distress behaviour was a response to the loss of control over his routine, and that he felt ashamed and unhappy when he hurt his cat and his Mum. These statements indicate Nick had some deep wishes: to have control over where he lived, to enjoy a stable routine and maintain relationships with his family. But Nick's family's attempts to support him were all rebuffed because his needs for autism-specific support had not, at this point, been identified by professionals. They were also told that Nick's need for routine and predictability did not demand 'special treatment' and that when Nick communicated his distress with anger and frustration he was simply being *manipulative*.

***

Nick: My family's voices and my voice had finally been listened to when the Crown Court Judge made the decision to make a court referral order to stay at a specialist unit for adults on the autistic spectrum that are going through the torment and trauma of distress behaviour meltdowns. My options were to spend another three weeks on remand in prison in Birmingham or to go back home again until my placement had been finalised. My social worker disapproved of the Court's decision to allow me to return home, saying I should have been remanded for another three weeks.

The idea of being remanded in prison for three weeks felt like eternity. One hour felt like one day being subjected to daily verbal abuse and physical threats from prison officers and inmates. I felt scared and intimidated sharing a cell with a complete stranger. I self-harmed cutting my left wrist with a razor blade out of view in the toilet cubicle. Should I terminate my life by cutting deeper had crossed my mind several times after enduring five months of turmoil at all three hostels.

The transition from my family home to the specialist unit was a gradual process. My family and I read through the Residential Therapeutic Campus brochure. A couple of days before my official sectioning and admittance I was shown around the unit I would be staying at. The Clinical Services Manager kindly made the 150-mile round day trip from my family home to see for myself the unit I would be staying at. I met and spoke to the nurses and was given a guided tour. All patients are allocated their own private bedroom with en-suite bathroom with a shower. At the hostels, I had to share the bathroom and toilets that were dirty, smelly and unhygienic.

Tuesday 21 June 2005: I was admitted to the unit under Section 3 of the Mental Health Act to a secure unit. Once my mood swings had stabilised, I was transferred to an open unit with fewer restrictions. My daily routine and structure returned. Engaging well with the nurses and patients, knowing what was going to happen a week in advance, lowered my anxiety levels immensely by following a weekly timetable. We were not cocooned all day inside the unit with regular interaction in public areas. Shopping, eating out, walking in the countryside and go-kart racing made the stay an uplifting experience. I felt a moment of sadness when I was fully discharged in January 2006 after the fun times I had with everyone at the unit.

I came out of my autistic shell after being discharged from the residential therapeutic unit with a new lease of life feeling newly born and rejuvenated. I was no longer stepping into my isolation SafeZone circle having the self-confidence to start engaging in public settings. My autistic shell had finally been broken away enabling me to achieve my personal goals in life. Going out on dates and getting into my first ever relationship was a huge confidence booster.

***

Nell and Chloe: Nick spent seven months at the specialist unit. Unlike the hostels where Nick had lived, he was not bullied and his specific needs were well understood and supported. It was structured and each day had a predictable routine. His medication was reviewed and he was taken off almost all the medication he had been taking. He was supported to learn new independent living skills. By the time he left, Nick describes being more independent than ever.

However, these gains came at a cost. Nick was deprived of his liberty and now holds a permanent criminal record as a result of the events leading up to his detention:

> ...we are all deeply distressed to learn that Nicky has been sent to Winson Green Prison following his appearance at the Magistrate's Court...We find it extremely disturbing and outrageous that Nicky is now being treated as a criminal when it is clear that his violent actions are due to his Asperger's and caused by the immense stress, huge levels of anxiety and frequent and sudden changes he has had to cope with over the last few months.[7]

Perhaps the most striking thing about Nick's story is how decisions which had far-reaching implications were made often under pressure, by officials who knew very little about Nick's life at that time or about the specific needs he had as a result of his autism. These decisions were reached by highly qualified professionals: social workers, housing officers, psychiatrists, working within systems which valued case management over empowering individuals.

It was an initial failure to listen to the voice of the disabled person and ensure that Nick's wishes were placed at the heart of the care-planning process that led to Nick's placement in a series of hostels where staff lacked the experience, training or time to support Nick effectively. The bullying and coercion Nick suffered was a consequence of this. This is not surprising. A large body of empirical evidence about coercion demonstrates that people often describe experiencing the highest degree of 'perceived coercion' when subject to informal coercion (Beck and Golowka, 1988; Monahan et al., 1995).

This was avoidable. Nick received excellent support in communicating his wishes and feelings from his sister and brother-in-law. This means we know from Nick's own accounts and the notes made by his family how Nick was feeling during his breakdown and what support Nick wanted. By the time the police, FMEs, AAs, duty solicitors, Crown Prosecution Service and others were involved, the freedom to reverse these earlier damaging decisions was over. The earlier opportunities to help Nick had been missed. It was only after conviction that Nick finally received the support he needed – at the price of a criminal record. If he had received the support he and his family had called for at the very beginning of these events, he would not have been left in the position he talks about in his story: unsupported, victimised and criminalised.

Nick's story demonstrates that effectively hearing people's voices can prevent these interventions having to be made within the CJS, at a significant cost to the individual's liberty and rights under Article 12 and 14 of the UN Convention on the Rights of Persons with Disabilities (CRPD). Article 14 CRPD prohibits depriving disabled people of their liberty on the basis of their impairment and the Committee's guidelines make clear that Nick's detention under the Mental Health Act was an abuse of human rights. Yet, whilst legally Nick's detention was wrong, it was ironically only at this point that Nick's voice was finally heard.

Although the judge in Nick's case ordered his detention, it was Nick who felt in control of the decision to accept treatment at the specialist unit. It is important to emphasise that not everyone who is detained by reason of their disability experiences positive treatment in this way. However, if we question Nick's decision to receive the treatment offered to him on this basis, are we not in effect undermining his capacity to make decisions, contrary to Article 12? What we should be questioning is why Nick only received the treatment he wanted when he had been detained for a criminal offence.

Nick's story demonstrates that solutions to violations of Article 14 may have their origins in Article 12, recognising the legal capacity of all disabled people. If someone is being deprived of their liberty because they are unhappy, or aggressive or frightened, is there a way to offer the individual support which includes their perspective? Even in coercive environments, such as psychiatric detention, individuals report feeling less coerced by care that maintains respect for their wishes and feelings than by care which excludes them from decision-making processes (Hoge et al., 1997; Katsokou et al., 2011).

In Nick's case, providing appropriate support that facilitated his participation in decision-making would have helped him to exercise that legal capacity. General support such as the provision of appropriate adults whilst in custody was simply not sufficient as it did not take into account his specific needs. Nick was ultimately barred from equal access to justice as he was unable to fully participate in the CJS; a right reaffirmed by Article 13. But, if Nick had been provided with tailored support appropriate to his needs he might not have been later detained contrary to Article 14.

There was never any question in Nick's story of his capacity to make decisions. The real question evident throughout his story is why this was never recognised by those who went on to make those decisions about him. Had Nick been allowed to exercise his capacity to make decisions about where to be treated in the first place, it is likely that his involvement in the CJS would have been avoided altogether. He need never have been in the position where he had to pay for his right to choose where to be treated at the cost of a criminal record.

Notes

1 In the UK, hostels provide supported accommodation for adults at risk of homelessness, or for adults with mental health needs or learning disabilities typically with support staff on site.
2 ABH is a criminal offence in England and Wales, contrary to s 47 of the Offences Against the Person Act 1861. Bodily harm is "any hurt or injury calculated to interfere with the health or comfort of the prosecutor. Such hurt or injury need not be permanent, but must ... be more than merely transient and trifling" (R v Donovan [1934] 25 CR App 1 R 1 CCA).
3 Force or Forensic Medical Examiners are now referred to as Appropriate Healthcare Professionals under the Police and Criminal Evidence Act 1984 Code C. They may attend police custody if a custody officer suspects a detainee is suffering from a physical injury or mental disorder (para 9.5 PACE Code C) and to conduct an assessment to determine whether they are fit to be interviewed or detained (para 12.3 PACE Code C).
4 The Police and Criminal Evidence Act 1984 Code of Practice C requires police officers to provide 'vulnerable' adults with an AA (para 3.15 PACE Code C). This can be a family member, social worker or volunteer (para 1.7 PACE Code C). AAs perform many functions including giving advice and assistance (para 3.18 PACE Code C) and observing when a detainee is cautioned or interviewed (paras 3.21 & 11.17 PACE Code C).
5 The Disclosure & Barring Service is a government agency in England and Wales which enables voluntary and paid employers to access applicants criminal records and which maintains a list of individuals barred from working with children and vulnerable adults. It is a legal requirement for employers in many sectors including child and adult care to seek disclosure of an applicant's criminal record before appointment, and it is a criminal offence for an employer to appoint a barred individual to certain roles or to fail to disclose evidence of abuse to the Disclosure and Barring Service.
6 Excerpt from notes made by Nick and his sister Bernadette on 06/09/2004.
7 Excerpt from letter sent by Nick's sister and brother-in-law on 14/05/2005.

Bibliography

Beck J, and Golowka E. (1988). A study of involuntary treatment in relation to Stone's 'thank you' theory. *Behavioral Sciences and the Law*, 6(4), pp. 559–566.

Hoge, S.K., Lidz, C.W., Eisenberg, M., Gardner, W., Monahan, J., Mulvey, E., Roth, L., and Bennett, N. (1997). Perceptions of coercion in the admission of voluntary and involuntary psychiatric patients. *International Journal of Law and Psychiatry*, 20(2), pp. 167–181.

Katsakou, C., Marougka, S., Garabette, J., Rost, F., Yeeles, K., & Priebe, S. (2011). Why do some voluntary patients feel coerced into hospitalisation? A mixed-methods study. *Psychiatry Research*, 187(1–2), pp. 275–282.

Monahan J. et al. (1995). Coercion and commitment: Understanding involuntary mental hospital admission. *International Journal of Law and Psychiatry*, 18(3), pp. 249–263.

5 Questions of criminal culpability and persons with disabilities

Amita Dhanda and Gábor Gombos

With greater freedom comes greater responsibility. This credo of liberal thought has been oft quoted in the context of disability rights ever since the United Nations Convention on the Rights of Persons with Disabilities (CRPD) recognised the legal capacity of persons with disabilities in all aspects of life and persons with disabilities and their representative organisations demanded that the right must be made available to all without exception. This assertion of universal application has been countered in several ways: by relying on the text of Article 12;[1] absence of express abolition of the institution of guardianship and the opening abyss of criminal culpability (Freeman et al., 2015).

This chapter is not aimed at deliberating on the presence and absence of universal legal capacity – a controversy which in our view General Comment No. 1 has already settled (Dhanda, 2016). Instead this chapter concentrates on the relationship between legal capacity and criminal culpability. Since Article 12(2) recognises the legal capacity of persons with disabilities on an equal basis with others, we begin this chapter by first inquiring into the relationship between legal capacity and culpability in non-disabled persons. We then ask whether the standards created for non-disabled persons can be applied as they are, or would they need to be customised for persons with disabilities. As the question of difference is not just to address the difference between the disabled and non-disabled but also extends to the differences between persons with disabilities, we next examine how the principles of universal design, accessibility and reasonable accommodation are integral to according a fair trial for persons with disabilities. Most expositions on criminal culpability operate on the presumption that in a criminal trial only one of the parties, whether the complainant or the accused, would be a person with disability. In this last section, we draw attention to the fair process requirements that need to be fulfilled when both complainant and accused are persons with disabilities. Failure to address this matter not only breaches the right to equality but could also result in disabled persons being played against each other.

Exceptions – exemptions to criminal culpability

As a general rule for criminal liability to be imposed, a wrongful act has to be accompanied with a wrongful intention. A wrongful act could *inter alia* happen without requisite intention; by mistake, in necessity, or due to grave and sudden provocation. The absence of the requisite wrongful intention either exempts the wrongdoer from criminal liability or reduces the extent of liability. These exemptions or exceptions are available for all non-disabled persons. The fact that non-disabled persons possess legal capacity does not deny them the benefit of these exceptions. The diktat of equality would ensure that these exceptions are also available to persons with disabilities. In contradistinction to these general principles of criminal liability, there is the special defence of insanity which exempts from criminal liability those persons who commit wrongful acts due to the unsoundness of their mind. For the defence to be available such unsoundness of mind is required to subsist at the time of the offence and be of the kind which is legislatively specified. The continuance of this defence, it is contended, shall be endangered if universal legal capacity with support is insisted upon (Freeman et al., 2015). The acceptance of the defence may result in acquittal but such acquittal in innumerable jurisdictions causes the acquitted to be detained in safe custody for indefinite duration. That the defence provides questionable protection can be surmised from the fact that it was largely pleaded in cases where the accused was charged with an offence which was punishable with death (Dhanda, 2000). Even a failed insanity defence plea has often resulted in commutation of the death sentence in countries which retained the death penalty. The defence has been in and out of the statute book in several jurisdictions;[2] even where retained, the defence has progressively gone into disuse with the abolition of the death penalty (Hathway, 2009). In such a situation to refer to the defence of insanity as a protection seems a misnomer. This is the reason why despite its many failings, Perlin (1996, 2017) takes issue with recommendations for the abolition of the defence of insanity. The defence, he holds, is still the best chance for persons with psychosocial and intellectual disabilities to obtain a fair deal from the criminal justice system. In making this argument, Perlin is not considering the stigma accompanying the defence and the manner in which its continuance hardens the barriers confronting universal legal capacity. This stigma and its impact on full personhood drives Minkowitz's (2014) argument on abolition. Significantly, neither Perlin nor Minkowitz believe that just retention or abolition would resolve matters. The retention or abolition need to be accompanied with other reforms in criminal justice to protect the human rights of persons with disabilities in the criminal justice process. We are more interested in those reforms and how they would protect the interests of persons with intellectual and psychosocial disabilities. We understand Perlin's concern but are of the view that gradualist gestures are not suitable for affecting paradigm shifts. To that limited extent and as part of a larger criminal justice reform we would advocate abolition of the defence of the insanity. To usher that reform, we would tread the path of equality and non-discrimination.

The right to equality would require that persons with disabilities are treated similarly to and yet not the same as non-disabled persons. This would mean that they are treated the same where possible and differently when needed. Difference in mind or body is not a ground to discriminate; but wherever it exists, it provides a reason to accommodate. And failure to provide reasonable accommodation according to the CRPD is discrimination on the basis of disability. The leading question then is what is reasonable? Dhanda (2017) in her exposition before the CRPD Treaty Body contended that the Committee on the Rights of Persons with Disabilities (the Committee) should find every strategy of inclusion to be reasonable, even when only one individual person with disability needs it (Stinneford, 2012). Further, procedures devised for non-disabled persons cannot be described as inclusive because persons with disabilities manage to make do with them. The exclusion experienced by disabled persons needs to be acknowledged and compensated in such a way as to effect inclusion. Any intervention which stops short of providing fair process to persons with disabilities would be unreasonable. The absence of appropriate education and training could result in wrongful, even criminal, conduct. When that happens, it is our contention that this failure of the State and its instrumentalities should be taken into account whilst determining culpability and meting out punishment to persons with disabilities. Only when such deficiencies in service provision are taken note of, can it be said that a fair trial was being provided to person with disabilities.[3]

The need to forge a connection between poor health and education services and criminal culpability is also needed because modern criminal law, unlike the traditional one, has increasingly ousted wrongful intention from the calculation of culpability. With the increasing use of the principle of strict liability, simply doing a wrongful act invites criminal liability. Without entering into a discussion on the desirability of these developments in criminal jurisprudence, we wish to point out that this model of criminal culpability relies upon social conditioning to curb wrongful conduct. Education is a major mode of inculcating such like conditioning. The denial of education or appropriate education is thus depriving a community of people to participate and interact with other people in the community. Or if such participation is allowed, within a minefield of strict liability offences, criminal law could be the new pathway to the exclusion of persons with disabilities. In order to create a level playing field for persons with disabilities, it is important that the differences in life opportunities between disabled and non-disabled people are taken note of in determining culpability. Failure to do so would be discriminating on the basis of disability, which has been rendered impermissible by the CRPD.

In elaborating on how criminal justice systems should be disability inclusive we have chosen to discuss criminal culpability and not criminal responsibility. The ascription of responsibility is not necessarily blameworthy. A person can be held responsible for not just the bad but also the good they do.[4] In comparison, to be found culpable is to be blamed for wrongdoing. A person can be held responsible without being found culpable. When should an action invite blame and when not are decisions which each society arrives at, keeping in view its own social exigencies. Such a classification of blameworthiness and exculpation exists for non-disabled people; a similar regime needs to be created for persons with disabilities. Whilst the grounds of exculpation may be similar; the justificatory element may draw from the lived lives of persons with disabilities. It would also be necessary to consider whether there is need to draw an additional list of mitigating factors keeping in view the stigma faced and exclusion experienced by persons with disabilities. Again though the grounds may be included due to persons with disabilities, their application should not be limited to them and may be extended to anyone to whose narrative of crime it may apply. Such distinctions need to be introduced because as Stinneford (2012) correctly contends, criminal law does not only regulate; it pours moral condemnation on the offender in the name of the community.

In this part of the chapter, we have pointed out how exemptions, exculpations and commutation are an integral part of criminal law jurisprudence. These complex patterns of culpability and exoneration bring home that societies do not handle wrongdoing only with punishment. Forgiveness, deferred punishment and acknowledging mitigating circumstances are all part of the package (Nussbaum, 2016). In comparison, the defence of insanity has operated as a zero-sum game, which disadvantages both the people to whom it was extended and the ones who were found to be not covered by it. The ones to whom the defence was found to apply, were in several jurisdictions subjected to the dangers of the near indefinite post-acquittal detention. And persons who were found to be not covered by the defence were left to fend for themselves with no organised support from the system (Hathway, 2009). We propose that the criminal justice system should acknowledge the difference of disability without breaching the right to equality and non-discrimination.

The comparison between non-disabled and disabled persons shows that the exemption regime created for non-disabled persons cannot simply be extended to persons with disabilities. In the next part it is our contention that keeping in view the wide diversity subsisting within disability, this disability inclusive exemption regime cannot be monolithic. The nature of that diversity and the various ways in which it has been normatively acknowledged shall be discussed in the next part.

Making room for the diversity in disability

The CRPD does not contain a definition of disability. Instead its preamble recognises that disability is an evolving concept which encapsulates a wide range of human diversity. The stated purpose of the CRPD is to promote, protect and ensure the full and equal enjoyment of all human rights by all persons with disabilities. The expansive nature of the protection is further underscored in Article 1. It states that persons with disabilities include 'those who have physical, mental, intellectual and sensory impairments which in interaction with various barriers may prevent their full and effective participation on an equal basis with others'. We recount the CRPD's declarations on diversity to highlight how the drafters of the Convention did not consider one size to fit all. Also, in Article 2 with denial of reasonable accommodation being characterised as discrimination on the basis of disability, a real effort was made to ensure that no one was left behind.

This commitment to diversity would need to be remembered at each point as the cross-cutting impact of the right to equality and non-discrimination is realised in all aspects of life. Amartya Sen (1995, 1997) in his seminal piece on equality had stressed that the right to equality has to be understood operationally. It is necessary to ask: 'equality of what?' In the context of criminal culpability, the CRPD's commitment to equality would require that all persons with disabilities, whether as complainants, accused or witnesses obtain a fair deal be it in investigation, trial or sentencing. In the first place, all of these systems need to make room for the modes and formats of communication used by persons with disabilities so that their voice is not muffled or silenced at any time. It is the principle of participation which is critical and not the technological medium through which it is undertaken that should be determinative. For example, whilst some persons with disabilities may have access to technologically sophisticated means of communication, others may be making do with more rudimentary methods. Even as every effort may be made to provide persons with disabilities with the technological aid that helps their maximum participation, the absence of the aid should not cause loss of participation. The critical question at all times should be how a person with disabilities can be accorded a hearing and not whether a particular means or method of communication is or is not available. We stress upon this difference in recognition of the fact that all countries are not at the same level of development and to name any one mode or means of communication, could result in exclusion even though the intention was to include. Thus, for example to provide for digital communication or information through Braille to an uneducated blind person who prefers to communicate through a personal assistant could result in exclusion. Just as not providing for a sign-language interpreter for a person with hearing impairment could be exclusionary, if the person with disability communicates through that medium. The need to ensure communication and participation should prevail each time. We make this point drawing analogically from Amartya Sen's exposition on relative and absolute poverty. Relative poverty is primarily seen as a comparison in commodities. Thus a person in a small house begins to feel poor when a larger house is built near his humble abode. Absolute poverty on the other hand is the absence of any kind of home or shelter. Sen (2001) speaks of situations where relative poverty in terms of commodities could result in absolute poverty in terms of capabilities. For example, when the standard of living in a society rises, then the same need may have to be fulfilled through a more expensive commodity. In such a society the denial of that upper end commodity would result in an absolute denial of the capability. We are making the same contention for persons with disabilities, only we are making it from both ends. We are seeking provision for the more sophisticated means of communication where needed and permission to use the more rudimentary one where required.

If customisation of modes, means, and formats of communication is one demand of fair process, then recognition of legal capacity with support is the other. Before the adoption of the CRPD, persons with mental, intellectual and developmental disabilities have been presumed to lack legal capacity which has resulted in: their trials being postponed if they were charged with crimes; their complaints being dismissed if they were complainants and their testimony being disbelieved if they were witnesses. In most jurisdictions, persons with the aforesaid impairments were not considered incapable by reason of the impairment alone. A conclusion of incapacity was reached if their impairment prevented them from performing a function essential to that context, thus for example a person with disability was considered incapable of standing trial if by reason of his or her disability they were unable to understand the nature of the charge, or instruct counsel, or put up a defence. However, since the impairment was the reason for the question of legal capacity to be raised at all, these provisions often worked to disqualify persons solely on the basis of their impairments, as once the fact of impairment was established, the dysfunctionality was presumed (Arstein-Kerslake et al., 2017).

With Article 12 of the CRPD recognising the legal capacity of persons with disabilities in all aspects of life and permitting the use of support without negating the use of legal capacity, these various provisions which allegedly protected by disqualifying are not endorsed by the CRPD. Instead the new paradigm requires that persons with disabilities should be allowed reasonable accommodation and provided support to participate in criminal justice proceedings whether as accused, complainant or witness. Information in plain language; non-confrontational cross-examination and mediated communication are some of the strategies, which have been permitted in some jurisdictions (Hepner et al., 2015). Efforts to prevent the participation of persons with intellectual disabilities and to treat them the same as children has been dispelled by the Indian Supreme Court who refused to accept specious 'mental age' arguments whereby the petitioner attempted to magnify the harm experienced by a young woman with cerebral palsy (*Eera through Manjula Krippendorf v Govt of NCT Delhi* (2017)).

We contended in the previous segment that the recognition of legal capacity requires impairment centric defences such as the defence of insanity to be abolished because they single out and discriminate. On similar reasoning, the prerequisites of criminal culpability (such as wrongful intention) and also the general defences have to be available to persons with disabilities on an equal basis with others. The demands of equality require persons with disabilities to be treated both same as the non-disabled and different. The plea for difference is compensatory in nature. We have contended that whilst determining criminal culpability, the failure to provide education and training to persons with disabilities and also other opportunities of capability development should be taken into account as mitigating factors (Hull, 1999). In this part, we have continued with the theme of sameness and difference by asking that persons with disabilities should have the right to participate in the criminal justice system on an equal basis with others, but this participation should be provided in such manner that it ensures real and not notional participation. Denial of appropriate means of communication or deprivation of legal capacity would be both impermissible.

In the first part of this chapter, the theme of equal basis with others was drawn upon to seek parity between the disabled and the non-disabled; in the second part we were pleading for customised opportunities to all persons with disabilities and in the last section we wish to address the *inter se* relations between persons with disabilities.

Criminal culpability when conflict arises within the disability community

This chapter has until now proceeded on this presumption that questions of criminal culpability of persons with disabilities shall arise only when one of the parties is a person with disability. This presumption arises from the belief that persons with disabilities are seeking entry into mainstream non-disabled society. As a result, conflict would arise between persons with disabilities and non-disabled persons. That disputes could arise between persons with disabilities is not envisaged, possibly because from the outside, the world of the disabled looks like one unvariegated whole. We have already discussed the diversity of impairments in the previous section, to which we can add the differences of race, gender, class, sexual orientation, region, and religion. These varied intersections could be fertile ground for both collaboration and conflict. This vast combine has huge possibilities of enhancing social capital; however, that is not the concern of this chapter. Insofar as we are concerned with the doing of criminal wrongs, in this part we concern ourselves with conflict between persons with disabilities. What should be the course of action when that happens? Should these *inter se* conflicts be treated differently from discords between disabled and non-disabled persons? The reason for asking this question is that when a person with a disability acts wrongfully against another person with a disability, he is often treated like a non-disabled person without support and without reasonable accommodation. We contend that such treatment of a person with a disability is also discrimination on basis of disability.

In order to explore the validity of our contention, it would be necessary to obtain information on how criminal disputes between the non-disabled are addressed. In the first instance victims or others are only obligated to report the perpetration of serious offences;[5] the duties of investigation, prosecution are the responsibility of the State. The complainant or victim can, if they so wish, supplement the prosecution efforts of the State if they so wish but the burden of obtaining accountability does not rest on the complainant or the victim. This quality of cognisability results in offences being prosecuted whenever discovered, whether or not the victim pursues the matter. Despite such evident leaning towards the victim, there are a range of principles which also look out for the accused. Amongst them are the presumption of innocence, the right to legal counsel, the right to a public hearing, and a reasoned judgment. We are aware of the fact that accused persons are not assured of these rights in all jurisdictions, but this is a normative analysis, not a realist one. Normatively, it is accepted that an accused should be accorded a fair trial before the deprivation of freedom. If such trial is not given and yet freedom is denied the unfairness of the process denudes it of legitimacy.

A fair trial is needed so that only the person who committed the offence is prosecuted and convicted for it. Since there is a social stake in nabbing the wrongdoer, often people are picked up before adequate verification. In the case of persons with disabilities, their vulnerability enhances the sense of outrage and hence greater urgency to book the wrongdoer. If this wrongdoer happens to be a person with disabilities, the granting of legal and personal support, reasonable accommodation, and inquiry into extenuating circumstances would take time. The desire for quick results, the need to reach out to the person with disabilities who is wronged, could cause cutting of corners. As vulnerability is the hallmark of disability to the non-disabled world, the person with a disability who is the alleged wrongdoer no longer seems vulnerable, which could result in a lower standard of proof, failure to provide reasonable accommodation and support and most importantly failing to inquire if there were any extenuating circumstances. As already stated, fair process requirements take note of the vulnerability of the accused in trials of the non-disabled accused, through the provision of legal protections including the presumption of innocence. This situational disadvantage along with the vulnerability of their impairment makes persons with disabilities who are accused of criminal wrongdoing doubly disadvantaged. It is important therefore that the fair process requirements of a trial involving persons with disabilities are expressly articulated. Failure to do so could cause their particular needs and vulnerabilities to be forgotten.

It has often been found that vulnerability is easier to accept in disadvantaged groups than excellence. The need to reduce these exceptional human beings to their vulnerability is often experienced and reported by the victims of racism, sexism, casteism, and ableism. Whilst the members of the marked view themselves as equal and hence entitled to equal respect and dignity, it is this respect and dignity that many members of the dominant group find more difficult to extend (Young, 2011). The demand for respect by one and the need to humiliate by the other creates a situation of endangerment for these persons with disabilities. Whilst challenging the prejudices of ableism they unwittingly get trapped by the self-same prejudices in being unable to seek the support and reasonable accommodation which is their due. Such support is not proactively extended by the prosecuting agencies as they wittingly or otherwise (maybe due to the wrongdoing) do not see the persons with disabilities as being in need of it. In order to minimise the dangers of the minefields of double consciousness, the need to extend such support and reasonable accommodation needs to be expressly stated. Double consciousness causes an excluded group to seek acceptance from the very community that is constantly serving it rejection (Hull, 1999). The desire to belong may cause a person with disabilities to be duped into serving the all-pervasive system of ableism. To protect all persons with disabilities from these ableist traps, it is important to expressly lay down the fair procedure standards to be followed in criminal proceedings involving persons with disabilities.

Conclusion

MacKinnon was once asked that if she was given an opportunity to feminise legal education, how would she go about it? Her response can be analogically extended to the inclusion projects of several disenfranchised groups. She would not, MacKinnon (1989) asserted, add women and stir. In this chapter, we have made a similar case in relation to persons with disabilities. We reject the add disability and stir approach. Instead, we ask that that both the normative and administrative regimes of the criminal justice system are re-examined and both questions of culpability and fair procedure re-designed keeping in mind the lived experience of persons with disabilities. Such first principles thinking is needed if persons with disabilities are not to be excluded a second-time round.

In undertaking this first principles thinking, the insights obtained in promoting inclusive education could be of some use. Educationists distinguish between segregation, integration and inclusion. This classification used by educationists also assumes relevance in the administration of the criminal justice procedure. The defence of insanity and the special procedures for the trials of "persons of unsound mind" exemplifies segregation. As both procedures single out persons with a psychosocial disability and treat them as distinct and different from other members of the populace. There are several accused persons that are unable to meaningfully participate in the criminal justice system due to illiteracy, poverty, not knowing the administrative language and so on. If these psychosocial factors are addressed as a whole, then sustainable support can be devised without pushing people out of the system.

If segregation is problematic then so is forcible mainstreaming. The strategy here is to do away with all accommodations and make persons with disabilities unmarked members of the criminal justice system. The difficulty with this strategy is that it totally denies the particular needs of accessibility, communication, and capacity support that may be needed by persons with disabilities. It has been conceded that with all their limitations, special procedures do a better of job of focussing on the particular needs of persons with disabilities. Yet persons with disabilities pay the heavy cost of stigma, isolation and oblivion to obtain these benefits whose actual provision is largely uncertain.

With the adoption of the CRPD, the United Nations has unequivocally pronounced that disability rights are human rights. Persons with disabilities are thus integral members of the human populace. It is therefore necessary to redesign the criminal justice system in full acknowledgment of their participation. We have flagged communication, legal and social support, customising general procedures to special needs by applying the principle of reasonable accommodation. Each of these inclusion procedures may be of use to members of the populace other than people with impairments. It is this dimension of disability rights which makes them sustainable as they can be used by all as and when required. Such use is supported by the pluralistic evolving model of the CRPD. The enterprise of inducting disability rights in the CRPD should be so undertaken that it humanises the system for all.

Notes

1 The text of the article requires states to provide for support and in the safeguards mentioned in Article 12(4) envision that the measures to aid the exercise of legal capacity shall 'apply for the shortest time possible' be 'subject to regular review'. The inclusion of these phrases, they reason, points to the inclusion of guardianship, albeit in the rarest of rare cases.

2 The defence has been abolished in several US states. A major difference between those abolitions and the present is that at that point the defence was withdrawn to uphold security of the State; and now abolition is being demanded so that the respect and dignity due to persons with disabilities is not compromised. For a detailed recount of the American engagement with the defence of insanity see (Hathway, 2009).

3 In the VOICES workshop on Criminal Responsibility it was unanimously felt by all participants that the failure to provide appropriate education and training and reasonable accommodation needs to be taken into account whilst determining criminal culpability and quantum of punishment.

4 The importance of this distinction was brought home to us from the presentation made by Professor Bebhinn Donnelly Lazarev from Swansea University at the VOICES Workshop on Criminal Responsibility on 23 September 2016. [online] Available at: https://www.youtube.com/watch?v=jZjabbVh9Oo&index=2&list=PLvKS9kpe3SYMPN5IifTq67N3LNXW9rnVE&t=23s [Accessed 31 Jan. 2018].

5 The Indian Criminal Procedure Code places a duty on citizens to report whenever a cognisable crime is committed. This obligation also extends to the victim of a crime.

Bibliography

Arstein-Kerslake, A., Gooding, P., Andrews, L., McSherry, B., (2017). Human rights and unfitness to plead: the demands of the Convention on the Rights of Persons with Disabilities. *Human Rights Law Review*, 17(3), pp. 399–419.

Dhanda, A., (2000). *Legal order and mental disorder*. Thousand Oaks, CA: Sage Publications.

Dhanda, A., (2016). From duality to indivisibility: mental health care and human rights. *South African Journal on Human Rights*, 32(3), pp. 438–456.

Dhanda (2017). In a class of my own Reasonable accommodation from a disability perspective. Presentations by invited speakers of the day of general discussion on the right of persons with disabilities to equality and non-discrimination. [online] Available at: http://www.ohchr.org/Documents/HRBodies/CRPD/EqualityNonDiscrimination/presentations/AmitaDhanda_NalsarUniversity.pdf [Accessed 22 Jan. 2018].

Freeman, M.C., et al., (2015). Reversing hard won victories in the name of human rights: a critique of the General Comment on Article 12 of the UN Convention on the Rights of Persons with Disabilities. *The Lancet Psychiatry*, 2(9), pp. 844–850.

Hathway, M., (2009). The moral significance of the insanity defence comment. *The Journal of Criminal Law*, 73(4), pp. 310–317.

Hepner, I., Woodward, M.N., Stewart, J., (2015). Giving the vulnerable a voice in the criminal justice system: the use of intermediaries with individuals with intellectual disability. *Psychiatry, Psychology and Law*, 22(3), pp. 453–464.

Hull, B.A., (1999). *Double-consciousness: W.E.B. DuBois and Frederick Douglass*. Henderson, TN: Freed-Hardeman University.

MacKinnon, C., (1989). Feminism in legal education. *Legal Education Review*, 1(1), pp. 85–96.

Minkowitz, T., (2014). Rethinking criminal responsibility from a critical disability perspective: The abolition of insanity/incapacity acquittals and unfitness to plead, and beyond. *Griffith Law Review: Special Issue – Disability at the Peripheries*, 23(4), pp. 434–466.

Nussbaum, M.C., (2016). *Anger and Forgiveness: Resentment, Generosity, Justice*. New York: Oxford University Press.

Perlin, M.L., (1996 – 1997). The borderline which separated you from me: the insanity defence, the authoritarian spirit, the fear of faking, and the culture of punishment. *Iowa Law Review*, 82, pp. 1375–1426.

Perlin, M.L., (2017). God said to Abraham/kill me a son: why the insanity defence and the incompetency status are compatible with and required by the Convention on the Rights of Persons with Disabilities and basic principles of therapeutic jurisprudence. *American Criminal Law Review* 54, pp. 477–520.

Sen, A., (1995). *Inequality Reexamined*. New York: Russell Sage Foundation and Clarendon Press.

Sen, A., (1997). *Choice, Welfare, and Measurement*. Cambridge, MA: Harvard University Press.

Sen, A., (2001). *Development as Freedom*. New York: Oxford University Press.

Stinneford, J.F., (2012). Punishment without culpability. *Journal of Criminal Law & Criminology*, 102(3), pp. 653–723.

Young, I.M., (2011). *Justice and the Politics of Difference*. Princeton, NJ: Princeton University Press.

6 Conclusion

Criminal responsibility

Anna Arstein-Kerslake

The recognition of a person with disability's criminal culpability on an equal basis with others is a particularly laden concept. This is largely due to the ever-pervasive prevalence of the charity model of disability. The charity model of disability views disability as a burden on society and something to be pitied. Those operating under this model view people with disability as deserving of charity. In the criminal justice system, we can see this model play out in the exclusion from criminal culpability on the basis of disability – for example, the insanity defence, and other similar legal mechanisms. Such laws view people with disability as incapable of understanding and controlling their own actions. As such, they must be looked upon with mercy and pity and we must not hold people with disability responsible for their actions in the same way that others are held responsible. This is a paternalistic, prejudiced, and discriminatory perspective of disability.

The reality of disability is much different from how a charity model presents it. Disability is varied. It is sometimes hidden. It is sometimes perceived to exist, when it actually does not. Its effects are unpredictable and as mysterious as the human personality or consciousness. Most importantly, it is merely an element of the human condition. The biology of our bodies and minds is unpredictable and diverse. Where our bodies or minds manifest a difference (or 'impairment') that runs up against socially constructed barriers, disability is created. This is the well-developed theory of the social model of disability, which holds that disability only exists because of a social world that is unwilling to bend and adapt to individual needs or the needs and desires of people with disability. Instead, it creates an artificial category of 'others' – people who do not fit exactly in to the structures that we have created; people with disability.

If disability is viewed from this social model perspective, it is no surprise that people with disability are overrepresented in the criminal justice system. As observed previously, prejudice and existing power structures play a large role in the modern penal system, and have done so for, arguably, their entire existence. If disability is a social construct emerging from disadvantage created by social barriers put in place by those in positions of power and privilege, it fits perfectly that the criminal justice system becomes the trap that people with disability end up in.

Social barriers, stigma, and prejudice are landing people with disability into criminal justice systems. The charity model's exculpation of people with disability from criminal culpability appears to be one, figurative, 'bone' thrown to people with disability that are entangled in such systems. It is quite clearly differential treatment – and treatment that amounts to inequality before the law, because people with disabilities are not respected as decision-makers on an equal basis with others. However, some would argue, the result is dismissal of punishment or partial punishment and dismissal of the burden of the criminal justice system. This, however, is a grave misperception, as is made evident by the work in this chapter. There is a worrying history of the criminal justice system maintaining and perpetuating marginalisation and contributing to the on-going social disadvantage of people with disability. Criminal law currently operates unequally, however excusing criminal culpability on the basis of disability may be exacerbating that inequality instead of mitigating it.

However, it must not be dismissed that people with disability continue to experience marginalisation and social barriers that often impact them greatly. There remains a lack of acceptance, understanding, and support when it comes to many disabilities – including Autism, as discussed in Nicholas' work. This may result in denial of the individual's rights, such as the right to liberty, the right to legal capacity, the right to reasonable accommodation – all of which were denied at different stages of Nicholas' experience. These denials, and the marginalisation that occurs alongside such denials, must be factored in to reform of the criminal justice system. As Amita and Gabor describe, the solution is not disability-specific exceptions to criminal culpability, it is exceptions to criminal culpability that are non-discriminatory, encompass a consideration of social disadvantage, and apply equally to all.

Part 2

Contractual capacity – inheritance, property and everyday decision making

7 Introduction to contractual capacity

Clíona de Bhailís

Contracts at their most basic level are about buying and selling either goods or services. The law regarding contracts is broadly developed through legislation and case law and, while no two legal systems are the same, there are common elements across jurisdictions including that most jurisdictions require of a certain level of cognitive ability to make a binding agreement. In this part of the book, we will read personal and professional perspectives from Kenya, Ireland, Bulgaria, the Czech Republic, and Australia. While a thorough examination of contract law and in particular contractual capacity and disability is beyond the scope of this chapter, it will clarify some basic elements so that the following chapters contributed by the pairs within the project are placed within the appropriate legal and human rights context.

Some of the stories in the following chapters deal with a contract on a basic or fundamental level while others deal with complex express terms. Some contracts are on the face of it simple transactions, for example buying a bus ticket, but come with a myriad of express and implied terms which make them more complex than any of us would consider when completing this often mundane task. Therefore, the ability to enter into valid and binding agreements impacts a person's ability to exercise a range of other rights guaranteed by the UN Convention on the Rights of Persons with Disabilities (CRPD) particularly her right to live independently and within the community under Article 19, her ability to participate in employment under Article 27 and potentially her right to personal mobility under Article 20, participation in cultural life, recreation and leisure under Article 30, and her right to health under Article 25.[1]

People with disabilities, in particular people with intellectual or cognitive disabilities, face a disproportionate level of discrimination and exclusion regarding entering into and exiting contracts. This can be in the form of formal or informal barriers. Informal barriers can be imposed by society, family, friends and supporters, as we will see in Chapter 7, by preventing a person with a disability from exercising any contracts in their daily lives through either restricting their access to money or preventing them from completing basic tasks or errands. Formal barriers to contract are restrictions on decision making in the form of plenary or partial guardianship and requirements for rationality and cognition imposed through the concepts such as an 'intentional meeting of minds' or mutual intention to create legal relations.[2]

As pointed out in Chapter 1, signing a contract amounts to an exercise of legal agency and because legal agency is just one element of the right to legal capacity, it is protected under Article 12 CRPD. Therefore, it is also a decision for which States are obligated to provide support. From this it can be surmised that to comply with Article 12, people with disabilities must be able to enter into and exit from contracts in the same ways as people without disabilities. For this to happen, the law of contract must recognise people with disabilities as legal actors with the intention to create legal relations. An essential part of this is ensuring that people have access to the appropriate supports and that third parties (those who they are contracting with) will be confident in entering into the agreement.

As we will see from the following chapters, the level and form of support an individual will require to complete a contract will vary depending on the individual. However, some commonly quoted examples of support include information on the terms in an accessible format, and the recognition of a trusted supporter as someone who can facilitate the completion of a binding agreement.

For some, particularly those with more complex support needs, the recognition of a trusted supporter will be key. Legal recognition of this support mechanism can provide certainty to the third party that he or she can enter into a binding agreement with an individual with a disability, which in turn ensures that people with disabilities are afforded the same opportunity to contract as people without disabilities, and also ensures that the person with a disability has their chosen and appropriate support available to them to examine the terms of the contract, for example the consequences of non-compliance or breach of contract for both parties.

As you read the stories and responses in this section it is important to not only look at, and learn from, the individual experiences – both the challenges and the triumphs – and the immediate solutions, but also to bear in mind the bigger picture: how can we ensure that people with disabilities are in a position to enter into and exit from contracts in the same was as people without disabilities? From this we must consider if this feat requires a radical overhaul of contract law as we know it. Or can it be achieved with minor adjustments to existing provisions? What role will other branches of law and equity play in this reform? Some would argue that disability-neutral solutions already exist for example, the concepts of unconscionable bargains, duress, and undue influence. Are these the best solutions?

Notes

1 In some countries, the document signed to indicate a person's consent to a medical procedure is a contract between the patient and the health service provider (Ruck Keene, 2016). Issues regarding consent to treatment are dealt with in Part 4 of this publication.

2 An intention to create legal relations is a fundamental element of contract law which operates on the basis of two strong rebuttable presumptions – that parties *do not* intend to create legal relations with regards to social and domestic agreements and that parties *do* intend to create legal relations with regards to commercial agreements. See for example, Chen-Wishart (2008).

Bibliography

Chen-Wishart, M. (2008) *Contract Law*. (New York, United States): Oxford University Press.

Ruck Keene, A. (2016). Re configuring contract law for purposes of the CRPD: a discussion paper. [online] Available at: http://www.mentalcapacitylawandpolicy.org.uk/wp-content/uploads/2016/11/Reconfiguring-contract-law-for-purposes-of-the-CRPD-Paper-Discussion-Paper-for-ERC-Voices-Workshop-November-2016.pdf [Accessed 31 Jan. 2018].

8 I have the strength to speak up for myself

Nikona nguvu ya kujiongelelea

Joy Rehema and Emer O'Shea[1]

This morning I woke in my apartment and decided to buy myself some new outfits. I purchased a beautiful long red dress and some new jeans with a top. As I walked around, I bought an ice-cream and then headed to Karate class. After class, I went for my driving lesson. I'm so excited that I will be able to get around independently. I just bought a new car and can't wait to collect it and show my friends. After a busy day, I headed home to quickly change into my new clothes before going to meet my friends. We went to a movie and then to a club where we danced the night away. We spent the night telling stories and laughing non-stop. It was so much fun. I'm so lucky to be able to choose what to do in my life, work in a job I love, earn enough money to buy myself new things and be surrounded by people who always support me and make me smile.

Sadly, that's not how I spent my day; that was a dream or maybe someone else's life story.

So now let me tell you the real story. My name is Joy, I was born in Nairobi and I'm in my early twenties. When I was young, probably around five, I was diagnosed with an intellectual disability and dyslexia. No-one ever actually explained this to me. It was just as I got older my mother said I never met my developmental goals when I was meant to, things like I started talking late for my age. I've no memory of having any tests done and I have never actually seen evidence of my diagnosis. I remember that I started in a mainstream school and was suddenly pulled out of my class. I was put in a special unit in the same grounds; it was very humiliating to be segregated. People called it "the dummy's class" just because you needed some help with things, they made jokes about me and I lost all my friends.

In the special unit, instead of giving me the help and support I needed to live independently, I was just labelled and left. I've never been recognised as a person with capabilities because of what was said when I was small and as I got older my family wouldn't bring me to have a disability assessment done. By getting the assessment I can get a disability card,[2] this card would help me to get the support I need to be an independent adult. I've been discriminated against all my life because of my intellectual disability and the stigma that's attached to having a disability in Kenya. I've felt excluded, scared, ignored, not good enough and let down, in my social world and by the formal systems that should have helped me.

Back as far as I can remember I've been treated differently from others, in every area of life. It's never felt as though this was for my own good. When I look at other people my age like my siblings I realise that my life has been very different from theirs. It's painful that they can go out when they want without getting permission, yet I can't leave the house without someone else's consent. While others in my family were encouraged and supported to do things or make choices, I was kept in doors to work, clean or prepare meals. I have been shouted at when things were not ready when others wanted them. I've even been physically hurt for not doing what others want. I get no opportunity to be a responsible adult. This is why I often feel sad, lonely and why I cry myself to sleep sometimes.

When I started school, l was given learning tools like building blocks, similar to everyone else, including my younger sister. As we got older, my sister was offered new learning opportunities in subjects like maths, chemistry and art among others but I remained playing with blocks until I finished school. In Kenya, you have to get a certificate when you leave school so you can get a job or go to college. I was not allowed to get my certificate because there is a written exam and the government would not give me any help to sit the exam because they saw no point when I have an intellectual disability.

So while others around me were beginning life as an adult, it was assumed that I never grew past being a child and was not capable of doing anything more with my life. Then I got the wonderful opportunity to join the training centre.[3] I finally got to try new things, I realised I enjoy beadwork and learning about human rights; I'm learning to speak up for myself and for my rights as a self-advocate. Now I know I'm good at things. I wish that everyone else could see that I have many skills. It's hard to show them who I really am though as they don't think I can do things as well as them or that I can understand things and have opinions. I'm always expected to accept what others decide is best for me.

Until I joined the training centre, I felt left behind in life. Growing up, I watched as my little sister was given money to go out or buy things like new clothes for herself yet I never picked out my own clothes or bought something outside of what I was told to get. My mother shopped for me and I often dreamed of the type of things I would actually like to wear; I think I would have a very different wardrobe. But it's not just my mother buying things for me that has been problematic. When I go to a shop to buy something, even just a carton of milk, I can be seen as someone to take advantage of. On several occasions, I've been given the wrong change by shopkeepers who are aware that I have a disability. This has created problems at home and it's very upsetting that people feel it is ok to steal from me.

Having little access to my own money has created many difficulties and stops my freedom to go places, to live outside my family home and to access supports like paying for a disability assessment myself. I really want to get a job so I can change my situation but no-one will hire me. In 2012, I tried to get some practical experience by joining an employment programme. I started a placement at a salon with an agreed wage and was very excited to learn. The salon owner had a child with a disability, so I thought she would be supportive, but she wasn't, and she didn't want to teach me anything. I worked long hours, often until late, which caused issues for me getting home safely. I wasn't given any wages, I was asked to buy things from my own money which was to benefit my placement and was to be reimbursed but nothing ever happened and they kept the money anyway. Another girl with an intellectual disability also worked there who was treated the same as me, but the other staff were not. I decided I didn't want to work there anymore because it wasn't helping me and I felt really bad going there. My centre tried to speak to the lady on my behalf about the money I was owed, but she wouldn't reply, so I got nothing. Looking back, I realise the owner completely abused her power and took advantage of my disability.

What little money I receive directly through the training centre or other means such as gifts, I have rarely kept for myself or got to decide how to spend it. On some occasions, members of my family have taken money without my consent and people have even emptied my bag out on the floor to take my money. I watch my sister having the freedom to pick a job to earn her own money. I see her experiencing life in such a beautiful way because of her freedom. It makes me feel bad that, whenever I can get a little bit of money myself, it has to go towards house funds, yet others can keep their money and decide what to do with it. Sometimes I don't see what the value is in having money when it feels like I have no choice about how to spend it anyway.

I thought if I got a bank account I could keep my money safe, but I didn't know how to set up an account on my own and so I asked the training centre staff to help me. This was not easy as I did not have my own documents for identification because even though I'm an adult my family hold all documentation relating to me. When I looked for these documents, my family said they wanted control of the account with access to the pin number if they were going to help me. This was the reason I wanted my own account, so no-one else could make all the decisions around my money anymore. Eventually, after my centre spoke to the bank, they agreed to let me open the account with a copy of my identity card. A support person from the centre comes to the bank whenever I want to withdraw money so it's safe. It's sad I had so much trouble getting my own account and it really upsets me that my family and other people don't treat me with respect.

The bank account is not the only process that was difficult to overcome. I dream of having the freedom to choose when to leave my house and of where to go without seeking permission. Because don't have choice, I was very happy when I was invited to Ireland for the ERC VOICES Project. I didn't realise that it would be so hard to get a passport to travel. To apply I had to get documents like my original birth certificate and a copy of my parents' identity cards. My family didn't want me to have a passport and it took time to convince them that like everyone else I am entitled to this document. Eventually they agreed to give me the information I needed but would not bring me to get the application or pay the fees so again I got help from the training centre. The forms were not very accommodating towards someone with intellectual disabilities so they helped me to complete them and also helped pay the fees. Even after getting my passport my mother wasn't going to give me permission to travel to Ireland and as I live under her roof I have little choice but to do as I am told. When I finally got consent my family assumed I would return from Ireland with money for them. When I returned with nothing they mocked me and didn't believe I went away which was hurtful. But it's not just international travel I have problems with; the local transport services do not understand disability and I get no support when I use them which makes independent mobility very difficult.

I believe in the saying "Pamoja na haki kuna majukumu. Ukiweka bidii utapata mazao, usipoweka bidii hautapata mazao." (With rights come responsibilities. If you put your effort in it will yield fruit; if you don't put any effort in you get nothing.) I try to live by this, but to get people to see I have rights is not easy and I am capable of understanding things and making decisions. Every little step towards independence, choice and legal recognition has been hard but I keep putting effort in. As a self-advocate, I now go to schools to talk to children with disabilities and their parents about how important it is to change how people with disabilities are treated. I can show them that we are smart and like everyone else sometimes we need help, but with the right supports we can exercise our rights on an equal basis with others.

For the first time ever in this year's Kenyan elections, I was able to vote to make a better future. I wasn't allowed to vote in the last elections but Kenya has now changed the system to make it accessible for people with disabilities to participate. I had to register with the commission beforehand and needed the training centre staff's help to do this. They also explained the voting process. The voting experience was beautiful. I woke early to join the queue of people. I didn't have many barriers at the polling station because of all the changes that were made through representatives of people with disabilities talking to the government beforehand.[4] I had to bring an identification document with me and if I had a disability card I could have moved to the front of the queue. I'm happy that I'm now able to give an opinion and be recognised to have capacity at a legal level in my own society.

Since joining this project, many changes have begun in my life. My family are slowly changing how they treat me. Although sometimes they still return to old ways of restricting what I do or saying mean things; now I ask why they are not nice to me because I don't like it and don't want to always feel stress. "Ukiwa na stress utapata magonjwa ya akili, kwa hio kaa mbali na stress." (With stress you will get mental illness, so stay away from stress). I now dare to hope that things will keep changing for the better since my mother didn't want me to join the project at the start but agreed after much persuasion and my sister is now volunteering at my training centre. I got consent to attend meetings and represent other persons with intellectual disabilities in Kenya through the centre. I now realise that people want to listen to me and that I deserve a better life. This is helping me find the strength to speak up for myself and fight for it. I no longer cry all the time and believe that I'm not as good as everyone else; instead I've started to laugh at problems and smile at those who cannot see me for who I really am.

I feel really happy about these changes. It's hard to put into words how important it is for me to be able to decide what to eat, what clothes to wear, who to spend time with or to deal with things that have a legal impact on my own life, as these are rights that many other people have already. It's very painful not to have any privacy and things of my own or not to be able to make choices about my own life. I want people to see me, not as a diagnosis or a burden and not as less than them, just as Joy.

***

My name is Emer, I'm from Ireland. While working with Joy on this project, we discussed what I was doing at Joy's age and I realised how different my experiences were. I got a job in retail when I left school and saved money to journey abroad. I had the freedom to travel to several countries with my sister and some friends. When I returned home from travelling, I got another job, moved in with friends in a rented property and went out whenever or wherever I wanted.

No two life experiences will ever be completely equal but it's a disturbing realisation that some people are not even being recognised before law or society as an individual human being.

By sharing this story, Joy has illustrated how a person's life is affected when they aren't given the opportunities which many take for granted, to exercise personal autonomy like choosing a place to live, and recognition of legal capacity by entering into a contract, no matter how small this may be. Society, government policies and the country's laws all affect the fundamental rights of persons with disabilities. Equality cannot be obtained without recognition of the individual's legal capacity and the provision of supports to exercise capacity in every aspect of life. Until things are changed to empower and support every person to exercise these rights, people that are in a situation such as Joy's will continue to face discrimination, oppression and abuse.

The aspects of Joy's life which she chose to share clearly highlight the need for a review of both the legal and societal attitudes towards persons with disabilities. Continuously people are required to enter into agreements of a legal nature both small and large, from purchasing products, opening bank accounts to obtaining documents of identification. Without legal recognition, a person suffers a 'civil death' wherein they are seen as an object not capable of participating in choices which affect their own lives (Quinn, 2015). Article 12 of the Convention on the Rights of Persons with Disabilities (2006) (CRPD), recognises the importance of equality before law in order to ensure the inherent rights of every individual is upheld. In 2008, Kenya ratified the CRPD. Under Article 2(6) of the Constitution of Kenya (2010), "any treaty or convention ratified by Kenya shall form part of the law of Kenya." Yet from Joy's experiences there seems to be some gaps between the Constitution, the national laws and society's attitude. Research has also shown that "people with intellectual disabilities experience greater restrictions, limitations and denial of their right to make decisions for themselves" (Mental Disability Advocacy Centre 2014, p. 1). Speaking to Joy, there are many areas of her life, both in everyday living and legal issues, where better supports could have been put in place.

From the beginning, Joy's story portrays the lack of inclusion that she's felt in her own life and the decisions which have affected it. To have doctors, teachers and family members discuss someone's capabilities, needs and future, without conversing with the person themselves, goes completely against a person-centred approach (O'Brien and Lovett, 2003). To also then be removed from a familiar class, segregated and mocked by former friends without understanding why this happened, would make the situation even more inconceivable, but this is what Joy experienced. Article 17 of the CRPD declares the integrity of a person should be protected. Article 24 recognises the right to inclusive education, yet without appropriate support within an inclusive school, these rights cannot be realised. After discussing this, Joy suggested that when a child is diagnosed with a disability the government should educate the family and advise what supports, services or documents are available that would benefit the child. By supporting the families to take positive action from the beginning, a person is more likely to have access to vital services or documents that will allow them to integrate into their community. This may also reduce the negative stigma that can be associated with disability.

Section 18 of the Kenyan *Persons with Disability Act 2003*, states that those with disabilities will receive formal education and be supported to complete exams. However, this legislation also still supports segregated education for people with disabilities under Section 18(3) which states 'Special schools and institutions, especially for the deaf, the blind and the mentally retarded, shall be established to cater for formal education, skills development and self-reliance'. It's within this segregated setting that people such as Joy are vulnerable to receiving substandard education which does not translate to equal recognition in law. Article 24 of the CRPD, notes that States should provide inclusive education systems that allow for lifelong learning, not merely when they first enter the education system. Unfortunately, despite education being an inherent human right, anyone who experiences educational exclusion as Joy did, will not be able to proceed to further education in the mainstream system.

Joy continuously displays enthusiasm to join the work force, earn an income, and contribute to her society. The Kenyan government has attempted to promote non-discrimination in the area of employment through Section 54(2) of the Constitution which declares that a percentage of all elective and appointive bodies should be made up of people with a disability. However Joy's experiences on the employment programme suggest that equal employment opportunities are not promoted at grassroots level as her employer showed prejudice and took advantage of Joy. By effectively obtaining equal access to the employment market, a person's life course projects towards a productive life, independent living and an increase of self-esteem and dignity (Gichuhi, 2014). Yet how are persons with disabilities meant to enter a sustainable job market when they receive a lower level of education and are not taught any professional skills? Perhaps the employment programme may have worked more efficiently if there were guidelines for employers, scheduled supervision meetings with the employer and Joy during the programme and direct payment of agreed wages to Joy's account so any disparity in wages are evident. In addition to a lack of education, a study by Opoku et al. (2017) found that other barriers to inclusion in the Kenyan employment market exist. Negative attitudes and perceptions of capacity, physical environmental barriers for instance access, ineffective legislation and inaccessible information on employment also contribute to this issue.

There is no consideration given to the additional direct and indirect costs of living with a disability as a contributing factor towards persons with disabilities disproportionately living in poverty (Devandas-Aguilar, 2016). Without a personal income, Joy's reliance on family for financial support places her within this risk of poverty. Supporting persons with disabilities to control their own financial affairs is a key commitment of Article 12, paragraph 5, of the CRPD; financial independence allows for independent choice like entering a property rental contract or in Joy's case freedom to finance a disability assessment and pay for her passport. In Kenya, the government has made moves towards financial support for persons with disabilities through the likes of the National Development Fund for persons who may require supports such as physical equipment but this does not provide any direct monetary support to the person. The UN Special Rapporteur notes that supports for persons with disabilities should encompasses a wide range of formal and informal interventions (Devandas-Aguilar, 2016). It also notes that for many, access to quality support is a necessary prerequisite for living and fully participating in their communities with choices equal to others. However, the fact that Kenya does not have a personal welfare support system for less advantaged parts of the population reduces independence and choice for many people. Relying on another to financially support you or having no access to money without another's consent also leaves people at risk of suffering neglect or of being under someone else's oppressive control.

The lack of documents officially stating her disability and support needs has made it more difficult for Joy to obtain her independence and exert her legal rights as an adult. This has resulted in difficulty accessing supports, informing people they need to explain things in a way she understands, or exercising her legal capacity to engage in contracts. As Joy stated, she is unable to apply for a disability card unless her family support her to go for an assessment, due to the financial costs involved and Joy may need help navigating the information required or the process. Although Joy is not under any formal guardianship or any other substituted decision-making order, she does not independently engage in the decisions and processes that impact her life socially or legally. While, in Kenya, people with intellectual disabilities are rarely put under formal guardianship[5], as a society it is generally regarded that while you live in the family home, you respect your parents' decisions and seek consent to engage in things outside the home, even as an adult. This de facto guardianship in families deprives a person with a disability of their ability to make choices and is an informal denial of the person's legal capacity (CRPD Committee, 2015, para. 23).

The lack of identification held by Joy herself and the lack of accessible information available on how to set up a bank account created a situation that left Joy no choice but to turn to the training centre for assistance, a support which others may not have available to them. It's important for organisations to realise that it can be society's intolerance of difference that creates the marginalisation of persons with disabilities (Oduor, 2016). Joy relayed that opening the bank account actually became one of the most positive experiences she has had when dealing with any form of authority. After the bank had engaged in disability awareness education through the training centre, she actually felt understood and supported by the person in the bank. It was unfortunate that the bank waited to be approached by the training centre rather than being proactive in developing its own awareness campaigns. If all services took time to educate staff on relaying information through different mediums and had easy read versions of information on their products or services it would promote a more inclusive and person-centred culture. Accurate and supportive explanations of information would also greatly reduce the risk of people signing legally binding forms or agreements that they do not properly understand.

Joy stated that obtaining a passport was a very difficult legal process to engage in. Despite being an adult and having the right for free movement protected by Article 18 of the CRPD, Joy had to get permission to get a passport. The application required information about the family which she didn't have and neither the application nor the information on how to complete it were available in an accessible format. Then, when Joy spoke to the immigration officer, they didn't know what an intellectual disability was and as they could not physically see a disability, they gave her no support at all. Several factors contributed to this negative experience for Joy. First, the lack of practical guidance for the staff on how to support a person with an intellectual disability and the lack of accessible information for this process created a barrier. Devandas-Aguilar's report (2016) indicates that many States do not allocate funding towards providing reasonable accommodation in relevant public institutions, which will only serve to prolong inequality. This raises the question of whether the State should provide additional funding to businesses and State agencies to educate staff and produce documentation in a variety of formats. This would ensure everyone could access all services they require like obtaining a passport. Lastly, the lack of recognition of Joy's legal capacity as an adult to obtain a passport and travel abroad without the consent of a parent once again reflects the informal denial of legal capacity that has been so prevalent throughout Joy's life.

In the area of elections, Kenya has clearly begun to genuinely recognise everyone's legal capacity, as the African Commission on Human and Peoples Rights were ahead of other regional bodies in addressing the exclusion of persons who were seen to be of 'unsound mind' from voting (Thuo, 2016). Under Section 3(1) of the Elections Act 2012 any adult citizen can exercise the right to vote.

The Elections (General) Regulations 2012 expands this to ensure no-one is excluded because of a disability. It states that reasonable accommodation must be made for people with a disability through supports. This may be through allowing a person with a disability to designate someone to assist them at a polling station or for those who cannot access the station for special reasons including disabilities, the commission may make provisions for the person to vote through election officials, observers. This is reflective of the positive experience that Joy had when voting recently. Further, the Kenyan Constitution Section 54(2) states that 5 per cent of elected representatives and public bodies should be persons with disabilities. However, Section 22(b) of the *Elections Act 2012* says in order to qualify for candidate nomination you must have a post-secondary school qualification. This stipulation would then actually prevent Joy or anyone else who experienced similar exclusion within the education system from becoming a nominee for election as a result of the State's failure to support them in school.

Joy has expressed determination and desire to embrace life, learn skills and participate in society. Yet despite this personal effort to succeed, it's clear that many external factors in her life are having a negative impact on attempts to achieve independence and full recognition of her legal capacity. These external barriers to equality are slowly being reduced and the CRPD is testament that external influences, self-advocates and international law, can impact on creating positive changes around the world.

The view that disability is a deficit and the person is the problem needs to be eradicated; we should instead identify and remove the socially constructed barriers that prevent persons with impairment from enjoying their human rights (Asia Pacific Forum, 2017). Without actively listening to personal experiences like Joy's and taking action, people with disabilities will continue to be marginalised and treated as less than equal throughout the world. Yet, by hearing and learning from the perspective of persons with disabilities, we can break down the barriers and recognition of every individual's legal capacity could be attained. As the former UN High Commissioner for Human Rights, Mary Robinson (2001) said 'Human rights are inscribed in the hearts of people; they were there long before lawmakers drafted their first proclamation.'

Notes

1 With special thanks to Fayel Haji and Elizabeth Kamundia for all their support throughout the project.

2 The Kenyan Persons with Disabilities Act 2003 requires the National Council for Persons with Disabilities to register persons with disabilities under section 7 (1)(c). Once registered, persons with disabilities are issued with a card that identifies them as persons with disabilities, i.e 'disability card'.

3 Kenya Association of the Intellectually Handicapped (KAIH).

4 United Disabled Persons of Kenya published their correspondence to political participants in relation to inclusive electoral reform, http://www.udpkenya.or.ke/pubs.php

5 The Mental Health Bill 2012 refers to people with "mental illness" in relation to guardianship laws not specifically people with an intellectual disability.

Bibliography

Asia Pacific Forum. (2017). *Human Rights and Disability: A Manual for National Human Rights Institutions.* [online] Available at: https://nhri.ohchr.org/EN/News/Documents/Human_Rights_and_Disability_Manual.pdf. [Accessed 19 Aug. 2017].

Committee on the Rights of Persons with Disabilities (2014). General Comment No. 1. Article 12: Equal Recognition Before the Law, UN Doc. No. CRPD/C/GC/1.

Committee on the Rights of Persons with Disabilities. (2015). *Concluding Observations in Relation to the Initial Report of Kenya* [online] Available at: http://tbinternet.ohchr.org/_layouts/treatybodyexternal/TBSearch.aspx?TreatyID=4&DocTypeID=5. [Accessed 5 Oct, 2017].

Devandas-Aguilar, C. (2016). *Report of the Special Rapporteur on the Rights of Persons with Disabilities.* [online] Available at http://www.un.org/ga/search/view_doc.asp?symbol=A/HRC/34/58. [Accessed 1 Dec. 2017].

Elder, B. C. (2015). Right to Inclusive Education for Students with Disabilities in Kenya. *Journal of International Special Needs Education*, 18(1), pp. 18–28.

Gichuhi, J. (2014). Disability and the Law: Assessing the Right of Persons with Disabilities to Employment in Kenya. *Kenya School of Law.* [online] Available at: http://www.kenyaschooloflaw.academia.edu/ [Accessed 25 Sept. 2017].

Kabutha Mugo, J. et al. (2010). *Testing Youth Transitions in Kenya: Are Young People with Disabilities Falling Through the Cracks?* Kenyatta University: Research Consortium on Educational Outcomes and Poverty.

Kamundia, E. (2012). Contemporary Housing Issues in a Changing Europe – Independent Living for People with Disabilities in Kenya: Charting the Way Forward. [online] Available at: www.nuigalway.ie/media/housinglawrightsandpolicy/Kamundia,-E-Independent-living-forpeople-with-disabilities-in-Kenya.doc. [Accessed 19 Aug. 2017].

Kamundia, E. (2016). The Right to Own and Manage Property and Finances by Persons with Psychosocial Disabilities in Kenya. *East African Law Journal*, Special Issue On Disability Rights, pp. 1–28.

Mental Disability Advocacy Center. (2014). *The Right to Legal Capacity in Kenya.* Budapest: Mental Disability Advocacy Center.

National Council for Persons With Disabilities. (2017). National Development Fund [online] Available at: ncpwd.wordpress.com/national-development fund for-persons-with-disabilities/ [Accessed 3 Sept. 2017].

O'Brien, J. and Lovett, H. (2003). *Finding A Way Toward Everyday Lives: The Contribution of Person Centered Planning.* Harrisburg, PA: Pennsylvania State Department of Public Welfare.

Oduor, R. (2016). Western Liberalism, African Communalism and the Quest for Adequate Ideological Foundation for the Recognition and the Protection of the Rights of Persons with Disabilities in Kenya. *East African Law Journal*, Special Issue On Disability Rights, pp. 29–49.

Opoku, M. P. et al. (2017). Access to employment in Kenya: the voices of persons with disabilities. *International Journal on Disability and Human Development*, 16(1), pp. 77–87.

Quinn, G. (2015). *From Civil Death to Civil Life – Perspectives on Supported Decision-Making for Persons with Disabilities.* [Presentation Talk], Tbilisi State University Georgia [online] Available at: https://www.nuigalway.ie/cdlp/documents/Tbilisi%20State%20University%20Talk%20GQfinal%20Dec%202015.pdf [Accessed 19 Jan. 2018].

Robinson, M. (2001). Speech at the Launch of the Global Initiative to End all Physical Punishment of Children. Geneva.

Stone-MacDonald, A. and Butera, G. (2014). *Cultural Beliefs and Attitudes about Disability in East Africa. Review of Disabilities Studies.* [online] Available at: http://www.rdsjournal.org/index.php/journal/article/viewFile/110/367. [Accessed 25 Sept. 2017].

Thuo, L. (2016). Implementation of political participation standards for persons with intellectual disabilities in Kenya. *Strathmore Law Journal*, 2(1), pp. 97–131.

9 Silenced, alone, powerless: My life as a Ward of Court in Ireland

Claire Hendrick and Donna McNamara

I grew up in Beaumont in Dublin, Ireland with my two brothers and mum and dad. My parents separated when I was 11. I was in a special class throughout school but I didn't know why. I was unaware that I had an intellectual disability until I was 23 years old. I found medical reports when I had to go through my mum's things when she had died. I was a little bit shocked but not surprised, I always had a feeling I was different from others but I do not think I have a disability and I don't call myself disabled.

When I finished school, I was my mum's full-time carer as she had a chronic illness. I was her carer for five years until she died in 2006. I came back from the shops one day and found her dead on the floor. The day mum died, my eldest brother came to the house to find my mum's will, which stated that both of my brothers should get €20,000 each and everything else was to be left to me, including the house. My two brothers promised me they would stick by what my mum wanted in the will. It went downhill from there as my mum hadn't signed the will. Three weeks after my mum died, my home was put up for sale against my wishes. I was left homeless. It took two or three years for the house to sell.

Our family solicitor made me a Ward of Court. He thought it was in my best interests at the time. The solicitor gave me a false impression of the benefits of it, saying I would be looked after. I had to go see a psychiatrist and psychologist about being assessed for being made Ward of Court. They check your mental abilities and said I was unable to look after my own affairs as I was vulnerable and still grieving for my mum. I was deemed incapable of looking after my own affairs. A lunatic in the eyes of the law.

On Christmas Eve in 2010, I became a Ward of Court. But I wasn't told about it until January because I rang the solicitor to ask for an update and he told me I had been made a Ward last month. After I was made a Ward of Court my life changed. All the decisions were made by the Office of the Ward of Court. After a while, my aunt and my cousin were allowed to make some decisions for me and they made up the Committee.[1] But, at first, all the decisions were made by workers in the Court office who didn't know me.

I couldn't have a relationship, go to the doctor or make decisions for myself. I didn't have access to my own money. I had a personal bank account for day-to-day spending, but the Court kept most of my money I inherited from the sale of my house. If I wanted to buy something for myself, I had to ask the Court for permission.

For my birthday, I wanted to buy a phone so I had to send details of the phone, the price, etc., to the Court and they took three weeks to reply to me. When I wanted to buy a pair of runners for €93, they said they were too expensive even though I loved them. If I wanted to go to the doctor, I had to let them know about it even though I have a medical card and do not need to pay to see a doctor. I still needed the permission of the Court Office before receiving any treatment. This caused problems for me because I need regular B12 injections every two weeks. If I had an accident and needed to see a doctor straight away, I'm not sure what I would have done. You must tell them everything in advance and they might not get back to you on time.

When I was a Ward, they were very strict about relationships. They carried out a full criminal background check on everyone I went out with. But how can you be in a relationship when the law doesn't let you?

During this time, I lived in Sophia Housing on Cork Street, on the south side of Dublin city centre. This is a supported housing service for people with alcohol issues, drug users and homeless people. I lived here for a year and a half. I wasn't happy living there; I wasn't eating and couldn't sleep. I wanted to live in my own house near my family on the north side of the city. At this stage, I was very unhappy and with the help of my aunt and cousin I went to the Court Office to ask if I could buy my own home with my money. I was told I couldn't because I was a Ward. They said I could move out of transitional housing and could move into rented accommodation. This was not easy though – how do you tell a landlord that you'll be getting the rent cheque from the High Court? How do you explain that? This made me feel like there was no point in me even existing – it just didn't make sense when it was my money but I couldn't access it.

I decided to challenge the Court office because I wanted to buy my own house. We had a meeting with my aunt and cousin and the support worker in the Court Office. I actually wanted to stay a Ward of Court because I wanted to be protected. If you own a home and have a disability, you are vulnerable. I was afraid someone would take advantage of me because I owned a house so I would have liked the protection of Wardship if something went wrong. They wouldn't agree to this though, so I decided in May 2012 to leave Wardship.

I got a solicitor to get out of Wardship. I ended up having to go back to the same psychologist and psychiatrist to get reassessed to confirm I was self-sufficient and no longer vulnerable. They said as long as I had legal support and help from my reliable family members I could leave the Ward of Court system. I got a phone call from my solicitor who told me that I would be released from Wardship on the 30 August 2012.

When I left Wardship, there were mixed views on what money I had left after the fees were taken out. I never knew it would be so expensive. It cost up to €20,000 in the end. That made it hard to look around for houses; I didn't have enough money for where I wanted to live near where I grew up with my family.

If I got the extra few quid from the Court I would've gotten a house I wanted. After much searching, I found a suitable house on the northside of the city. I went to the estate agent on my own the first time and had a look at a house. I said I needed to do this by myself. My cousin came with me the second time to see it and she told me to put an offer in and see what happens. We got a surveyor in and haggled with the estate agent so we got a good price. I never told them I had a disability. It was never an issue because I could pay in cash; I didn't need a mortgage so it was very straightforward.

My cousin came with me when I had to go to the solicitor to sign the deeds, get the keys and I made my own will to make sure it wouldn't happen again. My capacity was never questioned by the solicitor – it was the same firm that had helped me leave Wardship so they understood. They treated me like I was human. My cousin explained the contract for the sale of the home to me – she dealt with that because she understood it better.

The sale was finalised on Valentine's Day, February 2013, seven years after my mum died. I am now an independent member of society, managing my household and I have a childcare level 6 degree. I have a job, no mortgage and I'm doing what I love. My aunt and cousin still help me with big decisions when I ask them and we see each other regularly. No one else should ever have to go through Wardship again. Just because you have a disability does not make you any less human. You are a person with rights, but Wardship takes those away from you.

Now that I look back, Wardship is a disgrace. It is like mental torture. I was a prisoner. People are playing games with you every day. They take away your power, your power to make your own decisions. Living independently now with the support of my aunt and cousin is the best way for me. I would have preferred this all along and would have chosen this if I was offered it by the solicitor instead of being made a Ward. I'm now treated like a human being and I'm not a 'lunatic' any more.

***

Claire's story illustrates the legal barriers which arise for persons with disabilities who are subjected to guardianship and denied the right to make personal decisions. Claire's experience as a Ward of Court demonstrates how substitute decision-making regimes create a barrier to persons with disabilities from exercising their rights on an equal basis with others. Her transition from Wardship to independent living is an excellent example of how all persons, including persons with disabilities, can be supported to make decisions and enter into contracts. In 2007, Ireland became one of the first countries to sign the UN Convention on the Rights of Persons with Disabilities (CRPD), but at the time of writing remains one of the few countries yet to have ratified the treaty.[2] Ireland has yet to ratify the Convention but it is expected to take place in 2018, as such it is necessary to have regard to stories such as Claire's, to best realise the aims and objectives of the CRPD.

Guardianship law in Ireland

Article 12 of the CRPD requires States Parties to abolish all laws which permit substituted decision-making and replace them with supported decision-making alternatives (CRPD Committee, 2014, para. 28). One of the most common substituted decision-making models is guardianship, which is most commonly imposed by a Court to provide 'protection' for persons with disabilities (Dinerstein, 2012). In Ireland, the *Lunacy Regulation (Ireland) Act* 1871 introduced a complete substituted decision-making regime, known as Wardship, which deprived persons with disabilities (otherwise referred to as 'lunatics') of their fundamental human rights. This Act proved to be the ultimate barrier to Claire, as it prevented her from making decisions for herself in all circumstances.

A 'Ward' is defined in the Act as 'a person who has been declared to be of unsound mind and incapable of managing his person or property.' A status based assessment is undertaken to assess capacity which 'focuses on factors extraneous to the person, like having a disability of any kind, and assumes, without foundation, that incapacity is an inherent part of that status' (Keys, 2009). If an individual is deemed to lack capacity, they lose all subsequent rights to make all decisions for themselves. This understanding of capacity does not comply with the overarching principles endorsed within Article 3 of the CRPD, namely non-discrimination, respect for inherent dignity, personal autonomy and independence of persons (CRPD Committee, 2014, para. 4). Continued reliance on this approach further contradicts the guarantee provided under Article 12, which recognises that the legal capacity is an implicit component of the right to equal treatment before the law, which is a 'universal attribute inherent in all persons by virtue of their humanity and must be upheld for persons with disabilities on an equal basis with others' (CRPD Committee, 2014, para. 8).

In considering an application for Wardship, the High Court must also be satisfied that an individual is 'of unsound mind' and incapable of managing his or her affairs, as determined on the basis of medical evidence (Order 76 of the Rules of the Superior Courts, S.I. No. 15 of 1986). The Court must also be satisfied that it is necessary for the individual to be made a Ward for the protection of their person or property.[3] In Claire's case, she was advised that Wardship would be in her best interests as she had an intellectual disability and was unable to manage her share of the inheritance. While there are no legal impediments to a person with a disability inheriting property in Ireland, there is an increased possibility that the individual will be made a Ward following an inheritance (Lennon, 2014). This may be due to paternalistic or protectionist approach to disability, arising from the medical model of disability, which focuses on a person's impairment rather than the barriers imposed by society or the environment (Oliver, 1990).

There were no attempts made to explore alternative options before making the application for Wardship, such as providing bereavement counselling and offering supports such as how to manage finances, finding a home or how to apply for a job. Wardship was the only option considered and it resulted in the complete removal of Claire's human rights and independence. Usually an application for Wardship is initiated by a family member (Courts Service Ireland), but, in this case, the application was initiated by her family solicitor. This raises important ethical concerns and may contradict Article 13 of the CRPD, which provides a right of access to justice. Access to effective legal advice is an important component of ensuring access to justice (Flynn, 2015) and in this case it would have been preferable for Claire to have received independent advice in relation to her inheritance and to advise her on the implications of Wardship, which were not made fully clear to her at any point. The 1871 Act does not make it a requirement for a proposed Ward to receive legal advice, however a person can challenge the application in writing, and this is usually carried out by their solicitor (Office of the Wards of Court, 2003). This raises further concerns as Claire did not receive the necessary documents usually served on a Ward which outline their right to object and therefore, she missed her opportunity to challenge the application.

Being made a Ward is also very expensive; Claire was responsible for solicitor's fees, the costs of attending medical practitioners who assessed her mental capacity, and for annual fees from the Court Office. It is somewhat counterintuitive that an individual is expected to pay for their basic human rights to be taken from them, for the proposed purpose of being 'protected'. Furthermore, as a Ward, Claire was no longer entitled to access her money, which was invested and managed by the Office of the Ward of Court.[4] Due to the economic recession in Ireland in 2009–2010, Claire suffered a loss on the investment which subsequently made it difficult to find a home once she left Wardship. In total, the experience of being made a Ward resulted in a loss of €20,000; the likelihood of such costs was never outlined to her when she became a Ward. The management of Ward's funds has recently been criticised by Justice for Wards of Court, a group of representatives of persons under Wardship, who called for a judicial inquiry into the alleged misappropriation of funds (O'Brien, 2017; McLoughlin, 2017). However, it is unclear whether such a review will take place.

Contractual relationships

Claire's story demonstrates the conflict experienced by a person who has been made a Ward and the tension which arises between exercising one's personal free will against the discretion of the Court and the Committee of the Ward. Article 12 of the CRPD recognises all persons with disabilities are legal agents with the powers to make decisions with legal consequences, enter transactions and to create legal relationships (CRPD Committee, 2014, para. 12). However, traditionally persons with disabilities, especially those who have been admitted to guardianship, have been denied the opportunity to create and enter legal contracts. In keeping with the protectionist approach taken under the 1871 Act, a Ward is not entitled to enter into a legally binding contract without the permission of the Court.

The CRPD requires States Parties to put in place support structures to enable people to make their own decisions; such supports may differ depending on the needs of the individual in question. Article 12 does not specify the exact nature of what supports should be put in place, but it is recognised that supported decision-making arrangements are the most preferable including both formal and informal arrangements, of varying intensity depending on the circumstances involved (CRPD Committee, 2014, para. 17). Importantly, persons with disabilities must be allowed to decide the nature of the supports which should be provided, in accordance with their individual autonomy. If support is not requested or desired, the person's will and preferences must be respected. This is acknowledged in General Comment No. 1, which states that 'at all times, including in crisis situations, the individual autonomy and capacity of persons with disabilities to make decisions must be respected' (CRPD Committee, 2014, para. 18).

The nature of the contract will further dictate which supports should be put in place and they may vary depending on the nature of the contract in question. For example, a mobile phone contract which is only for two years' duration will require less extensive support than entering an agreement for the sale of a house – a contract that Claire fought to be able to sign as a Ward. In such cases, minimal supports were helpful for Claire to understand the terms of the contract and to be able to provide full and informed consent. In this regard, she relied upon her family members to support her and assist her, which is not unusual, as many people refer to their family or friends before making important decisions – this is not a support which is specific to persons with disabilities.

Claire was also unable to make straightforward decisions as a Ward. As she was not entitled to access her bank account, she repeatedly had to write to the Court for permission if she wanted to buy something, which compounded the difficulties faced by Claire. For example, if she wanted to purchase a pair of shoes for her birthday, she had to submit a request to the Court with a full explanation of why it was necessary and outlining the cost. If she wanted to purchase a mobile phone, the process became even more complicated as she would first have to receive permission to purchase the phone and second, it would have to be a pay-as-you-go phone as she could not enter a contract with any of the phone companies for a better smartphone.

For the purpose of Article 12, the most problematic element of Claire's story was her desire to remain in Wardship as she saw it as a means of protection. Claire tried to negotiate with the Court to be able to use her inheritance to purchase a home, while remaining a Ward of Court, but this was refused and she was advised that it was not possible for her to buy a home. Her main priority was to have more control over her life and most importantly, where she lived; but she was still hesitant about the lack of support and protection that would come from leaving Wardship. The cost of this 'protection', as she saw it, was the loss of all power and decision-making abilities over her own life, therefore she felt that it was worth taking the risk and decided to leave Wardship, with the support of her aunt and cousin.

Under the Ward of Court system, '[i]f a Ward has sufficient means, is able to reside in the community and does not have adequate or suitable accommodation, his or her funds can be used to purchase a house' (Office of the Wards of Court,

2003). It is unclear however if a Ward has ever been allowed to purchase property in Ireland and it would seem, following Claire's experience, that the Court has taken a protectionist stance in this regard as despite the published guidance referenced above, she was advised that it would not be possible to purchase a home.

Wardship is an indefinite order and there is no right to a regular review of one's status. To be released, a written request must be made to the Court by the Ward or by a solicitor on their behalf (Office of the Wards of Court, 2003). This will be followed by a medical assessment, to assess whether the individual is mentally capable of managing their affairs. Claire was advised to revisit the original psychiatrist and psychologist who had found her mentally incompetent in 2009, for her capacity to be reassessed. They determined that Claire was mentally competent and capable of managing her affairs, provided she received regular support from her family. While Claire had a positive relationship with her aunt and cousin, the lack of guidance regarding the nature of their support could have proved problematic in different circumstances as the law would look to her closest relatives as opposed to the people Claire would have wanted (her aunt and cousin). The requirement that Wards must be assessed by the same professionals demonstrates how arbitrary and subjective the process is. There is also no information available to explain how one can challenge this decision, or if such a right exists.

New legal framework

Supported decision-making has now been formally recognised by the Assisted Decision-Making (Capacity) Act 2015, which was introduced to facilitate Ireland's ratification of the CRPD.[5] This Act, when commenced, will introduce significant reforms in relation to decision-making. However, Wardship will not be abolished immediately; existing Wards will be reviewed within three years of the Act's commencement and will either be released (s. 55) or transferred into one of the other decision-making options provided under the Act (s. 49(2)(b) and 49(4)).

A presumption of capacity is contained in the Act and provides that capacity is always presumed unless the contrary can be shown (s. 8(2)). However, this inclusion is mitigated by the adoption of a functional test of capacity which is provided in section 3. A determination of incapacity will be made in circumstances when the individual is unable to understand the information relevant to the decision, to retain that information long enough to make a voluntary choice, to use or weigh that information as part of the process of making the decision, or to communicate his or her decision (whether by talking, writing, using sign language, assistive technology, or any other means) or, if the implementation of the decision requires the act of a third party, to communicate by any means with that third party. The inclusion of a functional test further violates Article 12 of the CRPD, as interpreted in the General Comment No. 1, which states that the functional test of capacity is flawed for two reasons – first, it is discriminatorily applied to persons with disabilities (CRPD Committee, 2014, para.15). The existence of disability-specific tests directly contradicts the ethos of the CRPD and the non-discrimination provision as provided in Article 2, as it specifically identifies the existence of disability as a ground to distinguish between persons. Second, the functional test also presumes to be able to accurately assess the intricacies of the human mind, and if an individual does not pass this assessment, their human rights are subsequently denied (CRPD Committee, 2014, para.15).

The 2015 Act also seeks in some limited ways to support persons with disabilities to exercise legal capacity and includes a principle of respect for 'will and preferences' inspired by Article 12. While this Act was not in force when Claire's capacity was questioned, it might have provided a more suitable solution to her situation. The Act recognises a form of supported decision-making, known as assisted decision-making, which is available for persons whose decision-making capacity is in question and allows them to enter into a decision-making assistance agreement (s. 10). This provision would allow individuals, including Claire, to nominate their chosen decision-making assistant(s) to provide support. This assistant may also ascertain the individuals' will and preferences in relation to a certain decision and can assist in communicating this decision (s. 14(c)). The inclusion of the will and preferences approach is a significant improvement and brings Irish law into closer alignment with Article 12. However, the law still contains substitute decision-making provisions (s. 38) and is therefore not fully compliant with the CRPD.

Final thoughts

There are a number of recommendations arising from Claire's story and her experience as a Ward. First, it is imperative that the Ward of Court system is abolished and the 1871 Act is repealed. While the 2015 Act has made significant reforms, Irish law remains non-compliant with Article 12 as interpreted by the CRPD Committee in General Comment 1, as it still retains a form of substituted decision-making through the continued reliance on Wardship and the use of decision-making representatives in section 38. In accordance with Article 12, substituted decision-making models should be replaced by supported decision-making arrangements, which will enable the individual concerned to exercise their right to legal capacity. This reform will require an extensive review of the supports in place to assist persons with disabilities to exercise their legal capacity.

For Claire, it is also important that people with disabilities can inherit property without difficulties or the risk of being exposed to Wardship. In light of Article 12(5), all appropriate steps must be taken to ensure that persons with disabilities have an equal right to own or inherit property. Appropriate supports should be made available to assist persons with disabilities to manage their finances and enter into contracts, such as a personal advocate service, which could be made available on a formal or informal basis to provide supports to persons with disabilities to enforce their rights and entitlements

(Flynn, 2013). The introduction of a service which provides supports such as accessible information, communication assistance and support for decision-making would also ensure the right of access to justice, which is provided for in Article 13.

Claire's story ultimately provides an insight into the barriers which exist for persons with disabilities with respect to inheriting a property, being made a Ward of Court and the process of exiting Wardship and purchasing your first property. For Claire, the overwhelming loss of control over the lives of persons with disabilities in Ireland is worrying; specifically, the extent of State control over the lives of people under Wardship. Now she has taken back control of her life, she has been able to enter into a relationship, go on holidays, start a college course, find a job and buy her first house. This story demonstrates that all persons can make decisions and we may all need a certain level of support to do so, but only if we choose to seek such supports. It also portrays the dangers of substituted decision-making and the need for persons with disabilities to have their legal capacity recognised and their will and preferences respected.

Notes

1 A Committee of the Ward may be appointed by the President of the High Court to act on behalf of the Ward. In most cases the Committee is made up of one person, but in Claire's case her aunt and cousin were appointed to this role to oversee her personal care on a day-to-day basis.

2 At present, just 14 signatory countries have yet to ratify the CRPD. See United Nations Office of the High Commissioner, Status of Ratification http://indicators.ohchr.org/

3 As Quinn (2009) explains, there is a deep connection between property and the concept of personhood. Indeed many of the early guardianship laws were introduced to protect assets or property rather than people, and applications for guardianship were in turn motivated by proprietary interests and to control assets.

4 Under the 1871 Act, the High Court is charged with managing the estate of all Wards of Court, which can be invested and administered for their benefit.

5 According to the Oireachtas Library and Research Service '[t]he overall objective of the Assisted Decision-Making (Capacity) Act 2015 (the Act) is to put in place a modern legislative framework to support those with capacity difficulties and which complies with the CRPD'.

Bibliography

Committee on the Rights of Persons with Disabilities (2014). General Comment No. 1. Article 12: Equal Recognition Before the Law, UN Doc. No. CRPD/C/GC/1.

Courts Service Ireland. (No date). *Wards of Court.* [online] Available at: http://www.courts.ie/offices.nsf/0/19111E254B2EF547802573D2006CCF26 [Accessed 18 Jan. 2018].

Dinerstein, R.D. (2012). *Implementing Legal Capacity Under Article 12 of the UN Convention on the Rights of Persons with Disabilities: The Difficult Road from Guardianship to Supported Decision-Making.* Human Rights Brief, 19(2), pp 8–12.

Flynn, E. (2013). Making human rights meaningful for people with disabilities: advocacy, access to justice and equality before the law. *The International Journal of Human Rights*, 17(4), pp. 491–510.

Flynn, E., (2015). *Disabled Justice? Access to Justice and the UN Convention on the Rights of Persons with Disabilities.* London: Routledge.

Inclusion Ireland. (2014). *Submission to the Department of Justice and Equality on the Proposed Amendment to the Criminal Law (Sexual Offences) Act 1993.* [online] Available at: http://www.inclusionireland.ie/submissions [Accessed 18 Jan. 2018].

Inclusion Ireland. (2016). *Capacity.* [online] Available at: http://www.inclusionireland.ie/capacity [Accessed 18 Jan. 2018].

Keys, M. (2009). Legal capacity law reform in Europe: an urgent challenge. In G. Quinn, L. Waddington and E. Flynn. Ed., *The European Yearbook of Disability Law, Volume 1.* Mortsel, Belgium: Intersentia, pp. 59–91.

Lennon, S. (2014). Making a will: what you should know. *Frontline. The Irish Voice of Intellectual Disability.* [online] (95). Available at: http://frontline-ireland.com/making-a-will-what-you-should-know/ [Accessed 18 Jan. 2018].

McLoughlin, G. (2017). *Anger after Wards of Court Funds Lost Cash. Irish Independent.* [online] Available at: https://www.independent.ie/irish-news/courts/anger-after-wards-of-court-funds-lost-cash-36248860.html [Accessed 24 Oct. 2017].

O'Brien, T. (2017). Courts Service rejects claims of significant losses in wards' funds. *Irish Times.* [online] Available at: https://www.irishtimes.com/news/ireland/irish-news/courts-service-rejects-claims-of-significant-losses-in-wards-funds-1.3252811 [Accessed 12 Oct. 2017].

Oireachtas Library and Research Service. (2017). *Assisted Decision-Making (Capacity) Act 2015: How Will it Work?* [online] Available at: https://www.oireachtas.ie/parliament/media/housesoftheoireachtas/libraryresearch/lrsnotes/Assisted-Decision-Making-(Capacity)-Act-2015.pdf [Accessed 18 Jan. 2018].

Oliver, M. (1990). *The Politics of Disablement.* London: Macmillan.

Quinn, G. (2009). *An Ideas Paper* (Seminar on Legal Capacity, European Foundation Centre Consortium on Human Rights and Disability). [online] Available at: http://www.inclusionireland.ie/sites/default/files/attach/basic-page/846/anideaspaperbygerardquinnjune2009.pdf [Accessed 18 Jan. 2018].

10 'The law is very complicated...'

Dermot Lowndes and Jan Strnad

JAN: Where does your story begin Dermot?

DERMOT: My life was OK but I got pretty fond of the booze 'cause I was arguing with my sister and she was telling me she owned the house. So, then my mother passed away in 2001 and she was telling me: 'Oh, you better move into the residential service because I do not want to look after you', you know.

Then we got, my other sister and me – we rang up our mother's solicitor. He set up and we had to meet him in Dublin Castle.[1] Because he was not too sure if the law, you know – the law for people with disabilities, if you are left property. There is a clause in it. It is very hard for a person with disability to understand that law.

So we went to the High Court, and then he rang us up and we went to Dublin Castle, to meet this legal girl. She was called the legal barrister and she told us, that under such a – I am not too sure really – under the 18 Act or something like that she said that we could sue our sister and get the property off her. But if the judge ruled in her favour, we would have to pay all the bills – that we would have to pay our solicitor and her solicitor and we could lose everything.

So my sister said no, and I asked the barrister, I said I have a disability and said could you take that and explain that to me and that's what she told me – that it was legal, that I could sue my sister but if the judge ruled against me and my other sister we would lose the case.

JAN: Where were you living at the time?

DERMOT: I was living with my sister and my mother. And then I moved to the house in Middle Third (housing estate) that was kind of sheltered housing... It was OK for a while but then I got really fed up and got really depressed, you know that type of thing, and then I went off. I went missing for a few days and then they moved me to a residential service.

JAN: Did you like living in the residential service?

DERMOT: When I moved there first, I wasn't very happy. I felt very bitter and I went off again. But the residential service helped me to get back on my feet.

JAN: Where would you have wanted to live if you had a real choice at that time?

DERMOT: In my mother's house, if I had a real choice.

JAN: And what was your mother's last will?

DERMOT: Her last will was that I was to stay there for five years, but then after that I don't know.

JAN: And was that respected?

DERMOT: No, no, because my sister kept telling me to move out. She wasn't going to ... that it wasn't her job to look after me and I felt very angry about it, you know, because I said to my mother's solicitor that she should have put it in the will that the place should have been sold and we would all get a dig out but then solicitor told me that because of the legal things the solicitor only does your mother's wishes, so you have to get another solicitor to, you know, clear all that and it costs you a good lot of money. So then my mother's solicitor said, oh, I can't get involved in this because of legal reasons. I will sort your mother's property and I will write your sister to say that she has to get a solicitor and that she owns the house. I will write to her to tell her that I carried out your mother's wish to the best of my ability, and blah blah blah ... He said you have to go and see some other solicitor, because of clash of interests. So my sister got the house.

JAN: So you did not get appropriate legal support?

DERMOT: No, no, not from the solicitor. I felt very angry that there is nobody, no legal person to give me a voice, you know, so that's what happened to me.

My sister from Cork tried to help us, but it was very, do you know, when you are a working-class person the law is very complicated and for a person with a disability it is very complicated as well. There is no legal advice for a person, or no private solicitor that can come and say, well, I'll do this for the person with a disability. Because they think, because you have the disability, that you don't understand the law because you have a disability.

JAN: Did you feel that you understood the situation and the options?

DERMOT: Yes, I understood what he was saying that we could have taken my sister to the court and sue her and we could have lost everything. And my sister would get the property and we get nothing but my mother's solicitor said he would sort it all out and he did and I got a small amount of money out of it, I think about €200 or so, but me and my sister now get on better so I'll leave it at that. I don't say anything. I don't mention about the house or anything.

Do you know, I feel very bitter, because the government are saying to people with disabilities that you have a right to live independently, to live in your community, to live in your area where you are from. But there is just no one to give you a legal advice and you feel very hurt and, you know, because there is no one and maybe residential services don't want to get involved in that because it could be a family thing and they do not want to get involved in legal things.

But there is no person. There is no Ombudsman for the person with a disability and I feel very bitter about that and I feel solicitors are very corrupt in Ireland. So, that is my story...

JAN: Did the barrister mention that you could also become Ward of Court?

DERMOT: No – no warning about a Ward of Court.

JAN: What really made you decide not to take the case?

DERMOT: Because, you see, my sister and me, we would have to get our solicitor and our barrister and we would have to argue the case, and you have to pay the solicitor and legal barristers. The costs would be €300 or maybe €400. And if you lose the case you have to pay everything (your sister's solicitor and your own) ...you have to pay legal fees.

If you are with disability, you have no ... there is no person to give you legal advice, you know, there is no ... you are afraid because your mother's solicitor is only doing your mother's wish. He is not here for your sister's wishes or yours. He carries out your mother's wish. He can't interfere.

JAN: What would have helped you to decide whether to take the case or not?

DERMOT: There should be a person who works with people with disabilities to help them understand the law, like an Ombudsman. The person should understand the law, and should understand people with disabilities, and they should be independent.

JAN: How was your life after that?

DERMOT: Well, it went very bad then. I got a bit depressed. I went out and slept rough but now... it's great now because I am on the National Platform of Self Advocates.[2] I am also on Inclusion Ireland,[3] so that is great now and I am kind of happy in myself.

I met the Platform 2 years ago. We are talking about people from all over the country fighting for persons with disability. We talk on radio and go to media. So, we are trying to change things but it's a struggle. It's not easy.

In Inclusion Ireland, I have been working there for four or five years. Inclusion Ireland has the Board of Directors and the Deputy Board. I am on the Deputy Board. We control and bring the agenda for directors. We talk to politicians, try to influence policies and so on.

JAN: How is your life now?

DERMOT: It's great, it is very good, I'm very happy. I go to Browne's for a cup of coffee and the chap that owns it runs a Halloween party every year and I do stewarding in the park. I do the same thing at Christmas.

***

Dermot's story, as he just presented it, is inspiring and illustrating in several aspects. It can be read both as a typical story of troubles with inheritance within a family and as a clear illustration of the interrelation between the basic rights of a man with disability as they are currently thematised in the Convention on the Rights of Persons with Disabilities (CRPD).

Dermot himself prefers not to look into the past and seek a legal remedy. He takes a different approach. He wants his story to prevent this happening again to people in the same situation.

My response respects this focus, although it cannot pass over certain issues. In this sense, it is not intended as an academic paper but as an attempt to reflect the complexity and interrelation of the legal and practical demands on the system of support in exercising legal capacity. It is trying to point out the key role of availability and quality of support in making decisions with legal consequences. Let's step a bit back together and try to see wider picture from perspective of the CRPD which in fact did not exist when Dermot was making one of the most crucial decisions of his life.

Equality before the law

Human rights of people with disabilities are not different from anyone else's, but something more has to be stated to reach them and to ensure they are not deprived of them. Although Ireland has not ratified the CRPD, this Convention arguably has not created any new rights in international human rights law. Since the CRPD simply restates how existing rights can be applied to persons with disabilities, I rely on its provisions here to consider how the State (in this case, Ireland) could have responded differently to Dermot's experience.

Article 12.5 CRPD compels the State to protect and ensure Dermot's right to own and inherit property. The State also has an obligation to ensure that he is not arbitrarily deprived of it in any way. One of the most important preconditions for an individual's ability to perform his rights is to be aware of them and to know the key remedies and their consequences.

Inheritance is a sensitive area by its nature. The need to consider legal solutions to conflicts or disputes comes at a vulnerable time following the loss of a loved one, and is difficult for everyone. If an individual feels that he has been unfairly treated, this situation can become extremely stressful for him.

At first sight, Irish law creates no direct barrier for people with disabilities to inherit property (Succession Act 1965). Dermot was therefore entitled to obtain his share according to his mother's last will. He was supposed to keep a right of residence in the house, where he had spent most of his life, for five years after her death. Technically, this right could also be given a monetary value and become the subject of a contract between all heirs. Although we do not know the exact reasons, it appears that this did not happen in this story, and Dermot's mother's wishes were not fulfilled.

Dermot's situation within the inheritance procedure required him to decide what to do when he felt he was not treated fairly. This decision was complex and likely to influence his future. There were at least two very important legal aspects that were not taken into consideration while Dermot was making the key decision described in his story.

The first is legal concept of 'proper provision' that could have possibly been used in his favour to mitigate the unfairness he felt regarding the distribution of the inheritance. In Irish law, there is no automatic right for a person to receive anything in their parent's will. However, the Succession Act 1965 recognises the moral duty of parents to provide for their children by making proper provision for them. That is to protect not only children under 18 years of age but everyone at a point in their life where they might reasonably expect support from their parents. Proper provision covers a duty to provide housing, alimentation and other support to ensure individuals' maintenance and advancement in life. If a court considers that a parent has not made proper provision for their child, then some money may be given to him or her from the deceased's assets. Claiming this entitlement is not easy and requires adherence to strict time limits and arguing specific conditions (s. 117, Succession Act 1965).

Pursuing his rights in the will could have presented a risk to Dermot's legal status. There were serious concerns regarding what would have happened if Dermot obtained part of estate or some compensation for his unrealised right of residence. Such inheritance could have become a reason for his legal capacity to be questioned on the basis that he would not be capable of managing his affairs.

Although Dermot was not made aware of this in the legal advice he received at the time, under Irish law he could have been made a Ward of Court (Regulation of Lunacy (Ireland) Act 1871). His affairs and decisions would be supervised and administered by the Court. That would present a serious intrusion to his rights and his life.[4]

From the story, it seems that Dermot was not made aware of all the opportunities and risks attached to his options that would enable him to assess them properly. He was however very aware of the risk of not being successful if he was to litigate his rights, and the financial costs that could then be imposed on him. Another question is whether the support to make this decision was available to him at the time.

Access to justice – availability, accessibility and non-discrimination of support

Legal procedures are usually complex and full of formalised steps and actions. For most people, it is very difficult to understand them. This is where various forms of support are necessary.

Under Article 12.3 CRPD, the State has a positive duty to provide access to support in the exercise of an individual's legal capacity, to perform his legal agency.

This leads us to question what support Dermot had and what would have helped him to realise and understand his rights and options and to make an informed choice. Key elements of any type of support to become effective are its availability and accessibility.

Availability of support

It appears from Dermot's story that legal advice was available for him and he tried to use it. There was a solicitor appointed and responsible for execution of Dermot's mother's last will and it seems that the standard legal procedure was adhered to. While the solicitor was responsible for carrying out Dermot's mother's wishes in the will, he would not have been able to represent Dermot in taking a case against his sister regarding the right of residence as this would have been a conflict of interest. He referred Dermot to the barrister he later met at Dublin Castle for independent legal advice.

Within the justice system, a barrister has a wide range of functions. First of all, she might explain to her client the situation and give a legal opinion on whether or not the client has a good legal case against the person with whom he has a dispute. If a client chooses to go to trial, the barrister drafts the necessary legal documents and represents him in court. A barrister may also negotiate the settlement of case instead of going to trial.[5] In the Irish system, individuals cannot engage barristers directly, as a barrister is engaged by the person's solicitor.

Dermot in his own words did not feel supported by the barrister. His decision of whether to take the case or not should be based on the barrister's expert explanation of all possible options and assessment of the probability of the case's success. In this sense, the barrister's advice becomes one of inputs to the process of making the decision. However, the support, which would have helped him to interpret the barrister's advice and to work with the gained information to make his decision was not present.

Under Article 13 CRPD States parties have an obligation to ensure that persons with disabilities have access to justice on an equal basis with others. The CRPD's addition in the field of access to justice is not innovative in requirements for legal proceedings themselves. Above all, Article 13 CRPD emphasises the key role of accessibility as a necessary precondition to enjoy this right. The Committee on the Rights of Persons with Disabilities (the Committee) is very clear in this point and assumes that there can be no effective access to justice if the services, information and communication which law-enforcement agencies and the judiciary provide are not accessible to persons with disabilities (CRPD Committee, 2014b, para. 37).

The recognition of the right to legal capacity is essential for access to justice in many respects (CRPD Committee, 2014a, para. 38). Recognition of legal personality would not suffice to ensure effective protection of an individual's rights without appropriate support enabling him to perform his legal agency.

Article 12 CRPD guarantees support in the exercise of legal capacity. Such support could take various forms, including recognition of diverse communication methods, procedural accommodation and other assistive methods. The judiciary must also be trained and made aware of their obligation to respect the legal capacity of persons with disabilities, including legal agency and standing (CRPD Committee, 2014a, para. 39).

In this context, the consequent requirement that States should provide resources to systems of supported decision-making to assist persons with disabilities to navigate existing legal systems seems to be very important (CRPD Committee, 2017, para. 56).

Lack of accommodation

In addition to the State's obligation to provide persons with disabilities with the support necessary to perform their legal capacity and secure access to justice, all professionals offering their services to the public are subject to the requirement of reasonable accommodation under Article 2 CRPD. Where a service to the public concerns a decision with legal consequences, the accommodation can be also understood as a form of support to the individual in making his decision.

By ensuring the accessibility of information and services in this field and protection against discrimination in their use, the State directly influences the terrain and space for the application of the CRPD's requirement to provide support to exercise legal capacity through law, policy and practice.

Article 2 CRPD defines reasonable accommodation as any 'necessary and appropriate modification and adjustments not imposing a disproportionate or undue burden, where needed in a particular case, to ensure to persons with disabilities the enjoyment or exercise on an equal basis with others of all human rights and fundamental freedoms'. Reasonable accommodation seeks to achieve individual justice in the sense that non-discrimination is ensured, taking the human dignity, autonomy, and choices of the individual into account (CRPD Committee, 2014b, para. 26).

Article 5 CRPD imposes an obligation on State Parties 'to take all appropriate steps to ensure that reasonable accommodation is provided'. Accommodation of this type is not unconditional – it is limited to forms and intensity that do not present an undue burden for the provider. If they do not, the denial of reasonable accommodation is understood as discrimination on the basis of disability.

The legal service Dermot received from the barrister is a mainstream type of support – generally used by any person in making decisions that require expert opinion in particular issues, e.g. law or medical treatment. To really benefit from it, persons with disability will often need reasonable accommodation or some type of additional support.

The legal advice that Dermot described does not seem to be tailored to a person with intellectual disability at all. The story shows no mark of reasonable accommodation – more time given to disclosing the relevant information adequately, use of plain language or any other means that could have easily adapted the procedure and information to his actual situation and needs. Legal advice was important but definitely not the only support he needed and no other form of support was in his reach at the time.

Accessibility of support

Under the current legal framework, we can find a strong connection to rights under Article 9 CRPD. The general right to accessibility requires States to identify and eliminate existing barriers and limits of services offered to the public.

Accessibility is related to groups and it has to be provided before a person with a disability wants to exercise the right, i.e. to use the service, on an equal basis with others. In interpretation of the Committee, it is necessary to establish minimum standards for the accessibility of different services provided by public and private enterprises for persons with different types of impairments. Minimum standards must be developed in close consultation with persons with disabilities and their representative organizations, in accordance with Article 4, paragraph 3, of the Convention (CRPD Committee, 2014b, para. 30). The lived experience of people facing these barriers in their everyday lives can help to encompass all the critical points.

An important factor in the means and quality of such support is also its independence. Dermot in fact had natural support at least from one of his sisters, however, very often family members are disqualified from offering support in decisions related to family issues and property due to perceived conflict of interest. The high probability of this conflict should be considered in designing forms of support to be offered to people with disabilities in similar situations.

In making his decision, Dermot had to contend with the consequences for his family relationships, options for new housing and other crucial issues for his future. Legal support is an important tool, but the sensitivity of these decisions in social and family environments requires further mediation or similar activities.

For all of these reasons, it seems clear that the support that would have helped Dermot to make the decision about pursuing his rights under his mother's will should be based on a variety of formal and informal sources and include a multidisciplinary approach.

The Committee uses the term 'supported decision-making regime' in the General Comment and gives it a broad scope. Based on this definition, a supported decision-making regime includes supported decision-making, decision-making assistance and broader support to exercise legal capacity, across a range of law, policy and practice (Gooding, 2015).

Decision-making is a process which varies according to individual needs, complexity and the importance of the decision to be made. Any system of support in decision-making should consist of various forms to help people in different situations. It has to reflect individual level of needs in the intensity of support that also varies in different times and situations. Michael Bach describes how the intensity of support needed can be addressed through a three-tiered approach as follows (Bach, 2014, pp. 9–11):

'Independent decisions' are made without supplementary support, using just consultations with natural supporters – family and friends. Crucial state intervention needed on this level includes the development of accessible environments with mainstream services built on principles of universal design and providing reasonable accommodations where necessary.

'Supported decisions' may require support in various steps in the process of decision-making from identifying the decision needed and gathering information, identification, consideration and choosing of alternatives, implementation of the decision and reviewing consequences where necessary. A wide scope of forms and tools of support can be combined. In this regard, the most important duty of States is to recognise or establish appropriate forms of supports to be addressed especially while informal support is not available or would not be sufficient for the individual.

'Representative decision-making' requires respect for an individual's right to appoint someone as an agent to make decisions that he defines on the base of the individual's will and preferences. The representative needs to know and be able to understand the individual's will and preferences and interpret them to third parties. Recognition of the status of such agency and providing appropriate safeguards to prevent abuse are the key challenges for the State.

Natural relationships are the key resource for support that should be primarily provided by the group of trusted people and professionals involved in care and support where necessary. Some persons providing support may need to obtain formal recognition of this role through approval or appointment by public authority.

In addition to Bach's proposed framework, tools of person-centred planning prove to be very valuable in providing support in decision-making.[6] Special care should be given to availability and accessibility of support or assistance in communication. Meaningful communication between the person, supporters and third parties is necessary for the performance of legal agency. Without that, the will and preferences of the person can easily remain unexpressed, ununderstood or misinterpreted.

Arstein-Kerslake and Flynn (2016) assess the main pros and cons of both formal and informal support. They point out that it is likely that the best system will include room for both informal supports with safeguards and non-invasive formal supports: 'Although the General Comment does not dictate that a system must include both forms of support, it leaves plenty of room for that eventuality' (Arstein-Kerslake and Flynn, 2016, p. 476).

Right to live in the community

The story clearly shows that the solution adopted in 2001 deeply influenced Dermot's life. Lack of appropriate and effective support in making this decision may have limited his choices and his life in the community.

Accessibility of support in exercising legal capacity and access to justice are closely related. In the words of the Committee to ensure equal and effective access to justice substantial rights to legal aid, support and procedural and age-appropriate accommodations are essential (CRPD Committee, 2017, para. 82).

Especially in making decisions with wide consequences for various aspects of a person's future, the access to a wide range of forms and types of support in the exercise of legal capacity is crucial. Supported decision-making in the sense of legally-recognised support measures is often necessary, but in many cases a broader array of measures and accommodations can be both necessary and sufficient. In Dermot's story, we can see a particular need for more accessible forms of information and for facilitation in seeking other available support services within his community.

It seems that the decision brought Dermot new challenges and led him out of his community to live in a residential service. The question is whether the decision not to struggle for his share in the family home became, in its time, the price he freely decided to pay for keeping his relationship with his family members, or whether it was just the result of inaccessibility of proper support. This type of dilemma shows that designing complex systems of support in decision-making is essential to ensure people in Dermot's situation equal enjoyment of their rights.

In this sense, Dermot lost a lot, but due to his character and attitude, definitely not everything. He overcame really bad times and kept a good relationship with his sisters. In addition, he is active now in advocacy and through his activities he helps other people.

Notes

1 Dublin Castle is the name of a complex of government buildings in Dublin, Ireland.
2 For more information see National Platform of Self Advocates [online] Available at: http://thenationalplatform.ie/ [Accessed 19 Jan. 2018].
3 For more information see Inclusion Ireland [online] Available at: http://www.inclusionireland.ie/ [Accessed 19 Jan. 2018].
4 This situation is described in another story in this book – 'Silenced, alone, powerless: my life as a Ward of Court in Ireland'.
5 For explanation of the roles of barristers within the Irish system of justice see the pages of The Bar of Ireland [online] Available at: https://www.lawlibrary.ie/About-Us/What-We-Do.aspx [Accessed 4 Nov. 2017].
6 For more information, see the recent project of Quip and partners – IDEA12 seeks to gather practical experience with use of these and contributes to awareness through creating inclusive trainings in support in decision making [online] Available at: http://www.kvalitavpraxi.cz/en/projects/current-projects/idea-12/ [Accessed 19 Jan 2018].

Bibliography

Arstein-Kerslake, A. and Flynn, E. (2016). The General Comment on Article 12 of the Convention on the Rights of Persons with Disabilities: A Roadmap for Equality Before the Law. *The International Journal of Human Rights*, 20(4), pp. 471–490.

Bach, M. (2014). Supported Decision Making Evolution of an Idea and Canadian Experience: Supported Decision-Making Models. [online] Available at: http://supporteddecisionmaking.org/sites/default/files/032614_transcript.pdf [Accessed 4 Jan. 2018].

Committee on the Rights of Persons with Disabilities. (2014a). General Comment No. 1. Article 12: Equal Recognition Before the Law, UN Doc. No. CRPD/C/GC/1.

Committee on the Rights of Persons with Disabilities. (2014b). General Comment No. 2. Article 9: Accessibility, UN Doc. No. CRPD/C/GC/2.

Committee on the Rights of Persons with Disabilities. (2017). Draft General Comment on Equality and Non- discrimination (Article 5). [online] Available at: www.ohchr.org/documents/HRBodies/CRPD/GCArt5.docx [Accessed 4 Nov. 2017].

Committee on the Rights of Persons with Disabilities. (2017). General Comment No. 5 on Living Independently and Being Included in the Community, UN Doc. No. CRPD/C/GC/5.

Gooding, P. (2015). Navigating the 'Flashing Amber Lights' of the Right to Legal Capacity in the United Nations Convention on the Rights of Persons with Disabilities: Responding to Major Concerns. *Human Rights Law Review*, 15(1), pp. 45–71.

11 Travel and dementia: one story, many rights

Helen Rochford-Brennan and Moira Jenkins[1]

My name is Helen Rochford-Brennan and I am participating in the VOICES project as a person living with dementia and as a dementia advocate. I have decided to focus on my right to travel and to free movement as a person living with a disability because over the last few years, I have come to the realisation that my right to travel is fundamental to me remaining a part of my community and contributing to wider society.

My advocacy work takes me all over Ireland and all over the world. It gives me hope and purpose and greatly improves my quality of life while living with dementia. For these reasons, my right to travel should not be restricted by disability-based discrimination when I travel.

I come from Tubbercurry in Sligo, but my working life has meant I spent many years abroad before returning home to settle in Ireland. Living in a rural part of Ireland makes my need to access transport even more important to combat isolation and loneliness. Many people with dementia don't want to travel far because of anxiety and don't travel alone. I enjoy and need to travel for my advocacy work to change the perception of dementia across the world. I often travel by myself, it is daunting. The main thing is I don't want to get lost. I have had to set my own standards as to how I should be treated as a person with dementia using transport services. I communicate and pre-book my assistance needs but too often my requests are ignored and when I ask for assistance, I am often greeted by a wheelchair on arrival, rather than what I actually need and requested, which is a person to accompany and guide me. All transport companies need to make dementia awareness a major part of their education and training for staff. Dementia is sometimes forgotten when we think of disabilities. It is a hidden disability and those of us living with dementia have a tendency to try to hide it more in order to be accepted.

I lived abroad for many years. I had a wonderful career in the corporate sector. Together with my husband Sean and our son Martin, we returned to Sligo where we ran a business in the tourism sector for a number of years and I later worked in the disability sector. I was a very active citizen serving on boards, and a promoter of human rights. This was my life before the irrevocability of a dementia diagnosis crept in.

A lot of my work in community development and the disability sector has been about human rights and advocating for the rights of others, but I write here today advocating for my own rights. In my mid-fifties, I started to experience memory problems and finally I was diagnosed with early-onset Alzheimer's in 2012 at the age of 62 while I was busy working and planning my retirement.

It was like a slow realisation that a creeping fog had descended on your life and it was there for good. My day-to-day tasks became worryingly challenging. First, it was forgetting words, stopping mid-sentence, wondering what I was about to say, searching, covering up, forgetting again. Simple tasks that I had been doing all my life became a chore, a worry. I found my slowed thinking very difficult to deal with. It impacted on me in many ways; such as trying to remember something I had read or newly learned, seeing words but being unable to reach them, forgetting events of a recent meeting, forgetting what people had asked me to do. I can still see the look on people's faces and feel the burning silence when the words failed to come to me at a meeting. I began forgetting names, covering up and trying to keep out of the limelight.

There is no way I can describe the shock of the day I received my diagnosis or the long lonely drive home from Galway to Sligo wondering how I was going to tell my husband and son. There was however, also a degree of relief in getting a diagnosis, as I really thought I was losing my mind. I don't remember the conversation with my family, but I do remember the pain.

Ask yourself this question, how do you tell your loved ones that within an undisclosed amount of time you will not be able to recognise them, nor retain any of the wonderful memories that you've banked along the way? I remember lying awake, staring into the blackness, wondering where do I go from here?

A flurry of visits to the doctor and the consultant followed, as I tried to come to terms with the diagnosis, but there was yet another blow to come. More bad news; the threshold age for early-onset Alzheimer's support is 65. For anyone diagnosed with early-onset dementia-related illnesses before their sixty-fifth birthday, there is nothing, and I mean nothing at all; no support services, nowhere to go, no one to give you advice or tips on how to proceed.

For me, having spent my adult life campaigning for human rights, this was inconceivable. I couldn't believe that because of a random number, I would be ignored. Worse still, that I would be refused all help and services. But I didn't have the strength or will to fight it. I retreated. I felt helpless for the first time in my life, no plan, no ideas, and no strategies.

Eventually, I got the courage to seek help and start telling people I had the condition. I looked up research being carried out through Trinity College which led to me to the Alzheimer's Society of Ireland and the newly formed Irish Dementia Working Group, a group of people living with dementia who advocate for their own rights. Until I reached out and got help, all I could see was the deepest grief imaginable, but somehow after I told people I could see some light. The Irish Dementia Working Group has given me a lifeline. It was a support at a time when there are virtually no supports for people under 65 with a diagnosis. In April 2016, when I was Chair, we published a Charter of Rights for People with Dementia[2] demanding the same human rights as every other citizen. The Charter is direction from people living with dementia on a rights-based approach to support and assistance.

Acceptance of my diagnosis has allowed me to go one step further and start to look for my human rights as a person with dementia who is also a mother, a wife, a sister, a community activist and a citizen. This is where my right to travel and to access public transport has been of primary importance to me as a person living with dementia.

I spend a lot of time travelling. I drive and I take my on-road driving assessment each year. I take quite a lot of taxis. I take a lot of trains and use public buses. I also fly. All these forms of transport bring different challenges for me.

Navigating public transport on my own can be hugely stressful. Travelling in rural Ireland is particularly challenging. You really need to work out your connections in advance. A lot of planning is necessary. For example, there was an unexpected stop and change of train once when I was travelling by train at night. We had to get onto a bus and then off the bus again and back on the train. This disruption was not communicated well. No one asked if there was anybody who needed help. There was no staff person available to me and instead I had to figure out what was happening on my own and decide whether to change train. I was raging with Irish Rail. It is not good for a person with dementia to sit at the back of the bus. Sometimes you have to ask where to get off. Drivers don't always want to assist you. It can depend on the mood of the driver. I have to say 'Look I have Alzheimer's.' You feel like pulling out your dementia card. I had a business card made up that says on the back 'I have Alzheimer's disease. Please be patient with me.'

My dementia advocacy work has taken me all over the world. In 2016 I travelled to London where I represented Ireland at a major health conference, I met the Queen of Spain when I represented the European Dementia Working Group for an award ceremony. I attended conferences in Switzerland and Austria and spoke about Human Rights at the European Parliament. My advocacy work has taken me to Copenhagen, Brussels, León, Lindau and beyond. In 2017, as the Chairperson of the European Dementia Working Group, I chaired a number of sessions and gave a plenary address at the 27th Alzheimer Europe Conference in Berlin in October 2017. My diary entries for September and October 2017 show a typical period of travel for me.

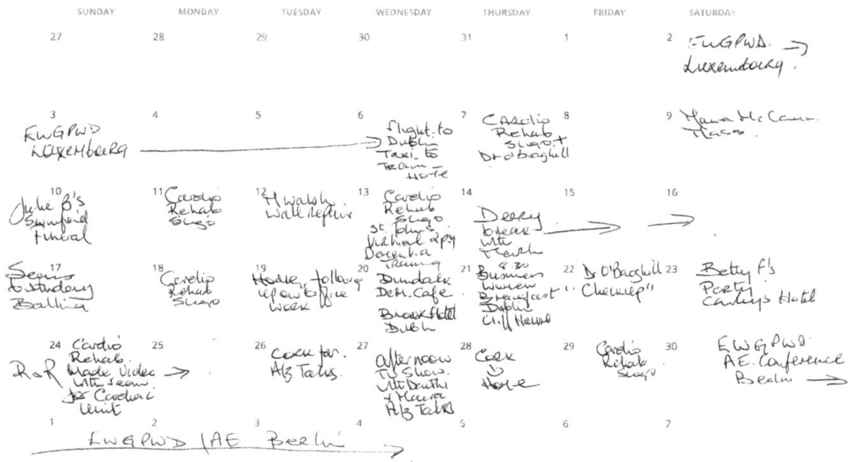

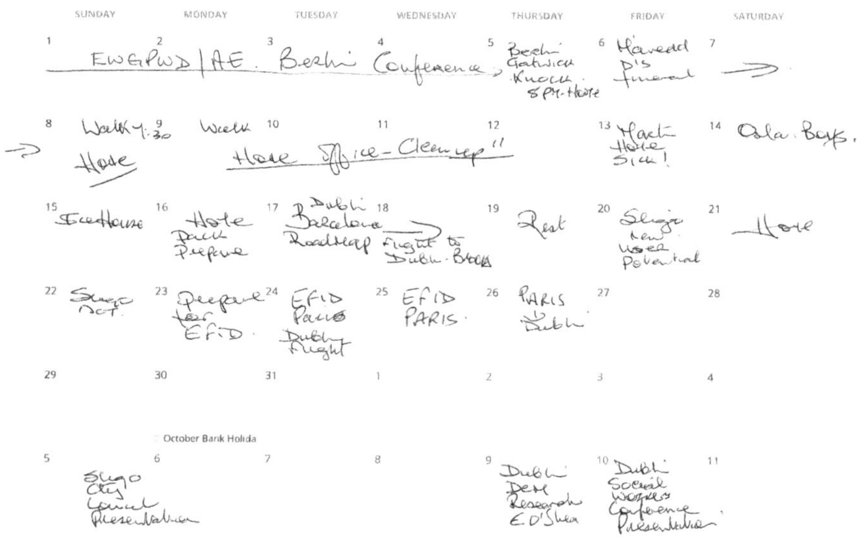

This international travel means that I use the airport very often. I think a lot of work needs to happen in terms of widening the understanding of dementia as a disability. Recently a form for assistance was returned to me headed 'Intellectual disability. Walker required.' Why is a label required, why not simply agree to provide the assistance requested? There is a lack of understanding of dementia and there is nothing for people with a cognitive disability. In some airports, pre-booked assistance doesn't happen or if it does it is only at the last minute. When I arrive at an airport, most of the time there is a wheelchair waiting for me and I have to explain that I don't need the chair but I do need someone with me. I have to explain that I can walk but that my anxiety is heightened and my cognitive ability to navigate a large airport is limited. Most of the time, individual staff get this but it is at a more strategic level that this learning needs to happen.

At a German airport in 2016, when the pre-arranged support failed to show up, the woman on the information desk personally accompanied me to the plane and asked a male passenger in the queue to assist me to board the plane. I had a contract for specific support but instead was left to the kindness of strangers. This is not equal rights. I should not be dependent on charity nor friendliness.

When travelling to speak at the European Parliament, I put in an application to an airline for assistance. I got a form back for my doctor to complete asking how long I had had the illness and what stage of the illness I was at. I contacted the airline and the female staff member said she was very aware of Alzheimer's and there was no way they could let someone with Alzheimer's travel alone. I recall pleading, saying I travelled all the time and starting to cry. She then talked to her boss, said 'you sound okay' and that I could go but I still needed to send in the form signed by my doctor. I had to book and pay for the appointment with my doctor and pay for the letter. How can someone make a decision about the state of my illness on the basis of a phone call? I did seek support to make a complaint about this incident and a national disability rights body would have taken it as a case but it is so stressful to complain.

I hope my stories have shown how important travel is to me personally but also as an advocate who wants to influence change for others living with dementia. This chapter has focused on travel to shine a human rights lens onto one part of my life but, as the chapter shows, there are many other aspects of my life that also need a human rights lens not least of which is my right to be active in my community, my right to work with support, my right to be heard, my right to live at home and my right to be respected and recognised as an equal human being.

***

Helen's story of diagnosis with early-onset Alzheimer's and struggle to continue to live independently and in her community provides a vital perspective on the support[3] people living with dementia require to exercise their human rights. Helen's experience when diagnosed was that dementia was not seen, nor responded to, as a disability with rights but as an illness affecting older people only. She was caught at an intersection of ableism and ageism – too young for dementia support services and not regarded as having a disability[4]. In the Republic of Ireland, the absence of a legal entitlement to community support too often results in segregation and institutionalisation of people with dementia and older people in long-term care facilities despite their preference to stay at home in the community (Donnelly et al., 2016). People living with dementia in Irish nursing homes do not appear to be regarded as people with a disability in a congregated setting with attendant CRPD rights.[5]

Helen's story demonstrates how the right to travel is fundamental to her continuing to live independently as an active contributor to her community but a continual struggle to realise. In order to live independently, to remain and be included in the community, to choose where and with whom to live and to have access to in-home and community support services (Article 19) people with dementia must have personal mobility (Article 20). The support paradigm inherent in the CRPD, as explained in the 2016 Report of the Special Rapporteur on the rights of persons with disabilities, frames independence as broader than self-reliance and as founded on interdependence. Despite caution (Series 2015, p. 81) the concept of relationality has been utilised as a lens by lawyers in the context of dementia care (Harding 2014, p. 379) but adopting a human rights approach to support 'opens the door for a societal dialogue about the interdependence of all individuals' (Flynn and Arstein-Kerslake 2014, p. 130). Responding to the external barriers to Helen's right to travel demands procedural accommodation for equality before the current law and a re-engineering of the law to make community living accessible to everyone.

Helen has applied her lifetime of professional and community activism experience to changing society's perceptions of and attitudes to people with dementia, primarily through telling her story. She refused to submit to a crisis narrative of dementia diagnosis meaning redundancy, dependency, unsustainable burden and threat. The Committee on the Rights of Persons with Disabilities, in its nascent jurisprudence, has highlighted that evidence of how inaccessibility affects the person's right to independent living is essential to determining a violation of rights.[6] The Committee has clarified that, in addition to the group *ex ante* accessibility requirements of Article 9, the individual right to personal mobility in Article 20 requires that medical assessments, availability of examinations, aids/adaptations/allowances relating to reasonable accommodation and personal mobility should be affordable and eligibility standardised and transparently applied. The Committee also recommended that States introduce a public budget for mobility requirements for people with disabilities.

Helen tells that she expressly contracts for the support she requires to travel in detail and in advance – but the contract is often not performed. In contractual terms, the express (written or discussed) and/or implied (read into the contract by law, custom or conduct) conditions of Helen's travel contracts were breached. To make rights real, there must be procedural support to secure an effective remedy in law (Lawson and Flynn 2013, p. 25; Bingham 2010, p. 85), specifically for enforcement of breach of contract.

Helen's stories of travelling expose a societal expectation that the person with dementia will adapt to existing conditions rather than a premise that disabling practices and processes must change in order to accommodate people with dementia (Bartlett and O'Connor 2010, p. 74). The amount of time Helen has to spend planning, negotiating, explaining, arranging, being assessed and complaining to be able to travel is discriminatory. While ostensibly about the needs of the traveller, most of the additional testing and third-party authorisation required of the person with a disability, including people living with dementia, primarily benefits or conveniences others. Having to sue to secure contractual compliance from transport service providers is impractical in terms of money, time and anxiety for most people. Civil legal aid is limited in Ireland and the current State scheme does not provide a statutory right to the 'procedural accommodation' envisaged in Article 13(1) of the CRPD to ensure effective access to justice by people with disabilities. While human rights organisations might support a test case on these issues, persons with disabilities should not be reliant on ad hoc support to have their rights vindicated.

Trains and buses

Helen tells of fragmented train and bus journeys causing her great stress, anxiety and loss of dignity. People with disabilities in Ireland still have to give 24-hour notice to secure assistance to travel by train.[7] In addition to the express terms for assistance Helen negotiates, Irish Rail passengers are also protected by Irish Rail's Customer Charter[8] and European Union regulations,[9] which imply further terms into the contract but the degree of complexity involved in reading implied terms into a contract reduces accessibility and awareness of rights.

Action: The State should require all transport providers include a right to compensation for any passenger where an agreed contractual condition for personal support was breached or the obligation to provide reasonable accommodation was not met. The State should provide support for persons with disabilities to exercise their rights when breaches occur, including civil legal aid for representation in court where necessary to sue for breach of contract or personal injuries. In addressing discriminatory outcomes by making a complaint and/or pursuing a legal remedy, some people will require procedural support and a statutory, independent advocacy service should be developed in tandem with the implementation of the Assisted Decision Making (Capacity) Act 2015 for people who do not have a volunteer decision-making assistant.

The proposed European Accessibility Act[10] may address some of the barriers faced by people with disabilities and older persons to accessible transport in Europe, though some forms of transport including local buses remain exempted. The Committee, in the first report on how the EU was complying with the Convention, recommended strengthening the monitoring of legislation to ensure effective and equal enjoyment of rights by all passengers with disabilities across the EU, including implementation of the European Mobility Card. In Ireland, providers of goods and services must provide reasonable accommodation to people with disabilities but only where less than a nominal cost is incurred,[11] which is non-compliant with the standard of reasonable accommodation that does not impose a disproportionate or undue burden in the CRPD and hence the EU.[12]

Airports and flying

Helen contracts for personal assistance when transiting airports and on flights but tells of breach in how these arrangements are ignored or misinterpreted, leaving her isolated and anxious.

Regulation (EC) No. 1107/2006 governs the rights of disabled persons and persons with reduced mobility when travelling by air in Europe. The Commission for Aviation Regulation is the National Enforcement Body in Ireland handling complaints. The Regulation prevents refusal of carriage (except in limited circumstances) and protects the right to assistance. The person must request assistance from an airline at least 48 hours prior to departure. Assistance is required to be provided from arrival at the airport and as necessary for embarkation, disembarkation and transiting through the airport.

Action: Assistance for people with a disability in making a complaint should be mandated in aviation contracts, including support to pursue civil compensation and access advisory opinions. A choice of contract type allowing the State or another third party to enforce breach should also be considered in line with reform of law on privity (Law Reform Commission, 2008).

Helen's story primarily tells of the hurdles faced by a person with dementia in exercising her right to travel where no formal challenge to her contractual capacity has been made. However, Helen has been asked for confirmation of her ability to travel independently from her doctor, rather than her own decision being respected. This was a direct denial of her contractual capacity on status grounds – because she disclosed her dementia diagnosis she was presumed to be unable to decide to travel on her own. The Republic of Ireland is poised to outlaw such status approaches to capacity with a functional approach to mental/decision-making capacity in the Assisted Decision-making (Capacity) Act, 2015.[13] The version of the functional approach in the Act requires a person to understand the nature and consequences of the decision. One wonders if anyone can fulfil the requirement to understand the consequences of a decision without the power to predict the future and it is as yet uncertain how the Act will be implemented.

What else could we nominate, beside decisions and intention, for the law to recognise as agency? Perhaps what matters is our aspirations – our desires. Respect for the will and preferences of the person, as enshrined in Article 12 and interpreted by the Committee in the first General Comment, will require private law reform, including options for legally enforceable agreements. The challenge is in making human rights and private law compatible (Collins, 2012).

We can create further choices between types of contracts and/or agreements to serve various purposes – what Dagan and Heller (2013) have termed 'freedom of contracts'. By demanding the State provide a choice of legal processes or spaces that encourage greater communication, cooperation and cumulative insight we can foster skills in the development of services that open community living to all. Ian Macneil's essential contract theory is seen as the exemplar of relational theories of contract (Macneil's 2001, cited in Mitchell 2013, pp. 171–199) and proffers a useful frame for reviewing the existing menu of contract types. Different relational contract types already exist over a continuum between the no community, arms-length, tick-the-agreed box, standard form contract requiring little or no intra-communication and the co-operative, exchange relations common in much commercial practice. Instead of rigidity of the express and implied terms at the time of the deal – *consensus ad idem* as a meeting of minds – the more relational contract requires accord on the core objectives or intentions of the parties, with details changing over time – an interpretation of *consensus ad idem* as agreement on the thing. A legally enforceable arrangement premised on a departure point of a shared sense of the aspiration, would allow understanding of evolving terms and conditions be assigned to an agent, statutorily appointed assistant or fiduciary and evolution rather than synchronically fixed terms and conditions. Realising universal legal capacity will require more than accommodation within existing parameters of contract law defences, in spite of academic and judicial effort (Varney, 2017).

Through their acts of citizenship, Helen and other people living with dementia are 'broadening the dementia debate' (Bartlett and O'Connor, 2010) in demanding transformation of community living and substantive equality. Social relationships and support should not be understood as merely constraining or enabling agency, but as constituting the very structure of agency and of citizenship itself (Burkitt 2016, p. 336). We must demand options for community-promoting legal relationships in private as well as public law if the voices of people living with dementia are to matter.

Notes

1 Helen and Moira acknowledge the support of Dr Margaret Crean in the writing of this chapter.

2 The charter was based on the Scottish Charter of Human Rights developed by the Cross-Party Group in the Scottish Parliament on Alzheimer's and informed by the *PANEL* approach endorsed by the United Nations.

3 On the meaning of support in the CRPD see the Report of the Special Rapporteur, Catalina Devandas Aguilar, on the rights of persons with disabilities 2017, A/HRC/34/58; General Comment No. 1 (2014) on equal recognition before the law, para. 17 and, General Comment No. 5 (2017) on article 19: Living independently and being included in the community, CRPD/C/GC/5.

4 '(...) older persons tend to be overrepresented in the disability community.' (World Health Organization and World Bank, 2011 cited in Devandas Aguilar (2017), Promotion and protection of all human rights, civil, political, economic, social and cultural rights, including the right to development, UN Doc. No. A/HRC/34/58). Neither people living with dementia of any age nor older persons were involved in the negotiation of the CRPD.

5 See Statement by Minister McGrath on Ratification of the UN Convention on the Rights of Persons with Disabilities, 3 Dec. 2017.

6 For example in the case of *Mr F vs Austria* (Communication No. 21/2014) the Committee found Austria had breached Article 5 (2) and Article 9 (1) and (2) (f) and (h) in not ensuring access to the public transport system for a person visually impaired. But it also found that there were insufficient elements to assess the extent to which

the failure to provide access 'affects his right to personal mobility and to live independently. Consequently the Committee is of the view that it cannot establish a violation of Articles 19 and 20 of the CRPD in this case' [para 8.8 of decision].

7 See M. O'Halloran (2017). Notice period of 24 hours for disabled to take trains 'unacceptable'. *Irish Times.* [online] Available at: https://www.irishtimes.com/news/politics/oireachtas/notice-period-of-24-hours-for-disabled-to-take-trains-unacceptable-1.3301401 [Accessed 19 Jan. 2018].

8 Irish Rail. 'Passenger Charter – Know your rights', [online] Available at: http://www.irishrail.ie. [Accessed 1 Dec. 2017].

9 See *EC Regulation 1371/2007.*

10 See 'Briefing EU Legislation in Progress'. 10 November 2017 [online] Available at: http://www.europarl.europa.eu/RegData/etudes/BRIE/2017/603973/EPRS_BRI(2017)603973_EN.pdf [Accessed 1 Dec. 2017].

11 The *Equal Status Acts 2000–2015* outlaw discrimination in all services that are generally available to the public, whether provided by the state or the private sector. These include transport and travel services. How to make a complaint under the Acts is explained on the website of the Workplace Relations Commission.

12 Article 2 of the CRPD defines reasonable accommodation as: 'necessary and appropriate modification and adjustments not imposing a disproportionate or undue burden, where needed in a particular case, to ensure to persons with disabilities the enjoyment or exercise on an equal basis with others of all human rights and fundamental freedoms.' The Irish Supreme Court arguably applied a broader definition of the reasonable accommodation duty under the *Equal Status Acts 2000–2015* in the case of *Kim Cahill v. Minister for Education and Science. 24.05.17.*

13 Section 3 of the *Assisted Decision-Making (Capacity) Act,* 2015 is the version referenced. The 2015 Act states that, when using a functional approach: '[A] person's capacity shall be assessed on the basis of his or her ability to understand, at the time that a decision is to be made, the nature and consequences of the decision to be made by him or her in the context of the available choices at that time.' See also Gibson (2017) on mental capacity as a site of negotiation on identity.

Bibliography

Alzheimer Society of Ireland and Irish Dementia Working Group (2016). *A Charter of Rights for People with Dementia.* [online] Available at: https://www.alzheimer.ie/getattachment/About-Us/Policy/Human-Rights/A-Charter-of-Rights-for-People-with-Dementia/Charter-of-Rights-for-People-with-Dementia.pdf.aspx [Accessed 28 Nov. 2017].

Bartlett, R. and O'Connor, D. (2010). *Broadening the Dementia Debate. Towards Social Citizenship.* Bristol: Policy Press.

Bingham, T. (2010). *The Rule of Law.* London: Penguin.

Burkitt, I. (2016). Relational agency: relational sociology, agency and interaction. *European Journal of Social Theory.* 19(3), pp. 322–339.

Collins, H. (2012). On the (In)compatibility of Human Rights Discourse and Private Law. LSE Law, Society and Economy Working Papers 7/2012. [online] Available at: www.lse.ac.uk/collections/law/wps/wps.htm [Accessed 3 Dec. 2017].

Committee on the Rights of Persons with Disabilities (2014). General Comment No. 1. Article 12: Equal Recognition Before the Law, UN Doc. No. CRPD/C/GC/1.

Committee on the Rights of Persons with Disabilities (2015). *Concluding Observations on the Initial Report of the European Union*, UN Doc. No. CRPD/C/EU/CO/1.

Committee on the Rights of Persons with Disabilities (2014). General Comment No. 2. Article 9: Accessibility, UN Doc. No. CRPD/C/GC/2.

Committee on the Rights of Persons with Disabilities (2017). General Comment No. 5 on living independently and being included in the community, UN Doc. No. CRPD/C/GC/5.

Dagan, H. and Heller, M. (2013). Freedom of Contracts. *SSRN Electronic Journal.* [online] Available at: https://papers.ssrn.com/sol3/papers.cfm?abstract_id=2325254 [Accessed 30 Dec. 2017].

Devandas Aguilar C. (2017). Report of the Special Rapporteur on the rights of persons with disabilities, Promotion and protection of all human rights, civil, political, economic, social and cultural rights, including the right to development. UN Doc. No. A/HRC/34/58.

Donnelly, S., O'Brien, M., Begley, E. and Brennan, J. (2016). 'I'd Prefer to Stay at Home but I Don't Have a Choice': Meeting Older People's Preference for Care: Policy, but What About Practice? University College Dublin. School of Social Policy, Social Work and Social Justice. [online] Available at: http://researchrepository.ucd.ie/bitstream/handle/10197/7670/IASW.AGE_ACTION.ASI.UCD_Research_Report_on_Care_of_Older_People_2016.pdf?sequence=1 [Accessed 30 Dec. 2017].

Flynn, E. and Arstein-Kerslake, A. (2014). The support model of legal capacity: fact, fiction, or fantasy?. *Berkeley Journal of International Law*, 32(1), pp. 124–143.

Gibson, D. (2017). Negotiating relationality: mental capacity as narrative congruence. *International Journal of Mental Health and Capacity Law*, pp. 49–68.

Harding, R. (2014). Dementia and carers: relationality and informal carers' experiences. In: C. Foster, J. Herring, J. and I. Doron, *The Law and Ethics of Dementia*. London: Bloomsbury Publishing, pp. 379–391.

Law Reform Commission (2008). Privity of Contract and Third Party Rights. Dublin.

Lawson, A. and Flynn, E. (2013). Disability and access to Justice in the European Union: implications of the UN Convention on the Rights of Persons with Disabilities. In: G. Quinn, L. Waddington and E. Flynn. Eds., *The European Yearbook of Disability Law, Volume 4*. Mortsel, Belgium: Intersentia, pp. 7–44.

Mitchell, C. (2013). Contract Law and Contract Practice: Bridging the Gap between Legal Reasoning and Commercial Expectation. London: Hart Publishing.

Series, L. (2015). Relationships, autonomy and legal capacity: mental capacity and support paradigms. *International Journal of Law and Psychiatry*, 40, pp. 80–91.

Varney, E. (2017). Redefining contractual capacity? the UN Convention on the Rights of Persons with Disabilities and the incapacity defence in English contract law. *Legal Studies*, 37(3), pp. 493–519.

World Health Organisation (2015). *Global action against dementia*. New York: World Health Organization

12 I had one dream – to buy a simple smartphone

Marieta Petrova and Aylin Yumerova

My name is Marieta Petrova. I'm 22 years old. I would like to share with you two stories of my life that show how my desire to buy something so simple, like a smartphone, brought me some problems because the legislation of my country couldn't protect my rights as I needed.

Currently, I live in a small town in northwestern Bulgaria – the city of Vidin, where I was born. When I was a little child, I grew up with my parents in our family house. But when I was about 3 years old, my parents separated. For a short period of time, I lived with my mother and her new husband, who often beat her. I was a silent witness to all this and I was feeling really scared. Later on, my grandmother took me and I moved to live with my father. Since that day I have not seen my mother. Life with my father was not very nice. He often yelled at me which I didn't like. He claimed that 'because of my state' I didn't have the right to make my own decisions for my life. Later, I found out that he was receiving social benefits because of having 'a child with intellectual disabilities'. This child was me! I didn't understand why he was getting social benefits for me, as he was spending the money only on himself, never even giving me pocket money. At that period of my life, I trusted nobody – not my father or my grandmother.

Since 2012, I have attended a Day Care Centre for Adults with Disabilities in Vidin where I met many new friends and supporters. Among them was Ivan[1] – a client of the Centre like me. One day, I heard that they had smartphones for sale and I decided to get my own phone. I shared this with Ivan and he offered to accompany me to the phone store. I was offered a smartphone for the amount of 20.00 leva (about €10) and my friend Ivan was ready to pay for it (because I didn't have any money on me). When I chose the phone, the shop assistant immediately asked for my ID card and gave me quickly some papers to sign. I didn't know what those papers were but I signed them and I took the phone.

After a couple of weeks, I received a letter with an invoice in it for the monthly payments on my account. It turned out that I had purchased the phone with a two-year contract for telephone services. Once they heard about my phone and the invoice, my father and grandfather got very angry. They told me that we couldn't afford to pay extra money for my phone bills because I was not working, nor receiving a disability pension. I had no income. My grandfather decided to take back the phone to the store. He tried to terminate the contract that I had signed without really knowing what it was for, but he was supposed to pay a penalty. In the end, he did not pay any penalty, but also did not take any document proving that the phone was returned. Four years later, in 2016, I received a call from the telephone company and I was told that I had owed money for the period of using the phone and for liquidated damages. I was very scared because I hadn't any idea that I owed money to the telephone company – during the previous years nobody had contacted me and informed me that I had monetary liabilities. I could not pay the requested amount because I didn't have enough income. However, by this time I had built a network of supporters around me who helped me to overcome this situation. With the support of my friends and professionals from the Day Care Centre, I managed to reach an agreement with the telephone company. One of my friends in the Centre, who also was my supporter, came with me to the phone store and helped me to clarify the case. We explained the situation to the shop assistant, representing the company, and we were advised to wait for the limitation to pass. So, we did. And in the end, I did not pay any money to the telephone company.

The second case happened in 2014. Back then, I was already living in the Sheltered House in Vidin with another five girls with intellectual disabilities. My birthday was getting closer and my friend Ivan asked me what I wanted for a birthday present. I said I would like to have a smartphone. I had not told anyone about our conversation. Then, Ivan decided to surprise me and went to a pawnshop and bought a phone for me. On the next day, after he gave me the present, everyone in the Day Care Centre was very curious to know how I could have such a beautiful phone. Finally, I told them the truth. After, we had a meeting with the persons I trusted and supported me most, and we discussed together the situation and what to do next. After the conversation with my supporters, I realised that I had made a mistake asking Ivan to buy me a smartphone. I knew that he, also like me – a guy with an intellectual disability who had very little income – could become an easy prey of bad people who wanted to take advantage of him. Ivan had spent almost his entire pension for my present, but he hadn't received any document for the money he paid. After a week, with the support of the Day Care Centre's staff who went together with Ivan to the pawnshop, he managed to get a cash note for the purchased phone and, thus, we realised how expensive it was. Fortunately, this time there were no serious legal consequences from the purchase – neither for Ivan, nor for me. I kept the phone as a present from my friend and on his birthday, I gave him a present in return. This case helped us to realise that when we wanted to buy something expensive, but we weren't confident if we could manage our money, we should seek support and advice from the persons we trusted. Since then, I count more on the support of my trusted persons from the Day Care Centre and Sheltered House when I have to take decisions and sign contracts. I invited these persons to be a part of my support network.

In 2015, I joined the Supported Decision-Making Project of the Bulgarian Association for Persons with Intellectual Disabilities (BAPID). With the help of my facilitator, I built my network of support, consisting of people whom I trust to support me in making decisions about my life. I think that if I had had a support network when I first bought the smartphone, I would have consulted some of my supporters in advance or asked someone among them to come with me and explain to me about the contract – what it meant and what would happen if I signed it – in order to get information on what decision I should take. Thus, I would not have been misled and would not have gone through all those fears and troubles. The same applies for the second story – if I had shared with one of my supporters that I needed a mobile phone, I know that together we'd have met to figure out a way to buy the phone with my own money.

Thanks to the people who support me today, I am now more confident and more responsible for my decisions! I am very happy and proud of myself. I want to tell everyone to believe in themselves, to search for support of trusted persons, not to be afraid to express their desires and fight for their dreams!

***

Marieta grew up in a challenging environment, as she describes in her story. Her father never encouraged her personal development and independence, just the opposite – throughout her childhood he kept Marieta in fear and dependence. Taking advantage of Marieta's disability, her father, who was her legal representative at the time, was receiving her social benefits on her behalf but spending the whole amount of the money for himself without taking care of her daily needs. Marieta's father got control of her life when Marieta was very young and this situation continued until she came of age. Despite her potential and learning skills, the lack of family support and necessary social care hindered Marieta from acquiring her budget management skills (especially how to save, manage and spend her own income), as well as how to develop self-confidence in taking independent decisions. At that time, there wasn't any strict control system by the responsible state authorities, for example the Social Assistance Directorate or the Child Protection Departments, to check whether Marieta was receiving the social benefits she was entitled to, and whether the money was spent to meet her specific needs as a person with a disability.

Case 1: the simple smartphone purchase

When the first case occurred – the signing of the two-year contract for purchase of a smartphone on deferred payments – for the very first time, Marieta acted independently according to her will and preferences. But there was a lack of support in exercising her right at the time of the purchase because she did not receive the needed information regarding the content of the contract, including information about what her obligations would be if she entered this contract, especially with regard to fixed-term payments on an instalment plan. Even if the shop assistant had noticed that Marieta and her friend both needed additional support and specific interpretation of the information about the contract conditions and the legal consequences in an easy to understand format, she did not provide it. The shop assistant's responsibility in this matter is separate to the company's obligation to make its services accessible to persons with disabilities. The requirement to make services accessible should include the provision of information in accessible formats – an obligation which the company did not fulfil in this case. Because of either misinformation between the parties, lack of special training of the telephone company's staff, or lack of awareness of how to trade with a diverse range of clients, including clients needing additional support, it seems that the shop assistant simply wanted to have the purchase contract signed as soon as possible and did not take any steps to ensure that Marieta or her friend understood the contract.

This case impacted on Marieta's relationships with her father and grandfather. They got angry with her because she purchased the smartphone, acting independently without their approval, neither taking into account the family's or her financial resources. As a person with intellectual disability, who was perceived by her family to be facing difficulties with managing her financial affairs, and in order to be protected from future purchases that could damage her financial situation, Marieta faced the risk of potentially being placed under guardianship under the national law. Technically, her father and grandfather could have brought an action before the court to place her under guardianship on the basis that she couldn't independently exercise her civil rights and carry on her own affairs and finances.[2] The legal provisions that allow this are provided in the Bulgarian Persons and Family Act (PFA). According to Article 5, paragraph 1 of the PFA: 'adults who, due to imbecility or mental illness, cannot take care of their issues, shall be placed under full guardianship and become incapacitated to act'. Under this type of guardianship, the guardian can carry out a broad range of legal actions on behalf of the person.

Paragraph 2 of Article 5 provides that 'adults with such sufferings, whose state of health is not so severe to be put under full guardianship, shall be placed under limited guardianship'. Under this type of guardianship, the individual can only take legal action with the consent of the guardian, but they can make simple small contracts themselves to meet their current needs and receive pay for their labour. People with intellectual disabilities, like Marieta for example, who owe money under civil contracts, can be brought before the court by their relatives to be put under guardianship in their best interests with the purpose to avoid damaging themselves. So, her family members could also have argued that option as a necessity to 'protect' Marieta's interests. But thinking about the words all together: 'interest', 'protection', 'limitation', 'become incapacitated', I asked myself, how can a limitation of the person's legal capacity to act independently provide protection for civil rights, when it gives the power to make decisions to another person? And the only answer I found was that there was no way to protect someone's interests if you deprive the person from his/her natural rights. It is not justice. And it shouldn't be in our value system. Because when it comes to who we actually protect, I think the answer is – society's rights and its comfort than the rights of the person.

Case 2: the possible solution – supported decision-making

When the second case occurred at the end of 2014, Marieta had already found a couple of new friends at the Day Care Centre and received full support of the social workers, psychologists and work therapists from the Centre. During this period, she increased her social skills and developed skills to make her own budget and to shop independently. She participated in a project for integrated employment and started to develop her working skills. Despite this, she still didn't have enough income to pay for the new smartphone she wanted because the amount of her social pension and salary only were covering the costs of the social services she was using and some daily needs. Also, she had not yet built a support network of trusted people, so she didn't share her wish with the staff members who could have helped her with savings and management of her financial resources.

One year later, in 2015, Marieta joined the supported decision-making pilot project of the RASPMD – a member organisation of the BAPID. Then, with the help of a social worker – her facilitator – she invited her friends, specialists and social workers to become a part of her informal support network. Thus, every time she has difficulties and needs support to make decisions on financial, contractual or health issues, she knows she can receive support from her network. Although there weren't any direct legal consequences for Marieta, the second story shows how her wish to buy something simple like a phone, for example, without asking for support or advice from her supporters, could have caused negative legal consequences for the third person – Ivan. His wish to purchase a phone, spending the whole amount of his monthly pension without getting any documents to prove his purchase, could also put him at risk of being placed under guardianship. And this is because his decision could be interpreted as 'wrong' and not in his 'best interests'.

To a great extent, these risks arose because of the lack of supportive legal framework and social system in Bulgaria that could protect both Marieta and Ivan from potential negative consequences of exercising their contractual rights. The existing legal system does not provide obligations for companies and traders to use appropriate methods to ensure that persons with disabilities have adequate support before entering into contracts. Reforms could include the adoption of legal obligations for traders to provide extra support and more information to persons with disabilities in a manner consistent with their needs, from one side, and the provision of legally recognised individual support measures, from the other. For example, Article 12, paragraph 3 of the UN Convention on the Rights of Persons with Disabilities (CRPD) provides that States Parties (such as the Republic of Bulgaria) shall take appropriate measures to provide access by persons with disabilities to the support they may require in exercising their legal capacity. Supported decision-making can take the form of a community-based skills building model of support, which empowers people with intellectual disabilities and mental health problems to make and communicate decisions about their lives.

Within the Bulgarian pilot project for supported decision-making, Marieta was helped to build her own support network of trusted persons who supported her in exercising her civil rights independently and finding the best solutions to the problems she faced. The facilitation of the building of a support network was actually a support measure implemented within the social work program of the Day Care Centre. As a result, by the end of 2016, she demonstrated enhanced self-confidence in exercising her civil rights in daily life, as a responsible person with respect to herself and the community. As it is evident from her words in the last two paragraphs of her story, supported decision-making helped her in the development of her personality. She is a quick learner and used her ability to learn from experience and apply the lessons learnt in life. Now, when Marieta faces difficulties in exercising her right to contract or managing her money, she seeks the assistance or advice of her trusted persons to make her own choices and act independently. And if in 2012 Marieta was provided with legally recognised support measures, the negative consequences (fear, panic, monetary obligations) for her would be completely avoided.

Empowerment through the supported decision-making made it possible for Marieta to rediscover the social world and herself as participant in that world. Both the spatial and the temporal boundaries of her private world are expanding very rapidly: she dares to explore social territories that were previously inaccessible to her, such as business relations, and make future plans, thus showing that a new life horizon is appearing before her.

Final thoughts

Five years after the ratification of the CRPD, the State of Bulgaria still hasn't adopted a system of appropriate measures into the national legislation to provide persons with intellectual disabilities with the support they may require in the exercise of their legal capacity, including the exercise of their contractual rights. If the telephone company had a legal obligatio, for which a penalty is envisaged, to provide Marieta with the necessary information and interpretations in an understandable way in order to clarify her all the contract clauses and give her enough time to consider, probably she would not have signed the first purchase contract and she would have been protected from affecting her contractual rights, as well as from the risk of being placed under guardianship due to a perceived inability to manage her financial affairs.

The revocation of guardianship by means of legislative changes and the validation of the new support measures will be a decisive U-turn in the national law. Irreversible societal change, however, requires a more sustainable transformation in the culture backed up by a constantly evolving legal and institutional framework. This could ensure the improvement of the system of community-based support and the evolution of the professional practice and ethics of the professions assisting in the process. The Council of Ministers, after three years of debate and three public consultation procedures, in 2016 made a proposal to change the legal framework through the adoption of the draft law of the Natural

Persons and Support Measures Act, which will now be placed again on the policy agenda. But whether this will become a solution, accessible to everyone, and will give legal guarantees for receiving support in a way ensuring that human rights of persons with disabilities are recognised and respected, depends on the legislative authority of the Republic of Bulgaria, which has also ratified the CRPD. Until that moment, Marieta and many other persons with intellectual disabilities like her will be waiting for legal reform to happen and will continue to advocate publicly for their human rights (such as civil and political rights) and fundamental freedoms.

Notes

1 Marieta's friend did not wish his his real name to be used therefore he is referred to here as Ivan.
2 According to Article 336, paragraph 1 of the Bulgarian Civil Procedure Code 'the spouse, close relatives, the prosecutor and anyone with a legitimate interest may apply to request the placing of a person under full or limited guardianship'.

13 From institutional life to home ownership: a personal story demonstrating the power of support to enable the exercise of legal capacity

Paul Alford and Michelle Browning

I was 19, going on 20, when I moved into Peamount Hospital[1] on 19 April 1983. I had moved there from a nursing home in Blackrock called St Augustine's, which was run by the St John of God Brothers. I had been working with the St John of God Brothers for two years as a cleaner doing long hours and not being paid the right money so I decided I wanted to leave. I didn't have anywhere else to go so I called a social worker who got me a bed at Peamount Hospital in Newcastle, County Dublin. The social worker told me I would be at Peamount for six months. It took me 32 and a half years to leave.

I had never lived with my family in the family home. My brother Jimmy told me I had bad health as a child and was in and out of hospital a lot. I grew up in a boarding school run by nuns in Baldoyle. At the school, we were abused and forced to do things we didn't want to do. I was punished if I got out of bed at night to go to the toilet. The nuns would stop me from going on outings or receiving money for the week. It was a hard life there.

When I moved to Peamount Hospital, I was the youngest person living onsite. I stayed at St. Brendan's for the first two years where I slept in a dormitory and had to have meals at certain times. You learned pretty quickly if you didn't eat what came out of the kitchen you would starve. The staff made big pots of tea and I wanted coffee. At 9pm each night was the last cup of tea and we were given two biscuits. After this time, we couldn't eat again until breakfast the following day at 8am. Each night we had to go to bed at 10pm and get up at 7am.

I loved travelling and when I moved into St. Brendan's, the staff told me I couldn't go out on my own without permission. I told the staff I already had a holiday booked to the Isle of Man and because it was paid for they couldn't stop me. They had meetings about me that I was never allowed to attend. Over time, they got to know me and my background and eventually they agreed to let me go. I had a great time away. They told me in the future I should tell them before I book. I chose to ignore their advice.

When I was living at St. Brendan's my mum and dad would come and visit on Sundays to have a chat and a cup of tea or a biscuit. Once every blue moon my three brothers and one sister would come to visit me. I used to have to get permission to leave Peamount and visit them at their home in East Wall, Dublin 3.

After my first two years in St. Brendan's in 1985, I moved to Pine Lodge, which was one of the bungalows at Peamount. I lived with nine other people. Occasionally, when I got to visit my family, I would catch the bus there and take my dad the Irish Independent newspaper and my mum custard creams for afternoon tea. I also liked catching the bus to visit my friend John Bradley and his family. John and I met in a park through listening to a show on Radio Dublin. We stayed in touch over the years writing letters and later in person. We would meet up in Dublin to visit the pub and come home late. I thought of John's family like my own family. I stayed with John and his family a lot over the years, I bought them Easter eggs and presents at Christmas. John's mum tells me she likes what I have done with my life. She would like the same thing for John.

In 1990, I moved to Aylmer Road, a residential house still part of Peamount, where I learned to cook, wash my own clothes and clean. Meal times were still set and I had to go to bed at 10pm every night. I shared a room at Aylmer Road with one other person.

During this time at Peamount, I had no choice in the work I did. We all had to work onsite at workshops or 'sweat shops' as they were called. I had two different jobs over the years. One was packing empty whiskey bottles in cardboard boxes and the other was tying up mushroom baskets and covering them in shrink-wrap. The supervisor of the workshop was a bully. She wouldn't allow me outside to have a smoke. At the time, I enjoyed smoking cigars and now I smoke a pipe. She would time people when they went to the toilet and if someone was late she would ring their house and threaten that they wouldn't get paid. When I worked there, I was paid 10 pence a day (10 cents), which was 50 pence a week (50 cents).

For a short time, I moved out of Peamount to work as a kitchen porter at a hotel in Wicklow. I had my own room there for six weeks but I couldn't stay because they told me I was too slow at the job. I was disappointed to have to return to Peamount.

In 2003, I got a job working in the office of a drama and performance group called Shadow Box on Saturdays. The job was in Bray, County Wicklow which meant commuting an hour and a half each way. I would answer calls, clean and go to the bank for them. I was paid more to do this job and also enjoyed doing it. When I did this work, it was the first time I could start to save money towards moving out of Peamount and into my own apartment.

The whole time I was living at Peamount, the organisation had been receiving my disability allowance and taking everything except €20 or €30 (pocket money). In 2005, the law changed[2] and it meant people in institutions were able to receive the money owed to them directly. A friend from Inclusion Ireland, Liza Kelly, helped me get the money I was owed. It took three years to get my money back but in 2008, I received a big cheque in my own name. Peamount had wanted me to deposit the cheque in the Bank of Ireland but I said no. I put the money in to the TSB bank myself. Later on, I decided to use that money to buy my own apartment.

Around this time at Peamount, the staff there started taking me to self-advocacy meetings once a month. It was at the Hill Street advocacy meeting that I was invited to be become part of an anti-bullying group run by the National Institute for Intellectual Disability at Trinity College Dublin (now known as Trinity Centre for People with Intellectual Disabilities). I travelled to their office in Dublin on the bus from Newcastle and it took me half an hour. The anti-bullying group was run by Stephen Curtis and Kelley Johnson. I didn't know when I joined the group that the support I would receive there would become very important in the future.

After a short while, I was approached by Inclusion Ireland to be on the RTÉ Three 60 programme.[3] The programme wanted to talk to people with disabilities who lived in institutions. Not long after doing this interview, I was offered a job at Inclusion Ireland working as an office assistant. Initially, I made many mistakes like sending letters to the wrong people because I didn't know how to read and write. I did not get a proper education at school. But Inclusion Ireland helped me find a course that would teach me how to read and write as an adult. I attended classes on Fridays for seven years so that now I can do my job well.

When Paddy Connolly became CEO of Inclusion Ireland, I got my own desk, computer and started interacting more with other staff members in the organisation. My hours were moved slightly earlier to help make the commute into town easier.

In 2009, I moved up the road to the Castle Lyons Apartments which was independent living accommodation run by Peamount. It was the first time while being a resident at Peamount I had my own room. I asked staff not to go into my room unless they had my permission because I was paying rent and had the right to my own privacy.

While at Castle Lyons, one of the three people in my part of the accommodation bullied me. She was very aggressive and would verbally attack me. We had a number of meetings and the staff told me things would change and they did for a little while, but then she went back to bullying me. The woman was in and out of hospital a lot and the stress of the situation caused my blood pressure to rise well over 200. During this time, I needed blood pressure medication to keep my blood pressure under control.

It took a long time for me to be able move out of Castle Lyons because I wanted to own my own home. The staff at Peamount kept suggesting options I didn't like for example, sharing with others and renting instead of me owning my own place. I said no because I wanted to live by myself in a place I owned.

One day while living at Castle Lyons, I went to a Genio[4] meeting with Paddy Connelly from Inclusion Ireland. People from Genio introduced me to Dr Bob McCormack from Possibilities Plus[5] and he organised a meeting with the staff at Peamount to make a plan about moving out. My brother Jimmy and his wife Bernie came to the meeting at Peamount. They were nervous about my idea to move out, but I decided that it was my life and I wanted to move. I asked Fiona Weldon, who took over from Stephen Curtis, supporting the anti-bullying group, to help me. Two people from the group had already moved in to their own places. Claire Finnigan from Possibilities Plus also had a lot to do with supporting me to move.

It took three years of meetings to help me get the money together to employ a direct support worker to help me live in my own place. Eventually, the Health Service Executive (HSE) provided some money and Peamount provided some. I had my own savings and decided to keep some for travelling and borrow some from the credit union to buy my apartment. Claire supported me to get the loan from the credit union. I needed her to explain to me what was happening with the loan and how it was going to work. I had borrowed money from the credit union before to go to Australia for holidays. Because I paid it off quickly, I had a good credit rating. The credit union never questioned my legal capacity and gave me approval for the loan without any hassle. Once I had the money, it also took time to find a place that was in the right location at the right price – near a bus route, safe area, shops and not more than €80,000.

I found my own apartment with the help of my friends Jim and Fiona in a small town called Navan in County Meath. Jim and Fiona supported me to meet the solicitor to sign the contract for the apartment. Fiona explained to the solicitor that I had a mild intellectual disability and that I had the capacity to sign the contract but I would need time to understand what was in it before I signed it. Initially, I found it hard to understand what the solicitor was talking about but with help from Jim and Fiona, I was able to understand it. Once I signed the contract, I was the proud owner of the apartment.

I moved into the apartment after some renovation on 11 January 2016. I really enjoy living there on my own. I get assistance from Brian, my direct support worker from Possibilities Plus, a few times a week and my friends, Jim and Fiona, twice a week. These supporters help me do things I can't do on my own like book holidays and buy a phone.

It was hard when I first moved into a new community. I found it difficult to find things to do and it was lonely living by myself for the first time. When I moved in, I got support for eight hours a week from Brian. Initially, I choose to use the support to get to know my new community. Brian helped me to find things in the community that I liked. I joined a local social club for people with disabilities where I made new friends and started going to bingo each week. After I had made new friends at the club and at bingo, I decided I wanted to use the support hours for different things like going to the gym and doing some work for the church. Currently, Brian and I are looking for a local pub where they play Irish music.

I have learned how to do lots of new things like cleaning my own home, cooking and baking, how to change a light bulb and budgeting. I like being busy and knowing what I am doing each week. I am starting to arrange my own doctor's appointments. I have found living on my own has been good for my health. My blood pressure is not high anymore because I am no longer feeling stressed.

I feel much happier now in my new life. I have reconnected with my brother and his family. We went away together to Graceland this year because I love Elvis Presley. I feel lucky to have such great friends. Some live close to my new home and others are further away and I speak to them on the phone. I think it is important that people with disability can do the things they want to do, live where they want to live with the support they need.

***

Paul Alford's story offers a number of important insights into the enablers and barriers people with cognitive disabilities face in exercising their right to live in the community and own property. Prior to Paul being able to exercise his legal capacity, there were significant social and environmental barriers that needed to be overcome. There were personal barriers such as illiteracy and a lack of confidence, social barriers such as isolation from long-term institutionalisation, and resource constraints such as difficulty accessing individualised funding. The social and environmental barriers Paul encountered represented a mountain he had to climb with the support of some important people and processes. The help he received to sign the contract for the property and obtain a loan from the credit union were the final steps in a long climb to the summit of the mountain.

In Ireland, there are still over 3,000 people who live in institutions who want to be able to live their own life, in their own home (Fleming et al., 2016). Despite de-congregation being a policy agenda in Ireland for the last six years (Health Service Executive, 2011), social and environmental barriers have prevented de-institutionalisation from occurring for many people with intellectual disabilities. Paul and I hope that by sharing his experiences, people in Ireland and other parts of the world may be better placed to move into a home of their choosing in the community. We hope that changes in community expectations will make it less necessary for people with cognitive disabilities to have to climb mountains to be able to exercise their right to own their own home.

Personal barriers

Institutional life has been described as a 'trap' that mindlessly imposes 'segregation and supervision on people who require accommodation and assistance' (O'Brien, 2005, p. 260). Living in an institution for the majority of Paul's life had a significant impact. It limited the opportunities he had to learn to read and write, affected his self-confidence and prevented him from developing an understanding of his rights as a citizen. For Paul, the rigid routine of life at Peamount undermined his ability to express his individual preferences and make decisions. Paul experienced punishment when he tried to assert his independence and make choices about how he wanted to use his time.

A key turning point in Paul's journey was becoming involved with the anti-bullying group at Trinity College. This group offered Paul the opportunity to learn about his rights and develop skills in self-advocacy. It also connected him with peers who had similar goals and who became trusted friends. Paul met other people who dreamed of leaving congregated care and who also eventually moved into their own homes. These relationships offered Paul the opportunity to discover new things about himself. He developed a stronger sense of who he was and what he wanted out of life. He also developed greater confidence in his ability to speak up and ask for what he wanted. When Paul experienced bullying at Peamount, he had the courage to speak out against it. His complaints were often ignored but he didn't give up asking for what he knew was right.

> The institution wants to silence you; find safe ways to use your voice and don't give up just because others don't act on your messages.
>
> (O'Brien, 2005, p. 268)

Paul was never subject to a legal order that determined he was incapable of exercising his legal capacity. Even so, the staff at Peamount questioned his capacity to make decisions about his life. In spite of the scepticism of staff, Paul believed he was capable of living independently in the community, and developed financial literacy, by having his own bank account and borrowing money to go on holidays. These actions led to him having a good credit rating and paved the way for him to be able to borrow money from the credit union to be able to purchase his own home.

> The institution makes decisions for you to protect you from risks; see yourself as a decision-maker and take risks to improve the chances of getting what you want
>
> (O'Brien, 2005, p. 268)

Social barriers

Social isolation and segregation from the wider community creates a significant barrier for people wanting to move out of institutional life. A defining characteristic of institutional life is 'social distance' (Mansell and Beadle-Brown, 2010, p. 105). This distance makes connecting with supporters and allies who would be able to provide independent assistance difficult for people living in institutions. Additionally, the people who work in institutions typically see residents as 'less valuable' than other people (Mansell and Beadle-Brown, 2010, p. 105). The culture of institutional settings reinforces negative attitudes about the residents living in them. This was certainly the case for Paul as the staff at Peamount were unable to see him as someone who was capable of living independently in the community. For years, their low expectations and negative beliefs prevented Paul from being given the opportunity to explore community living. The experiences of people such as Paul moving out of institutions highlight 'how important it is for people with intellectual disabilities to have family or advocates or friends to support them in moving out' (Johnson, 2005, p. 146).

An important strategy Paul employed, which significantly contributed to his success leaving the institution, was gathering a group of people around him that he trusted. Without realising it, Paul formed a circle of support. During his involvement in the anti-bullying group and his employment at Inclusion Ireland

Paul connected with people who became friends and allies. They listened to the dreams he had for his life, respected his wishes, encouraged him to ask for what he wanted and motivated him to continue when things became difficult. These people, as Paul would describe them, became his 'champions' and 'fighters'. Without these advocates, Paul would not have been able to achieve his goal to move out of the institution. These important people had skills, access to resources and social connectedness that allowed Paul to successfully obtain the individualised funding he needed to be able move out.

> The institution wants to own you and your past; tell and retell your own story to yourself and anyone you can trust to listen ... The institution wants to own your future; keep your dream alive and guard it from people who would try to kill it.
>
> (O'Brien, 2005, p. 269)

Article 12 of the CRPD outlines the importance of people with disability receiving support to exercise their legal capacity (Committee on the Rights of Persons with Disabilities, 2014). For many people with intellectual disability having supporters who listen, respect, and encourage them to communicate and act on their will and preferences is a central to being able to exercise their legal rights.

Financial barriers

Moving from an institution requires 'the commitment of resources to support people in new ways to make and act on decisions about moving to new housing arrangements of their choice' (Fisher et al., 2015, p. 69). Once Paul was linked in with the right people, he needed to obtain the financial resources to leave Peamount. This involved a number of important processes. Paul needed individualised funding that would enable him to be supported to live independently in the community. Paul was linked in with the organisation Possibilities Plus that advocated for him to obtain individualised funding and supported him to engage in a person centred planning process. Advocacy groups in Ireland have demanded that the Irish Government lives up to its commitment to implement policy-based recommendations for individualised funding, which are necessary to accelerate the process of de-institutionalisation (Fleming, McGilloway and Barry, 2016). For Paul, the process of obtaining individualised funding took 3 years and a significant amount of advocacy. This seems too long and unreachable for many people who are less well connected.

A successful transition to community-based services needs to be 'carefully planned around the needs and wishes of individual people and then continually monitored and adjusted as people's needs and wishes change' (Mansell and Beadle-Brown, 2010, p. 109). Possibilities Plus engaged in a thorough discovery process (person centred planning process) with Paul. This involved identifying his priorities, needs and all the options available to him in the community. Paul's priority was living in his own home. At the time, there was a shortage of public housing which meant Paul had to wait over eight years to obtain property in this way. Luckily, for Paul his tendency towards saving, his good credit rating and a change in the law in 2006 meant he had the funds to explore purchasing his own home. For many people coming out of institutions, public housing would be their only viable option.

In 2006, the Irish Government recognised that people like Paul had been overcharged fees by the institutions in which they lived for many years. The Health (Repayment Scheme) Act was created to enable people who had been charged unlawfully to live in institutions to have their money returned. Paul was supported by staff at Inclusion Ireland to apply for redress. The application was successful and when Paul received a large lump sum of money, he used that as a deposit to purchase his home. Without the introduction of the Health Repayment Scheme, Paul might never have been able to afford to purchase his own home.

Support with communication

Many people in institutions have higher support needs whether because of the nature of their intellectual and physical disabilities, their perceived challenging behaviour or social impairments (Mansell and Beadle-Brown, 2010). As a result, people with higher support needs often experience worse outcomes than people who require less support (Felce and Emerson, 2001). A model of decision-making support called 'supported decision-making' has been promoted internationally as a means of enabling people with disabilities to exercise their legal decision-making rights (Committee on the Rights of Persons with Disabilities, 2014) and has been used in Australia to improve the outcomes of people with high support needs in the context of de-institutionalisation (Fisher et al., 2015). Supported decision-making was the means by which people with high support needs were assisted to identify and communicate their preferences around moving in to the wider community (Fisher et al., 2016). A practice framework was developed to help decision-making facilitators provide decision-making support to residents at a large institution in New South Wales, Australia (Bigby and Douglas, 2015). Project facilitators had three roles to: work with families and staff to develop their skills and confidence as decision-making supporters, help to build a network of supporters for people with limited family connections, and, if necessary, build relationships with and act directly as decision-making supporters for people who have no network beyond paid support staff (Bigby and Douglas, 2015). The practice framework involved steps in supporting decision-making, principles and strategies for practice. It seems the use of supported decision-making in the context of de-institutionalisation may ensure the rights of residents to participate in decision-making and have their will and preferences direct their transition to living in the community. While this framework is yet to be formally evaluated, other trials of practice in Australia have demonstrated support for decision-making has positive outcomes for decision makers and supporters (Bigby et al., 2017). Positive outcomes include decision makers becoming more confident making decisions with support, experiencing greater autonomy and participating in a wider range of activities (Bigby et al., 2017). Given growing evidence regarding the benefits of supported decision-making, people with intellectual and other forms of cognitive disability would benefit from the practice becoming more widely available to support their self-determination and the exercise of their right to legal capacity.

Support to exercise legal capacity

Paul's legal capacity was not a significant barrier to him acquiring his own home. His solicitor and credit union did not question his legal capacity because he was well supported to understand the legal contracts by his supporters. Through receiving support, Paul was able to the sign the relevant documents, exercise his legal capacity, and become a homeowner. Many people with intellectual and other cognitive disabilities do not have adequate support to understand legal contracts. Paul's experience exemplifies the significant role informal support can have in assisting a person with intellectual disability to move from being incapable of exercising their legal capacity independently to being able to do so with the right support. Without this support, Paul would likely have been denied the right to own property. Paul's story demonstrates the importance of this type of decision-making support being available to all people with intellectual and cognitive disabilities to ensure they are able to exercise their human rights (Committee on the Rights of Persons with Disabilities, 2014).

Perhaps, the greatest challenge Paul faced in exercising his legal capacity were the attitudes and limited beliefs of the staff at Peamount who were in positions of power. Gaining the freedom to choose his own home was brought about by challenging the attitudes and beliefs others had about his capacity and finding people who could help him acquire the skills and resources he needed to realise his goal.

Support through law reform

The law must ensure it is accessible for all and, where there are injustices such as unfair payment for work or unlawful charges in relation to accommodation, it holds individuals, organisations and governments accountable. It must ensure people with cognitive disabilities are provided with access to the services and support they need to be able to move out of institutions. Services need to listen to the priorities and needs of each person and support them to develop important skills they were unable to acquire in the institutional environment such as literacy, financial acumen, self-advocacy and the safety to speak out against bullying and harassment. Governments need to ensure people with cognitive disabilities have access to individualised funding and appropriate housing alternatives to congregate care. To ensure this occurs, the law must reflect a new rights-based paradigm of disability and drive cultural changes that reflect this new paradigm such as de-institutionalisation, and individualised and person centred approaches to providing accommodation and support.

Notes

1 Peamount Healthcare was founded in 1912 as a Tuberculosis (TB) Sanatorium. Services for people with intellectual disabilities were established in 1963 following a request from the Department of Health to accommodate persons with intellectual disabilities. Taken from the Peamount Healthcare website on 8 July 2016 [online] Available at: http://www.peamount.ie/our-services/information-on-services-for-health-professionals/residential-services/ [Accessed 19 Jan. 2018].

2 The Health (Repayment Scheme) Act 2006 was created to enable people who had been charged unlawfully to live in institutions to have their money returned. The scheme was administered in accordance with the provisions of the Health Repayment Scheme Act 2006 (Act No. 17 of 2006). In total, 35,417 applications were received under the scheme and 19,809 claimants received a repayment. The total amount repaid by the Irish government was €448.7million. Information obtained from Health Services Executive (2018). Health Repayments Scheme [online] Available at: http://hse.ie/eng/services/list/4/olderpeople/healthrepaymentscheme.html [Accessed 19 Jan. 2018].

3 Three 60 was a lifestyle program shown on RTÉ, Ireland's national television and radio broadcaster in the mid-2000s. Paul Alford was interviewed by the program to discuss his limited wage working in the sheltered workshop. The program sought to explore whether people with intellectual disabilities can be supported to manage their own money, what role sheltered workshops have in modern day society, and how people in residential care can be supported to pay their bills and contribute to the household in an independent manner. Paul's interview was aired on Monday 8 August 2005, at 7.30pm. See RTÉ (2005). Three 60 [online] Available at: https://presspack.rte.ie/2005/08/08/three-60-15/ [Accessed 19 Jan. 2018].

4 Genio is a not for profit organisation in Ireland that brings together government and philanthropy to develop, test and scale cost-effective ways of supporting disadvantaged people to live the lives they want in the community. Genio works with people with disability, people with dementia and people with mental health issues to transform services, and ensure the community-living options they fund are self-directed.

5 Possibilities Plus is a community organisation, which offers support brokerage to people with disability to enable them to control their resources and live the life they want. A support broker works with the person with disability to identify their hopes and dreams, their circle of support, and develop a support plan based on their goals that can be resourced by their individualised funding. Possibilities Plus is based in County Kildare. For more information see Possibilities Plus. (2018). http://possibilitiesplus.ie/ [Accessed 19 Jan. 2018].

Bibliography

Bigby, C. and Douglas, J. (2015). Support for decision making – a practice framework. Living with Disability Research Centre, La Trobe University.

Bigby, C., Douglas, J., Carney, T., Then, S., Wiesel, I., & Smith, E. (2017). Delivering decision-making support to people with cognitive disability – what has been learned from pilot programs in Australia from 2010–2015. *Journal of Social Issues, 52*(3), pp. 222–240.

Committee on the Rights of Persons with Disabilities (2014). General Comment No. 1. Article 12: Equal Recognition Before the Law, UN Doc. No. CRPD/C/GC/1.

Felce, D. and Emerson, E. (2001). Living with support in a home in the community: predictors of behavioural development and household and community activity. *Mental Retardation and Developmental Disabilities Research Reviews,* 7(2), pp. 75–83.

Fisher, K.R., Lutz, D., Gadow, F. Robinson, S. and Gendera, S. (2015). A transformative framework for deinstitutionalisation. *Research and Practice in Intellectual and Developmental Disabilities*, 2(1), pp. 60–72.

Fleming, P. McGilloway, S. and Barry, S. (2016). The successes and challenges of implementing individualised funding and supports for disabled people: an Irish perspective. *Disability and Society,* 31(10), pp. 1369–1384.

Health Service Executive. (2011). *Time to Move on From Congregated Settings.* A Strategy for Community Inclusion. Report of the Working Group on Congregated Settings. [online] Available at: http://www.hse.ie/eng/services/list/4/disability/congregated settings/congregatedsettingsreportfinal.pdf [Accessed 21 May 2017].

Johnson, K. (2005). Moving out: a reflection. In: K. Johnson and R. Traustadóttir (Eds.). *Deinstitutionalization and People with Intellectual Disabilities: In and Out of Institutions.* London: Jessica Kingsley Publishers, pp. 145–154.

Mansell, J. and Beadle-Brown, J. (2010). Deinstitutionalisation and community living: position statement of the Comparative Policy and Practice Special Interest Research Group of the International Association for the Scientific Study of Intellectual Disabilities. *Journal of Intellectual Disability Research,* 54(2), pp. 104–112.

O'Brien, J. (2005). Out of the Institution Trap. In: K. Johnson and R. Traustadóttir (Eds.). *Deinstitutionalization and People with Intellectual Disabilities: In and Out of Institutions.* London: Jessica Kingsley Publishers, pp. 259–273.

14 Conclusion

Contractual capacity

Clíona de Bhailís

The stories and responses in the preceding chapters are set in varied, and at times, vastly different contexts – culturally, legally, socially and personally. It may be surprising therefore, that beyond links to Article 12 of the UN Convention on the Rights of Persons with Disabilities (CRPD), there are many other common themes, shared issues, and linked solutions.

The most striking of these themes is the link between contractual capacity, Article 12 CRPD, and Article 19 CRPD. Claire, Paul and Dermot all share experiences which show how the denial of legal capacity or a lack of support to exercise legal capacity could have a monumental impact on a person's ability to exercise their right to choose where and with whom to live. For Claire, this independence was achieved after successfully challenging her plenary guardianship, known as Wardship in Ireland, and choosing her own support. She achieved her dream of owning her own home with the support of family and friends. This was after, as discussed in Chapter 9, escaping a system which was designed as a protectionist structure to safeguard a 'vulnerable' individual but which in reality left her homeless, without proper supports or access to her basic rights. Although Dermot didn't encounter a formal denial of legal capacity, his story highlights the lack of options available to people with disabilities and the importance of knowledgeable support. In Chapter 13 too, both Paul and Michelle stress how crucial his 'champions' were to Paul realising his right to live independently.

Without equal recognition of legal capacity and Article 12, realising the right to live independently and as part of community is almost impossible. Overall it is clear that a lack of choices, restricting individuals' opportunities to make choices and not being included in the community becomes a never-ending circle where if people with disabilities are not given the opportunities to make decisions for their lives, use support and take risks they may not be in a position to see the opportunities available to them and achieve their independence.

The second overarching theme in this part of the book is how contract law interacts with the minor aspects of daily life and the impact this can have. From purchasing a smartphone, to arranging a flight, to buying a dress or a pair of shoes, contract law impacts on all of us. However, as the personal experiences and responses have shown us, these simple transactions are laden with additional barriers for people with cognitive disabilities in particular. Joy and Marieta's accounts of a lack of support and opportunities to build basic skills in financial decision-making highlight how informal barriers to decision-making can impact on a person's legal capacity. In both Chapter 8 and Chapter 12, the authors acknowledge the need for support but also for opportunities to develop trusted networks and decision-making skills and resources. Financial decision-making and budgeting are skills everyone needs time to develop and ones for which most people use some form of support. However, in reality, people with intellectual disabilities are denied these opportunities all too often. Helen's story demonstrates the importance of terms within a contract and perhaps support of a different kind. For Helen, to take even a short trip on public transport engages a myriad of express and implied contractual terms in relation to accessibility, reasonable accommodation and support. The terms of the contract which mandate that a company provides these services, and perhaps more so their enforceability, are central to her independence. In Chapter 11, national, regional and international law is drawn together to advocate for a reliable system with enforcement mechanisms for when companies do not fulfil their responsibilities under a contract.

In the introduction to this part of the book readers were asked to consider the bigger picture – the need to either radically reform or reimagine existing elements of contract law to ensure that people with disabilities, and in particular people with cognitive disabilities, have the ability to enter into and exit from contracts on an equal basis with people without disabilities. In the preceding chapters, the solutions and recommendations put forward are, understandably, as varied as the experiences. Some advocate for specific and exacting changes to legislation where others call for a more general change to societal attitudes. However, what they do agree on is the need for support – be it personal or professional, the need for opportunities and choices, the need for equal recognition and the need for their voices to be respected. Therefore, while even when combined, the chapters have not outlined detailed recommendations on how to reform the entire contract law system. They have shown both the need for reform and that if the appropriate supports are available, people with disabilities can, and should, contract on an equal basis with others. With this in mind, we hope this represents the start of the conversation and the road to reform.

Part 3

Relationships and consent to sex

15 Introduction to relationships and consent to sex

María Laura Serra

By providing a theoretical analysis to a practical issue, this chapter will outline the core issues regarding sexuality and the right to have intimate relationships for persons with intellectual disabilities.

There are some legal and social barriers that interact with each other creating situations of discrimination and oppression for persons with disabilities. Owing to prejudice and stigma, persons with disabilities *do not fit* in the dominant group, where the white, bourgeois, heterosexual and able man is the lighthouse from which the centre of society was designed, and, therefore the abstract subject of law and only holder of rights.

Through the voices of the storytellers, in the next chapters, we will be able to perceive how social and legal barriers interact and reinforce each other. Legislation has a social impact, and the law legally protects some social prejudices that dominant society has about persons with intellectual disabilities in terms of intimate relationships and sexuality. In this sense, WHO and UNFPA (2009) state that persons with disabilities may be denied their right to establish relationships or may be forced into unwanted marriages.

Sexuality can never be separated from the person, nor can it be conceived as a secondary or marginal theme. 'Sexuality is the stamp of adult life' (Kulick and Rydström, 2015). It contributes to living independently and being included in the community. Hence, the development of sexuality is not entirely related to what the sexual activity entails, but also to the person's social relations and social environments. Equally important, sexual activity, as well as intimacy beyond sexuality, means a contribution to personal maturity, a better adaptation to life and greater interpersonal communication, this is, to personhood.

The CRPD, as a human rights treaty, has the clearest language in terms of sexual and reproductive health, as well as family, parenthood, and relationships. In any case, these needs and desires must be recognised and be treated in the context of pleasure and not only in the context of reproduction. Consent to sex and relationships should be treated on an equal basis for all persons, with and without disability. However, there are legal barriers which have a huge impact on persons with intellectual disabilities when it comes to their sexuality and intimate relationships. Some of the legal barriers presented in the Irish legal background, where both storytellers come from, are related to the criminalisation of sexuality. In this regard, Arstein-Kerslake and Flynn (2016) stated that 'these laws presume that people with cognitive disabilities are vulnerable'. As Sarah will show in her response, the law and the information available from the various state departments is unclear and this lack of clarity could have serious consequences for persons with intellectual disabilities. It is unclear how capacity is assessed and by whom. The lack of clarity of the law could lead to a violation of the rights to have sexual relationships as well as get married.

The denial of legal capacity is a predominant factor in each of these violations of rights regarding intimacy and sexuality. The legal capacity of persons with disabilities must be recognised in law but also in practice so that they can develop their own destinies from their own bodies and relationships.

In the meantime, social barriers through prejudices, stigmas, and stereotypes create unsafe spaces where persons with disabilities are being disciplined in their sexuality as well in their personal relationships. There are cultural expressions of the dominant group being disseminated and these are transformed into the *normal* or universal expressions. These cultural expressions are related to some stereotypes that usually are ascribed to persons with disabilities (Chappell, 1998). These stereotypes could disempower the person's agency. As Young (1990) argues, 'stereotypes permeate society in such a way that they are not perceived as questionable'. Clear evidence of how stereotypes permeate all aspects of society are the existence of legislation, court rulings and/or statements that restrict will and preferences, criminalise sexuality and to some extent could ban marriage of persons with intellectual disabilities. With this approach, we can comprehend how sexuality as well as intimacy in relationships, are not conceived as subjective experiences for persons with disabilities.

Persons with disabilities have the right to make decisions about their own bodies and intimacy with dignity, freedom, and autonomy. This does not mean without support. Disciplining sexuality and relationships and restricting choices and support, produces a process of dehumanisation where the dignity of risk is not granted. According to Habermas (2010), the idea of human dignity is the conceptual hinge that connects the morality of equal respect for everyone with positive law and democratic law-making in such a way that their interplay could give rise to a political order founded upon human rights.

In the CRPD, dignity is mentioned repeatedly. It plays a preponderant role and is the core concept needed to eliminate social disadvantages and promote human rights and fundamental freedoms so that persons with disabilities can restore their autonomy. The recognition of human rights is linked with the guarantee to the realisation of a dignified life. Lack of recognition means living below the requirement of that dignified life, without sexuality nor relationships freely consented to.

16 'My sister is married. Why can't I get married?'

Maria Mahony and Sarah Richardson

My name is Maria Mahony, I was born in Dublin in July 1970. I'm a Leo! I went to school in Raheny.

This is me with my mum, dad and godmother ready for my communion. I love my family.

I grew up to be a gymnast and went to the Special Olympics in America. I brought home five medals for Ireland.

I went to college to study hairdressing and graduated in 2012. I met Paul at the day centre we both go to, and we fell in love.

Paul asked me to marry him and I said yes.

We got married to each other but it was only when we played Sky and Sophie in Mamma Mia.

I went to look at engagement rings for Paul and me. The man in the shop wouldn't let me try on the ring. He said: 'You can't get married, you're too.

young'. He said it to my face. The cheek of him! He should mind his own business. I'm 47!! I left the shop. It wasn't very nice.

I want to marry Paul but I can't. My sister got married, why can't I get married? I was a bridesmaid in pink. My older sister got married too, and my brother who lives in England.

I met Paul 6 years ago, we've been together for three years. I love the face off him. He's very good-looking. He's my type. Paul has proposed to me lots of times. I always say yes to him.

I spoke up at Inclusion Ireland recently. I said I want my own house. I want to cook dinners. I want to be with my boyfriend. I love going to his house for dinner. I like to watch telly with him in his room.

If I was married I could live with Paul. I could watch telly with him. I might go to the pictures with him. I'd go for a drink with him.

Paul makes me happy, I like his face, I love the face off him.

I learned about sex on a course in Coolock. I learned about the pill and if you take it you don't have babies. I know about having babies. I don't want a baby. I want to have sex without having a baby. I wanted a baby but not now, I'm too old. I'm big enough and old enough to have sex. I don't know why they won't let me.

Sex is about love. Kissing in the centre – it's not allowed, so we go outside. I don't want to get in trouble. I'd love to get married. The important thing about marriage is love and being kind.

It's my body, my choice!

***

Responding to Maria's question

'My sister got married, why can't I get married?' seems to be the most important question to address. It is something that is clearly personally important to Maria but, in addressing the question, legal and social factors will need to be considered; marriage is both a legal commitment and a personal one that takes place within a social environment. I want to explore 'who' or 'what' is preventing Maria from getting married and under what legitimacy? Do any such barriers exist or are they only perceived?

Maria is an adult woman, an Irish citizen. She also has a disability. She holds rights laid down in various treaties including the right to recognition before the law and the right to marry. She is guaranteed these rights under various International Human Rights Treaties which Ireland has signed up to (European Convention on Human Rights, Convention on the Rights of Persons with Disabilities, and the International Convention on Civil and Political Rights for example); she also holds rights domestically through the Irish constitution. The Irish constitution contains fundamental rights including protection of the family (Article 41). The Irish courts' interpretation of these rights has resulted in the recognition of associated rights not expressly set out in the constitution, which includes the right to marry. The Department of Foreign Affairs and Trade on its website states that 'Ireland is committed to having human rights both at the heart of both our national and foreign policy. Ireland is committed to creating the conditions in which these rights can be realised.'

What are Maria's rights under the Convention for the Rights of Persons with Disabilities (CRPD)?

At the time of writing, Ireland is a signatory to the CRPD which means it has given a preliminary endorsement of the Convention. Signing does not create a binding legal obligation but it does demonstrate the State's intent to examine the treaty domestically and consider ratifying it. It also obliges the State to refrain from acts that would defeat or undermine the treaty's objective and purpose, which is to promote, protect and ensure the full and equal enjoyment of all human rights and fundamental freedoms by all persons with disabilities, and to promote respect for their inherent dignity.

Of particular relevance in addressing the question are Articles 12 and 23. Article 12 guarantees equal recognition before the law for all persons with disabilities, who should also enjoy legal capacity on an equal basis with others. Importantly, it also identifies the State as being responsible for taking appropriate measures to provide access to support that people with disabilities might need in order to exercise their legal capacity.

Article 23 guarantees the right of people with disabilities to marry with the usual caveat that free and full consent of both parties is required; it also requires the State to take effective and appropriate measures to eliminate discrimination against people with disabilities in matters relating to marriage.

Marriage is the legally or formally recognised union of two people as partners in a personal relationship so what are the legal requirements and are there any legal barriers to Maria being able to get married?

In order to meet a legal requirement, one must have legal personhood to exercise legal capacity. Article 12 of the CRPD states that 'persons with disabilities have the right to recognition everywhere as persons before the law… [and] *enjoy* legal capacity on an equal basis with others in all aspects of life'. This opens the door to *enjoying* rights to do things including the right to marry, buy somewhere to live and vote. There is no requirement in human rights law to demonstrate anything other than being a member of the human race in order to claim legal personhood. Series (2015) states that human rights approaches connect legal personality to any *human,* regardless of their individual capacities. Therefore, legal personhood cannot be withdrawn using any status approach e.g. having a disability. In fact, there is a duty upon the State to 'take appropriate measures to provide access by persons with disabilities to the support they may require in exercising their legal capacity'.

Stavert, McGregor and Martin (2016) state that legal capacity has been described in a number of ways. Series (2015) points out that law and legal scholarship recognises a diverse family of legal practices concerned with the concepts of 'legal personality' and 'legal capacity' which govern whether and how different entities may enjoy legal rights and duties. To be clear, I will be adopting the interpretation of Article 12 issued by the UN Committee on the Rights of Persons with Disabilities General Comment No. 1 (CRPD Committee, 2014, para.13) as follows:

> Legal capacity is the ability to hold rights and duties (legal standing) and to exercise these rights and duties (legal agency).

Having established that Maria is a person entitled to human rights on an equal basis with other persons and who has legal capacity, meaning she is the holder of rights and should be able to exercise her rights, including the right to get married, there would appear to be no legal barrier.

What are the legal requirements in order to get married in Ireland?

In order to get married in Ireland, the parties must be over 18 and there must be no impediment to marriage (section 2(2), Civil Registration Act 2004 as amended). An impediment includes being already married or being related by blood or marriage to each other (section 2(a)). Maria and the person she wants to marry are both over the age of 18. Neither of them has been married before and neither are they related by blood or marriage.

Another impediment to marriage is the Marriage of Lunatics Act 1811, describing itself as 'an Act further to prevent the Marriage of Lunatics'. The language and purpose of the Act created 206 years ago in the reign of George II could certainly be considered archaic. A 'lunatic' is not defined in this Act, but a person who is considered a 'lunatic' is prevented from marrying unless declared sane by the Lord Chancellor. This is still technically in force despite the fact that Ireland has no Lord Chancellor who could declare parties sane.

Before getting married, parties must also give three months' notification of the marriage to a civil registrar (section 46). Interestingly, the 2004 Act does not discuss the requirement for parties to give free consent to the marriage, although this is a principle of common law, which will be referred to later.

As part of the notification process, parties must sign a declaration that there is no impediment to the marriage (section 46). After this, anyone can object to the proposed marriage, if they believe there is an impediment. For example, if someone believes this would be a 'marriage of lunatics' they can lodge an objection with An t-Ard-Chláraitheoir (the Chief Registrar) and must provide a certificate from a registered medical practitioner to support their objection (section 58(11)). The Chief Registrar will adjudicate the objection and if found valid, will direct that the marriage is not performed. If invalid, the marriage will proceed. In performing the marriage ceremony, the solemniser must be satisfied that 'the parties to the marriage understand the nature of the marriage ceremony and the declarations' they make (section 51(2)(d)), which are that there is no impediment to the marriage, and that they accept each other as husband and wife, or spouse (section 51(4)).

When the Assisted Decision-Making Capacity Act (2015) enters into force, section 7 will repeal the Marriage of Lunatics Act. The 2015 Act also amends the Civil Registration Act and makes it an explicit requirement that both parties have mental capacity to marry (section 2(2) 2004 Act as amended). A lack of capacity in this sense is considered an impediment to marriage. Once the 2015 Act is in force, objections to a potential marriage on the basis that one or both parties lack capacity must be accompanied by a copy of the declaration or order from the Circuit Court which verifies the lack of capacity. However, a solemniser can still refuse to perform a marriage where he or she believes that one or both parties do not understand the marriage ceremony or the declarations they are making.

It is perhaps because Ireland is currently at a crossroads in repealing old laws and bringing in new ones that there are differing interpretations of the requirements that appear on governmental and NGO websites which can cause confusion.

For example, according to Citizens Information Ireland (2016) the legal pre-requisites for marriage contain just three rules. To contract a legally valid marriage in Ireland, the parties to the marriage must have the capacity to marry each other, freely consent to the marriage and observe the necessary formalities. This guidance goes on to state that;

> ...free consent may be absent if, 'at the time of the marriage, a person is suffering from intoxication, brain damage, mental disability or insanity to the extent that he/she is not able to understand the implications of marriage'.

By providing these specific examples, there is the potential to single out people using, amongst other language, the rather derogatory and potentially confusing label of 'mental disabilities'. This could lead to a status based assessment of the individual's mental capacity. The Civil Registration Act (2004) clearly states a registered solemniser shall not solemnise a marriage unless he or she is satisfied that the parties to the marriage understand the nature of the marriage ceremony. Therefore, this applies to everyone and does not single out those who may have a brain injury, intellectual disability, mental ill health or perhaps even have had a few drinks before the ceremony.

Citizens Information Ireland (2016) also states that;

> To be legally entitled to marry, both parties must also have the mental capacity to understand *the nature of* marriage.

So, in this interpretation freely consenting requires 'understanding *the implications of* marriage', whilst having mental capacity requires 'understanding *the nature* of marriage'. Perhaps this is a semantic difference, but, as has already been pointed out, the 2004 Act does not discuss the requirement for parties to give free consent to the marriage; therefore, there is no definition of what exactly someone has to demonstrate.

So, a potential barrier is identified; a problem arises in that in the interpretation of the law one of the 'legal requirements' to marry appears to be based on the ability to demonstrate 'understanding of the implications of marriage' if, amongst other things, you have a 'mental disability'.

What is a mental disability? There is no clear definition with different terms being used by different governmental departments and professionals, e.g. learning difficulty, learning difficulties, learning disability, mental handicap, mental disability, mental disorder, etc. In Ireland the terminology commonly adopted in legislation and by non-governmental organisations including, most importantly, by advocacy organisations such as Inclusion Ireland, is 'intellectual disability'.

Whatever the terminology used, and it is important, there is already confusion evident which could lead to a test that does not apply to those who do not have a learning or intellectual disability. Whilst referring to the use of terminology, the use of the term 'suffering' in the guidance is also negative implying pain, discomfort and/or an ongoing sense of hopelessness. It is pejorative language often employed when writing about people with disabilities and is not respectful of people's inherent dignity.

When anyone's capacity is questioned, there needs to be a robust legal framework in place to support the person whose capacity is in question. I will refer to the law in England as this is the country I live in, and so am most familiar with the principles and some of the challenges of implementation. There is a presumption of capacity in English law – the Mental Capacity Act (2005) (MCA). This Act states it is the responsibility of the person who is questioning an individual's capacity to demonstrate they do not have it, rather than the person having to prove they have. However, this is done by applying a two stage assessment. Stage one determines whether the person has an impairment of, or disturbance in the functioning of the mind or brain. Stage two is a functional assessment of capacity. The functional test requires the person to demonstrate they can understand the information needed to make a decision, retain the information for long enough to make a decision, evaluate or weigh up the information, understand the effect of not making a decision and communicate that decision. There has been much criticism of the MCA, the overwhelming view from academic legal scholars and Disability Rights UK is that the MCA is not compliant with the CRPD. Criticisms include that it permits legal capacity to be denied on the dual basis of mental incapacity and disability and the definition of mental incapacity in s.2 (1) of the MCA violates the anti-discrimination provisions of CRPD Article 5, specifically in its restriction of mental incapacity to those who suffer from an 'impairment of, or a disturbance in the functioning of, the mind or brain' (Disability Rights UK, 2017). There are examples of the MCA being used inappropriately to conduct invasive assessments of capacity with regards to the right to marry (Ryan, 2014).

The same principles with regards to the definition of capacity and the four-stage functional assessment also apply in the Assisted Decision-Making (Capacity) Act (2015) (although the direction on decision-making when a lack of capacity has been established is on the individual's will and preference rather than the sometimes subjective best interests used in the MCA (2005)).

However, there is further confusion as to whether the Assisted Decision-Making (Capacity) Act can be used to assess someone's mental capacity with regards to the right to marry with many references found online, e.g. an article by published the Law Society Gazette in March 2016 stating 'the Act defines capacity in relation to decision-making and explicitly sets out that it does not apply to capacity or consent required in relation to marriage' (Butler, 2016, p. 44). A factsheet explaining the remit of the Assisted Decision-Making Capacity Act published by Inclusion Ireland (2016) states that decisions relating to marriage or divorce, adoption, jury membership and sexual relationships are covered by different laws.

While there are separate laws on these issues, the Assisted Decision-Making Capacity Act, does, as discussed above, amend the Civil Registration Act in relation to capacity to marry. This change was made in a later reading of the Bill,[1] so that it will, in the future, be used to assess mental capacity with regards to the right to marry; but again, this information is not readily accessible.

According to Inclusion Ireland (2016):

> there is no provision to assess capacity to marry prior to the marriage of two persons. Typically an assessment of a person's capacity to marry is made upon the breakdown of a marriage. At present there are no reported cases of annulment of marriage on the basis that a person lacked capacity because of intellectual disability. Once a person can be found to understand the nature and effect of getting married then s/he can be said to possess the capacity to marry.

This is supported by Matthews (2015) who states that 'In Ireland, some marriages have been nullified due to the inability of one of the parties to consent to the marriage due to mental illness, but there is no case law on the capacity to consent to marriage on the part of older persons with dementia, or those with intellectual disabilities.'

However, there is further guidance on getting married found on the website of the Department of Social Protection (2017) which states an impediment to marriage is that 'one or both parties are incapable by reason of intellectual disability or mental illness of understanding the nature and effect of the marriage contract, a medical report is required to establish the facts in such cases'. This would appear to be referring to the provisions of the Civil Registration Act (2004) (Section 58(11)) that an objection on the grounds that the marriage would be void by virtue of the Marriage of Lunatics Act shall be accompanied by a certificate of a registered medical practitioner supporting the objection, which is still technically in force.

In short, it's all very confusing, with different interpretations and guidance found on a number of different governmental and NGO websites and very little, if any, of the information is accessible to someone with an intellectual disability.

Let's talk about sex

The issues regarding the right to marry go hand in hand with the right to have a sexual relationship and a family. Maria explained she had attended two courses on sexual education in the recent past 'I learned about sex and babies. I love to talk about sex, I can have sex if I want, I can speak for myself. It's my choice, it's my body.' On Paul, she says: 'Paul makes me happy, I like his face, I love the face of him.' However, there is an underlying tension that Maria struggles to resolve. Whilst on one hand Maria uses the language of empowerment, 'it's my body, it's my choice, I can have sex if I want, I can speak for myself' she also states 'I'm big enough and old enough to have sex. I don't know why they won't let me. Sex is about love. Kissing is allowed. But we can't go there. I don't want to get in trouble.' There is clearly a feeling that she shouldn't have sex, that it is something that would get her into trouble.

If Maria and her boyfriend wanted to pursue a sexual relationship outside of marriage until as recently as March 2017 they could potentially have been committing a criminal offence. The Criminal Law (Sexual Offences) Act 1993 section 5 criminalised specific forms of sexual activity with people with intellectual disabilities. It states:

> A person who –
>
> a has or attempts to have sexual intercourse, or
> b commits or attempts to commit an act of buggery,
>
> with a person who is mentally impaired (other than a person to whom he is married or to whom he believes with reasonable cause he is married) shall be guilty of an offence.

For the purposes of this Act the definition of a person who is 'mentally impaired' only applied to people 'incapable of living independently and protecting themselves from exploitation' which appears to be a rather subjective definition. This is another piece of law that has been very recently replaced by the Criminal Law (Sexual Offences) Act 2017. Whilst consensual sexual intercourse between two people with intellectual disabilities with sufficient 'mental capacity' has now been decriminalised; Inclusion Ireland (2017) feels the new Act has not gone far enough stating it is narrow, paternalistic and protective and is not compatible with the CRPD as it categorises people with intellectual disabilities as 'protected persons', applying a special status that is clearly not disability-neutral.

Sexuality and intellectual disability is still a very taboo issue. There has been much research undertaken to show that people with intellectual disabilities do not experience the same level of sexual and relationship education as those of their peers. They are overprotected, infantilised or desexualised, and have less experience of relationships and therefore fewer opportunities to learn (Dukes and McGuire, 2009).

There are clear examples of this in Maria's story. 'I went to a shop with my keyworker to look at engagement rings. The man in the shop said I wasn't old enough'. Maria is clearly old enough. The man must know this but for some reason he finds it so difficult to comprehend that Maria could have a relationship like anyone else. He treats her like a child, both placing her in the age range of a child, although she is clearly an adult woman, and speaking to her like she is a child. We are usually only ever told we are not old enough to do something when we are children. In just four words 'You're not old enough', he disempowers her removing her dignity as an adult woman, the right to make her own decisions and her power as a customer. If she cannot even own her age, how can she own an engagement ring? The cognitively abled able-bodied male has access to power, capital, decision-making, education, resources and public space as opposed to the woman with intellectual disability who has been desexualised and infantilised.

Another very striking example is when Maria and Paul are cast as Sophie and Sky in a production of Mamma Mia. Sophie is the young bride and Sky is her fiancé, and, in the film, they get married. They were cast as a couple to play a couple getting married. Literally, you can 'play' at being married but you can't in reality. Again, there is a disempowering and infantilising discourse occurring here. Children play act, dress up and pretend to do things that grown-ups do, partly as a preparation for growing up, but people with intellectual disabilities are prevented from growing up and treated as eternal children.

A systematic review conducted by Harfleet and Turner (2016) of peer reviewed and grey literature focussing only on papers written in the UK and Ireland looked at the barriers or challenges to people with learning disabilities developing sexual/romantic relationships. They found, not surprisingly, a multitude of barriers or challenges that fit into three broad categories – barriers as a result of society and people's attitudes; barriers related to the support provided to people with learning disabilities and additional barriers to specific groups of people with learning disabilities. Interestingly there were no legal barriers. There is clear evidence of parents, teachers and staff being resistant to people with learning disabilities having sex or relationships at all, staff holding the view that relationships should be limited (e.g. kissing/holding hands is OK, but sex is not) or even ended. Maria gave me an example of this when she was told that she and Paul were not to kiss in the day centre they attended because it was not 'appropriate'. Maria said 'Kissing in the centre – it's not allowed, so we go outside'.

The lack of clarity and guidance available on governmental websites along with the very recent decriminalisation of consensual sexual intercourse and recent repeal of other outdated laws could perhaps, not surprisingly, lead to a risk-averse, over-protective approach to personal relationships from disability service staff. Overprotection of people with learning disabilities and a culture of sexual disempowerment has been well documented (McCarthy, 1999; Hollomotz, 2011; Fitzgerald and Withers, 2013).

Harfleet and Turner (2016) also found there were limitations in sex education, including lack of evidence-based sex education tools and resources as well as a lack of information, training and resources to support people to develop relationships. Again, this is reflected in Maria's experience. I asked Maria if she had learned about sex whilst at school? 'No, nothing.'

The Irish Family Planning Association (2007) acknowledge in their briefing paper on sexuality and disability that the discourse in Ireland surrounding sexuality and disability is largely paternalistic and concentrates primarily on issues of protection. This discourse is reinforced formally by legislation and public policy and informally by the social perpetuation of stereotypes and myths, such as the example given earlier by the denial of Maria's age perpetuating the 'eternal child' myth. Alexander and Taylor Gomez (2017) attempt to address some of the issues. They ask:

> We teach people many life skills; everything from cleaning their teeth to understanding public and private spaces. Why do we not routinely teach people to have healthy and intimate relationships? Why are the values and beliefs of disability service staff paramount for this particular issue, when we are supposed to be person-centred regarding everything else?

The role of the State in providing support

Returning to the provisions of the CRPD, Article 12, it is the responsibility of the State to take appropriate measures to provide access by persons with disabilities to the support they may require in exercising their legal capacity. In this instance in order to exercise her right to marry which requires the exercise of legal capacity Maria has to jump over the hurdles put before her solely because she has an intellectual disability.

Gewirth (1998) argues that individuals have rights to whatever is necessary to achieve the purposes of their action because without such guarantees they may not be able to function effectively at all (i.e. they will be unable to successfully realise their goals). Harnacke (2012) writing about the CRPD from the perspective of Nussbaum's (2001) capabilities approach supports this view stating, 'An individual who needs more resources to attain a certain capability (capability being defined by Nussbaum as what people are able to do and to be) also has a legitimate claim to the development of that capability.' If the current status quo requires Maria to demonstrate understanding of the implications and/or nature of marriage then before making any assessment of Maria's understanding, there needs to be an offer of accessible information and education provided on the implications of marriage. This would support Article 12 paragraph 3 which recognises that States' parties have an obligation to provide persons with disabilities access to the support necessary to enable them to make decisions that have legal effect, which they can choose to accept or decline.

The duty should not be on Maria to prove she understands the implications of marriage but on the State to ensure she has access to resources needed for her to enter into marriage if she chooses with the person she chooses to marry. Neither should her decisions be held up to closer scrutiny than anyone else. She should be allowed to take risks and make mistakes, like everyone without an intellectual disability can. The concept of the dignity of risk was first articulated by Perske (1972).

Overprotection may appear on the surface to be kind, but it can be really evil. An oversupply can smother people emotionally, squeeze the life out of their hopes and expectations, and strip them of their dignity. Overprotection can keep people from becoming all they could become. Many of our best achievements came the hard way: we took risks, fell flat, suffered, picked ourselves up, and tried again. Sometimes we made it and sometimes we did not. Even so, we were given the chance to try.

How many people get married or enter civil partnerships with far less to prove? Maria might find two months, two years or 20 years on she has made a mistake, fallen out of love, fallen in love with someone else or just grown apart from the person she married, and if that happens she should be able to start over again, like the other 103,895 people who are divorced in Ireland (Central Statistics Office). Before that though, she has the right to join the other 1,792,150 people who are married... and you never know, she might just live happily ever after with the person she married.

Recommendations

Ensure advice and guidance on governmental websites reflects the current changes to the law and make it clear which laws now apply. There is a lot of confusing information little, if any, of which is actually accessible to people with intellectual disabilities. People cannot exercise their rights if they are not aware of them. The law itself does not appear to put barriers in the way; rather there are some extremely conservative interpretations of it.

Ensure supports are put in place to enable people with intellectual disabilities to make their own decisions. The full implementation of the Assisted Decision-Making (Capacity) Act (2015) should assist with this, but be aware of lessons learned from implementation of the MCA (2005). There is much evidence that professionals do not always understand it and apply it in the wrong way. There needs to be education for all; first, for people who may be subject to the Act, they need to know it is there for them, advocates, professionals and families.

Include evidence-based relationship and sexual education in the curriculum for all children and young people with intellectual disabilities and within the provision offered by adult services. This should not be delivered by the staff who work in those services to ensure there is no hidden agenda and people feel free to speak about anything they want to.

Ensure all language used on public information sites is neutral, avoiding use of terminology such as 'suffering' or 'mental disability'.

Finally, man from the shop, remember the customer is always right!

Note

1 For more information, see Seanad Debates (2015) Assisted Decision-Making (Capacity) Bill 2013: Committee Stage [online] Available at: http://www.oireachtas.ie/documents/amendments/2015/b8313d-sc10.pdf [Accessed 19 Jan. 2018].

Bibliography

Alexander, N. and Gomez, M.T. (2017). Pleasure, Sex, Prohibition, Intellectual Disability, and Dangerous Ideas. *Reproductive Health Matters*, 25(50), pp. 114–120.

Butler, K. (2016). In What Capacity? Law Society Gazette March 2016. pp. 44–46. [online] Available at: http://www.gazette.ie [Accessed 18 Jan. 2018]

Citizens Information. (2016). Legal Prerequisites for Marriage. [online] Available at: http://www.citizensinformation.ie/en/birth_family_relationships/getting_married/legal_prerequisites_for_marriage.html [Accessed 19 Jan. 2018].

Department of Employment Affairs and Social Protection. (2017). Getting Married. [online] Available at: http://www.welfare.ie/en/Pages/Getting_Married.aspx [Accessed 19 Jan. 2018].

Disability Rights UK. (2017). CRPD Shadow Report England And Wales. [online] Available at https://www.disabilityrightsuk.org/news/2017/january/disabled-people-tell-un-committee-uk-failing-international-rights-convention [Accessed 19 Jan. 2018].

Dukes, E. and McGuire, B.E. (2009). Enhancing capacity to make sexuality-related decisions in people with an intellectual disability. *Journal of Intellectual Disability Research*, 53(8), pp. 727–734.

Fitzgerald, C. and Withers, P. (2013). 'I don't know what a proper woman means': what women with intellectual disabilities think about sex, sexuality and themselves. *British Journal of Learning Disabilities*, 41 (1), pp. 5–12.

Gewirth, A. (1998). *Self-fulfillment*. Princeton, NJ: Princeton University Press.

Harfleet, N. and Turner, S. (2016). Supporting people with learning disabilities to develop sexual and romantic relationships. National Development Team for Inclusion (NDTi). [online] Available at: http://www.ndti.org.uk [Accessed 19 Jan. 2018].

Harnacke, C. (2012). Capability and disability: the CRPD from the perspective of the Capabilities Approach in J. Anderson and J. *Phillips, Disability and Universal Human Rights: Legal, Ethical and Conceptual Implications of the Convention on the Rights of Persons with Disabilities*. Utrecht. Netherlands: Human Rights.

Hollomotz, A. (2011). Learning Difficulties and Sexual Vulnerability: A Social Approach. London: Jessica Kingsley.

Inclusion Ireland. (2016). Assisted decision making factsheet. [online] Available at: http://www.inclusionireland.ie/sites/default/files/attach/basic-page/991/assisted-decision-making-act-factsheet.pdf [Accessed 19 Jan. 2018].

Inclusion Ireland. (2017). Press Release. [online] Available at: www.inclusionireland.ie/content/media/1608/provisions-new-sexual-offences-bill-are-narrow-protective-and-paternalistic [Accessed 19 Jan. 2018].

Irish Family Planning Association. (2007). Disability and sexuality briefing report. [online] Available at: https://www.ifpa.ie/Media-Info/Publications/Publications-Reports/Sexuality-and-Disability [Accessed 19 Jan. 2018].
Matthews, F. (2015). Cognitive impairment and the capacity to marry. *Irish Journal of Legal Studies*, 5(2), pp. 52–83.
McCarthy, M. (1999). *Sexuality and Women with Learning Disabilities*. London: Jessica Kingsley.
Nussbaum, M. (2001). *Women and Human Development*. Cambridge: Cambridge University Press.
Perske, R. (1972). The dignity of risk and the mentally retarded. *Mental Retardation*, 10(1), pp. 24–28.
Ryan, F. (2014). Couples with learning disabilities face unfair wedding bar. *The Guardian* 17 June. [online] Available at: https://www.theguardian.com/society/2014/jun/17/couples-learning-disabilities-denied-marriage-sexual-relations [Accessed 19 Jan. 2018].
Series, L. (2015). Relationships, autonomy and legal capacity: mental capacity and support paradigms. *International Journal of Law and Psychiatry*, 40, pp. 80–91.
Stavert, J., McGregor R., and Martin W. (2016). Support for the exercise of legal capacity. Essex Autonomy Project. [online] Available at: https://autonomy.essex.ac.uk/wp-content/uploads/2016/11/ThreeJurisdictionsProject_briefingpaper4_supportfor excerciseoflegalcapacity.pdf [Accessed 19 Jan. 2018].

17 Dreaming of travelling – dreaming of freedom

Ronnie Harris and Jana Offergeld

Jana: This chapter is about Ronnie's story, about his life with his fiancée Denise and about his unfulfilled wish to travel overseas with her. Ronnie told me that he applied to the VOICES project to be supported to reach out to his family and express his desire to travel. He also wanted to raise awareness about the obstacles he faces to living independently. We decided to present Ronnie's story in a series of letters. The first eight letters summarise our Skype correspondence over the space of a year. Additionally, Ronnie wanted to add three more letters and use them to communicate aspects of his story that were particularly important to him: one letter addressed to his fiancée Denise, another letter to society in general and, last but not least, – a letter to his brother Damian.

***

Dear Jana,

My name is Ronnie and I live in Dublin.

I love music. My favourite singer is Elvis. I am pretty good at bowling. Once I even competed in the Special Olympics in China! I like to go out, go shopping and watch football – just living a normal life.

My fiancée Denise and I live together in Darndale, a rough area of Dublin.

Right now, we are living in a temporary flat far away from the bus station. When it rains, we get wet because the roof leaks! The lamps also need to be fixed. I hope we can move back to our old place soon. The old flat needed to be renovated and we were told to move into a temporary home.

I work at a community centre as a volunteer. I keep the centre clean and tidy. I pick up garbage off the streets.

I like my job. I like talking to people on the streets. I like meeting dogs when picking up the garbage. But I do not get paid for working there.

I have another job as a relief worker at the Sudocrem factory. They call me in, when someone is sick.

This job does not pay much and I never know when I will be called. So, it is hard to make plans that involve money!

I want to talk about my wish to travel overseas with Denise. I love travelling, but my family will only let me travel with a group, not with my fiancée.

I hope this project can help me to make my wish a reality.

Ronnie

Dear Ronnie,

Thank you for your letter. I hope you were able to move back into your place by now!

I feel like I have to apologise to you. When you first told me about your problem, I didn't quite understand. I thought: Couldn't they just travel in Ireland instead?

Then I realised: I love travelling myself. And it would be the worst if someone told me: you are not allowed to travel.

We share a passion for getting to know new places. So, I should be the first to understand your wish to travel overseas!

I am trying to understand your problem better. I wonder: Why doesn't your family want you to travel with Denise?

Maybe you could tell me a bit more about your family, too.

Looking forward to hear from you soon!

Jana

Dear Jana,

Thanks for your letter.

Denise and I are still living in the temporary flat. We really don't like staying here. It is very far away from the community centre and the factory where I work.

They keep on saying: you will be able to move back soon! But nothing happens. My mother and father have passed away.

I have four sisters and three brothers. My sisters all live near or in Dublin. Two of my brothers have moved down south. I don't see them much. My brother Damian lives in our family home in Dublin.

I don't see my family too often. Sometimes I miss them. And sometimes, I am annoyed with them.

My brothers and sisters are looking out for me. They often worry about me.

They often tell me what to do. And sometimes, they make decisions on my behalf. For example, they decide: 'You cannot travel with Denise'.

See, it is not about Denise. My family gets along great with her. I think it's because they are worried. They think I cannot take care of myself. They only let me travel overseas on a group holiday for people with disabilities. I really don't like group holidays!

I know family members worry about each other but I wish my brothers and sisters would take my wish to travel more seriously. I want them to trust Denise and I, that we can travel by ourselves.

I hope all is well with you over there in Germany. I would love to visit you one day!

Ronnie

Dear Ronnie,

Thanks for telling me a bit more about your family. Seven siblings, that is quite a big family.

When you say, your family is looking out for you, what do you mean?

I would say, my family is looking out for me too, but I am pretty sure it's not the same situation. I still don't quite understand: Why can they tell you not to travel overseas with Denise?

Under the Irish Law, a person with disabilities sometimes is a 'Ward of Court'.[1]

Being a Ward of Court means that a court has decided: This person cannot make decisions by himself. The court then orders: Your sister or brother can make decisions on your behalf.

Then your siblings can decide: Ronnie cannot travel on his own.

Before you become a Ward, two doctors have to talk to you. And the court has to let you know. An officer has to tell you: you are a Ward of Court.

Did this ever happen? Do you know if you are a Ward?

Best wishes,

Jana

Dear Jana,

I am sorry, I don't remember ever going to court. I don't think I ever spoke to any doctors about becoming a Ward of Court.

When my mother passed away, we had to sell the house.

My brothers and sisters started looking out for me. They have always taken care of things for me. And they have always told me what to do.

They look after my money. And sometimes they buy me clothes or stuff. They are taking turns.

I have a bank account. Denise helps me with this; she is my bank lady.

There is not a lot of money in the account. Sometimes I also ask my family for money. When I need money for travelling, I also ask them.

Right now, Damian is the one who is taking care of me. I like Damian a lot. Talk to you soon!

Ronnie

Dear Ronnie,

Thanks for clarifying this! It doesn't sound like you were ever made a Ward of Court. Maybe your siblings are looking after your money? I cannot be sure, though.

But now I understand your situation a lot better!

Right now, you have to ask your siblings for their OK, when you plan a holiday. But you also have to ask them for the money to travel, don't you?

I can imagine: you don't want to pick fights with your sisters and brothers. They are important to you. But you also want to be able to travel with your fiancée Denise.

I understand this is a tricky situation.

Have you talked about this with any of your brothers and sisters?

Best,

Jana

Dear Jana,

How are you keeping? I have some good news and some bad news.

The good news: we were finally able to move back into our renovated flat. I am so relieved! It was especially hard on Denise to live in this run-down place.

The bad news: I will once again go on a group holiday this year. Denise will travel to Spain with a friend, but without me.

I talked about this with my sisters the other day. And spoke to Damian on the phone. But they still haven't changed their minds.

Now, staff from my service provider have asked me: 'Ronnie, do you want to come with us to Barcelona?' I said yes. I guess a group holiday is still better than staying home alone.

They say the group will be small. But I bet, it won't.

They will give me more information about the trip. Then I have to give the information to my brother Damian. He will probably give his OK, because I am travelling with a group. Then he will give me the money for the trip.

I still haven't given up hope. I want to travel without a group. One day, I want to take Denise on a trip. Just the two of us!

I want to use this book to change things and to tell everyone how I feel. To tell people to take me seriously and let me live my life. To tell Denise how much I want to travel with her. And to explain to my family, why this is so important to me.

That's why I wanted to be part of the project.

Bye for now,

Ronnie

Dear Ronnie,

I understand. I hope I can help you with this plan.

We talked about this in our last Skype chat: You want to write a letter to Denise and a letter to your brother Damian.

I will help you write the letters.

I hope you can come visit me in Germany one day!

Best,

Jana

Dear Denise,

We have been living together for a long time. Maybe for 12 or 13 years.

But we met long before that!

I know, the last year has not been easy. We had to live in that dodgy flat. It wasn't easy living there!

I am so happy, we were finally able to move back into our renovated flat.

My biggest wish is to be able to travel with you! I am worried that not travelling together and spending so much time apart from each other is bad for our relationship.

You love travelling and so do I and you are my favourite travel partner.

Instead, I have to go on group trips, while you travel with friends. This makes me really sad. My family is worried. They think we cannot travel on our own. They say: 'What if you get sick, Ronnie? What if there is an emergency?'

But I am not worried. I know in the EU, we could go to a hospital if there is an emergency. And we could take care of each other. And you have been travelling without a group lots of times. I am sure you could show me how to get around.

I wanted to take part in this project and write this chapter, because I hope it will help to change things. I hope to be able to travel with you soon.

Love,

Ronnie

Dear Society,

In my life, I have had many experiences where I felt: I am not being taken seriously. I am not being treated as an adult.

When I got engaged to my fiancée Denise, people didn't take us seriously. I bought a ring anyway and proposed to her on one knee!

It took me a long time to move in with Denise. I had to move to a residential facility first. At the facility, they made me practice how to live independently. I had to prove that I could cook and clean. They said it would be only for a short period of time, but it felt like I stayed there much longer!

It is very hard to live independently when you don't earn a lot of money. I have two jobs at the moment, but I hardly get paid. My family supports me with money.

I feel like every time I try to live on my own terms, society has me jumping through hoops before giving me the chance to do what I want. Sometimes, I am worried that I might have to move back to a residential service one day.

I'm not asking for anything over the top. I just want to live a normal life with my fiancée.

Cheers,

Ronnie

Dear Damian,

I am writing you this letter because I know you always look after me. I feel very close to you.

I am presenting my story in the VOICES project, because I want to change my life. I want to use this book to talk to you and our other siblings.

We have talked about my wish to travel with Denise before. But every time we talk about this, you say: 'You have to travel with a group, Ronnie. It is too dangerous for you and Denise to travel on your own.' And you ask: 'What if you get sick? What if there is an emergency?'

I know you and the others have always worried about me and still do. But I really need you to understand: it is very important to me to be able to travel with Denise. And to travel without a group.

I hate travelling with a group. They always say: it will be a very small group. But then, we end up being many more people. There are strict time schedules. When travelling with a group, I cannot decide, where I want to go. What I want to see. Who I want to be with. Or even when to get up!

I know, Denise and I are able to travel in the Irish countryside. But I need some change! We are always going to the same places. We are always seeing the same things. I want to see other countries. I want to learn about new things.

Denise loves going overseas too. She spends a lot of holidays without me. It is not good for our relationship, if we never travel together. That worries me.

I would love to prove that I can travel without a group. Alfredo, my supporter at the centre, could accompany me. We can practice together: how to book a flight and hotel, how to get to the airport. I might need support with some things. But Denise or Alfredo could help me. We could plan for emergencies.

When I dream of travelling, I dream of choosing where to go and how to spend my days. I want to experience new things and make new memories.

When I dream about travelling, I dream of what it's like to be free.

I hope you understand this. And I hope you can support me.

Your brother,

Ronnie

***

What is Ronnie's story about?

There is an aspect of Ronnie's story that surprised me. Even though his legal capacity has not been formally restricted, his right to decide how he wants to live his life is significantly impaired within informal spheres. Since the adoption of General Comment No. 1 (GC No.1) by the UN Committee on the Rights of Persons with Disabilities (the Committee), the debate around Article 12 has mainly focused on the 'hard cases', for example when a person is in a coma and cannot communicate wishes and preferences in regard to medical treatment or financial affairs (Freeman et al., 2015; de Bhailís and Flynn, 2017). While these cases highlight important legal issues that need to be considered in the implementation of the Convention of the Rights of Persons with Disabilities

(CRPD), the one-sided debate has also led to the neglect of other important challenges directly linked to the respect of individual autonomy: the prevailing practices and informal barriers that prevent people with disabilities from making self-determined decisions regarding their everyday lives (Inclusion International, 2014). I will argue that these are good examples of the domination that persons with disabilities often still experience (Arstein-Kerslake and Flynn, 2017; O'Shea, 2015) and that paternalistic attitudes, particularly towards people with cognitive impairment, play a significant role in this respect.

My first task as a respondent was to check Ronnie's legal situation. If Ronnie was a Ward of Court, his family would not only have been able to deny his wish to travel but also would have authority on decisions regarding Ronnie's wedding plans, his place of residence and other crucial areas of life. But it soon became clear that the barriers preventing him from travelling as he chooses are not of legal nature. His legal capacity has not been restricted formally and thus, his family is not in the legal position to make this decision in his place.

While identifying the exact reasons behind Ronnie's inability to travel as he chooses was surprisingly complex, three interlinked factors play a major role: the financial dependence on his family, the lack of external support and the prevailing doubts about his ability to travel and live independently. Despite several attempts, I have been unable to understand Ronnie's financial situation in detail, particularly, if his siblings manage money that has been placed in a trust for Ronnie's benefit. This makes it difficult to answer important questions and find solutions to his situation. Ronnie emphasised that his current job[2] does not provide him with sufficient income to pay for a holiday and that he has to ask his siblings for money instead. This fact significantly interferes with his travel plans and general opportunities for independent living. Yet, it is evident that money is not the only barrier, as he has travelled overseas before and has another group trip planned for summer holidays. Another crucial factor is that his siblings deny their consent out of worry for his safety. Their reluctance to let Ronnie travel with his fiancée seems to be based on their assumption that he is unable to travel without an organised group and without the supervision of professional staff. They have told Ronnie they are afraid that he might fall ill and would not know what to do in the case of such an emergency. Ronnie himself does not share these worries, but acknowledges that he needs support in preparing for the trip, managing his holiday finances and in finding his way around while travelling. He argues that Denise could help him should problems occur, as she frequently travels without formal support. While Ronnie has voiced his desire repeatedly, so far, all respective discussions with his siblings seem to have been rather brief and without consideration of different options that might help to eliminate or reduce their fears. Instead, he is only provided with the financial support he requires when travelling with a group and professional supervision. Ronnie himself is worried that his inability to travel with Denise is harming their relationship, as she is travelling with friends instead and he is unable to share these experiences with her. Overall, he finds it hard to live 'a normal life' with his fiancé and feels like their relationship often is not taken seriously by his social environment.

Ronnie's situation seems to fit what O'Shea describes as 'microdomination', applying the republican political philosophy to the situation of disabled persons whose everyday choices are restricted in the scope of their support system: 'the capacity for decisions to be arbitrarily imposed on someone, which, individually, are too minor to be contested in a court or a tribunal, but which cumulatively have a major impact on [their] life' (O'Shea, 2015, p. 136). Dependency and domination are fundamentally interlinked. In family relationships, dependency commonly carries an emotional dimension regardless of any legal or financial pressures. Family conflicts carry the risk to minimise or remove social and emotional support. As Arstein-Kerslake and Flynn (2017, p. 32) argue, 'if an individual perceives a great cost in exiting a particular relationship, they may be considered dependent on that relationship, regardless of whether their perception is accurate'. In Ronnie's case, even if he decides to go on a trip with his fiancé against his family's will, he would not be able to do so without support. By his own account, he needs help with saving up money and booking transport and accommodation. Additionally, his capacity might be questioned by others, e.g. the airline or airport staff, and therefore, he might be hindered in arranging the trip himself.

Ronnie's motivation behind participating in the VOICES project was to secure help in communicating his wishes with his siblings and in pursuing his goal to travel with Denise. This speaks to the fact that he lacks access to respective support within his community. From his point of view, the inability to travel poses a significant dilemma that negatively impacts on his relationship with his fiancée. But his formal and informal support network does not seem to take the urgency of his wish seriously and thus, to provide him with assistance in its realisation. Overall, 'not being taken seriously' was a reoccurring theme in Ronnie's recollections as we talked about negative reactions to his engagement, his struggles to find a paid job and the constantly lingering risk of having to move back to a residential service. These experiences illustrate a challenge people with intellectual disabilities face to this day: the continuing devaluation of their choices and personhood, based on commonly unconscious paternalistic assumptions about their capabilities (Goffman, 1967).

A human rights-based perspective

Paternalistic attitudes stand in stark contrast with the human rights-based approach to disability promoted in the CRPD, which aims to abolish the stigma and resulting discrimination against people with disabilities. From a human rights perspective, the need for support does not justify the restriction of someone's rights and choices. When we apply the CRPD[3] to Ronnie's situation, two articles seem of particular relevance: Article 3, highlighting the '(a) Respect for (…) individual autonomy including the freedom to make one's own choices' as one of the general principles of the convention, and Article 19 on the right to 'Living independently and being included in the community'. Ronnie's desire to travel overseas with his fiancée can be regarded as a choice of lifestyle protected under the right to independent living. As emphasised in General Comment No. 5 of the CRPD (GC No. 5), individual choice is not limited to the place of residence but includes all aspects of a person's living arrangements, the daily schedule and routine as well as a person's way of life (15 a)). Interestingly, Ronnie's description of his experiences on group holidays mirrors descriptions of institutionalization in the GC 5: 'lack of control over day-to-day decisions, lack of choice over whom to live [and travel] with, rigidity of routine irrespective of personal will and preferences, identical activities in the same place for a group of persons under a certain authority (...)' (CRPD Committee, 2017, para. 16 c).

The applicability of Article 12 on 'Equal recognition before the law' is less obvious, considering that Ronnie is not formally denied his legal capacity. Arstein-Kerslake and Flynn (2017) point out that people with cognitive disabilities face a particular risk of being denied decision-making in informal spheres and argue that even in regard to decisions that do not have legal consequences, people with disabilities are sometimes forced to assert legal agency because they live in a relationship of domination. This seems to apply to Ronnie's situation, as he is prevented from travelling according to his choices despite having full legal capacity. So far, he has not attempted to exercise his legal agency in regard to travelling alone with Denise. Apart from his financial situation, this can be explained by the lack of support he faces to implement his decision, as well as the fact that he values his relationship with his siblings and does not want to go against their wishes.

Are there solutions?

While a legal framework providing formal regulation and monitoring could protect Ronnie from family interference in his decision-making, it would also allow state intervention in the most private spheres of life. This seems intrusive in itself and therefore problematic (Arstein-Kerslake and Flynn, 2017). However, Ronnie should be able to make a formal complaint, if his family is denying him access to his own financial assets to prevent him from travelling according to his choices, if he desires to.

To what extent the new Assisted Decision-Making (Capacity) Act 2015 could improve Ronnie's situation, remains to be seen. The law was enacted in 2015 but has not fully commenced yet. It would enable Ronnie to choose someone outside of his family as a decision-making assistant. However, several challenges remain: first, he would need to select a person that would accept his request to be his assistant. The law prohibits professional staff affiliated with the person to become assistants to prevent undue influence[4]. While Ronnie is open to the idea of having someone outside his family to support him in his decisions, he can only think of professional supporters as possible candidates. Second, he does not need support in the decision-making process but in communicating his decisions and in turning them into actions. When we discussed what he believed he might need to travel outside group holidays, he came up with a couple of ideas, e.g. creating a plan for emergencies in consultation with his fiancée, bringing a personal assistant on the trip or identifying support structures in the destination country prior to the trip. The support would have to encompass such practical steps.

As the barriers Ronnie faces in regard to his choices of independent living are not of legal nature, the solution might not be a legal one either. Generally, Ronnie's story indicates that he currently knows of no person or organisation that could help him realise his wish to travel with Denise. The recent report of the Special Rapporteur on the Rights of Persons with Disabilities (Human Rights Council, 2016) addresses the interplay between the lack of support in communities, the missing political interest to change this and the denial of autonomy and choice (para. 15). It points out that this dynamic forces people with disabilities to be dependent on (both formal and informal) forms of support that come along with a restriction of an individual's decision-making opportunities (para. 19) and calls states to '[d]esign support systems so that they enable direct choice and control to be exercised by persons with disabilities' (UNHRC, p. 21). Such support could enable Ronnie to prioritise his choices, address his concerns about how not travelling together negatively impacts his relationship with Denise with his siblings and other support persons, and – last but not least – develop a travel plan. One source of such support might be the National Advocacy Service for People with Disabilities in Ireland, which seeks to support people with disabilities in making decisions about their lives and in communicating choices with families and professionals.[5]

Prevailing societal attitudes and stigma might be the most compromising factors hindering Ronnie from travelling and living as he chooses. At the same time, they seem to be the most resistant and cannot be tackled by legal reforms alone. While active awareness-raising about persons with disabilities' right to independent living and the ongoing respective barriers they face is a crucial strategy to avoid experiences as presented in Ronnie's story, the abolition of attitudinal barriers also has an interrelated dynamic: the more people with disabilities are enabled to live in the community according to their own choices as citizens, co-workers, neighbours and co-vacationers, the more society's perceptions will change. This was what Ronnie emphasised repeatedly in our conversations and his presentations at workshops throughout the VOICES project. In the end, we all share the same desire to live our lives according to our own choices and with our loved ones regardless to our different support needs, capabilities and preferences.

Notes

1 Wardship is the Irish guardianship system for adults (and children) regulated under the Lunacy Regulation (Ireland) Act 1871.
2 Ronnie fills in for workers on sick leave in a factory and thus has no regular income.
3 While Ireland has not ratified the CRPD yet, the government has been taking steps in order to align national legislation with this international treaty ever since it came into force in 2006.
4 Assisted Decision Making (Capacity) Act 2015, s. 11(f) and s. 13(4)(f).
5 See the website Citizensinformationboard.ie. *National Advocacy Service for People with Disabilities – Citizens Information Board.* [online] Available at: http://www.citizensinformationboard.ie/en/services/advocacy/ [Accessed 8 Dec. 2017].

Bibliography

Arstein-Kerslake, A. and Flynn, E. (2017). The right to legal agency: domination, disability, and the protections of Article 12 of the Convention on the Rights of Persons with Disabilities. *International Journal of Law in Context*. Special Issue: Legal Capacity and Human Rights, pp. 22–38.

de Bhailís, C. and Flynn, E. (2017). State of the art – literature to date on Article 12. *International Journal of Law in Context*. Special Issue: Legal Capacity and Human Rights, pp. 22–38.

Devandas-Aguilar C. (2016). Report of the Special Rapporteur on the rights of persons with disabilities, promotion and protection of all human rights, civil, political, economic, social and cultural rights, including the right to development. UN Doc. No. A/HRC/34/58.

Freeman, M.C. et al. (2015). Reversing hard won victories in the name of human rights. A critique of the General Comment on Article 12 of the UN Convention on the Rights of Persons with Disabilities. *The Lancet Psychiatry*, 2(9), pp. 844–850.

Goffman, E. (1967). *Stigma. Notes on the Management of Spoiled Identity*. London: Penguin.

Inclusion International (2014). *Global Report on the Right to Decide*. [online] Available at: http://inclusion-international.org/wp-content/uploads/2014/06/Independent-But-Not-Alone_-final.pdf [Accessed 8 Dec. 2017].

O'Shea, T., (2015). Disability and Domination: Lessons from Republican Political Philosophy. *Journal of Applied Philosophy*, 35(1), pp. 133–148.

UN Committee on the Rights of Persons with Disabilities (2014). General Comment No. 1 Article 12 equal recognition before the law. UN Doc. No. CRPD/C/GC/1.

UN Committee on the Rights of Persons with Disabilities (2017). Draft General Comment No. 5 on Living independently and being included in the community. [online] Available at: http://www.ohchr.org/EN/HRBodies/CRPD/Pages/DGCArticle19.aspx [Accessed 8 Dec. 2017].

18 Conclusion

Relationships and consent to sex

María Laura Serra

The storytellers in this section of the book are from the same social and legal context. Both are from Ireland, affected by the same legal definitions and stigmas, living in a country that until now has not ratified the CRPD. Through their voices, Ronnie and Maria show that sexuality and intimacy are not just about their bodies or just a biological need. Their experiences are about social encounters, interdependency and their opportunity to live a life independently. It is true that human lives are not homogenous in any society stratified by gender, disability, and other factors of identity and, therefore each of their experiences is unique. Nevertheless, because both storytellers share a social and legal context, I decided in these few paragraphs find some common patterns and try to deconstruct them, using the CRPD as a lighthouse.

The first pattern that I found is that the oppression that both storytellers are discussing occurs in the private sphere, making it difficult to detect. The situation is intensified when those discriminatory practices are socially accepted and legally protected. The second pattern is that society and family are the two subjects that Ronnie and Maria choose to speak to. Meanwhile, the respondents, Sarah and Jana, pointed to the State and the justice system through the law.

State, law, society, and family, represent the power that underpins legal and social barriers, as well as structural oppression.

Family: through Ronnie's letter to his brother and with Maria's question about why she cannot get married while her sister is already married, we are able to acknowledge how important the role of their family is in their lives. They are trying to get their families on board with this simple plan of having a life on their own with the support that they need. In this way, Maria and Ronnie are not denying the need for support but asking to exercise their right to choose, having opportunity to make mistakes: the possibility of the dignity of risk. Interpersonal relationships between persons with disabilities and their families and service providers influence their daily life experiences. In this regard, families and service providers need to know how to support a person without paternalistic preconceptions. A change of mentality is necessary. In this way, Ireland' ratification of the CRPD could trigger this necessity of changing the approach.

Law: the two pair chapters stress the fact that the legal capacity of the storytellers has not been formally denied. However, their right to decide about their intimacy is prohibited due to the huge impact of legal barriers. There is an archaic way of seeing consent to sex and relationships in Irish law that allows creating an unsafe space for persons with intellectual disabilities.

The CRPD Committee's jurisprudence states that 'support in the exercise of legal capacity must respect [their] rights' as well that 'the best interest of the person is replaced [through the CRPD] by will and preferences' (CRPD Committee, 2014). However, these solutions have to come with a change in social policies. In this regard, the same Committee (2016) has stated that 'lack of awareness training and policies to prevent harmful stereotyping by public officials, be it teachers, health service providers, police officers, prosecutors, judges, and the public at large can often lead to individual instances of violations of rights'. Although here the CRPD Committee is talking about structural or systemic discrimination against women with disabilities, we can extend this assumption to all persons with disabilities. There is a necessity not to undermine personhood and autonomy for persons with intellectual disabilities.

Society: even if the entire Irish society does not know Ronnie and Maria, it is one of the main oppressors regarding sexuality and intimate relationships. Prejudices, stigmas and, therefore discrimination, are not created out of nowhere. In the collective imaginary, a person with an intellectual disability is perceived as unable to make decisions about their intimacy, incapable of controlling desires and unable to have an intimate life, lived with subjectivity and pleasure. Through Maria and Ronnie's voices, we can understand how these misconceptions must be deconstructed. They identify stigmas and prejudices. Young (1990) explains that structural oppression does not refer to the power of a tyrant with selected and isolated policies but to systemic constraints, designating disadvantage through the daily life of a well-intentioned liberal society. Disadvantage and injustice are what Maria and Ronnie are living in terms of developing their sexuality and relationships. The embedded laws, habits, and symbols, underlie the rules of institutions and the collective consequences of what it means to unquestioningly adjust to these rules and habits is a constant in both stories.

State: the two pair chapters trigger the idea that the State needs to look further than traditional ways of approaching autonomy and legal capacity of persons with intellectual disabilities. There is an idealisation of the human based on ableist standards.

There is a distorted image of persons with intellectual disabilities and an objectification of the social role they are expected to fulfil. It seems that the self of persons with intellectual disabilities is somehow weak or even non-existent. Thus we can invade the person's space and create a 'protective wall that has enabled massive interventions in the rights and liberties of the person (...)' (Quinn, 2015).

Taking into account the radical reframing that the disabled community has given to the meaning of protection in order to change that objectification, the consideration of subjects of rights rather than objects of charity, we need to address the fact that 'our subjective lives, our autonomous selves, are in part a function of our inter-subjective lives (...)' (Quinn, 2015). We need to discuss the mechanisms that we can use to respect our common goal and interest: to respect and guarantee a substantive equality for persons with intellectual disabilities in all aspects of life, including sexuality and relationships.

Bibliography

Committee on the Rights of Persons with Disabilities (2014). General Comment No. 1. Article 12: Equal Recognition Before the Law, UN Doc. No. CRPD/C/GC/1.

Committee on the Rights of Persons with Disabilities (2016). General Comment No. 3. Article 6: Women and girls with disabilities, UN Doc. No. CRPD/C/GC/3.

Quinn G. (2015). The autonomy of the Treaty Drafting Process – Lessons for the Age Treaty from the Drafting of the UN Disability Treaty. In: R. Ruebener, T. Do and A. Taylor, eds. *International and Comparative Law on the Rights of Older Persons.* Lake Mary, FL: Vandeplas Publishing, pp. 1–17.

Young, I. (1990). *Justice and the Politics of Difference.* Princeton, NJ: Princeton University Press.

Part 4

Consent to medical treatment – mental health and forced treatment

19 Introduction to consent to medical treatment

Eilionóir Flynn

In this part of the edited collection, the pair chapters document how the consent of people with psychosocial disabilities has routinely been ignored, devalued and overridden in the specific context of the mental health system. Although to some extent these experiences can be viewed as a unique product of the mental health system, they also contain much which can be transferrable to other aspects of healthcare provision and practice. They also provide a stark demonstration of the need for reform, not just in psychiatry, but in the health system as a whole.

The specific context of coercion within the mental health system must be acknowledged at the outset before turning to the perspectives provided in the following chapters. Globally, mental health laws still permit forced psychiatric treatment and deprivation of liberty in psychiatric settings. These practices and the laws that permit them are in clear violation of the CRPD. The Committee on the Rights of Persons with Disabilities has routinely criticised these practices and informed States of the need to abolish these coercive regimes and replace them with systems of healthcare that are based on free and informed consent of the individual. Scholars of the CRPD reaffirm that it is not possible to obtain free and informed consent within a system that maintains coercion as an option (Minkowitz, 2006; Gooding, 2015; Brosnan and Flynn, 2017). This is one of the greatest challenges for law and policy reform in order to achieve compliance with the CRPD.

A core question posed in the theoretical framework of the VOICES project, as described in Chapter 1, was as follows: 'How can we ascertain whether an individual is giving free and informed consent (necessary to make an action legally binding), without engaging in a functional assessment of that person's mental capacity?' In answering this question, the VOICES project seeks to move away from laws that embed a functional assessment of mental capacity as a prerequisite for the recognition or respect for the exercise of legal capacity, in accordance with General Comment 1. Elsewhere, members of the VOICES team have set out one possible means of achieving this in the specific context of consent to medical treatment (Brosnan and Flynn, 2017). Our proposal states that in order to obtain free and informed consent to treatment, the law must first recognise the individual's legal capacity, and ensure the absence of coercion. Recognition of legal capacity in this context means that refusals of treatment must be respected, regardless of the perceived or actual mental capacity of the individual. It also requires respect for the individual's will and preferences and recognition of the validity of any support mechanism that the individual wishes to use to reach a decision concerning medical treatment. Instead of engaging in functional assessments of the individual's mental capacity, those proposing to provide the relevant treatment must instead determine what support, if any, the individual wishes to use in making the decision, and ensure such support is provided. In keeping with the requirements of General Comment 1 (CRPD Committee, 2014), the individual must also be free to refuse any offer of support in making the decision.

Our approach draws on feminist thinking about freedom to negotiate in the context of consent (Anderson, 2004) – which pays attention to the power imbalances between the person and the medical system, and requires work to minimise these imbalances and ensure that the healthcare system does not employ coercive methods which amount to undue influence or duress on the individual making the decision. While we acknowledge that in the context of medical treatment it is impossible to remove these power imbalances entirely, we believe that by drawing attention to them, we can work to minimise their impact.

Before we can progress work to redefine the law's approach to consent to medical treatment (including mental health treatment) in accordance with human rights norms, it is important to confront the lived realities of the present, and fully understand the opportunities and barriers to making the paradigm shift the CRPD requires. The pair chapters in this section provide a stark reminder of the realities we are currently facing around the world. The pairs describe experiences in a range of different countries (Australia, India, Ireland), the use of formal and informal coercion in psychiatric practice, the role of family members and friends in colluding with, or challenging, mental health professionals, and the sources of support they found within and outside the mental health system that enabled them to express their views and make their voices heard.

In reading the pair chapters that follow it is important to consider how we might design systems of support that respect will and preferences even in times of crisis and distress, how we might communicate with people experiencing distress to understand their will and preferences and how we can work to eliminate coercion and forced treatment in psychiatry and other aspects of the healthcare system. These stories and responses can help to clarify our thinking about the work which remains to be done in order to achieve the vision of the CRPD – a world where forced treatment is no longer permissible, and the exceptionality which has persisted in psychiatric practice, reinforced by coercive mental health laws, has disappeared.

Bibliography

Anderson, M.J. (2004). Negotiating sex. *Southern California Law Review*, 78, pp. 1401–1438.

Brosnan, L. and Flynn, E. (2017). Freedom to negotiate: a proposal extricating 'capacity'from 'consent'. *International Journal of Law in Context*, 13(1), pp. 58–76.

Committee on the Rights of Persons with Disabilities (2014). General Comment No. 1. Article 12: Equal Recognition Before the Law, UN Doc. No. CRPD/C/GC/1.

Gooding, P. (2015). Navigating the 'flashing amber lights' of the right to legal capacity in the United Nations Convention on the Rights of Persons with Disabilities: Responding to major concerns. *Human Rights Law Review*, 15(1), pp. 45–71.

Minkowitz, T. (2006). The United Nations Convention on the Rights of Persons with Disabilities and the right to be free from nonconsensual psychiatric interventions. *Syracuse Journal of International Law & Commerce*, 34, pp. 405–428.

20 This is not a story: from ethical loneliness to respect for diverse ways of knowing, thinking and being

Cath Roper and Piers Gooding

This is not a proper story. Stories should have beginnings middles and ends, but here, nothing quite fits. The characters are the State and I, but there is no plot, no arc, because experience, body and emotion are a cavernous, shapeless, hungry, lonely, wordless, unprocessed source.

There is a cupboard I can (usually) *choose* to open or close. Within its darkest recesses are partial memories spanning 13 years – some drugged memories faintly strobing, echo-y, foggy and dimly lit, many sharper incidents like short films, some on repeat like broken technology. And some moments are like shameful violent cellular shocks that ambush me. Like being in a focus group, body suddenly shaking, as a psychiatrist earnestly argues it is possible to seclude someone using 'recovery principles'.

Here is what I know and what matters to me:

1 People subject to mental health laws (MHL) can be detained against their will.
2 Needles, pills, electro-convulsive therapy and other psychiatric treatment can be given without the consent of the person.
3 In the face of refusal, treatment will be administered with violence.
4 That violence will not be seen for what it is, rather it will be re-interpreted as 'necessary' for health and wellbeing.
5 All of these are little known facts 'out there'.
6 These facts matter.

For the first 22 years, the State and I had an uneventful relationship. He was just there in the background. Not something to think about.

But after a relationship breakup, with my first long-term boyfriend, things went downhill. It was 1985. My shared house disbanded and I was couch surfing, and occasionally staying with my ex. I was falling deeper and deeper into a bad place and was losing a lot of weight. One morning, from his place, about 4am, I became very scared, mistrustful, and phoned for an ambulance to take me to a hospital. When the ambulance arrived, they found I was dehydrated and not making sense. So, they took me to a psychiatric hospital where I thought I would be helped. I knew about therapeutic communities. I couldn't go on like I was – I was starting to imagine myself hanging, or cutting my arms in the bath tub. The 'State will provide', I thought, 'and help make me better'.

I remember the showers were communal, in a hexagon shape, in the middle of the bathroom, the doors only covering our torsos. Tiles were coming off the walls. There was no therapeutic community, nothing to do, except go for walks and smoke cigarettes. I was scared – the person I shared a room with told me she was a witch. Someone kept stealing my clothes. Or was I stealing other people's clothes? Was I someone else? Was I two people? These were real experiences, ones I vividly remember, wanted to remember, accept and learn from, even if they were occasionally scary. For me, this was never a medical situation.

Hospital admissions

Each year I would be put in a psychiatric hospital, in wintertime, usually for about six weeks. The hospitalisations were always without my consent. I always resisted. That meant often the police were involved. These were the days of the stand-alone hospitals just before de-institutionalisation. The inner-city hospital complex was Edwardian. It had well-tended rose gardens and was surrounded by parklands. Sometimes in the evening you could hear the animals from the zoo just down the road. The outer suburbs hospital was surrounded by native bush. In those days, as long as you were in 'low dependency' in an open ward, you could go for walks during the day – the doors were not locked except at night. But if you were on a locked ward, or you were in high dependency (HD), a locked smaller section within the ward, you could not get out.

Needles and pills

During the first admission, I was an elderly woman who had been in the French resistance in the Second World War. Because I wasn't able to talk, the psychiatrist gave me a chemically induced abreaction (like a truth drug) which involved having a drip put in my arm. He asked me questions which I groggily gave answers to. A few days later, when he wanted to perform the same treatment but this time in front of his students, I said no. I went to my primary nurse and asked if he could stop the procedure from happening again. Although this nurse went with me to the meeting with the psychiatrist to support me, it was clear that the procedure would go ahead without my consent. It was a highly intrusive treatment. I was afraid of injections, and I did not like not being in control of what I said.

As I write now, I see that even by his own logic, this doctor had no right to perform the treatment because by now I was speaking and not 'catatonic'. There was no 'therapeutic' value in the treatment – he just wanted his students to have an opportunity to see the experiment performed. That was during the first hospitalisation, which lasted for about three weeks. After that, the State's relationship with me deteriorated.

The drugs took away sensation, slowed thinking and caused internal alienation which was horrifying, like missing myself, watching myself die. Did they want part of me to die? Was it some form of eugenics? But, why would they? What was so despicable about me? There were numerous instances of being dragged into seclusion by five nurses, held face down on a bare mattress, pants removed, being injected and then passing into unconsciousness. In these moments, my relationship with the State was severed as I realised that He both sanctioned and administered this violence.

Because it was known that I did not want treatment, the constant threat of forced injections and seclusion edged my time in hospital. Even asking a question about what medications I was taking could result in a forced injection and seclusion. It seemed I was not capable of 'making it easier on myself' or 'learning to play the game' by acquiescing, so as to avoid the violence. I felt the portrayal staff had of me is that I brought the violence on myself, by refusing, which caused them frustration as they then had to go to violent lengths to administer treatment. Beneath this, there could be no construction of me as a choosing individual (who might refuse) allowed, serving a twofold purpose: refusals could be characterised as further symptoms, and the violence of treatment administration could be justified.

Very early on, I realised that people on the outside were not appalled by the violence. In fact, they didn't see the violence. They saw it as an equation, that the treatment was doing me good. It protected me from myself. In this sense, everyone around me colluded. They saw it as an unfortunate necessity, that I had to go through in order to become 'my old self again'. But I *was* that self that went through strange experiences. I swallowed the story that I was mentally ill and I swallowed the pills. It lasted many years. The State had me under His thumb. It wasn't until I met activists in the early 1990s that I began to find another voice, breathe life into buried stories, hear and read the stories of others.

Assailable

Being repeatedly and violently subject to treatments I did not want taught me that I was helpless. My body was not my own. It had no integrity. I was assailable. I could not give effect to my refusals: the dawning that no help would come to release me; nobody was outraged; the helpers were the ones holding me down. People who apparently loved me thought this was necessary. Will can be violated. Skin can be punctured, brain, body, mind changed. Reflecting on his experience at Auschwitz, Jean Améry writes about 'the first blow' of torture:

> The boundaries of my body are also the boundaries of my self. My skin surface shields me against the external world. If I am to have trust, I must feel on it only what I want to feel...At the first blow, however, this trust in the world breaks down. The other person, opposite whom I exist physically in the world and with whom I can exist only as long as he does not touch my skin surface as border, forces his own corporeality on me with the first

> blow. He is on me and thereby destroys me...If no help can be expected, this physical overwhelming by the other then becomes an existential consummation of destruction altogether.
>
> (Améry, 1980, p. 28)

In Améry's account the torturer means deliberate harm. The torturer is an individual but also an arm of the State. It is not just the permeability of the skin and self at stake after the first blow, it is the relationship with the State that could sanction it, 'trust in the world breaks down'. Ordinary expectations are destroyed irretrievably, causing an 'existential consummation of destruction altogether'. The violence engaged in, in the name of the State, under mental health laws, is not intended to harm, in the way that Améry's torturer and the State that sanctioned it, absolutely intended obliteration. But nevertheless, the State does harm and any denial of harm is an additional harm. Violence is not justifiable, nor is it ever necessary. Once perpetrated, it does not go away and must be acknowledged for what it is, if the 'consummation of destruction altogether' is to be avoided.

Dehumanisation

On a locked admissions ward, I had been put into HD 'for my own protection' because there was a male on the unit who thought I was his wife. While in HD, I kept asking to be able to do my hand-washing because I had run out of underwear. Finally, the Charge Nurse took me to the laundry room. He sexually assaulted me there. For many years, nobody around me believed what happened, not other staff, or family or friends. A few years later, I was told I was going back to the same hospital where I had been sexually assaulted, where the perpetrator still worked, even though I had thought it was written on my file that I should not be admitted there.

The State over-rode my will, my refusals, with impunity, violently entering my body, mind and spirit. He constructed me as a non-autonomous person, who did not know what was in my own interests (Liegghio, 2013). We demonstrate respect for persons when we respect the decisions of others (Harris, 1985). The State failed to demonstrate respect for my personhood, my humanness, in denying my refusal of treatment. In this process, I became 'other', in danger of being perceived as an object or animal (Lammers and Stapel, 2010). It is not surprising that a failure to respect people's decisions, and thus a failure to demonstrate respect for them as persons, leads to de-humanisation.

As knowers and tellers

My relationship with the State was also characterised by less obvious violence. Like all colonial forces, the State took away language, thieving meaning away and re-presenting it – in this case, as illness and malady. Between the State and the surrounding culture is a mutually agreed illness narrative concerning people like me. In that story, one's thinking is faulty, one's imagination is not to be trusted, one's feelings, unfathomable. One is *essentially* 'apart from' others.

Miranda Fricker uses the term 'testimonial injustice' to explore how the testimony of individuals belonging to particular groups may be disqualified:

> Testimonial injustice occurs when prejudice causes a hearer to give a deflated level of credibility to a speaker's word.
>
> (Fricker, 2007, p. 1)

Fricker goes on to say that to be given credence as a knower and teller is essential to human value and when speakers are wronged in their capacity as knowers and tellers, it may interfere with their self-development, and they may be 'prevented from becoming who they are' (p. 5). When our position as tellers/knowers is doubted, we may be susceptible to doubting what we know, or even, *if* we know at all (Roessler, 2015).

For a person subject to MHL, the potential consequences of living in social contexts where our experiences are not primarily understood as *breaches of human rights* must also be considered. Stauffer (2015) describes 'ethical loneliness' as '...a condition undergone by persons who have been unjustly treated and dehumanised by human beings and political structures, who emerge from that injustice only to find that the surrounding world will not listen to or cannot properly hear their testimony...' (p. 1). In this instance, the 'political structure' is MHL. That the grand narrative, 'mental illness', eclipses other narratives, contributes to ways in which the surrounding world 'cannot properly hear' divergent stories, and stories of violence. The violence cannot, then, properly be contextualised. We lack the language to tell, and our testimony and knowledge is doubted. The resulting alienation is 'ethical loneliness'.

Beyond not having credence bestowed on us, because we are seen as 'irrational', is a critique asking, 'What then, are the costs to individuals and cultures that seek to narrow down, limit ways of knowing and being in the world, to the rational, the "sane"'? We survey each other for signs of falling off very binding logic/rational tracks. The cultural power of 'sanity', is its synonymity with what it is to be a human. This tyranny of needing to have the 'right consciousness' causes a form of testimonial injustice for those who are dubbed outside of its borders. For those who don't meet its criteria, life can be stultifying, dehydrating, even unbearable. And finally, it is this tyranny of needing to have the right consciousness which serves to justify the violence of forced treatment enacted upon mad people – because (at least at times) we palpably/visibly live with a different consciousness and must be brought back into the fold.

But, what if this was a world with no corralling of what can be believed, where everything is as real as everything else, a world where we had broken out of mechanistic ideas about persons as bounded, rational, internally consistent, and we embraced diversity in ways of being and knowing, as we are starting to, for example, embrace cultural and identity diversity in other areas. We would embrace metaphoric/poetic ways of knowing/being. We would avoid subjecting people to the tyranny of some cultural sanity and we would not lock them up and force treatment on them.

What is the role of law reform in 'coming clean' about violence, in ending it? What plans are there for redress? In the meantime, in order to protect against 'ethical loneliness', space for many more stories to be told is still needed, to render visible the 'harder to see' violence and its consequences, so that the 'surrounding world' will learn to hear and understand.

***

To move from Cath's writing to 'lessons for law and policy' feels uncomfortable, like a strange shift in register. Efforts to problem-solve so easily suck the oxygen from personal reflections, just as Cath's piece is not a story, nor is this an academic paper. Our dialogue is the unusual terrain of the VOICES project, which invites participants to experiment with form in an attempt to discover new concepts. Cath's work expands this discovery, offering much more than I can respond to in any depth here.

In the brief space I do have, I want to engage with the idea of 'body and emotion as source', a concern that seems intrinsic to the form of Cath's writing itself. Her fusion of testimony and theory starts with 'cavernous, hungry, lonely, wordless, embodied, unprocessed' experience. From a critical literary perspective, this could be read within a tradition of post-structuralist and feminist writing, for which Jane Gallop's (1990), *Thinking Through the Body* is often seen as a founding text. From a legal perspective, to which I will turn here, Cath's writing could be read as a strong claim for an embodied account of personhood and legal capacity. By this I mean a view of the legal subject – the imagined person around which the law is organised – that is truer to life as it is lived. In contrast, current legal responses to mental distress, disablement, 'madness', and so on, appear to rest on an idealised view of human beings as 'free' and liberal subjects.

Ngaire Naffine (2003, pp. 362–364), in her investigation into 'who and what counts as a 'person' in law and who does not', concluded that the idealised figure at the heart of Western law today is the 'responsible subject'. This 'classic contractor' is 'rational and therefore responsible'. He enters legal contracts that demarcate clear boundaries of responsibility. This formulation is particularly useful for servicing contracts: clearly defined actors help to indicate who is legally relevant to a decision, and who is not.

The problem is, no one really lives up to this ideal. Humans are interdependent and relational (Series, 2015), not purely autonomous and isolated; they are driven by emotion and irrationality, not pure reason and logic. Inserting the responsible subject into health law has meant that the moment a person loses 'capacity to consent', she or he loses a degree of legal relevance. Beyond this point, one becomes a 'cognitive foreigner' (Bach, 2017), for whom rights are suspended. From here, the potential for domination, testimonial injustice and ethical loneliness increase, as Cath's account shows.

In the *Mental Health Act 1986* (Vic), to which Cath was subject, the key criteria for intervention was that:

(a) the person appear[ed] to be mentally ill;
(b) the person's mental illness require[d] immediate treatment …; and
(c) … the treatment of the person [wa]s necessary for his or her health or safety … or for the protection of members of the public.

(*Mental Health Act 1986* (Vic) s8)

These criteria create a form of institutional discrimination by creating different rules for those who satisfy the metrics of a psychiatric diagnosis, even an apparent diagnosis.

Under the Act, a diagnosis provides grounds to assess a person's apparent risk of harm to herself/himself and others. Yet, a mounting body of evidence suggests that experts' ability to accurately assess risk is often greatly exaggerated or entirely unsubstantiated (Callaghan, Ryan and Kerridge, 2013). On the matter of self-harm, there is some evidence indicating that coercion may even increase the risk of self-harm and suicide by compelling people who fear involuntary commitment to conceal their suicidal thoughts, hence cutting off the potential for support (Stefan, 2016). On the matter of public protection, there are many examples of people without a psychosocial disability who manifestly pose a greater risk of harm to others, such as young men consuming alcohol or known perpetrators of intimate-partner violence. Yet, these groups do not face formal, group-based restrictions on liberty and autonomy.

Once the criteria of diagnosis and risk are satisfied under mental health law – or if the person is deemed to 'require immediate treatment' – rights to liberty and consent to medical intervention can be restricted. This combination of risk assessment followed by pre-emptive detention and forced psychiatric intervention is not applied to any other group in society (though an exception here, perhaps rather tellingly, appears to be convicted sex offenders, and to some extent, asylum seekers and suspected terrorists).

What is the basis for the differential treatment?

I will suggest two possible answers to this question. One possibility goes to the commonly-held view that there 'really is something special about mental illness, that people are not their normal selves when acutely ill', as one prominent psychiatrist puts it (Burns, 2010, p. 34). If this claim is accepted then not only is it reasonable to suspend a person's rights to liberty, to informed consent and equal treatment before the law; it is *necessary* to uphold the rights of the person's 'normal self' to health, physical and mental integrity, and even the right to life. But if the claim of exceptionalism is rejected, then those subject to forced psychiatric intervention can be not only seen to face violations of liberty and autonomy rights, but also rights concerning physical and mental integrity, freedom from abuse, violence and exploitation, and even freedom from torture, cruel, inhuman and degrading treatment (Méndez, 2013).

In other words, the extent to which the 'responsible subject' is accepted as a foundational norm, and the extent to which distress, disorder and disablement are seen to sever ties to this norm, determines the extent to which non-consensual psychiatric intervention is viewed as liberal, compassionate and humanist, or its opposite – illiberal, cruel, and a violation of fundamental rights.

There is another possibility, and one which is more troubling than a disagreement about the nature of distress and human freedom. If it is accepted that the responsible subject is a fiction, helpful in some areas of law but unhelpful in others, then its imposition on people with disability and requirement that they meet its impossible demands, starts to seem at some level, like an act of domination. It would not be the first time in history that those with political, economic and social power might arbitrate legal personhood by determining who may claim rights. Aboriginal people in British colonies in the nineteenth century, for example, faced a complete (or near-complete) lack of legal personality (see Aboriginal Protection Act 1869 (Vic) No. 349). Married women faced similar restrictions in common law well into the twentieth century (Shelley, 1989). Such groups simply lacked the 'right to claim rights' in many areas of life, which continues for other groups today. Is it possible that a similar dynamic is at play with mental health law?

Those who answer in the affirmative, might point to the questionable scientific standing of risk assessments, imposed prejudicially on an already marginalised group. They might ask, as Cath does, what it is that is so frightening about distress, disorder and disablement to justify this exceptional treatment? They might look to the anti-torture framework, as Tina Minkowitz (2007) and others have done, and call for a moratorium on all forced treatment and reparations for survivors. They might justifiably see mental health law as a veil to legitimise the prejudicial control of a confusing and objectionable minority – an outwardly rational act that paradoxically, conceals irrational, State-based violence.

This view might seem like a stretch to some, but major UN agencies and a range of human rights commentators are increasingly heading in this direction.[1] In one recent example, the Special Rapporteur on the Right to Health, Dainius Pûras (2017) argued that the medical profession had unduly attributed characteristics that 'othered' people with psychiatric diagnoses from some presumed (and often unstated) norm. He criticised the 'reductionist biomedical paradigm that has contributed to the exclusion, neglect, coercion and abuse of people with … psychosocial disabilities' (para. 8) that have informed 'legal 'exceptions' [that] *normalized coercion in everyday practice*' (para. 23) (emphasis added). Instead of providing an accountability mechanism, mental health law has 'legitimize[d] coercion and further isolate[d] people within mental health systems from access to justice' (para. 52). This causes 'mistrust … and has made many turn away, fearful of seeking help within mainstream mental health services' (para. 65).

Cath extends an account of these harms beyond mere mistrust or aversion to services, conveying a severing of ties between citizen and State, between self and body, a profound act of alienation. The State also crumbles in this account, its legitimacy undermined by a failure to maintain a protective sphere around the individual. 'Care', which is meant to drive mental health law, is replaced by an interference that seems shaming, coercive and punishing.

How have governments responded to the challenge of the CRPD? The picture is mixed. In Germany, for example, the CRPD sparked a major reduction in non-consensual psychiatric interventions (Federal Constitutional Court (Germany), 2011; Zinkler, 2016). Elsewhere, forced interventions not only continue but their rates expand. Britain, for example, has seen a 47% increase in reported rates of detention under mental health legislation in the decade to 2016 (National Health Service, 2016). Today, a person admitted to a British mental health ward is more likely to be detained than not, particularly if you are a woman or person of colour (Health and Social Care Information Centre, 2015). This latter point highlights dimensions of gender, race and class that are beyond the scope of this response. Outside the hospital, compulsory intervention in people's homes is increasing in most jurisdictions where it is permitted.[2] In Victoria, where most of Cath's and my exchanges took place, forced community interventions are reported to have reached the highest rate per capita in the world (Light et al., 2012).

These paradoxical directions offer part of the answer to Cath's question, 'What role for the law?'

Law is a structure that generates domination through reductive accounts of agency and personhood, distress and disablement, while also providing a terrain of resistance relied on regularly by disabled communities. Current struggles at the national and international-level suggest we are currently in a period of flux. Multiple layers of law are in operation, and tension.

Consider the European Convention on Human Rights, which prohibits discrimination on 'any ground such as sex, race, colour, language, religion, political or other opinion' (Article 14), yet tolerates rights exceptions for those of 'unsound mind', who are grouped with 'alcoholics', 'drug addicts or vagrants' and 'persons [detained] for the prevention of the spreading of infectious diseases' (Article 5(1)(e)). In contrast, the CRPD explicitly rejects all cognitive thresholds to claiming rights. The CRPD aims to 'promote, protect and ensure … all human rights and fundamental freedoms by *all* persons with disabilities, and to promote respect for their *inherent* dignity' (Article 1) (emphasis added). These small differences signify a major change.

The participatory development of the CRPD meant people with disabilities could bring their testimonial knowledge and theoretical sophistication to bear on a successful claim for more embodied formulations of personhood and legal capacity. At a minimum, such accounts would seemingly require recognition that distress and disablement are part of human diversity, that each of us in a human body is entitled to legal capacity, and that the boundaries of the body need to be respected on an equal basis with others. Translating this shift into domestic law will be challenging given the deep roots of the responsible subject in popular culture, political theory, law and science (Bach, 2017).

Cath's writing offers a form of 'narrative agency' (Lucas, 2016) that can account for the current contradictions in law. She draws ethical loneliness and testimonial injustice out and into the light. Cath's work acknowledges the sheer extent to which people are shaped by power relations, but in a way that remains invested in the subject's emancipatory potential to confront and change those imbalances, and the myths that feed them. The result is a profound act of mutual recognition, solidarity and conversation.

Notes

1 See for example Méndez (2013, para. 81); CRPD Committee, (2014, para. 25 and 42); Office of the High Commissioner for Human Rights, (2015).
2 See for example Johnson (2013).

Bibliography

Améry, J. (1980). *At the Mind's Limits, Contemplations by a Survivor on Auschwitz and its Realities* (trans. Rosenfeld, S. and Rosenfeld, S.P.) Bloomington, IN: Indiana University Press.

Bach, M. (2017). Inclusive Citizenship: Refusing the Construction of 'Cognitive Foreigners' in Neo-liberal Times. *Research and Practice in Intellectual and Developmental Disabilities*, 4(1), pp. 4–25.

Burns, T. (2010). Mental Illness is Different and Ignoring Its Differences Profits Nobody. *Journal of Mental Health Law* (special edition), pp. 34–39.

Callaghan, S., Ryan, C., and Kerridge, I. (2013). Risk of Suicide is Insufficient Warrant for Coercive Treatment for Mental Illness. *International Journal of Law and Psychiatry*, 36(5–6), pp. 374–85.

Committee on the Rights of Persons with Disabilities (2014). *General Comment No 1: Article 12: Equal Recognition Before the Law.* UN Doc. No. CRPD/C/GC/1.

Federal Constitutional Court (Germany), (2011). 'Press Office – Press Release No 28/2011 of 15 April 2011, Order of 23 March 2011', 2 BvR 882/09.

Fricker, M. (2007). *Epistemic Injustice: Power and the Ethics of Knowing.* (New York, United States): Oxford University Press.

Gallop, J. (1990). *Thinking Through the Body.* New York, United States: Columbia University Press.

Harris, J. (1985). *The Value of Life: An Introduction to Medical Ethics.* London: Routledge.

Health and Social Care Information Centre. (2015). *Inpatients Formally Detained in Hospitals Under the Mental Health Act 1983 and Patients Subject to Supervised Community Treatment, England – 2014–2015, Annual figures* (National Health Services, London).

Johnson, S. (2013). Can We Reverse the Rising Tide of Compulsory Admissions? *The Lancet* 381(9878), pp. 1603–1604.

Lammers, J. and Stapel, D.A. (2010). Power Increases Dehumanization. *Group Processes & Intergroup Relations*, 14(1), pp. 113–126.

Liegghio, M. (2013). A Denial of Being: Psychiatrisation as Epistemic Violence. In: LeFrancois, B.A., Menzies, R., Reaume, G., eds., *Mad Matters: A Critical Reader in Canadian Mad Studies*, Toronto, Canada: Canadian Scholars' Press Inc, pp. 122–129.

Light, E. et al. (2012). Community Treatment Orders in Australia: Rates and Patterns of Use. *Australasian Psychiatry,* 20(6), pp. 478–482.

Lucas, S.D. (2016). *The Primacy of Narrative Agency: A Feminist Theory of the Self* (PhD Thesis, University of Sydney, Sydney).

Méndez, JE. (2013), *Report of the Special Rapporteur on Torture and Other Cruel, Inhuman or Degrading Treatment or Punishment,* UN Doc A/HRC/22/53.

Minkowitz, T. (2007), The United Nations Convention on the Rights of Persons with Disabilities and the Right to Be Free from Nonconsensual Psychiatric Interventions. *Syracuse Journal of International Law and Commerce,* 34(2), pp. 405–428.

Naffine, N. (2003). Who Are Law's Persons? From Cheshire Cats to Responsible Subjects. *The Modern Law Review,* 66(3), pp. 362–364.

National Health Service (2016). *Community and Mental Health Team, NHS Digital, Inpatients Formally Detained in Hospitals under the Mental Health Act 1983, and Patients Subject to Supervised Community Treatment Uses of the Mental Health Act: Annual Statistics, 2015/16.* [online] Available at: www.content.digital.nhs.uk [Accessed 18 Jan. 2018].

Office of the High Commissioner for Human Rights, (2015). *'Dignity Must Prevail' – An Appeal to Do Away with Non-consensual Psychiatric Treatment World Mental Health Day.* [online] Available at: http://www.ohchr.org/en/NewsEvents/Pages/DisplayNews.aspx?NewsID=16583&LangID=E [Accessed 18 Jan. 2018].

Pûras, D. (2017). *Report of the Special Rapporteur on the right of everyone to the enjoyment of the highest attainable standard of physical and mental health.* UN Doc. No. A/HRC/35/2.

Roessler, B. (2015). Autonomy, Self-Knowledge, and Oppression. In: Oshana, M.A.L., ed., *Personal Autonomy and Social Oppression, Philosophical Perspectives,* New York: Routledge, pp. 65–68.

Series, L. (2015). Relationships, Autonomy and Legal Capacity: Mental Capacity and Support Paradigms. *International Journal of Law and Psychiatry,* 40, pp. 80–91.

Shelley, M.L. (1989). *Feminism, Marriage, and the Law in Victorian England.* Princeton, NJ: Princeton University Press.

Stauffer, J. (2015). *Ethical Loneliness, The Injustice of Not Being Heard.* New York: Columbia University Press.

Stefan, S. (2016). *Rational Suicide, Irrational Laws: Examining Current Approaches to Suicide in Policy and Law.* New York: Oxford University Press.

Zinkler, M. (2016). Germany without Coercive Treatment in Psychiatry: A 15 Month Real World Experience. *Laws,* 5(1), pp. 15–21.

21 Getting sucked out of the black hole of India's legal mental health machinery

Lavanya Seshasayee and Maths Jesperson

Based on the Mental Health Act of 1987, my parents were given full power by my psychiatrist to confine me within the limits of their residence for a year, in 1997–1998. My psychiatrist refused to offer me the hope that someday I could recover. She was only consenting to confine me within my parents' residence. I wasn't witnessing the rising sun, the hope that I, someday could lead a productive life. There was no hope for me in that medical chamber. A chamber reeking of forced psychiatry. 'Do I have to die without my dreams ever being achieved?' I was sobbing helplessly.

All the doc did was to stare and ask my mother 'Does she cry like this very often?' And my mother said 'YES, AND I HAVE NO IDEA WHAT I SHOULD DO WITH HER!' My psychiatrist then said, 'I'll start her on an antidepressant – Prodep – 10 mg in the morning after breakfast and 10 mg in the night before she sleeps – let's see how this works on her! And yes, Risperidone will take care of her cognitive distortions.'

'But doctor, doctor!!! If I had a friend, whose shoulder I could lean upon, my difficulties will go. Will you be that friend? A friend for a lifetime? Will you love me and care for me?' Now my psychiatrist truly felt I was acting silly. She thought I was expecting a bit too much of her.

'Oh, you have such a nice mother Lavanya! I have to see hundreds of patients like you. I have research to conduct, conferences to attend, papers to present, theories and scientific stuff to catch up with, lectures to give, classes to take and PhD students to guide. No dear! All I can do for you is devote 10 minutes a week. I'll listen to you and medicate you! You can't really expect anything beyond that!'

'Medicate, medicate, medicate! Is that all? Yes Doctor, in short, I am a pest, an unwelcome pest, a pest with a brain to be medicated and no feelings at all. It's OK doctor, I'll resign myself to this fate!'

Again, I wept bitterly.

'Now, Lavanya, you are being paranoid', said the doctor, before she called the next patient in.

'This is clearly an assembly line of patients – a medical assembly line' thought I, when I sat weeping in the auto-rickshaw with my mother beside me, with nobody to comfort me and help reinforce the idea that I deserved and could have a wonderful future.

A mother who had no idea of how to care for a child who was a girl. A girl child who needed help and support. A mother who couldn't stand independence and growth in her children – especially her daughter. For that was what my mother had been just then. A mother who had liked her timid son, my brother, because he had clung to her apron strings.

But if my mother died, I would not have anybody else to turn to either. I had become dependent and been made helpless by my mother. Again, I wept bitterly. My mother had been told by the doctor that what I was in need of was a 'rest cure'. However, the 'rest cure', – being confined at home – hardly helped me to rest. This was what I had become just because I had trusted the medical system too much. 'Nobody should have to go through what I am going through', I thought.

I had started a course at college but was badly bullied and became scared to attend my classes after a year and a half of studying at the college. Even this could have been overcome, if I had been allowed to go to college and attend my classes and lessons after the first time I failed in my exams, but my mother didn't trust me to complete the course. Nor did my doctor. Nor did my father. And that had been their major undoing.

The people with psychosocial disabilities in India had begun asking themselves, who they really were. The system had traumatised them so much that they lacked a sense of identity. Hans Georg Gadamer's (1996) all too crucial concern about whether the doctor can take away the illness of the patient without taking away their personhood had been very clearly left unaddressed.

Even where 'patients' were 'cured' they were not empowered. They were not healed. They did not achieve personal recovery. They just existed. There were burning questions if the Mental Health Act of 1987 was a disability rights law at all.

Now I am in my room, where I am being confined.

This seems like the very opposite of Paradise.

Up and down, up and down. I perambulate up and down my room just like the peripatetic philosophers of Greece. I am certainly not one among the famous five.

Forward 2 3 4
Backward 1 2 3 4
Left 2 3 2
Right 3 2 4

And sometimes it is

Right 1 2 3 2 and yet,
At other times, it is
Left 1 3 2 4

'Society ought to be kinder to the mentally disturbed – to the persons with schizophrenia,' I find myself saying, again and again.

To the wall clock,
To the pencil stand,
To the pen stand,
(They are my friends).

To the long steel glasses on my dusty table, cluttered with all kinds of stuff that I might need. Old diaries that I might need. For reference, of course. I'm a voracious diary writer. Things must be placed in their exact and right context. Who said what, to whom and when.

Separate the past from the present, the present from the future, and the past from the future. No, I am not imagining things. I know perfectly well (for some time), where I should draw the borderline that separates imagination from reality. It scares me, because I am still in my senses. Not totally oblivious of things I see around me, of things happening around me.

Suddenly I am back in my own world – my world, where beginnings coincide with ends, collide with ends, and curl up with ends. Hazily, mistily, vaguely and confusedly. Where colours blend with one another so delicately that one can hardly make out their borders or boundaries or edges. A world, where emotion unfalteringly thumbs her fruity nose at logic and makes her fumble, and slips out of her arms greasily, and smiles an unctuous smile. It is a land of imprisonment – and yet a land of freedom. Paradoxically enough. It is a land to which lots have escaped, and a land, which very few people have the fortune to come back from. And the few, who do come back, do so with great difficulty. I make desperate attempts to feel secure in a tacitly insecure world. I do in fact watch TV programs and read all the artists' names – the characters, their real names, the names of the script-writers, directors, make-up experts and cinematographers aloud, literally everything that comes on screen, every letter and every number, to find simplicity in a sordidly complex universe. 'I will be a writer one day' I tell my relatives, when they question me. My caregivers hadn't made the right decisions. Was I to blame?

The creepy, crawling sensations begin to come back. They begin to spread all over my body. I start shivering and crying. It is a torture, but I hardly know how to overcome it. Neither deep breathing exercises nor medication seems to help me. My very existence becomes a torture. Can't somebody help me? Is there no solution at all? Must I be doomed to lead this kind of a life – every hour, every minute, and every second? Isn't it a shame on society's part to be doing this to an individual? 'My lord, my lord, why have you forsaken me?' say I, even as I stare imploringly at the idol of the deity in my room.

And the stone idol coldly stares back at me.

The onus to change and recover always lay on the individual and never on the caregivers, who made me the way I was, and who were never assigned any responsibility or standard to change their behaviour too or at least to help induce recovery in me. All they needed to be responsible for was to ensure that the 'patient' (as I was called then) took her medication. For even when 'the patient' decided to recover, she needed support.

I did not feel good at all and began dreading the passing of each night into new day. I hated clocks. For they reminded me that time was passing.

In the familial realm – or at least in my family – being a wife and a mother or being trained to be a wife and a good mother, were the only roles being conceptualised for women back then. And women who became hysterical or schizophrenic supposedly did so because they refused to accept these God-given, God-ordained roles. This was the reality that made my mother think a professional education for a girl was a waste of money! Also, my mother thought the psychiatrist knew more about me than I knew about myself.

I did however, succeed to rebuild my life from scratch and to take back my full legal capacity through education. But first came survival, for that was the primordial instinct. I asked my mother to re-parent me. And my mother seemed to be conveying the following message – tell me where and how you need security my baby. I see you have a need. Let me meet your need my little one. I will do all I can to help you survive.

I could for the first time feel the heartbeat of the maternal figure who at the end of the day would show herself to be the only person with a heart. A heart that was forever beating for my well-being. The maternal quintessence of a being that truly cared. For we had been part of a common biological ecosystem. An ecosystem that manifested itself and existed before I was even born. While I was a foetus. It was just that it had existed. Nothing more. Nothing less. Love ruled here and not the ego.

My mother did bother about justice after I confronted her; now that she had done all she had wanted to do to me. She felt sorry for me, her crazy daughter. My mother now understood my anger. She saw through it very clearly. Still she initially attributed the illness to her daughter's faulty genes. I was to take some time to dispel this dirty idea that was so victim blaming.

As mother and daughter, we spent a whole lot of time weeping in each other's arms because my mother's intestines squeezed in pain every time I wept and asked her 'Mummy who will care for me after you die?'

All of a sudden, it became crystal clear to my mother as to what she had really reduced me to. At least she bothered to admit this at the conscious level. This saved me. My mother understood the need to be human and humane with me. She acknowledged the need to save me – her dying daughter – from a morbid civil and living death. She stopped behaving in ways that irritated me. Or using words that were sure to cause a relapse. She understood the need to allow me, her daughter, to pursue my own dreams. For people with schizophrenia are hypersensitive. Social medicine needed to be provided. Along with psychotropic medication only if psychotropic medication were to be needed. It was of paramount importance for the people around the affected individual to change.

This was exactly where psychiatry failed in its role to facilitate recovery.

My mother and I spent those months combating stigma. I had lost everything I had in life. So, had my mother.

My mother and I slogged together – we trudged through the sludge, through the seemingly endless mire of dirt. Ours was a heart-rending fight against the world and the disabling social environment. My mother was now my strongest ally.

The mother figure held out her strong hand for her baby daughter to clutch. The baby daughter clutched her mother's hand finger by finger until she steadied herself and was capable of supporting herself.

Together we studied the academic lessons, sang to one another, and watched movies of disabled kids who had found it most difficult to move their muscles even, initially but had done something great and extraordinary with their lives.

I sat on my mother's lap 8 hours each day and studied my academic lessons. My mother, the Great Caregiver, practised Zen Buddhism. She also patiently listened and listened to every word of what I read out. For I had to read my lessons aloud to be able to concentrate. My mother agreed to do this and a lot more for me. She monitored my nutrition intake meticulously and celebrated every academic victory of mine.

One step at a time our souls communed with each other.

And then something magical happened! I recovered from 'schizophrenia'. I proved for the umpteenth time in history that 'mental illness' wasn't mental illness really! That it was a myth and that the condition could be reversed.

When my mother phoned my psychiatrist to tell her I had done my BA and MA degrees and a lot more, all that my psychiatrist did was to ask a silly-ridiculous question: 'How did she do it? Did you take her to a different psychiatrist?'

I then did my PhD wherein I was to link up Women's Studies with Psychology and other Mental Health Sciences. I clearly conceptualised my support system, Feminist Self Advocacy (FSA)[1], for psychosocially disabled women. FSA gave me wings to fly. With that came newfound confidence. Boundless confidence. I was able to travel to several countries on my own and take part in international conferences with other professionals who were on the frontiers of mental health science and cutting-edge user-survivor research. They were the leading lights in mental health. I questioned them, debated with them, learned from them, reasoned with them, agreed with them many a time and tore them apart when I thought I needed to.

A girl who had once upon a time been scared to travel to the bus stop nearest her house on account of a devastating mental illness was now flying across rivers and deserts, mountains and valleys, continents and oceans. Fly? It wasn't just that.

I soared into the high heavens.

All a consequence of a super sensitive caregiver who learned exactly where, when and how to let go. MAATHRU DEVO BHAVA! One's mother is one's Goddess.

The results of supported decision-making as against substituted decision-making were there for the entire world to see!

***

Lavanya's story is a good illustration of the importance of the UN Convention on the Rights of Persons with Disabilities' (CRPD) paradigm shift from control to self-determination. When it comes to persons with psychosocial disabilities, the reaction from psychiatrists, politicians and common people is often that the CRPD is unrealistic, that it is a theoretical construction, made by human rights lawyers, who know nothing about the reality of persons with severe mental health problems (Freeman et al., 2015; Dawson, 2015). But Lavanya's story shows that they are wrong, and that the CRPD approach is realistic.

In Lavanya's story, many of the articles of the CRPD are violated. But her story also shows something more: that the prevalent methods of control not only violate fundamental human rights principles but are also detrimental and anti-therapeutic. These coercive measures are legitimised as being 'for your own good', but Lavanya's story shows that they just make everything much worse. Despite their lack of any real rationale, these practices are still carried out everywhere.

Lavanya was studying at college, when a combination of factors in her personal life – as well as the general cultural and social situation for women in India – drove her into a severe state of distress, where she was on the brink of a mental breakdown. Her mother brought her to a female psychiatrist, an understandable reaction for a parent worrying about her child. She trusted the seeming professionalism of the psychiatrist, and followed the advice given to her, not knowing that psychiatrists are no experts at all on human distress, and that their treatment methods are anti-therapeutic.

Lavanya wanted to go back to college and continue her studies, but the psychiatrist thought it would only make her psychiatric condition worse. Instead she told Lavanya's mother to keep her daughter confined at home for one year. The ignorant psychiatrist thought that this would give Lavanya the rest she needed to recover, but in reality, it only made things worse. If Lavanya in the beginning was only on the brink of a mental breakdown, the decisions made by the female psychiatrist and her parents, drove her into a psychosis, into compulsive rituals, a deep depression and finally into a catatonic state of mind.

What saved Lavanya's life and finally brought her back to normal life and back to her studies, was that she succeeded to convince her mother to make a turnaround from substitute decision-making to supported decision-making – in accordance with Article 12 CRPD.

Substituted decision-making is when a disabled person is denied legal capacity, and the decisions about her are made by another person against her own will – by a guardian, a psychiatrist or another family member. In supported decision-making, the disabled person still makes the decisions herself, but a support person can help her to formulate her decisions, and to communicate them to others (CRPD Committee, 2014, paras. 27–29).

Lavanya wanted to go back to college, but her mother first made a decision against her will to stop this and confined her in the family's home. Later her mother realised that this was wrong, and instead supported Lavanya's own decision – which she did in a very active way, by helping Lananya to regain her studying skills, step by step. When Lavanya retrieved her rights to exercise her legal capacity, things started to go right. She resumed her studies at college, and quickly made an astounding academic career.

The situation in India differs in many aspects from the situation in Western Europe, although much is the same. The main difference is the more prominent role for the family and the collective, compared with the very individualistic lives in Western Europe. When I discuss the CRPD with Indian psychiatrists, they always mention that in India they have to reason with the whole family and not just with the patient. Because of this, it is a bit difficult to distinguish what in Lavanya's story is dependent on the general praxis of Indian family life – which is taken for granted – from what is regulated by law. However, the CRPD is not only targeting legislation but also social praxis.

What is most striking in Lavanya's story is the violation of Articles 12 and 14 of the CRPD. The psychiatrist told her parents to keep Lavanya confined at home for one year, thus preventing her from going back to college. The psychiatrist did not transfer power to Lavanya's parents in a strict legal way. Instead, she utilised the traditional power of Indian parents over their children, which continues even when they are grown-up.

In any case, confining Lavanya in her family's home for a year is a violation of Article 14(1)-(b), which says 'that the existence of a disability shall in no case justify a deprivation of liberty', which is exactly what happened in Lavanya's case. It doesn't matter if the confinement was at a psychiatric institution, or at home. Regardless, it is a deprivation of Lavanya's liberty, justified by her psychosocial disability.

Something similar can be said about the psychiatrist and Lavanya's parents preventing her from going back to college. As Lavanya is explicitly saying that she wants to continue her studies, but the psychiatrist and her parents hinder it, this is a clear violation of Article 12 on the right to self-determination 'in all aspects of life', and also on Article 24 on the right to education. It does not matter that the psychiatrist just utilised the traditional power of Indian parents. Article 12 also prohibits informal denials of legal capacity, including those involving the traditional powers of the family (CRPD Committee, 2014, para. 26).

The whole arrangement, made up by Lavanya's psychiatrist and family, is also a violation of Article 19(a), which says that the State shall ensure that 'persons with disabilities have the opportunity to choose their place of residence and where and with whom they live on an equal basis with others and are not obliged to live in a particular living arrangement'. What this means is specified by the UN Committee on the Rights of Persons with Disabilities (the Committee) in its General Comment No. 5 on living independently and being included in the community: 'the right to independent living refers to an individual dimension, as a right to emancipate oneself without being denied access and opportunities' (CRPD Committee, 2017, para. 19). This right must be protected also in informal settings, like families: 'Even if no formal laws are in place, other persons, such as families, caregivers or local authorities, sometimes exercise control and restrict an individual's choices by acting as substitute decision makers' (CRPD Committee, 2017, para. 26).

Much in Lavanya's story is universal. It could happen anywhere on the globe – as the consultation with the psychiatrist, which would occur in a similar way in Western Europe. But there are other elements in her story that are related to a cultural and social context in India, which is very different. To illuminate this, I will make some comparisons with Sweden, where I live.

In India, as in many other countries, parents pay for higher education for their children. Lavanya's parents were in control of the money and could decide to terminate her course at college without her consent. When she had fallen into this confused state of mind, they thought it was just a waste of money to let her continue her studies, and, further, that it was not as profitable to invest money in a daughter's education as in a son's. Lavanya was denied the opportunity to make her own decision about her studies – whether this denial was based on a legal framework or on economic control.

In Sweden, all studies at colleges and universities are free, and students can easily borrow money from the State for their daily living. If this had been the case also in India, Lavanya could have resumed her studies at college, without being dependent on her parents and their decisions. The only way for the psychiatrist to hinder it, would have been to confine Lavanya in a psychiatric institution, but also that would had been hard to do.

This shows that in India it is not enough to change the legislation, when implementing human rights for disabled persons according to the CRPD. It also needs general, social reforms. Despite this, there are many steps that can be taken immediately.

What obviously are lacking in India are independent support structures. Lavanya had no one else to turn to beside the psychiatrist and her parents – for advice, for information on her human rights, for help to get these rights respected, for support in formulating her own decisions, in communicating them to others and to get them realised.

If something like the Swedish Personal Ombudsman system is implemented in India, Lavanya's peers can avoid being stuck in similar, locked situations. The Personal Ombudsman is recognised by international bodies as a good example on supported decision-making – in accordance with Article 12(3) CRPD.[2] A personal ombudsman works 100% on the commission of his clients only, and only carries out what his clients ask him to do.[3] There is also a lack of economic support outside the family. To be able to live independently in the community according to Article 19 CRPD, persons with psychosocial disabilities in India need to get some basic economic support from the government. Otherwise the right to live in the community will only be a phrase on a paper.

Lanaya's story shows not only that several specific Articles (12, 14, 19) of the CRPD were violated. It also illustrates that these articles are interrelated. For example, Article 19 on living independently and being included in the community cannot be realised without Article 12 on the right to exercise legal capacity being respected at the same time. And these two articles cannot be realised if Article 14 on the right to liberty and security is violated.

Notes

1 For more information regarding Feminist Self Advocacy see the online publications by the Center for Global Mental Health, available at: http://www.centreforglobalmentalhealth.org/sites/www.centreforglobalmentalhealth.org/files/uploads/documents/1B%20Service%20user%20experience-%20Seshasayee.pdf>

[accessed 18 Dec. 2017]; and Youth Ki Awaaz, available at: https://www.youthkiawaaz.com/2015/06/personal-story-of-living-with-schizophrenia/ [accessed 18 Dec. 2017], respectively.

2 As presented in 'The World Report on Disability', published by the World Health Organization and the World Bank in 2011.

3 For more details on the Personal Ombudsman see Jesperson (2007) and Jesperson (2016).

Bibliography

Committee on the Rights of Persons with Disabilities. (2014). *General Comment No 1: Article 12: Equal Recognition Before the Law.* UN Doc. No. CRPD/C/GC/1.

Dambrot, F., & Reep, D. C. (1993). Overview of feminist therapy: a treatment choice for contemporary women. *The Journal of Training & Practice in Professional Psychology,* 7, pp. 10–25.

Dawson, J. (2015). A realistic approach to assessing mental health law compliance with the UNCRPD. *International Journal of Law and Psychiatry,* 40, pp. 70–79.

Enns, C.Z. (1997). Feminist Theories and Feminist Psychotherapies: Origins, Themes, and Variations. New York: Harrington Park Press.

Foucault, M. (1989). Madness and Civilization: A History of Insanity in the Age of Reason, (trans. Howard, R.), New York: Vintage.

Freeman, M.C. et al. (2015). Reversing hard won victories in the name of human rights: a critique of the General Comment on Article 12 of the UN Convention on the Rights of Persons with Disabilities. *Lancet Psychiatry,* 2(9), pp. 844–850.

Gadamer, H.-G. (1996). *The Enigma of Health: The Art of Healing in a Scientific Age.* Stanford, CA: Stanford University Press.

Jesperson, M. (2007). Personal ombudsman in Skåne. A user-controlled service with personal Agents. In: P. Lehmann and P. Stastny, eds., *Alternatives Beyond Psychiatry,* Berlin: Peter Lehmann Antipsychiatrieverlag, pp. 299–304.

Jesperson, M. (2016). The personal ombudsman: an example of supported decision-making. In: J. Russo and A. Sweeney, ed., *Searching for a Rose Garden: Challenging Psychiatry, Fostering Mad Studies,* Wyastone Leys: PCCS Books, pp. 134–141.

UN Committee on the Rights of Persons with Disabilities (2017), *General Comment No. 5 on living independently and being included in the community.* UN Doc. No. CRPD/C/GC/5.

World Health Organization and World Bank, (2011). *The World Report on Disability.* p. 138. [online] Available at: http://whqlibdoc.who.int/publications/2011/9789240685215_eng.pdf [Accessed 18 Jan. 2018].

22 Consent is more than just yes or no

Fiona Anderson and Bo Chen

First admission interview

I distinctly remember the first mood swing episode began on Friday 16 December 1988 coinciding with the onset of my menses. The first thing I noted was this strange sensation in my head which I describe as having a hive of drones continually buzzing and in 1994 was advised that it was agitation linked to a 'mixed affective mood swing' and I was swinging from low to high mood cycles throughout the day and extremely unpleasant symptom. I sensed something was amiss as over the following months my behavioural pattern became erratic and irrational. I was in a highly charged mental, emotional and physical disarray and frame of mind when I was confronted by seven medical personnel in a confined space and found the atmosphere smothering for my first admission interview and terrified of finding myself in this position. This interview is for all intents and purposes an assessment of legal capacity mixed with subtle coercion. The interview consisted of four main questions fired at me from three medics sitting opposite me at a table and designed to determine my lucidity, concentration, memory and thought process and can still recall these questions and my responses. The interview commenced with the question 'What is the price of the Irish Independent?' My response was immediate: '85 pence'. The medics seemed surprised that I was correct. This was followed by the request to count back from one hundred in sevens. I halted a few times within a timed minute, making mistakes in my calculations. This, in my mind, was more a reflection of my poor mathematical ability under pressure and not my lucidity, concentration or pressure of thought. For the third question, I was given a name and address to recall 10 minutes later.

The fourth question was 'Is anyone putting thoughts into your head?' My responses sewed me up. I acknowledged I had some irrational thought processes and beliefs. By the time it got to this final question I would have said anything to get out of that room and was in great distress. This line of questioning was a subtle form of coercion to sign myself in as a voluntary patient. At that moment, I thought if I showed any sign of dissent or lack of cooperation, hovering over my head was the prospect of 'involuntary detainment'. Consultant psychiatrists had a broad range of powers and authority under the Mental Health Treatment Act 1945 and at their whim could wield their authority. The legislation provided no protection for involuntary detained persons and there was no provision for an independent psychiatric review or tribunal. Under this Act, Consultant Psychiatrists could authorise the involuntary detention of a person for up to three months and no questions or explanations were required. Retaining full legal capacity to consent to medical treatment was an unknown concept when I was admitted in 1989, and my naivety was evident as I thought there would be some element of discussion and choice about the proposed medication regime. I sought information on the medication to be commenced but all I was told was 'It is non-addictive.' I was admitted to the unit and had all of my clothes removed and locked away for several days. As a voluntary patient, I questioned this practice. I remember feeling humiliated, embarrassed and dehumanised in front of visitors. In the beginning, I requested that nobody, not even my closest friends, were to be told where I was. However, I was spotted in the unit and this went viral within 24 hours.

***

The first and most intuitive question raised by Fiona's story is why an admission interview was needed when she sought help on a voluntary basis. Fiona mentioned that her interview was essentially an assessment for legal capacity. As a result of the interview, if a person was assessed as lacking mental capacity, his or her legal capacity would be denied accordingly and substituted decisions could be made against the person's wishes. The decision Fiona made before the interview was to seek care in hospital, and she felt more distressed facing the unfriendly environment and questions. She was aware that her answer to the last question was deemed 'irrational' but never got another chance to make her true voice properly heard. The 'irrationality' under distress, however, did not make her decision to seek help invalid or lead to her admission being refused by the hospital. Instead, even if she planned to sign in voluntarily, Fiona had to 'cooperate' with the seven interviewers, avoiding worse attitudes and arrangement associated with their power of involuntary commitment. Fiona was still under coercion at the very beginning when she walked into the mental health system, making the idea of voluntary treatment in a system that maintains involuntary detention and forced treatment a fiction. The fact that Fiona was not really free to choose her treatment but assessed as a voluntary patient echoes the appeal that the focus should shift from standards of involuntary treatment to providing voluntary, accessible and quality services (McSherry, 2010).

The purpose served by the admission interview and the arrangements afterwards correspond with what Goffman (1961) describes as 'leaving off' self-identity and control of life outside the total institution and 'taking on' the new world within. The 'leaving off' is usually done by depriving people of their personal possessions embedded with emotional investments. When Fiona was locked up and required to remove all her clothes, this created fear, loss and mortification even more directly. The admission interview, however, was a performance displaying the institution's authority, including the power to determine Fiona's 'lucidity, concentration, memory and thought process'.

As a result of the deinstitutionalisation movement in the West, the number and size of psychiatric institutions has been reduced. The unequal nature of psychiatric services has been less altered. Under the Irish Mental Health Act 2001, for example, even a voluntary patient is still subject to explicit coercive power as he or she could be detained or refused permission to leave hospital based on psychiatric assessments (Mental Health Act 2001, s. 23–24). On the other hand, however, services based on free and informed consent, as required by multiple Articles of the UN Convention on the Rights of Persons with Disabilities (CRPD), are largely underfunded. It is reasonable to assume that if Fiona and other service users had access to peer-led services, that could better understand and address the common distress and fear they experienced, there would be fewer obstacles between services and people in need.

The training video

In the summer of 1994, I was admitted to the psychiatric unit as a voluntary patient and again all of my clothes were removed and locked away for several days stirring again the feelings of humiliation, embarrassment and dehumanisation. Worse was yet to come. There was a practice used in the mental health services and the unit at the time. I had heard previously of this practice on the grapevine. A few days after my admission, a medic approached me and I was requested to participate in a training video. I understood the concept behind the request and the purpose of the video. A carrot was dangled before me to gain agreement – if I participated, I could get my clothes back. I was very sick as I was experiencing a 'mixed affective mood swing' and swinging from low to high throughout the day in a very distressed and agitated state. I was particularly vulnerable and had a persistent buzzing sensation in my head. I was manipulated and blackmailed into agreeing. I felt I was in no position to argue and could not be guaranteed the treatment I would receive if I refused. The concept of informed consent in mental health services still did not exist in practice and there was no written consent given or asked for. I invariably said yes and my clothes were returned immediately. I was escorted by a nurse 500 metres to the larger institution to record the video. I was left outside a room specifically designed for this video session. When I entered the room and took my seat I noticed one video camera facing me and another facing a young medic. There were microphones and the medic had an earpiece prompting him with the questions to ask. My attention was drawn to five heavy-duty spotlights shining down on me which caused huge distress. Perspiration began to roll off me from the intense heat the spotlights generated. The training video consisted of a role-play of the admission interview I experienced before on several occasions with the same four main questions as my first admission interview.

I could reel off my responses, as by this stage I had learned the appropriate responses to give. Adding to my distress was my rather unkempt state and appearance as I weighed 18 stone at the time. When the video was completed I ambled back to the unit and a fuss was made of the fact that I had not been accompanied by a staff member. An assumption was made. I might have absconded! Several years later in the medical records I received, my distress from the spotlights was recorded and an inaccurate entry states that my clothes were returned two days later. I made a written complaint about this, and the medic who responded stated that participation in such training is indeed voluntary and no manipulation, blackmail or bargaining chip is ever used. I might have been very sick but I make no false assertion regarding the methods employed to get a positive response. In my written complaint, I listed all the file notes that had not been supplied and a further search was undertaken. When I asked the institution for the files they told me that these records were either 'missing' or 'could not be found'! Apparently, the training video was destroyed a month after it was made. Later in 2010, when I was admitted to a psychiatric unit for a fortnight, I was requested twice to participate in training videos with young medics. I refused as I was not prepared to put myself in that position and go down a similar road again.

***

Fiona's story reflects a typical scenario where consent was sought under domination (Arstein-Kerslake and Flynn, 2017). Fiona agreed to the proposal of participating in the training video out of fear that she would not receive treatment she needed and would never get back her clothes. The consent was sought by medical professionals who had total control of her life within the institution, including deprivation of liberty authorised by the Mental Treatment Act 1945. The power and authority here were visible and no effective external constraint could be expected, at least by Fiona who could not escape from the domination. However, the obvious domination did not prevent the medical professionals from going through the performance of gaining her consent.

How could a genuine and meaningful consent be sought then? A theoretical framework of consent has been provided elsewhere by the VOICES Project (Brosnan and Flynn, 2017). Applying this approach to Fiona's case, her legal capacity should be recognised, and adequate information on the environment, her role and her right to stop recording etc., should be provided in an accessible manner. A negotiation in which Fiona could choose from different options and express her will and preference on a voluntary basis should be actively initiated by the medical professionals. In order to ensure the voluntariness and authenticity of consent, coercion should also be eliminated and power imbalances should be minimised. However, this would have been impossible to achieve in practice not only in Fiona's story 20 years ago but also in most countries worldwide that permit formal coercion in mental health services through mental health legislation.

The legitimacy of mental health laws has long been debated, and the CRPD provides a new source of international human rights law into the battle-field. The CRPD Committee keeps recommending to State Parties to abolish coercive mental health laws in concluding observations and General Comment No.1. Service models without involving coercion have been studied and promoted by civil society organisations (Minkowitz, 2017). Despite the growing jurisprudence and literature on the CRPD and mental health law, Fiona's home country, Ireland, is still upholding the Mental Health Act 2001 which grants coercive power to psychiatry. It may be the reality that the debate will continue and the current law will not be changed overnight. However, at least, new legislation should reaffirm that any consent under the domination created by coercive mental health laws cannot be free and informed. Therefore, Fiona's consent to the participation for training video under coercion for example, should not be regarded as genuine and meaningful in the eyes of the law.

Lithium therapy

In October 1990, someone in my life noted my diagnosis of 'bi polar affective disorder' and spoke to my medical team, thinking lithium would be the best treatment for me. I felt I was just lumbered with this label and not considered as an individual with my own unique personality and character traits. I was lumped into a box with everybody with the diagnosis. Although I was a capable adult of 25 years of age, the mental health services discussed my treatment with this person in my life without my consent, contravening my privacy and confidentiality. The medic held discussions with this person; however, I was not present or even invited to be included and was left sitting in the alcove in the corridor of the unit. When I spoke to the medic, I requested that my illness and treatment plan was not to be discussed with anyone else. This was blatantly ignored and the medic continued to hold a further conversation with that person. I was upset by this intervention and instead of focusing on my justifiable emotional response from the invasion of my privacy, the dosage of my medication was increased. Whilst in theory I was given the time to consider going on lithium in the end there didn't seem to be any other option. From my own research, years later, I discovered lithium has an adverse impact on the renal system and that this was well known in the scientific literature, but I was not told of the health risks to my kidney function by the medics when commencing treatment. Under pressure in March 1991, I was admitted to the psychiatric unit to undergo the preliminary tests for the lithium treatment. These tests consisted mainly of a 24-hour urine collection sample recording the ability of the renal system to flush out the residue of the lithium. Due to the damage lithium can cause to the kidney function and thyroid it is important to have three monthly blood serum tests to gauge the therapeutic dosage level. A serum reading above 1 indicates lithium toxicity and requires the dosage to be reduced.

Even one bout of lithium toxicity can cause severe irreversible damage to the renal system resulting in chronic kidney disease (CKD). I attended a medical specialist regarding my polycystic ovarian syndrome (PCOS) etc., in 2000. It came to their attention that I was leaking protein and blood from my kidneys but they associated it with my diabetes. They prescribed another medication, Tritace, for the kidney function and from my own research I discovered it adversely interacts with lithium. I did not take it as it leads to toxicity. Several months later, I had a series of recurring kidney infections and experienced lithium toxicity at the same time, so my doctor reduced the dosage. Over the years there were several opportunities for various health professionals treating me to recognise my kidney function levels were impaired by lithium, but no one made the connection. Each health professional was working in a separate area. They did not join forces or attempt to organise and provide a coordinated multidisciplinary or interdisciplinary approach to my situation. This might have led to an earlier recognition of the impact the lithium was having on my kidney function. It was only years later when I received my medical files that I discovered that the psychiatrists had recorded information related to my kidney problems and yet continued the lithium treatment regardless. In early 2006, another one of my specialists undertook a 24-hour urine collection sample and a month later advised not to wait any longer to deal with my impaired kidney function. After 17 years on lithium, despite my repeated concerns to a wide variety of health professionals about its impact on my kidneys, it was only after the intervention of two other allied medical healthcare specialists in April 2007 that the decision to stop lithium was made. There have been a number of consequences of the mismanaged lithium therapy and the damage to my renal function is irreversible. I have daily chronic pain issues and due to my renal dysfunction, I am not permitted to take any pain killers.

I am reliant on regular steroid trigger point injections to get some form of pain relief. I have three monthly blood tests to monitor my renal function. I now receive a holistic and coordinated multidisciplinary team approach from the medical and psychiatric specialists including my main healthcare practitioners rather than fragmented and segregated care. In the Irish public health system, mental health services are divided into geographical regions and sectors and you must attend the psychiatrist in the sector you reside. This creates a problem if you don't gel with the practitioner and have no other option unless you can afford to go privately or have private health insurance and can select a consultant of your own choice.

Champix therapy

In August 2008, I requested one of my consultants to refer me to the smoking cessation nurse. At this appointment, we discussed ways for me to quit my smoking habit. I was provided with a leaflet about the medication Champix. As I read, my attention was immediately drawn to the first major side-effect: mood swings. I brought this to the notice of the nurse. I highlighted my mental health disorder. This medication interferes with the functioning of the brain and it was assessed as a high risk to my mental health and was not prescribed. A year later I returned to one of my specialists and even before the consultation, it appeared a decision had already been made to prescribe Champix. Again, I immediately pointed out my mood swing disorder. However, no discussion or adequate risk assessment was undertaken by the medics. The medics did not have the courtesy, decency or manners to converse with me. In hindsight with my knowledge I should have gone with my gut instinct that this medication was not suitable for me. I brought the prescription to one of my healthcare professionals and they expressed the same concerns. I felt obligated to comply with the medication as I was of the belief that non-compliance would impact on my future treatment with these medics and felt that my consent was not considered. The adverse consequences of taking this medication were not adequately assessed. One of my healthcare professionals issued a warning that at the first sign of a mood swing episode it was to be ceased. In early November 2009, there was a noticeable switch in my mood balance but I did not recognise this mood change until the end of that month. I stopped the Champix but it was too late and the mood swing took off. At the same time PCOS kicked in. A litany of obstacles, calamities and adverse chain of events ensued. By August 2010, I was highly anxious, mentally stressed, emotionally and physically drained bruised and battle worn. The mood swing continued to escalate. I was admitted to a psychiatric unit later that year for a fortnight.

For various reasons, it was necessary to move home and I was referred to the mental health services of the region and sector I moved into. I attended the day centre as an outpatient twice a week. At the end of October 2010 my mother died after a short illness. I was emotionally, mentally and physically bereft. I felt isolated and abandoned by everyone in my grief. After mum's death, the mood swing became more intense and I was hospitalised for seven months between May and December 2011. I either had to swim or sink.

Epilim therapy

During 2011, my psychiatrist suggested using Epilim which is an epileptic medication as a mood stabiliser. I was provided with an information leaflet to read and make an informed decision. Despite being ill my legal capacity and capability to consent were not questioned. I read the information and decided against it at that point in time. This time my decision was respected. I had previously reacted negatively to two other epileptic drugs: one for my mood disorder and the other for my chronic pain and thought I would react to this medication as well. Several years later my psychiatrist suggested Epilim again. My psychiatrist said: 'You are an intelligent and bright young woman' and advised me to research this medication. I was given space and time to make a fully informed decision. Therefore, I weighed all the pros and cons, having read all that I could, making a final decision to reject the treatment. The lithium therapy had left a rather bitter aftertaste. The possible liver damage from Epilim was at the forefront of my mind and I could not risk adding to my medical conditions. I advised the psychiatrist of my decision which was respected. There was no attempt by the psychiatrist to influence me or try to change my mind. There was a very apparent clear contrast with the approach by this psychiatrist regarding Epilim when compared to the circumstances surrounding the lithium therapy.

***

From Fiona's negative and positive experiences of making decisions about medical treatment, it is obvious that things would have ended up better if doctors were willing to listen to her and trust her in understanding information and reaching her own decisions. It is particularly worth noting that all of this happened without any functional capacity assessment. None of these treatments was authorised when Fiona was an involuntary patient under the Mental Health Act 2001 and therefore, each treatment required informed consent from Fiona, just as any other treatment decision in a general healthcare setting would. The functional assessment of mental capacity has been enshrined in Irish case law as a precondition for providing valid consent to medical treatment, for example in *Fitzpatrick v. FK* (2008). Even though some of Fiona's treatment occurred prior to 2008, the functional assessment of mental capacity had already been developed in English case law and could potentially have applied to Fiona. Regardless of academic debates or practical difficulties around the permissibility of the functional approach, what matters to Fiona is that her legal capacity was not denied when she refused to take the Epilim therapy after research. One can argue that Fiona's positive experience was only possible because the disabling law did not jump in as a barrier, declaring Fiona to lack 'mental capacity' or encouraging medical professionals to override her decision by arranging a capacity assessment.

Although the Assisted Decision-Making (Capacity) Act 2015 will not alter the main provisions in the Mental Health Act 2001, the role of the new piece of legislation in the Irish context becomes an interesting question, as voluntary users of mental health services could be affected by the 2015 Act. Will there be more service users who can make informed decisions about their own treatment and get their voices heard, or less? Will the Act remind medical professionals that there is a legal tool they can use to legally override or ignore the voices of service users? Or, will the decision-making supports provided by the Act and its new principle of respect for 'will and preferences' rather than best interests benefit the communication and mutual trust between service users and providers? These questions can only be answered by the Act's implementation.

On the other hand, whether meaningful consent is possible also depends on the operation of the medical system. As mentioned above, capacity law and mental health law create a power-imbalanced mental health system which service users are unable to escape from. However, there are also other practical and attitudinal factors affecting effective and meaningful communication and consent. For example, Fiona mentioned that in the public health system in Ireland, there is only one psychiatrist per region, so it is very difficult for service users to express any dissent to their psychiatrists. The lack of alternatives to the designated psychiatrists enhances the authority of psychiatrists and therefore there is arguably less room for service users' participation in treatment decision-making. Fiona's voice was further ignored, or marginalised at least, by the fact that her specialists appeared to have more concerns about the hierarchy among medical departments (this may explain why an interdisciplinary team was never formed), rather than listening to Fiona's opinion or decision. Because of these barriers, Fiona's lithium dose was not stopped until another doctor intervened, although Fiona was fully aware of its side effects and strongly against its use in the first place. The false documentation provided by medical professionals in her files made it harder for Fiona to make any complaint. The same problems may also exist to some degree in not only psychiatry but all medical spheres. However, mental health service users usually face more barriers because of the stereotype of incapacity, and therefore need more support in making their voices heard and decisions respected (Arstein-Kerslake and Flynn, 2017).

Solving these practical and attitudinal barriers is a big project, requiring more attention and investment from the whole society. What is key, however, is to ensure the service users' involvement at all levels, including policy-making, training for medical professionals, and delivery of service on a daily basis. However, the power imbalances have been commented on as the 'primary obstacles' to service users' involvement in Irish mental health system (Brosnan, 2012). The new human rights approach provides critical understanding and aims to reform oppressive psychiatry and its coercive mental health laws. The CRPD also requires in Article 4 that, in all decision-making processes concerning issues relating to persons with disabilities, 'States Parties shall closely consult with and actively involve persons with disabilities, including children with disabilities, through their representative organizations.' A similar requirement is also provided in Article 33. The status of service users' organisations in policy-making and monitoring may be enhanced by this piece of legally binding international human rights law, and the Committee on the Rights of Persons with Disabilities (the Committee) will become a new platform for advocacy. But this potential will not become reality unless Ireland ratifies the CRPD first and implements it faithfully.

***

For these years I have seen too many service users just following whatever they are told by health professionals and being very passive in any engagement. I hope measures could be adopted to empower service users to become more active in their care plan, because in my experience the importance of information, communication, and mutual trust between my doctors and myself cannot be overstated. Service users need to be informed, trusted and involved in our treatment plan. When we have more people engaging as much as we can, the system is more likely to be altered.

As a result of many previous good and bad interactions in decision-making, there have been improvements in obtaining informed consent, policies, procedures and practices for admission as a 'voluntary patient'. The mental health services also have improved their form and techniques of interviews. Now a service user is less likely to confront so many doctors and nurses or silly questions as I did. The practice of removing clothing has also ceased for 'voluntary patients' but still exists in involuntary procedures. It is a humiliating, embarrassing, degrading and dehumanising practice. I do not think this issue can be solved as long as the coercive mental health system exists.

***

Fiona tells us her story to ensure that what happened to her should not happen to others again. This purpose has been partly fulfilled as several years later the mental health services Fiona was attending have introduced a lithium policy, including an information booklet, a detailed consent form which must be signed by the patient, a diary for recording lithium serum test results, and a record card in an emergency advising on lithium. In addition, an independent advocacy service has become available in Ireland, and service users can now be supported in speaking out and claiming their entitlements (Independentadvocacy.ie, 2017). But these progresses should not be the end. In order to promote meaningful change, more work needs to be done following a human rights approach.

Bibliography

Arstein-Kerslake, A. and Flynn, E. (2017). The right to legal agency: domination, disability and the protections of Article 12 of the Convention on the Rights of Persons with Disabilities. *International Journal of Law in Context*, 13(1), pp. 22–38.

Brosnan, L. (2012). Power and participation: an examination of the dynamics of mental health service-user involvement in Ireland. *Studies in Social Justice*, 6(1), pp. 45–66.

Brosnan, L. and Flynn, E. (2017). Freedom to negotiate: a proposal extricating 'capacity' from 'consent'. *International Journal of Law in Context*, 13(1), pp. 58–76.

Goffman, E. (1961). Asylums: Essays on the Social Situation of Mental Patients and Other Inmates. Piscataway, NJ: AldineTransaction.

Independentadvocacy.ie. (2017). *What is Independent Advocacy?* [online] Available at https://sites.google.com/site/independentadvocacyireland/ [Accessed 11 Dec. 2017].

McSherry, B. (2010). The right of access to mental health care: voluntary treatment and the role of law. In: B. McSherry and P. Weller, eds., *Rethinking Rights-based Mental Health Laws*. Oxford: Hart, pp. 379–396.

Minkowitz, T. (2017). CRPD and transformative equality. *International Journal of Law in Context*, 13(1), pp. 77–86.

23 The humour in my tumour: respecting legal capacity in health-care decision-making

Reshma Valliappan and Roxanne Mykitiuk

The reversible madness – 2011

convulsions of the normal

by Val Resh on Monday, May 23, 2011 at 5:25pm

> This entry was taken from my facebook update, written in a state of anger using my Sony Ericsson mobile as I lay in bed experiencing bouts of convulsions. I was using social media for my advocacy work and found it important that my readers knew what was transpiring in my life that very minute since I had no support from anyone during those hours.

please ignore the typos as ive having a ifficult time to type using bothn hands.

21st May 2011, Saturday evening

My hands started shaking, i cud feel my entire right body throbbing, and spasms like insects moving through my arm, and waist, and breast, legs, toes, buttocks and yes my bloody groin. BUt its was only the right side of body that had to bear this.

I thought having a shower might help...maybe I was being stressed and been lying down too much.

i cudnt operate the shower as earlier as my right hand culdn't grip the handle...so i had my shwr with the left. I got dressed, and as I was applying my kajal,[1] my entire right just got numb and started shaking horrible. My fingers gt into a weird fold and i called for my mom. M<y sister="" and="" mom="" didnt="" knpw="" what="" was="" going="" on="" put="" my="" a="" chair="" right="" body="" shaking="" i="" couldnlt="" beat="" the="" pain.="" had="" tears="" rollingdown="" because="" this="" has="" never="" happoened.="" called="" dad...he="" came="" they="" trying="" to="" calm="" me="" down.="" it="" got="" worse="" when="" holding="" as="" no="" control="" over="" hand="" lept="" hitting="" mom.="" told="" them="" stay="" away="" let="" sit.="" dad="" psychiatrist="" took="" valium.="" rushed="" ratna="" hospital.="" happened="" at="">

/rushed to casualty ward, they took my ecg, sugar test,bp. my hand was still mving without me wanting to move it.

First dr ask my dad for history. Dad says 'history of schizophrenia' 'reyes syndrome' as a child. Then they ask me for any complaints... i say 'I've been having fever bouts for the last month, im either constipated or

(*Continued*)

otherwise.' Ma said, 'She's had a right shoulder muscle pull giving her trouble for very often. Next mrning i ask dad, what the doctors said ;They said it is psychological. I asked 'Based on what? that I'm bloody schizo?'so dad n i not talking

Tday 1pm: Went with my ma to a family physician who was in charge of the report from those nght shift doctors;.He checked my joints with the usual hammer and said 'all ok' nthing to worry bout.

Doc Asked 'What medications are you taking?'

I 'None'

He 'Then you'r ok. u can go'

I 'but this doesnt explain the numbness and what im feeling inside'

He 'If someone is going to call me at 9pm and worry her parents and have everyne run around for her and then not take the medications, then the next time dont bother calling me coz i just wont answer.

I 'No, why shud i just take the medicatiosn when those doctors ruled me of as a psychologicial problem without paying attention to the complaints i gave them.!?!

He' 'I am not interested with your dialougue with them. i was callked for help and u refused the treatment'

I was bpoiling alot by then to say anything after this! I said 'FUCK U' and stood up. Opened the door and said 'you people shud learn to not discriminate the mentally ill'

got home. ma came later and we had a fight. so now we arent talking.

Apparently those night shift doctors never told my physician about the fever and shouder.

Suffering smothering system – 2013

A year and a half after my craniotomy, my seizures were still not under control by the medications prescribed. It was 23 June 2011 when I had to undergo surgery for the removal of a meningioma which was growing over the left hemisphere of my brain. The surgery could not be delayed as the tumour had begun affecting my body physically and delay in its removal could lead to irreversible brain damage. The prognosis given to me was that I needed a full year of being seizure free before the medications could be reduced. My diet, lifestyle, work, social, emotional, mental, physical, spiritual life got overturned by the invasion of a few little buggers by the name of Levera and Gabapentin.[2] I was worse off than before.

Everything became over stimulated. The surgeon said it was a side effect of the which in itself is a trauma for the brain to have the skull opened up. Added to the removal of a creature sitting on top of my brain and pressing it down for years (since they couldn't tell how long the tumour was growing on top of my left hemisphere). It appeared that the tumour had made its home on my brain and now its removal was like forcing an abusive lover to leave its home. And like most abusive lovers who come back, there was no certainty it would not return, though after six years it has not been back.

A physician, Dr. X, explained that after my, my wonderful crazy brain showed scar tissue. It was natural that it would, and that the scar tissue would have memories of the tumour. This in turn would affect what the brain would remember, which means even if there is no tumour, the brain could think the tumour is still there and go on experiencing seizures.

Dr. X said I have to keep taking these medications and I can't stop them as I did with my meds for schizophrenia giving the same prognosis: 'Until you are free from seizures for an entire year, only then can there be a reduction of the meds which again have to be monitored, as just one seizure in itself means another relapse to work with'.

'But that means meds for life', I said. 'Cause everything can cause a seizure including working on my laptop, indigestion, chocolates, working out, dehydration, anger, heat, dance floors, martial arts, tai chi, alcohol, dancing, hopping, lights, cinemas, Xbox, television, music, pranayama[3]...am I supposed to not breathe at all then? If I can't do everything in life, then what's the point in having one?'

He looked at me with no certainty to my question but said 'Well, you'll have to figure it out then and work with your neurologist.'[4]

It was very distressing that I had to live with this new brain problem now. Mr. Scar Epilepsy wasn't really a nice guy. I thought my life was really over and no one could understand why I was reacting the way I did. It was very easy for them to say take it in your stride, you've already gone through other stuff in life...this should be easy. It was very easy for them to have a list of expectations, questioning my strength during adversity, since I was quite a goof all the time and saw humour in everything. But at that point in my life, I was trying to come to terms with the ever strange brain problems with which my life was presented, and the walk was a very lonely one, as the disabling nature of it is never visible to others...I began withdrawing more from everyone.

I had messaged my neurologist late evening on a Saturday. I asked what would happen if someone consumed all the Frisiums,[5] anti-anxieties and anti-epileptics with alcohol. My neurologist messaged back, but I passed out trying to read the message and woke up in a very strange place with my limbs tied up, an extension wire sticking out of my hand, and everything was white (well that's what it looked like). I thought the aliens attached me to some device and were transferring their consciousness through my arms.

As I opened my eyes and made some gibberish sounds, my mother walked up and placed her hand on mine 'Reshma, can you hear me?' I looked at her with acknowledgement and asked her what happened. Why was she looking so sad? I had some memory of something but I don't know what that something was and what that memory was. Mom said, 'You tried taking your life Reshma.'

I heard that and fell asleep again only to awaken later with nurses all around me and the doctor having a conversation with my mom and dad. I woke up again but I sounded different. I asked for something but my mother couldn't understand what I was saying.

I threw a fit demanding that I get out of that place. My folks said I couldn't, as I have to be in hospital. Mom calmed me down and tried narrating to me the details of what had transpired. 'You took all your pills Resh and we had to rush you to the hospital. Then you also bit your sister on her hand and she cried because she was surprised you would do that. The mamas (hospital ward men) … 5 of them had to hold you down because you refused to calm down. The doctor was finding it difficult because you were being very violent so they had to tie you down to the bed but even then you managed…' and poof! I fell asleep again.

I kept going in and out of consciousness those few days until a sedative was given, only then would I remain asleep for long hours. I woke up again and looked around me. I was still lying on bed with my legs tied but arms loose. My mom narrated what happened.

'Resh, you had taken the rod that was holding your drip and sat on your bed moving it around and hitting everything. None of us were there as we went home because we were told you were fast asleep. Thankfully, the evening nurse was just signing out but upon hearing the commotion she rushed in to your room. She sat with you for an hour at least and waited for me to come back. She told the other nurses to leave as she knew they would react in fear and wouldn't understand, so she decided to wait until you calmed down.'

'Who was she Mom, did you ask for her name?' I enquired.

'No, I was so shocked and confused so I just thanked her and forgot to ask for her details' Mom said.

'But she was like an angel sent for you Resh. If she wasn't around then the hospital would again trouble us and involve the police.'

I do recollect the nurse holding my palm and standing very close to my bed to avoid being hit by the rod since I was still holding it. That was a smart thing she did since the rod, being long, wouldn't have been able to hit her as she was so close to me. She managed to talk me through the reasons I was swinging the rod and establish communication with me. After this she asked if I could give her the rod since my saline drip was all over the floor and that would complicate things for me. I knew she was telling me the truth as I was feeling giddy, exhausted and thirsty, and even if it wasn't the truth, my body was not able to hold on to the rod or to sit up any longer.

So I gave her the rod. She called in a nurse to replace my drip and clean the place while holding my palm and talking to me. Then she fed me some water and said they will need to put in a sedative as they might be afraid that I'll end up hurting myself or others again. She asked me if she can do it herself and continued 'Trust me okay. This will help you rest a little as you have exhausted yourself so much with the swinging. I'll wait with you until your family members come in.' I said yes and by the time I was looking for more words I had already passed out.

My ex-psychiatrist was worried as to why I pulled such a stunt and got violent throughout my admission. My first counsellor who was just driving through that locality had received a message from my mother and decided to drop in to visit me. Mom said, 'Resh, your counsellor looked very worried and didn't know what or how to help you.'

The unknown nurse who took responsibility at such a moment to care and stand by me speaks for all other 'strangers' in the world who, when given the power of care, will do something about it. We've always thought about care being a job of the treating doctor and other white coats who check you out and give you a prescription…unfortunately or fortunately. But I see care as a full circle existing within a community and there are many different players in a community. Most certainly these players would not be able to play their roles if their lives and capacity to make decisions were controlled by another authority. B ut when there is no second or third authority in the room they pretty much can choose to care for you with kindness and compassion and enable you to still feel you are capable of choice. How else can we translate or show care towards a mind that is running amok?

My experience after this attempt was followed with more 'unique' experiences of violence to self. A visiting psychiatrist watched me get a seizure in front of her. When it was over, she stood and chatted with me and then told my mom 'This isn't a symptom of schizophrenia. I'm seeing with my own eyes how painful the seizure is for her and she *is* able to communicate to me.'

When she said that, I was so grateful my mom heard it from her and told my dad too. But, I had been saying the same thing for some time and no one believed me, including my treating neurologist. I could only be believed when another doctor said the same thing. So evidently, my sanity does rely on another authority.

It is easy to wipe the wounds and clean the blood of an injured arm and gently blow on to a wound so that it doesn't burn and hug the person to make them feel secure and safe, and even sing them lullabies as they sleep. But this method might not be possible for someone who does not like touch to begin with and has too many thoughts about the world around her and speaks a very different language. Care, choice and capacity are spoken about in the English language and this is very limiting because English is a language and not the measure of compassion, communication or of intelligence.

I always ask others to learn some autism, some schizophrenia, some depression, or some seizures and then communicate to me and others in those languages and see if they can do it. And if they can't, then they can't place such linguistic expectations on us to be in a position to communicate ourselves. Even MBA students have to enrol in workshops and classes to learn about 'Communication' but nobody questions their capacity to make decisions if they are unable to communicate and deliver a presentation at a board meeting. What is this communication that the mental-health sector is referring to? And how is that determining my ability to choose for my care?

Care as many of us know of it does not exist in 'Mental-Health Care'. This term itself implies that you are caring only for the state of the person's mentality and not for the person as an entity in their own right.

***

Reshma's story illustrates the discriminatory and prejudicial health-care services and treatment that persons regarded as lacking capacity are subject to as they navigate a health-care system that is more intent on reinforcing dynamics of power than listening and attending to the health needs of the person with a disability. Yet, while her narrative is cautionary and critical, it is also instructive and hopeful.

Reshma's narrative, while grounded in Article 12 of the Convention on the Rights of Persons with Disabilities (CRPD) which recognises the right to legal capacity on an equal basis with others without discrimination on the basis of disability, also engages those of Article 25 and the relationship between the two. Article 25 of the CRPD provides a fundamental right for persons with disabilities to the highest attainable standards of health without discrimination on the basis of disability and therefore, the right to seek medical care and receive it on an equal basis with others. Reshma sought treatment for physical symptoms that were causing her significant distress and were subsequently determined to be caused by a brain tumour. However, Reshma was denied basic medical care and her novel physical symptoms were immediately attributed to her schizophrenia without apparent further investigation. This failure to investigate and treat constitutes discrimination on the basis of her disability and is a violation of her human rights as protected by Articles 12 and 25 of the CRPD as demonstrated below.[6]

Article 12 CRPD guarantees persons with disabilities the right to equal recognition before the law and the right to enjoy legal capacity on an equal basis with others in all aspects of life. It is the right to have one's decisions legally recognised. Reshma's decision not to take medication prescribed for schizophrenia was not accepted and respected by the physician. Instead, the physician implied that Reshma would be denied any further medical care for her current symptoms until she complied with a pharmaceutical-based treatment course for her psychiatric condition. Thus, Reshma would have had to take drugs against her will and preferences, to access standard medical care. In addition, by not respecting her legal capacity regarding Reshma's decision not to take drugs for her schizophrenia, the physician further discriminated against Reshma in regards to other aspects of her health, including investigation of a new set of symptoms and signs that ultimately should have led to an earlier diagnosis and treatment of Reshma's brain tumour and thus less pain, anguish and complications for her.

After Reshma's surgery for a brain tumour, which was delayed because the doctors attributed her report of new symptoms to her schizophrenia and her refusal to take medications for its treatment, one of the subsequent complications of the surgery was seizures. Even when it should have been clear to Reshma's physicians that not respecting her will and preferences in decision-making regarding taking medications for schizophrenia led to a delay in the diagnosis of her brain tumour, Reshma's self-determination in health-care decision-making was again denied when she developed the surgical complication of seizures and she was hesitant to take drugs for this potential complication of the late diagnosis. Reshma was provided only one option for treatment – medication for her seizures. She made clear expressions of her desire for another treatment route and expressed significant concerns about the only treatment option that was offered and the implications this would have for her quality of life.

Within a framework for consent that complies with international human rights standards including Article 12(1) of the International Covenant on Economic, Social and Cultural Rights (1966), the Convention on the Elimination of All Forms of Discrimination against Women (1979), the Convention on the Rights of the Child (1989) and the CRPD (2006), Brosnan and Flynn (2017) propose several essential elements that must be present for valid consent to be ascertained. These elements include the recognition of legal capacity, freedom to negotiate, provision of information, respect for will and preference and voluntariness (Brosnan and Flynn, 2017). The authors state that there is an obligation on the individual proposing to act upon the body of another to ensure that this person has all the relevant information about the action to which she is being asked to consent (Brosnan and Flynn, 2017). As argued by Morrison et al. (2012), in the medical context, the provision of sufficient information would require the treating mental-health professional to disclose all possible side effects of the proposed medication or treatment procedure, in a manner accessible to the person.

An important objective in the process of obtaining consent is the elimination of conditions that would vitiate valid consent, which include the threat of coercion or force on the decision. This concern is especially relevant in the context of consent to medical treatment, where an inherent power imbalance exists between patient and physician. Gaventa (2006) describes three forms of power that exist in relation to decision-making in the medical treatment context: visible, hidden, and invisible. Commentators have discussed how through 'hidden power', medical professionals can control the agenda and influence what information is brought to the decision-making table when treatment decisions are being made (Brosnan and Flynn, 2017). Indeed, some physicians may choose to withhold information on potential side effects of medications, in order to ignore that the patient could cope without medication (Brosnan and Flynn, 2017).

As Reshma tells us in her story, she was not fully informed of the side effects of the anti-epileptic medication she was prescribed for her seizures, the benefits of taking such medication or what the possible effects of not taking the medication would be. Given Reshma's clearly stated (and acted upon) preferences regarding the use of anti-psychotics, coupled with her articulated concerns about the implications of taking anti-seizure medications on her quality of life, the physician's response to Reshma's concerns about the anti-epileptic medication that '*well, you'll have to figure it out then* (emphasis added) and work with your neurologist,' appears to undermine Reshma's ability to make informed choices because her physician is not prepared to discuss treatment options nor to engage in a discussion of the consequences of not taking anti-epileptics. Rather than exploring the negative side effects and consequences of taking anti-epileptics, the possible alternatives to anti-epileptics or the consequences of a choice not to take them, with Reshma, her physician ignored the requirements for valid consent, asserting his power, and ignoring Reshma's expressed preferences.

Not all of Reshma's encounters with health-care providers were negative. In her story, the respect afforded her by one of her nurses, following her suicide attempt, illustrates a course of action that adheres to the mandates of

Article 12 of the CRPD. In this instance, the nurse respected and affirmed Reshma's legal capacity, rather than disputing it, and worked with her, creating the conditions of support, respect and trust in which Reshma was able to communicate her consent and make decisions about her own life. Article 12(3) of the CRPD creates the obligation for States to provide support for the exercise of legal capacity, as opposed to permitting State actors to discriminatorily intervene in the lives of persons with disabilities. This nurse's interaction with Reshma provides evidence that practices involving respectful communication and trust can be used as alternatives to forced medication of individuals experiencing emotional distress. Open dialogue is one communication-based approach that involves the individual experiencing psychosocial crisis, their friends and family members, and mental-health professionals in a partnership approach to the recovery process.[7] The nurse achieved success by inviting Reshma to be part of the process of diffusing the crisis and helping her understand the reasons for her actions. As demonstrated here, open dialogue is only successful if the environment is perceived as 'safe', a condition the nurse established by asking others to leave, thereby providing Reshma the space in which to make her own decisions.

Reshma's experience with this particular nurse is consistent with a framework for consent to medical treatment that upholds the human rights obligations under the CRPD (Article 25(d) requires health-care professionals to provide care on the basis of 'free and informed consent'). Such a framework requires that consenting parties must have the freedom to negotiate and the freedom to refuse in the context of medical treatment. The process of obtaining valid consent requires active communication between the parties, and the individual who proposes to administer the treatment must provide all the necessary information about the treatment in a manner that is accessible to the patient – this includes offering a range of meaningful choices.

In Reshma's story, the nurse asked Reshma for her consent (and left open the possibility of refusal) before administrating a sedative and provided information about how the treatment would benefit her. The nurse communicated with Reshma in a clear, calm and truthful manner, which was accessible to Reshma in her agitated state. The nurse's course of action provided Reshma the freedom to negotiate as a request for consent implies the right for refusal and Reshma was also given the option to wait for her family to arrive before making a decision. The nurse waited for an active response from Reshma. As Reshma tells us, the nurse cared with 'kindness and compassion' and enabled her 'to still feel'... 'capable of choice. How else can we translate or show care towards a mind that is running amok?'

Reshma recommends that mental-health actors translate the care they provide in a manner that is meaningful and accessible to the individual with the disability. Article 12 of the CRPD creates a State obligation to provide mechanisms of support to persons with disabilities while General Comment No. 1 specifies that the types of support will differ based on individual needs but must always respect the rights, will and preference of the individual (CRPD Committee, 2014, paras. 12–15). As Bach and Kerzner (2010) remind us, the paradigm of the right to legal capacity under Article 12 includes an inquiry into the supports and accommodations required to exercise and maximise legal capacity. Moreover, expressions of an individual's choice and capacity must be understood and interpreted generously. As stated in General Comment No. 1, the obligation for support also includes using non-traditional communication methods to allow people to convey their will and preferences. The manner in which an individual chooses to communicate cannot be used as a means to assess or deny legal capacity (CRPD Committee, 2014, para 17). Article 12 recognises that there are different ways in which people communicate and make decisions and General Comment No. 1 definitively states that 'perceived or actual deficits in mental capacity [may not] be used as a justification for denying legal capacity' (CRPD Committee, 2014, para. 13). Indeed, in her story, Reshma implores health-care workers and others to learn 'some autism, some schizophrenia, some depression, or some seizures and then communicate to me and others in those languages and see if they can do it' as a means of challenging and expanding rigid conceptions of capacity.

On 6 July 2017, Reshma and I met to discuss her story. In that conversation, she advocated passionately for alternative approaches to treatment for individuals experiencing mental-health crises. We noted that in the West, family group conferencing involves a gathering of an individual's family and friends to support that individual in making decisions with the aim of rebuilding harmony within the community. The process is premised on building a partnership between family, community leaders and professionals from state agencies based on open communication with an emphasis on supported decision-making and crisis prevention (Santegoeds). Reshma emphasised that Article 19 of the CRPD, the provision that guarantees all individuals the right to choose where to live, including the right to live independently and the right to be included in the community, intersects with Articles 12 and 25, to create in practice, a right to a circle of support. She explained that she experiences something like this positive circle of support within Indian culture and within her community. Reshma suggests that by embracing a social model of disability, which acknowledges that social determinants can cause disability, and certainly exacerbate its effects and meaning, being supported by an empowering community of people who see her as a legal agent in that community – who accept her – and therefore participate in facilitating her emotional physical and spiritual needs, her capacity is enabled by living in such a community. As examples of those whose supports have facilitated her capacity in this way, Reshma includes: her parents, counsellor, many friends, her partner, and psychiatrist – whose approach to her, she said, allowed her to live as a legal entity in the community.

It is well established that determinants of positive health include adequate housing, education, employment and social inclusion (Canadian Mental Health Association, 2008). Reshma is surrounded by a vast social network of family and friends who accept her and participate in facilitating her emotional, physical, and spiritual needs. The unconditional support she receives from an empowering community enables her inclusion in the community as a legal agent. Reshma's positive experience within a culture (and family dynamic) that support her self-determination highlights the importance of the same values enshrined in the CRPD to provide the support and safeguards necessary to allow individuals to exercise legal capacity and to require states to promote these values in legislation, policy and practice.

Notes

1 Kohl or eyeliner.
2 Levera and Gabapentin are anti-seizure medications.
3 Pranayama is a yogic breathing exercise that consists of different breathing techniques and impacts food choices.
4 My neurologist and Dr. X played an important role in my care and management though I never liked their back and forth inquiry of my schizophrenia.
5 Frisium is a medicine under the class of benzodiazepines used in the treatment for seizures.
6 India has subsequently enacted mental health legislation which guarantees persons with disabilities the right to equality and non-discrimination in the context of medical treatment, Mental Health Care Act, 2017.
7 Open dialogue as a formal practice was developed by Jaakko Seikkula and Marku Suttela. Although it is a practice used in the Western context, the nurse who engages with Reshma in India intuitively follows many of the same principles and practices associated with this method in her interactions with Reshma. What is regarded as alternative in one culture may be normative in another. For further discussion of open dialogue, see opendialogueapproach.co.uk (2017).

Bibliography

Bach, M. and Kerzner, L. (2010). A New Paradigm for Protecting Autonomy and the Right to Legal Capacity. *Law Commission of Ontario.* [online] Available from: http://www.lco-cdo.org/disabilities/bach-kerzner.pdf [Accessed 29 Oct. 2017].

Brosnan, L. and Flynn, E. (2017). Freedom to Negotiate: A Proposal Extricating 'Capacity' From 'Consent'. *International Journal of Law in Context,* 13(1), pp. 58–76.

Canadian Mental Health Association. (2008). What Is the Fit Between Mental Health, Mental Illness and Ontario's Approach to Chronic Disease Prevention and Management? [online] Available at: https://ontario.cmha.ca/documents/what-is-the-fit-between-mental-health-mental-illness-and-ontarios-approach-to-chronic-disease-prevention-and-management/ [Accessed 17 Aug. 2017].

Committee on the Rights of Persons with Disabilities. (2014). *General Comment No. 1 – Article 12: Equal Recognition Before the Law.* UN Doc. No. CRPD/C/GC/1.

Gaventa, J. (2006). Finding the Spaces for Change: A Power Analysis. *IDS Bulletin,* 37, pp. 23–33.

Morrison, A.P., Hutton, P., Shiers, D. and Turkington, D., (2012). Antipsychotics: Is It Time to Introduce Patient Choice? *The British Journal of Psychiatry,* 201(2), pp. 83–84.

opendialogueapproach.co.uk. (2017). Open Dialogue UK. [online] Available from: http://opendialogueapproach.co.uk/ [Accessed 17 Aug. 2017].

Santegoeds, J. Respecting Persons and Dealing with Diversity in Psychosocial Crisis Situations – Experience-based Development of an Alternative to Forced Psychiatric Interventions. [online] Available from: http://www.mindrights.org/Preliminary%20article_experience%20based%20development%20of%20the%20Eindhoven%20Model.pdf [Accessed 29 Oct. 2017].

24 Conclusion

Consent to medical treatment

Eilionóir Flynn

While the pair chapters in this part of the book are drawn from vastly different legal, political and cultural contexts, many common themes can be seen across these different experiences. A constant theme in the storytellers' experiences is the provision of 'consent' under duress – due to fear of what might happen if they refuse (Fiona), or the knowledge that their refusals will not be respected (Cath), and coercion will be imposed. Many of the chapters describe the use of coercion outside the context of involuntary detention – including as a 'voluntary' patient (Fiona and Reshma) and within the realm of the family (Lavanya).

These chapters also highlight the sources of support drawn on by those with lived experience of the mental health system – including the support of peers (Chapter 20), unexpectedly supportive allies within the healthcare system (Chapter 23), family and friends. Many also acknowledge the barriers that family members presented to respect and recognition of the individual's legal capacity – and in some cases a dramatic shift in the role of family members occurred which enabled them to move from imposing substitute decision-making to facilitating supported decision-making (Chapter 21). Two chapters further highlight how the existence of a mental health label or diagnosis adversely impacted on the provision of physical healthcare – contributing to misdiagnosis or delayed treatment for serious physical health conditions (Chapters 22 and 23).

Reflecting on the chapters as a whole, it is worth noting that all the storytellers who shared their experiences in this section of the book are women. While some specifically identify a gender dimension to their experience (Chapter 21), others have not prioritised or focused much on this. However, all of these women have developed in their chapters, together with their respondents, a clear vision of what needs to change to make sure that what they experienced does not happen again. It is interesting to note that much of the literature on alternatives to coercion in psychiatry has also been developed by women, especially by women survivors of psychiatry (e.g. Santegoeds, 2017; Mead, 2014). The chapters in this section of the book make an important contribution to survivor literature as well as to research on how to fully implement the UN Convention on the Rights of Persons with Disabilities.

An overarching theme that emerges from all these chapters is the need to ensure that people are listened to, believed and respected when they describe their experiences of distress. Reshma describes how she asks others 'to learn some autism, some schizophrenia, some depression, or some seizures and then communicate to me and others in those languages' (Chapter 23). If we accept the idea that disability, including psychosocial disability, is a social construction (Oliver 2013; Beresford 2002) then it follows that the onus should be on society to change and adapt to make space for the full inclusion and equal participation of persons with disabilities. We should not require persons with disabilities to fit any arbitrary 'ideal' of the good citizen (often understood as the heterosexual, white, middle class, man) in order to recognise and respect their human rights. The chapters in this part of the book vividly describe how much work is needed to achieve this.

Many of those who are sceptical of the radical shift which the CRPD requires have argued that the idea of an absolute prohibition on coercion and forced treatment is an impossible goal, and that those who support such an approach are merely idealistic dreamers, divorced from the harsh realities of the current system (Freeman et al., 2015). Such sceptics argue that coercion will always be needed, as those who are in crisis cannot be trusted to make decisions for themselves (Dawson, 2015). However, the chapters in this part of the book tell quite a different story – it is precisely those who have experienced the reality of current oppressive regimes who are best placed to show others why and how things need to change. In all these chapters, the storytellers have recounted how, in the midst of crisis and emotional distress, they were still clearly communicating their will and preferences, and could still identify what supports, if any, they wanted to use to express their wishes and ensure their decisions were respected. With the knowledge and experience of these storytellers and respondents, we can see that much more is possible than we might previously have expected. While we should not underestimate the challenge of implementing the ideals of the CRPD, the stories and responses contained in these chapters turn our spark of hope for how this might be achieved into a brightly burning flame.

Bibliography

Beresford, P. (2002). Thinking about 'mental health': Towards a social model. *Journal of Mental Health*, 11(6), pp. 581–584.

Dawson, J. (2015). A realistic approach to assessing mental health laws' compliance with the UNCRPD. *International Journal of Law and Psychiatry*, 40, pp. 70–79.

Freeman, M.C., Kolappa, K., de Almeida, J.M.C., Kleinman, A., Makhashvili, N., Phakathi, S., Saraceno, B. and Thornicroft, G. (2015). Reversing hard won victories in the name of human rights: a critique of the General Comment on Article 12 of the UN Convention on the Rights of Persons with Disabilities. *The Lancet Psychiatry*, 2(9), pp. 844–850.

Mead, S. (2014). Intentional peer support: an alternative approach. [online] Available at: http://www.intentionalpeersupport.org/ [Accessed 31 Jan. 2018).

Oliver, M. (2013). The social model of disability: thirty years on. *Disability & Society*, 28(7), pp. 1024–1026.

Santegoeds, J. (2017). Position d'ENUSP opposée à la contrainte en psychiatrie, position basée sur l'expérience. *L'information psychiatrique*, 93(7), pp. 579–586.

25 Freedom: a work in progress

Rusi Stanev and Sheila Wildeman[1]

> I had a lot of dreams, but then I was put in the institution, and then I had only one dream – to be free – and nothing else. All my thoughts were around this.
>
> (Rusi Stanev in conversation with Sheila Wildeman, 19 July 2016)

An untimely death

Rusi Stanev, survivor of an intransigent system of guardianship and institutionalisation, victor in a ground-breaking disability rights case against Bulgaria at the European Court of Human Rights (ECtHR), my partner in this writing project and (for too short a time) my friend, died on 9 March 2017, before our chapter could be completed. He was 61. Questions have been raised about the appropriateness of the care Rusi received in his final days; at the time of finalising this chapter, a formal inquest into the circumstances of his death had not issued a decision.[2] But whether or not Rusi Stanev's death is proven to be connected to specific failings on the part of one or more state-backed authorities, it cannot in any straightforward sense be attributed to 'natural causes'.

Rather, Rusi Stanev's death, like his life, must be understood against the background of the deeply entrenched injustices – structural, systematic – dealt him over a lifetime. In short, psychosocial disability functioned over Rusi Stanev's lifetime not as a throughway to respectful and responsive supports but rather as a means of legitimising progressively more intense subjection to a coordinate set of harms – deprivation of liberty, forced medication, legal incapacitation, and with these, consignment to deep poverty and social stigmatisation – making his early death as wholly predictable (Thornicroft, 2011; Westman et al., 2012) as it was unjust.

What was less predictable was Rusi Stanev's rise to fame on the world stage as a human rights hero (Lewis, 2012). Even those who did not know Rusi personally will likely, if they have even passing familiarity with the world of disability rights advocacy, have encountered *Stanev v Bulgaria* (2012). This was the first judgment of the ECtHR to recognise placement in a social care home by a guardian as a deprivation of liberty, and to recognise conditions in a social care home as cruel and inhuman treatment. The judgment affirmed, moreover, the right of those consigned to guardianship and institutional social care to directly access the courts in order to assert their rights.

Few, however, are familiar with the frustrating sequelae of *Stanev v Bulgaria* as these played out in Rusi Stanev's life. The stark reality is that when he died, Rusi was still under guardianship and still in an institution. His situation had in certain key respects improved. But he continued to be denied the right to make the most basic decisions about his life without the co-signature of his guardian(s), and the right to live in the community on equal terms with others. Those who celebrated *Stanev v Bulgaria* and who seek to bring about fundamental social change through human rights must ask: What accounts for this disappointing end to Rusi Stanev's story?

This chapter makes the barest of starts in answering that question. Its primary aim is to celebrate, and mourn, Rusi Kosev Stanev's remarkable life: his rising up despite and against the profound forms of subordination to which he was subjected. It is composed of fragments of Rusi's writing that he produced through the VOICES project, including in the last weeks before his death, and Sheila's responses to those fragments. Its subject – our subject – is Rusi Stanev's unfinished project: freedom.

Stanev v Bulgaria revisited: Rusi Stanev's story

"We are here to die"

My name is Rusi Stanev and I am from the town of Ruse. In 2000, as my sister wanted to take my house, she put me under guardianship. She wanted to remove me from the house.

Residence at Pastra

On 12 December 2002, I was sent to Pastra institution. There I met people who were very ill. I asked someone, 'Why are we here?' and he stated: 'We are here to die.'

In 2004, two young women came and they recorded a video of me. I spoke in front of the camera and said that defenders of human rights should be there.

Then another woman came and helped me to write a request for the prosecutor to lift the guardianship. She promised to give it to him, as I was imprisoned in Pastra institution. The most terrible place – 106 people were imprisoned there.

This is how my road to Strasbourg started.

***

Advocates and academics around the world have told and retold Rusi Stanev's story: the foundation for *Stanev v Bulgaria* (2012), a leading judgment in international human rights law on the rights of persons under guardianship consigned to institutional living, or social care.[3] Rusi's account begins with his placement under guardianship – or 'partial guardianship,' which in Bulgaria is a status requiring a guardian's co-consent to give effect to legal transactions. The guardian first appointed on Rusi's file in 2002 was a municipal official in his home town of Ruse whom he never met, then or since. It was she who decided, six days into her appointment, to send Rusi to the Pastra Institution for Men with Psychiatric Disorders: a remote institution in the Rila mountains some 400 kilometres from his home.

The judgment in *Stanev v Bulgaria* makes note of the illegality, even under prevailing Bulgarian law, of the contract for services through which Rusi's placement was secured and his disability pension diverted to institutional authorities. That contract was signed by the municipal guardian and the institutional director, with no consent on Rusi's part despite the statutory requirement of co-consent. This was enough, according to the Strasbourg Court, to establish an illegal deprivation of liberty and so a breach of Article 5 of the ECHR (*Stanev v Bulgaria*, paras. 143 and 150). In time, the role of Rusi's guardian was transferred to the director of the institution, whose consent was then required in order for Rusi to enter into contracts (including for residential care or tenancy elsewhere) or to secure legal representation.

The Strasbourg Court's judgment further describes (and finds to substantiate a breach of the ECHR's Article 3) a litany of grim facts about the conditions Rusi endured in Pastra. This is something that Rusi chose not to elaborate on much. Then again, it is difficult to imagine a more effective way of relaying the horror he must have felt upon arriving at this strange and threatening place than his account of the response he was given (by a nameless 'someone') when he sought the reason for banishment: 'We are here to die.'

In his own, concise account, Rusi compares the many painful details of his story to the plot essentials: familial betrayal and institutional abuse, carried out with the complicity of judicial and administrative authorities and those responsible for delivery of social care. It is not often that those so dealt with have the opportunity to tell their side of the story. In November 2016, at a VOICES workshop, we were asked to respond to certain creative writing prompts: 'I wish,' 'I get so frustrated when', and things along those lines. Rusi became increasingly agitated and left the room. He said: 'How can someone be an "I" when they are not even a person?' That Rusi identified the hero in his story as himself is perhaps the most important result of his involvement in this project. ('I spoke in front of the camera and said that human rights defenders should be there').

Then again, Rusi was very careful, over many years, to remain the active centre of his life. This was reflected in the extraordinary efforts he made each day to remove himself from the daily drugging, torpor and despair that marked life at Pastra. The director kept control of his identity papers, so impeding his ability to travel far or make significant transactions (the one time Rusi failed to return from a permitted absence to Ruse, he was apprehended by police and returned to Pastra by institutional staff – a fact that contributed to the Strasburg court's determination that his placement there constituted a deprivation of liberty). However, he was nonetheless frequently permitted to walk the many kilometres into the village where he 'provided domestic help to villagers or carried out tasks at the village restaurant'. Indeed, sometimes Rusi walked a further 10 kilometres to the famous Rila Monastery, where he would pass the time 'talking with the foreigners' (as he put it) – accepting their stray coins and cigarettes. The physical stamina and strength of will this took is difficult to imagine, but it explains in part how Rusi Stanev managed to survive Pastra, and, moreover, to keep his memories of what happened there relatively intact while so many others (including those subjected to the daily doses of anti-psychotic medications his early departures enabled him to avoid) could not.

The picture reproduced below is Rusi's rendition of the figures he would draw over and over on the road as he travelled from the institution in the woods to the village, the restaurant, the monastery – and back again to hell. He drew it during a session when Rusi, Aneta Genova (Rusi's Mental Disability Action Centre (MDAC) lawyer since 2005, and our joint interpreter and supporter during this

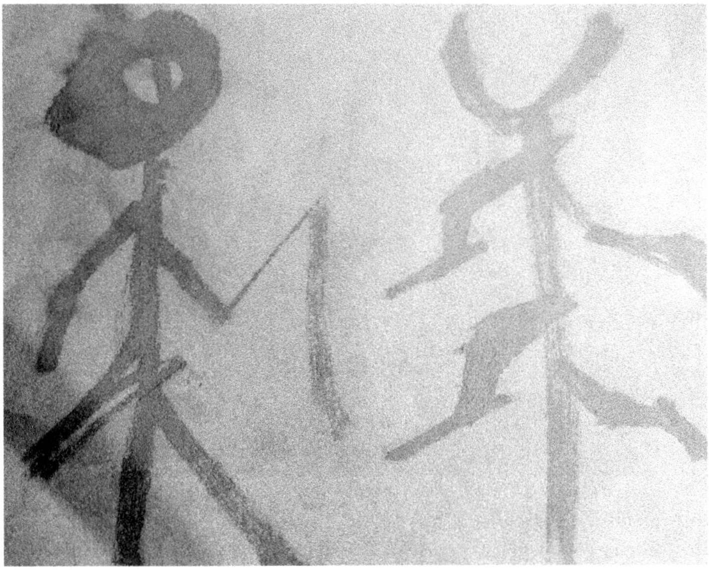

Rusi Stanev - Figures on the Road from Pastra.

project) and I enjoyed some down time in Galway. Sometimes I see in this image a symbol of force and violence and domination; other times I see Rusi's indomitable spirit: his will to bring into being a kind of communion with others, a kind of reciprocity, a dance.

After Strasbourg

I won the case in Strasbourg. The court decreed this home was in reality a prison.

I was released from Pastra after the court decision, but nevertheless my guardianship hasn't been lifted and formally persists.

So, as I am still under guardianship, I need a lawyer who will be able to lift my guardianship. But I have obstacles in court. It appears that I need a guardian. The court requires a guardian's signature to validate the contract with the lawyer and give her power to act as my attorney. It's only me who can decide who my lawyer will be and who to believe. It isn't fair somebody else gets to decide if I need a defence and who can defend me. I am forbidden only because I am under guardianship.

In Bulgaria, they still build defended homes for people with disabilities and under guardianship in depopulated areas. I am in a such place now.

I am not an object. They can't move me where they want. I am a human being and I need my freedom and people to communicate with.

***

Aneta Genova and Rusi Stanev in Strasbourg.
Photo credit: Validity Foundation (formerly the Mental Disability Advocacy Centre).

Rusi Stanev in front of the European Court of Human Rights, 2009.
Photo credit: Validity Foundation (formerly the Mental Disability Advocacy Centre).

For all its importance in extending human rights oversight to the context of social care, the Strasbourg Court's judgment in *Stanev v Bulgaria* failed to take on Rusi's central arguments (made via Aneta Genova and other MDAC counsel). Those arguments sought to conjoin the principle of least restriction on liberty with positive duties on the state (grounded in Article 8 of the ECHR, and in Articles 12, 14 and 19 of the CRPD) to fashion autonomy-respecting supports for choice and independent living in the community (Flynn, 2016; Nelson, 2012). In effect, the judgment imposed requirements of procedural legitimacy (e.g., access to the courts, and requirements that involuntary social care placements be backed by proper medical documentation) without fundamentally disturbing the premises of disability-based deprivation of liberty and legal capacity in Bulgarian guardianship and social care law.

Rusi's account focuses on the failure of his win in Strasbourg to register his life in the manner he had believed that it would. The Strasbourg Court ordered the Bulgarian authorities to re-examine his social care placement 'without delay in the light of the findings of th[e] judgment' (*Stanev v Bulgaria*, 2012, para. 257). Yet in March 2011, prior to the judgment's release, Rusi had already been transferred to a 'centre for temporary placement' in Ruse: a facility 'located within the grounds of a psychiatric hospital' (Mental Disability Advocacy Centre, 2015). In October 2011, he was transferred to a so-called 'family-type' facility again situated inside a psychiatric hospital. Here Rusi's freedom was even more restricted than at Pastra: '[H]e even had to ask for the staff's permission and assistance to go into the yard of the hospital, since the doors were locked.' Moreover, '[t]here were no specific programs for reintegration, nor any rehabilitation services provided for him on the basis of his individual needs'. While it appears that Rusi signed a contract agreeing to this placement, it is not clear under what circumstances he signed it, nor whether any alternatives were presented (Mental Disability Advocacy Centre, 2015).

Subsequent developments in Rusi's journey through the world of Bulgarian social care reinforce the thinness of the distinction between formal and *de facto* deprivation of the capacity and opportunity to choose (Kukova, 2011). Following expulsion from the 'family-type' hospital-based facility (for breaking institutional rules) and a short-lived attempt to live on his own in the community, Rusi moved through a series of social care placements, punctuated by periods of living on the street. Most recently he was placed in another 'family-type' facility, now just outside the spa town of Dolna Banya. Here, Rusi reported, the conditions were more comfortable than in other institutions of that type in which he had lived. But he still required permission to come and go, and the facility was a few kilometres from the town – isolated and hidden away in a manner that he experienced as punishing and stigmatising. Again, his situation was such that he could not interact on equal terms with others, or assume control over his living environment in a fashion others take for granted.

A further layer of frustration following the judgment in *Stanev v Bulgaria* involved Rusi's continued subjection to partial guardianship and the intransigence of Bulgaria's guardianship regime more generally. In 2017, Bulgaria has still not altered its guardianship law to bring it into compliance either with the ruling in *Stanev v Bulgaria*[4] or with the CRPD (Mental Disability Advocacy Centre, 2016, 2017; Committee of Ministers, 2017). This is despite a law reform process and resultant bill that received the backing of several prominent disability rights organisations and appeared initially to have had significant support from government.

The lack of meaningful change to state laws following *Stanev v Bulgaria* was mirrored in Rusi's life in the Kafkaesque nature of the legal processes through which he attempted to dissolve his partial guardianship. Perhaps the most perplexing element of this part of Rusi's story is the fact that, on repeated occasions and even for years at a time, his formal subjection to guardianship persisted despite the absence of a guardian with authority to act in his case (a turn of events loosely explained by Rusi's periodic shifts in municipal residency and attendant shifts in administrative responsibility for his guardianship). This meant that Rusi was, for extended periods since 2000, without any formal mechanism for obtaining the co-authorisation required to enter into legal transactions, including contracts for social care or residential placements or – critically – legal representation.

Viewed against this absurdist background, it is perhaps no surprise that Rusi's attempts to challenge his partial guardianship were stymied at every turn. In February of 2012, officials at the Ministry of Justice wrote to the prosecutor's office in Ruse requesting commencement of a process to lift Rusi's guardianship. The prosecutor declined, arguing that neither the Strasbourg Court's judgment nor the Ministry's request constituted a valid basis for commencing such proceedings in Bulgarian law. Following that, with Aneta's assistance, Rusi began the complex and circuitous process of attempting to have the guardianship dissolved. Near the beginning of that process, they learned that Rusi had been without a guardian (although he remained under guardianship) since November of 2012, and so was formally without the power to commence legal proceedings (MDAC, 2015).

Rusi persisted. A new guardian was appointed in May of 2014 – a member of a supported living association in Pazardzhik Municipality, where Rusi was then residing. Still, a number of preliminary procedural difficulties prevented the hearing of his application for two full years. At least three times, the Regional Courts to which Rusi applied, declined jurisdiction in favour of alternative Regional Courts. There was further wrangling around the appropriate defendant, required payment of court fees, and failure to inform Rusi (or his counsel) of the noted changes in venue. When finally, the Pazardzhik court assumed jurisdiction, it decided of its own accord that it required an independent psychiatric opinion for which Rusi must pay.

These procedural obstacles were accompanied by more substantive ones, primarily the entrenched attitudes of court-appointed experts for whom Rusi's historical psychiatric diagnosis, legal incapacitation and institutionalisation appear to have supported an effectively irrebuttable presumption that he could not manage his own affairs. In May 2016, the Pazardzhik court issued a decision upholding Rusi's guardianship. It stated that what Rusi and his counsel had fundamentally failed to understand was that guardianship is a protective, not a repressive institution. Imposition of a guardian in Rusi's case was, quite simply, for his own good. The periods during which Rusi had been without a guardian and/or tried to live outside an institution had been marked by instability. He thus required a guardian, reasoned the court, not least to ensure his compliance with institutional rules.

Rusi, with Aneta's help, appealed this decision. Yet the problem was that Rusi was once again (since leaving Pazardzhik) without anyone in the role of his guardian and so was precluded from initiating this legal action. Eventually a new guardian was appointed. Then came another blow: in February 2017, the appellate court denied the appeal. As MDAC's recent submissions to the CRPD Committee relate, Rusi 'was in the process of preparing another appeal to the Supreme Court when he passed away. Now, after his death, the case can no longer be continued' (Mental Disability Advocacy Centre, 2017)

Thus, it appears that *Stanev v Bulgaria,* wherein Rusi Stanev established deprivation of liberty and exposure to cruel and inhuman treatment along with illegal obstruction of his right to access the courts, was in the end of little use in protecting him from Bulgaria's coordinate regimes of guardianship and institutionalisation. This should inspire serious and careful reflection on the strategies adopted by human rights advocates to effect individual and systemic change.

The path of hope (freedom-in-reciprocity)

Two core concepts emerge out of Rusi's late writings. He was no longer writing about his journey out of Pastra or his human rights victory. Rather, he was peeling away those parts of his life to re-engage with his life before guardianship and before – was there ever a time before institutional time? He was engaging, I believe, with fragments of his past in which he saw some hope: some lessons to help reorient and advance the fight against intransigent guardianship and institutionalisation.

I have selected two fragments of Rusi's late writing that speak to two critical elements of that fight – or rather, critical elements of the reciprocity that is arguably a precondition of freedom. These elements are recognition and resistance. More specifically, the excerpts selected foreground the act of recognising the other through a gift, and of asserting one's difference and one's resistance in the dually creative and destructive form of a prank.

The gift

The work that Rusi, Aneta and I did together in preparation for the presentation we gave in Galway in November of 2016 was deep work. It began with gifts. Rusi had been clear about what an appropriate gift would be, and I was grateful for the guidance, as, despite my 49 years, I remain uninitiated in many things, one being the purchase and consumption of cigarettes. I acquired an entire crate of Marlboro Golds at the duty free on my way through Boston – an acquisition that appeared wholly satisfactory when produced in Galway. Rusi in turn gave me a delicate, shiny, red and gold embossed pen stamped with the brand name 'piano' which I thought exquisite. He also gave me a couple of postcards showing the resort town of Dolna Banya, the centre of which was a few kilometres from the social care home in which he was then residing. We would meet there in the summer we said, Aneta, Rusi and me, and explore and write together.

When we parted after that emotional second meeting in Galway (it was emotional at least for me – indeed I surprised Rusi and myself by weeping most unbecomingly through our joint presentation), I said I would send Rusi a gift at Christmas time. What he wanted was very clear: more cigarettes. Too late I learned that it was illegal to send tobacco (or alcohol, or firearms) through the post from Canada. In an effort to make up for my blunder – and no longer in time for Christmas, indeed just barely in time for New Year's Day – I sent an inexpensive watch (in Galway, Rusi had kept pulling at my arm to see my watch), some chocolates, a grand and ornate leather notebook, and somewhere in all that, a few illicit cigars.

What follows is his response to me, which I did not receive until after his death, when the notebook was found among his things. Aneta's friends Milena and Barry translated what he had written inside. I call this initial excerpt 'The gift', and I read it as a meditation on the roots of freedom, or freedom-in-reciprocity.

> *Rusi Kosev Stanev's notebook*
> *for keeping in touch with Sheila who is from the country of Canada.*
> *I will be writing about my past.*

Hello Sheila!!!

Sheila, right now it is 3pm Bulgarian time and I am sitting down to write you about some of my memories from my past, while in Canada right now it is the middle of the night and you are sleeping.

Sheila, first of all I would like to wish you a Happy New Year 2017 and hope that you have much success in your work.

I know that you know that I am in an institution and that you empathise with me.

Thank you so much for the New Year's present that you sent me. Nobody has ever given me a grand present like that before except for when I was a young student and I received a package from the USSR – a red 'pioneer' bandana and a T-shirt and other things that I don't remember as it was a long time ago. Sheila, later on I personally tied the very same red bandana around my sister's neck and shoulders when she graduated from the 2nd grade.

A memory of mine from my school years is about how the 'Radetski' ship was rebuilt in the ship-building factory. Our grade was granted the honour of climbing on board the ship and to sail all the way to the city of Kozlodui and back. I still remember how somebody broke a bottle of champagne on the bow of the 'Radetski' ship and then how the ship slid along some rails into the Danube River.

***

Early in our conversations, Rusi was very careful to establish how things stood between us as we entered into this work together. He did this by telling me some stories about work he had done for friends over the years: a man from Ruse with considerable wealth and status whom he had helped make wine; the owner of the café near Pastra where he had gone to do odd jobs in exchange for food and coffee or alcohol, a little money. Rusi and I both understood that what he had of value to share with me were his stories. As he had done many times in his life, he had identified what others valued among the things he had to offer. Indeed, he had a knack for effecting exchanges in conditions resistant to his participation and devaluing of his labour. In this way, he was able, throughout his life, to establish relationships of reciprocity, of mutual recognition and respect, across extraordinary imbalances of power.

The idea of the gift – of striking reciprocal relationships across difference through careful consideration of what is valued by the other, by imagining oneself enjoying a gift they would enjoy – is something Rusi has left me with to think hard about as I and others confront the question of how to disrupt the seemingly intractable logic of guardianship and institutionalised social care. Reciprocal gifting seems to me a device through which we might begin to revisit relationships of charity or control, or for that matter, devalued wage-labour, in a manner that shifts the basic assumptions of contract (use of the other as an instrument of one's own good) to an alternative imperative involving recognition of the other as a site of innate moral value. This was a shift in orientation about which Rusi was slowly tutoring me in the time I knew him: a lesson to be learned not at the level of theory but at the level of doing, of giving – of micropolitics.

Gifting, as I am positioning it here, stands outside the economy of instrumental exchange and is grounded instead in a felt imperative to fashion creative ways of recognising the other as unique and of value. Yet there are tensions in this idealised way of conceiving relationships of care, support, or co-creation. That is, the economy of gifting seeks to transcend and yet is inevitably shaped by dominant (neoliberal) institutional structures and norms. (Buch, 2014). Indeed, Rusi's emphasis on gift-giving was informed at least in part by his having been *forced* into a gift economy – his having been consigned to legal incapacity and abject poverty, and so to live on the remains of the wealth generated by others' valued work and instrumental exchanges.

Ultimately, Rusi's story of gifting speaks not only to the ways we structure our intimate or private relationships but also to what it means to be gifted by the state. Young Rusi's excitement on receiving the uniform of the Young Pioneers is shadowed by the knowledge that this gift was at the same time an instrument of control, a demand for conformity. Might a gift from the state (and if so, in what circumstances might it) function not as a tool of control but as a gesture of recognition, an acknowledgement of one's moral importance? Might a gift from the state (taking the form, say, of a guaranteed basic income) function to enact reciprocity, both vertically (with authorities) and horizontally (among citizens)? The tender gesture with which Rusi regifted his scarf (fitting it around the neck of the sister who would later send him away) bespeaks the vicissitudes of power and vulnerability that mark our lives: the ways (as Martha Fineman (2010) has observed) we move in and out of positions of power and vulnerability – a fundamental fact of the human condition that public policy should reflect. At the same time, this tender gesture speaks to the ways we are eased into, and invite others into, allegiance with the institutions that produce our subordination.

All these insights are set into motion, kaleidoscope-like, by Rusi's reflections on the theme of gifts. They arguably bear relevance to the pressing imperative of operationalising the CRPD's Article 12 through the fashioning of regimes of 'supported decision-making', and moreover that of integrating Articles 14, 19 and 5 to underwrite a state duty to provide community-based options for residency and care, so as to eradicate or render obsolete rights-denying disability-based deprivation of liberty.

A prank (school days)

I was sent to a school where I studied for two years through the end of 8th grade. [...] [I]t was located in a village 30 km from the city – the village was called Tabachka within the district of Ruse, and the school's name was Maksim Gorki. Sheila, I have both good and bad memories from this school. The school was famous for the mischief (of its students) and the following punishments imposed by the director, Tsvetan. The wire fence around the school was 1 km in diameter. This fence was used as a disciplinary measure in cases of misdemeanour as the entire grade would be made to do laps around the fence if we broke the rules, and then we would go and eat breakfast.

I have one memory from my chemistry class about how the product 'sodium' would explode when mixed with water. Once, with one of my friends and classmates, Lyubcho, who was stronger than me and who protected me from getting beaten by the other students, we stole a piece of this miraculous sodium from a flask where it was stored in the lab. Then we waited and when there was no one else in the bathroom we placed it into the toilet, watched it swirl around in the water, and then it exploded quite violently. This happened after the end of the day's classes and after the director, Tsvetan, had already gone home. Every now and then, the entire grade had to do laps around the fence in the morning as punishment and sometimes we had to do as many as five laps! At the same time, one of us would herd the cows. [...]

***

This story of a childhood prank serves as a necessary complement to the earlier passages on gifting. Rusi's time spent at the Maksim Gorki school – a reform school, located 30 km from the nearest village – of course foreshadows his time in Pastra. It was in this sense the start of a long road of institutionalisation.

Yet Rusi disrupts this apparent foreshadowing and lays a path toward freedom: now through the mechanism of a prank. His story of making the toilets explode with the help of some sodium and his friend Lyubcho comes off as an ode to creative resistance – to making use of what is at hand to make trouble. I will leave the reader to consider the claim that resistance, like recognition, is necessary to reciprocity. In short, I take this further story from Rusi's youth as a reminder that our relationships (including relationships of care and support) must make space for difference, for resistance: for the mystery of other minds and others' rich interior lives.

A work in progress

I must conclude this chapter here, though there is so much more I would like to say and to know about Rusi Stanev's life story, his many stories.

What I will remember most about Rusi Stanev was his fierce will to arrive at a point in his life when he could freely offer others his friendship and his love and be recognised in return for who he was: to be loved back. He walked miles in search of community, and still, at the time of his death, had not arrived. His time bumming cigarettes and coins off foreigners at the monastery in Rila offered those tourist-pilgrims (though they likely did not see it) a profane illumination of the world we have created – one that could consign Rusi Stanev to the special circle of hell that lies at the intersection of legal incapacity and institutionalisation. Rusi made his way up the highway to that sacred place at great cost. His teaching was profound. But it was not understood.

This brings me back to the question: if a man like Rusi Stanev remained under guardianship and was institutionalised to the end of his life, despite a victory at the European Court of Human Rights, what good are human rights?

The answer, I think, must run deeper than accommodating difference so as to enable equal access to the ('free') market. This chapter, in the spirit of the VOICES project and of the CRPD, suggests that we share responsibility to create the conditions of freedom-in-reciprocity. This sets us (as Rusi has set us) on a path no less daunting than rethinking the ethical foundations of the social and legal order. The groundwork for such efforts may be discerned in theories that urge a shift from a neoliberal ethos of independence (obscuring the ways that all choices are grounded in supportive conditions and options) to a radical egalitarian ethos of interdependence. Rusi Stanev's stories of forging reciprocity across

Rusi Stanev's grave - Dolna Banya.

difference bring these theories to earth – asking us what we are willing to give in order to recognise the deep humanity of the other.

Notes

1 Sadly, Rusi Stanev died during the course of the VOICES project. Sheila finished this chapter in memory of him. Rusi's text is in *italics* and is drawn from his presentations to the public workshops for the project and his writing for the chapter before he died. Sheila's text reflects on Rusi's writing and draws on her conversations with him since April 2016, when they were paired up through the VOICES project. The support and friendship extended by Aneta Genova to Rusi (over many years) and to Sheila (over the course of this project) made these conversations possible and serves as the foundation for the chapter as a whole. Thanks to the other participants in the VOICES workshops, and to the many people who met with Aneta and Sheila in Bulgaria in July 2017, including in particular Krassimir Kanev and Slavka Kukova of the Bulgarian Helsinki Committee. Translation of Rusi's writing in Part 1 was done by Tsvetelina Kanazirska, and in Part 2, by Barry Feno and Milena Mileva-Feno. Special thanks also to Liz Brosnan, Clíona de Bhailís, Maria Laura Serra, Amita Dhanda and Eilionóir Flynn.

2 Communications with Aneta Genova, July and November 2017. See also MDAC et al. (2017, para. 29).
3 'Social care home' signifies a publicly funded residential facility for persons lacking other means of accessing long-term care and support (Bulgarian Helsinki Committee, 2002, p. 5).
4 See also *Stankov v. Bulgaria* [2015] ECHR 276.

Bibliography

Benjamin, W. (1969). Franz Kafka: On the Tenth Anniversary of His Death. *Illuminations* New York, United States: Schocken Books, p. 116.

Buch, E. (2014). Troubling Gifts of Care: Vulnerable Persons and Threatening Exchanges in Chicago's Home Care Industry. *Medical Anthropology Quarterly*, 28(4), pp. 599–615.

Bulgarian Helsinki Committee. (2003). Archipelago of the Forgotten – Social Care Homes for People with Mental Disabilities in Bulgaria. Sofia: Bulgarian Helsinki Committee.

Council of Europe, Committee of Ministers. (2017). Notes and Decisions on Individual and General Implementation of *Stanev v Bulgaria*. [online] Available at: http://hudoc.exec.coe.int/eng?i=004-3767 [Accessed 24 Jan. 2018].

Fineman, M.A. (2010). The Vulnerable Subject and the Responsive State. *Emory Law Journal*, 60, pp. 251–275.

Flynn, E. (2016). Disability, Deprivation of Liberty and Human Rights Norms: Reconciling European and International Approaches. *International Journal of Mental Health and Capacity Law*, 22, pp. 75–101.

Kukova, S. (2011). Fundamental Rights Situation of Persons with Mental Health Problems and Persons with Intellectual Disabilities: Desk Report Bulgaria. (Commissioned by the European Union Agency for Fundamental Rights. Bulgarian Helsinki Committee) [online] Available at: http://www.humanconsultancy.com/downloads/320-bulgaria-desk-report-fundamental-rights-situation-of-persons-with-mental-health-problems-and-persons-with-intellectual-disabilities [Accessed 24 Jan. 2018].

Lewis, O. (2012). Stanev v. Bulgaria: On the Pathway to Freedom. *Human Rights Brief* 19(2), pp. 2–7.

Mental Disability Action Centre. (2015). Information on The Implementation of the European Court of Human Rights Judgment of 17/01.2012 in Stanev v Bulgaria, no. 36760/06 by Bulgaria Regarding the Individual Measures Ordered by the Court. DH-DD(2015)454.

Mental Disability Action Centre. (2016). Communication from NGO (Mental Disability Advocacy Centre (MDAC)) (14/04/2016) on General Measures in the Cases of Stanev and Stefan Stankov against Bulgaria (Applications No. 36760/06, 25820/08). DH-DD(2016)515.

Mental Disability Action Centre, Global Initiative on Psychiatry, and Bulgarian Centre for Not-for-Profit Law. (2017). NGO information to the United Nations Committee on the Rights of Persons with Disabilities For consideration at the 18th session when it will adopt a list of issues on the initial report of The Republic of Bulgaria under the Convention on the Rights of Persons with Disabilities. [online] Available at: http://tbinternet.ohchr.org/Treaties/CRPD/Shared%20Documents/BGR/INT_CRPD_ICO_BGR_28482_E.docx [Accessed 24 Jan. 2018].

Nelson, L. (2012). Stanev v. Bulgaria: The Grand Chamber's Cautionary Approach to Expanding Protection of the Rights of Persons with Psycho-social Disabilities. [online] Available at: https://www.escr-net.org/node/375437 [Accessed 24 Jan. 2018].

Thornicroft, G. (2011). Physical Health Disparities and Mental Illness: The Scandal of Premature Mortality. *British Journal of Psychiatry*, 199(6), pp. 441–442.

Westman, J., Gissler, M., and Wahlbeck, K. (2012). Successful Deinstitutionalization of Mental Health Care: Increased Life Expectancy Among People with Mental Disorders in Finland. *European Journal of Public Health*, 22(4), pp. 604–606.

26 Overall conclusion

Eilionóir Flynn

An impression that strikes me at the end of this edited collection is of a loud and vibrant chorus of voices – person after person speaking up and saying, 'this happened to me too'. The injustice of denying the recognition of legal capacity becomes ever clearer, the more stories we hear, the more we get to know the people behind those stories. Time and time again, as people tell their stories throughout this project, those who hear and bear witness to those stories reassure them 'of course this should not have happened to you'. In our decision to publish so many stories in one place, we hope that you as readers will share this 'of course not' reaction. The more people who think 'well of course this shouldn't have happened to Nick, or Claire, or Maria, or Cath', then the more we can gain support for the idea that this should never happen to anyone, ever.

Our goal throughout this project has been to give people space to describe their own experiences and own their own stories. In part, this is why it has been so important for everyone to publish under their own names, as co-authors of each of the chapters. Through this process, we want to restore the power that has been taken away from people when others have told their stories for them. All of us will naturally describe ourselves very differently from how other people might think of us. The disparity between the descriptions of people in medical case notes, in court judgments, in the case files of social services, and in the descriptions, which appear in the pair chapters throughout this volume is incredibly stark and important.

This edited volume is just the beginning of what we hope will become a much greater part of the research and scholarship on the right to legal capacity. In this book, we focused on four aspects of the right to legal capacity protected by Article 12 of the UN Convention on the Rights of Persons with Disabilities (criminal responsibility, contract, consent to sex and relationships, and consent to medical treatment) but there are many more – and even those discussed here have many more dimensions than we had time to explore in this project. There are also many more and diverse perspectives and experiences than those which have been included in this collection which deserve to be documented, considered and responded to.

What messages can we take away from these stories and responses? First, the acknowledgement that realising the universal right to legal capacity is not an impossible pipe dream but an urgent necessity. Second, that those who have experienced rights violations are best placed to imagine better and design a more equal, just and compassionate world. And third, that we need our allies in this struggle from all walks of life – peers, friends, family members, health and social care professionals, researchers, activists, artists, journalists, lawyers, judges, legislators and policy-makers. Many of the storytellers and respondents in this volume fulfil one or more of these personal and professional roles, but we also need to bring others beyond the project into this conversation and along this journey of change. This work is necessary to spread the message of Article 12 and the Convention as a whole, about respecting the autonomy, integrity and dignity of all human persons, with and without disabilities.

Index

Note: Page numbers followed by 'n' refer to notes

For Product Safety Concerns and Information please contact our EU representative GPSR@taylorandfrancis.com
Taylor & Francis Verlag GmbH, Kaufingerstraße 24, 80331 München, Germany

www.ingramcontent.com/pod-product-compliance
Ingram Content Group UK Ltd.
Pitfield, Milton Keynes, MK11 3LW, UK
UKHW011004180926
475701UK00004B/552

* 9 7 8 0 3 6 7 4 7 3 7 0 9 *

SCIENCES

Geoscience, Field Director – Yves Lagabrielle

The Surface of the Lithosphere and the Biosphere, Subject Head – François Baudin

Interactions between the Geosphere and the Biosphere

Coordinated by

Karim Benzerara

Christophe Thomazo

iSTE

WILEY

First published 2025 in Great Britain and the United States by ISTE Ltd and John Wiley & Sons, Inc.

ISTE Ltd
27-37 St George's Road
London SW19 4EU
UK

www.iste.co.uk

John Wiley & Sons, Inc.
111 River Street
Hoboken, NJ 07030
USA

www.wiley.com

Library of Congress Control Number: 2024949159

British Library Cataloguing-in-Publication Data
A CIP record for this book is available from the British Library
ISBN 978-1-78945-203-7

ERC code:
PE10 Earth System Science
PE10_5 Geology, tectonics, volcanology
PE10_6 Palaeoclimatology, palaeoecology
PE10_9 Biogeochemistry, biogeochemical cycles, environmental chemistry
PE10_12 Sedimentology, soil science, palaeontology, earth evolution
LS8 Environmental Biology, Ecology and Evolution
LS8_1 Ecosystem and community ecology, macroecology
LS8_2 Biodiversity

Contents

Introduction

Christophe THOMAZO[1] **and Karim BENZERARA**[2]
[1] *Laboratoire Biogéosciences, University of Burgundy, Dijon, France*
[2] *IMPMC, UMR 7590, CNRS, Sorbonne Université, Paris, France*

The division of the Earth into compartments, each with their own dynamics but still interacting with one another, is a key principle in biogeochemistry, which aims to understand how the Earth functions and how it has evolved over geological time, as well as to predict how it will evolve in the future. These compartments are called "spheres" and can be delimited differently and at different scales depending on the questions asked (Figure I.1). We regularly see the terms atmosphere, hydrosphere, lithosphere or biosphere as constituents of the Earth system[1]. At smaller scales, we can also consider the troposphere and the stratosphere when we are more specifically interested in the functioning of the atmosphere, or the lithosphere and the asthenosphere for the study of plate tectonics. At other scales, we can define the pedosphere when studying soils. Reference to the anthroposphere designates the compartment influenced by anthropogenic activities. In this book, we understand the geosphere as the set of solid, gaseous and liquid compartments composing the Earth. Thus, the geosphere brings together the oceanic and continental lithospheres, the even more internal parts, namely the mantle and the core as well as the most superficial parts constituting the hydrosphere and the atmosphere. The term biosphere, a concept introduced for the first time in the natural sciences in 1875 by

1 Term designating all geospheres and biospheres formalized during a congress organized by NASA in the 1980s as a scientific disciplinary field in its own right aimed at understanding and mechanistically quantifying the interactions between spheres and their impacts.

Interactions between the Geosphere and the Biosphere,
coordinated by Karim BENZERARA and Christophe THOMAZO.

Eduard Süß, professor of paleontology at the University of Vienna, designates all living beings.

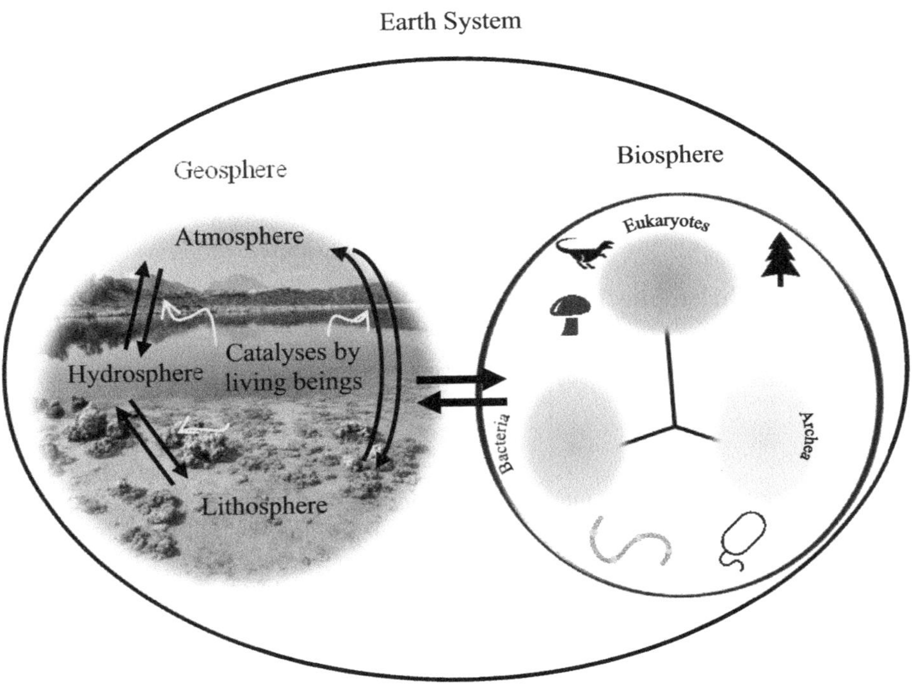

Figure I.1. *A representation of a biogeochemical cycle (e.g. of carbon but it could be for many other chemical elements) involving different reservoirs and in particular the geosphere and the biosphere, all making up the Earth system. The geosphere is itself made up of different reservoirs such as the atmosphere, the hydrosphere or the lithosphere. The biosphere is a reservoir in itself, but living organisms also catalyze transfers between reservoirs. For a color version of this figure, see: www.iste.co.uk/benzerara/geosphere.zip*

The existence of interactions between these two compartments has been suspected since the 16th century, when debates on the origin of oil, used for more than 3,000 years, began. It was Andreas Libavius, a German chemist and doctor, who, in 1597, was one of the first to suggest an organic origin of petroleum corresponding to ancient tree resin. In 1757, Mikhail Lomonosov clarified this theory and proposed that liquid petroleum and bitumen came from the transformation of plant organism remains at depth, under the effect of increasing temperature and pressure. Joint observations using geological (oil found in the center of sedimentary basins) and geochemical approaches (the isotopic composition of oil is the same as that of the surface biosphere, and all oils contain very specific molecules called porphyrins, which derive from chlorophyll) confirmed four centuries later the hypotheses of Libavius and Lomnosov on its biological origin. However, it was Vladimir Verdnasky, an illustrious Russian scientist in his time (1863–1945), who theorized these interactions between the geosphere and biosphere by emphasizing the role of life (and human beings) as a geological force (Verdnasky 1986). These ideas formed the foundations of the discipline, biogeochemistry, which has since continued to develop.

When the two editors of this book were studying at French universities, courses combined life sciences and Earth sciences, with the particular objective of training secondary school teachers. This coupling seemed to come directly from the traditional alliance of the natural sciences, which had generated much knowledge in both biology and geology in the era of Jean-Baptiste Lamarck, Georges-Louis Leclerc de Buffon, Georges Cuvier or Charles Darwin. However, specialization in scientific research further separated biology and geology and a few rare lessons in ecology and paleontology made it possible to note the obvious links between these two scientific fields.

The influence of the geosphere on living organisms generally seems the most obvious. In ecology, the concept of fundamental ecological niche is associated with the surrounding abiotic conditions, themselves partly imposed by the geosphere. The biotope is a geographical area defined by relatively homogeneous physical and chemical properties. Associated biotope and biocenosis form an ecosystem. There is a roughly latitudinal distribution of large vegetation covers on the Earth's surface, from tundra and taiga at high latitudes to tropical forests, including temperate forests and savannahs. This distribution is controlled by the climate, itself controlling the properties of the soil, which imposes local living conditions. Few places seem uninhabitable on Earth. Indeed, since the 1960s, we have known about ecosystems developing in hydrothermal environments at the bottom of the ocean in the absence of light. The temperature limit of life appears to be approximately 120°C, which can be reached in environments under a relatively high pressure such as at the bottom of the oceans. We also find traces of life in the coldest deserts in Antarctica or the hottest and driest deserts such as the Atacama. Only a few hypersaline, hyperacidic and (hyper)hot lakes in Ethiopia do not seem to support life.

On the other hand, the influence of the biosphere on the geosphere may seem less obvious at first glance. Indeed, the difference in scale (in size and over time) between organisms such as bacteria and a mountain makes it difficult to imagine how the former could influence the latter. And yet, in the 1960s, James Lovelock and Lynn Margulis jointly developed a revolutionary idea, outlined in the Gaia hypothesis (Lovelock and Margulis 1974). This hypothesis suggests that Earth's living organisms collectively regulate the planet's conditions, including the chemical composition of the atmosphere, creating a stable and hospitable environment for life. They thus envisaged the Earth as a self-regulating system, in which life itself influences the geosphere, and in particular, climate.

Although such a global interaction between the biosphere and geosphere remains debated, we will see in the first chapter that the influence of the biosphere on the geosphere can be studied on a more local scale, notably through mineral dissolution processes. This process ensures the cycling of chemical elements, including those essential to life, releasing them into the soil, whose fertility is thus impacted. Despite all of our knowledge, predicting the dissolution rate of minerals is still difficult and although the influence of life on these rates has been determined in certain cases, quantifying it on a global scale is a current issue. A large quantity of these chemical elements released by minerals will, after having transited or not through the biosphere, reach the hydrosphere (rivers, lakes, streams and oceans). There, they can be re-trapped in de novo minerals and participate in redistributing matter, sometimes by creating resources of interest to humans, such as iron or phosphorus deposits, for example.

The second chapter addresses another action of the biosphere on the geosphere: the formation of minerals by living beings or biomineralization. We will see that from a very early point in the Earth's history, organisms have impacted the formation of minerals. On the one hand, this has had repercussions on the functioning of living organisms and the history of life. But in return, biomineralization also seems to have played a role in the evolution of the chemical functioning of the Earth's surface by notably lowering the concentration of certain chemical species in the oceans.

Stromatolites are emblematic examples of rocks formed by life. These "living stones" have been observed in geological records as old as 3.5 billion years. The third chapter will explain the mechanisms involved in their formation, and the information obtained from the study of ancient stromatolites will provide knowledge about the history of life. Stromatolites are mainly formed by diverse microbial ecosystems that transform their immediate chemical environment. The identification of these microbes and their geochemical functions through their metabolisms requires the use of molecular biology methods, whose methodological progress over the past decades has revolutionized our knowledge of the diversity of living organisms. The fourth chapter will explain this approach as well as how we can obtain valuable information about the history of life from studying the diversity of living beings today.

The most obvious manifestation of the role of life in the transformation of the Earth throughout its history is the protracted oxygenation of the atmosphere, which remarkably expanded during the Great Oxidation Event, nearly 2.3 billion years ago and has allowed over the last 600 million years for the development of sulfate-rich oceans as well as the development of eukaryotes, including plants and animals. This chemical revolution followed a biological innovation: the appearance of oxygenic photosynthesis. The fifth chapter will detail how this event became engrained in the geological record, how it was dated and will specify the links between this biological innovation and the chemical evolution of the geosphere. Beyond the provision of a new molecule abundant in the atmosphere (the dioxygen molecule), this event profoundly disrupted the chemical functioning of the Earth's surface and in particular the cycle of other chemical elements such as carbon and nitrogen, of biological and climatic importance.

Thus, the sixth chapter will explain the functioning of the current carbon and nitrogen cycles and how we can try to reconstruct their functioning in the past. We will learn that living beings once again play a key role in these global cycles. The study of biogeochemical cycles requires the manipulation of a variety of tools including measuring abundance ratios between different isotopes of chemical elements. This leads to the definition of reservoirs represented schematically by "boxes", which interact with each other via flows of molecules whose speciation can change during transfer. The variation over time of a physico-chemical (or biological) parameter, for example, temperature, can intensify a flow. In turn, this intensification can induce modifications, which in return will increase even more or, on the contrary, reduce this same flow. We thus see the establishment of positive or negative feedback loops, making the prediction of the evolution of the Earth system after a disturbance or change unintuitive. Therefore, to make these predictions, it is necessary to conduct a modeling approach to evaluate the relative importance of different processes in the evolution of a geochemical compartment.

The purpose of the seventh chapter will be to explain the different types of modeling currently used to understand the disruptions in geosphere/biosphere interactions occurring within the Earth system, for example, the climatic consequences of the colonization of continents by plants more than 450 million years ago and the geological causes of the mass extinctions, which affected living organisms. Different interaction loops stabilized the Earth system and maintained life over long periods of geological time, but this couple also evolved to become what it is today. Current anthropogenic disturbances could in turn destabilize this system. The extent of these changes and the future feedback, beyond the direct threats to human civilizations, however, remain uncertain.

Finally, the eighth chapter will dive further into the changes in biodiversity over geological time, including episodes of extinction and diversification of living organisms which testify to multiple interactions between the biosphere and the geosphere.

Ultimately, this book will be an opportunity to become more aware of the diversity of concepts, knowledge and know-how that must be mobilized to study the interactions between the geosphere and the biosphere. This is the very essence of a so-called interdisciplinary field, which here involves the use of notions from physics, chemistry, biology and of course, geology. In addition, we will note that life does not exist separate from planet Earth. The two are strongly intertwined, and the evolution of the first has influenced the history of the second and vice versa. The different chapters are independent and have been written by different authors, thus offering an overview of the multidisciplinary nature of this field of study.

The interactions between the geosphere and the biosphere certainly took place very early on in the history of the Earth. Understanding them is a necessity to better assess what a habitable and inhabited planet is. This is key for the search for extraterrestrial life.

References

Lovelock, J.E. and Margulis, L. (1974). Atmospheric homeostasis by and for the biosphere: The Gaia hypothesis. *Tellus*, 26(1–2), 2–10.

Vernadsky, V.I. (1986). *The Biosphere*. Copernicus, New York.

1

Weathering of Rocks by Living Organisms

Bastien WILD[1] and Damien DAVAL[2]
[1] *Princeton University, USA*
[2] *ISTerre, CNRS, Université Grenoble Alpes, Gières, France*

1.1. Rock weathering in the critical zone

The critical zone constitutes the outermost layer of the continental crust. It extends from the top of the canopy to the lower limit of surface aquifers, down to several hundred meters deep. This particular zone, where "rocks meet life", is at the basis of most surface ecosystems. It is the locus of countless couplings between chemical, biological, physical and geological processes, the understanding of which is crucial for pressing environmental and societal challenges. Critical zone preservation is necessary to achieve sustainable development goals and preserve landscapes and biodiversity (Brantley et al. 2007; Gaillardet 2023).

Rock weathering is a key process in the functioning of the critical zone. It encompasses all processes that lead to the progressive breakdown of rocky substrates. It results from physical and chemical processes, driven by planetary scale forcings (tectonics, climate cycles generated by solar radiation). Fluxes[1] of matter induced by weathering processes, also referred to as *denudation fluxes*, are either

---

1. Flux of matter corresponds to a quantity of material moving from one compartment to another per unit area and per unit time.

Interactions between the Geosphere and the Biosphere,
coordinated by Karim BENZERARA and Christophe THOMAZO.

(i) in solid forms (sediments, suspended matter), which correspond to erosion processes; or (ii) in dissolved forms (ions, colloidal particles), which correspond to chemical weathering. Weathering in the broad sense designates the combination of both physical processes of fragmentation (erosion) and chemical processes of dissolution/precipitation of minerals (chemical weathering). The combination of these processes is at the origin of the progressive transformation of the bedrock into "soil".

Rocks freshly exposed by tectonic processes are out of thermodynamic equilibrium with respect to the conditions prevailing on the Earth's surface and therefore weather chemically. In addition to this spontaneous process, living organisms can contribute directly or indirectly to rock weathering (van Breemen et al. 2000a; Lapanje et al. 2012; Uroz et al. 2015). The "chemical" or "biological" weathering of rocks thus constitutes a fundamental step in numerous geochemical processes, such as the geological carbon cycle (Beaulieu et al. 2012) or the supply of inorganic nutrients to the critical zone (Olsson et al. 1996; White et al. 2012).

In this chapter, we will focus especially on mineral dissolution, defined by the chemical reaction between an aqueous fluid and a solid ("primary phase"), responsible for the transfer of elements – in the form of ions for instance – into solution, before their possible incorporation into a "secondary" mineral phase. First, we will discuss the parameterization of mineral dissolution kinetics[2] and the associated molecular mechanisms to evidence factors controlling the intensity of chemical weathering fluxes. The importance of life in weathering processes will then be highlighted, as well as the underlying bio-weathering mechanisms. Finally, we will evaluate the impact of mineral weathering on microbial communities in the environment.

1.2. Parameterization of mineral dissolution rates

Before quantifying the contribution of living organisms to rock weathering fluxes, we will see how the reactivity of minerals in contact with an aqueous solution is translated into equations. This subject has been a matter of scientific debate for more than half a century. Mineral dissolution rate laws currently used to model weathering fluxes on large temporal and spatial scales often have an empirical basis (Lüttge 2006), even if a mechanistic framework underlies some of the terms of these rate laws (Schott et al. 2009). Such a comprehensive law is detailed below. The basic principle is that a mineral dissolves at its surface, i.e. the interface between the mineral and the solution surrounding it. Figure 1.1 provides a

2. The kinetics of a reaction corresponds to the rate law.

simplified representation of the mineral surface, showing the dissolution processes at different scales.

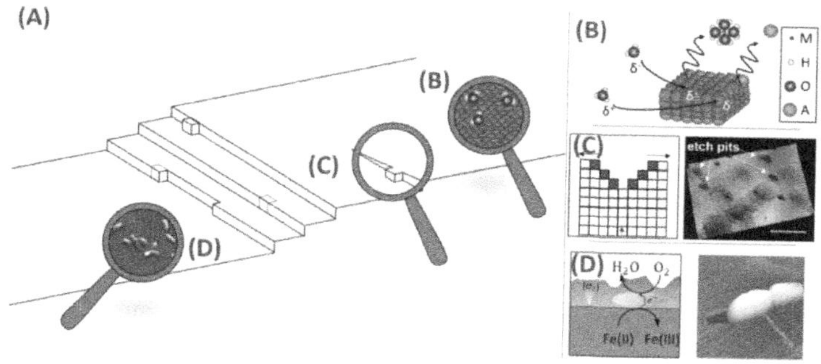

Figure 1.1. *(A) Simplified representation of dissolution processes at the fluid–mineral-(living organism) interface from the atomic scale to the micrometer scale. (B) At the atomic scale, dissolution can be described as resulting from the sum of the nucleophilic attacks of the negatively polarized part of a reactant (e.g. oxygen atoms of a water molecule) on the metal centers of the solid and the electrophilic attacks of the positively polarized part of a reagent (e.g. hydrogen atoms of hydronium ions) on the anionic centers of the solid (e.g. oxygen atoms). (C) At the atomic scale, defects in the crystal structure, such as dislocations*[3]*, represent preferential dissolution sites. On a cross-sectional representation of the fluid–mineral interface, the dissolution propagates preferentially along the dislocation line (red arrow), generating reactive steps (colored sites), allowing propagation of the dissolution over the surface (black arrows) and the development of etch pits (corrosion) (see the corresponding image, representing the topography of a dissolved calcite surface at far-from-equilibrium conditions: scale bar = 2 µm). (D) At the micron scale, microorganisms can promote the dissolution of minerals (Image A). The action of microorganisms can then also be a driving force for pitting, as illustrated in the image on the right, taken by atomic force microscopy, illustrating the biodissolution of a calcite surface by cells of the bacteria Shewanella sp. (taken from Luttge et al. 2005). For a color version of this figure, see www.iste.co.uk/benzerara/geosphere.zip*

1.2.1. *General equation*

Aagaard and Helgeson (1982) laid the foundations of mineral dissolution rate laws, which is still the most commonly used today:

$$R_{min} = k_{min}.S(\xi).e^{-E_a/RT}\prod_i[a_i]^{j_i}.\left(1-e^{\Delta_r G/RT}\right) \quad [1.1]$$

3. A dislocation is a linear defect in the stacking of atoms in a crystal, inducing a discontinuity in the organization of the crystal structure.

The parameters of this equation are detailed in the following: R_{min} is the dissolution rate of a mineral, expressed as a quantity of material per unit of time. This rate is equal to the product of five different terms. k_{min} is the dissolution rate constant specific to each mineral. S is the "effective" mineral surface, in contact with the solution and this effective surface is a function of ξ, which is the progress of the dissolution reaction (i.e. a parameter describing the evolution of the dissolution reaction from its initial state to the final state). The larger the surface area of the mineral in contact with the fluid, the faster the dissolution. The parameter E_a refers to the activation energy[4] of the process, and R and T are, respectively, the ideal gas constant and the temperature. The term $\prod_i [a_i]^{j_i}$ accounts for the catalytic or inhibitory effect of certain species (denoted i) in solution, such as H^+ or Al^{3+}. Finally, the last multiplicative term of the equation, $(1 - e^{\Delta_r G/RT})$, accounts for the thermodynamic driving force of the dissolution process. The parameter $\Delta_r G$ corresponds to the Gibbs free energy of the reaction (also referred to as "undersaturation"). It depends on the concentrations of the dissolved chemical species constituting the mineral phase. When these are very low, the solution is very undersaturated or far from equilibrium and $\Delta_r G$ is negative. When this parameter is negative, the dissolution reaction is therefore thermodynamically favorable and the dissolution rate R_{min} is nonzero. The reaction stops when the equilibrium between the solution and the solid is reached ($\Delta_r G = 0$ and therefore $(1 - e^{\Delta_r G/RT})$ becomes zero). The relationship (E1) is often broken down into three distinct equations corresponding to mechanisms prevailing under acidic, neutral and basic pH conditions. The different terms of this equation are further explained and discussed in the following sections.

1.2.2. *Dissolution rate constant (k_{min})*

The dissolution rate constant reflects the ease with which hydrolysis of a mineral occurs. All things being equal, the dissolution rate constants of major rock-forming minerals on Earth span over 10 orders of magnitude depending on the mineral considered. Silicates are the least reactive minerals (Figure 1.2(A)). It is the nature of the chemical bonds in minerals, and in particular the energy of these bonds, that controls the intrinsic value k_{min}. For isostructural minerals, i.e. with the same atomic structure but a different chemical composition, a mineral will have a dissolution rate constant that is higher as the binding energy involving the cation is low

4. The activation energy of a process corresponds to the energy that needs to be provided to a chemical system for this process to take place. This is also equivalent to the variation in free energy between the transition state of the system (maximum free energy) and the initial state of the system.

(and therefore, the ionic radius will be high) (see Figure 1.2(B)). This explains the greater reactivity of calcite ($CaCO_3$) compared to magnesite ($MgCO_3$), or that of wollastonite ($CaSiO_3$) compared to enstatite ($MgSiO_3$). Indeed, the ionic radius of Ca is ~ 33% greater than that of Mg, and the Ca–O bond energy is therefore lower than that of Mg–O. For silicates, Si–O is the strongest bond in the crystal lattice and therefore determines the value of the dissolution rate constant. This explains that the more polymerized a structure is (i.e. the more second Si neighbors a Si atom will have), the more difficult it is to extract the Si from the structure. Therefore, the corresponding k_{min} and the dissolution rate under the given conditions are lower (Figure 1.2(C)). This explains, for example, why olivine (orthosilicate or nesosilicate, devoid of Si–O–Si bonds) has a higher rate constant than albite (tectosilicate, corresponding to a completely polymerized structure).

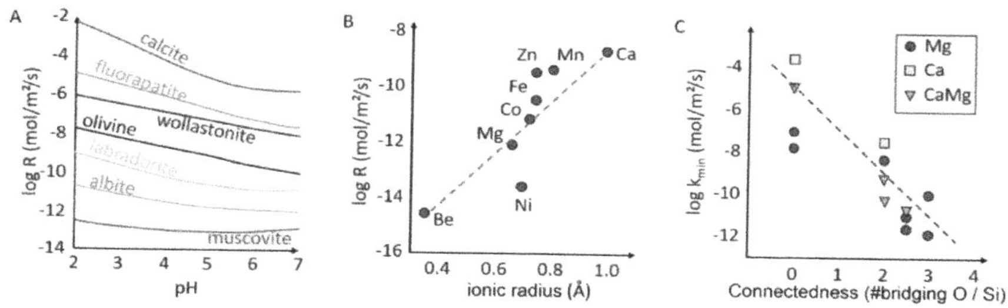

Figure 1.2. *(A) Logarithm of the dissolution rate (R) of different common minerals as a function of pH (adapted from Rimstidt (2015)). (B) Logarithm of the dissolution rate of orthosilicates (M_2SiO_4) at pH 2 depending on the ionic radius of the M^{2+} cation (adapted from Casey and Westrich (1992)). (C) Dissolution rate constants of silicates (in log) as a function of the degree of polymerization of their structure (adapted from Criscenti et al. (2006)). For a color version of this figure, see www.iste.co.uk/benzerara/geosphere.zip*

1.2.3. "Effective" surface area between the fluid and the mineral (S)

The "effective" surface area refers to the proportion of the surface area of a mineral that is involved in the dissolution reaction. This surface is estimated either by assuming an average grain size and an ad hoc geometry (often spherical), or by gas adsorption as a monatomic layer of the gas molecule on the mineral grains analyzed (Brunauer et al. 1938). The evolution of the surface during the progress of the reaction is generally described according to the following relation:

$$S(\xi) = S_0.(m/m_0)^p \quad [1.2]$$

where S_0 and m_0 are, respectively, the surface area and the initial mass of the mineral considered, m is the mass of the mineral at a given time during the dissolution process, and p is a dimensionless coefficient varying between 2/3 for spherical particles to 1 for a distribution of nonspherical particles. We frequently encounter the approximation of a linear dependence of the surface with respect to the progress of reaction (m/m_0), so that the relation (E1) is then reduced to a first-order differential equation, in a perfectly identical manner to the kinetic laws describing the consumption of a single reagent in the case of an elementary reaction (i.e. occurring in a single step, without a reaction intermediate).

Concretely, defining the effective surface is still an unresolved challenge for weathering modeling. This parameter is a very strong adjustment variable for reactive transport modeling[5], likely to be reduced by several orders of magnitude in order to align the simulations with the actual reactivity measured in the field (e.g. Aradóttir et al. 2012).

1.2.4. *Specific effect of species dissolved in solution* ($\prod_i [a_i]^{j_i}$)

The hydronium (H_3O^+ or H^+) and hydroxide (OH^-) ions are undoubtedly those whose effect on the kinetics of mineral dissolution has been the most studied. Generally, in the acidic pH range, the dissolution rate increases as the pH decreases (Figure 1.2(A)). This may be linked to the weakening of M–O–M' bonds (M and M' being cations), resulting from the attack of H^+ ions on the oxygen atoms at the surface of the mineral (Xiao and Lasaga 1994) (Figure 1.1(B)). The effect of OH^- ions does not follow a simple general rule: while the dissolution rate of quartz and aluminosilicates significantly increases at basic pH (Figure 1.2(A) and 1.3(A)), no increase in rate is observed for carbonates and non-aluminous silicates (Figure 1.2(A)).

Furthermore, many organic molecules present in natural waters have one or more chelating functional groups. This is particularly the case for carboxylic acids. The complexation of these ligands on the surface of minerals can thus accelerate their dissolution rate (Figure 1.3(B)). According to the pK_a of the acid considered, the dissolution of minerals in an acidic medium can therefore result from the simultaneous electrophilic attack of protons on the oxygen atoms and the nucleophilic attack of ligands on the cationic centers on the surface of the mineral

5. Reactive transport models are numerical models coupling the transport of dissolved chemical species in fluids with chemical reactions taking place within these fluids.

(Figure 1.1(B)). Thus, at a constant temperature and far from an equilibrium, the overall dissolution rate of the reaction will be written as the sum of the contribution of protons and ligands to the hydrolysis of the mineral (e.g. Wogelius and Walther 1991):

$$R_{min}/S = k_{H^+}.[H^+]^{n_{H^+}} + k_{L^-}.[L^-]^{n_{L^-}} \quad [1.3]$$

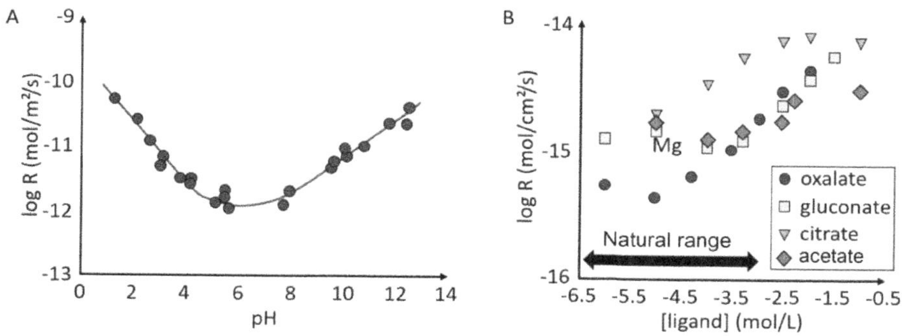

Figure 1.3. *(A) Dissolution rate of albite as a function of pH (adapted from Blum and Lasaga (1988)). (B) Dissolution rate of diopside at 25 °C for different concentrations of organic ligands (adapted from Golubev and Pokrovsky (2006)). For a color version of this figure, see www.iste.co.uk/benzerara/geosphere.zip*

1.2.5. *Effect of deviation from thermodynamic equilibrium ($\Delta_r G$)*

The most commonly used relationship to link the rate of dissolution of minerals (R_{min}) with $\Delta_r G$ (the Gibbs free energy of the dissolution reaction) imply that R_{min} is proportional to $(1 - e^{\Delta_r G/RT})$. This comes from the transition state theory, developed by Eyring (1935). The transition state or "activated complex" is a transitional state between the reactants (here the mineral phase which dissolves) and the products (the species in solution), where the energy of the reactant–product system is at its maximum. The reader is invited to refer to the article by Lasaga (1981) for a more detailed explanation. Its application to the kinetics of mineral dissolution is based on the (questionable) hypothesis that the hydrolysis reaction is comparable to an elementary reaction (i.e. that on the microscopic scale, it takes place in one single step, without going through the formation of a reaction intermediate). If this relationship makes it possible, operationally, to take into account the effect of the saturation state of the fluid on the dissolution rate of a mineral, it nevertheless reduces the complexity of the fluid–mineral interface to a simple collision between two molecules. This simplification is the cause of significant gaps between R_{min}-$\Delta_r G$ relationships predicted theoretically and those resulting from experimental work (section 1.2.7.1).

1.2.6. *Effect of temperature (T)*

Like any chemical reaction, the hydrolysis of a mineral is a thermally activated process, i.e. dependent on temperature. For a given fluid composition, the dependence of the dissolution rate on temperature is relatively well described by the Arrhenius relation:

$$\frac{d\ln R_{min}}{dT} = \frac{E_a}{RT^2} \qquad [1.4]$$

The activation energy (E_a) associated with dissolution varies with the nature of the mineral and the pH range considered, and typically ranges from ~ 15 to ~ 100 kJ/mol (Palandri and Kharaka 2004). In the framework of the transition state theory, the activation energy of a chemical reaction is the standard enthalpy change from reactants to activated complex (Lasaga 1981), i.e. the difference between the bond energies involved in the formation of the activated complex and the energies of the reactant bonds to be broken. Therefore, experimentally determined activation energies may provide information on the nature of the rate-limiting steps of the dissolution reactions (the breakdown of the activated complex is this limiting state). In practice, things are more complicated. Activated complexes are formed by adsorption and/or exchange reactions occurring on specific surface sites. Thus, the experimentally measured activation energy is the result of the contribution of two terms: (i) the contribution of the enthalpy of formation of the specific surface site where the adsorption and/or exchange reactions occur; and (ii) the activation energy of the activated complex (Casey and Sposito 1992). In the end, we generally speak of the apparent activation energy (which includes several terms) when we quantify the dependence of the dissolution rate of minerals on temperature.

1.2.7. *Uninformed factors in the general equation*

The relation (E1) corresponds to the "conventional" equation of mineral reactivity. However, this relationship does not take into account a certain number of parameters playing a potentially important role in reactivity, which are briefly reported below.

1.2.7.1. *Crystal defects*

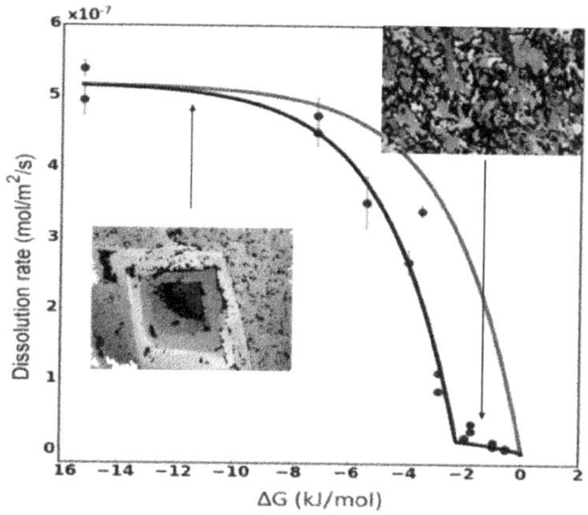

Figure 1.4. *Calcite dissolution rate as a function of Gibbs free energy. For ΔG > -6kJ/mol, the nucleation of etch pits is no longer spontaneous, leading to a drop in the dissolution rate (adapted from Bouissonnié et al. (2018)). The experimental relationship (black curve) then deviates from that resulting from the transition state theory (red curve). For a color version of this figure, see www.iste.co.uk/benzerara/geosphere.zip*

Crystal defects (dislocations, vacancies) (see Figure 1.1) on the surface of a mineral can greatly contribute to the total dissolution flux. Defects such as dislocations are high energy points likely to be preferentially attacked during dissolution, generating characteristic geometric figures on the surface of the material called "etch pits" (Figures 1.1(C) and 1.4). When an etch pit forms at a dislocation site, it becomes a continuous source of step propagation on the surface of the mineral, thus participating in the progressive retreat of the surface (Lasaga and Lüttge 2001). Lasaga and Blum (1986) showed that the opening of an etch pit was spontaneous for any value of $\Delta_r G$ lower than the $\Delta_r G$ of pit nucleation (ΔG^{crit}), i.e. in reaction conditions sufficiently far from the thermodynamic equilibrium, or in other words when the fluid in contact with the mineral is very undersaturated with respect to the mineral as would be the case for a very dilute solution, for example. This results in two distinct kinetic regimes, for which the dissolution rate at $\Delta_r G < \Delta G^{crit}$ can be up to three orders of magnitude higher than for $\Delta_r G > \Delta G^{crit}$. The direct observation of a drop in rate associated with surfaces free of etch pits has been well documented for both silicates (Pollet-Villard et al. 2016) and carbonates (Bouissonnié et al. 2018). On the other hand, such an effect cannot be reproduced using the transition state theory (Figure 1.4), which is usually implemented in reactive transport codes.

1.2.7.2. *Formation of surface-altered layers rich in silica*

The dissolution of silicates in an acidic to neutral environment forms silica-rich surface layers with a nano- to micrometric thickness (Hellmann et al. 2012). Such layers can hinder dissolution: recently, Wild et al. (2016) proposed that the less aggressive the weathering conditions were (e.g. for pH close to neutrality), the more likely such layers were to be passivating, i.e. preventing the fluid from accessing to the unweathered (pristine) surface of the silicates. The main consequence of silicate passivation by silica layers lies in an (apparent) shift in the thermodynamic driving force of the reaction: macroscopically, the dissolution reaction can slow down or even stop while the fluid is still largely undersaturated with respect to the primary silicate. Alternative formalisms to equation [1.1] exist to account for this effect (Daval et al. 2013), but are currently not incorporated in reactive transport codes.

1.2.7.3. *Mechanical effects*

Finally, it is important to specify that the description of the kinetics summarized above was developed in the context of free mineral surfaces, devoid of any extrinsic volume (and therefore mechanical) constraint. However, it frequently happens (see section 1.4.5 for examples relevant to biodissolution) that dissolution takes place under mechanical stress (i.e. with local excess pressures exerted on the mineral surface). A mechanical stress induces an increase in the chemical potential of the interface between the solid under stress and the fluid (Hellmann et al. 2002). This will result in a diffusive flux of dissolved species from the stressed interface to the free interface. Therefore, the increase in the solubility of the surface under stress coupled with the diffusive flux can be responsible for an increase in the dissolution rate of the surface concerned.

1.3. Modeling rock chemical weathering in the critical zone

1.3.1. *A classic, essentially abiotic approach*

Mineral reactivity in the field can be modeled using so-called "reactive transport" codes. These numerical models make it possible to simulate physicochemical conditions prevailing in the environment, to deduce parameters such as the chemical saturation of environmental solutions with respect to the mineral phases (and thus $\Delta_r G$), and therefore to calculate dissolution rates based on kinetic rate laws derived from laboratory experiments (see section 1.2). A multitude of reactive transport codes following this general scheme are used to quantitatively model-weathering fluxes on large spatial and temporal scales: PROFILE (Warfvinge and Sverdrup 1992); KIRMAT (Gerard et al. 1996); WITCH (Godderis et al. 2006); or CrunchFlow (Steefel et al. 2015) for instance, each with its specificities. These models are, however, all based on modeling the evolution of the water–rock interaction from input parameters such as the chemical composition of the system solutions or the reactive surface area of each mineral phase present in the system at the initial state. The fundamental relationship governing the exchanges of matter between solid and aqueous phases and common to all of these codes is the classic dispersion–advection–reaction equation, where the reactivity of a rock is described as a result of the reactivity of the constituting minerals (adapted from Steefel and Maher (2009)):

$$\frac{\partial(\emptyset C_i)}{\partial t} = \nabla \cdot (\emptyset D_i \nabla C_i) - \nabla \cdot (\emptyset \mathbf{u} C_i) - \sum_{n=1}^{N_r} \nu_{in} R_n - \sum_{m=1}^{N_m} \nu_{im} R_{min,m} \quad [1.5]$$

The first two terms on the right-hand side of equation [1.5] characterize the transport of solutes (diffusion and advection, respectively) and the following two, their production or consumption (reactivity or source terms, resulting from rate laws such as that described in section 1.2). The parameter ϕ is the porosity, C_i is the concentration of the species i, t is the time, D_i is the diffusion coefficient of the species i, $\mathbf{u}$ is Darcy's velocity, R_n and R_{min} are the rates of the N_r homogeneous reactions and N_m is the heterogeneous reactions (i.e. fluid/solid), affected by stoichiometric coefficients ν_{in} and ν_{im}.

These models therefore make it possible, in theory, to predict the mineral reactivity of natural systems (Beaulieu et al. 2012). However, it has been shown that data from mineral dissolution experiments in a laboratory implemented in these models commonly overestimate field measurements by up to five orders of magnitude (White and Brantley 2003). As a result, this imposes adjustments to other parameters in the model such as specific surface areas, for example, to reproduce field measurements (Godderis et al. 2006). However, these adjustments are not particularly justified by the observations. The precise cause of this laboratory-field difference gap is still unknown.

The contribution of living organisms is implemented in these models in an empirical manner (i.e. these models are based on field data to account for the increase in weathering rates by living organisms) (e.g. Beerling et al. 2020), without seeking to take into account the details of the underlying mechanisms. However, there are, on the other hand, "mechanistic" models, which account for the impact of life on the different parameters mentioned above, such as pH or saturation but in an extremely simplified way (e.g. Calabrese et al. 2017). Overall, at present, the modeling of chemical weathering within the critical zone overlooks the direct contribution of living organisms to the dissolution of minerals.

1.3.2. *Weathering by living organisms: why be interested in microorganisms?*

While elements such as carbon, nitrogen and phosphorus constitute the main "building blocks" of organic matter, inorganic macronutrients such as potassium, magnesium and calcium are essential for the development of ecosystems. In the critical zone, these chemical elements are mainly stored in two distinct compartments: biomass (Johnson 2014) and cation exchange phases such as the clay–humic complex (Lucas et al. 2011), which defines the association of organic matter to clays in soils, and has a strong ion retention capacity. These chemical elements are largely recycled by microbial litter degradation processes (van der Heijden et al. 2013). For systems at steady state, whose incoming and outgoing element fluxes no longer vary with time, the loss of inorganic nutrients leached by gravity out of the system is compensated by a gain via atmospheric inputs (aerosols) and the chemical weathering of so-called "primary" mineral phases (Ranger and Turpault 1999).

The "classic" abiotic understanding of inorganic nutrients cycling in the critical zone implicitly considers that biosphere depends on the release rate of nutrients during the abiotic dissolution of minerals, which is, in turn, dictated by ambient physicochemical properties prevailing in the environment considered. A growing number of studies tends to emphasize the active role of living organisms, and in particular microorganisms, in controlling inorganic nutrient fluxes within the critical zone. Notably, it has been demonstrated that fungi (Gadd 2007) or bacteria (Uroz et al. 2009a) contributed to the alteration of minerals (see section 1.5), ensuring the supply of ecosystems with inorganic nutrients, in addition to atmospheric inputs (Ranger and Turpault 1999). More generally, bioweathering capabilities were evidenced for the main components of biomass such as bacteria (Uroz et al. 2015) or large groups of eukaryotes including fungi (Courty et al. 2010), plants (van Hees et al. 2006) and animals (Dorn 2014).

Microorganisms are key in the mobilization of inorganic nutrients and their transfer to ecosystems. First of all, they occupy a strategic position at one end of the food web that structures these ecosystems. The mineral–bacteria–fungi–plant continuum formed around the ectomycorrhizal complex of the rhizosphere (see section 1.3.3) is one of the best-known examples. In addition to this strategic position at the interface between biosphere and lithosphere, microbial communities are particularly versatile and can respond to plant stimuli, on the one hand (see "mineral continuum–bacteria–fungi–plants"), and adapt to the mineral environment, on the other hand (see the concept of "mineralosphere" in section 1.5.1).

The influence of microorganisms on dissolution kinetics was evidenced in the laboratory with approaches classically used to track mineral dissolution in vitro, consisting of the following elemental release from fresh mineral surfaces in solution. Biotic dissolution processes were thus reproduced directly, by adding to the fluid various microbial species known for their weathering properties such as bacteria *Burkholderia* sp. (Barker et al. 1997; Welch et al. 1999), *Paenibacillus polymyxa* (Vasan et al. 2001), *Bacillus subtilis* (Song et al. 2007), fungi *Paxillus involutus* (Bonneville et al. 2009) or *Talaromyces flavus* (Li et al. 2016). The bioweathering action was also quantified indirectly by adding to the fluid some chemical reagents produced by living organisms, with known mineral weathering properties. Molecules tested encompassed organic acids and chelating molecules (see section 1.4.4). These in vitro experiments have made it possible to put forward an overall catalytic role for the action of microorganisms on mineral dissolution reactions (see below). However, knowledge of the effective distribution of these microbial actors (Uroz et al. 2009a) in the field, or of their action in "real" conditions (Jones et al. 2003), is still in its infancy.

The active participation of microorganisms in mineral weathering processes in the field has only recently been evidenced, in particular by the pioneering work of Bennett et al. (1996). Their conclusions were established on the basis of strong correlations observed between the nature of primary minerals incubated in the laboratory or in the aquifer of an experimental site and their degree of microbial colonization. The authors suggested that the colonization of minerals by microorganisms did not occur randomly, but via selection by the properties (e.g. chemical composition) of the mineral substrate (Bennett et al. 1996) or its mineral inclusions (Rogers et al. 1998). In other words, certain mineral phases and/or certain contents of mineral inclusions in mineral phases favor microbial colonization over others. Further observations made it possible to interpret the biotic acceleration of weathering induced by this colonization as a result of chelating biomolecules secreted near cells attached to the surface, with the goal of extracting nutrients such as phosphorus or iron from the mineral matrix (Bennett et al. 2001; Rogers and Bennett 2004). These results, mainly based on microscopic observations, have laid the qualitative foundations for our understanding of the biotic contribution to mineral weathering in situ and the impact of microorganisms on chemical weathering fluxes. In quantitative terms, a very strong variability is observed among the values reported for the increase in the dissolution rates related to the presence of microorganisms. Such a variability is in fact expected given the high diversity of contexts studied, approaches used, as well as the relatively small number of studies carried out to date. No clear acceleration was evidenced in the case of the olivine weathering by microbial communities originating from the A horizon of a forest soil (Wild et al. 2018, 2021). On the other hand, an acceleration factor ("biotic"/"abiotic") of 1.5 was measured for the bacterial weathering of biotite in the presence of *B. subtilis* (Hopf et al. 2009). An acceleration factor of 3 was evidenced for the weathering of glass by *P. aeruginosa* (Perez et al. 2016), 5 for the weathering of hornblende by bacteria of the genus *Streptomyces* (Liermann et al. 2000) and up to 2 orders of magnitude for the action of *Paxillus involutus* hyphae on biotite (Bonneville et al. 2011) or for silicate weathering (feldspar, biotite) in bacterial cultures from various pedological contexts (Barker et al. 1998). A virtually infinite acceleration factor was observed in the case of magnetite reduction to iron hydroxide by *Shewanella putrefaciens* (Etique et al. 2016).

1.3.3. *How do microbial alteration processes occur in different types of ecosystems?*

Although the isolated action of certain microbial strains allows for the mobilization of nutrients from primary phases, recent studies highlight the importance of a combined and synergistic action of bacterial and fungal weathering contributions for a certain number of ecosystems. This is particularly true in the context of the bacteria–fungi–plant symbiotic system (van Scholl et al. 2008) or subsurface syntrophic systems (Lau et al. 2016).

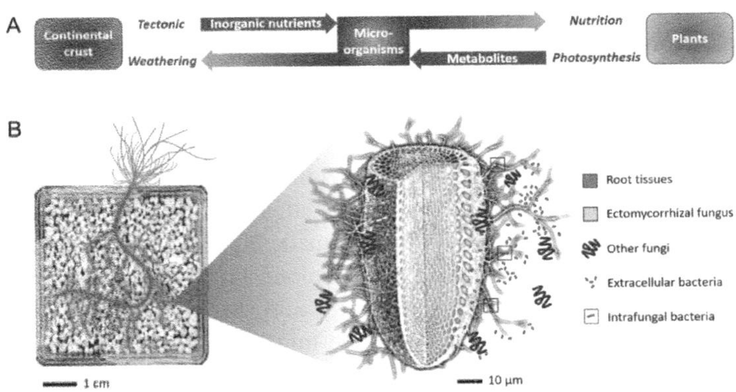

Figure 1.5. *Schematic representation of the contribution of microorganisms to the weathering of the continental crust and nutrition of surface ecosystems in the context of the rhizosphere (A); structure and composition of the mycorrhizal complex (B) (adapted from Frey-Klett (2005) and Bonneville et al. (2011)). For a color version of this figure, see www.iste.co.uk/benzerara/geosphere.zip*

The mineral–bacteria–fungi–plant continuum revolves around the symbiotic mycorrhizal relationship, established between most terrestrial plants and a mycorrhizal fungal counterpart located at the level of their root system (Smith and Read 1997). This generates a system of mutually beneficial nutrient exchanges between these different individuals and contributes to elemental cycles, as presented in Figure 1.5. The photosynthetic partner provides its symbionts with organic molecules resulting from its primary production, which serve as sources of energy. In exchange, the fungal partner explores the surrounding soil to extract nutrients and water and exchanges them with the plant (Frey-Klett et al. 2007). In the case of trees, this reciprocal-nutrient exchange generally takes place in the Hartig network, composed of hyphae inserted between the epidermal and cortical cells of the plant. In addition, so-called "mycorrhiza helper" bacteria play a key role in these fluxes (Frey-Klett et al. 2007), in particular by promoting the mobilization of inorganic nutrients such as phosphorus from primary minerals (Toro et al. 1997). This type of system allows for an efficient translocation of nutrients along the mineral–bacteria–fungus–plant chain, without passing through the surrounding ambient environment, which can be the scene of fierce competition for limiting nutrients. The effectiveness of this type of cooperation has been demonstrated in the case of the symbiosis between *Pinus sylvestris* and *Paxillus involutus*, where the synergistic action of the plant with its fungal symbiont allows for better adaptation to a deficiency than in the case where each of these two partners is separately subjected to the same stressful situation (Van Scholl et al. 2006).

The mechanisms for allocating carbon resources from plants to their symbionts also enable plants to exert control over microbial populations in the rhizosphere by selecting microorganisms from which they can derive the best benefit (Zhalnina et al. 2018), particularly in terms of nutrient uptake (Frey-Klett and Garbaye 2005). For instance, it was shown that young Scots pine shoots increased their allocation of carbon resources to the hyphae in contact with minerals presenting a nutritional content of interest (Heinonsalo et al. 2004; Rosling et al. 2004a). To this basic structure are added a multitude of mycorrhiza helper bacteria (MHB), which participate in the process of mobilizing inorganic nutrients and perform other beneficial functions for the fungus, such as nitrogen fixation by diazotroph species[6], or for the plant by producing growth factors (Frey-Klett et al. 2007). It was shown that ectomycorrhiza fungi were capable, in turn, of selecting bacteria specialized in the extraction of inorganic nutrients from primary minerals (Calvaruso et al. 2007; Uroz et al. 2007), but less effective in the degradation of organic matter, which is

6. Diazotrophy is the metabolic capacity of certain prokaryotes to fix atmospheric dinitrogen in a biologically useful form of nitrogen (ammonium ions).

then carried out by fungi (Uroz et al. 2012, 2013). Both in the case of plants and fungi, control over microbial populations can be achieved by providing different energy sources (different types of carbohydrates) (Hameeda et al. 2006) or other elements (different types of nitrogen compounds, in particular) (Wu et al. 2008). Finally, such cooperation in the mobilization of inorganic nutrients was also evidenced in the case of systems such as lichens (Banfield et al. 1999).

The relative contribution of mineral weathering to the functioning of ecosystems gets larger in the so-called aphotic zone, which corresponds to the portion of the lithosphere disconnected from photosynthesis processes. These environments – which account for nearly 15% of the terrestrial biomass, and more than 80% of bacteria and archaea (Bar-On and Milo 2019) – are usually characterized by nutrient deficiency (oligotrophy). These ecosystems are referred to as the *deep biosphere.* Such harsh conditions require the implementation of complex survival strategies among subsurface microbial communities, culminating in the establishment of syntrophic relationships (i.e. strict symbiosis relationships), which optimizes the exploitation of the flow of energy and allows certain metabolic pathways to overcome the thermodynamic limitations imposed by environment (Lau et al. 2016). These environments thus host particular microbial communities, such as lithoautotrophic microbial subsurface ecosystems[7], which constitute their biomass by chemosynthesis[8], by exploiting the sources of inorganic carbon and energy present in these environments (e.g. by oxidation of methane under anaerobic conditions, oxidation of sulfur by denitrification, autotrophic methanogenesis or sulfate reduction). These ecosystems are based on the exploitation of their mineral environment. This may explain why the mineralosphere concept was primarily developed by studies on subsurface aquifers (Bennett et al. 1996; Jones and Bennett 2014). These environments also constitute a probable ground for the development of life on Earth more than three billion years ago (Fredrickson and Balkwill 2006).

Ultimately, cooperation processes can occur at various scales, from the mineralosphere to the ecosystem level, and from continental surfaces to the deep subsurface.

Given the potential contribution of living organisms to global weathering fluxes, it therefore appears essential to consider mechanisms mobilized by microorganisms to promote rock weathering.

---

7. Lithoautotrophic organisms use inorganic compounds as their sole carbon source.
8. Chemosynthesis is the production of organic matter using chemical energy from the oxidation of reduced chemical compounds. It differs from photosynthesis, which uses light as an energy source.

1.4. Mechanisms associated with microbial dissolution

There are multiple mechanisms involved in the microbial weathering of rocks and all of the different modes of mineral reactivity (acid–base, chelation or redox mechanisms) are exploited. Certain microorganisms are capable of locally controlling the chemical potential of the reactive species involved.

1.4.1. *Biofilms and micro-environments*

Microorganisms are known for their ability to escape the bulk physico-chemical conditions imposed by their surrounding environment by establishing biofilms at fluid–mineral interfaces (Flemming and Wingender 2010). These micro-environments allow them to locally control the chemical potential of the species present in order to provide conditions (in terms of relative humidity pH, etc.) favorable to their survival and thriving. These microenvironments also shield organisms from changes in environmental conditions (droughts or fluctuations in the composition of solutions). While the secretion of extracellular polymeric substances (EPS), mainly composed of polysaccharides, constitutes the structure of the biofilm and maintains its mechanical consistency, the simultaneous production of organic acids locally impacts the reactivity of mineral interfaces (Barker et al. 1998). It was thus shown that microorganisms were capable of locally controlling parameters important for mineral reactivity, such as redox (Fredrickson et al. 1998; Newman and Kolter 2000), pH (Barker et al. 1998; Li et al. 2016) or even fluid–mineral contact (see phenomena of "hydraulic decoupling" (Flemming and Wingender 2010)).

1.4.2. *Redox reactions*

The use of elements with several degrees of oxidation (such as iron or manganese) constitutes one of the primary drivers of the dissolution of minerals by microorganisms. For example, the reduction of insoluble Fe(III) (i.e. Fe^{3+}) in Fe(II) (i.e. Fe^{2+}), much more soluble, by bacterial iron reduction, leads to the destabilization of mineral phases carrying Fe(III), resulting in an increase in their dissolution rate. Associated electron transfers fuel redox reactions within microorganisms which draw their energy from them. In the case of iron reduction, bacteria release electrons by oxidation of organic carbon (electron donor) and these electrons are routed to Fe(III) phases, which serve as the final electron acceptor. When elements involved are very insoluble (such as Fe(III)), direct contact between iron-reducing bacteria and ferric minerals may be required to achieve electron transfers. This is the case, for example, for bacterial species of the genus *Geobacter*, for which the reduction of Fe(III) to Fe(II) is mediated by enzymes called cytochromes located on the external wall of their membrane. In environments lacking electron acceptors, it has also been shown that certain iron-reducing bacteria (e.g. *Shewanella*) can produce *nanowires* ensuring electron conduction from their cell wall to the mineral substrate. Alternatively, electron transfers can also be achieved without direct contact. Bacteria then use endogenous (e.g. flavins) or exogenous (e.g. humic substances) intermediate molecules as electron shuttles (see Miot and Etique (2016) for more details).

1.4.3. *Acidolysis*

Acid–base hydrolysis processes are among the most commonly studied mechanisms for silicate dissolution. These processes can be promoted by microorganisms, in particular by the production of organic acids (Drever and Stillings 1997). Such molecules can be secreted by many species of bacteria and fungi. Furthermore, mineral hydrolysis reactions can also be indirectly promoted by bacterial metabolism, such as respiration processes producing CO_2 and nitrification, which produces nitrous acid (HNO_2). These two metabolic by-products tend to acidify their surrounding environment (Uroz et al. 2009a).

1.4.4. *Ligands*

The secretion of chelating organic compounds such as ethylenediaminetetraacetic acid (EDTA) or diethylenetriaminepentaacetic acid (DTPA) can also promote the dissolution of primary minerals by shifting chemical equilibria. This effect can occur indirectly, by chelation of the reaction products, shifting the thermodynamic equilibrium of the dissolution reaction towards the consumption of reactants. This is the case for siderophores, known for their iron chelating properties (Buss et al. 2007; Ahmed and Holmstrom 2015). These molecules are produced relatively ubiquitously by bacteria or fungi (Saha et al. 2013) and may exhibit exceptionally high iron association constants ($\log(K) = 12 - 52$) (Neilands 1982). By complexing Fe(III), these molecules remove the dissolved Fe(III) from the solution and promote the dissolution of the ferric phases. Chelating molecules can also increase dissolution rates through the formation of surface complexes (see Golubev and Pokrovsky (2006) and section 1.2.4).

1.4.5. *Mechanical effects*

Mechanical processes can also be mobilized by microorganisms in rock weathering. This is for instance the case of constraints induced by turgor pressure during the growth of fungal hyphae. These pressures, which can reach up to 20 MPa (Howard et al. 1991), were reported to induce an increase in mineral dissolution as mentioned previously (section 1.2.7.3). The mechanical stresses involved could be sufficient to locally distort the mineral crystal lattice, facilitating its chemical weathering (Bonneville et al. 2009). Such mechanisms were highlighted in the case of the weathering of lizardite, one of the polymorphs of serpentine, by *Talaromyces flavus* (Li et al. 2016) or *Paxillux involutus* (Bonneville et al. 2009). These processes can also physically breach or crack the material, thus generating additional surface area (Li et al. 2016). The increase in reactive surface, which is fresher and therefore has maximum reactivity, also increases weathering.

1.5. Biotic weathering by microorganisms

Several bacterial and fungal taxa directly or indirectly associated with mineral weathering have been identified, as reviewed in the following sections. One classical way to relate microorganisms and mechanisms involved in weathering consists of identifying microbial phylotypes[9] present in environmental samples. The application of genomic sequencing methods paved the way to linking the chemical composition of minerals (and therefore their nutritional potential or their toxicity) and the structure of microbial communities (Gleeson et al. 2005; Benzerara et al. 2006; Gommeaux et al. 2010). The recent introduction of more advanced techniques of metagenomics (see Chapter 4), based on direct sequencing of total DNA from environmental samples, allowed for a semi-quantitative and relatively exhaustive characterization of metabolic pathways and functional diversity. This has opened new perspectives in understanding the role of microorganisms in various geochemical cycles (Anantharaman et al. 2016), including those involving mineral weathering (Uroz et al. 2015, 2016).

1.5.1. *The mineralosphere*

Beyond the weathering action of bacteria on minerals, several studies have suggested a specific influence of minerals on the structure of microbial communities located in their direct vicinity. First, in natural settings, it was demonstrated that the properties of the mineral substrate (i.e. its chemical composition and its structure) constitute a structuring parameter for microbial (Uroz et al. 2012) and fungal (Gleeson et al. 2005) communities. This was observed in a wide diversity of environments, including subglacial environments (Mitchell et al. 2013), forest soil profiles (Uroz et al. 2012) or surface aquifers (Bennett et al. 2001). These field

9. A phylotype is a grouping of phylogenetically close individuals.

observations were also supported by results from laboratory experiments, which made it possible to establish a formal link between the structuring of bacterial communities and the properties of mineral substrates, colonized according to their nutritional potential (e.g. P, Fe) (Phillips-Lander et al. 2014), or deleterious effect (e.g. release of Al^{3+}, toxic for certain species) (Jones and Bennett 2014). In the latter case, the community can be structured by the selection of resistant species and/or by more complex mechanisms underlying the cooperation between species to reduce the effects of the toxic metal. This is particularly the case for the sulfate-reducing bacterium *Desulfococcus* (Jones and Bennett 2014), or the strain *Pseudomonas fluorescens* (Appanna et al. 1995), which has the capacity to neutralize local aluminum toxicity. It was shown that this can lead to the over-representation of these species in communities associated with aluminum-bearing mineral phases (Jones and Bennett 2014). Aluminum is also known for its inhibitory effect on the kinetics of Ca or Mg assimilation at the root cell wall (Finlay 1995; van Scholl et al. 2008). In response to an excess of Al^{3+}, certain tree species are capable of producing small organic acids (citrates, oxalates) in order to complex the excess aluminum. This mechanism can be further exacerbated in the case of a symbiosis with ectomycorrhizal fungi, such as *Suillus variegatus*, *Rhizopogon roseolus* (Ahonen-Jonnarth et al. 2000) or *Paxillus involutus* (Rudawska and Leski 1998).

Overall, based on these observations, it was hypothesized that a fraction of the critical zone would thus be under the direct influence of the release of nutrients or toxic elements from minerals (Uroz et al. 2015). This particular compartment of the critical zone, at the direct interface with primary minerals, was initially introduced under the term "stonesphere" (Certini et al. 2004). Its definition was then refined with the concept of mineralosphere, by analogy with other ecological niches such as the rhizosphere (Uroz et al. 2009a, 2012, 2015). The mineralosphere can therefore be defined as "the volume of soil in the critical zone under the influence of the nutritive and toxic elements contained in minerals" (Uroz et al. 2015). This emerging concept, when confirmed, would extend the range of interactions between microorganisms and mineral phases beyond microbial weathering, recognizing the existence of a feedback of mineral properties on the bacterial and fungal communities in the critical zone.

1.5.2. *Bacteria*

An increasing number of bacteria with particularly effective weathering capabilities such as certain members of the genus *Collimonas* (Uroz et al. 2009b) are identified each year in the literature. This section provides a summary of the main bacterial genera concerned (Uroz et al. 2009a, 2015, Sokolova 2011). A striking point in this table is the universality of the mechanisms involved (e.g. production of siderophores or organic acids) and the ubiquity of the weathered mineral phases. Classical approaches leading to the compilation of the tables below mostly relied on microbial taxonomy. By contrast, more recent studies increasingly focus on the analysis of functions present in the total genome of environmental samples using metagenomic methods (and possibly gene expression using metatranscriptomics) instead of determining the taxonomy of the species or genera present through the sequencing of 16S or 18S rDNA-type identity genes (Napieralski et al. 2019).

Microorganisms	Example (genus)	Altered phases	Possible or supposed weathering mechanisms
α-Proteo-bacteria	*Labrys* (Uroz et al. 2009a); *Rhanella* (Kim et al. 1998); *Rhizobium* (Kim et al. 1998); *Sphingomonas* (Calvaruso et al. 2007; Uroz et al. 2007)	Phosphates, biotite, hydroxyapatite	Production of gluconic acid and siderophores
β-Proteo-bacteria	*Burkholderia* (Ullman et al. 1996; Barker et al. 1998; Welch et al. 1999; Kim et al. 2005; Vassilev et al. 2006; Calvaruso et al. 2007; Uroz et al. 2007; Wu et al. 2008; Lepleux et al. 2012); *Collimonas* (Calvaruso et al. 2007; Uroz et al. 2007; Lapanje et al. 2012); *Janthinobacterium* (Uroz et al. 2009a; Frey et al. 2010); *Cupriavidus metallidurans* (Ullman et al. 1996; Olsson-Francis et al. 2010; Cockell et al. 2020)	Biotite, phosphates, bytownite, feldspar, granite, basalt	Production of siderophores, gluconic acid, oxalic acid and hydrogen cyanide

δ-Proteobacteria	*Azotobacter* (Page and Huyer 1984; Page 1987); *Geobacter* (Childers et al. 2002)	Pyrite, glauconite, olivine, goethite, limonite, hematite, apatite, granite	Production of gentisic acid and siderophores, redox activity
γ-Proteobacteria	*Acidithiobacillus* (Mustin et al. 1992; Vera et al. 2013); *Pseudomonas* (Puente et al. 2004, 2009; Uroz et al. 2005, 2007; Hameeda et al. 2006); *Serratia* (Krishnaraj and Goldstein 2001; Hameeda et al. 2006); *Shewanella* (Kostka et al. 1996; Lower et al. 2001; Dong et al. 2003; Davis et al. 2007)	Pyrite, biotite, phosphates, limestone, apatite, granite, basalt, marble, limestone, smectite	Siderophore production, gluconic acid production, redox activity
Gram-positive bacteria	*Arthrobacter* (Ullman et al. 1996; Barker and Banfield 1998; Kalinowski et al. 2000; Frey et al. 2010); *Bacillus* (Hameeda et al. 2006; Song et al. 2007; Puente et al. 2009); *Paenibacillus* (Modak et al. 1999; Vasan et al. 2001; Uroz et al. 2009a); *Staphylococcus* (Lee and Stotzky 1999; Puente et al. 2009; Uroz et al. 2009a), *Streptomyces* (Liermann et al. 2000; Brantley et al. 2001; Faramarzi and Brandl 2006)	Hornblende, bytownite, feldspar, granite, biotite, limestone, apatite, granite, basalt, marble (calcite, dolomite), phosphates, bauxite	Production of organic acids, siderophores and hydrogen cyanide

Table 1.1. *Main bacteria studied for their weathering properties*

1.5.3. *Fungi*

As with bacteria, the colonization of the natural environment by fungi is, among other things, directed by the nutrient content of minerals (Rosling et al. 2004b). Table 1.2 brings together the main fungal species with proven bioweathering activity (Courty et al. 2010; Gadd 2010; Sokolova 2011). As for bacteria, this bibliographic summary highlights the universality of the weathering mechanisms used and the ubiquity of the weathered phases.

Microorganisms	Example (genus)	Altered phases	Possible or supposed weathering mechanisms
Ascomycetes	*Aspergillus fumigatus* (Daghino et al. 2008; Favero-Longo et al. 2009); *Aspergillus Niger* (Rossi 1978; Sayer et al. 1997; Gadd 2007; Wei et al. 2012; Sun et al. 2013); *Cenococcum geophilum* (Haselwandter and Winkelmann; Yuan et al. 2004); *Verticillium leptobactrum* (Daghino et al. 2008, 2009)	Chrysotile, crocidolite, potassium feldspars, olivine, dunite, serpentine, muscovite, spodumene, kaolin, nepheline, cuprite, galena, rhodochrosite, tartar, leucite, birnessite, vermiculite, phlogopite	Siderophores, organic and carbonic acids.
Basidiomycetes	*Paxillus involutus* (Berzelius 1835; Wallander and Wickman 1999; Ahonen-Jonnarth et al. 2000; Arvieu et al. 2003; van Hees et al. 2003; Rosling et al. 2004b; Van Scholl et al. 2006; Bonneville et al. 2009, 2011; Saccone et al. 2012; Schmalenberger et al. 2015); *Piloderma croceum* (Mahmood et al. 2001; Glowa et al. 2003; Van Scholl 2006); *Rhizopogon roseolus* (Ahonen-Jonnarth et al. 2000; Arvieu et al. 2003); *Schizophyllum commune* (Wengel et al. 2006; Kirtzel et al. 2017)	Phlogopite, quartz, K-feldspar feldspar, apatite, phosphate, marble, biotite, microcline, muscovite, chlorite, marble, slate	Oxalic, citric and malonic acids, biomechanical constraints, redox activity, carbonic acid

Table 1.2. *Main fungi studied for their weathering properties*

1.6. What quantitative impact do living organisms have on mineral dissolution?

Throughout this chapter, we describe weathering processes from the stance of one of its main steps: the dissolution of minerals. We have provided the foundations of abiotic parameterization to the reader, while reporting the evidence that has been collected so far on the possible impact of living organisms, and in particular, microorganisms, on the kinetics of mineral weathering. In this section, we will summarize the current position of the scientific community on the relative contribution of living organisms to mineral dissolution, and more generally, to mineral weathering on Earth. The knowledge generated by scientific research is in constant progress and we will see here that answers to several key questions are still to be validated. We also present some of the challenges in quantifying the impact of life, and some possible avenues to overcome them.

1.6.1. *An absence of scientific consensus*

Living organisms, and microorganisms in particular, are fundamental in the surface geochemical cycle of numerous chemical elements: it is estimated that nearly two-thirds of the minerals known on Earth are the direct or indirect result of biochemical processes (Hazen et al. 2008). However, the quantitative contribution of living organisms to weathering remains unknown.

If we were to roughly divide the driver of weathering into abiotic contribution, microbial contribution and contribution of macroorganisms, it is generally accepted that vegetation has played a major role in weathering over geological time scales. The appearance of plant roots during the Devonian (–420 to –360 million years ago) correlated with an abrupt drop in atmospheric CO_2, has often been taken to illustrate this assertion (Berner 1997). Modeling of the external carbon cycle during the Phanerozoic has independently confirmed the primordial role of plants in stimulating weathering and the associated CO_2 consumption (Berner 1991) (see Chapter 7). In fact, vegetation stabilizes soils by retaining particles generated by physical erosion while acting as a "sponge", able to increase the surface area and the contact time between the liquid and solid phases (Schwartzman and Volk 1989). Current models of soil profile weathering on a continental scale can no longer ignore the major role played by vegetation.

The position of the scientific community about the relative contribution of microorganisms to vegetation is much less consensual. We note that weathering under plant cover can be considered as the result of the effect of root networks as well as the microbial communities associated with them. Comparing the weathering fluxes of areas differing only by their vegetation cover, all other things being equal (lithology, topography and climatic regime of the areas studied) is a possible method to clarify this point. While, for example, Moulton and Berner (1998) measured that the weathering intensity of basalts under forests was only two to five times greater than the weathering intensity of basalts covered only with mosses and lichens, this difference could reach a factor of 10 in the context of Hawaiian basalts (Ford Cochran and Berner 1996).

Finally, the lack of consensus is even more obvious if we consider the contributions of microorganisms comparatively to a purely abiotic contribution. Thus, early modeling by Schwartzman and Volk (1989) defends the idea that life as a whole (micro- and macroorganisms) is responsible for a weathering flux 100–1,000 times greater than that of purely abiotic weathering. If the ratio of the contribution of macroorganisms to microorganisms is 2–10 (see above), then the specific contribution of microorganisms should be 9–330 times greater than that of the abiotic flux. These estimates do not correlate well with some observations suggesting that weathering under lichen is essentially identical to the weathering of supposedly sterile basalts ("barren") as reported in Ford Cochran and Berner (1996), thus raising a real paradox. In addition, estimates of weathering fluxes linked to tubular weathering textures and whose biological origin is still controversial (see section 1.6.2) vary from 0.5% (Smits et al. 2005) to 50% (van Breemen et al. 2000b) of the total flux, again highlighting the lack of certainty as to the quantitative contribution of microorganisms to dissolution rates in the natural environment.

1.6.2. *Obstacles in assessing the microbial contribution*

A major difficulty in determining the contribution of living organisms to weathering on Earth comes from the fact that it requires an abiotic control, which does not really exist given the omnipresence of life on the Earth's surface. This justifies the development of an appropriate methodological approach. Quantifying the impact of life will therefore require us to solve a series of problems, still not fully elucidated, among which:

(i) *The clear definition of a "weathering biosignature"*: at present, there is no consensus on whether characteristic imprints of the action of life exist. Yet, this would make it possible to assess the extent of the contribution of living organisms to weathering. For example, morphological criteria such as the presence of etch pits or tubular microchannels in naturally weathered silicate materials are often considered biodissolution fingerprints (e.g. Thorseth et al. 1995; Bennett et al. 1996; Jongmans et al. 1997; Fisk et al. 1998). However, the determination of biosignatures based on the microtopography of naturally weathered samples has often proven equivocal.

For example, Fisk et al. (2013) showed that etch pits and microchannels similar to those attributed to microbial activity in basalt glass can be reproduced by abiotic dissolution experiments. In the same vein, the criteria of "size and shape" for etch pits, sometimes interpreted as resulting from microbial weathering (Thorseth et al. 1995; Bennett et al. 1996) can also be reproduced abiotically (Grandstaff 1986; Daval et al. 2013). Finally, none of the rare detailed studies at the nanoscale (including for instance the study of surface layers located between the microorganisms and the weathered silicate surface), revealed chemical signatures specific to bioweathering (Benzerara et al. 2005). These questions therefore remain open.

(ii) *Upscaling laboratory measurements of microbial weathering stimulation*: a significant number of experimental studies dedicated to quantifying the impact of microorganisms on the weathering rate of minerals have focused on quantifying the effect of the biomolecules secreted (in particular, organic ligands). While such molecules can have a significant effect on the reactivity of minerals (see section 1.2.4), several studies agree that their characteristic concentrations in soil solutions are too low to have a significant impact on mineral reactivity (Drever and Stillings 1997; Golubev and Pokrovsky 2006). Experiments carried out with microbial strains partly made it possible to more accurately estimate the actual impact of microorganisms in contact with minerals. However, the representativeness of the reference strains used in the laboratory is increasingly questioned. Although this problem has been gradually resolved, thanks to the recent introduction of high-throughput sequencing methods allowing a semi-quantitative metagenomic approach to microbial communities, the identification of mineral weathering actors in natural conditions is still in its infancy (Uroz et al. 2009a, 2015). In addition, laboratory cultures (i) are limited to species that we know how to cultivate, (ii) promote/amplify the extent of microorganism–mineral contacts (and therefore overestimate the microbial contribution to weathering) and (iii) do not account for the complex feedback loops that can exist within microbial communities. Behaviors observed in culture can differ from behavior and functions expressed within a complex microbial community (Nadell et al. 2016). In addition, bioweathering functions identified in pure cultures can in fact be the consequence of metabolic processes completely independent of the weathering processes. In general, the production of organic ligands by bacteria can respond to matter other than mineral reactivity and their secretion should therefore be interpreted with caution. This is particularly the case for certain siderophores such as vibrioferrin or pyoverdine. Despite the role of iron chelates with which siderophores are associated by default and which promotes the dissolution of iron-bearing minerals (section 1.3.4), they can also be used by certain microorganisms to inhibit quorum sensing mechanisms[10]

10. Quorum sensing is a type of chemical communication between cells, allowing them to detect and respond to variations in cell density.

(Dembitsky et al. 2011) or other inter-cell signaling functions (Nadal Jimenez et al. 2012), therefore with no apparent link with mineral dissolution. Similarly, low molecular weight organic acids produced by a broad spectrum of bacterial and fungal species can serve a large number of functions, related or not to inorganic nutrient cycling in the critical zone. This is, for instance, the case for oxalic acid, which promotes the dissolution of certain minerals, but which is also involved in the extraction of calcium from cell walls (Dutton and Evans 1996), in organic matter degradation processes such as hemicellulose decomposition and cellulose depolymerization (Green et al. 1991). This analysis highlights the absence of a clear link between the secretion of organic molecules with reactive properties, as observed using in vitro approaches, and possible mineral weathering properties in the field.

(iii) *Considering the complexity of the mineral surface in the field*: apart from a few rare studies (Wild et al. 2018), the vast majority of work dedicated to the study of biodissolution uses freshly ground mineral substrates. The reactivity of such substrates is potentially much greater than that of minerals weathered over geological time scales (Vance et al. 2009), such that most of the work carried out to date completely ignores the effects of "aging" of the mineral surfaces and in particular the effects of passivation by surface layers that we mentioned in section 1.2.7.2.

1.6.3. *Towards new protocols to measure microbial contribution to weathering?*

Conventional methods to estimate the weathering rate in the field provide an integrated vision of weathering processes but do not make it possible to distinguish the different weathering processes at work, such as biological versus abiotic (Sverdrup et al. 2002). From this perspective, the detailed understanding of weathering mechanisms in general seems illusory. In particular, the part represented by biotic weathering processes, although potentially predominant in the most superficial parts of the Earth's crust, still remains poorly understood.

On the one hand, a bottom-up approach allows for the identification of potential bioweathering agents and associated biomolecular mechanisms through laboratory experiments under controlled conditions, but its relevance in the field remains uncertain. On the other hand, the top-down approach aimed at determining bioweathering processes in situ, comes up against the intrinsic complexity of the natural environment, preventing the unequivocal identification of biotic weathering agents in the field and the quantification of their action in situ. Concerning the bottom-up approach, we noted above (i) the uncertainties regarding constraints in the laboratory and (ii) the possible gap between the processes observed under controlled conditions in vitro and the processes at work within complex microbial communities. For the top-down approach, the absence of an initial sterile or unweathered surface adds ambiguity when determining bioweathering agents and mechanisms. This is demonstrated in particular by controversies surrounding "rock-eating fungi" (Jongmans et al. 1997; van Scholl et al. 2008), or biotic weathering of basaltic glasses in an oceanic context (Torsvik et al. 1998; Benzerara et al. 2007). In each of these contexts, weathering patterns either at the mineral surface ("etch pit" type) (see Figure 1.1) or within the solid (tubular structures) have been highlighted, without a real consensus on their biological or non-biological origin.

While qualitative estimates of field weathering could be obtained through observations of mineral surfaces with electron microscopy (Rogers and Bennett 2004; van Scholl et al. 2008), the use of incubated minerals in soil profiles made it possible to obtain quantitative estimates based on topographical analyses, while overcoming the limitations mentioned above. Thus, Quirk et al. (2012) incubated fresh muscovite surfaces in situ whose initial topography was known, in the rhizosphere of trees belonging to different functional groups (Gymnosperms and Angiosperms). Characterizing the depressions located under the fungal hyphae, which colonized the muscovite surfaces after a certain incubation period, made it possible to quantify the rate of microbial dissolution as well as reactivity conditions representative of the environment. Likewise, similar experiments set up in a beech forest provided weathering fluxes related to the colonization of olivine surfaces by fungal hyphae belonging to the genus *Verticillium* (Wild et al. 2021). These experiments also allowed us to quantify their relative contribution to the total weathering flux by comparing the amplitude of the "underhyphae" depressions to the retreat of the surface linked to the dissolution of the mineral in contact with soil solutions. This in situ incubation approach should allow for the emergence of new data sets including fluxes, agents and mechanisms of biotic weathering, necessary for a more detailed understanding of bioweathering.

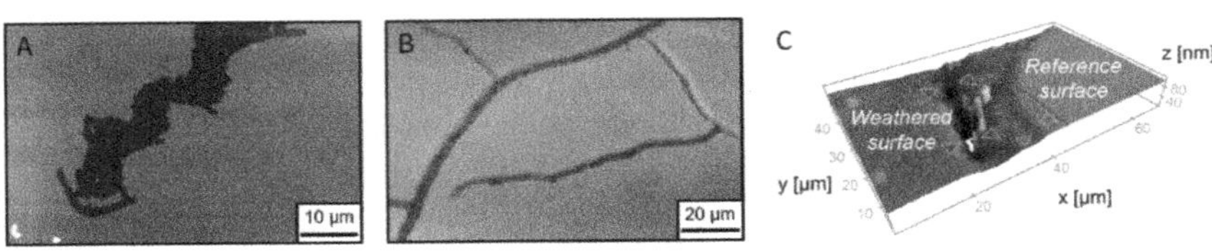

Figure 1.6. *Imprints left by the action of fungal hyphae on chlorite surfaces in mesocosm experiments For a color version of this figure, see www.iste.co.uk/ benzerara/geosphere.zip*

COMMENT ON FIGURE 1.6.– *(A) At the surface of muscovite (B) and on olivine minerals, (C) samples incubated in situ (images adapted from Gazzè et al. (2012), Quirk et al. (2012) and Wild et al. (2021), respectively). The step indicated by the blue arrows in (C) is related to the dissolution of the mineral in contact with soil solutions, while the green arrows indicate the mark left by the action of a fungal hypha.*

1.7. Conclusion

In this chapter, we described, on the molecular scale, how minerals dissolve and how rate laws were developed for such dissolution reactions. This made it possible to better understand how living organisms could a priori influence the dissolution rates of minerals, for example, by locally modifying the pH, by releasing organic ligands which chelate metals, by fueling transfers of electrons produced or consumed by their metabolism, or by inducing mechanical stress.

To date, "reactive transport" codes aiming to model mineral reactivity in the field only consider the contribution of living organisms in a very indirect way. However, the amplifying effect of life on the dissolution rates of minerals now seems well established by laboratory experiments or in situ incubations of well-characterized mineral surfaces. The biodissolution process sometimes involves synergies between fungi, bacteria and plants, particularly in the context of the rhizosphere and there is a great taxonomic diversity of bacteria and fungi that seem particularly effective in promoting mineral dissolution. This helps ensure the supply of inorganic nutrients to ecosystems, and this interaction between minerals and microorganisms could thus truly result from evolutionary selection having led to more or less specific colonization and weathering strategies.

By what multiplicative factor have microorganisms amplified mineral dissolution on Earth? This question remains a major enigma in current research. However, we have seen that the coupling of mineralogical, geochemical and biological methods could answer this enigma in the future.

As highlighted in this chapter, mineral dissolution is only one facet of rock weathering. Due to dissolution in particular, the solutions become enriched in dissolved elements, which may lead to conditions of supersaturation with respect to new mineral phases. This can result in the precipitation of secondary phases. Here again, this process of mineral precipitation can be influenced by life. Such biomineralization processes are discussed in the second chapter.

1.8. References

Aagaard, P. and Helgeson, H.C. (1982). Thermodynamic and kinetic constraints on reaction-rates among minerals and aqueous solutions. 1. Theoretical considerations. *American Journal of Science*, 282(3), 237–285.

Ahmed, E. and Holmstrom, S.J.M. (2015). Microbe-mineral interactions: The impact of surface attachment on mineral weathering and element selectivity by microorganisms. *Chemical Geology*, 403, 13–23.

Ahonen-Jonnarth, U., Van Hees, P.A.W., Lundstrom, U.S., Finlay, R.D. (2000). Organic acids produced by mycorrhizal *Pinus sylvestris* exposed to elevated aluminium and heavy metal concentrations. *New Phytologist*, 146(3), 557–567.

Anantharaman, K., Brown, C.T., Hug, L.A., Sharon, I., Castelle, C.J., Probst, A.J., Thomas, B.C., Singh, A., Wilkins, M.J., Karaoz, U. et al. (2016). Thousands of microbial genomes shed light on interconnected biogeochemical processes in an aquifer system. *Nature Communications*, 7, 13219. doi: 10.1038/ncomms13219.

Appanna, V.D., Finn, H., Pierre, M.S. (1995). Exocellular phosphatidylethanolamine production and multiple-metal tolerance in *Pseudomonas fluorescens*. *FEMS Microbiology Letters*, 131(1), 53–56.

Aradóttir, E.S.P., Sonnenthal, E.L., Björnsson, G., Jónsson, H. (2012). Multidimensional reactive transport modeling of CO_2 mineral sequestration in basalts at the Hellisheidi geothermal field, Iceland. *International Journal of Greenhouse Gas Control*, 9, 24–40.

Arvieu, J.C., Leprince, F., Plassard, C. (2003). Release of oxalate and protons by ectomycorrhizal fungi in response to P-deficiency and calcium carbonate in nutrient solution. *Annals of Forest Science*, 60(8), 815–821.

Banfield, J.F., Barker, W.W., Welch, S.A., Taunton, A. (1999). Biological impact on mineral dissolution: Application of the lichen model to understanding mineral weathering in the rhizosphere. *Proceedings of the National Academy of Sciences*, 96(7), 3404–3411.

Barker, W.W. and Banfield, J.F. (1998). Zones of chemical and physical interaction at interfaces between microbial communities and minerals: A model. *Geomicrobiology Journal*, 15(3), 223–244.

Barker, W.W., Welch, S.A., Banfield, J.F. (1997). Biogeochemical weathering of silicate minerals. *Reviews in Mineralogy and Geochemistry*, 35(1), 391–428.

Barker, W.W., Welch, S.A., Chu, S., Banfield, J.F. (1998). Experimental observations of the effects of bacteria on aluminosilicate weathering. *American Mineralogist*, 83(11–12 Part 2), 1551–1563.

Bar-On, Y.M. and Milo, R. (2019). Towards a quantitative view of the global ubiquity of biofilms. *Nature Reviews Microbiology*, 17(4), 199–200.

Beaulieu, E., Godderis, Y., Donnadieu, Y., Labat, D., Roelandt, C. (2012). High sensitivity of the continental-weathering carbon dioxide sink to future climate change. *Nature Climate Change*, 2(5), 346–349.

Beerling, D.J., Kantzas, E.P., Lomas, M.R., Wade, P., Eufrasio, R.M., Renforth, P., Sarkar, B., Andrews, M.G., James, R.H., Pearce, C.R. et al. (2020). Potential for large-scale CO_2 removal via enhanced rock weathering with croplands. *Nature*, 583(7815), 242–248.

Bennett, P.C., Hiebert, F.K., Choi, W.J. (1996). Microbial colonization and weathering of silicates in a petroleum-contaminated groundwater. *Chemical Geology*, 132(1–4), 45–53.

Bennett, P.C., Rogers, J.R., Choi, W.J. (2001). Silicates, silicate weathering, and microbial ecology. *Geomicrobiology Journal*, 18(1), 3–19.

Benzerara, K., Menguy, N., Guyot, F., Vanni, C., Gillet, P. (2005). TEM study of a silicate-carbonate-microbe interface prepared by focused ion beam milling. *Geochimica et Cosmochimica Acta*, 69(6), 1413–1422.

Benzerara, K., Chapon, V., Moreira, D., Lopez-Garcia, P., Guyot, F., Heulin, T. (2006). Microbial diversity on the Tatahouine meteorite. *Meteoritics & Planetary Science*, 41(8), 1249–1265.

Benzerara, K., Menguy, N., Banerjee, N.R., Tyliszczak, T., Brown, G.E., Guyot, F. (2007). Alteration of submarine basaltic glass from the Ontong Java Plateau: A STXM and TEM study. *Earth and Planetary Science Letters*, 260(1–2), 187–200.

Berner, R.A. (1991). A model for atmospheric CO_2 over phanerozoic time. *American Journal of Science*, 291(4), 339–376.

Berner, R.A. (1997). The rise of plants and their effect on weathering and atmospheric CO_2. *Science*, 276(5312), 544.

Berzelius, J.J. (1835). *Théorie des proportions chimiques, et table analytique des poids atomiques, des corps simples et de leurs combinaisons les plus importantes*. Didot, Paris.

Blum, A. and Lasaga, A. (1988). Role of surface speciation in the low-temperature dissolution of minerals. *Nature*, 331, 431–433.

Bonneville, S., Smits, M.M., Brown, A., Harrington, J., Leake, J.R., Brydson, R., Benning, L.G. (2009). Plant-driven fungal weathering: Early stages of mineral alteration at the nanometer scale. *Geology*, 37(7), 615–618.

Bonneville, S., Morgan, D.J., Schmalenberger, A., Bray, A., Brown, A., Banwart, S.A., Benning, L.G. (2011). Tree-mycorrhiza symbiosis accelerate mineral weathering: Evidences from nanometer-scale elemental fluxes at the hypha–mineral interface. *Geochimica et Cosmochimica Acta*, 75(22), 6988–7005. doi: 10.1016/j.gca.2011.08.041.

Bonneville, S., Bray, A.W., Benning, L.G. (2016). Structural Fe(II) oxidation in biotite by an ectomycorrhizal fungi drives mechanical forcing. *Environmental Science & Technology*, 50(11), 5589–5596.

Bouissonnié, A., Daval, D., Marinoni, M., Ackerer, P. (2018). From mixed flow reactor to column experiments and modeling: Upscaling of calcite dissolution rate. *Chemical Geology*, 487, 63–75.

Brantley, S.L., Liermann, L., Bau, M., Wu, S. (2001). Uptake of trace metals and rare earth elements from hornblende by a soil bacterium. *Geomicrobiology Journal*, 18(1), 37–61.

Brantley, S.L., Goldhaber, M.B., Ragnarsdottir, K.V. (2007). Crossing disciplines and scales to understand the critical zone. *Elements*, 3(5), 307–314.

Brunauer, S., Emmet, P.H., Teller, E. (1938). Adsorption of gases in multmolecular layers. *Journal of the American Chemical Society*, 60, 309–319.

Buss, H.L., Lüttge, A., Brantley, S.L. (2007). Etch pit formation on iron silicate surfaces during siderophore-promoted dissolution. *Chemical Geology*, 240(3–4), 326–342.

Calabrese, S., Parolari, A.J., Porporato, A. (2017). Hydrologic transport of dissolved inorganic carbon and its control on chemical weathering. *Journal of Geophysical Research: Earth Surface*, 122(10), 2016–2032.

Calvaruso, C., Turpault, M.-P., Leclerc, E., Frey-Klett, P. (2007). Impact of ectomycorrhizosphere on the functional diversity of soil bacterial and fungal communities from a forest stand in relation to nutrient mobilization processes. *Microbial Ecology*, 54(3), 567–577.

Casey, W.H. and Sposito, G. (1992). On the temperature-dependence of mineral dissolution rates. *Geochimica et Cosmochimica Acta*, 56(10), 3825–3830.

Casey, W.H. and Westrich, H.R. (1992). Control of dissolution rates of orthosilicate minerals by divalent metal-oxygen bonds. *Nature*, 355, 157–159.

Certini, G., Campbell, C.D., Edwards, A.C. (2004). Rock fragments in soil support a different microbial community from the fine earth. *Soil Biology & Biochemistry*, 36(7), 1119–1128.

Childers, S.E., Ciufo, S., Lovley, D.R. (2002). Geobacter metallireducens accesses insoluble Fe(III) oxide by chemotaxis. *Nature*, 416(6882), 767–769.

Cockell, C.S., Santomartino, R., Finster, K., Waajen, A.C., Eades, L.J., Moeller, R., Rettberg, P., Fuchs, F.M., Van Houdt, R., Leys, N. et al. (2020). Space station biomining experiment demonstrates rare earth element extraction in microgravity and Mars gravity. *Nature Communications*, 11(1), 5523.

Courty, P.E., Buee, M., Diedhiou, A.G., Frey-Klett, P., Le Tacon, F., Rineau, F., Turpault, M.P., Uroz, S., Garbaye, J. (2010). The role of ectomycorrhizal communities in forest ecosystem processes: New perspectives and emerging concepts. *Soil Biology & Biochemistry*, 42(5), 679–698.

Criscenti, L.J., Kubicki, J.D., Brantley, S.L. (2006). Silicate glass and mineral dissolution: Calculated reaction paths and activation energies for hydrolysis of a Q^3 Si by H_3O^+ using ab initio methods. *The Journal of Physical Chemistry A*, 110(1), 198–206.

Daghino, S., Martino, E., Vurro, E., Tomatis, M., Girlanda, M., Fubini, B., Perotto, S. (2008). Bioweathering of chrysotile by fungi isolated in ophiolitic sites. *FEMS Microbiology Letters*, 285(2), 242–249.

Daghino, S., Turci, F., Tomatis, M., Girlanda, M., Fubini, B., Perotto, S. (2009). Weathering of chrysotile asbestos by the serpentine rock-inhabiting fungus *Verticillium leptobactrum*. *FEMS Microbiology Ecology*, 69(1), 132–141.

Daval, D., Hellmann, R., Saldi, G.D., Wirth, R., Knauss, K.G. (2013). Linking nm-scale measurements of the anisotropy of silicate surface reactivity to macroscopic dissolution rate laws: New insights based on diopside. *Geochimica et Cosmochimica Acta*, 107(0), 121–134.

Davis, K.J., Nealson, K.H., Luettge, A. (2007). Calcite and dolomite dissolution rates in the context of microbe-mineral surface interactions. *Geobiology*, 5(2), 191–205.

Dembitsky, V.M., Al Quntar, A.A.A., Srebnik, M. (2011). Natural and synthetic small boron-containing molecules as potential inhibitors of bacterial and fungal quorum sensing. *Chemical Reviews*, 111(1), 209–237.

Dong, H.L., Kukkadapu, R.K., Fredrickson, J.K., Zachara, J.M., Kennedy, D.W., Kostandarithes, H.M. (2003). Microbial reduction of structural Fe(III) in illite and goethite. *Environmental Science & Technology*, 37(7), 1268–1276.

Dorn, R.I. (2014). Ants as a powerful biotic agent of olivine and plagioclase dissolution. *Geology*, 42(9), 771–774.

Drever, J.I. and Stillings, L.L. (1997). The role of organic acids in mineral weathering. *Colloids and Surfaces A: Physicochemical and Engineering Aspects*, 120(1–3), 167–181.

Dutton, M.V. and Evans, C.S. (1996). Oxalate production by fungi: Its role in pathogenicity and ecology in the soil environment. *Canadian Journal of Microbiology*, 42(9), 881–895.

Etique, M., Jorand, F.P.A., Ruby, C. (2016). Magnetite as a precursor for green rust through the hydrogenotrophic activity of the iron-reducing bacteria *Shewanella putrefaciens*. *Geobiology*, 14(3), 237–254.

Eyring, H. (1935). The activated complex and the absolute rate of chemical reactions. *Chemical Reviews*, 17, 65–82.

Faramarzi, M.A. and Brandl, H. (2006). Formation of water-soluble metal cyanide complexes from solid minerals by *Pseudomonas plecoglossicida*. *FEMS Microbiology Letters*, 259(1), 47–52.

Favero-Longo, S.E., Castelli, D., Fubini, B., Piervittori, R. (2009). Lichens on asbestos–cement roofs: Bioweathering and biocovering effects. *Journal of Hazardous Materials*, 162(2), 1300–1308.

Finlay, R.D. (1995). Effects of acid deposition and tropospheric ozone on forest ecosystems in Sweden. *Ecological Bulletins*, 44, 197–214.

Fisk, M.R., Giovannoni, S.J., Thorseth, I.H. (1998). Alteration of oceanic volcanic glass: Textural evidence of microbial activity. *Science*, 281(5379), 978–980.

Fisk, M.R., Crovisier, J.-L., Honnorez, J. (2013). Experimental abiotic alteration of igneous and manufactured glasses. *Comptes rendus geoscience*, 345(4), 176–184.

Flemming, H.-C. and Wingender, J. (2010). The biofilm matrix. *Nature Reviews Microbiology*, 8(9), 623–633.

Ford Cochran, M. and Berner, R.A. (1996). Promotion of chemical weathering by higher plants: Field observations on Hawaiian basalts. *Chemical Geology*, 132(1), 71–77.

Fredrickson, J.K. and Balkwill, D.L. (2006). Geomicrobial processes and biodiversity in the deep terrestrial subsurface. *Geomicrobiology Journal*, 23(6), 345–356.

Fredrickson, J.K., Zachara, J.M., Kennedy, D.W., Dong, H., Onstott, T.C., Hinman, N.W., Li, S.-M. (1998). Biogenic iron mineralization accompanying the dissimilatory reduction of hydrous ferric oxide by a groundwater bacterium. *Geochimica et Cosmochimica Acta*, 62(19–20), 3239–3257.

Frey, B., Rieder, S.R., Brunner, I., Ploetze, M., Koetzsch, S., Lapanje, A., Brandl, H., Furrer, G. (2010). Weathering-associated bacteria from the Damma glacier forefield: Physiological vapabilities and impact on granite dissolution. *Applied and Environmental Microbiology*, 76(14), 4788–4796.

Frey-Klett, P. and Garbaye, J. (2005). Mycorrhiza helper bacteria: A promising model for the genomic analysis of fungal-bacterial interactions. *New Phytologist*, 168(1), 4–8.

Frey-Klett, P., Garbaye, J., Tarkka, M. (2007). The mycorrhiza helper bacteria revisited. *New Phytologist*, 176(1), 22–36.

Gadd, G.M. (2007). Geomycology: Biogeochemical transformations of rocks, minerals, metals and radionuclides by fungi, bioweathering and bioremediation. *Mycological Research*, 111, 3–49.

Gadd, G.M. (2010). Metals, minerals and microbes: Geomicrobiology and bioremediation. *Microbiology*, 156(3), 609–643.

Gaillardet, J. (2023). *La Terre habitable. Ou l'épopée de la zone critique*. La Découverte, Paris.

Gazzè, S.A., Saccone, L., Vala Ragnarsdottir, K., Smits, M.M., Duran, A.L., Leake, J.R., Banwart, S.A., McMaster, T.J. (2012). Nanoscale channels on ectomycorrhizal-colonized chlorite: Evidence for plant-driven fungal dissolution. *Journal of Geophysical Research: Biogeosciences*, 117(G3). doi: 10.1029/2012JG002016.

Gerard, F., Clement, A., Fritz, B., Crovisier, J.L. (1996). Introduction of transport phenomena into the thermo-kinetic code KINDIS: The code KIRMAT. *Comptes rendus de l'Academie des sciences. Serie II. Sciences de la terre et des planètes*, 322(5), 377–384.

Gleeson, D.B., Clipson, N., Melville, K., Gadd, G.M., Mcdermott, F.P. (2005). Characterization of fungal community structure on a weathered pegmatitic granite. *Microbial Ecology*, 50(3), 360–368.

Glowa, K., Arocena, J., Massicotte, H. (2003). Extraction of potassium and/or magnesium from selected soil minerals by Piloderma. *Geomicrobiology Journal*, 20(2), 99–111.

Godderis, Y., Francois, L.M., Probst, A., Schott, J., Moncoulon, D., Labat, D., Viville, D. (2006). Modelling weathering processes at the catchment scale: The WITCH numerical model. *Geochimica et Cosmochimica Acta*, 70(5), 1128–1147.

Golubev, S.V. and Pokrovsky, O.S. (2006). Experimental study of the effect of organic ligands on diopside dissolution kinetics. *Chemical Geology*, 235, 377–389.

Gommeaux, M., Barakat, M., Montagnac, G., Christen, R., Guyot, F., Heulin, T. (2010). Mineral and bacterial diversities of desert sand grains from South-East Morocco. *Geomicrobiology Journal*, 27(1), 76–92.

Grandstaff, D.E. (1986). The dissolution rate of forsteritic olivine from Hawaiian beach sand. In *Rates of Chemical Weathering of Rocks and Minerals*, Colman, S.M. and Dethier, D.P. (eds). Academic Press, Orlando.

Green, F., Larsen, M.J., Winandy, J.E., Highley, T.L. (1991). Rolle of oxalic acid in incipient brown rot decay. *Material Und Organismen*, 26(3), 191–213.

Hameeda, B., Reddy, Y.H.K., Rupela, O.P., Kumar, G.N., Reddy, G. (2006). Effect of carbon substrates on rock phosphate solubilization by bacteria from composts and macrofauna. *Current Microbiology*, 53(4), 298–302.

Haselwandter, K. and Winkelmann, G. (2002). Ferricrocin – An ectomycorrhizal siderophore of *Cenococcum geophilum*. *Biometals*, 15, 73–77.

Hazen, R.M., Papineau, D., Bleeker, W., Downs, R.T., Ferry, J.M., Mccoy, T.J., Sverjensky, D.A., Yang, H. (2008). Mineral evolution. *American Mineralogist*, 93(11–12), 1693–1720.

Heinonsalo, J., Hurme, K.R., Sen, R. (2004). Recent C-14-labelled assimilate allocation to Scots pine seedling root and mycorrhizosphere compartments developed on reconstructed podzol humus, E- and B-mineral horizons. *Plant and Soil*, 259(1–2), 111–121.

Hellmann, R., Wood, S.A., Renders, P.J.N., Gratier, J.-P., Guiguet, R. (2002). Experimental pressure solution compaction of chalk in aqueous solutions: Part 1. Deformation behavior and chemistry. In *Water-Rock Interactions, Ore Deposits, and Environmental Geochemistry: A Tribute to David A. Crerar*, Hellmann, R. and Wood, S.A. (eds). The Geochemical Society, Washington, D.C.

Hellmann, R., Wirth, R., Daval, D., Barnes, J.-P., Penisson, J.-M., Tisserand, D., Epicier, T., Florin, B., Hervig, R.L. (2012). Unifying natural and laboratory chemical weathering with interfacial dissolution–reprecipitation: A study based on the nanometer-scale chemistry of fluid–silicate interfaces. *Chemical Geology*, 294–295, 203–216.

Hopf, J., Langenhorst, F., Pollok, K., Merten, D., Kothe, E. (2009). Influence of microorganisms on biotite dissolution: An experimental approach. *Geochemistry*, 69, 45–56.

Howard, R.J., Ferrari, M.A., Roach, D.H., Money, N.P. (1991). Penetration of hard substrates by a fungus employing enormous turgor pressures. *Proceedings of the National Academy of Sciences of the United States of America*, 88(24), 11281–11284.

Johnson, D.B. (2014). Biomining–biotechnologies for extracting and recovering metals from ores and waste materials. *Current Opinion in Biotechnology*, 30, 24–31.

Jones, A.A. and Bennett, P.C. (2014). Mineral microniches control the diversity of subsurface microbial populations. *Geomicrobiology Journal*, 31(3), 246–261.

Jones, D.L., Dennis, P.G., Owen, A.G., Van Hees, P.A.W. (2003). Organic acid behavior in soils – Misconceptions and knowledge gaps. *Plant and Soil*, 248(1–2), 31–41.

Jongmans, A.G., Vanbreemen, N., Lundstrom, U., Vanhees, P.A.W., Finlay, R.D., Srinivasan, M., Unestam, T., Giesler, R., Melkerud, P.A., Olsson, M. (1997). Rock-eating fungi. *Nature*, 389(6652), 682–683.

Kalinowski, B.E., Liermann, L.J., Brantley, S.L., Barnes, A., Pantano, C.G. (2000). X-ray photoelectron evidence for bacteria-enhanced dissolution of hornblende. *Geochimica et Cosmochimica Acta*, 64(8), 1331–1343.

Kim, K.Y., Jordan, D., Krishnan, H.B. (1998). Expression of genes from *Rahnella aquatilis* that are necessary for mineral phosphate solubilization in *Escherichia coli*. *FEMS Microbiology Letters*, 159(1), 121–127.

Kim, Y.H., Bae, B., Choung, Y.K. (2005). Optimization of biological phosphorus removal from contaminated sediments with phosphate-solubilizing microorganisms. *Journal of Bioscience and Bioengineering*, 99(1), 23–29.

Kirtzel, J., Siegel, D., Krause, K., Kothe, E. (2017). Stone-eating fungi: Mechanisms in bioweathering and the potential role of laccases in black slate degradation with the basidiomycete Schizophyllum commune. In *Advances in Applied Microbiology*, Sariaslani, S. and Gadd, G.M. (eds). Academic Press, Cambridge, MA.

Kostka, J.E., Stucki, J.W., Nealson, K.H., Wu, J. (1996). Reduction of structural Fe(III) in smectite by a pure culture of *Shewanella putrefaciens* strain MR-1. *Clays and Clay Minerals*, 44(4), 522–529.

Krishnaraj, P.U. and Goldstein, A.H. (2001). Cloning of a *Serratia marcescens* DNA fragment that induces quinoprotein glucose dehydrogenase-mediated gluconic acid production in Escherichia coli in the presence of stationary phase *Serratia marcescens*. *FEMS Microbiology Letters*, 205(2), 215–220.

Lapanje, A., Wimmersberger, C., Furrer, G., Brunner, I., Frey, B. (2012). Pattern of elemental release during the granite dissolution can be changed by aerobic heterotrophic bacterial strains isolated from Damma glacier (central Alps) deglaciated granite sand. *Microbial Ecology*, 63(4), 865–882.

Lasaga, A.C. (1981). Transition state theory. In *Kinetics of Geochemical Process*, Lasaga, A.C. and Kirkpatrick, R.J (eds). Mineralogical Society of America, Chantilly.

Lasaga, A.C. and Blum, A.E. (1986). Surface chemistry, etch pits and mineral-water reactions. *Geochimica et Cosmochimica Acta*, 50(10), 2363–2379.

Lasaga, A.C. and Lüttge, A. (2001). Variation of crystal dissolution rate based on a dissolution stepwave model. *Science*, 291, 2400–2404.

Lau, M.C.Y., Kieft, T.L., Kuloyo, O., Linage-Alvarez, B., Van Heerden, E., Lindsay, M.R., Magnabosco, C., Wang, W., Wiggins, J.B., Guo, L. et al. (2016). An oligotrophic deep-subsurface community dependent on syntrophy is dominated by sulfur-driven autotrophic denitrifiers. *Proceedings of the National Academy of Sciences*, 113(49), E7927.

Lee, G.H. and Stotzky, G. (1999). Transformation and survival of donor, recipient, and transformants of *Bacillus subtilis* in vitro and in soil. *Soil Biology & Biochemistry*, 31(11), 1499–1508.

Lepleux, C., Turpault, M.P., Oger, P., Frey-Klett, P., Uroz, S. (2012). Correlation of the abundance of Betaproteobacteria on mineral surfaces with mineral weathering in forest soils. *Applied and Environmental Microbiology*, 78(19), 7114–7119.

Li, Z.B., Liu, L.W., Chen, J., Teng, H.H. (2016). Cellular dissolution at hypha- and spore-mineral interfaces revealing unrecognized mechanisms and scales of fungal weathering. *Geology*, 44(4), 319–322.

Liermann, L.J., Kalinowski, B.E., Brantley, S.L., Ferry, J.G. (2000). Role of bacterial siderophores in dissolution of hornblende. *Geochimica et Cosmochimica Acta*, 64(4), 587–602.

Lower, S.K., Hochella, M.F., Beveridge, T.J. (2001). Bacterial recognition of mineral surfaces: Nanoscale interactions between *Shewanella* and α-FeOOH. *Science*, 292(5520), 1360–1363.

Lucas, R.W., Klaminder, J., Futter, M.N., Bishop, K.H., Egnell, G., Laudon, H., Hogberg, P. (2011). A meta-analysis of the effects of nitrogen additions on base cations: Implications for plants, soils, and streams. *Forest Ecology and Management*, 262(2), 95–104.

Lüttge, A. (2006). Crystal dissolution kinetics and Gibbs free energy. *Journal of Electron Spectroscopy and Related Phenomena*, 150(2–3), 248–259.

Lüttge, A., Zhang, L., Nealson, K. (2005). Mineral surfaces and their implications for microbial attachment: Results from Monte Carlo simulations and direct surface observations. *American Journal of Science*, 305(6–8), 766–790.

Mahmood, S., Finlay, R.D., Erland, S., Wallander, H. (2001). Solubilisation and colonisation of wood ash by ectomycorrhizal fungi isolated from a wood ash fertilised spruce forest. *FEMS Microbiology Ecology*, 35(2), 151–161.

Miot, J. and Etique, M. (2016). Formation and transformation of iron-bearing minerals by iron(II)-oxidizing and iron(III)-reducing bacteria. In *Iron Oxides: From Nature to Applications*, Faivre, D. (ed.). Wiley-VCH, Weinheim.

Mitchell, A.C., Lafreniere, M.J., Skidmore, M.L., Boyd, E.S. (2013). Influence of bedrock mineral composition on microbial diversity in a subglacial environment. *Geology*, 41(8), 855–858.

Modak, J.M., Vasan, S.S., Natarajan, K.A. (1999). Calcium removal from bauxite using *Paenibacillus polymyxa*. *Minerals & Metallurgical Processing*, 16(4), 6–12.

Moulton, K.L. and Berner, R.A. (1998). Quantification of the effect of plants on weathering: Studies in Iceland. *Geology*, 26(10), 895–898.

Mustin, C., Berthelin, J., Marion, P., Dedonato, P. (1992). Corrosion and electrochemical oxidation of a pyrite by thiobacillus-ferrooxidans. *Applied and Environmental Microbiology*, 58(4), 1175–1182.

Nadal Jimenez, P., Koch, G., Thompson, J.A., Xavier, K.B., Cool, R.H., Quax, W.J. (2012). The multiple signaling systems regulating virulence in *Pseudomonas aeruginosa*. *Microbiology and Molecular Biology Reviews*, 76(1), 46–65.

Nadell, C.D., Drescher, K., Foster, K.R. (2016). Spatial structure, cooperation and competition in biofilms. *Nature Reviews Microbiology*, 14(9), 589–600.

Napieralski, S.A., Buss, H.L., Brantley, S.L., Lee, S., Xu, H., Roden, E.E. (2019). Microbial chemolithotrophy mediates oxidative weathering of granitic bedrock. *Proceedings of the National Academy of Sciences*, 116(52), 26394–26401. doi: 10.1073/pnas.190997011.

Neilands, J.B. (1982). Mocrobial envelope proteins related to iron. *Annual Review of Microbiology*, 36, 285–309.

Newman, D.K. and Kolter, R. (2000). A role for excreted quinones in extracellular electron transfer. *Nature*, 405(6782), 94–97.

Olsson, B.A., Bengtsson, J., Lundkvist, H. (1996). Effects of different forest harvest intensities on the pools of exchangeable cations in coniferous forest soils. *Forest Ecology and Management*, 84(1–3), 135–147.

Olsson-Francis, K., Van Houdt, R., Mergeay, M., Leys, N., Cockell, C.S. (2010). Microarray analysis of a microbe-mineral interaction. *Geobiology*, 8(5), 446–456.

Page, W.J. (1987). Iron-dependent production of hydroxamate by sodium-dependent azotobacter chroococcum. *Applied and Environmental Microbiology*, 53(7), 1418–1424.

Page, W.J. and Huyer, M. (1984). Derepression of the Azotobacter-Vinelandii siderophore system, using iron-containing minerals to limit iron repletion. *Journal of Bacteriology*, 158(2), 496–502.

Palandri, J.L. and Kharaka, Y.K. (2004). A compilation of rate parameters of water–mineral interaction kinetics for application to geochemical modeling. Open File Report, U.S. Geological Survey, Menlo Park.

Perez, A., Rossano, S., Trcera, N., Huguenot, D., Fourdrin, C., Verney-Carron, A., Van Hullebusch, E.D., Guyot, F. (2016). Bioalteration of synthetic Fe(III)-, Fe(II)-bearing basaltic glasses and Fe-free glass in the presence of the heterotrophic bacteria strain *Pseudomonas aeruginosa*: Impact of siderophores. *Geochimica et Cosmochimica Acta*, 188, 147–162.

Phillips-Lander, C.M., Fowle, D.A., Taunton, A., Hernandez, W., Mora, M., Moore, D., Shinogle, H., Roberts, J.A. (2014). Silicate dissolution in Las Pailas Thermal Field: Implications for microbial weathering in acidic volcanic hydrothermal spring systems. *Geomicrobiology Journal*, 31(1), 23–41.

Pollet-Villard, M., Daval, D., Fritz, B., Knauss, K.G., Schäfer, G., Ackerer, P. (2016). Influence of etch pit development on the surface area and dissolution kinetics of the orthoclase (001) surface. *Chemical Geology*, 447, 79–92.

Puente, M.E., Bashan, Y., Li, C.Y., Lebsky, V.K. (2004). Microbial populations and activities in the rhizoplane of rock-weathering desert plants. I. Root colonization and weathering of igneous rocks. *Plant Biology*, 6(5), 629–642.

Puente, M.E., Li, C.Y., Bashan, Y. (2009). Rock-degrading endophytic bacteria in cacti. *Environmental and Experimental Botany*, 66(3), 389–401.

Quirk, J., Beerling, D.J., Banwart, S.A., Kakonyi, G., Romero-Gonzalez, M.E., Leake, J.R. (2012). Evolution of trees and mycorrhizal fungi intensifies silicate mineral weathering. *Biology Letters*, 8(6), 1006–1011. doi: 10.1098/rsbl.2012.0503.

Ranger, J. and Turpault, M.P. (1999). Input-output nutrient budgets as a diagnostic tool for sustainable forest management. *Forest Ecology and Management*, 122(1–2), 139–154.

Rimstidt, J.D. (2015). Diffusion control of quartz and forsterite dissolution rates. *Applied Geochemistry*, 61, 99–108. doi: 10.1016/j.apgeochem.2015.05.020.

Rogers, J.R. and Bennett, P.C. (2004). Mineral stimulation of subsurface microorganisms: Release of limiting nutrients from silicates. *Chemical Geology*, 203(1–2), 91–108.

Rogers, J.R., Bennett, P.C., Choi, W.J. (1998). Feldspars as a source of nutrients for microorganisms. *American Mineralogist*, 83(11–12), 1532–1540.

Rosling, A., Lindahl, B.D., Finlay, R.D. (2004a). Carbon allocation to ectomycorrhizal roots and mycelium colonising different mineral substrates. *New Phytologist*, 162(3), 795–802.

Rosling, A., Lindahl, B.D., Taylor, A.F.S., Finlay, R.D. (2004b). Mycelial growth and substrate acidification of ectomycorrhizal fungi in response to different minerals. *Fems Microbiology Ecology*, 47(1), 31–37.

Rossi, G. (1978). Potassium recovary through leucite bioleaching: Possibilities and limitations. In *Metallurgical Applications of Bacterial Leaching and Related Microbiological Phenomena*, Murr, L.E. and Torma, A.E. (eds). Academic Press, New York.

Rudawska, M. and Leski, T. (1998). Aluminium tolerance of different *Paxillus involutus* Fr. strains originating from polluted and nonpolluted sites. *Acta Societatis Botanicorum Poloniae*, 67(1), 115–122.

Saccone, L., Gazzè, S.A., Duran, A.L., Leake, J.R., Banwart, S.A., Ragnarsdottir, K.V., Smits, M.M., Mcmaster, T.J. (2012). High resolution characterization of ectomycorrhizal fungal-mineral interactions in axenic microcosm experiments. *Biogeochemistry*, 111(1–3), 411–425.

Saha, R., Saha, N., Donofrio, R.S., Bestervelt, L.L. (2013). Microbial siderophores: A mini review. *Journal of Basic Microbiology*, 53(4), 303–317.

Sayer, J.A., Kierans, M., Gadd, G.M. (1997). Solubilisation of some naturally occurring metal-bearing minerals, limescale and lead phosphate by *Aspergillus niger*. *FEMS Microbiology Letters*, 154(1), 29–35.

Schmalenberger, A., Duran, A.L., Bray, A.W., Bridge, J., Bonneville, S., Benning, L.G., Romero-Gonzalez, M.E., Leake, J.R., Banwart, S.A. (2015). Oxalate secretion by ectomycorrhizal *Paxillus involutus* is mineral-specific and controls calcium weathering from minerals. *Scientific Reports*, 5(1), 12187.

Schott, J., Pokrovsky, O.S., Oelkers, E.H. (2009). The link between mineral dissolution/precipitation kinetics and solution chemistry. *Thermodynamics and Kinetics of Water-Rock Interaction*, 70, 207–258.

Schwartzman, D.W. and Volk, T. (1989). Biotic enhancement of weathering and the habitability of Earth. *Nature*, 340(6233), 457–460.

Smith, S.E. and Read, D. (1997). *Mycorrhizal Symbiosis*, 2nd edition. Academic Press, London.

Smits, M.M., Hoffland, E., Jongmans, A.G., Van Breemen, N. (2005). Contribution of mineral tunneling to total feldspar weathering. *Geoderma*, 125(1–2), 59–69.

Sokolova, T.A. (2011). The role of soil biota in the weathering of minerals: A review of literature. *Eurasian Soil Science*, 44(1), 56–72.

Song, W., Ogawa, N., Oguchi, C.T., Hatta, T., Matsukura, Y. (2007). Effect of *Bacillus subtilis* on granite weathering: A laboratory experiment. *Catena*, 70(3), 275–281.

Steefel, C.I. and Maher, K. (2009). Fluid–rock interaction: A reactive transport approach. *Reviews in Mineralogy and Geochemistry*, 70(1), 485–532.

Steefel, C.I., Appelo, C.A.J., Arora, B., Jacques, D., Kalbacher, T., Kolditz, O., Lagneau, V., Lichtner, P.C., Mayer, K.U., Meeussen, J.C.L. et al. (2015). Reactive transport codes for subsurface environmental simulation. *Computational Geosciences*, 19(3), 445–478.

Sun, L., Xiao, L., Xiao, B., Wang, W., Pan, C., Wang, S., Lian, B. (2013). Differences in the gene expressive quantities of carbonic anhydrase and cysteine synthase in the weathering of potassium-bearing minerals by *Aspergillus niger*. *Science China Earth Sciences*, 56(12), 2135–2140.

Sverdrup, H., Hagen-Thorn, A., Holmqvist, J., Wallman, P., Warfvinge, P., Walse, C., Alveteg, M. (2002). Biogeochemical processes and mechanisms. In *Developing Principles and Models for Sustainable Forestry in Sweden*, Sverdrup, H. and Stjernquist, I. (eds). Springer Netherlands, Dordrecht.

Thorseth, I.H., Furnes, H., Tumyr, O. (1995). Textural and chemical effects of bacterial activity on basaltic glass: An experimental approach. *Chemical Geology*, 119(1), 139–160.

Toro, M., Azcon, R., Barea, J.M. (1997). Improvement of arbuscular mycorrhiza development by inoculation of soil with phosphate-solubilizing rhizobacteria to improve rock phosphate bioavailability (P-32) and nutrient cycling. *Applied and Environmental Microbiology*, 63(11), 4408–4412.

Torsvik, T., Furnes, H., Muehlenbachs, K., Thorseth, I.H., Tumyr, O. (1998). Evidence for microbial activity at the glass-alteration interface in oceanic basalts. *Earth and Planetary Science Letters*, 162(1–4), 165–176.

Ullman, W.J., Kirchman, D.L., Welch, S.A., Vandevivere, P. (1996). Laboratory evidence for microbially mediated silicate mineral dissolution in nature. *Chemical Geology*, 132(1–4), 11–17.

Uroz, S., Chhabra, S.R., Camara, M., Williams, P., Oger, P., Dessaux, Y. (2005). N-Acylhomoserine lactone quorum-sensing molecules are modified and degraded by *Rhodococcus erythropolis* W2 by both amidolytic and novel oxidoreductase activities. *Microbiology*, 151(10), 3313–3322.

Uroz, S., Calvaruso, C., Turpault, M.P., Pierrat, J.C., Mustin, C., Frey-Klett, P. (2007). Effect of the mycorrhizosphere on the genotypic and metabolic diversity of the bacterial communities involved in mineral weathering in a forest soil. *Applied and Environmental Microbiology*, 73(9), 3019–3027.

Uroz, S., Calvaruso, C., Turpault, M.-P., Frey-Klett, P. (2009a). Mineral weathering by bacteria: Ecology, actors and mechanisms. *Trends in Microbiology*, 17(8), 378–387.

Uroz, S., Calvaruso, C., Turpault, M.P., Sarniguet, A., De Boer, W., Leveau, J.H.J., Frey-Klett, P. (2009b). Efficient mineral weathering is a distinctive functional trait of the bacterial genus *Collimonas*. *Soil Biology & Biochemistry*, 41(10), 2178–2186.

Uroz, S., Turpault, M.P., Delaruelle, C., Mareschal, L., Pierrat, J.C., Frey-Klett, P. (2012). Minerals affect the specific diversity of forest soil bacterial communities. *Geomicrobiology Journal*, 29(1), 88–98.

Uroz, S., Ioannidis, P., Lengelle, J., Cébron, A., Morin, E., Buée, M., Martin, F. (2013). Functional Assays and metagenomic analyses reveals differences between the microbial communities inhabiting the soil horizons of a Norway Spruce Plantation. *PLOS ONE*, 8(2), e55929.

Uroz, S., Kelly, L.C., Turpault, M.P., Lepleux, C., Frey-Klett, P. (2015). The mineralosphere concept: Mineralogical control of the distribution and function of mineral-associatec bacterial communities. *Trends in Microbiology*, 23(12), 751–762.

Uroz, S., Oger, P., Tisserand, E., Cebron, A., Turpault, M.P., Buee, M., De Boer, W., Leveau, J.H.J., Frey-Klett, P. (2016). Specific impacts of beech and Norway spruce on the structure and diversity of the rhizosphere and soil microbial communities. *Scientific Reports*, 6, 1–11.

Van Breemen, N., Finlay, R., Lundstrom, U., Jongmans, A.G., Giesler, R., Olsson, M. (2000a). Mycorrhizal weathering: A true case of mineral plant nutrition? *Biogeochemistry*, 49(1), 53–67.

Van Breemen, N., Lundstrom, U.S., Jongmans, A.G. (2000b). Do plants drive podzolization via rock-eating mycorrhizal fungi? *Geoderma*, 94(2–4), 163–171.

Van Der Heijden, G., Legout, A., Pollier, B., Mareschal, L., Turpault, M.P., Ranger, J., Dambrine, E. (2013). Assessing Mg and Ca depletion from broadleaf forest soils and potential causes – A case study in the Morvan Mountains. *Forest Ecology and Management*, 293, 65–78.

Van Hees, P.A.W., Godbold, D.L., Jentschke, G., Jones, D.L. (2003). Impact of ectomycorrhizas on the concentration and biodegradation of simple organic acids in a forest soil. *European Journal of Soil Science*, 54(4), 697–706.

Van Hees, P.A.W., Rosling, A., Finlay, R.D. (2006). The impact of trees, ectomycorrhiza and potassium availability on simple organic compounds and dissolved organic carbon in soil. *Soil Biology & Biochemistry*, 38(7), 1912–1923.

Van Scholl, L., Smits, M.M., Hoffland, E. (2006). Ectomycorrhizal weathering of the soil minerals muscovite and hornblende. *New Phytologist*, 171(4), 805–814.

Van Scholl, L., Kuyper, T.W., Smits, M.M., Landeweert, R., Hoffland, E., Van Breemen, N. (2008). Rock-eating mycorrhizas: Their role in plant nutrition and biogeochemical cycles. *Plant and Soil*, 303(1–2), 35–47.

Vance, D., Teagle, D.a.H., Foster, G.L. (2009). Variable Quaternary chemical weathering fluxes and imbalances in marine geochemical budgets. *Nature*, 458(7237), 493–496.

Vasan, S.S., Modak, J.M., Natarajan, K.A. (2001). Some recent advances in the bioprocessing of bauxite. *International Journal of Mineral Processing*, 62(1–4), 173–186.

Vassilev, N., Vassileva, M., Nikolaeva, I. (2006). Simultaneous P-solubilizing and biocontrol activity of microorganisms: Potentials and future trends. *Applied Microbiology and Biotechnology*, 71(2), 137–144.

Vera, M., Krok, B., Bellenberg, S., Sand, W., Poetsch, A. (2013). Shotgun proteomics study of early biofilm formation process of *Acidithiobacillus ferrooxidans* ATCC 23270 on pyrite. *Proteomics*, 13(7), 1133–1144.

Wallander, H. and Wickman, T. (1999). Biotite and microcline as potassium sources in ectomycorrhizal and non-mycorrhizal *Pinus sylvestris* seedlings. *Mycorrhiza*, 9(1), 25–32.

Warfvinge, P. and Sverdrup, H. (1992). Calculating critical loads of acid deposition with PROFILE – A steady-state soil chemistry model. *Water Air and Soil Pollution*, 63(1–2), 119–143.

Wei, Z., Kierans, M., Gadd, G.M. (2012). A model sheet mineral system to study fungal bioweathering of mica. *Geomicrobiology Journal*, 29(4), 323–331.

Welch, S.A., Barker, W.W., Banfield, J.F. (1999). Microbial extracellular polysaccharides and plagioclase dissolution. *Geochimica et Cosmochimica Acta*, 63(9), 1405–1419.

Wengel, M., Kothe, E., Schmidt, C.M., Heide, K., Gleixner, G. (2006). Degradation of organic matter from black shales and charcoal by the wood-rotting fungus Schizophyllum commune and release of DOC and heavy metals in the aqueous phase. *Science of the Total Environment*, 367(1), 383–393.

White, A.F. and Brantley, S.L. (2003). The effect of time on the weathering of silicate minerals: Why do weathering rates differ in the laboratory and field? *Chemical Geology*, 202(3–4), 479–506.

White, A.F., Schulz, M.S., Vivit, D.V., Bullen, T.D., Fitzpatrick, J. (2012). The impact of biotic/abiotic interfaces in mineral nutrient cycling: A study of soils of the Santa Cruz chronosequence, California. *Geochimica et Cosmochimica Acta*, 77, 62–85.

Wild, B., Daval, D., Guyot, F., Knauss, K.G., Pollet-Villard, M., Imfeld, G. (2016). pH-dependent control of feldspar dissolution rate by altered surface layers. *Chemical Geology*, 442, 148–159.

Wild, B., Imfeld, G., Guyot, F., Daval, D. (2018). Early stages of bacterial community adaptation to silicate aging. *Geology*, 46(6), 555–558.

Wild, B., Imfeld, G., Daval, D. (2021). Direct measurement of fungal contribution to silicate weathering rates in soil. *Geology*, 49, 1055–1058.

Wogelius, R.A. and Walther, J.V. (1991). Olivine dissolution at 25°C: Effects of pH, CO_2, and organic acids. *Geochimica et Cosmochimica Acta*, 55, 943–954.

Wu, L., Jacobson, A.D., Hausner, M. (2008). Characterization of elemental release during microbe-granite interactions at T = 28 degrees C. *Geochimica et Cosmochimica Acta*, 72(4), 1076–1095.

Xiao, Y. and Lasaga, A.C. (1994). Ab initio quantum mechanical studies of the kinetics and mechanisms of silicate dissolution: H+(H3O+) catalysis. *Geochimica et Cosmochimica Acta*, 58(24), 5379–5400.

Yuan, L., Huang, J., Li, X., Christie, P. (2004). Biological mobilization of potassium from clay minerals by ectomycorrhizal fungi and eucalypt seedling roots. *Plant and Soil*, 262, 351–361.

Zhalnina, K., Louie, K.B., Hao, Z., Mansoori, N., Da Rocha, U.N., Shi, S., Cho, H., Karaoz, U., Loqué, D., Bowen, B.P. et al. (2018). Dynamic root exudate chemistry and microbial substrate preferences drive patterns in rhizosphere microbial community assembly. *Nature Microbiology*, 3(4), 470–480.

2

Biomineralization: The Formation of Minerals by Living Organisms

Karim BENZERARA
IMPMC, UMR 7590, CNRS, Sorbonne Université, Paris, France

2.1. Introduction

Living organisms frequently form minerals. This may seem surprising at first. Indeed, we tend to associate minerals with inorganic or inanimate matter, unlike life, which we associate more with animate and organic matter. Three kingdoms have long been distinguished, notably in Linnaeus' *Systema naturae*: mineral, plant and animal. And yet, as we will see in this chapter, a diversity of living beings has formed numerous minerals called biominerals, as well as numerous rocks on the Earth's surface over geological time. The so-called biomineralization process is thus a key player in geosphere/biosphere interactions. The term biomineralization, designating the formation of minerals by living organisms, appeared for the first time in 1970 in the literature (Dauphin 2023). However, the scientific study of these processes and the mineral structures formed by living organisms is much older. We can cite, for example, the drawings of skeletons and bones by Leonardo da Vinci at the end of the 15th century, then the studies of the microscopic structure of bones by Havers in 1691. Studies of different biomineralization systems multiplied in the 18th century (Dauphin 2023).

Let us define the key terms in this chapter. A crystal is most often a solid, whose constituent atoms or molecules are arranged periodically in space (Figure 2.1).

Interactions between the Geosphere and the Biosphere,
coordinated by Karim BENZERARA and Christophe THOMAZO.

Atoms and molecules are arranged in planes, spaced at defined distances and intersecting at very precise angles. We are surrounded by crystals every day, such as quartz crystals making up the sand on beaches, halite crystals in table salt, diamond in a ring, graphite in a pencil tip, crystals of semiconductors in electronics or, even (but less classically), a crystal of proteins (or DNA) synthesized in the laboratory. The crystalline state is opposite to the amorphous (or vitreous) state, which characterizes a solid with atoms that are not periodically arranged as mentioned above (Figure 2.1). The glass in a window, the frustule of diatoms or even the radiolarian test are examples of an amorphous state with an elementary chemical composition (SiO_2) identical to that of a quartz crystal. In reality, we understand that intermediate states exist between the perfect crystal and the entirely amorphous state: these are solids in which we can find a locally periodic arrangement of atoms (on the scale of a few nanometers/micrometers) but whose periodicity is lost on a larger spatial scale. The way in which atoms are arranged, called its structure, is important to know because it governs all of the physical, optical and chemical properties of the solids in question.

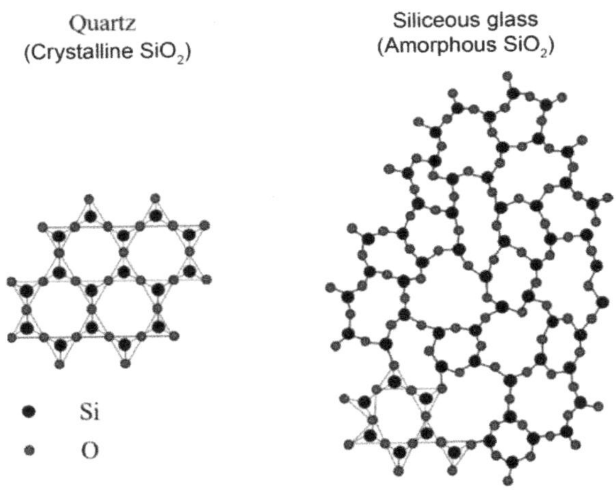

Figure 2.1. *Organization at the atomic scale of atoms in a crystalline solid (quartz mineral) and an amorphous solid (siliceous glass). For a color version of this figure, see www.iste.co.uk/benzerara/geosphere.zip*

The term "mineral" is more ambiguous. It is sometimes used, notably by chemists, in the sense of an inorganic compound (as in "mineral matter"), in opposition to organic, which includes compounds formed from reduced carbon. On the other hand, for a mineralogist, "mineral" is an abbreviated way of saying a "mineral species" and in this case the definition is very strict, laid down by the International Mineralogy Association. It is a solid of which there is at least one occurrence in nature (a mineral species cannot be solely synthetic) and which is characterized by a given chemical composition and crystal structure (for more details, read Box 2.1). It is in this sense that we will use the term mineral in this chapter. We then give a name to this mineral species: for example, quartz, calcite, aragonite, etc. In this sense, a "mineral" (in the sense of a mineral species) is necessarily crystalline. Still according to this meaning, the molecules constituting the mineral can be inorganic or organic. There are thus mineral species composed of organic molecules, such as weddellite, a mineral composed of calcium oxalate dihydrate, a major component of some kidney stones. Finally, we understand that if we have well-crystallized solids, we can sometimes extend this notion of mineral (in the sense of the mineralogist) to compounds that are not necessarily perfect crystals; this is, for example, the case for opals. Minerals formed by living organisms are often poorly crystalline compounds. Finally, note that minerals are constituents of rocks, whether magmatic, metamorphic or sedimentary. Therefore, dealing with the formation of minerals by life means questioning the formation of rocks by life.

In this chapter, we will explain how living organisms can form minerals and rocks, before showing that there has been a great diversity of biomineralizing organisms throughout geological time. Finally, we will discuss a certain number of effects that this biomineralization process has on the functioning of the Earth system and on living organisms themselves.

New mineral species are named and classified following their examination by a commission within the International Mineralogical Association (Nickel and Grice 1998). A new mineral species is defined on the basis of the description of a specimen in a natural object, terrestrial or extraterrestrial, with a new structure and/or chemical composition. Solids formed specifically by humans are not considered minerals, unless they are formed indirectly through the transformation of pre-existing minerals following anthropogenic activities. The rules herein are subject to interpretation and may change. More generally, certain rules stipulate that a substance that is only of biological origin and does not have a "geological" occurrence cannot be defined as a mineral species. Here again, the example of hazenite ($KNaMg_2(PO_4)_2,14H_2O$) and the great prevalence of certain phases in life question this rule. Finally, except in special cases, only crystalline phases generally make it possible to define a mineral species. To date, there are nearly 5,900 mineral species.

There are then different ways of classifying mineral species. One of these classifications, established by the mineralogist James Dwight Dana in the mid-19th century, sorts species first according to their chemistry and then according to their atomic structure. We thus have an initial division into nine sets on the basis of chemistry

(01. native elements, 02. sulfides, 03. oxides and hydroxides, 04. halides, 05. carbonates–nitrates–borates, 06. sulfates–chromates–selenates, 07. phosphates–arsenates–vanadates, 08. silicates, 09. organic minerals). Then, within each division, there are several subdivisions on a chemical or structural basis. Within carbonates, we distinguish anhydrous carbonates with the simple formula ACO_3; within this subdivision, the calcite group, which is in fact a set of mineral species with different chemistries (e.g. calcite *s.s.* – $CaCO_3$, magnesite – $MgCO_3$, siderite – $FeCO_3$, etc.) but all with the same atomic symmetries (defined by what we call a space group).

Other classifications might be possible for other perspectives. For example, Cleland et al. (2021) proposed a classification of mineral species based on their geological history (date of appearance, abundance over geological time, etc.).

Box 2.1. *Mineral species, definition and classification*

2.2. Diversity of biominerals and biomineralizing organisms

Biominerals cover a great diversity of mineral species, and are formed by a very broad diversity of biomineralizing organisms, distributed across all kingdoms of life. Attempts to list them remain tentative, as new biomineralization examples are discovered each year (Lowenstam 1981). Lowenstam and Weiner (1989) counted more than 60 mineral species found among biominerals and already noted the progressive increase in this list over time (Table 2.1). Hazen and Morrison (2022) count 77 mineral species involved as biominerals and nearly 2707 whose formation is more or less directly influenced by the action of living organisms. These mineral species are distributed across most of the 10 known mineral classes (e.g. native elements/sulfides/oxides and hydroxides/carbonates/sulfates, etc.). Moreover, Ehrlich et al. (2008) counted among the biomineralizing organisms, approximately 128,000 species of molluscs, 800 species of corals, 5,000 species of sponges including 525 silicifying ones, 700 species of green, red or brown calcifying algae, more than 300 species of benthic foraminifera, and 200,000 species of diatoms. The number of species of biomineralizing bacteria has not been quantified to date. Making progress on how biomineralization works in a given organism is a long-term task, as we will see later. Also, the concepts of biomineralogy have progressed greatly on the basis of a few model biomineralizing organisms. However, it is still difficult to assess how the diversity of living organisms affect the formation of minerals. Here, it is a question of studying diversity from another angle: how do we recognize a biomineralizing organism, and/or what distinguishes it from a non-biomineralizing organism? What are the differences between biominerals and their abiotic structural counterparts?

	Formula	Examples of organisms		Formula	Examples of organisms
Native elements			Phosphates		
a or y sulfur (Rosickyite)	S	Cyanobacteria, sulfur-oxidizing bacteria	Fluoroapatite	$Ca(PO_4)_3F$	Sharks, parrot fish
Carbonates			Struvite	$Mg(NH_1)(PO_4).6H_2O$	Fungi, ureolytic bacteria
Calcite	$CaCO_3$	Numerous protists, algae, metazoa, plants, bacteria	Vivianite; amorphous iron phosphate, hydroxyapatite	$Fe_3(PO_4)_2.8H_2O$ and $FePO_4$	Iron-reducing bacteria, polychaete annelids
Aragonite	$CaCO_3$	Mother-of-pearl from many mollusks, corals		$Ca_2(PO_4)_3(O11)$	Vertebrate skeletons, bacteria, plant trichomes
Vaterite	$CaCO_3$	Rhodophytes, mollusks	**Sulfides**		
Monohydrocalcite	$CaCO_3H_2O$	Mollusks, chordates, cacti, bacteria	Acanthite	Ag_2S	Fungi, bacteria
Dolomite and high Mg calcite	$CaMg(CO_3)_2$	Ants, bacteria	Greigite	Fe_3S_1	Magnetotactic bacteria
Amorphous calcium carbonate	$CaCO_3H_2O$	Mollusks, corals, algae, bacteria	Orpiment	As_3S_3	Bacteria
Siderite	$FeCO_3$	Iron-reducing bacteria	Pyrite	FeS_2	Sulfur-reducing bacteria
Sulfates			**Hydroxydes**		
Barite	$BaSO_4$	Euglenzoa, foraminifera, haptophytes	Birnessite	$NAMn_4O_8.3H_2O$	Various bacteria
Celestite	$SrSO_4$	Euglenozoa, charophytes, cilia	Ferrihydrite	$Fe_{4-s}(OH,O)$	Chitons, various bacteria, ferritin from animals and plants

	Formula	Examples of organisms		Formula	Examples of organisms
Native elements			Phosphates		
Jarosite	$KFe_3(SO_4)_2(O11)_6$	Fungi, iron-oxidizing bacteria	Goethite	a-FeO(O11)	Limpet radulas, bacteria
Oxides			**Organic minerals**		
Magnetite	Fe_3O	Chiton, pigeons, social insects, humans, bacteria	Whewellite	$CaC_2O_1.H_2O$	Bacteria, plants, fungi, animals including humans
Silicates			Guanine	$C_511_3(N11_2)N_4O$	Various animals including chameleons
Amorphous Silica	$SiO_2.nlI_2O$	Diatoms, radiolarians, plants, bacteria	**Chlorides**		
Stevensite	$(Ca, NA)_xMg_{3-x}(SI_2O_{10})(OH)_2$	Bacteria	Atacamite	$Cu_2Cl(OH)$	Glycera annelid mandibles

Table 2.1. *Non-exhaustive list of biominerals illustrating their diversity, heir chemical composition and some biological organisms forming them*

2.2.1. *Who are the biomineralizing organisms?*

2.2.1.1. *Prokaryotes*

A very wide diversity of prokaryotes, notably bacteria, are capable of forming minerals. This is partly linked to their great metabolic diversity, much greater than that observed in eukaryotes. As bacteria can (i) significantly modify the pH of their environment, (ii) catalyze the redox transformations (reduction and/or oxidation) of most chemical elements such as carbon, iron, manganese, arsenic, selenium or uranium, or (iii) catalyze reactions involving biologically important elements such as phosphorus or sulfur, they can induce the formation of a very wide diversity of biominerals. Biomineralizing bacteria are today identified in different ways: they can be isolated from the environment and their capacity to biomineralize is then evaluated in laboratory cultures. Their identification often involves sequencing an identity gene such as the gene encoding 16S ribosomal RNA (16S rDNA). Otherwise, they can be identified directly in their environment by DNA amplification of a sample and mass sequencing of the DNA (metagenome).

What is difficult is then linking the microscopy observation of a biomineralizing cell with one of hundreds or thousands of DNA sequences. The use of fluorescent nucleic acid probes hybridizing specifically to the 16S rDNA sequence of interest and observations using epifluorescence microscopy (fluorescence in situ hybridization (FISH) technique) helps to make this connection. Finally, when genes indicating the ability of an organism to biomineralize have been identified, as is the case in magnetotactic bacteria, which biomineralize intracellular iron oxides, it is then possible to search for them in a metagenome. However, it should be noted that today, only a very small proportion of the diversity of biomineralizing prokaryotes is known. We can cite the example of bacteria that promote the formation of kidney stones from an infection (Figure 2.2). Kidney stones (renal lithiasis) are mineral precipitates (often oxalates, or different phosphate phases) forming in the bladder and sometimes leading to significant pain due to obstruction of the urinary tract. Some stones are of infectious origin, formed by bacteria that hydrolyze urea (ureolytic bacteria), thus leading to a sharp increase in urine pH and the release of ammonium ions. This promotes the precipitation of a magnesium ammonium phosphate mineral: struvite. It has, however, been noted that other stones could also be of infectious origin but not linked to ureolytic strains; however, the identity of the bacteria involved remains unknown to this day.

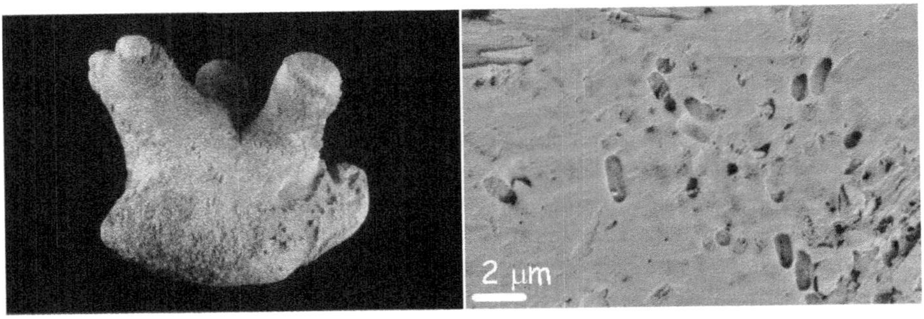

Figure 2.2. *Left: macroscopic photograph of a kidney stone of infectious origin (type IVb according to Letavernier et al. (2023)). These stones measure several millimeters to centimeters. Right: scanning electron microscopy photograph of bacterial imprints in a kidney stone of infectious origin (Livrozet et al. unpublished). For a color version of this figure, see www.iste.co.uk/benzerara/geosphere.zip*

2.2.1.2. *Eukaryotes*

Biomineralization is present in most eukaryotic phyla. Many unicellular organisms (protists) as well as many metazoans (animals), fungi and plants can biomineralize (Figure 2.3). Often, biomineralization is an integral part of the biology of these organisms, with dedicated genetics. The biominerals produced then have a defined function, in particular support and/or protection in the case of so-called skeletal biominerals. The census of biomineralizing species is probably more complete than among prokaryotes, even if there are many unknown biomineralizing protists. The diversity of mineral phases produced is less than in prokaryotes, particularly because of a more restricted metabolic diversity in eukaryotes. The main types of skeletal mineral phases formed are: different polymorphs of calcium carbonates, calcium phosphates (mainly hydroxyapatite), and amorphous silica (opal). The biomineralization of amorphous silica is one of the most widespread taxonomically. It is mainly observed in diatoms and silicoflagellates, two groups of unicellular freshwater and marine algae, as well as radiolarians, which are part of marine animal plankton (Marron et al. 2016). Many land plants can also biomineralize amorphous silica (phytoliths). Finally, although this is rarer in animals, it is found in a certain number of sponges and some arthropods. Later in the chapter, we will explain how the biomineralization of silica is so widespread in the oceans, although dissolved silica is not. The biomineralization of calcium phosphates, often in the form of hydroxyapatite (but there are other mineral phases also containing calcium and phosphates) concerns the formation of the vertebrate endoskeleton (Murshed 2018) as well as the shell of certain brachiopods. It remains very rare among protists. Finally, the biomineralization of calcium carbonates, mainly in the form of calcite or aragonite, is a very abundant process on Earth today and leads to the formation of external structures in certain sponges (calcite), cnidarians (corals that form aragonite), brachiopods and many molluscs (calcite and/or aragonite) or in arthropods (calcite). The structures can be internal as in echinoderms or tunicates. Finally, many protists biomineralize calcium carbonates, mainly calcite, for example, foraminifera, coccolithophorids or some amoebae.

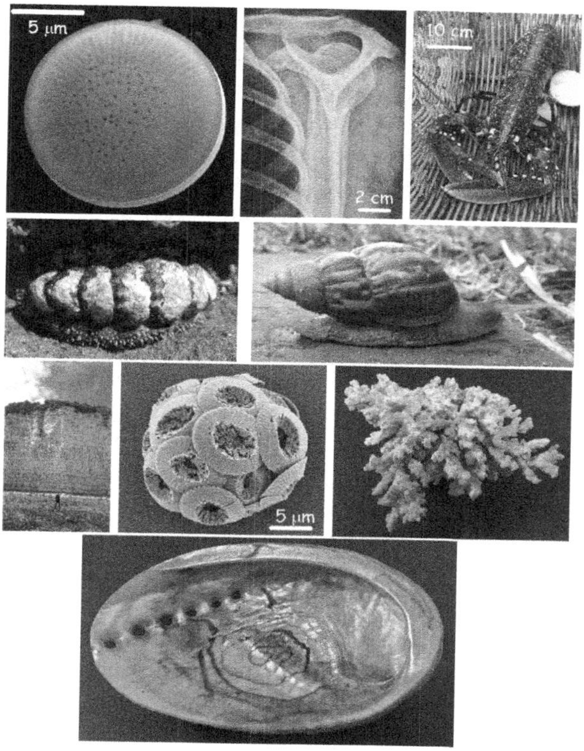

Figure 2.3. *From right to left, top to bottom: scanning electron microscopy image of a diatom frustule (amorphous silica); radiograph of a human shoulder (hydroxyapatite); photograph of the calcified shell of a lobster (calcite, apatite carbonate, amorphous calcium carbonate); photograph of a chiton (aragonite shell and magnetite radula); photograph of the shell of a gastropod (aragonite); limestone cliffs of Etretat made up of the accumulation of coccoliths (calcite); scanning electron microscopy image of a coccosphere (calcite); photograph of a coral after cleaning it with bleach (aragonite); mother-of-pearl from the shell of an abalone (aragonite). For a color version of this figure, see www.iste.co.uk/benzerara/geosphere.zip*

2.2.2. *What are the differences between biominerals and their abiotic counterparts?*

No mineral species has been described only in living organisms, except according to Yang et al. (2011), hazenite, a phosphate phase, but this remains an extremely rare phase, whose abiotic occurrences are yet to be discovered. Consequently, if we simply characterize an atomic structure and a chemical formula, i.e. what defines a mineral species, there is nothing to distinguish a biomineral from an abiotic mineral. Could other properties, such as the morphology of minerals, their textural arrangement, the presence or absence of defects, their trace element composition or even their isotopic composition be unique to biominerals? Some authors answer yes to this question. In this case, these signatures could be identified in ancient and/or extraterrestrial rocks to highlight the past presence of life. However, other authors, noting that living organisms do nothing but follow the laws of physics and chemistry and that it is difficult to prove that something does not exist (i.e. an abiotic mineral with the same properties), think that there is probably no parameter which, alone, can be an absolute criterion of biogenicity (Benzerara et al. 2019). However, whatever the answer to the previous question, living organisms imprint their activity in the properties of the biominerals formed. In other words, if these properties are not unique to living things, we nevertheless expect to find them in biominerals. Here are some (non-systematic) properties of biominerals: (i) it is common to find poorly crystalline or amorphous phases within biominerals. The fact that these phases are often unstable but can be stabilized by living organisms can explain why we find amorphous phases more often associated with life. These amorphous phases have been described as precursors to many carbonate and phosphate skeletal biominerals (Gower 2008). (ii) Many biominerals contain organic matter. The location of these organic molecules is still under debate: are they included within the structure of minerals? Or, more likely, do they surround the nanocrystals agglomerated to form biominerals? The organic matter contents are not necessarily very high (sometimes no more than 5% of the total mass), but this is enough to give them particular mechanical properties, in particular remarkable resistance to fracture. This is the case, for example, of mother-of-pearl in molluscs (Meyers et al. 2013). (iii) In the case of biominerals formed intracellularly, their chemical composition, controlled by that of the intracellular solution, is different from the chemical composition of a mineral that would have formed outside the cell. Consequently, if we know the composition of the extracellular solution (which is difficult in the case of a geological sample), a deviation from the expected chemical equilibria can be a sign of a role of biology. Thus, it was shown that the intracellular magnetites of magnetotactic bacteria had a very different trace element chemical composition from what was expected compared to the chemistry of the extracellular environment (Amor et al. 2015). In addition, the isotopic composition of biominerals can also be different from that of minerals forming in the absence of organisms, particularly when the molecules forming these minerals are metabolized by the organism. (iv) A number of biominerals have very different morphologies from those of their abiotic counterparts. For example, the calcite crystals making up certain coccoliths formed by unicellular algae are single crystals with an anvil shape (at least for one of the forms of the algal lifecycle), very different from the classic calcite rhombohedrons (Houdan et al. 2004). (v) Finally, biominerals can be arranged in specific assemblages. For example, a systematic hierarchical structuring from the nanoscale to the macroscopic scale has been described in many skeletal biominerals. These biominerals are composed of calcium carbonate or phosphate nanocrystals that arrange and orient themselves crystallographically to form mesocrystals, which can themselves be oriented in particular ways, relative to each other to form a macroscopic structure (Dove 2010). Bones are another example of such hierarchical structuring in which nearly seven levels of structuring have been identified (Figure 2.4). This starts from apatite nanocrystals oriented in relation to each other along collagen fibers synthesized by osteoblasts, to form lamellae on a micrometric scale with elongation directions varying from one lamella to another. These lamellae form osteons on a scale of a few hundred micrometers, which themselves are grouped within the bone structure. Proteins other than collagen also participate in the overall structure, such as osteocalcin, which is attached to collagen via osteopontin.

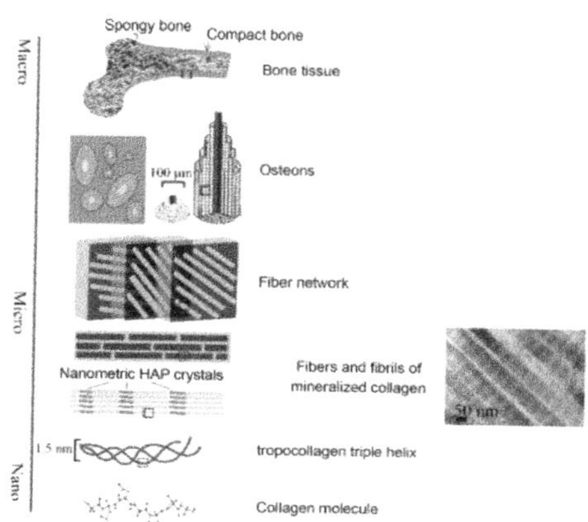

Figure 2.4. *Some levels of the hierarchical structure of a bone. Bone tissue is made up of structural units called osteons, which result from a stack of layers formed by a network of collagen fibers, mineralized by hydroxyapatite. These fibers are themselves an arrangement of collagen fibrils which correspond to a helical arrangement of collagen molecules. Transmission electron microscopy image of non-mineralized collagen fibers (copyright, © Louisa Howard). For a color version of this figure, see www.iste.co.uk/benzerara/geosphere.zip*

2.3. Biomineral formation mechanisms

2.3.1. *How are minerals formed?*

2.3.1.1. *Minerals precipitate from saturated or supersaturated aqueous solutions*

The formation of a mineral is a chemical reaction whose reactants are the chemical species (molecules, ions, atoms) in solution constituting the mineral. For example, calcite, $CaCO_3$ chemical composition in the trigonal crystal system, can be formed by the precipitation of dissolved Ca^{2+} and CO_3^{2-} ions in an aqueous medium. We can write the reaction as:

$$(CaCO_3)_c \rightleftarrows Ca^{2+} + CO_3^{2-} \qquad [2.1]$$

where the *c* subscript denotes calcite. For the other $CaCO_3$ polymorphs (vaterite, aragonite), the chemical equation would be written in the same way and only the subscript would change. This reaction E_0 reflects the dissolution of calcite when read from left to right, and the precipitation of calcite from right to left. An equilibrium constant, denoted K_s, also called solubility constant is associated with it, whose value varies with temperature and pressure but not according to the concentrations of the species in solution. Furthermore, this constant imposes, in thermodynamic equilibrium, the following relationship:

$$K_s=(aCa^{2+})_{eq}*(aCO_3^{2-})_{eq}/(CaCO_3c)_{eq} \qquad [2.2]$$

where $(a)_{eq}$ designates the activity of a chemical species when equilibrium is reached. By approximating the activities of the chemical species to the concentrations (noted in brackets []), as well as the activity of the solid ($CaCO_3c$) to 1, we obtain the following expression for the solubility constant:

$$K_s=[Ca^{2+}]_{eq}*[CO_3^{2-}]_{eq} \qquad [2.3]$$

We see that at the thermodynamic equilibrium between calcite and dissolved Ca^{2+} and CO_3^{2} ions, the product of the concentrations of ions in solution is equal to a “constant” (at a given temperature and pressure). In other words, if we note the coexistence in a solution between a mineral species and its dissolved constituent chemical species and we postulate the existence of a thermodynamic equilibrium (we then say that the solution is saturated), then we can deduce the value of the product of the concentrations of the chemical species in question. At 25°C and ambient pressure, vaterite is more soluble than aragonite (i.e. at equilibrium, the product of the Ca^{2+} and CO_3^{2} concentrations is higher for vaterite than for aragonite), which is itself more soluble than calcite. If thermodynamic equilibrium prevailed systematically, it would then become simple to predict whether a mineral precipitates (or not) from the moment we know the composition of the solution in question.

In reality, many aqueous solutions (lakes, oceans, rivers, etc.) are not at thermodynamic equilibrium with respect to the precipitation reaction of calcium carbonates. Despite an obvious oversaturation of the solution, no precipitation is observed. It takes time, sometimes a lot, for the reaction to take place: it is limited kinetically. This may be linked to the presence of precipitation inhibitors and/or to the fact that the probability that one of the mineral formation steps takes place is low. We then introduce the notion of saturation index of a solution, which is expressed as follows:

$$\Omega=[Ca^{2+}]*[CO_3^{2-}]/K_s \quad [2.4]$$

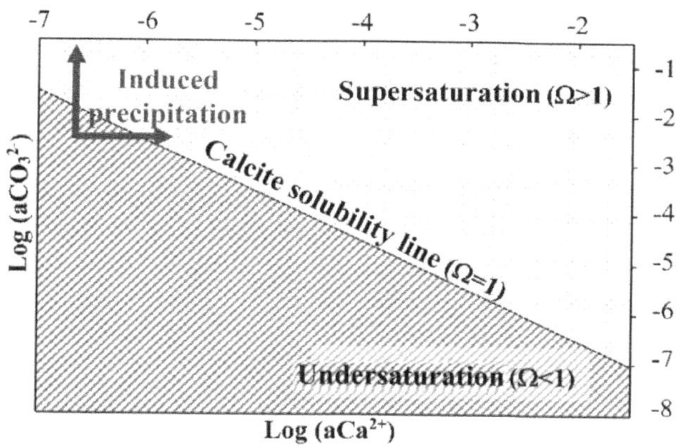

Figure 2.5. *Calcite solubility diagram. We represent the logarithm of the activity of the Ca^{2+} ions (x-axis) as a function of the logarithm of the CO_3^{2-} ion activity (y-axis), measured in a solution. The solutions align with the solubility line of calcite when there is equilibrium between these solutions and calcite (with a zero saturation index, Ω=0). Solutions are undersaturated (Ω<0) when solutions appear below the line in this diagram. In this case, no precipitation of calcite can happen. Solutions are supersaturated (Ω>0) when they are above and there can be precipitation. It is clearly seen that an increase in the activity of Ca^{2+} and/or CO_3^{2-} ions favors precipitation, the latter possibly being due to the increase in pH and/or the concentration of dissolved inorganic carbon (red lines). For a color version of this figure, see www.iste.co.uk/benzerara/geosphere.zip*

The saturation index is the ratio between the actually measured ionic product of Ca^{2+} and CO_3^{2-} and the solubility constant (which would be the ionic product at equilibrium). This can be understood as the deviation of the system from equilibrium (we saw in Chapter 1 the parameter $\Delta_r G$ which is directly connected to Ω). When Ω is less than 1, we say that the solution is undersaturated. According to thermodynamics, calcite should dissolve in such a solution. This is the scenario mainly addressed in Chapter 1 of this book. When Ω is greater than 1, we say that the solution is oversaturated. According to thermodynamics, the calcite should then precipitate.

Ultimately, we understand that any phenomenon increasing the concentration of Ca^{2+} and/or CO_3^{2-} ions can therefore make it possible to move from an undersaturated solution, where calcite cannot precipitate, to an oversaturated solution where calcite can precipitate and therefore promote the formation of this mineral (Figure 2.5).

Additionally, it has been measured that the higher the saturation index of a solution, the higher the precipitation rate of calcite (van der Weijden and van der Weijden 2014). This reflects the greater propensity of a solution to precipitate calcite when it is further from equilibrium (toward supersaturation). Thus, in a supersaturated solution, any process increasing the concentration of Ca^{2+} and/or CO_3^{2-} ions accelerates the calcite precipitation reaction. Finally, the concentration of carbonate ions (CO_3^{2-}) depends on the concentration of hydrogen carbonate (or bicarbonate ions, HCO_3^-) and pH according to the constant of the following acid–base reaction:

$$HCO_3^- \rightleftarrows H^+ + CO_3^{2-} \quad [2.5]$$

whose equilibrium constant is written as:

$$K_{a2}=[H^+]_{eq}*[CO_3^{2-}]_{eq}/[HCO_3^-]. \quad [2.6]$$

Bicarbonate ions are the major form of dissolved inorganic carbon for pHs between 6.4 and 10.3 at 25°C. Thus, we deduce from the previous relationship that any process increasing (i) the pH, or (ii) the concentration of dissolved inorganic carbon (sum of all the acid–base species of the carbonate system) at a constant pH, increases the concentration of carbonate ions and therefore promotes calcite precipitation.

2.3.1.2. *Minerals nucleate and then grow after passing an activation energy threshold*

We can consider the formation of a mineral from another point of view (but completely complementary) consisting of describing the energetic evolution of the solution–mineral system during mineralization. Nucleation is the step during which chemical species in solution bind to form the first mineral embryos (or nuclei). When this takes place within the solution, we refer to homogeneous nucleation. When nucleation takes place in contact with a surface, we refer to heterogeneous nucleation. During homogeneous nucleation, chemical species begin to interact with each other rather than with solvent molecules. If these new interactions are energetically more favorable, this process is then accompanied by a loss of free enthalpy[1] ($\Delta G<0$), the amplitude of which depends on the quantity of chemical species interacting in the nucleus formed. This quantity is equal to the volumetric concentration of the species in the mineral formed, multiplied by the volume of the nucleus.

By contrast, on the surface of the nucleus, chemical species interact with the other internal chemical species in the nucleus as well as with the external solvent. The interaction with the solvent is destabilizing (due to surface tension) and is accompanied by a gain in free enthalpy, the amplitude of which, this time, depends on the surface of the nucleus.

In total, the variation in free enthalpy during nucleation is the sum of the two terms mentioned below, the first being a function of the volume, the second of the surface of the nucleus (Figure 2.6). The volume increases more slowly than the surface area in the first stages of particle growth, so the enthalpy variation is initially positive for small nuclei and then becomes negative (and therefore favorable) for increasingly larger nuclei. Once the maximum enthalpy, called the energy threshold, has been crossed, the nucleus is then stable and nucleation occurs.

All processes modifying surface tension, in particular stabilizing the surface of nuclei during heterogeneous nucleation, promote this initial stage of mineral formation by lowering the nucleation energy threshold.

1 Free enthalpy is a thermodynamic parameter characterizing the propensity of a system to evolve spontaneously or not toward another state. The variation in free enthalpy ΔG is sometimes referred to as "difference from equilibrium".

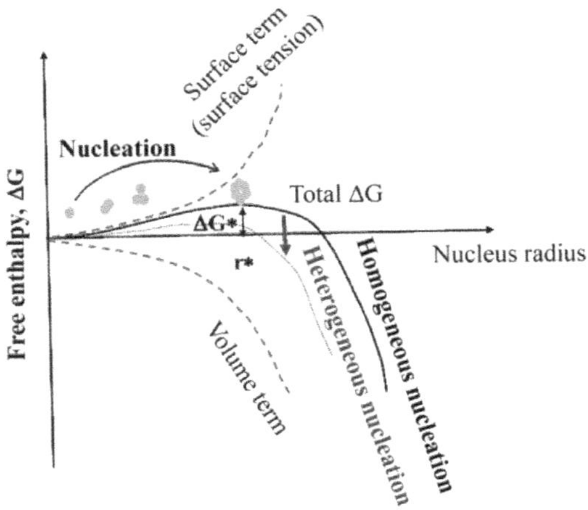

Figure 2.6. *Graph showing the evolution of the free enthalpy during the precipitation of a mineral by homogeneous nucleation (black curve) and heterogeneous nucleation (red curve). We distinguish in this energy balance the contribution of the nucleus surface area, which is positive and increases as a function of the radius squared, from the volume contribution (interactions between crystal components) which is negative and contributes as r^3. The sum (total ΔG) passes a maximum (activation threshold, ΔG*) reached at a critical radius. For smaller radii, we define homogeneous nucleation. For larger radii, there is growth of the nucleus. In heterogeneous nucleation (on a surface), the activation energy decreases. For a color version of this figure, see www.iste.co.uk/benzerara/geosphere.zip*

2.3.2. *Principles of action of living organisms on the formation of minerals*

2.3.2.1. *Biologically induced, influenced or controlled mineralization*

The preceding sections have allowed us to understand the different processes by which living beings promote the formation of biominerals. There are several types of mechanisms (Figure 2.7) (Görgen et al. 2020).

In the first types, living beings modify the chemical parameters of an aqueous solution due to their metabolic activity. For example, various metabolisms can, under certain conditions, lead to an increase in the pH of a solution. This is particularly the case for oxygenic photosynthesis (i.e. the metabolism which, thanks to light energy, reduces the CO_2 into organic carbon while releasing O_2 by oxidation of water molecules). Other metabolisms such as ureolysis (hydrolysis of urea releasing ammonia) or even anoxygenic photosynthesis, for example, can also lead to an increase in the pH of a solution. This increase in pH modifies the saturation of the solution in relation to certain mineral phases such as carbonates as explained above. An undersaturated solution can thus become saturated or oversaturated. Or, if the solution was already saturated, its saturation may increase which accelerates precipitation. In this case, we refer to induced biomineralization.

Secondly, some organic molecules synthesized by living beings can promote the nucleation of minerals by reducing surface tension on the surface of the nuclei. This is possible in a solution that is otherwise already saturated or oversaturated. The organism in this case does not need to be metabolically active (it may even be dead). This is what is known as influenced biomineralization. Extracellular polymers, also known as exopolymeric substances (EPS), mainly polysaccharides formed by many bacteria, can play this role. Proteins such as collagen formed by animals may play a similar role in the formation of skeletons.

Finally, the third type of biomineralization is known as controlled biomineralization. This mode overlaps with the two principles already stated, namely the modification of the chemical conditions of the precipitation medium, possibly associated with the synthesis of molecules that modify the nucleation of minerals. But in this case, all of the processes are under strict and specific genetic control. These biomineralization processes can take place intra- or extracellularly (the intercellular case, for example, can occur between the cells of a tissue) and the mineral formed has an adaptive function for the organism.

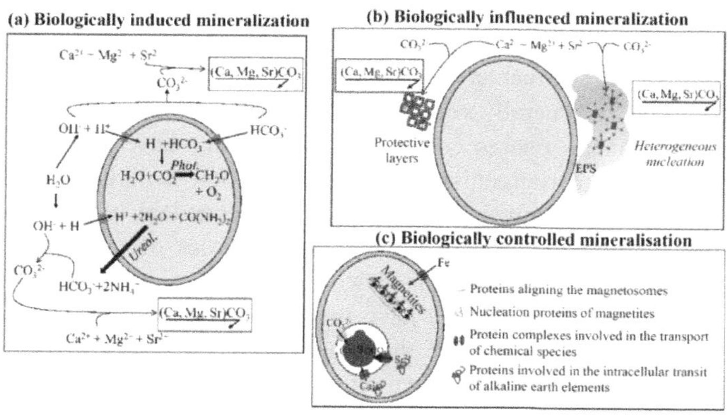

Figure 2.7. *The different categories of biological mineralization: example of (a) carbonate precipitation by biologically induced mineralization (Ureal: Urealoysis) and by (b) biologically influenced mineralization. Example of (c) the controlled biomineralization of magnetites and carbonates by a bacteria. For a color version of this figure, see www.iste.co.uk/benzerara/geosphere.zip*

Different metabolisms are accompanied by the consumption of protons (or production of hydroxyls). Organisms induce, at least locally, an increase in pH due to these metabolisms, which favors the precipitation of mineral phases such as carbonates or phosphates. Here are some examples:

$HCO_3^- + H_2O = CH_2O + O_2 + OH^-$ oxygenic photosynthesis (cyanobacteria, algae, plants)

$2H_2 + HCO_3^- = CH_2O + H_2O + OH^-$ anoxygenic photosynthesis (various bacteria)

$R\text{-}NH_2 + H_3O^+ = R\text{-}OH + NH_4^+$ ammonification of amino acids (many organisms)

$2CO(NH_2)_2 + 6H_2O = 2HCO_3^- + 4NH_4^+ + 2OH^-$ ureolysis (bacteria)

$5\ HS^- + 2\ NO_3^- + 7\ H^+ = 5\ S^0 + N_2 + 6\ H_2O$ sulfoxidation producing elemental sulfur (bacteria)

$HCO_3^- + 4H_2 = CH_4 + 2H_2O + OH^-$ methanogenesis (archaea)

Box 2.2. *Metabolisms inducing the precipitation of carbonate (or phosphate) minerals*

2.3.2.2. *Examples of biomineralization processes*

2.3.2.2.1. Biologically induced and influenced mineralization of carbonate and silicate phases in stromatolites

Stromatolites are sedimentary formations, most often mainly composed of carbonates, formed by generally very diverse microbial assemblages (Chapter 3). In many cases, the mineral phases constituting these rocks have precipitated in situ under the action of microorganisms. This precipitation is likely the result of a mixture of purely abiotic precipitation (entirely independent of microorganisms), induced mineralization linked to the metabolic activities of microorganisms and finally influenced mineralization linked to EPS, in particular. Stromatolites are particularly interesting because they have been found in the geological record for more than 3.5 billion years and are therefore among the oldest traces of mineral formation by the biosphere. For a long time, stromatolites have been associated with cyanobacteria, i.e. bacteria carrying out oxygenic photosynthesis. Cyanobacteria trap and transform CO_2 by this metabolism, i.e. subtract from the surrounding solution the most acidic form of the system $CO_2/HCO_3^-/CO_3^{2-}$. As a result, they tend to increase the pH of the surrounding solution, which increases the saturation of the solution with respect to the carbonated mineral phases, leading in favorable cases to their precipitation. However, with advances in molecular biology (Chapter 4), it has been noted that there are many other microorganisms associated with stromatolites. Among these microorganisms, some have metabolisms that can also induce an increase in pH. This is the case, for example, of anoxygenic photosynthesis, methanogenesis or certain metabolisms oxidizing reduced sulfur. Alongside this so-called induced mineralization, it has been suggested that EPS may have a crucial role in the formation of these rocks, for example, by lowering the nucleation energy threshold of calcium carbonate minerals, thereby accelerating the kinetics of this process.

Conversely, in certain cases, these EPS, by complexing Ca^{2+} can reduce its activity and inhibit its precipitation. Thus, influenced mineralization and induced mineralization can coexist. In addition, it has been shown that certain bacteria, also found in the biofilms of certain stromatolites, biomineralize carbonates in a controlled manner but their quantitative contribution to the formation of these rocks remains unknown (Couradeau et al. 2012). Finally, in recent years, it has been discovered that a significant fraction of certain stromatolites was composed of hydrated magnesium silicates, also possibly formed by induced and/or influenced mineralization, illustrating the diversity of mineral phases that can form (Zeyen et al. 2015).

2.3.2.2.2. Biologically controlled mineralization of magnetites by bacteria

There is another well-known case of controlled biomineralization in bacteria: that of intracellular magnetic crystals (Lefevre and Bazylinski 2013). These so-called magnetotactic bacteria are phylogenetically diverse and synthesize magnetite crystals (Fe_3O_4 in the cubic system) or greigite (Fe_3S_4), within intracellular vesicles called magnetosomes (Figure 2.8). The crystals formed have very controlled sizes and shapes and align into one or more intracellular chains. This control allows optimization of the magnetic properties of these mineral assemblies, used by bacteria as magnetic field sensors. These bacteria can thus swim by orienting themselves along the lines of the Earth's magnetic field which, in the northern hemisphere, plunge downward. These bacteria complete this magnetic guidance by detecting oxygen gradients, which allows them to stop their progression when the oxygenation conditions are most favorable to their physiology. Indeed, these bacteria are most often microaerophilic, i.e. they need a little bit of oxygen but not too much. Others are strictly anaerobic.

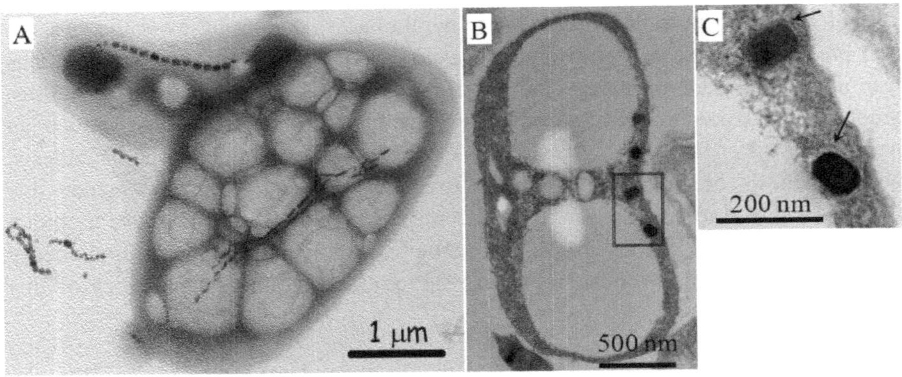

Figure 2.8. *(A) Transmission electron microscopy image showing two different magnetotactic bacteria as well as chains of magnetosomes (very dark particles) extracted from other cells. The top bacterium has a single chain of prismatic magnetosomes extending between the two ends of the cell. This cell also contains electron-dense (dark) inclusions at each of its ends, likely phosphorus-rich inclusions. The bottom bacterium shows two chains of magnetosomes with a so-called "bullet" morphology. It also contains numerous electron-transparent inclusions, likely lipid-rich inclusions. (B) Transmission electron microscopy image of a magnetotactic bacterial cell cut by ultramicrotomy. The electron-dense objects (dark on the right) are magnetite crystals. (C) Enlargement of an area containing two magnetites. The lipid membrane forming the two magnetosomes can be observed in certain locations (arrows)*

In order to form these intracellular crystals, magnetotactic bacteria use a set of specific proteins. These proteins are encoded by several dozen genes grouped within the genome of these bacteria in a genomic island. These proteins are involved, for example, in (i) the formation of intracellular compartments where crystals nucleate, (ii) the formation of a cytoskeleton allowing their alignment, (iii) the establishment of molecular sites favoring crystal nucleation, (iv) iron transporters and proteins catalyzing iron redox transformations (Figure 2.7(c)). We do not yet know all the stages of the biomineralization of these crystals within these bacteria, in particular the function of all the genes grouped in the genomic island, nor their diversity within the taxonomic diversity of magnetotactic bacteria. This remains the challenge of active research in the field of biomineralogy at the interface with microbiology.

2.3.2.2.3. Skeletal biomineralization in metazoans

Besides prokaryotes, protists, plants and animals also form biominerals, many of which ensure the maintenance and/or physical protection of organisms. This is known as skeletal biomineralization, external (exoskeleton) or internal (endoskeleton) to the body, which is invariably controlled. Here again, much research is currently being carried out on the processes involved in the diversity of biomineralizations in eukaryotes. We will not discuss them in detail here, and readers should refer to specific publications for more details (Marin et al. 2014; Murshed 2018; Drake et al. 2020). Nevertheless, we can note some general principles and overviews of these processes. Whether it is the shell of an egg, the bone of a vertebrate or the shell of a mollusc, skeletal biominerals are composite structures composed of a matrix of organic molecules, interpenetrated by nano- to micrometric mineral phases. Their formation involves various organic molecules synthesized by an organism (Figure 2.9): (i) matrices of extracellular hydrophobic organic molecules that structure the architecture of the skeleton (e.g. chitin, collagen). They ensure this function by controlling the growth of biominerals, in particular their crystallographic orientation and thus acting as a template. (ii) In addition, other macromolecules (proteins and others), often rich in acidic functional groups (e.g. carboxylic functions), catalyze the nucleation of a given mineral phase. In corals, proteins rich in acid functional groups (notably aspartic acids) are likely involved in directing biomineralization toward a specific polymorph of $CaCO_3$, in this case, aragonite. The most important macromolecules forming organic matrices in the living world are chitin and collagen. Chitin is a polysaccharide formed by the polymerization of N-acetylglucosamine monomers, linked by a saccharide bond[2]. It is the most abundant polymer after cellulose. It forms the matrix of the exoskeleton of crustaceans, mineralized by calcite, and it has also been identified in the mother-of-pearl (aragonite) of molluscs. Collagen, on the other hand, is a fibrillar protein that is organized at different scales: the fundamental unit is tropocollagen, a protein rich in glycine- and proline-type amino acids. Tropocollagen fibers assemble into collagen fibrils. These fibrils assemble themselves into collagen fibers. Once again, this structural macromolecule is the most abundant protein in the animal kingdom. It forms the mineralized matrix of bones in vertebrates and is secreted by connective tissue cells. In addition to these macromolecules, skeletal biomineralization processes involve changes in the chemical composition of the aqueous biomineralizing solution, whether intracellular or extracellular. For example, in corals, the formation of the skeleton is carried out within the extracellular calcification environment, isolated from seawater in particular by an epithelial tissue, the calicoblastic ectoderm. Cells of this epithelium secrete the extracellular organic matrix as well as modify the chemical composition of the calcification medium, in particular by raising the concentrations of dissolved inorganic carbon and Ca^{2+} and the pH, so that it becomes more strongly saturated with respect to the aragonite (Sevilgen et al. 2019). Finally, in certain cases, biomineralization

2. A saccharide or glycosidic bond is a covalent bond between oses (or monosaccharides), which are the monomers of carbohydrates.

inhibitors seem to be involved (Marin et al. 2016). Indeed, the organic mineralization matrices are bathed in supersaturated solutions and the inhibitors prevent anarchic precipitation outside of these matrices. Consequently, biomineralization is controlled by the localized degradation of inhibitors. Thus, in vertebrates, it has been suggested that polymers of orthophosphate ions (PO_4^{3-}), notably pyrophosphates, are inhibitors of the formation of apatite and that the action of enzymes hydrolyzing these polymers (phosphatases) induces tissue mineralization (Reznikov et al. 2020).

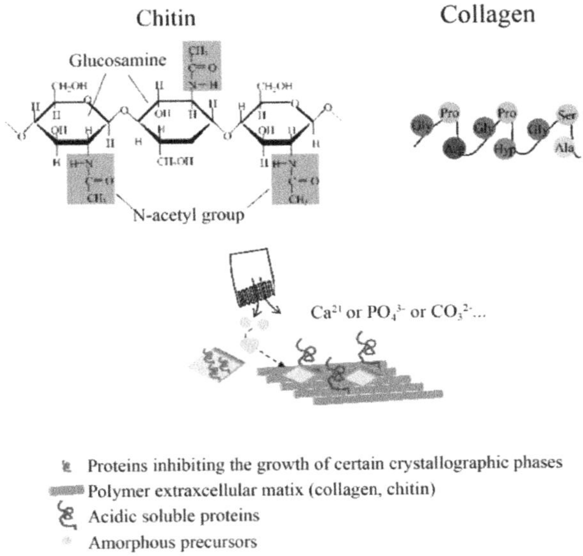

Figure 2.9. *Chitin and collagen, two main biological macromolecules involved in skeletal biomineralization. For a color version of this figure, see www.iste.co.uk/benzerara/geosphere.zip*

2.3.3. *Methods for studying biomineralization*

This general framework for understanding the role living organisms play in the formation of minerals has fueled and is fueled by numerous studies aimed at identifying the molecules involved in and the byproducts of biomineralization. These studies use know-how as diverse as bioinformatics, molecular biology, biochemistry as well as materials sciences or geochemistry. Biomineralogy is therefore an eminently interdisciplinary field.

2.3.3.1. *Biological methods*

Biomineralizing organisms can be studied in their natural environment or, for a certain number of them, cultivated in the laboratory, allowing physiological analyses at the organism, tissue or cell level. The molecules involved in biomineralization can be identified at different levels: the search for genes with functions specific to biomineralization (genomics) and the demonstration of their function (genetics); the study of the expression of these genes through the quantification of messenger RNA (transcriptomics); the study of proteins catalyzing the key chemical reactions of biomineralization, ensuring the nucleation of mineral phases, or even controlling their growth (proteomics). Since "omics" approaches have experienced considerable technological growth in recent years (Chapter 4), applications in the field of biomineralization have increased considerably.

Let us take one example among many others of an approach aimed at better understanding a biomineralization system (Figure 2.10). In 2012, a cyanobacterium (*Gloeomargarita lithophora*; see Chapter 4) was discovered in a lake in Mexico, that of biomineralized intracellular granules of amorphous $CaCO_3$ (Couradeau et al. 2012). The extracellular formation of calcium carbonates by cyanobacteria has been known for a long time and considered as a typical case of biologically induced mineralization, oxygenic photosynthesis, leading to alkalinization of the extracellular environment and therefore precipitation of carbonates. However, with *Gloeomargarita*, this was a very different scenario since the biomineralization was intracellular. Thus, many questions arose: was this a very atypical case of biomineralization, or even unique among cyanobacteria? Is this an old process? What is the degree of control by bacteria? Initially, the systematic observation by microscopy of 68 phylogenetically diverse strains of cyanobacteria available in the cyanobacteria collection at the Pasteur Institute, revealed intracellular amorphous carbonates in eight of them (Benzerara et al. 2014). The entire genome sequences of six of these cyanobacteria, available in public databases, were then compared to those of 50 strains that do not form intracellular calcium carbonates (Benzerara et al. 2022). First, the coding sequences (or CDS for coding DNA sequences), i.e. the portions of genes translated into proteins, were identified in these genomes. There were 523,683 CDS in total. A single group of so-called orthologous sequences (i.e. coming from the same ancestral gene) was detected in all intracellular $CaCO_3$-forming cyanobacteria, while these sequences were absent in cyanobacteria not forming intracellular $CaCO_3$. A group of orthologous sequences were involved here, because the sequences of these CDS are not strictly identical between organisms, even if they have the same evolutionary origin. Indeed, mutations accumulated during evolutionary history, following the divergence from their common ancestor between the lineages (Chapter 4). More differences appear, the older the divergence as well as when the mutation has a low impact on the functioning of the encoded protein; in fact, deleterious mutations are generally counter-selected and disappear. It should also be noted that an organism that does not form intracellular $CaCO_3$ may likely have genes necessary (but not sufficient) for biomineralization. Thus, the approach presented only gives an incomplete picture of the mechanisms. Once a group of orthologous sequences has been identified, it is then possible to search for it in public databases to see if this gene is already known, which allows its function to be deduced. In the example presented, we found no known homologous function genes. Different approaches can then be carried out to identify the function of this gene: for example, in a genetic approach, delete this gene within a mutant strain and observe how this affects the ability of these bacteria to form carbonates; or, insert this gene into a mutant, overexpress it to mass produce the protein, which can then be extracted and purified in order to study its atomic structure and chemical properties.

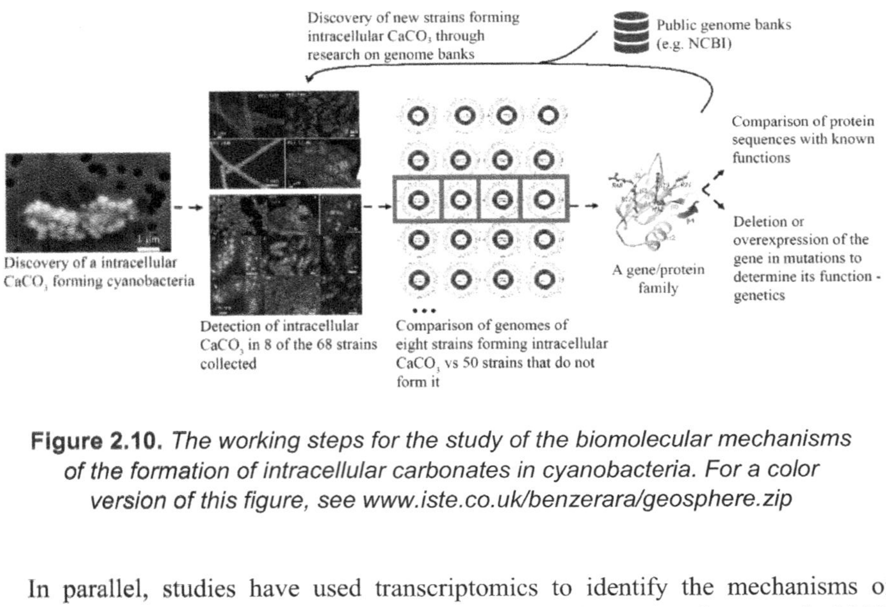

Figure 2.10. *The working steps for the study of the biomolecular mechanisms of the formation of intracellular carbonates in cyanobacteria. For a color version of this figure, see www.iste.co.uk/benzerara/geosphere.zip*

In parallel, studies have used transcriptomics to identify the mechanisms of biomineralization (Herlitze et al. 2018; Maas et al. 2018; Zhao et al. 2018; Salamanca-Díaz et al. 2022). For example, the comparative study of gene expression (i) between different tissues (biomineralizing or not), (ii) at different developmental stages of an organism, or (iii) under different environmental conditions, favorable or not to biomineralization. Since it is a single organism, the set of genes is the same, but it is possible that in the first case, the genes involved in biomineralization are strongly transcribed (in RNA), while being little or not transcribed in the second case (inducible genes). Comparison of transcripts between the two conditions thus makes it possible to identify genes involved in biomineralization. It should be noted, however, that the transcription of certain necessary genes can be constant whatever the conditions (constitutive genes), which does not then allow us to conclude which genes are involved in biomineralization. Finally, proteomics is another approach that has been used extensively to identify proteins involved in biomineralization. In this case, the proteins trapped within the biominerals are extracted and then identified by mass spectrometry. The working hypothesis is that if these proteins are trapped within biominerals, it is because they can contribute to their formation.

2.3.3.2. *Methods of material physics and chemistry*

Independently or in parallel with the approaches outlined above, we use tools to accurately characterize biominerals and associated cells. A large number of microscopy or spectroscopy techniques are particularly useful for biomineralization research, and it is impossible to cover them exhaustively here (DiMasi and Gower 2014; Table 2.2). No technique provides all of the desired answers, and it is therefore useful to know the advantages and limitations of each, and at the same time to develop protocols for correlations. The choice of technique must be guided by the type of information sought. Thanks to these techniques, it is today possible to obtain a very wide variety of information on mineral phases, whether their identification via the chemical bonds that compose them (Raman or infrared spectroscopy), their atomic structure and their crystallographic orientation (X-ray or electron diffraction techniques), the chemical composition of main elements or elements in trace quantities (notably X-ray fluorescence) or the isotopic composition of most of the chemical elements that compose them (mass spectrometer). Likewise, it is possible to characterize the chemical and biological environments of these biominerals, locate specific molecules, measure chemical parameters using fluorescent probes and identify the functional groups of organic molecules using certain spectroscopy techniques (infrared, X-rays, etc.). It is also possible to identify chemical interactions between organic molecules and minerals (nuclear magnetic resonance spectroscopy or NMR). For almost all of these techniques, we can turn to a spatially resolved analysis in the case of a very heterogeneous sample or a very precise analysis (little noise/error in the measurement itself) but poorly spatially resolved, which can be interesting in the case of a homogeneous sample.

> There are many microscopy techniques used to study biomineralization. They are distinguished by the nature of the light source used, the penetration depth into the sample and their spatial resolution; they provide different types of information. Photon microscopy uses photons in the visible wavelength range as a light source. Lateral spatial resolution is generally limited to about 200 nm. Confocal laser scanning microscopy (CLSM) uses excitation by monochromatic light (e.g. via a laser) and detects fluorescent light emitted from a thin layer of the sample at a chosen depth. This fluorescence

emission can be intrinsic to the sample (autofluorescence), linked, for example, to cell pigments. Alternatively, the technique can be used to localize fluorescent probes introduced into the sample and designed to (i) hybridize to specific molecules, including specific RNA sequences (FISH techniques), or (ii) react to local physicochemical conditions, by emitting light whose intensity or color vary with, for example, pH or the concentration of certain ions. Other microscopies use X-rays as a light source which, depending on their wavelength, penetrate more or less into the material. These X-rays can be produced by laboratory sources or large particle accelerators called synchrotrons. Certain X-ray microscopies allow the three-dimensional reconstruction of samples (tomography) with spatial resolutions as low as a few nanometers. Others couple with imaging, a spectroscopic analysis of the sample providing an identification and quantification of the chemical elements present and/or for a given element, its speciation, i.e. the state of oxidation of the element and the chemical bonds involved. Finally, certain approaches allow the characterization of the atomic structure of biominerals (crystallography) based on the way in which X-rays are scattered. Electron microscopy is widely used in biomineralogy. Electrons, whatever their energy, are strongly absorbed by matter. Thus, these microscopes operate under a high vacuum and require suitable preparation protocols for the prior dehydration of the sample without altering it too much. Scanning electron microscopy (SEM) uses so-called primary electrons as a light source whose energy is often less than 20 keV (i.e. accelerated under a voltage of 20 kV) and which are focused on the surface of the sample. It detects different signals produced including low energy secondary electrons, delivering information about the surface of the sample and making it possible to observe the topography of the sample with lateral spatial resolutions down to 1 nm. Backscattered electrons, with an energy close to that of primary electrons, mainly provide chemical imaging. Finally, the SEM detects in parallel the X-rays emitted by fluorescence, which provide access to the elementary chemical composition of the sample. Transmission electron microscopy (TEM) differs from SEM in that it uses higher energy electrons as a light source (e.g. 200 keV) to study thin samples of approximately a few hundred nanometers thick. TEM also provides a diversity of data, including images with (sub-)atomic resolution, elementary chemical maps, the atomic structure of minerals by electron diffraction or high-resolution imaging, or even the speciation of chemical elements using electron energy loss spectroscopy. Finally, ion probes use a focused ion beam that ionizes the sample material. Secondary ions are sorted according to their mass-to-charge ratio by a mass spectrometer, providing elemental or isotopic imaging. In recent years, cryoscopic methods have developed. These make it possible to analyze vitrified samples via these different techniques, i.e. frozen in amorphous water ice after being cooled very quickly to the temperature of liquid nitrogen, often under pressure. This offers the possibility of preserving biomineralized samples, very often hydrated, in a quasi-native state (i.e. preserving the ultrastructure).

Box 2.3. *Some microscopy techniques to study biomineralization*

Technique	Spatial scale	Information
Raman spectroscopy	Micrometer	Vibrational spectroscopy, identification of molecules and minerals
Infrared spectroscopy	From several hundred nanometers to the centimeter	Vibrational spectroscopy, identification of molecules and minerals
X-ray fluorescence	Micrometers to the centimeter	Quantified elementary analyses
Mass spectrometry	Several tens of micrometers (laser ablation) to a few millimeters or centimeters	Isotope analysis
NMR spectroscopy	Millimeters/centimeters	Specific-element analyses, chemical speciation, chemical bond identification
X ray diffraction	Several hundred micrometers to centimeters	Mineral analyses, interatomic distance and angles
Confocal laser scanning microscopy (CLSM)	Up to 200 nm x-y	3D imaging of autoflourescing cells, localization of specific fluorescent probes, DNA sequences, or specific chemical conditions
Flourescence in situ hybridization (FISH)	Up to 200 nm x-y	Identification of specific nucleic sequences
SEM	To the nanometer	Nanoscale topographic imaging, imaging of textural relationships between minerals, chemical element analysis, characterization of crystallographic orientations
TEM	To the Angstrom	Nanoscale imaging, crystallographic analyses by electron diffraction, chemical element analyses, chemical speciation analyses by spectroscopy

Table 2.2. *Some analytical techniques used for the study of biominerals*

2.4. Impact of biomineralization on how the Earth functions

Living organisms have had a significant influence on the chemistry of the Earth's surface. For example, the appearance of oxygenic photosynthesis in cyanobacteria led to the oxygenation of the atmosphere (Chapter 5). This has had significant repercussions on the oxidation state of metals such as iron, and consequently their solubility and availability in oceans. Biomineralization also has an influence on the geochemical functioning of the Earth's surface. Indeed, by trapping chemical elements from their dissolved form into solids, biomineralization participates in local and global geochemical cycles. Thus, the availability of certain polluting metals, particularly when in trace quantities, can be significantly affected by the activity of microorganisms inducing their biomineralization. For example, it was shown that iron- and/or arsenic-oxidizing bacteria were responsible for the very effective trapping of arsenic (between 20% and 60% in 30 meters) in sediments of the Reigous stream (Gard) through biomineralization, irrigating mining waste-rock rich in arsenic (Casiot et al. 2003). It has also been shown that certain cyanobacteria could selectively and effectively trap radioactive isotopes such as radium 226 or strontium 90 by biomineralization, and could thus be used to decontaminate water polluted by these isotopes (Mehta et al. 2019). Many other similar cases have been described in the literature. These repercussions can also be quantitatively significant on a global scale, even when these processes are catalyzed by microorganisms whose size is small. The most commonly cited example is that of the silicon cycle, which is the second most abundant element on Earth. Despite many uncertainties, here is the broad outline of what we think we know about the evolution of this cycle over geological time (Figure 2.11; Conley et al. 2017). In the Precambrian, the concentration of dissolved orthosilicic acid (H_4SiO_4) in the ocean was 10 times higher than today, and during at least part of the Precambrian, the cycle was mainly controlled by abiotic processes. At this concentration, the ocean was saturated with respect to amorphous silica and there was likely an abiotic precipitation of massive sedimentary deposits of silica called cherts. There could also have been precipitation of authigenic clays (notably hydrated magnesium and/or iron silicates) in the water column. Since orthosilicic acid can cross membranes, it was likely toxic to cells and we imagine that in order to regulate the intracellular concentration of Si, efficient transporters were selected to expel the Si out of the cells. Then, organisms appeared using Si to synthesize biominerals. These processes of uptake of an element, which changes from toxic to a nutrient, is accompanied by an active uptake (i.e. consuming energy and taking place against the chemical gradient) and a reduction in its concentration in the ocean. The first organisms to biomineralize silica may have been silicifying sponges, forming siliceous spicules. Although these organisms likely appeared well before this, their oldest traces known to date, in the form of submillimeter spicules, date from the transition between the Ediacaran and the Cambrian, almost 540 Ma ago (Chang et al. 2019). Radiolarians appear in the Cambrian, but it was not until the Ordovician that they became important components of the marine silica cycle. Finally, diatoms appeared during the Mesozoic, as well as particularly efficient transporters with a strong affinity for orthosilicic acid, so much so that it was during their expansion in the Cenozoic that ocean concentrations of orthosilicic acid decreased drastically to the very low modern concentrations (a few micromoles at the ocean surface) (Conley et al. 2017). We can thus see how the Si cycle has changed from a predominantly abiotic control to control by biosilicification.

Oceanic concentrations of orthosilicic acid thus become limiting for organisms that require this element and with transporters with lower affinities than those of diatoms: sponges then move from continental ridges to deeper areas where Si concentrations are higher; radiolarians use less silica (their skeleton becomes thinner) except in upwelling zones[3] where silica is less limiting; the diversity of sponge spicules decreases (Knoll 2003). It is possible that the impact of life on the concentration of dissolved Si in the oceans became significant as soon as at the end of the Archaean, since Si transporters homologous to those of silicifying protists were found in bacteria (Conley et al. 2017) and it has been shown that certain bacteria can also biomineralize amorphous silica intracellularly (Li et al. 2022).

Finally, it should be noted that diatoms represent nearly 20% of primary (organic carbon) production (Knoll and Kotrc 2015). By biomineralizing silica, they become heavier and are more likely to fall to the seabed after death, more effectively transferring the organic matter into the sediments. They thus increase the export of marine primary production to the ocean floor, hence a coupling with the carbon cycle. On the other hand, despite the large mass of carbonate sediments formed by biomineralization, it is today considered that living organisms have not had as strong an impact on the calcium and/or bicarbonate contents of the oceans as that observed for silica. Nevertheless, it is clear that carbonate sediments on present-day Earth and throughout the Phanerozoic are overwhelmingly biogenic. Striking examples are those of reef formations, or chalk cliffs formed by the accumulation of coccoliths (Figure 2.3).

3. An upwelling designates an upwelling of deep, cold and nutrient-rich water at certain coasts. These upwellings of nutrient-rich water are generally accompanied by a significant increase in biological productivity.

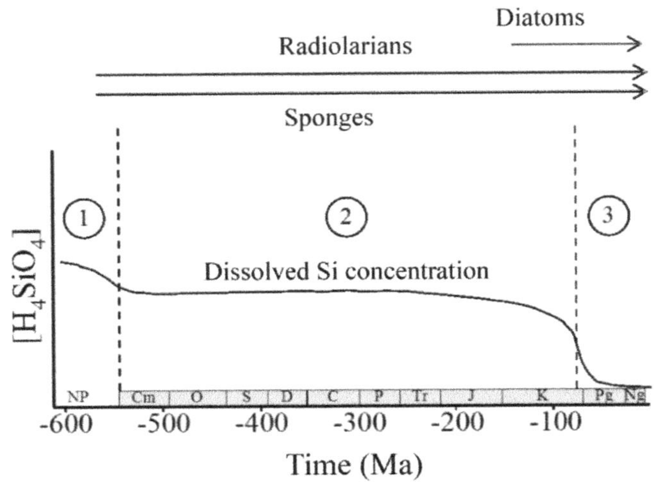

Figure 2.11. *Evolution of the concentration of dissolved silica in the oceans over geological time. During an initial phase, this concentration is mainly controlled by abiotic reactions. Then, after the appearance of radiolarians and sponges, these organisms control the dissolved silica concentration to a lower value (phase 2). Finally, during a third phase, following the advent of diatoms, the concentration of dissolved silica drops further. For a color version of this figure, see www.iste.co.uk/benzerara/geosphere.zip*

2.5. Impact of biomineralization on the functioning of living organisms

In return, biomineralization also influences the functioning of living organisms. Firstly, biomineralizing organisms themselves. In some cases where biomineralization is induced or influenced, it is suggested that the precipitation of minerals that encrust the cells may be lethal, because the mineral crust formed limits on the exchange of nutrients between the cells and the outside and/or the crystals may damage the membranes. Consequently, certain microorganisms have developed strategies to keep the nucleation of minerals away from the cells to prevent this encrustation. This is the case for bacteria of the *Gallionella* or *Leptothrix* genera, for example, which live in iron-saturated solutions and produce extracellular polymers promoting the nucleation of iron oxyhydroxides (Figure 2.12). Moreover, in the case of controlled biomineralizations, these have a biological function that increases the selective value of organisms (Cosmidis and Benzerara 2022). The cost of forming biominerals is likely lower than that of an equivalent organic structure, hence the advantage of producing them (Raven et al. 1999). This function may have changed over time. For example, the formation of intracellular magnetites by magnetotactic bacteria could have allowed detoxification of intracellular iron for these bacteria before they used them as a compass. In the same way, the siliceous spicules of sponges could have provided a supporting function before that of defense against predators. The expansion of skeletal biominerals could have had several consequences on the history of life: accompanying the development of larger organisms (which also implies the development of other biological structures); better resistance to predation, leading in turn to the selection of adapted structures in predators, thus following the Red Queen hypothesis in evolutionary biology.

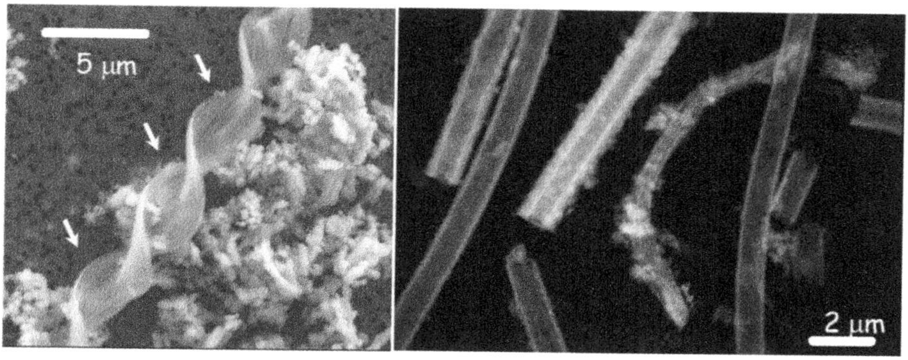

Figure 2.12. *Iron-oxidizing bacteria forming extracellular polymers to localize biomineralization beyond cells. Left: scanning electron microscopy image (secondary electron mode) of a twisted polymer biomineralized by iron-rich phases (arrows), formed by bacteria of the* Gallionella *genus. The cell, not visible here, is attached to one end of the twist. In the background, we see the ~200 nm pores of the filter on which the sample was collected. Right: transmission electron microscopy image (STEM mode) showing polymeric tubes encrusted by iron-rich phases, formed by bacteria of the genus* Leptothrix. *Cells not visible here grow inside the tubes*

2.6. Evolutionary history of biomineralization processes

There are two sources of information allowing us to reconstruct the history of biomineralization processes: (1) the study of the fossil record, consisting of searching for fossil organisms associated with biomineralized phases. This approach provides a lot of information as well as having limits, in particular because diagenetic processes can sometimes (i) reveal minerals not formed by biomineralization but which can be confused; (ii) dissolve them. Thus, Westacott et al. (2021) show that the apparent increase in diatom abundance in the Cenozoic is partly linked to the fact that diatom frustules were not preserved in older times due to the chemical conditions that prevailed. Likewise, in plants, it is difficult to identify the initial traces of silicification (Trembath-Reichert et al. 2015). (2) A second approach involves establishing the phylogenetic links of current living beings, particularly those that are relatively divergent, in order to infer the biomineralizing capacities of their common ancestor. Here again, knowledge of functional genes serving as markers of the biomineralization processes can also be a useful aid in reconstructing the evolutionary history of the biomineralization process.

We know very little about the oldest biomineralizing organisms, but the traces of stromatolites and the ancestral nature of the formation of intracellular minerals (magnetites in certain bacteria, carbonates in cyanobacteria) indicate that these processes are very ancient (Figure 2.13). Biologically controlled or induced mineralization processes may have participated in the formation of large sedimentary deposits, from banded iron formations (BIFs) to certain phosphorite deposits. However, we still too often limit the history of biomineralization to that of skeletal biomineralization in eukaryotes. This is mainly because it is better understood. This reached its climax during the Cambrian explosion, a brief period of time during which living organisms appeared (Marin et al. 2014). Weakly mineralized skeletons, such as that of *Cloudina*, are observed in the fossil record at the end of the Ediacaran (630–542 Ma). Then, within 25 Ma, a small duration for geological time scales, most of the known skeletal forms appear, i.e. more than 178 architectures recognized in marine animals. Numerous mineralized structures appeared at this time, including spicules, spines, scales, or shells, etc., composed of diversified mineral phases (mainly carbonates, phosphates or silica) in most metazoan phyla. Overall, biomineralization has been shown to arise independently in animals many times, but all with a common basis (Murdock 2020). This common base results from a set of pre-existing genes, called "the biomineralization toolbox". These genes, which appeared during the Precambrian, some possibly in prokaryotes, were therefore present in the non-biomineralizing common ancestor of metazoans. It has been proposed that some of these recruited genes initially encoded proteins inhibiting biomineralization, at a time when environmental conditions (notably ocean chemistry) were conducive to spontaneous mineralization and were toxic to cellular interiors. Later, these cellular components, for example, ionic pumps extracting ions outside the cell, controlled biomineralization, for example, by operating in the other direction and importing these ions. Additionally, early animals may have had less strict control over the formation of biomineralized structures. This would explain a greater initial disparity in the architecture of biomineralized structures and the mineralogical nature of biominerals, which depended on the aqueous chemistry of the environment in which they appeared. Then, these biominerals were used for defense against predation. Biological control became increasingly more prevalent as the evolutionary history of biomineralizing organisms progressed. Other events followed in the history of biomineralization: the appearance of massive carbonate skeletons in the Ordovician (notably articulated brachiopods, octocorals, bryozoans), then the development of reefs in the Devonian and Carboniferous periods. While in the Paleozoic, biomineralization by benthic organisms dominated, large-scale biomineralization by planktonic organisms expanded in the Mesozoic: coccolithophorids from the Triassic with a peak at the end of the Cretaceous, then planktonic foraminifera and finally diatoms. Several biological innovations may have caused the development of these biomineralizing organisms, such as the use of new polymers for biomineralization such as polysaccharides in coccolithophorids and polyamines in diatoms.

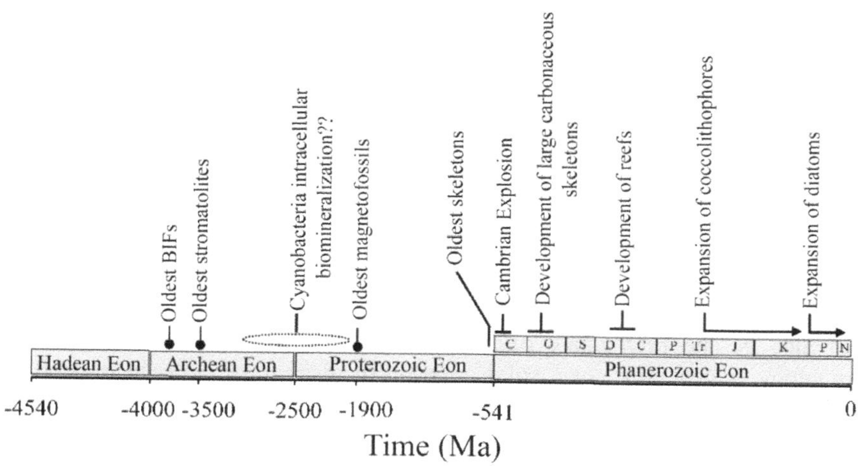

Figure 2.13. *Some stages of the geological history of biomineralization. For a color version of this figure, see www.iste.co.uk/benzerara/geosphere.zip*

2.7. Applications of biomineralogy

The study of minerals formed by living beings motivates numerous disciplinary fields and diverse applications (De Muynck et al. 2010; Dhami et al. 2013). We only mention a small part of it here. For fundamental research, biominerals are used for the reconstruction of past physicochemical conditions at the Earth's surface, including ocean paleo-salinities, paleo-pH and paleo-temperatures. For example, trace element compositions or isotopic composition of carbon, oxygen or other chemical elements can be measured in biominerals formed by planktonic or benthic marine organisms. The isotopic composition of oxygen ($\delta^{18}O$) of carbonates formed by foraminifera depends on the oxygen isotopic composition of the water in which they lived (which in turn depends on the volume of ice sheets at the time they lived) and the temperature of the water when the biomineral formed. Thus, provided that the isotopic composition of the oceans at the time of interest is known, these measurements provide a real paleo-thermometer.

Biominerals also have the advantage of telling us about the history of life. Organic matter composing unicellular or multicellular living beings is very labile on the geological time scale and is very rarely preserved, particularly for the most ancient periods, which would nevertheless inform us about the first moments of the history of life and/or possible traces of life on other planets such as Mars. By contrast, minerals formed by living things and their imprints are often more resistant to degradation and are preserved. This is how many stages in the history of life have been documented using vertebrate skeletons. During the Cambrian explosion, traces of so-called small-shelled fauna are entirely known to us through biominerals. Regarding the search for traces of life in very ancient rocks from the Archaean Eon and/or on Mars, certain strategies aim to find minerals with characteristics indicative of the involvement of living things (Benzerara et al. 2019). Thus, in 1996, researchers claimed to have observed submicrometric magnetite crystals in a Martian meteorite, with structural and chemical properties characteristic of life. This led them to propose the presence of traces of past life on Mars almost 4 billion years ago. However, other studies subsequently showed that some of these properties could also be the prerogative of purely abiotic magnetites. In the same way, morphology is generally not a solid criterion to distinguish between mineral and living organisms, since there are biomorphs, i.e. abiotic objects with a morphology similar to that of living organisms. The difficulty here is demonstrating the uniqueness of properties imprinted by living organisms without having exhaustively studied all the possibilities offered by the non-living. This is the challenge in continuing research on this subject. Beyond these fundamental aspects, biominerals are also of interest to the medical field. This is the case for certain pathologies, such as kidney stones (lithiasis). The formation of some of these stones is induced by bacterial infections which, for example, by hydrolyzing urea, lead to an increase in urine pH and thus the precipitation of ammonia–magnesium phosphates such as struvite (Letavernier et al. 2023). Conversely, the study of the mechanisms involved in the normal functioning of biomineralization can inspire treatment strategies. The idea of bioinspiration is that over billions of years, natural selection has optimized processes allowing the formation of functional structures, in this case biominerals (Sanchez et al. 2005). For example, the osteogenic properties of corals inspire bone tissue reconstruction strategies (Petite et al. 2000). The synthesis of certain nanomaterials with exceptional physical or chemical properties is inspired by living organisms. This is the case for magnetite crystals formed by magnetotactic bacteria, which have very interesting magnetic properties, particularly relevant for developing hyperthermia treatments, i.e. the local heating of tumor cells inducing their elimination (Gandia et al. 2019). There are many other examples, such as the use of the formation of minerals by bacteria to depollute water, consolidate soils or sediments via their biocementation or even renovate deteriorated facades.

2.8. Conclusion

We have seen that living organisms share very close connections with minerals, since their origins. Many organisms induce the formation of minerals with strong control over the structural, physical and chemical properties of the biominerals produced. The modification of aqueous chemistry at the microenvironment level or the synthesis of biomolecules affecting the nucleation of mineral phases are among the main ways of intervention by living organisms in these processes. This has led to a diversification of mineral species observed on the Earth's surface as well as major changes in geochemical cycles, such as that of silicon in the oceans. In return, many mineral species play key roles in the biology of organisms with diverse functions ranging from detoxification to mobility along magnetic field lines to skeletal support or protection against predators.

The formation of biominerals follows the laws of physics and chemistry in a similar way to abiotic minerals, but the biological catalysis involved can impart special properties that allow biological processes to be traced. Ultimately, it appears that biomineralogy is eminently interdisciplinary and requires the joint use of approaches from biology, chemistry and materials physics. This is also, despite the importance of the processes concerned and the relative age of the questions asked, a field still under development, which will undoubtedly generate new knowledge in the years to come (see videos of the seminars of Biomin IMPMC, https://www.youtube.com/@biomin_impmc9013).

2.9. References

Amor, M., Busigny, V., Durand-Dubief, M., Tharaud, M., Ona-Nguema, G., Gélabert, A., Alphandéry, E., Menguy, N., Benedetti, M.F., Chebbi, I. et al. (2015). Chemical signature of magnetotactic bacteria. *Proceedings of the National Academy of Sciences*, 112, 1699–1703. doi: 10.1073/pnas.1414112112.

Benzerara, K., Skouri-Panet, F., Li, J., Férard, C., Gugger, M., Laurent, T., Couradeau, E., Ragon, M., Cosmidis, J., Menguy, N. et al. (2014). Intracellular Ca-carbonate biomineralization is widespread in cyanobacteria. *PNAS*, 111, 10933–10938. doi: 10.1073/pnas.1403510111.

Benzerara, K., Bernard, S., Miot, J. (2019). Mineralogical identification of traces of life. In *Biosignatures for Astrobiology*, Cavalazzi, B. and Westall, F. (eds). Springer, Cham, 123–144. doi: 10.1007/978-3-319-96175-0_6.

Benzerara, K., Duprat, E., Bitard-Feildel, T., Caumes, G., Cassier-Chauvat, C., Chauvat, F., Dezi, M., Diop, S.I., Gaschignard, G., Görgen, S. et al. (2022). A new gene family diagnostic for intracellular biomineralization of amorphous Ca carbonates by cyanobacteria. *Genome Biology and Evolution*, 14, evac026. doi: 10.1093/gbe/evac026.

Casiot, C., Morin, G., Juillot, F., Bruneel, O., Personné, J.-C., Leblanc, M., Duquesne, K., Bonnefoy, V., Elbaz-Poulichet, F. (2003). Bacterial immobilization and oxidation of arsenic in acid mine drainage (Carnoulès creek, France). *Water Research*, 37, 2929–2936. doi: 10.1016/S0043-1354(03)00080-0.

Chang, S., Zhang, L., Clausen, S., Bottjer, D.J., Feng, Q. (2019). The Ediacaran–Cambrian rise of siliceous sponges and development of modern oceanic ecosystems. *Precambrian Research*, 333, 105438. doi: 10.1016/j.precamres.2019.105438.

Cleland, C.E., Hazen, R.M., Morrison, S.M. (2021). Historical natural kinds and mineralogy: Systematizing contingency in the context of necessity. *Proceedings of the National Academy of Sciences*, 118, e2015370118. doi: 10.1073/pnas.2015370118.

Conley, D.J., Frings, P.J., Fontorbe, G., Clymans, W., Stadmark, J., Hendry, K.R., Marron, A.O., De La Rocha, C.L. (2017). Biosilicification drives a decline of dissolved Si in the oceans through geologic time. *Frontiers in Marine Science*, 4, 397.

Cosmidis, J. and Benzerara, K. (2022). Why do microbes make minerals? *Comptes Rendus. Géoscience*, 354, 1–39. doi: 10.5802/crgeos.107.

Couradeau, E., Benzerara, K., Gerard, E., Moreira, D., Bernard, S., Brown, G.E., Lopez-Garcia, P. (2012). An early-branching microbialite cyanobacterium forms intracellular carbonates. *Science*, 336, 459–462. doi: 10.1126/science.1216171.

Dauphin, Y. (2023). A brief history of biomineralization studies. *ACS Biomaterials Science & Engineering*, 9(4), 1774–1790. doi: 10.1021/acsbiomaterials.1c01385.

De Muynck, W., De Belie, N., Verstraete, W. (2010). Microbial carbonate precipitation in construction materials: A review. *Ecological Engineering, Special Issue: BioGeoCivil Engineering*, 36, 118–136. doi: 10.1016/j.ecoleng.2009.02.006.

Dhami, N.K., Reddy, M.S., Mukherjee, A. (2013). Biomineralization of calcium carbonates and their engineered applications: A review. *Frontiers in Microbiology*, 4, 314. doi: 10.3389/fmicb.2013.00314.

DiMasi, E. and Gower, L.B. (eds) (2014). *Characterization of Biominerals and Biomimetic Materials*. CRC Press, Boca Raton. doi: 10.1201/b16621.

Dove, P.M. (2010). The rise of skeletal biominerals. *Elements*, 6, 37–42. doi: 10.2113/gselements.6.1.37.

Drake, J.L., Mass, T., Stolarski, J., Von Euw, S., van de Schootbrugge, B., Falkowski, P.G. (2020). How corals made rocks through the ages. *Global Change Biology*, 26, 31–53. doi: 10.1111/gcb.14912.

Ehrlich, H., Koutsoukos, P.G., Demadis, K.D., Pokrovsky, O.S. (2008). Principles of demineralization: Modern strategies for the isolation of organic frameworks: Part I. Common definitions and history. *Micron*, 39, 1062–1091. doi: 10.1016/j.micron.2008.02.004.

Gandia, D., Gandarias, L., Rodrigo, I., Robles-García, J., Das, R., Garaio, E., García, J.Á., Phan, M.-H., Srikanth, H., Orue, I. et al. (2019). Unlocking the potential of magnetotactic bacteria as magnetic hyperthermia agents. *Small*, 15, e1902626. doi: 10.1002/smll.201902626.

Görgen, S., Benzerara, K., Skouri-Panet, F., Gugger, M., Chauvat, F., Cassier-Chauvat, C. (2020). The diversity of molecular mechanisms of carbonate biomineralization by bacteria. *Discover Materials*, 1, 2. doi: 10.1007/s43939-020-00001-9.

Gower, L.B. (2008). Biomimetic model systems for investigating the amorphous precursor pathway and its role in biomineralization. *Chemical Reviews*, 108, 4551–4627. doi: 10.1021/cr800443h.

Hazen, R.M. and Morrison, S.M. (2022). On the paragenetic modes of minerals: A mineral evolution perspective. *American Mineralogist*, 107, 1262–1287. doi: 10.2138/am-2022-8099.

Herlitze, I., Marie, B., Marin, F., Jackson, D.J. (2018). Molecular modularity and asymmetry of the molluscan mantle revealed by a gene expression atlas. *Gigascience*, 7, giy056. doi: 10.1093/gigascience/giy056.

Houdan, A., Billard, C., Marie, D., Not, F., Sáez, A.G., Young, J.R., Probert, I. (2004). Holococcolithophore-heterococcolithophore (Haptophyta) life cycles: Flow cytometric analysis of relative ploidy levels. *Systematics and Biodiversity*, 1, 453–465. doi: 10.1017/S1477200003001270.

Knoll, A.H. (2003). Biomineralization and evolutionary history. *Reviews in Mineralogy and Geochemistry*, 54, 329–356. doi: 10.2113/0540329.

Knoll, A.H. and Kotrc, B. (2015). Protistan skeletons: A geologic history of evolution and constraint. In *Evolution of Lightweight Structures: Analyses and Technical Applications*, Hamm, C. (ed.). Springer Netherlands, Dordrecht, 1–16. doi: 10.1007/978-94-017-9398-8_1.

Lefevre, C.T. and Bazylinski, D.A. (2013). Ecology, diversity, and evolution of magnetotactic bacteria. *Microbiology and Molecular Biology Reviews*, 77, 497–526. doi: 10.1128/MMBR.00021-13.

Letavernier, E., Bazin, D., Daudon, M. (2023). Description of stone morphology and crystalluria improve diagnosis and care of kidney stone formers. *Healthcare*, 11, 2. doi: 10.3390/healthcare11010002.

Li, J., Liu, P., Menguy, N., Zhang, X., Wang, J., Benzerara, K., Feng, L., Sun, L., Zheng, Y., Meng, F. et al. (2022). Intracellular silicification by early-branching magnetotactic bacteria. *Science Advances*, 8, eabn6045. doi: 10.1126/sciadv.abn6045.

Lowenstam, H.A. (1981). Minerals formed by organisms. *Science*, 211, 1126–1131. doi: 10.1126/science.7008198.

Lowenstam, H.A. and Weiner, S. (1989). *On Biomineralization*. Oxford University Press, New York.

Maas, A.E., Lawson, G.L., Bergan, A.J., Tarrant, A.M. (2018). Exposure to CO2 influences metabolism, calcification and gene expression of the thecosome pteropod Limacina retroversa. *Journal of Experimental Biology*, 221, jeb164400. doi: 10.1242/jeb.164400.

Marin, F., Le Roy, N., Marie, B., Ramos-Silva, P., Bundeleva, I., Guichard, N., Immel, F. (2014). Metazoan calcium carbonate biomineralizations: Macroevolutionary trends – challenges for the coming decade. *Bulletin de la Société Géologique de France*, 185, 217–232. doi: 10.2113/gssgfbull.185.4.217.

Marin, F., Bundeleva, I., Takeuchi, T., Immel, F., Medakovic, D. (2016). Organic matrices in metazoan calcium carbonate skeletons: Composition, functions, evolution. *Journal of Structural Biology, Biomineralization*, 196, 98–106. doi: 10.1016/j.jsb.2016.04.006.

Marron, A.O., Ratcliffe, S., Wheeler, G.L., Goldstein, R.E., King, N., Not, F., de Vargas, C., Richter, D.J. (2016). The evolution of silicon transport in eukaryotes. *Molecular Biology and Evolution*, 33, 3226–3248. doi: 10.1093/molbev/msw209.

Mehta, N., Benzerara, K., Kocar, B.D., Chapon, V. (2019). Sequestration of radionuclides radium-226 and strontium-90 by cyanobacteria forming intracellular calcium carbonates. *Environmental Science & Technology*, 53, 12639–12647. doi: 10.1021/acs.est.9b03982.

Meyers, M.A., McKittrick, J., Chen, P.-Y. (2013). Structural biological materials: Critical mechanics-materials connections. *Science*, 339, 773–779. doi: 10.1126/science.1220854.

Murdock, D.J.E. (2020). The 'biomineralization toolkit' and the origin of animal skeletons. *Biological Reviews*, 95, 1372–1392. doi: 10.1111/brv.12614.

Murshed, M. (2018). Mechanism of bone mineralization. *Cold Spring Harbor Perspectives in Medicine*, 8, a031229. doi: 10.1101/cshperspect.a031229.

Nickel, E.H. and Grice, J.D. (1998). The IMA commission on new minerals and mineral names: Procedures and guidelines on mineral nomenclature. *Mineralogy and Petrology*, 64, 237–263. doi: 10.1007/BF01226571.

Petite, H., Viateau, V., Bensaïd, W., Meunier, A., de Pollak, C., Bourguignon, M., Oudina, K., Sedel, L., Guillemin, G. (2000). Tissue-engineered bone regeneration. *Nature Biotechnology*, 18, 959–963. doi: 10.1038/79449.

Raven, J.A., Evans, M.C.W., Korb, R.E. (1999). The role of trace metals in photosynthetic electron transport in O2-evolving organisms. *Photosynthesis Research*, 60, 111–150. doi: 10.1023/A:1006282714942.

Reznikov, N., Hoac, B., Buss, D.J., Addison, W.N., Barros, N.M.T., McKee, M.D. (2020). Biological stenciling of mineralization in the skeleton: Local enzymatic removal of inhibitors in the extracellular matrix. *Bone*, 138, 115447. doi: 10.1016/j.bone.2020.115447.

Salamanca-Díaz, D.A., Ritschard, E.A., Schmidbaur, H., Wanninger, A. (2022). Comparative single-cell transcriptomics reveals novel genes involved in bivalve embryonic shell formation and questions ontogenetic homology of molluscan shell types. *Frontiers in Cell and Developmental Biology*, 10. doi: 10.3389/fcell.2022.883755.

Sanchez, C., Arribart, H., Giraud Guille, M.M. (2005). Biomimetism and bioinspiration as tools for the design of innovative materials and systems. *Nature Materials*, 4, 277–288. doi: 10.1038/nmat1339.

Sevilgen, D.S., Venn, A.A., Hu, M.Y., Tambutté, E., de Beer, D., Planas-Bielsa, V., Tambutté, S. (2019). Full in vivo characterization of carbonate chemistry at the site of calcification in corals. *Science Advances*, 5, eaau7447. doi: 10.1126/sciadv.aau7447.

Trembath-Reichert, E., Wilson, J.P., McGlynn, S.E., Fischer, W.W. (2015). Four hundred million years of silica biomineralization in land plants. *Proceedings of the National Academy of Sciences*, 112, 5449–5454. doi: 10.1073/pnas.1500289112.

van der Weijden, C.H. and van der Weijden, R.D. (2014). Calcite growth: Rate dependence on saturation, on ratios of dissolved calcium and (bi)carbonate and on their complexes. *Journal of Crystal Growth*, 394, 137–144. doi: 10.1016/j.jcrysgro.2014.02.042.

Westacott, S., Planavsky, N.J., Zhao, M.-Y., Hull, P.M. (2021). Revisiting the sedimentary record of the rise of diatoms. *Proceedings of the National Academy of Sciences*, 118, e2103517118. doi: 10.1073/pnas.2103517118.

Yang, H., Sun, H.J., Downs, R.T. (2011). Hazenite, KNaMg2(PO4)2·14H2O, a new biologically related phosphate mineral, from Mono Lake, California, U.S.A. *American Mineralogist*, 96, 675–681. doi: 10.2138/am.2011.3668.

Zeyen, N., Benzerara, K., Li, J., Groleau, A., Balan, E., Robert, J.-L., Estève, I., Tavera, R., Moreira, D., López-García, P. (2015). Formation of low-T hydrated silicates in modern microbialites from Mexico and implications for microbial fossilization. *Frontiers in Earth Science*, 3. doi: 10.3389/feart.2015.00064.

Zhao, R., Takeuchi, T., Luo, Y.-J., Ishikawa, A., Kobayashi, T., Koyanagi, R., Villar-Briones, A., Yamada, L., Sawada, H., Iwanaga, S. et al. (2018). Dual gene repertoires for larval and adult shells reveal molecules essential for molluscan shell formation. *Molecular Biology and Evolution*, 35, 2751–2761. doi: 10.1093/molbev/msy172.

3

Microbialites in the Fossil and Current Record

Emmanuelle VENNIN[1], Anthony BOUTON[2], Pierre BOUSSAGOL[1] and Pieter T. VISSCHER[3]

[1] *Laboratoire Biogéosciences, University of Burgundy, Dijon, France*

[2] *University Bourgogne Franche-Comté, Besançon, France*

[3] *University of Connecticut, Storrs, USA*

3.1. Introduction

Since we have established the principles governing biomineralization in the previous chapters, we will now discuss an example of rock formed by living organisms: microbialites. Microbialites are organo-sedimentary deposits that result from the activity of benthic microbial communities (Figure 3.1). The formation of microbialites occurs through the trapping of detrital sediments and/or in situ precipitation (also referred to as authigenic) of minerals (Burne and Moore 1987). Thus, microbialites result from the lithification of microbial mats, which are complex ecological structures composed of different microbial communities that interact with each other (e.g. Dupraz et al. 2009). These microbial communities are composed of a wide diversity of bacteria but sometimes also micro-eukaryotes, such as diatoms. Interactions between the different communities, as well as environmental parameters, will lead, depending on the case, to the precipitation and/or dissolution of minerals (Dupraz et al. 2011). A net result in favor of precipitation will lead to the formation of microbialites. Microbialites most often form carbonate edifices (Reitner et al. 1996), although some can also be composed of silica (Walter et al. 1972), sulfates (Rouchy and Monty 2000) or phosphates

Interactions between the Geosphere and the Biosphere,
coordinated by Karim BENZERARA and Christophe THOMAZO.

(Krajewski et al. 2000). Currently, mineralizing or non-mineralizing microbial mats develop in environments as diverse as lagoons, salt or freshwater lakes, rivers or reef cavities and show great tolerance to variations in temperature, salinity or dissolved nutrients (Della Porta 2015). Also, microbialites from the geological record particularly interest us. These archives, both biological and sedimentary, are one of the oldest traces of life on Earth (Schopf et al. 2007). In addition, they record major events in the evolution of planet Earth (section 3.5.2), the most significant of which is undoubtedly the Great Oxygenation Event, approximately 2.4 billion years ago (see Chapter 5). This event saw an increase in the oxygen content of the atmosphere, produced by cyanobacteria carrying out oxygenic photosynthesis (Planavsky et al. 2014; Schopf 2014). In addition, microbial biocenoses react remarkably to biological crises (Bourillot et al. 2010; Vennin et al. 2015) and are frequently the first to recolonize ecological niches deserted by eukaryotes (Riding 2006).

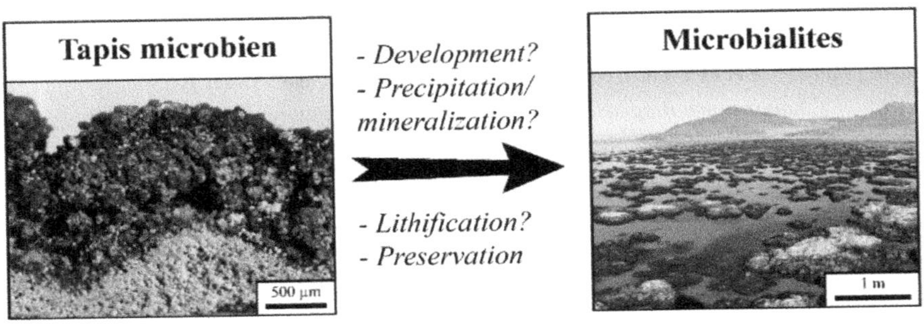

Figure 3.1. *Photos of microbial mats and microbialites. The former becomes the latter when it lithifies by in situ precipitation and/or trapping of detrital particles. This leads to better preservation in the geological record. For a color version of this figure, see www.iste.co.uk/benzerara/geosphere.zip*

3.2. Microbialites: a continuous archive of Earth's history

3.2.1. *Historical meaning of terms*

Microbialites have long been classified as algal limestones (Johnson 1961). The microbial communities composing them often include abundant cyanobacteria, previously called "blue-green" algae (Carr and Whitton 1982). However, while algal limestones are essentially composed of algal skeletons, microbial limestones are not! In 1967, Aitken proposed the term cryptoalgal sedimentary rock, which was replaced by cryptomicrobial in 1986 (Kennard and James 1986), then abandoned it in favor of microbialites, which now refer to microbial components generally and not just to cyanobacteria (Burne and Moore 1987). However, the definition proposed by these authors is very close to that proposed by Awramik and Margulis (1974) for stromatolites. In order to avoid the use of multiple terms for the same definition and because stromatolites meet different descriptions – such as (1) microbial and laminated (Krumbein 1983), (2) microbial but not necessarily laminated (Awramik and Margulis 1974) and (3) laminated but not necessarily biogenic (Semikhatov et al. 1979) – the term stromatolite is now restricted to laminated mineralized microbial structures. Thus, the term microbialite is now a general term grouping all microbial benthic deposits, marine or lacustrine, such as stromatolites (laminated), thrombolites (clotted), dendrolites (arborescent) or leiolites (without specific internal structures) (Riding 2011). The term microbialite has also been applied to authigenic accumulations of carbonates in which microbes are found, such as tufa, travertine, speleothem, spring deposits or hydrothermal vents. However, an inherent difficulty in using this term is recognizing the biogenic origin of the rocks. This difficulty appeared as early as the original publication of Kalkowsky (1908) who, for the first time by studying stromatolites dated to the Triassic, suggested a biogenic origin for the formation of microbialites. The controversy confronting a biotic/abiotic origin arose and continues to this day. Thus, for these carbonate objects and particularly for Precambrian structures, confirming biogenicity is a challenge (Grotzinger 1988). It is even more difficult since microbialites can sometimes present a certain hybridity by combining carbonates of abiotic origin, others of microbial origin or others formed by nonmicrobial eukaryotes (Riding and Virgone 2020; Vennin et al. 2021).

3.2.2. *Classification criteria for microbialites*

There is diversity in the classification of microbialites. We highlight this because the use of standard terminology when describing microbialites facilitates comparisons with information available in the literature. First of all, microbial carbonates can be subdivided into "bioconstruction" when biotic structures are built and bioaccumulation when carbonate grains are accumulated in continuous beds or levels often composed of oncoids (Vennin et al. 2019). Microbialites are then described according to four observational scales (Shapiro 2000) (Figure 3.2): (1) the megastructure refers to the organization of different structures, which can be called bioherms or biostromes; (2) the macrostructure refers to the morphology of an individualized structure (in this context, morphological descriptions alone are typically used to qualify and identify microbialites (Figure 3.3)); (3) the mesostructure is used to describe the internal structures of a macrostructure, which are visible to the naked eye; and (4) the microstructure corresponds to the microscopic details observed under a petrographic microscope or by scanning electron microscopy.

The characterization of microbialites by microscopy methods makes it possible to identify the presence of microorganisms (fossils), and metagenomic methods make it possible to characterize the incredible diversity of microbes participating in their formation (see Chapter 4).

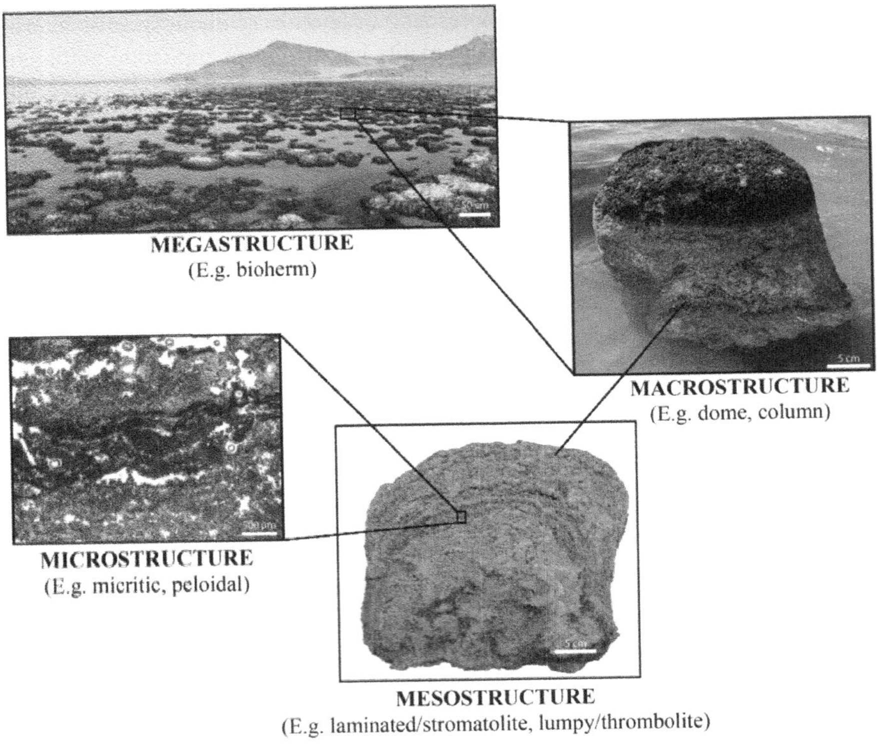

Figure 3.2. *Parameters for describing microbialites from the Great Salt Lake in Utah (USA) at four different scales. For a color version of this figure, see www.iste.co.uk/benzerara/geosphere.zip*

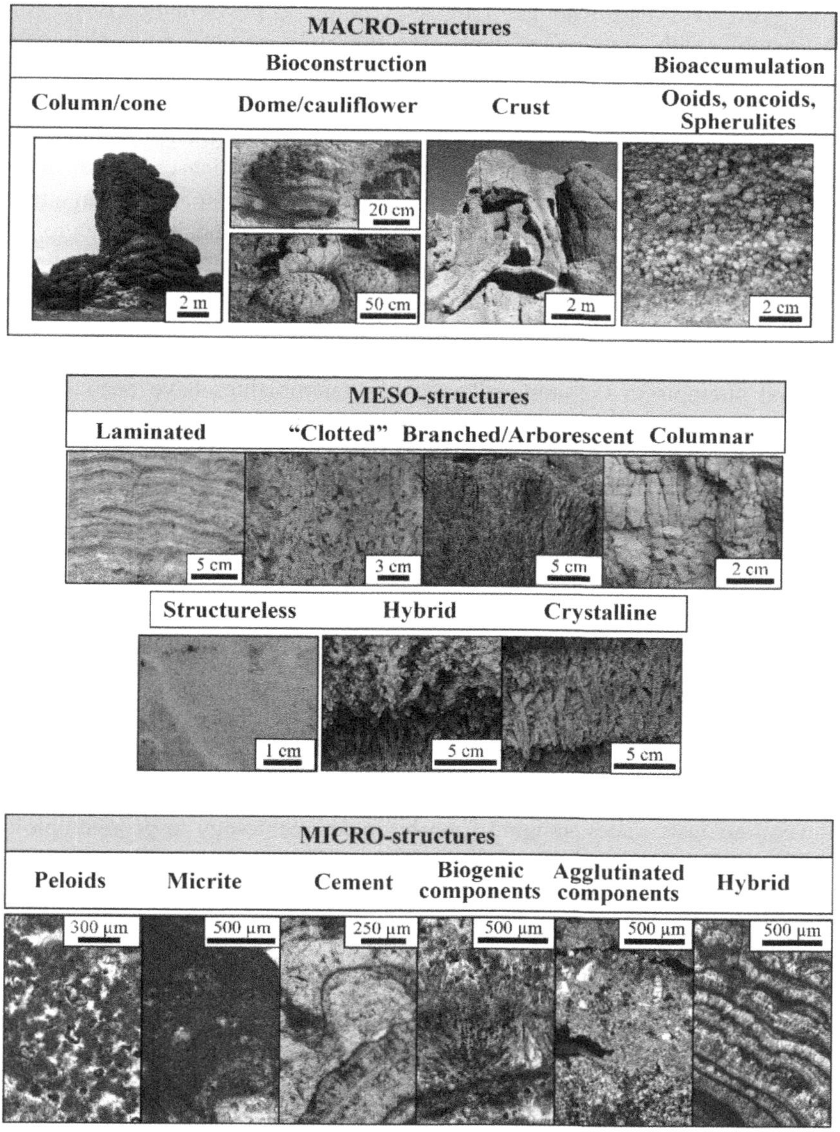

Figure 3.3. *Illustrated examples of macro-, meso- and micro-structures. For a color version of this figure, see www.iste.co.uk/benzerara/geosphere.zip*

The most used classification for the description of microbialites refers to the mesostructure, with four main types (Figure 3.3): stromatolites (laminated); thrombolites (clotted); leiolites (structureless); and finally dendrolites (branching/ arborescent) (Dupraz et al. 2011). This scale appears to be the most appropriate: on the one hand, it is easily visible in the field (unlike the microstructure, which requires microscopy techniques and the macrostructure, which can be difficult to identify in a two-dimensional section). These different mesostructures can alternate within the same macrostructure, thus forming a composite structure. The classifications proposed in this work use objective- description criteria that allow for the characterization of carbonate deposits independently of their depositional environment.

Several attempts to taxonomically classify microbialites have been made for biostratigraphic purposes. The condition for their use was that the microbialites follow a Darwinian evolution, that they are unique, recognizable and limited in time (Semikhatov and Raaben 2000; Shapiro 2007). This meets the definition of a stratigraphic fossil, and it is especially for Precambrian stromatolites that taxonomic classifications have been proposed (Bertrand-Sarfati and Walter 1981; Semikhatov and Raaben 2000; Zaitseva et al. 2016). Grey and Awramik (2020) provide a historical review of the use of microbialites in stratigraphy and suggest using the terms "group" and "form" rather than genera and species for these objects composed of a great diversity of microorganisms.

3.2.3. *Tools and methods for characterizing microbialites*

Several analysis scales, ranging from basin sedimentology to geomicrobiology, are necessary to understand these complex objects in detail. In addition, microbialites are widely diverse both in age and nature. The choice of analysis technique therefore depends on the scientific questioning (Figure 3.4).

Microbialite analysis generally begins with field studies. A hierarchical approach to characterization can be conducted from megastructure to microstructure. Mapping (using satellite, aerial or geological images) with a geographic information system (GIS) allows for spatialization of microbial objects. At the outcrop scale, the characterization of structures involves estimating their size, shape, spacing and geometric relationships with the surrounding sediments. At the object scale, new characteristics such as the nature of the surfaces, the characterization of mesostructures and the degree of preservation provide additional diagnostic elements. Sometimes, sawing and polishing of samples provide a truly spectacular observation window. A serial debitage of the structures allows access to a three-dimensional geometry. The microstructures are visualized by the production of thin sections and petrographic studies, or by 3D imaging using tomography methods such as CT scan (Bourillot et al. 2020). In addition to these field observations, a statistical approach to the object morphology can be implemented to establish classifications. Different attributes are used for the parameterization of microbial structures based on the profile, diameter, degree of curvature of the laminae and their thickness when observed, etc. More sophisticated quantitative approaches of mathematical modeling have been applied to microbialites, in particular on morphogenesis. These approaches have made it possible to discuss their biotic/abiotic character (Grotzinger and Rothman 1996), or to specify the relationships between microbes, sediments, and physical and chemical factors in the environment. As it is necessary to place these objects in their context, a hydrogeological and geochemical characterization of the water associated with microbial mats can be carried out directly in the field or in the laboratory for temperature, pH, partial pressure of CO_2 (pCO_2), conductivity, and major ion concentrations ($Ca^{2+,}$ Mg^{2+}, Na^+, K^+, Cl^-, NO_3^-, SO_4^{2-}, HCO_3^{2-}). The saturation indices (see Chapter 2) of the different mineral phases can be modeled using the Pitzer database (1979) in the PhreeqC software.

At a finer scale, the mineralogy of microbialites can be obtained using X-ray diffraction (XRD) analyses, quantification of total carbonates by calcimetry (using a Bernard calcimeter, for example) and Fourier transform infrared spectroscopy (FTIR). To obtain more information than by optical microscopy, thin sections can be subjected to observations by confocal laser scanning microscopy (CLSM), Raman spectrometry, cryo-scanning electron microscopy (cryo-SEM) and environmental SEM coupled with spatially resolved elemental analysis by X-ray spectrometry (SEM–EDS). Geochemical tools, particularly stable isotopes, provide information on the formation methods of microbialites and their biogenicity (see Chapter 6) (Thomazo et al. 2009). Microbial mats can also be subject to molecular biology analyses aimed at characterizing the associated microbial diversity (see Chapter 4) to better understand the direct or indirect impact of microorganisms on the precipitation or dissolution of minerals. Other methods can be used to highlight the metabolic activity of microorganisms at the mat scale. Oxygen, sulfide and pH-concentration profiles can be obtained using polarographic microelectrodes combined with a picometer (Visscher et al. 2000). Measurements are performed during the day in natural light and at night. The sulfate-reducing activity of microbial mats can be measured using the silver foil technique (Visscher et al. 2000). Silver foils are applied to a section of a fresh sample and lead to the reduction of sulfates that react with silver to form Ag_2S. The physicochemical properties of the extracellular polymeric substance (EPS) present in the mats can be obtained by extraction and purification to estimate the abundance (Smith et al. 1986) and the calcium binding capacity of the EPS (Braissant et al. 2009).

Finally, dating is important to understand the evolution of microbial deposits over time. It can be obtained by indirect methods called relative methods using fossil indicators when these are present (biostratigraphy), paleomagnetic dating or absolute radiochronology. However, even if it is possible to make direct measurements on microbialites using radiocarbon measurements present in carbonates (^{14}C) or using the U-Th isotope system, the latter remain quite uncertain and it is preferable to date the fossils or associated minerals. For example, the incorporation of CO_2 of deep volcanic or metamorphic origin, or from the recycling of carbonates results in a modification of the ages obtained by the ^{14}C method. In the continental domain, the use of several dating tools makes it possible to overcome these possible reservoir effects, which can modify the proportions of radiogenic carbon (Bouton et al. 2016). U-Pb dating of calcites is an emerging approach made possible by the development of femtosecond laser ablation coupled with plasma source mass spectrometry (fs-LA-ICP-MS), which allows in situ U-Pb dating at a high spatial resolution (~ 20 μm) for low-concentration minerals (Li et al. 2014).

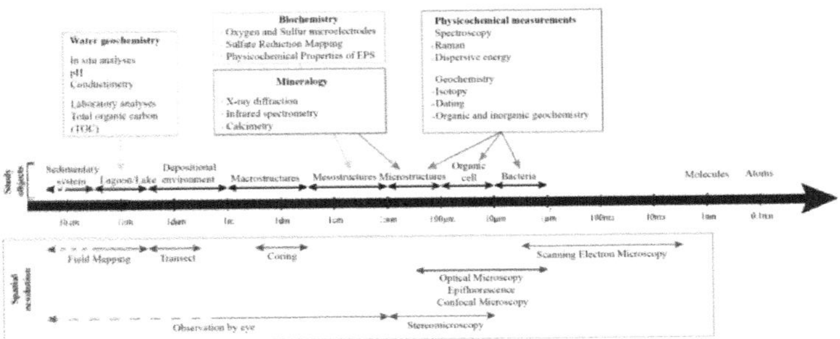

Figure 3.4. *Techniques for studying microbialites across scales. For a color version of this figure, see www.iste.co.uk/benzerara/geosphere.zip*

3.2.4. *Temporal and environmental distribution of microbialites*

3.2.4.1. *Throughout Earth's history*

Microbialites have been found in the sedimentary record since the Archean (Allwood et al. 2007). The oldest stromatolites date back to about 3.5 Ga (Stal 2012). They have been observed in the Pilbara Craton, Australia (e.g. Warrawoona Supergroup, or Strelley Pool) (Lowe 1980) and Kaapvaal, South Africa/Swaziland (Swaziland Supergroup) (Byerly et al. 1986). Laminated (stromatolitic) forms are abundant in these Archean deposits but contain only rare microfossils, and their biogenicity is therefore difficult to demonstrate (Hofmann 2000). Even if microfossils from this period are preserved, they cannot be unequivocally associated with cyanobacteria and could correspond to microorganisms developing other metabolisms such as anoxygenic photosynthesis or a chemosynthetic metabolism. Towards the end of the Mesoarchean, the morphologies of microbialites diversified (Lepot 2020) leading to the appearance and predominance in the Proterozoic of thrombolytic morphologies between 2.3 and 1.9 Ga (Barlow et al. 2016). Several nonexclusive mechanisms have been proposed to explain this change in dominant morphology-based studying modern examples: (i) a disorganization of laminated structures by the action of eukaryotic organisms or macrophytes (Tarhan et al. 2013); (ii) grazing by protozoa (Bernhard et al. 2013); and/or (iii) the involvement of specific cyanobacterial filaments that induce a typical fan-shaped distribution observed in current marine thrombolites from the Bahamas (Planavsky et al. 2009). Furthermore, transformations during early and late diagenesis of mineral precipitates can modify or even erase microbial structures at all scales of observation and the mineral and isotopic composition (Pace et al. 2016).

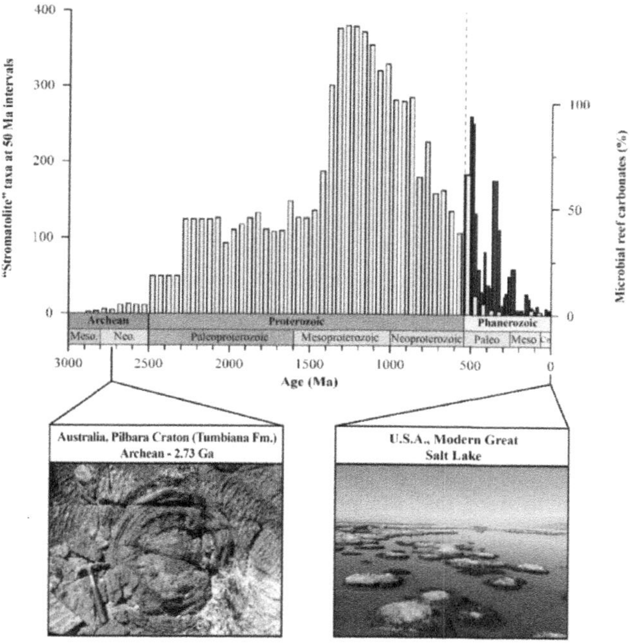

Figure 3.5. *Evolution of the "taxonomic" diversity of microbialites over geological time. The white bars represent the diversity of stromatolites (left scale), while the black bars indicate the relative abundance of microbial reef carbonates (right scale); Paleo: Paleozoic, Meso: Mesozoic, Cn: Cenozoic. For a color version of this figure, see www.iste.co.uk/benzerara/geosphere.zip*

Awramik (1971) was one of the first to provide a representation of the abundance of stromatolites by measuring the diversity of genera and morphological "species". These studies focus mainly on the Neoproterozoic, and it was not until the 1990s (1992–1993) that Riding observed the variations in the abundance of calcified cyanobacteria during the Phanerozoic. Then, databases established by Arp et al. (1998), Kiessling and Flügel (2002) and Kiessling et al. (2002) showed the secular variations in the distribution of microbial carbonates. These variations are plotted in Figure 3.5 and suggest a decline in microbial marine carbonates since the beginning of the Paleozoic.

3.2.4.2. *At all latitudes and in all depositional environments*

When the physicochemical conditions are met, microbialites can form at all latitudes (Figure 3.6). Microbial mats colonize many marine and continental environments (Figure 3.7). In continental environments, microbial mats have been found in hot (De Winder et al. 1990) and cold (Vincent et al. 1993) deserts; at high altitudes (Bougeault et al. 2019) (despite severe desiccation and low water conditions); caves and karst areas (Griffiths et al. 1987); in freshwater rivers and lake systems (Roche et al. 2019); and in hypersaline (Vennin et al. 2019) or hyper-alkaline waters (Gérard et al. 2018). They are also found in hot (Fouke et al. 2000) and cold (Takashima et al. 2011) springs, glacial lakes covered with ice in Antarctica (Mackey et al. 2015) and some calcrete-type soils[1] (Zhou and Chafetz 2009).

In marine environments, they are generally observed in coastal areas under the influence of tides, leading to fluctuations in salinity, temperature and immersion that limit the development of many metazoans (Stal 2012) as well as in more open marine environments (Reitner 1993). They also colonize lagoons and coastal lagoons (Bouton et al. 2016), dolomitic lagoons (Vasconcelos and McKenzie 1997) and hypersaline marine environments (Oren 2009).

It is interesting to note that the preferred environments of microbialites have evolved over time and while today they are mainly limited to continental environments (Figure 3.6), they populated the seas and oceans of the Precambrian. Furthermore, also note that the physicochemical conditions existing on the Earth's surface have changed drastically since the beginning of the history of our planet. Modern microbialites are therefore probably not faithful witnesses of the oldest microbialites, particularly regarding the metabolisms involved.

---

1. In pedology, this term designates a type of conglomerate, which, following the contribution of infiltration water, is cemented by limestone.

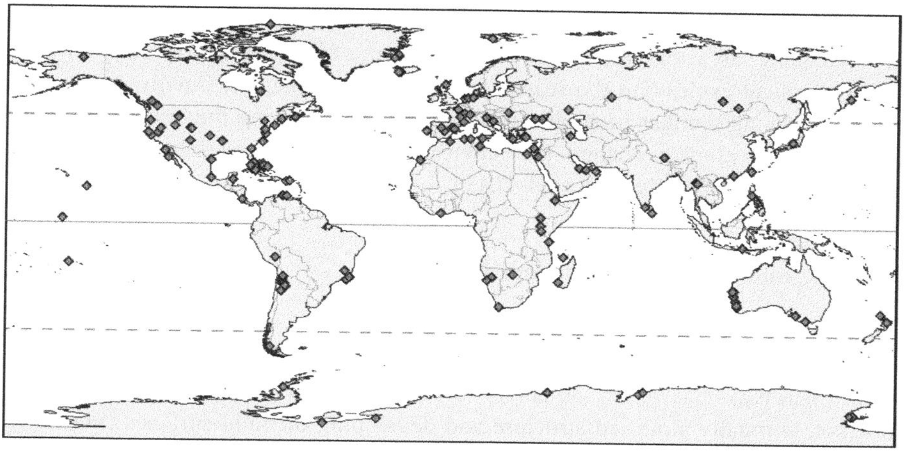

Figure 3.6. *Spatial distribution of known microbialites. For a color version of this figure, see www.iste.co.uk/benzerara/geosphere.zip*

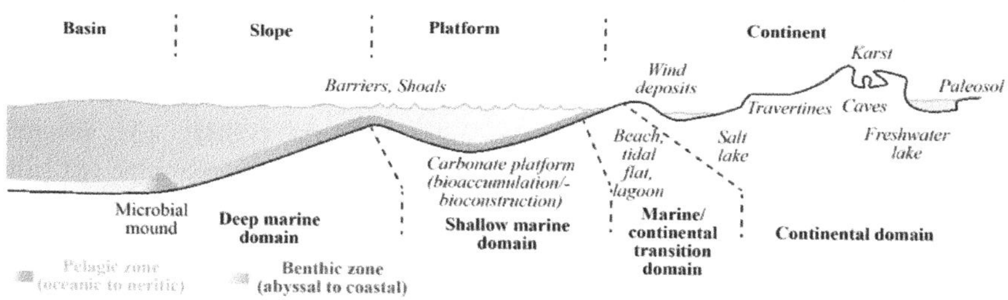

Figure 3.7. *Diversity of microbialite formation environments. For a color version of this figure, see www.iste.co.uk/benzerara/geosphere.zip*

3.2.5. *Fundamental, applied and societal implications of the study of microbialites*

Microbial deposits have been a focus of interest for many oil companies since the discovery of many petroleum reservoirs in relation to these deposits. For example, lacustrine microbialites have been linked to economically important petroleum systems such as the Lower Cretaceous “pre-salt” systems found offshore Brazil and Angola (Awramik and Buchheim 2012) and the Eocene Green River Formation in Utah, USA (Hurst et al. 2018). This has sparked a search for the best modern and/or fossil analogues to better understand the formation of these deposits

(Roche et al. 2018). But beyond this economic stake, modern microbialites represent an invaluable area of interest for research into the history of early life or biogeochemical cycles and the search for life on other planets. Finally, for several years, a growing number of studies have focused on bettering the understanding of the impact of climate change and environmental events associated with these microbial ecosystems (Reinold et al. 2019).

3.3. How microbialites are formed

3.3.1. *From microbial mats to microbialites*

A microbial mat is an assembly of microorganisms forming a physically coherent, vertically stratified structure and developing on solid surfaces (Stal et al. 1985) (Figure 3.1). Although they are part of biofilms, microbial mats are frequently dissociated from them due to their internal stratification, complexity and size. The microbial mat forms an ecosystem whose number of species frequently exceeds several thousand in an area restricted to a few millimeters (Papineau et al. 2005). Microbial mats have high metabolic diversity, determined by the availability of various environmentally controlled electron donors and acceptors (Wong et al. 2018). The microbial diversity of the mat can be grouped into six functional groups according to the dominant metabolism: (1) oxygenic phototrophs (e.g. cyanobacteria); (2) anoxygenic phototrophs (e.g. purple sulfur bacteria (PSB)); (3) anaerobic heterotrophs (e.g. sulfate reducers, methanogens); (4) aerobic heterotrophs; (5) sulfur oxidizing bacteria; and (6) fermenters (Dupraz and Visscher 2005; Dupraz et al. 2009). These different functional groups of bacteria are established within an exopolymeric organic matrix (extracellular polymeric substance (EPS), mainly secreted by cyanobacteria, as well as to a lesser extent by other microorganisms composing the microbial mat, such as sulfate-reducing bacteria (Braissant et al. 2007). This exopolymeric matrix stabilizes the microbial mat (Decho and Kawaguchi 1999) and also protects the microorganisms against external stresses by guaranteeing them an adequate microenvironment (Costerton and Stoodley 2003). EPS also promotes the trapping of suspended particles and therefore the fixation of allochthonous grains within the microbial mat (Gerdes 2010).

This trapping and binding mechanism is sometimes important in the formation of microbialites (e.g. Playford 1990). Suarez-Gonzalez et al. (2019) point out that this process is quite rare in modern and fossil environments and is mainly observed in environments under tidal influences. The factors governing this process are the presence of grains, the energy of the environment, the presence of EPS with strong adhesive capacities and water saturation too low to cause mineral precipitation (see Chapter 2). Lithification of trapped grains occurs due to the formation of micritic cements around the grains or thin micritic layers sealing the lamina (unlithified uncemented laminae). Cementation is induced by the in situ precipitation of minerals (often carbonates) often corresponding to a biotic process. In the formation of microbialites, often a mixture of (i) biologically induced precipitations resulting from the metabolic activity of microorganisms and (ii) biologically influenced precipitations, particularly in relation to EPS, which dominate (see Chapter 2) (Figure 3.8). These different mineralization processes are not limited to the cementation of grains but are responsible for most of the precipitation of mineral structures preserved in microbialites.

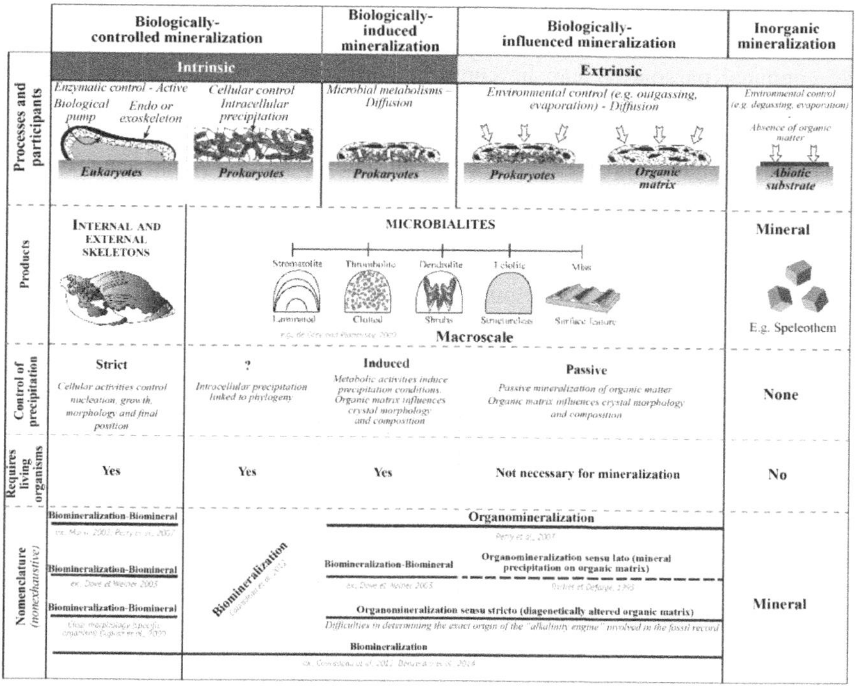

Figure 3.8. *Precipitation mechanisms involved in the formation of microbialites (modified from Dupraz et al. 2009)*

3.3.2. *Chemical conditions favorable to mineralization*

Calcium carbonate ($CaCO_3$) corresponds to one of the most frequently encountered mineral phases in microbialites. The precipitation/dissolution equilibrium of carbonate phases can be written as:

$$Ca^{2+} + 2HCO_3^- \leftrightarrows CaCO_3 + CO_2 + H_2O$$

Depending on the saturation state of the solution (Chapter 2), there will either be precipitation (supersaturated solution), or dissolution (undersaturated solution), or equilibrium between the two (saturated solution). The formation of microbialites therefore depends on this saturation state of the solution: it must be favorable to precipitation to form these mineralized objects. From a chemical point of view, the precipitation of calcium carbonate depends mainly on (i) the activity of carbonate ions (CO_3^{2-}) which itself depends on the concentration of bicarbonate ions (HCO_3^-) and the pH and (ii) of Ca^{2+} ion activity. The first is very often directly linked to a chemical parameter called the alkalinity of the solution. The activity of the Ca^{2+} ions can also be seen as the availability of calcium ions. We will see in the next part how these chemical parameters can be controlled intrinsically in the microbial mat or extrinsically.

In addition to constraining precipitation/dissolution processes, chemical conditions condition the mineralogy of microbialites, from the precipitation of the early minerals to their evolution during diagenesis. For example, a sufficient concentration of orthosilicic acid (H_4SiO_4) frequently leads to the precipitation of a Mg–silicate phase. Recently recognized (Burne et al. 2014; Zeyen et al. 2015), this silicate phase is sometimes considered to be a precursor to the formation of microbialites. Then, the Mg/Ca ratio of the surrounding solution controls the nature of the carbonate phase formed. When this ratio is moderate, calcite precipitates. It becomes magnesium at higher Mg/Ca ratios. Beyond a certain threshold, aragonite takes precedence. This is linked to the fact that the precipitation kinetics of calcite are then very disadvantaged by high Mg contents while that of aragonite is not affected since Mg does not enter into the structure of aragonite. Finally, when the Mg/Ca ratio of the solution becomes very high, magnesium carbonates form. Dolomite precipitation occurs early in mineralogical history, at the boundary between mineralization and early diagenesis. The partial dissolution of the previously precipitated mineral phases (Mg-Si and aragonite), under very slightly acidic pH conditions (approximately 6.5), leads to a significant accumulation of Mg^{2+} and Ca^{2+} cations, most likely promoting the precipitation of dolomite.

3.3.3. *Controlling factors of microbialite formation*

As mentioned above, the precipitation of calcium carbonates depends on the saturation state of the solution, itself a function of the Ca^{2+} and CO_3^{2-} ion activities. The alkalinity of a solution is approximately the sum of the bases in a solution that can be converted to uncharged species by the addition of a strong acid. Alkalinity acts as a buffer by neutralizing acids, stabilizing the pH. In many environments, the predominant base is the bicarbonate ion and thus alkalinity is related to the activity of the carbonate ions.

Overall, we see that the availability of Ca^{2+} ions and alkalinity are two important factors. We will discuss the different processes that can influence one, the other or both parameters. To do this, we distinguish between intrinsic (linked to the metabolism of microorganisms) to the microbial mat, extrinsic (not linked to microorganisms but of local origin), and external (dependent on external environmental parameters on a global scale) processes (Figure 3.8).

– *Intrinsic parameters* (Figure 3.9): the metabolic activities of the different microbial communities making up the mat can locally modify these conditions. The microbial mat is the site of many chemical reactions, resulting from the metabolism of each microbial population. A micro-environment is thus created at the level of the microbial mat. The chemical conditions that prevail there are specific to it, often very different from the surrounding environment, even if the latter remains the primary controlling factor. Certain microbial metabolisms impact the alkalinity of the environment (Figure 3.9): an increase in this will promote the precipitation of carbonates, while a decrease will be more conducive to dissolution. The precipitation of minerals within a microbial mat ultimately results from the balance between environmental conditions and metabolic interactions between the different microbial communities.

Photosynthesis is a metabolic process that induces conditions favorable to the precipitation of carbonates (Visscher et al. 1998; Dupraz et al. 2009). Photosynthesis can be oxygenic (e.g. cyanobacteria) or anoxygenic (e.g. purple anoxygenic bacteria). Sulfate reduction can also, under certain conditions, be favorable to the precipitation of carbonates.

Other metabolisms, however, such as aerobic heterotrophs, fermenters and sulfur oxidizing bacteria, under certain conditions promote the dissolution of carbonates.

These precipitation behaviors can be reversed during day/night cycles, as for phototrophic organisms, which see their metabolisms change in the absence of light, switching from photosynthesis to fermentation (e.g. Dupraz et al. 2009).

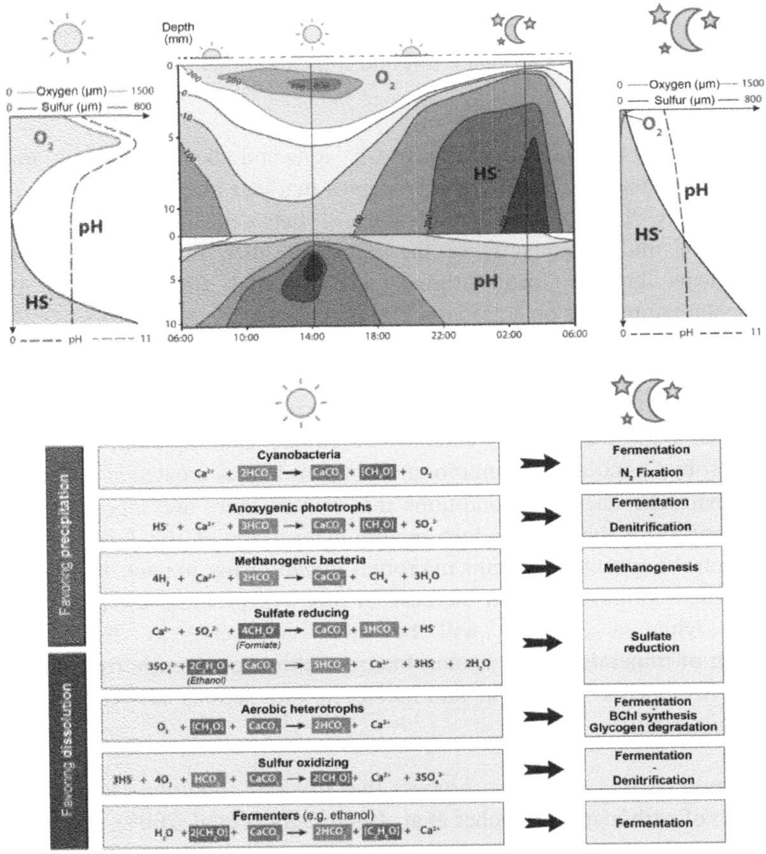

Figure 3.9. *Intrinsic, metabolic parameters of a biofilm controlling the precipitation and dissolution of carbonates during a day/night cycle. Top left (day) and right (night) show the O_2 and pH profiles as a function of depth according to the two lines indicated in the central figure and according to the same depth scale (from 0 to ~ 10 mm depth) (modified from Dupraz et al. 2009). For a color version of this figure, see www.iste.co.uk/benzerara/geosphere.zip*

– *Extrinsic parameters* (Figure 3.10): many abiotic processes can affect microbial communities. These act on the presence and development of microbial mats and biofilms, directly or indirectly (by changing the physicochemical gradients of the environment), and consequently, influence the intensity of mineralization. Among these processes, there are hydrodynamics (disaggregation of mats and biofilms, modification of the pCO_2 and pH), temperature variations (that promote or inhibit the development of microbial mats or modify thermodynamic equilibrium), variations in the radiation balance (light intensity, UV exposure, etc.), the evaporation/precipitation ratio (hydration/desiccation or variation in salinity), sedimentary inputs (act on the sanding rate, abrasion or even turbidity), bathymetry, accommodation or even wind direction.

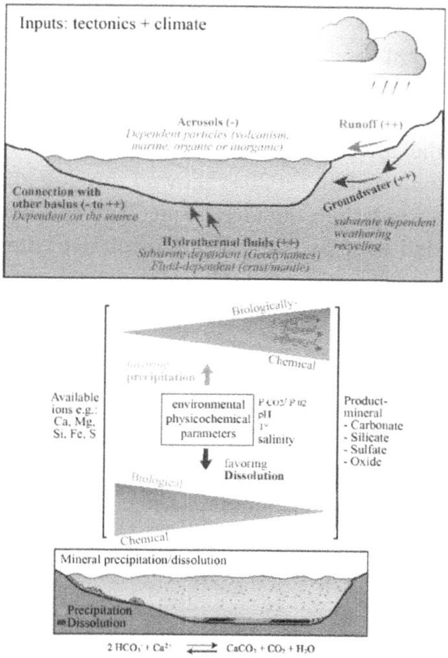

Figure 3.10. *Extrinsic and external parameters to biofilms influencing the formation of microbialites. For a color version of this figure, see www.iste.co.uk/benzerara/geosphere.zip*

Intrinsic and extrinsic parameters affect the biotic and abiotic processes involved in the mineralization of microbial mats and the role of their immediate environment (Figure 3.8). Although these parameters are controlled at the local scale (micro-environment in the case of intrinsic parameters; immediate environment in the case of extrinsic parameters), more global (climate), regional (tectonics, substrate lithology, volcanism, etc.) or local (faults, topographies, substrate, etc.) control factors will also act, on a large scale, on the modalities of carbonate precipitation (Figure 3.10).

– *External parameters* (Figure 3.10): climate is a global factor whose variations are recorded in the characteristics, textures, mineralogy and sedimentation rates of microbial carbonate deposits. Climate variations can be recorded on a seasonal scale (Arenas et al. 2015), as well as on a larger scale, particularly in ancient deposits. These parameters impact the saturation of solutions, their origins and flow rates (position and erosion rate; Evans 1999), and hydrodynamics (Viles et al. 2007). The geodynamic context controls the structuring of basins, the potential for preservation of sedimentation by the subsidence rate, the rejuvenation of watersheds and therefore the extent of exposed rocks, as well as underground drainage, and in particular the characteristics of aquifers. These parameters, coupled with the lithology of the rocks, consequently, influence the chemical composition of the waters and therefore the mineralization potential (pH, pCO_2, ion concentrations) (Teboul et al. 2016). Bouton et al. (2020a) showed through a "source-to-sink" study that carbonate precipitation within the Great Salt Lake endorheic basin is controlled by the amount of Ca^{2+} delivered by watershed erosion over time.

Furthermore, in lacustrine domains, hydrothermalism causes changes in water chemistry, sometimes promoting carbonate precipitation, with abiotic and biotic influences (Arp et al. 1999). At the regional or local scale, volcanism has a direct impact on subaerial and lacustrine deposits, particularly in rift systems (Wright 2012), where it contributes to changes in the physicochemical parameters of water (Armienta et al. 2008). However, the influence of hydrothermalism and/or volcanism on the development, mineralization and diagenesis of microbial carbonates is difficult to confirm in the fossil record even if, for example, the general neritic carbonate production of the Middle Cretaceous results from significant volcanic degassing (Pohl et al. 2020).

Finally, we see that in the case of microbial mats, alkalinity is controlled at different scales, from the global environment (external factors) – where it will be promoted by degassing processes, evaporation, or alkaline water inputs – to the microenvironment (extrinsic and intrinsic factors) – where certain metabolic processes (e.g. photosynthesis) promote its increase. The sum of these processes forms the "alkalinity engine" (Dupraz et al. 2009) and therefore participates in the precipitation of microbial carbonates.

3.3.4. *Environmental conditions favorable to the development of microbialites*

Microbialites can have different geometries depending on depth, from isolated mounds to platform geometries in marine or continental domains (Figure 3.11). The production rate of these microbial structures is fairly constant over a wide range of environments and depths. Production is efficient from shallow platform domains such as Shark Bay in Australia, to depths of over 500 m around methane vents (Peckmann et al. 2001). However, their distribution is particularly sensitive to wave action as highlighted by their preferential distribution on platforms, in protected areas or at slope breaks as illustrated by numerous Carboniferous, Triassic and Jurassic examples (Della Porta et al. 2004; Kenter et al. 2005).

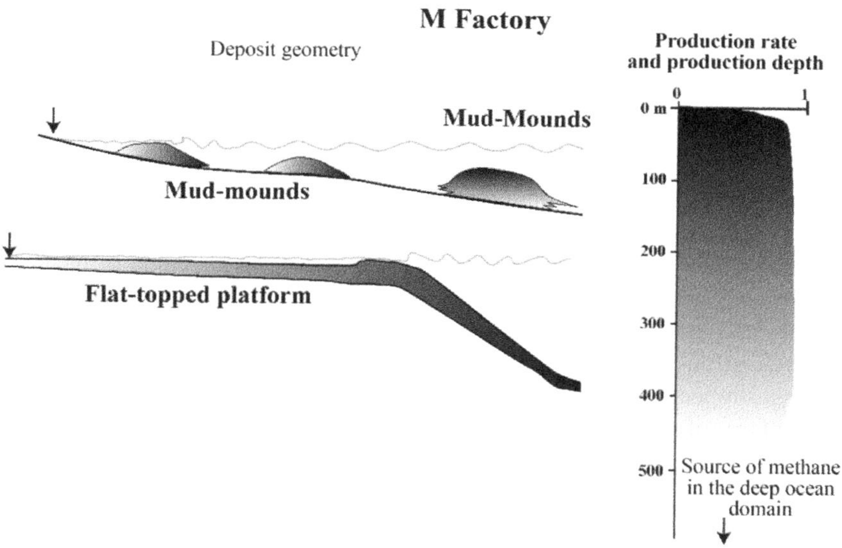

Figure 3.11. *The microbialite factory (M-factory). Left: influence of depth on the geometry of deposits: mud-mounds are mounds. Flat-topped platforms are flat deposits. Right, graph showing the relationship between the production rate of carbonate deposits (x-axis) and depth (y-axis). By comparison, the production rate of the tropical factory (e.g. corals, algae) does not exceed a few tens of meters of depth. For a color version of this figure, see www.iste.co.uk/benzerara/geosphere.zip*

The development of microbial mats and their lithification are also influenced by the physical and chemical properties of the substrate, in particular the grain size and the stability of the sediments constituting the substratum (Roche et al. 2019). For example, filamentous cyanobacteria form mats more rapidly on a fine fraction (< 125 m) than on larger particles (Rozenstein et al. 2014). Furthermore, the absence of microbialites growing on mud, silt or sand in riverbeds is due to a low lithification potential of microbial mats under these conditions (Roche et al. 2019).

Harder and more extensive substrates favor the perennial development of microbial mats and therefore give rise to more stable microbialites (Moore and Burne 1994). Also, increasing substrate roughness improves the growth rate of microbial mats and microbialites (Roche et al. 2018). Turbulence and surface flow velocity of microbialites affect mat colonization rates by grazing organisms (Bouton et al. 2016). Finally, substrate chemistry can affect microbial community colonization, mineralization capacity and preservation potential (Gradziński 2010). For example, microbial deposits develop more rapidly on limestone substrates than on copper, due to the toxicity of the metal (Parsiegla and Katz 2000).

Several global parameters also impact the formation of microbialites. Thus, Figure 3.12 relates the variations in the abundance of microbialites over time, the variations in the saturation index of the oceans in relation to calcite, the major periods of extinction, the variations in the diversity of metazoans and the variation curve of the atmospheric content of CO_2. The inverse relationship between variations in the abundance of microbialites and that of the diversity of metazoans tends to highlight the close link between a reduction in the abundance of microbial carbonates and the expansion of metazoans (Riding 2006). Several causes may be hidden behind this inverse relationship: some metazoans consume microbial mats (notably gastropods), their abundance could reduce the quantity of microbial mats, and therefore of microbialites. A second effect is linked to the ability of microorganisms to adapt to changing or even extreme conditions (T°, salinity, exposure to light, O_2, water level variation, etc.). These conditions can be harmful to more complex metazoans, allowing them to colonize environments where flora–fauna diversity will be low.

Fluctuations in the abundance of microbial carbonates accompany changes in ocean saturation with respect to carbonate phases (Riding and Liang 2005), even if the variations over geological time of the pH, the ionic composition of the oceans and the level of atmospheric CO_2 need to be further refined. In general, the diversity of microbial carbonates increases when ocean saturation is high and metazoan diversity is low. Thus, the Cambro-Ordovician (Lower Ordovician), Silurian, Late Devonian and periods following the extinctions at the end of the Permian and Jurassic record an increase in the abundance of microbial bioconstructions. Some of these periods also correspond to major biodiversity crises (Sepkoski 1997), with often high temperatures having favored an increase in the saturation of the oceans with respect to carbonate phases and a precipitation of carbonates (Veizer et al. 2000). However, a clear anomaly is observed during the Cretaceous between 120 and 80 Ma with a low abundance of microbial carbonates despite a high saturation index.

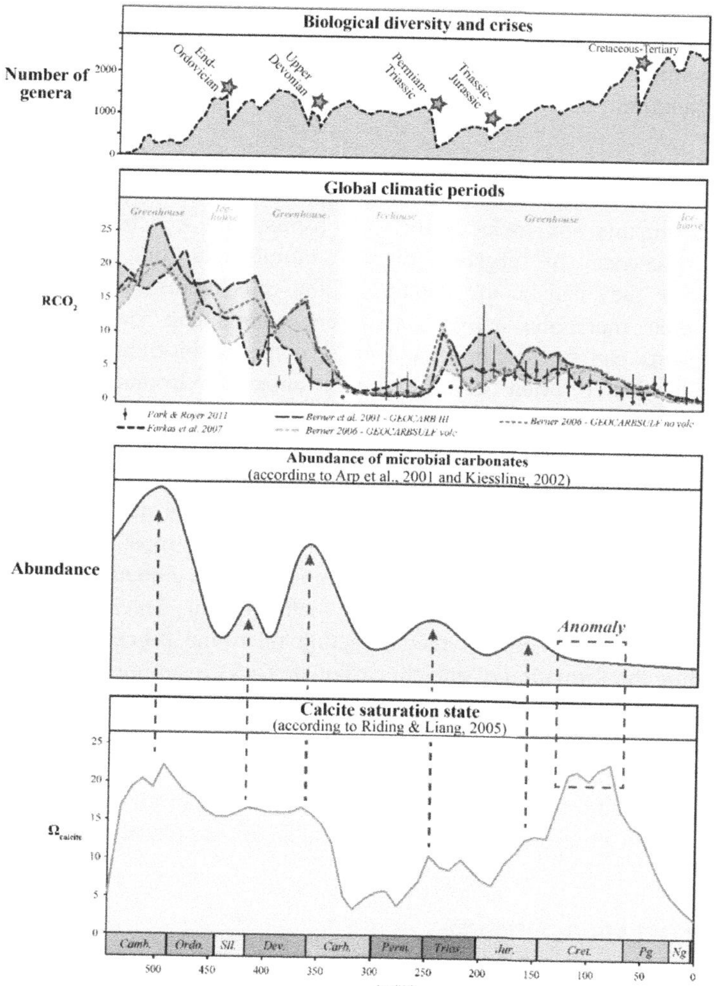

Figure 3.12. *Comparison of (i) the variation in the diversity (number of genera) of metazoans during the Phanerozoic, allowing us to identify the major biodiversity crisis; (ii) the variation in the atmospheric content of CO_2 (RCO_2) according to different models; (iii) the variation in the abundance of microbial carbonates (microbialites); and (iv) the variation in the saturation index of the oceans in relation to calcite ($\Omega_{calcite}$). Apart from an anomaly in the Cretaceous (see the dotted box), the high values of the saturation index and the abundance of microbial carbonates are synchronous. For a color version of this figure, see www.iste.co.uk/benzerara/geosphere.zip*

3.4. Preservation of microbialites in the fossil record

Microbialites have been well preserved in the fossil record for over 3.5 billion years. Dissolution, brecciation, boudinage, for example, can greatly blur their record.

Traces of microorganisms that built the microbialites can be preserved in minerals, sediments and rocks in different forms: they can be morphological or chemical (presence of organic matter, biominerals or particular isotopic compositions); they can be the remains of the cells themselves or more indirect traces of their metabolic activity. Different components or properties of the microorganisms can be fossilized: (1) cells, colonies, biofilms/mats, EPS (fossil organic molecules are often best preserved in anoxic environments where they are protected from aerobic microbial degradation); (2) the chemical composition of the various structural elements, including organic molecules and other essential elements; and (3) traces of their metabolic activity leading to the fractionation of elements such as C, S, O, N, P and Fe. Whether they are part of their metabolic activity or a side effect of their protective mechanism, most microbes have the ability to use or concentrate various metal cations in trace amounts. The detection of these trace elements, made possible by technological developments in recent decades, is a powerful tool for reconstructing microbial processes as well as for understanding the formation of ancient carbonate rocks resulting from the activity of microbes (Webb and Kamber 2004). Indirectly, microorganisms are also characterized by (4) the effects of their physical presence and metabolic products on their environment, in particular through the formation of microbially induced sedimentary structures (MISS). The latter are observed in all sediments and rocks formed in aquatic environments from the Archean to the present day (Noffke 2021).

3.4.1. *Preservation potential*

The resistance of microbial structures to physical, chemical and biological degradation determines their preservation potential (Figure 3.13). In most cases, the latter will be a function of the degree of lithification of the structures: lithification allows for better resistance to physical and biological degradation processes. The greater the intensity of lithification and the faster its kinetics, the more effective the preservation. While intrinsic and extrinsic factors have an essentially local impact (i.e. at the scale of the microbial structure), external/environmental control factors have a much broader influence. The physical, chemical and biological conditions of the environment will therefore play a significant role in the distribution and preservation of microbial mats in the form of microbialites.

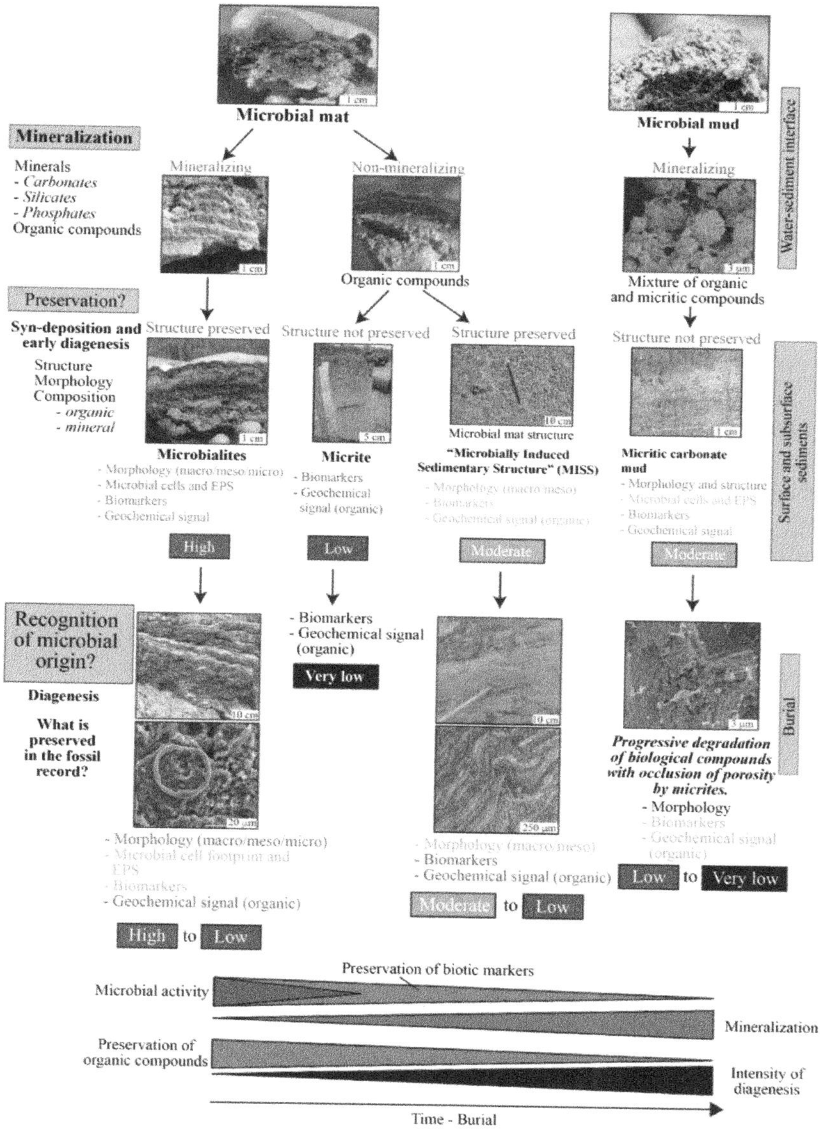

Figure 3.13. *Assessment of the preservation potential of microbial mats from their formation to the recording of diagenesis using current (Cuba, France) and fossil (USA, Spain) examples. For a color version of this figure, see www.iste.co.uk/benzerara/geosphere.zip*

Here are some external factors impacting the potential for early preservation of microbial structures. Grazing predation by protozoa, gastropods or shrimps leads to a reduction in microbial mats and reduces the potential for early preservation (Bernhard et al. 2013). Conversely, grazers sometimes play a role in ecosystem stability (van Gemerden 1993), and microbialites may have provided refuges for early protists (Bernhard et al. 2013) and metazoans (Gingras et al. 2011; Tarhan et al. 2013). Microbial mats are frequently present in extreme environments (Des Marais 1995; Visscher et al. 2010), in which most predators and/or competitors are absent (Garrett 1970). Furthermore, hydrodynamics is a physical factor that strongly impacts the preservation of microbial mats undergoing mineralization. Storms and hurricanes, and the resulting agitation of the environment, can both affect preservation: this can be positive when the mats become covered by bioclastic sands, but it can also be negative when the hydrodynamics erode the microbial structures. When the agitation becomes too great and the mats are not mineralized, they will most often be torn off to produce oncolithic sand. The destruction of microbial mats and microbialites can be favored by desiccation episodes, or by freezing and thawing under the effect of temperature variations (cryofracturing and cryoturbation) (Bougeault et al. 2019).

3.4.2. *Early diagenesis, late diagenesis*

"Diagenesis" refers to a series of "post-depositional" processes that have a significant impact on the chemical, mechanical and petrophysical properties of carbonate sediments (Bathurst 1982). Diagenesis of microbial structures can lead to the disappearance and/or modification of organic signals (morphology, organic structures, chemical and isotopic signature). Since the microbial mat is mainly organic, it is rarely preserved in the fossil record. In some unusual cases, exceptional taphonomic conditions allow for the preservation of intact cells and even the structure of EPS (Lepot et al. 2008). During diagenesis, organic matter is transformed mainly into carbon dioxide (CO_2) or methane (CH_4), and in some cases incomplete degradation can lead to enrichment of the sediment with organic matter (Bouton et al. 2020b). Evidence for the existence of the microbial mat or biofilm is then generally indirect.

In contrast to the abundant literature on diagenesis in marine environments, the scarcity of studies in continental areas is surprising, especially since diagenesis begins very early in these environments from fluids whose properties are very close to those responsible for the formation of carbonates. It therefore becomes difficult to determine when primary mineralization ends and diagenesis begins. Experimental techniques have been implemented in the laboratory or in the field to understand the transitional stages between the primary mineralization of microbial mats and their transformation during diagenesis (Benzerara et al. 2006; Burne et al. 2014; Pace et al. 2016).

Late diagenesis typically occurs at depths greater than 1.5 km. Due to fluid–rock interactions, late diagenetic pore fluids differ significantly from fluids associated with depositional environments (e.g. Milliken 2014). Late diagenesis often alters the sedimentary, chemical and isotopic record, and microbial structures are often difficult to individualize or are even erased.

3.5. Examples illustrating the diversity of microbialites in current and fossil environments

To illustrate the variability and diversity of microbialites in different current depositional environments and for key periods in the history of our planet, several examples are illustrated below.

3.5.1. *Examples of current microbialites*

Great Salt Lake, an example of lacustrine microbialites

The Great Salt Lake in Utah is a shallow (< 10 m) hypersaline endorheic lake, the remains of the ancient mega-lake Bonneville (which was more than 300 m deep). It is home to one of the largest populations of mineralizing microbial communities in the world (Figures 3.2 and 3.5). Their existence has been known for over 80 years through the pioneering work of Eardley (1938), who already emphasized the presence of microbial bioherms along the shallow margins of the lake. Microbialites have formed throughout the history of this hypersaline lake (Bouton et al. 2016), dated to 11,500 years ago $^{14}C_{BP}$.

The Great Salt Lake is a unique and ideal example to study environmental and anthropogenic influences on the occurrence and distribution of microbial deposits in a shallow mid-latitude area. Microbial mats and microbialites exhibit high morphological diversity, commonly related to associated microbial communities. This observed morphological diversity appears to be largely related to the accommodation space (i.e. available for sedimentation). In addition, climatic (e.g. water level variations) and tectonic (e.g. syn-sedimentary faults) parameters play a dominant role in the spatial distribution of observed microbial structures. Other more local factors, such as the nature of the substrate (gravity deposits), may also modify this distribution.

Shark Bay marine microbialites, present-day analogues of ancient stromatolitic deposits?

The Hamelin Pool microbial deposits (Shark Bay, Western Australia) are spectacular in the morphological diversity of their structures and microbial communities involved in the production of internal fabrics. They have long been compared to the diversity of Proterozoic structures, before the decline of microbialites recorded during the Paleozoic. Their existence in Australia has been known since the 1950s as indicated by the work of Playford and Cockbain (1976).

The Hamelin Pool microbial carbonate system developed in response to a slow and gradual change in environmental conditions. It results from the transformation of an almost open marine system into a restricted bay enclosed to the east, south and west and semi-enclosed to the north by an algal carbonate bank ("Faure Bank"), with abnormal salinity (66 psu) (Suosaari et al. 2016), as well as high alkalinity and evaporation (Logan et al. 1961). The oldest microbial deposits are dated to 2,000 years ago, well after the major Holocene sea level rise approximately 6,800 years ago. It is in this hypersaline environment with low eukaryotic diversity that organosedimentary deposits are formed resulting from the trapping and precipitation of carbonates of biological origin and where accretion processes surpass erosion (Logan et al. 1961). Among the microbial deposits, Jahnert and Collins (2013) recognize stromatolitic structures (composed of mats, domes and columns), thrombolytic forms (pustular) and crypto-microbial crusts. Optical microscopy analyses make it possible to identify micrites of microbial origin, resulting either from the activity of heterotrophs (notably sulfate-reducing organisms), or from phototrophic organisms or from precipitation within the EPS during the remineralization of organic matter. Furthermore, carbonate precipitation is favored by local saturation conditions that may be linked to the high evaporation of this shallow bay, conducive to degassing or to subsurface alkaline inputs (Burne et al. 1982). These studies show that the mineralization potential is linked to the nature and composition of the microbial mats, themselves dependent on local conditions (seasonality influencing temperature and salinity).

3.5.2. *Ancient microbialites: some key periods of Earth's history recorded by microbial deposits*

The Precambrian: deciphering biogenicity?

One of the most emblematic microbialite deposits of the Archean is the Tumbiana Formation (Australia) (Figure 3.5), which formed in a giant lake 2.72 Ga ago (Coffey et al. 2013). This deposit reveals laminated microbialites ("stromatolites") with very diverse morphologies (columns, domes, stratiforms and cones), comparable to that observed later during the Proterozoic. Due to weathering and diagenesis effects, defining the biogenicity of these deposits is still a challenge that requires the coupling of different analytical techniques. At the microstructural level, sinuous palisade structures attributed to filaments, now filled with calcite, are frequently observed in stromatolitic laminae (Buick 1992) and are strongly reminiscent of the bundles of cyanobacterial filaments encrusted with micrites observed in various modern examples (Monty 2012). Some tufted structures resemble structures recognized in modern microbial mats, probably indicating the presence of cyanobacteria (Flannery and Walter 2012). Within these Archean objects, the presence of aragonitic nanostructures associated with organic matter and microcrystalline calcites are interpreted as evidence of precipitation induced by the activity of microbes (Lepot et al. 2008). These deposits also contain metabolic signatures within three types of organic matter: aromatic compounds associated with quartz are interpreted as markers of anaerobic methane oxidation; organic globules found only in carbonate laminae also resulting from anaerobic methane oxidation; the presence of pyrobitumen with carbon isotopic compositions attributed to photo- or chemotrophic metabolisms (Thomazo et al. 2009). Tumbiana stromatolites contain abundant fenestrae-type structures (Flannery and Walter 2012), which could represent relics of ancient di-oxygen gas bubbles of photosynthetic origin or heterotrophic degradation products trapped by microbial mats (Monty 2012). These structures could also result from desiccation/flooding cycles, cavities resulting from the degradation of clusters of non-lithified microbial colonies or dissolution structures linked to microbial activity (Monty 2012).

Still on the Australian craton, the Dresser Formation, of approximately 3.5 Ga, has yielded samples through drilling that have been protected from surface weathering. These samples contain objects, interpreted as biogenic, in particular pyrites whose sulfur isotopic composition is compatible with biological activity (Baumgartner et al. 2020) and objects interpreted as remains of mineralized biofilms. In addition, nanoparticles and calcareous fibers in the pyrites are interpreted as the remains of extracellular polysaccharide (EPS) from microbial biofilms (Baumgartner et al. 2019). It should be noted, however, that the hydrothermal context associated with the development of these stromatolites could also induce biomorphic structures (Buick et al. 1981).

The oldest forms resembling stromatolites appear in Isua metamorphic deposits (Greenland) dated to 3.7 Ga (Nutman et al. 2016). The biogenicity of these structures, however, has been questioned (Allwood et al. 2018) and it has been suggested that they are late fluidization structures or tectonic boudinage structures (Zawaski et al. 2020).

A transitional period: Cambrian–Ordovician

Microbial carbonates (stromatolites, thrombolites) generally dominated reefs from the Ediacaran (Neoproterozoic) to the Early Ordovician. A major decline in stromatolite abundance and diversity is believed to have occurred at the beginning of the Phanerozoic, linked to the explosion of metazoan diversity (Walter and Heys 1985). This Cambrian transition period, however, shows a significant microbial component marked by the preservation of thrombolytic and dendrolitic structures. Microbial fossils in these rocks, called calcimicrobes (with species names given as *Renalcis* or *Epiphiton* among others) are often associated with calcified metazoans (*Archaeocyaths*, coralomorphs) in the Lower Cambrian bioconstructions. The Middle and Upper Cambrian is marked by the development of dendrolite-type microbial structures (Riding 1991) in association with stromatolites and thrombolites. Dendrolites exhibit unlaminated mesostructures dominated by calcimicrobe clusters. After the decline of *Archaeocyaths*, microbial carbonates continued to dominate reefs during the Middle and Late Cambrian, a period long considered to represent a major gap in the development of metazoan reefs (Riding 1991). Geochemical analyses suggest that the increase in dissolved oxygen in the oceans during the Ediacaran–Cambrian transition was followed by a widespread trend towards marine hypoxia–dysoxia[2] during the Middle–Late Cambrian. The Ordovician is marked by the appearance of stromatoporoids.

While considering the main features of microbial structures at the Precambrian–Paleozoic transition, Knoll et al. (1993) proposed an alternative explanation for the increase in calcimicrobes in relation to the decrease in cement precipitation on the seafloor and in the water column. The development of calcified microfossils would be linked to the emergence of carbonate skeletons involving changes in the saturation state of the oceans. However, these authors do not question the influence of the role of metazoans on the distribution of microbial mats through the processes of grazing, bioturbation and competition for space. Furthermore, the continued evolution of bioturbation in the Cambrian seems to have contributed to the elimination of microbial mats on shallow subtidal seafloors as observed in the Neoproterozoic.

Microbialites, indicators of crisis and recovery of post-crisis ecosystems: example of the Permo-Triassic crisis

Microbialites are frequently documented following several mass extinctions (i.e. Permian–Triassic transition), calling into question the environmental parameters

2. Dysoxia results from the mismatch between oxygen consumption and its supply, causing alterations in cellular metabolism.

controlling their development (Riding and Liang 2005). The Sonoma Foreland Basin (western United States) provides excellent and extensive deposits of Early Triassic microbial carbonates. This basin records the aftermath of the end-Permian mass extinction (Raup and Sepkoski 1982) and the subsequent Early Triassic recovery (of biodiversity) over a period of 1.5 Ma (see Chapter 8). This recovery is often considered to be longer (about 5 Ma) and associated with persistent and severe environmental stresses attributed to major climatic, oceanographic and biogeochemical perturbations. The Early Triassic microbial deposits, resembling Precambrian microbialites, therefore create "anachronistic" features. However, recent studies in the western basin of the United States have documented the site of these microbial deposits in association with abundant and diverse fossil content composed of echinoderms, ostracods, gastropods, bivalves, sponges, brachiopods and vertebrate remains (e.g. Vennin et al. 2015). This therefore calls into question the common interpretations of these microbial deposits as corresponding to particular deleterious environmental conditions.

3.6. Conclusions

Understanding microbialites requires a paradigm shift, and the analysis at all scales in space and time of these biomineralized objects that are located at the interface between the biosphere and the geosphere. A good understanding of the formation and preservation mechanisms of microbial mats and microbialites highlights the importance of microbial communities on Earth. Despite abundant literature, many questions remain unanswered, including (but not limited to):

– determination of criteria for differentiating biotic structures from abiotic structures;

– the degree of influence of biotic processes on the formation of microbialites, their shape and specific characteristics, such as microstructure;

– the influence of intrinsic factors over environmental abiotic factors in the formation and preservation of microbialites (extrinsic, local and global);

– the link between biological methods that allow communities to be characterized in detail, metabolisms and the mineral products obtained leading to the formation of microbialites of varied sizes and shapes.

The extreme conditions that prevail today in some regions of our planet, such as the Atacama Desert, seem close to those of the primitive Earth and could resemble those of other planets such as Mars. The search for such objects on Mars has been mentioned as one of the avenues to follow in the search for traces of ancient life. Is the construction of such structures by living things a "systematic" property of living things?

3.7. References

Aitken, J.D. (1967). Classification and environmental significance of cryptalgal limestones and dolomites, with illustrations from the Cambrian and Ordovician of southwestern Alberta. *Journal of Sedimentary Research*, 37(4), 1163–1178.

Allwood, A.C., Walter, M.R., Burch, I.W., Kamber, B.S. (2007). 3.43-billion-year-old stromatolite reef from the Pilbara Craton of Western Australia: Ecosystem-scale insights to early life on Earth. *Precambrian Research*, 158(3–4), 198–227.

Allwood, A.C., Rosing, M.T., Flannery, D.T., Hurowitz, J.A., Heirwegh, C.M. (2018). Reassessing evidence of life in 3,700-million-year-old rocks of Greenland. *Nature*, 563(7730), 241–244.

Arenas, C., Auqué, L., Osácar, C., Sancho, C., Lozano, M., Vázquez-Urbez, M., Pardo, G. (2015). Current tufa sedimentation in a high discharge river: A comparison with other synchronous tufa records in the Iberian Range (Spain). *Sedimentary Geology*, 325, 132–157.

Armienta, M.A., Vilaclara, G., De la Cruz-Reyna, S., Ramos, S., Ceniceros, N., Cruz, O., Aguayo, A., Arcega-Cabrera, F. (2008). Water chemistry of lakes related to active and inactive Mexican volcanoes. *Journal of Volcanology and Geothermal Research*, 178(2), 249–258.

Arp, G., Hofmann, J., Reitner, J. (1998). Microbial fabric formation in spring mounds ("microbialites") of alkaline salt lakes in the Badain Jaran sand sea, PR China. *Palaios*, 13(6), 581–592.

Arp, G., Reimer, A., Reitner, J. (1999). Calcification in cyanobacterial biofilms of alkaline salt lakes. *European Journal of Phycology*, 34(4), 393–403.

Awramik, S.M. (1971). Precambrian columnar stromatolite diversity: Reflection of metazoan appearance. *Science*, 174(4011), 825–827.

Awramik, S.M. and Buchheim, H.P. (2012). The quest for microbialite analogs to the South Atlantic Pre-Salt carbonate hydrocarbon reservoirs of Africa and South America. *AAPG, Houston Geological Society Bulletin*, 55(1), 21–27.

Awramik, S.M. and Margulis, L. (1974). Definition of stromatolite. *Stromatolite Newsletter*, 2, 5.

Barlow, E., Van Kranendonk, M., Yamaguchi, K., Ikehara, M., Lepland, A. (2016). Lithostratigraphic analysis of a new stromatolite–thrombolite reef from across the rise of atmospheric oxygen in the Paleoproterozoic Turee Creek Group, Western Australia. *Geobiology*, 14(4), 317–343.

Bathurst, R. (1982). Genesis of stromatactis cavities between submarine crusts in Palaeozoic carbonate mud buildups. *Journal of the Geological Society*, 139(2), 165–181.

Baumgartner, R.J., Van Kranendonk, M.J., Wacey, D., Fiorentini, M.L., Saunders, M., Caruso, S., Pages, A., Homman, M., Guagliardo, P. (2019). Nano–porous pyrite and organic matter in 3.5-billion-year-old stromatolites record primordial life. *Geology*, 47(11), 1039–1043.

Baumgartner, R.J., Fiorentini, M.L., Van Kranendonk, M.J., Martin, L., Jeon, H., Pages, A., Wacey, D. (2020). Sulfidization of 3.48 billion-year-old stromatolites of the Dresser Formation, Pilbara Craton: Constraints from in-situ sulfur isotope analysis of pyrite. *Chemical Geology*, 538, 119488.

Benzerara, K., Menguy, N., López-García, P., Yoon, T.-H., Kazmierczak, J., Tyliszczak, T., Guyot, F., Brown, G.E. (2006). Nanoscale detection of organic signatures in carbonate microbialites. *Proceedings of the National Academy of Sciences*, 103(25), 9440–9445.

Bernhard, J.M., Edgcomb, V.P., Visscher, P.T., McIntyre-Wressnig, A., Summons, R.E., Bouxsein, M.L., Louis, L., Jeglinski, M. (2013). Insights into foraminiferal influences on microfabrics of microbialites at Highborne Cay, Bahamas. *Proceedings of the National Academy of Sciences*, 110(24), 9830–9834.

Bertrand-Sarfati, J. and Walter, M. (1981). Stromatolite biostratigraphy. *Precambrian Research*, 15(3–4), 353–371.

Bougeault, C., Vennin, E., Durlet, C., Muller, É., Mercuzot, M., Chavez, M., Gérard, E., Ader, M., Virgone, A., Gaucher, E.C. (2019). Biotic–abiotic influences on modern Ca–Si-rich hydrothermal spring mounds of the Pastos Grandes Volcanic Caldera (Bolivia). *Minerals*, 9(6), 380.

Bourillot, R., Vennin, E., Rouchy, J.-M., Blanc-Valleron, M.-M., Caruso, A., Durlet, C. (2010). The end of the Messinian Salinity Crisis in the western Mediterranean: Insights from the carbonate platforms of south-eastern Spain. *Sedimentary Geology*, 229(4), 224–253.

Bourillot, R., Vennin, E., Dupraz, C., Pace, A., Foubert, A., Rouchy, J.-M., Patrier, P., Blanc, P., Bernard, D., Lesseur, J. (2020). The record of environmental and microbial signatures in ancient microbialites: The terminal carbonate complex from the Neogene basins of southeastern Spain. *Minerals*, 10(3), 276.

Bouton, A., Vennin, E., Pace, A., Bourillot, R., Dupraz, C., Thomazo, C., Brayard, A., Désaubliaux, G., Visscher, P.T. (2016). External controls on the distribution, fabrics and mineralization of modern microbial mats in a coastal hypersaline lagoon, Cayo Coco (Cuba). *Sedimentology*, 63(4), 972–1016.

Bouton, A., Vennin, E., Amiotte-Suchet, P., Thomazo, C., Sizun, J.P., Virgone, A., Gaucher, E.C., Visscher, P.T. (2020a). Prediction of the calcium carbonate budget in a sedimentary basin: A "source-to-sink" approach applied to Great Salt Lake, Utah, USA. *Basin Research*, 32(5), 1005–1034.

Bouton, A., Vennin, E., Thomazo, C., Mathieu, O., Garcia, F., Jaubert, M., Visscher, P.T. (2020b). Microbial origin of the organic matter preserved in the Cayo Coco Lagoonal Network, Cuba. *Minerals*, 10(2), 143.

Braissant, O., Decho, A.W., Dupraz, C., Glunk, C., Przekop, K.M., Visscher, P.T. (2007). Exopolymeric substances of sulfate-reducing bacteria: Interactions with calcium at alkaline pH and implication for formation of carbonate minerals. *Geobiology*, 5(4), 401–411.

Braissant, O., Decho, A.W., Przekop, K.M., Gallagher, K.L., Glunk, C., Dupraz, C., Visscher, P.T. (2009). Characteristics and turnover of exopolymeric substances in a hypersaline microbial mat. *FEMS Microbiology Ecology*, 67(2), 293–307.

Buick, R. (1992). The antiquity of oxygenic photosynthesis: Evidence from stromatolites in sulphate-deficient Archaean lakes. *Science*, 255(5040), 74–77.

Buick, R., Dunlop, J.S.R., Groves, D.I. (1981). Stromatolite recognition in ancient rocks: An appraisal of irregularly laminated structures in an Early Archaean chert-barite unit from North Pole, Western Australia. *Alcheringa*, 5(3), 161–181.

Burne, R.V. and Colwell, J.B. (1982). Temperate carbonate sediments of northern Spencer Gulf, South Australia: A high salinity 'foramol' province. *Sedimentology*, 29(2), 223–238.

Burne, R.V. and Moore, L.S. (1987). Microbialites: Organosedimentary deposits of benthic microbial communities. *Palaios*, 2(3), 241–254.

Burne, R.V., Moore, L.S., Christy, A.G., Troitzsch, U., King, P.L., Carnerup, A.M., Hamilton, P.J. (2014). Stevensite in the modern thrombolites of Lake Clifton, Western Australia: A missing link in microbialite mineralization? *Geology*, 42(7), 575–578.

Byerly, G.R., Lower, D.R., Walsh, M.M. (1986). Stromatolites from the 3,300–3,500-Myr Swaziland Supergroup, Barberton Mountain Land, South Africa. *Nature*, 319(6053), 489–491.

Carr, N.G. and Whitton, B.A. (1982). *The Biology of Cyanobacteria*, volume 19. University of California Press, Oakland.

Coffey, J.M., Flannery, D.T., Walter, M.R., George, S.C. (2013). Sedimentology, stratigraphy and geochemistry of a stromatolite biofacies in the 2.72 Ga Tumbiana Formation, Fortescue Group, Western Australia. *Precambrian Research*, 236, 282–296.

Costerton, J.W. and Stoodley, P. (2003). *Microbial Biofilms: Protective Niches in Ancient and Modern Geomicrobiology*. Kluwer, Dordrecht.

Decho, A.W. and Kawaguchi, T. (1999). Secretions using N anoplast® resin. *BioTechniques*, 27, 1246–1252.

Della Porta, G. (2015). Carbonate build-ups in lacustrine, hydrothermal and fluvial settings: Comparing depositional geometry, fabric types and geochemical signature. *Geological Society London Special Publications*, 418(1), 17–68.

Della Porta, G., Kenter, J.A., Bahamonde, J.R. (2004). Depositional facies and stratal geometry of an Upper Carboniferous prograding and aggrading high-relief carbonate platform (Cantabrian Mountains, N Spain). *Sedimentology*, 51(2), 267–295.

Des Marais, D.J. (1995). The biogeochemistry of hypersaline microbial mats. In *Advances in Microbial Ecology*, Jones, J.G. (ed.). Springer, Boston. doi: 10.1007/978-1-4684-7724-5_6.

Dupraz, C. and Visscher, P.T. (2005). Microbial lithification in marine stromatolites and hypersaline mats. *Trends in Microbiology*, 13(9), 429–438.

Dupraz, C., Reid, R.P., Braissant, O., Decho, A.W., Norman, R.S., Visscher, P.T. (2009). Processes of carbonate precipitation in modern microbial mats. *Earth-Science Reviews*, 96(3), 141–162.

Dupraz, C., Reid, R.P., Visscher, P.T., Reitner, J., Thiel, V. (2011). Microbialites, modern. *Encyclopedia of Geobiology*, 617–635.

Eardley, A.J. (1938). Sediments of Great Salt Lake, Utah. *AAPG Bulletin*, 22(10), 1305–1411.

Evans, J.E. (1999). Recognition and implications of Eocene tufas and travertines in the Chadron formation, White River Group, Badlands of South Dakota. *Sedimentology*, 46(5), 771–789.

Flannery, D.T. and Walter, M.R. (2012). Archean tufted microbial mats and the Great Oxidation Event: New insights into an ancient problem. *Australian Journal of Earth Sciences*, 59(1), 1–11.

Fouke, B.W., Farmer, J.D., Des Marais, D.J., Pratt, L., Sturchio, N.C., Burns, P.C., Discipulo, M.K. (2000). Depositional facies and aqueous-solid geochemistry of travertine-depositing hot springs (Angel Terrace, Mammoth Hot Springs, Yellowstone National Park, USA). *Journal of Sedimentary Research*, 70(3), 565–585.

Garrett, P. (1970). Phanerozoic stromatolites: Noncompetitive ecologic restriction by grazing and burrowing animals. *Science*, 169(3941), 171–173.

Gérard, E., De Goeyse, S., Hugoni, M., Agogué, H., Richard, L., Milesi, V., Guyot, F., Lecourt, L., Borensztajn, S., Joseph, M.-B. (2018). Key role of alphaproteobacteria and cyanobacteria in the formation of stromatolites of Lake Dziani Dzaha (Mayotte, Western Indian Ocean). *Frontiers in Microbiology*, 9, 796.

Gerdes, G. (2010). What are microbial mats? In *Microbial Mats*, Seckbach, J. and Oren, O. (eds). Springer, Dordrecht.

Gingras, M.K., MacEachern, J.A., Dashtgard, S.E. (2011). Process ichnology and the elucidation of physico-chemical stress. *Sedimentary Geology*, 237(3–4), 115–134.

Gradziński, M. (2010). Factors controlling growth of modern tufa: Results of a field experiment. *Geological Society London Special Publications*, 336, 143–191. doi: 10.1144/SP336.8.

Grey, K. and Awramik, S.M. (2020) *Handbook for the Study and Description of Microbialites*. Geological Survey of Western Australia, Perth.

Griffiths, M.S., Gallon, J.R., Chaplin, A.E. (1987). The diurnal pattern of dinitrogen fixation by cyanobacteria in situ. *New Phytologist*, 107(4), 649–657.

Grotzinger, J.P. (1989). Facies and evolution of precambrian carbonate depositional systems: Emergence of the modern platform archetype. In *Controls on Carbonate Platforms and Basin Development*, Crevello, P.D., Wilson, J.L., Sarg, J.F., Read, J.F. (eds). SEPM Society for Sedimentary Geology, Tulsa.

Grotzinger, J.P. and Rothman, D.H. (1996). An abiotic model for stromatolite morphogenesis. *Nature*, 383(6599), 423–425.

Hofmann, H. (2000). Archean stromatolites as microbial archives. In *Microbial Sediments*, Riding, R.E. and Awramik, S.M. (eds). Springer, Berlin, Heidelberg.

Hurst, P.B. (2018). An analysis of caddisfly larval cases from bioherms in the Upper Green River Formation, White Hill Cuesta, Ephraim, Utah. Senior Independent Study Thesis, 8183, The College of Wooster, Wooster [Online]. Available at: https://openworks.wooster.edu/independentstudy/8183.

Jahnert, R.J. and Collins, L.B. (2013). Controls on microbial activity and tidal flat evolution in Shark Bay, Western Australia. *Sedimentology*, 60(4), 1071–1099.

Johnson, J.H. (1961). Jurassic algae from the subsurface of the Gulf Coast. *Journal of Paleontology*, 37(1), 147–151.

Kalkowsky, E. (1908). Oolith und Stromatolith im norddeutschen Buntsandstein. *Zeitschrift der deutschen geologischen Gesellschaft*, 68–125. doi: 10.1127/zdgg/60/1908/68.

Kennard, J.M. and James, N.P. (1986). Thrombolites and stromatolites: Two distinct types of microbial structures. *Palaios*, 1, 492–503.

Kenter, J.A., Harris, P.M.M., Della Porta, G. (2005). Steep microbial boundstone-dominated platform margins – Examples and implications. *Sedimentary Geology*, 178(1–2), 5–30.

Kiessling, W. and Flügel, E. (2002). Paleoreefs – A database on Phanerozoic reefs. In *Phanerozoic Reef Patterns*, Kiessling, W., Flügel, E., Golonka, J. (eds). SEPM Society for Sedimentary Geology, Tulsa. doi: 10.2110/pec.02.72.0077.

Kiessling, W., Flügel, E., Golonka, J. (2002). *Phanerozoic Reef Patterns*. SEPM Society for Sedimentary Geology, Tulsa.

Knoll, A.H., Fairchild, I.J., Swett, K. (1993). Calcified microbes in Neoproterozoic carbonates: Implications for our understanding of the Proterozoic/Cambrian transition. *Palaios*, 8(6), 512–525.

Krajewski, K., Leśniak, P., Łącka, B., Zawidzki, P. (2000). Origin of phosphatic stromatolites in the Upper Cretaceous condensed sequence of the Polish Jura Chain. *Sedimentary Geology*, 136(1–2), 89–112.

Krumbein, W. (1983). Stromatolites – The challenge of a term in space and time. *Precambrian Research*, 20(2–4), 493–531.

Lepot, K. (2020). Signatures of early microbial life from the Archean (4 to 2.5 Ga) eon. *Earth-Science Reviews*, 209, 103296. doi: 10.1016/j.earscirev.2020.103296.

Lepot, K., Benzerara, K., Brown, G.E., Philippot, P. (2008). Microbially influenced formation of 2,724-million-year-old stromatolites. *Nature Geoscience*, 1(2), 118–121.

Li, Q., Parrish, R., Horstwood, M., McArthur, J. (2014). U–Pb dating of cements in Mesozoic ammonites. *Chemical Geology*, 376, 76–83.

Logan, B.W. (1961). Cryptozoon and associate stromatolites from the recent, Shark Bay, Western Australia. *The Journal of Geology*, 69(5), 517–533.

Lowe, D.R. (1980). Stromatolites 3,400-myr old from the Archean of Western Australia. *Nature*, 284(5755), 441–443.

Mackey, T., Sumner, D., Hawes, I., Jungblut, A., Andersen, D. (2015). Growth of modern branched columnar stromatolites in Lake Joyce, Antarctica. *Geobiology*, 13(4), 373–390.

Milliken, K. (2014). A compositional classification for grain assemblages in fine-grained sediments and sedimentary rocks. *Journal of Sedimentary Research*, 84(12), 1185–1199.

Monty, C. (ed.) (2012). *Phanerozoic Stromatolites: Case Histories*. Springer, Berlin, Heidelberg.

Moore, L.S. and Burne, R.V. (1994). The modern thrombolites of Lake Clifton, Western Australia. In *Phanerozoic Stromatolites II*, Bertrand-Sarfati, J. and Monty, C. (eds). Springer, Dordrecht. doi: 10.1007/978-94-011-1124-9_1.

Noffke, N. (2021). Microbially induced sedimentary structures in clastic deposits: Implication for the prospection for fossil life on Mars. *Astrobiology*, 21(7), 866–892.

Nutman, A.P., Bennett, V.C., Friend, C.R., Van Kranendonk, M.J., Chivas, A.R. (2016). Rapid emergence of life shown by discovery of 3,700-million-year-old microbial structures. *Nature*, 537(7621), 535–538.

Oren, A. (2009). Saltern evaporation ponds as model systems for the study of primary production processes under hypersaline conditions. *Aquatic Microbial Ecology*, 56(2–3), 193–204.

Pace, A., Bourillot, R., Bouton, A., Vennin, E., Galaup, S., Bundeleva, I., Patrier, P., Dupraz, C., Thomazo, C., Sansjofre, P. (2016). Microbial and diagenetic steps leading to the mineralisation of Great Salt Lake microbialites. *Scientific Reports*, 6(1), 1–12.

Papineau, D., Walker, J.J., Mojzsis, S.J., Pace, N.R. (2005). Composition and structure of microbial communities from stromatolites of Hamelin Pool in Shark Bay, Western Australia. *Applied and Environmental Microbiology*, 71(8), 4822–4832.

Parsiegla, K.I. and Katz, J.L. (2000). Calcite growth inhibition by copper (II): II. Effect of solution composition. *Journal of Crystal Growth*, 213(3–4), 368–380.

Peckmann, J., Reimer, A., Luth, U., Luth, C., Hansen, B., Heinicke, C., Hoefs, J., Reitner, J. (2001). Methane-derived carbonates and authigenic pyrite from the northwestern Black Sea. *Marine Geology*, 177(1–2), 129–150.

Pitzer, K.S. (1979). Relativistic effects on chemical properties. *Accounts of Chemical Research*, 12(8), 271–276.

Planavsky, N., Reid, R., Lyons, T., Myshrall, K., Visscher, P. (2009). Formation and diagenesis of modern marine calcified cyanobacteria. *Geobiology*, 7(5), 566–576.

Planavsky, N.J., Reinhard, C.T., Wang, X., Thomson, D., McGoldrick, P., Rainbird, R.H., Johnson, T., Fischer, W.W., Lyons, T.W. (2014). Low Mid-Proterozoic atmospheric oxygen levels and the delayed rise of animals. *Science*, 346(6209), 635–638.

Playford, P.E. (1990). Geology of the Shark Bay area, Western Australia. *Research in Shark Bay*, 13–31 [Online]. Available at: https://library.dbca.wa.gov.au/FullTextFiles/015200.002.pdf.

Playford, P.E., Cockbain, A.E., Druce, E.C., Wray, J.L. (1976). Devonian stromatolites from the Canning basin, Western Australia. In *Developments in Sedimentology*, Walter, M.R. (ed.). Elsevier, Amsterdam.

Pohl, A., Donnadieu, Y., Godderis, Y., Lanteaume, C., Hairabian, A., Frau, C., Michel, J., Laugie, M., Reijmer, J.J., Scotese, C.R. (2020). Carbonate platform production during the Cretaceous. *GSA Bulletin*, 132(11–12), 2606–2610.

Raup, D.M. and Sepkoski Jr, J.J. (1982). Mass extinctions in the marine fossil record. *Science*, 215(4539), 1501–1503.

Reinold, M., Wong, H.L., MacLeod, F.I., Meltzer, J., Thompson, A., Burns, B.P. (2019). The vulnerability of microbial ecosystems in a changing climate: Potential impact in Shark Bay. *Life*, 9(3), 71.

Reitner, J. (1993). Modern cryptic microbialite/metazoan facies from Lizard Island (Great Barrier Reef, Australia) formation and concepts. *Facies*, 29(1), 3–39.

Reitner, J., Paul, J., Arp, G., Hause-Reitner, D. (1996). Lake Thetis domal microbialites – A complex framework of cacified biofilms and organomicrites (Cervantes, Western Australia). In *Globale und regionale Steuerungsfaktoren biogener Sedimentation*, Reitner, J., Neuweiler, F., Gunkel, F. (eds). Georg-August-Universität Göttingen, Göttingen. doi: 10.23689/fidgeo-1817.

Riding, R. (1991). Classification of microbial carbonates. In *Calcareous Algae and Stromatolites*, Riding, R. (ed.). Springer, Berlin, Heidelberg.

Riding, R. (1992). Temporal variation in calcification in marine cyanobacteria. *Journal of the Geological Society*, 149(6), 979–989.

Riding, R. (1993). Phanerozoic patterns of marine $CaCO_3$ precipitation. *Naturwissenschaften*, 80(11), 513–516.

Riding, R. (2006). Microbial carbonate abundance compared with fluctuations in metazoan diversity over geological time. *Sedimentary Geology*, 185(3–4), 229–238.

Riding, R. (2011). The nature of stromatolites: 3,500 million years of history and a century of research. In *Advances in Stromatolite Geobiology*, Reitner, J. Quéric, N.-V., Arp, G. (eds). Springer, Berlin, Heidelberg.

Riding, R. and Liang, L. (2005). Geobiology of microbial carbonates: Metazoan and seawater saturation state influences on secular trends during the Phanerozoic. *Palaeogeography, Palaeoclimatology, Palaeoecology*, 219(1–2), 101–115.

Riding, R. and Virgone, A. (2020). Hybrid carbonates: In situ abiotic, microbial and skeletal co-precipitates. *Earth-Science Reviews*, 208, 103300.

Roche, A., Vennin, E., Bouton, A., Olivier, N., Wattinne, A., Bundeleva, I., Deconinck, J.-F., Virgone, A., Gaucher, E.C., Visscher, P.T. (2018). Oligo-Miocene lacustrine microbial and metazoan buildups from the Limagne Basin (French Massif Central). *Palaeogeography, Palaeoclimatology, Palaeoecology*, 504, 34–59.

Roche, A., Vennin, E., Bundeleva, I., Bouton, A., Payandi-Rolland, D., Amiotte-Suchet, P., Gaucher, E.C., Courvoisier, H., Visscher, P.T. (2019). The role of the substrate on the mineralization potential of microbial mats in a modern freshwater river (Paris Basin, France). *Minerals*, 9(6), 359.

Rouchy, J.M. and Monty, C. (2000). Gypsum microbial sediments: Neogene and modern examples. *Microbial Sediments*, Riding, R.E. and Awramik, S.M. (eds). Springer, Berlin, Heidelberg, 209–216.

Rozenstein, O., Zaady, E., Katra, I., Karnieli, A., Adamowski, J., Yizhaq, H. (2014). The effect of sand grain size on the development of cyanobacterial biocrusts. *Aeolian Research*, 15, 217–226.

Schopf, J.W. (2014). Geological evidence of oxygenic photosynthesis and the biotic response to the 2400–2200 Ma "Great oxidation event". *Biochemistry (Moscow)*, 79(3), 165–177.

Schopf, J.W., Kudryavtsev, A.B., Czaja, A.D., Tripathi, A.B. (2007). Evidence of Archean life: Stromatolites and microfossils. *Precambrian Research*, 158(3–4), 141–155.

Semikhatov, M.A. and Raaben, M.E. (2000). Proterozoic stromatolite taxonomy and biostratigraphy. In *Microbial Sediments*, Riding, R.E. and Awramik, S.M. (eds). Springer, Berlin, Heidelberg.

Semikhatov, M.A., Gebelein, C., Cloud, P., Awramik, S., Benmore, W. (1979). Stromatolite morphogenesis – Progress and problems. *Canadian Journal of Earth Sciences*, 16(5), 992–1015.

Sepkoski, J.J. (1997). Biodiversity: Past, present, and future. *Journal of Paleontology*, 71(4), 533–539.

Shapiro, H.M. (2000). Microbial analysis at the single-cell level: Tasks and techniques. *Journal of Microbiological Methods*, 42(1), 3–16.

Shapiro, J.A. (2007). Bacteria are small but not stupid: Cognition, natural genetic engineering and socio-bacteriology. *Studies in History and Philosophy of Biological and Biomedical Sciences*, 38(4), 807–819. doi: 10.1016/j.shpsc.2007.09.010.

Smith, G.A., Nickels, J.S., Kerger, B.D., Davis, J.D., Collins, S.P., Wilson, J.T., McNabb, J.F., White, D.C. (1986). Quantitative characterization of microbial biomass and community structure in subsurface material: A prokaryotic consortium responsive to organic contamination. *Canadian Journal of Microbiology*, 32(2), 104–111.

Stal, L.J. (2012). Cyanobacterial mats and stromatolites. In *Ecology of Cyanobacteria II*, Whitton, B. (ed.). Springer, Dordrecht.

Stal, L.J., van Gemerden, H., Krumbein, W.E. (1985). Structure and development of a benthic marine microbial mat. *FEMS Microbiology Ecology*, 1(2), 111–125.

Suarez-Gonzalez, P., Arenas, C., Benito, M.I., Pomar, L. (2019). Interplay between biotic and environmental conditions in pre-salt Messinian microbialites of the western Mediterranean (Upper Miocene, Mallorca, Spain). *Palaeogeography, Palaeoclimatology, Palaeoecology*, 533, 109242.

Suosaari, E.P., Reid, R.P., Araujo, T.A.A., Playford, P.E., Holley, D.K., Mcnamara, K.J., Eberli, G.P. (2016). Environmental pressures influencing living stromatolites in Hamelin Pool, Shark Bay, Western Australia. *Palaios*, 31(10), 483–496.

Takashima, C., Okumura, T., Nishida, S., Koike, H., Kano, A. (2011). Bacterial symbiosis forming laminated iron-rich deposits in Okuoku-hachikurou hot spring, Akita Prefecture, Japan. *Island Arc*, 20(2), 294–304.

Tarhan, L.G., Planavsky, N.J., Laumer, C., Stolz, J., Reid, R. (2013). Microbial mat controls on infaunal abundance and diversity in modern marine microbialites. *Geobiology*, 11(5), 485–497.

Teboul, P.-A., Durlet, C., Gaucher, E., Virgone, A., Girard, J.-P., Curie, J., Lopez, B., Camoin, G. (2016). Origins of elements building travertine and tufa: New perspectives provided by isotopic and geochemical tracers. *Sedimentary Geology*, 334, 97–114.

Thomazo, C., Pinti, D.L., Busigny, V., Ader, M., Hashizume, K., Philippot, P. (2009). Biological activity and the Earth's surface evolution: Insights from carbon, sulfur, nitrogen and iron stable isotopes in the rock record. *Comptes Rendus Palevol*, 8(7), 665–678.

Van Gemerden, H. (1993). Microbial mats: A joint venture. *Marine Geology*, 113(1–2), 3–25.

Vasconcelos, C. and McKenzie, J.A. (1997). Microbial mediation of modern dolomite precipitation and diagenesis under anoxic conditions (Lagoa Vermelha, Rio de Janeiro, Brazil). *Journal of Sedimentary Research*, 67(3), 378–390.

Veizer, J., Godderis, Y., Francois, L.M. (2000). Evidence for decoupling of atmospheric CO_2 and global climate during the Phanerozoic eon. *Nature*, 408(6813), 698–701.

Vennin, E., Olivier, N., Brayard, A., Bour, I., Thomazo, C., Escarguel, G., Fara, E., Bylund, K.G., Jenks, J.F., Stephen, D.A. (2015). Microbial deposits in the aftermath of the end-Permian mass extinction: A diverging case from the Mineral Mountains (Utah, USA). *Sedimentology*, 62(3), 753–792.

Vennin, E., Bouton, A., Bourillot, R., Pace, A., Roche, A., Brayard, A., Thomazo, C., Virgone, A., Gaucher, E.C., Desaubliaux, G. (2019). The lacustrine microbial carbonate factory of the successive Lake Bonneville and Great Salt Lake, Utah, USA. *Sedimentology*, 66(1), 165–204.

Vennin, E., Bouton, A., Roche, A., Gérard, E., Bundeleva, I., Boussagol, P., Wattinne, A., Kolodka, C., Gaucher, E., Virgone, A. (2021). The Limagne Basin: A journey through modern and fossil microbial deposits. *Bulletin de la société géologique de France*, 192(1), 41–76. doi: 10.1051/bsgf/2021030.

Viles, H.A., Taylor, M.P., Nicoll, K., Neumann, S. (2007). Facies evidence of hydroclimatic regime shifts in tufa depositional sequences from the arid Naukluft Mountains, Namibia. *Sedimentary Geology*, 195(1–2), 39–53.

Vincent, W.F., Castenholz, R.W., Downes, M.T., Howard-Williams, C. (1993). Antarctic cyanobacteria: Light, nutrients, and photosynthesis in the microbial mat environment. *Journal of Phycology*, 29(6), 745–755.

Visscher, P.T., Reid, R.P., Bebout, B.M., Hoeft, S.E., Macintyre, I.G., Thompson, J.A. (1998). Formation of lithified micritic laminae in modern marine stromatolites (Bahamas): The role of sulfur cycling. *American Mineralogist*, 83(11–12 Part 2), 1482–1493.

Visscher, P.T., Reid, R.P., Bebout, B.M. (2000). Microscale observations of sulfate reduction: Correlation of microbial activity with lithified micritic laminae in modern marine stromatolites. *Geology*, 28(10), 919–922.

Visscher, P.T., Surgeon, T.M., Hoeft, S.E., Bebout, B.M.,Thompson Jr., J., Reid, R.P. (2002). Microelectrode studies in modern marine stromatolites: Unraveling the Earth's past? In *Environmental Electrochemistry: Analyses of Trace Element Biogeochemistry*, Taillefert, M. and Rozan, T. (eds). Oxford University Press, New York.

Visscher, P.T., Dupraz, C., Braissant, O., Gallagher, K.L., Glunk, C., Casillas, L., Reed, R.E. (2010). Biogeochemistry of carbon cycling in hypersaline mats: Linking the present to the past through biosignatures. In *Microbial Mats*, Seckbach, J. and Oren, A. (eds). Springer, Dordrecht.

Walter, M.R. and Heys, G.R. (1985). Links between the rise of the metazoa and the decline of stromatolites. *Precambrian Research*, 29(1–3), 149–174.

Walter, M.R., Bauld, J., Brock, T.D. (1972). Siliceous algal and bacterial stromatolites in hot spring and geyser effluents of Yellowstone National Park. *Science*, 178(4059), 402–405.

Webb, G.E. and Kamber, B.S. (2004). Biogenicity inferred from microbialite geochemistry. *Microbiology Australia*, 25(1), 34–35.

de Winder, B., Matthijs, H.C., Mur, L.R. (1989). The role of water retaining substrata on the photosynthetic response of three drought tolerant phototrophic micro-organisms isolated from a terrestrial habitat. *Archives of Microbiology*, 152, 458–462.

Wong, H.L., White, R.A., Visscher, P.T., Charlesworth, J.C., Vázquez-Campos, X., Burns, B.P. (2018). Disentangling the drivers of functional complexity at the metagenomic level in Shark Bay microbial mat microbiomes. *The ISME Journal*, 12(11), 2619–2639.

Wright, V.P. (2012). Lacustrine carbonates in rift settings: The interaction of volcanic and microbial processes on carbonate deposition. *Geological Society London Special Publications*, 370(1), 39–47.

Zaitseva, T., Semikhatov, M., Gorokhov, I., Sergeev, V., Kuznetsov, A., Ivanovskaya, T., Melnikov, N., Konstantinova, G. (2016). Isotopic geochronology and biostratigraphy of Riphean deposits of the Anabar Massif, North Siberia. *Stratigraphy and Geological Correlation*, 24(6), 549–574.

Zawaski, M.J., Kelly, N.M., Orlandini, O.F., Nichols, C.I., Allwood, A.C., Mojzsis, S.J. (2020). Reappraisal of purported ca. 3.7 Ga stromatolites from the Isua Supracrustal Belt (West Greenland) from detailed chemical and structural analysis. *Earth and Planetary Science Letters*, 545, 116409.

Zeyen, N., Benzerara, K., Li, J., Groleau, A., Balan, E., Robert, J-L., Estève, I., Tavera, R., Moreira, D., López-García, P. (2015). Formation of low-T hydrated silicates in modern microbialites from Mexico and implications for microbial fossilization. *Frontiers in Earth Science*, 3, 64.

Zhou, J. and Chafetz, H.S. (2009). Biogenic caliches in Texas: The role of organisms and effect of climate. *Sedimentary Geology*, 222(3–4), 207–225.

4

Molecular Approaches for the Study of Phylogenetic and Functional Diversity of Living Organisms

Miguel INIESTO[1], Ana GUTIÉRREZ-PRECIADO[1], Thomas BACCHETTA[2], David MOREIRA[1] and Purificación LÓPEZ-GARCÍA[1]

[1] CNRS, Université Paris-Saclay, France

[2] Laboratoire MAP, UMR 5240, CNRS, Université Claude Bernard Lyon 1, Villeurbanne, France

4.1. Classifying and understanding living organisms

Understanding the diversity of living organisms and their functions is essential to understand their interactions with the geosphere and their impact on the major cycles of chemical elements, which are called biogeochemical cycles. Indeed, living organisms are systems transforming energy and matter, which, far from thermodynamic equilibrium, reproduce and evolve by natural selection. These transformations of matter and energy in cells are what we refer to as metabolism. These often alter the physicochemical environment, i.e. the biotope, in which biological communities develop, forming, overall, an ecosystem. Multicellular animals, plants and fungi are important components of today's terrestrial ecosystems. However, in recent decades, it has become clear that microorganisms have a major role in the biogeochemical cycles (Azam and Malfatti 2007; D'Hondt et al. 2019). Not only is the vast majority of terrestrial biological diversity found in the microbial world,

Interactions between the Geosphere and the Biosphere,
coordinated by Karim BENZERARA and Christophe THOMAZO.

but so is the diversity of energy and carbon metabolisms. Thus, while most eukaryotes (including animals and fungi) derive their energy from the oxidation of organic matter, using O_2 as an electron acceptor (aerobic respiration), and plants are also capable of photosynthesis (fixing the CO_2 in the form of organic matter using light energy and the Calvin cycle), prokaryotic microorganisms (archaea and bacteria) are able to draw their energy from a wide range of oxidation–reduction (redox) reactions and fix the CO_2 by using various biosynthetic pathways (Madigan et al. 2014). Even today, new microbial lineages are being discovered with previously unsuspected metabolic capacities, such as the ability to couple manganese oxidation and autotrophic CO_2 fixation (Yu and Leadbetter 2020). Aerobic respiration is accompanied by many modes of anaerobic respiration in archaea and bacteria, which use a wide variety of organic (organic acids, dimethyl sulfoxide, etc.) and inorganic electron acceptors (CO, CO_2; oxidized forms of Fe, S, N, Mo, Se, As, U, etc.). Therefore, archaea and bacteria are at the forefront of interactions with the mineral world, being able to alter mineral surfaces (bio-corrosion or biodissolution, see Chapter 1) to facilitate the release of metals or, conversely, inducing the precipitation of minerals (see Chapter 2).

In this chapter, we will briefly review the methods that currently allow us to characterize the diversity of microbial communities and their metabolic potential in the natural environment. As an example, we will focus on the study of microbialites, complex and ancient ecosystems where microorganism–mineral interactions are particularly intertwined.

4.1.1. *Taxonomy and classification systems of organisms*

Humans have been observing and trying to categorize nature for a very long time. Taking up Greek concepts, notably those of Aristotle and Plato, the medieval vision is that of the *Scala Naturae*, where different categories of beings are classified following a linear hierarchy according to their degree of complexity. At the bottom of the scale are minerals, followed by plants, animals, humans and, in the upper layers, supernatural beings. It was the Swedish naturalist Carl Linnaeus (1707–1778) who laid the foundations of the modern classification system. He introduced the Latin binomial nomenclature system of species and classified them in a hierarchy of nested categories, from species to phylum. These initial classifications are based on the resemblance of phenotypic traits[1], but do not include an evolutionary vision of the living. It was not until the arrival of Charles Darwin and the formulation of the theory of evolution by natural selection (Darwin 1859) that the idea of a phylogenetic classification of living organisms, i.e. based on the relationships of kinship between species, came to light. We owe the first sketch of the evolutionary process to Charles Darwin, in the form of a

1. The phenotype groups together all the observable characteristics of an organism.

tree structure; it reflects the divergence between species that transform over time. Later, it would be understood that Charles Darwin's intuition was correct. The first universal tree of life, which attempts to account for the relationships of kinship between organisms, was produced by Haeckel (1866) based on morphological observations. It was divided into three major kingdoms: animals, plants (including at the time blue-green algae that would later be recognized as bacteria: cyanobacteria) and a group called protists, which grouped together essentially large unicellular species. Bacteria (Monera) only appear in Haeckel's tree at the base. Here, we have a gradualist vision of life, which progresses from "simple" to "complex", from "primitive" to "evolved". Other later visions also based on observable phenotypic and ecological traits reproduce the same gradualist vision of life, such as the classification into five kingdoms (animals, plants, fungi, protists – here referring to unicellular eukaryotes – and bacteria) by Whittaker (1959) in which, again, bacteria appear at the base of the tree of life.

The major problem with all these traditional classifications is that morphology is not a sufficiently informative criterion to differentiate between very small microorganisms with relatively little variation in morphology. As a result, other so-called "operational" classifications began to be applied to bacteria. This is the case for "numerical" taxonomy, which took into account metabolic properties (production of gas or acid, type of respiration, transformed substrates, etc.) of clonal populations of bacteria isolated in laboratory culture media to classify these microbial species into similar functional categories. However, these classifications were not "natural", i.e. not based on criteria of evolutionary kinship. In the mid-1960s, it was considered impossible to establish a true universal phylogenetic classification of living organisms (Stanier et al. 1970).

4.1.2. *Molecular phylogeny and the tree of life*

Zuckerkandl and Pauling (1965) published an article entitled "Molecules as documents of evolutionary history" that would become the founder of a young discipline, molecular phylogeny. The proposition is simple: evolutionary information accumulates in the sequence of biopolymers, that of the nucleotides of DNA and RNA and that of the amino acids of proteins. Woese and Fox (1977) would exploit this idea to construct a phylogenetic tree of life using as a universal marker: the RNA of the small ribosome[2] subunit (16S rRNA for prokaryotes, 18S for eukaryotes; S, for Svedberg, the unit of the centrifugation sedimentation coefficient used to purify these molecules). Time showed the usefulness of this molecule as a marker of cellular

2. Ribosomes are organelles composed of RNA and proteins that ensure the translation of messenger RNA into proteins within cells. They have two subunits distinguished by their size.

identity, which is still used today. This molecule is an essential part of cells; it is responsible for the synthesis of proteins and is therefore highly conserved. This makes it possible to reliably align the sequences of even very distant species, while having variable regions that make it possible to differentiate groups of sequences (therefore, species) according to their similarity. The first universal phylogenetic tree reconstructed from 16S/18S rRNA sequences contained, but a priori very diverse, species: animals, plants, fungi and bacteria with varied properties. The observed relationships correlated well with what was expected for a group of methanogenic species or those from extreme environments (hot, salty) that stood out from the classic bacteria, forming a separate group. Called archaea and considered a third primary kingdom (Woese and Fox 1977), they later became one of the three domains of living organisms (Archaea, Bacteria and Eukarya) (Figure 4.1) (Woese et al. 1990).

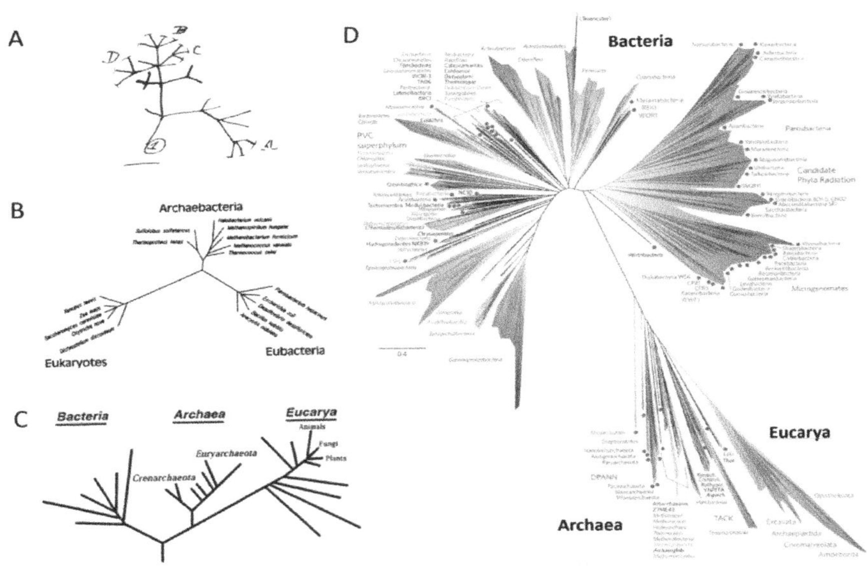

Figure 4.1. *Diversity and evolution of life exemplified by phylogenetic trees. A, tree structure showing the process of species transformation by Charles Darwin (1859). B and C, universal phylogenetic trees based on the RNA sequences of the small subunit of the ribosome produced by Carl R. Woese showing the three primary kingdoms (B), later renamed domains (C) of life. The tree shown in C is rooted in the branch of the Bacteria. D, recent universal tree of life based on the sequences of several ribosomal proteins; the red dots indicate environmental lineages (phylums) with no cultured representatives (Hug et al. 2016). For a color version of this figure, see: www.iste.co.uk/benzerara/geosphere.zip*

Today, with technological improvements, sequencing genomes is easy. We can therefore combine evolutionary information from several conserved genes coding for proteins and not just the 16S/18S rRNA gene. The phylogenetic trees thus obtained (which are often called phylogenomic) are generally more robust. Thus, the tree of life has been enriched with data from several thousand species (Figure 4.1D).

4.1.3. *Analysis of diversity based on phylogenetic identity marker genes*

Beyond the possibility of reconstructing molecular phylogenies and establishing a natural classification of living organisms, the analysis of 16S rRNA gene sequences has also opened the door to exploring microbial diversity in natural ecosystems. Indeed, microbiologists have long realized that only a very small proportion of microorganisms present in a natural sample could be cultivated and therefore studied in the laboratory (approximately 1% with variations depending on the type of environment). The analysis of specific identity marker genes makes it possible to overcome this constraint. It is sufficient to lyse the cells of the natural sample, to purify the community DNA and then to amplify and sequence the 16S rRNA genes present in the community. The analysis of the sequences makes it possible to arrange them in a phylogenetic tree and classify the organisms that they represent in already known groups or, even, define new ones if their evolutionary distance with those already described is relatively high.

The characterization of microbial diversity by these molecular methods dates back to the end of the 1980s. At the time, and until the development of mass sequencing methods at the beginning of the 21st century, we had to clone[3] copies of gene fragments amplified by PCR (polymerase chain reaction) using primers (oligonucleotides used to initiate the polymerization reaction by pairing with the target sequence) specific to bacteria or archaea. Each colony of the bacterium *Escherichia coli* transformed with a plasmid[4] containing an environmental 16S rRNA gene fragment carried a single gene. Each of these colonies had to be subcultured and the cloned genes sequenced using the Sanger method (reads of the order of 1,000 nucleotides). The sequences were then manually compared with those existing in the public sequence database GenBank (https://www.ncbi.nlm.nih.gov/) and classified by similarity to known sequences and/or by reconstruction of a phylogenetic tree that included reference sequences. All sequences that shared more

3. Cloning consists of identically multiplying a particular sequence of DNA present within a collection of different sequences.

4. A plasmid is a circular DNA molecule capable of autonomous replication within a cell and not essential to its survival.

than 97–98% identity were classified together as Operational Taxonomic Units (OTUs) supposed to represent the species level (Figure 4.2). These early studies, carried out on marine plankton, led to the discovery of new groups of bacteria, such as the Pelagibacteriales (SAR11) (Giovannoni et al. 1990), or archaea, such as Nitrososphaera (Group I, also called Thaumarchaeota) or Poseidoniales (Group II and III) (DeLong 1992; Fuhrman et al. 1992). Subsequently, numerous molecular characterization studies of the diversity of prokaryotes have enriched databases with thousands of environmental sequences and the discovery of many new groups of archaea and bacteria. Specific databases for 16S rRNA molecules that only keep very good quality sequences and offer classification tools, such as the SILVA database (Quast et al. 2013; Yilmaz et al. 2014), have emerged.

Early studies of unicellular eukaryote diversity by molecular methods based on the amplification and sequencing of the 18S rRNA gene only appeared about 10 years after those on prokaryotes. Here again, sequence analysis immediately showed the effectiveness of the approach and the existence of new eukaryotic lineages, typically small in size and with simple morphology (López-García et al. 2001; Moon-van der Staay et al. 2001; Moreira et López-García 2002).

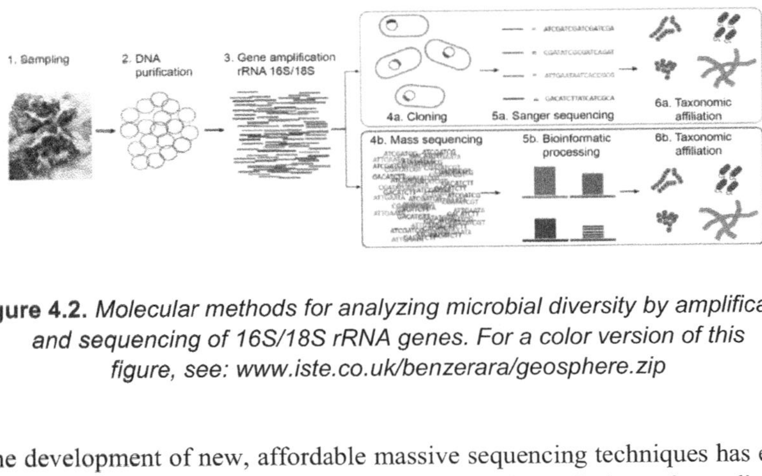

Figure 4.2. *Molecular methods for analyzing microbial diversity by amplification and sequencing of 16S/18S rRNA genes. For a color version of this figure, see: www.iste.co.uk/benzerara/geosphere.zip*

The development of new, affordable massive sequencing techniques has enabled the molecular analysis of microbial diversity (often also called metabarcoding) with unprecedented depth[5]. These methods, such as the Illumina method (producing short sequences, 100–300 base pairs or bp), generate billions of sequences. It is therefore no longer possible to manually analyze the sequences produced. The amplified products are directly sequenced (without a cloning step), and the sequences are then

5. Sequencing depth (also called coverage) is the ratio between the length of all the sequences read end to end and the length of the target genome.

processed by bioinformatics tools that are constantly improving. Typically, after a cleaning step for low-quality sequences, the sequences of the two reading strands (forward and reverse) are assembled, and then grouped by similarity to form OTUs with desired identity percentages (e.g. 97%) or to define Amplicon Sequence Variants (ASVs, equivalent to OTUs defined at 100% identity) (Figure 4.2). The use of ASVs (Callahan et al. 2016) is now favored because they allow inter-study comparison, even though ASVs can subsequently be grouped into more inclusive OTUs. There are bioinformatics pipelines that allow the chaining of different sequence processing programs; QiiME is one of the most widely used programs (Caporaso et al. 2010; Estaki et al. 2020).

4.1.5. *Metagenomics and other "omics" approaches*

While metabarcoding of 16S/18S rRNA genes can reveal the microbial diversity of an ecosystem, including the presence of previously unknown lineages, it does not provide direct information on the functions of this diversity, except for certain phylogenetic groups that are always associated with the same metabolisms. This is the case for cyanobacteria, which, with rare exceptions, all perform oxygenic photosynthesis. On the contrary, other lineages, such as alphaproteobacteria, have very varied metabolisms (anoxygenic photosynthetic, chemolithoautotrophic, heterotrophic), and it is therefore more difficult to associate a typical metabolism with them. In the case of newly identified lineages, without cultivated representatives, this is impossible. One possibility is therefore to sequence all the genomes present in a natural sample and to predict the function of the protein-coding genes by similarity with known and annotated genes (with an associated function). This metagenomic approach consisting of directly sequencing purified DNA from a natural sample has been widely developed with mass sequencing techniques, even though the early studies used the Sanger method (Venter et al. 2004) (Figure 4.3). Thus, metagenomics or environmental genomics developed at the dawn of the 21st century.

In practice, from the billions of sequences generated for a metagenome, bioinformatics tools are applied to eliminate poor-quality sequences and then assemble the obtained (short) sequences into contigs, i.e. longer fragments, using similarity criteria on regions that overlap over a certain length. The greater the depth (quantity) of the sequence and/or the less diverse the community, the longer the assembled contigs. In general, microbial communities are very diverse and contain thousands of species (this is the case for microbialites, see section 4.2), generating an enormous variety of contigs. These contigs can contain one or more complete genes, which can be annotated by comparison with known genes in databases. It should be noted, however, that a large proportion of genes in metagenomes are orphans (do not resemble any other known genes) or resemble known genes whose function is unknown (hypothetical function). As was already the case at the beginning of metagenomics (Yooseph et al. 2007), we are still far from having explored the genetic space of microbial communities. From the contigs obtained, two approaches can be used. The first is to study the functions encoded in the contigs of the metagenome. This gives us access to the metabolic pathways and their relative abundance in the ecosystem, while freeing ourselves from the organisms that carry them. This is how, for example, the importance of phototrophy in the oceans, based on proteorhodopsin (not associated with photosynthesis), was discovered (Venter et al. 2004). In general, the functions associated with an ecosystem tend to be more often conserved than the taxa carrying these functions (Louca et al. 2016a, 2016b). The other approach involves reconstructing the genomes of the microorganisms present in the community from the metagenomes; here, we refer to metagenome-assembled genomes (MAGs). To do this, we exploit the compositional biases inherent in each genome or group of phylogenetically close genomes (their "grammar"). The contigs are therefore grouped according to the frequency of different k-mers (k-letter words, the letters being the nucleotide bases that make up the DNA; *k* can vary to find an optimal separation of contigs in groups). If the same organisms are found in several samples with different relative abundances, we can co-assemble the different metagenomes and also exploit the differences in overlap using software such as Anvi'o (Eren et al. 2015).

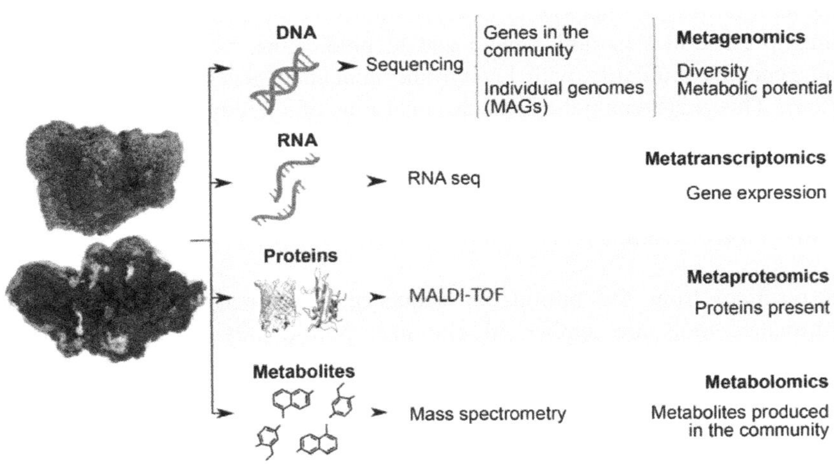

Figure 4.3. *"Omics" methods for studying metabolic functions and other traits encoded in microbial communities. For a color version of this figure, see: www.iste.co.uk/benzerara/geosphere.zip*

The reconstruction of MAGs from metagenomes has allowed the discovery of new lineages not necessarily well represented in metabarcoding databases because their rRNA sequences are divergent (Eloe-Fadrosh et al. 2016; Parks et al. 2017). For example, this approach highlighted the existence of a clade of bacterial phyla, the CPR (Candidate Phyla Radiation), which represents approximately 15–25% of known bacterial diversity (Brown et al. 2015; He et al. 2021). Phylogenetic trees can also be reconstructed using conserved protein genes from MAGs of uncultivated lineages, leading to a more realistic view of the tree of life (Hug et al. 2016). The Genome Taxonomy Database (GTDB) initiative even proposes a new, more streamlined taxonomic classification, based on a definition of phyla consistent with an equivalent phylogenetic depth, which incorporates all environmental lineages (Rinke et al. 2021).

Metagenomes provide access to the metabolic potential of microbial communities, but genes can be expressed (or not) depending on different constraints. Metatranscriptomics, i.e. the sequencing of RNA molecules present in the cell, provides access to messenger RNA (mRNA) and therefore to the expression of the functional potential of cells. These approaches have also enabled the discovery of small transcripts that play regulatory or unknown roles (Shi et al. 2009). The presence of mRNA is often taken as an indicator of the presence of active communities, for example, the subsurface (Orsi et al. 2013). Less developed, the integration of metaproteomic data (sequencing of proteins in a community) and metabolomic data (analysis of metabolites) with data from other "omics" is promising for understanding the functioning and ecology of microbial communities (Franzosa et al. 2015; Louca et al. 2016c) (Figure 4.3).

4.2. Microbial diversity associated with microbialites

Microbialites are sedimentary rocks formed under the influence of complex microbial communities in terms of phylogenetic and functional diversity (see Chapter 3) (Riding 2000; Dupraz and Visscher 2005). Most microbialites are composed of carbonates, and the microbial ecosystem they form is generally based on photosynthesis as the main form of primary production, and is logically found in the photic zone. But there are also authigenic carbonates associated with chemolithotrophic communities in the deep ocean (Bailey et al. 2009; Last et al. 2012). Microbialites can be laminated (stromatolites) or granular in structure (thrombolites). Fossil stromatolites are abundant in the geological record. The oldest records suggest the presence of life as early as 3.4 Ga (Tice and Lowe 2004; Allwood et al. 2006), but after a long peak in abundance during the Proterozoic, they declined since the Cambrian explosion about 500 Ma ago (Awramik 1971;

Altermann et al. 2006). Currently, even though they are rarer than in the past, microbialites still form in marine and continental contexts (coastal ponds, alkaline or karst lakes). These microbialites are analogues of fossil stromatolites, and their study can be useful for understanding the formation process and constraining the interpretation of fossil objects.

But, precisely, how are microbialites formed? Existing data suggest that, beyond the aggregation of mineral particles by filamentous cyanobacteria (particularly the order Oscillatoriales), which is sometimes important in a marine context (Paerl et al. 2001; Suarez-Gonzalez et al. 2019), these structures are formed mainly by the in situ precipitation of carbonates (Altermann et al. 2006). This precipitation must be favored by the physicochemical conditions of the environment, in particular by the supersaturation of the solutions with respect to the carbonate phases. This supersaturation itself depends on the CO_3^{2-} ion concentration (favored at high pH), and in cations, generally Ca^{2+} and Mg^{2+} (see Chapter 2). But microorganisms, through their metabolism, can in turn alter these abiotic conditions and promote the precipitation of carbonates by increasing the surrounding pH and/or by providing nucleation centers (Benzerara et al. 2006; Braissant et al. 2007; Obst et al. 2009; Decho 2010). For biology, the first question to be resolved is that of the diversity of microorganisms associated with microbialites and their relative abundance, i.e. to determine the structure of the microbial communities. This is the question addressed in this section.

4.2.1. *Environmental context and sampling*

Modern stromatolites can occur in marine environments; they are found in some rather tropical regions and in coastal lagoons sometimes connected to the sea. For a long time, the best studied have been those of Shark Bay, in Australia (Logan 1961; Reid et al. 2003) and those of Highborne Cay in the Bahamas (Dravis 1983; Reid and Browne 1991). However, microbialites (stromatolites or thrombolites) are also found in various alkaline continental lakes and ponds (Figure 4.4), such as the Pavilion Lake in Canada (Brady et al. 2009) and Alchichica in Mexico (Kazmierczak et al. 2011), and sometimes in karst environments, such as Ruidera in Spain (Santos et al. 2010). But they are also found in saline or hypersaline contexts, often in desert areas, such as Cuatro Ciénegas in Mexico (Souza et al. 2006), and/or in very high altitude areas, such as those of salt ponds ("salt flats") and lakes in the Andes (Vignale et al. 2021). These systems are also subject to strong ultraviolet radiation. Overall, the presence of microbialites has been described in more than 50 continental systems with a pH ≥ 7, but with varied hydrochemistry and salinity (Caumartin et al. 2023), although this inventory is surely far from exhaustive. In a recent study of a series of crater lakes located in the Mexican Transvolcanic Belt, whose chemical characteristics place them along an increasing gradient of alkalinity[6], there is a strong correlation between alkalinity, growth and the aspect of microbialites (Zeyen et al. 2021). These abiotic conditions can therefore locally favor the precipitation of carbonates, but they also influence the nature of the microbial communities that settle there. Are there particular microorganisms that favor the formation of microbialites under these conditions? How do microbial communities vary according to the physicochemical factors and the mineralogy of these systems?

To explore these questions, it is essential to collect as much information as possible on the physicochemical environment where the microbialites are found at the time of sampling, for the purpose of analyzing the associated microbial communities. It is necessary to know the season, date and time of sampling, and also their depth, since many parameters will correlate with these factors (level of irradiation, circadian cycle, seasonal stratification of certain lakes, nutrient supply, etc.). Physicochemical parameters such as pH, conductivity or salinity, dissolved oxygen or redox potential can be measured in situ using multiparameter probes, ideally along the water column (in the case of very deep lakes). Chemical analyses can then be carried out on water filtered on site through filters with a porosity of 0.2 μm, which excludes most bacteria and other microorganisms and prevents them altering the chemical composition of the solutions during storage. These different measurements can then be analyzed with data on the composition of microbial communities through multivariate statistical analyses to highlight possible correlations.

The collection of microbialite samples for microbial diversity analysis should be done with caution to prevent contamination by dust or other materials containing microorganisms exogenous to the microbialites (Figure 4.4). Handlers should wear gloves when fragmenting microbialites with pre-sterilized tools and place them in sterile tubes or containers. These samples should be fixed immediately to freeze the microbial communities as they are at the time of collection, by freezing in liquid nitrogen[7] or, more easily in the field, by chemical fixation, typically by immersion in ethanol (molecular biology grade) or other fixatives such as RNAlater™. The samples thus fixed can subsequently be stored at -20 or -80°C for years.

6. Alkalinity is the ability of water to neutralize acids and is the sum of the charges of weak bases. In many environments, it is roughly equivalent to the concentration of hydrogen carbonate ions (HCO_3^-).

7. At ambient pressure, nitrogen becomes liquid below about 196°C.

Figure 4.4. *Lakes of the Mexican Transvolcanic Region hosting microbialites. Photos of Lakes Tecuitlapa, Patzcuaro, Alchichica and Atexcac, and fragments of microbialites collected aseptically for the study of microbial communities. For a color version of this figure, see: www.iste.co.uk/benzerara/geosphere.zip*

4.2.2. Composition of microbial communities associated with microbialites through molecular tools

Microorganisms associated with microbialites were first analyzed using optical and/or scanning electron microscopy. They allowed the detection of numerous microorganisms, but, among the prokaryotes, only the species of cyanobacteria could be distinguished because of their larger size and their morphological variety (Doemel and Brock 1974; Dravis 1983; Kempe et al. 1991; Laval et al. 2000; Reid et al. 2000; Riding 2000; Kazmierczak and Kempe 2006). Various eukaryotes were also detected very early on in these systems (Des Marais 1990). From the first molecular analyses of microbial diversity, it became clear that these communities were very complex, comprising tens or even hundreds of OTUs defined at 97–98% identity, and that cyanobacteria were only one component of these communities (Paerl et al. 2001; Neilan et al. 2002; Burns et al. 2004; López-García et al. 2005; Couradeau et al. 2011). Subsequently, molecular metabarcoding analyses led to a much better quantification with approximately 2,000–4,000 OTUs, depending on the studies and the sequencing depth (Farias et al. 2013; Mobberley et al. 2013; Iniesto et al. 2020). However, only a fraction of these OTUs are relatively abundant. Eukaryotes have been studied somewhat less than prokaryotes and often independently, although some studies characterize them simultaneously on the same samples (Perkins et al. 2012; Iniesto et al. 2020). The primers used to amplify fragments of the 16S rRNA gene are often "universal" in that they amplify genes from archaea and bacteria at the same time. This allows us to observe that bacteria are very largely dominant, with archaea being rare (generally below 3–5% of prokaryotes, except in hypersaline systems that contain a relatively large fraction of halophilic archaea). The 18S rRNA genes, which are slightly larger, must be amplified with primers specific for eukaryotes. Therefore, the relative proportion of eukaryotes to prokaryotes using the number of amplified copies as an approximation cannot be estimated by amplicon sequencing. However, the identification of marker genes in metagenomes where the entire community DNA is randomly sequenced allows us to show that eukaryotes are also in the minority compared to bacteria, even though their proportion fluctuates depending on the samples, generally between 5 and 10%, occasionally more (Breitbart et al. 2009; White III et al. 2015; Saghaï et al. 2016).

Among the major groups systematically and predominantly associated with all the microbialites analyzed, we find cyanobacteria and also bacteria belonging to the Alphaproteobacteria (a fairly large fraction of which is affiliated with genera of anoxygenic photosynthetic bacteria), Planctomycetes and Bacteroidetes. The members of these latter phyla are probably involved in the degradation of polysaccharides (and in particular extracellular polymeric substances or EPS) produced by cyanobacteria. Then, we find a wide variety of other phyla and several classes of Proteobacteria (Gamma-, Beta- and sometimes Deltaproteobacteria, the latter involved in sulfate reduction). Members of *Chloroflexi* affiliated with genera of anoxygenic photosynthetic organisms are also sometimes found (Perkins et al. 2012; Farias et al. 2013; Iniesto et al. 2020; Saghaï et al. 2020). Among the eukaryotes in the structure of microbialites, we often find green algae (Chlorophyta) and/or diatoms (Bacillariophyta, Ochrophyta). Then, we easily detect typically grazing protists (ciliates, flagellates belonging to various taxa), which feed on the cells on the surface of the microbialite (Perkins et al. 2012; Farias et al. 2013; Iniesto et al. 2020).

The composition of microbial communities associated with microbialites can be compared more precisely by measuring the Bray–Curtis distance[8] between communities from OTU presence/absence matrices and their relative frequency (Bray and Curtis 1957). These distances can then be used to perform multivariate statistical analyses and assess the influence of different physicochemical parameters on community structure. It can be seen that the microbial communities of the microbialites of Lakes Alchichica and Atexcac in Mexico are closer to each other than to the microbial communities of other lakes in Mexico. These canonical correspondence analyses (CCAs) correlate positively with the Mg/Ca ratio,

8. The Bray–Curtis distance is an index used to assess the dissimilarity between two microbial communities.

conductivity and carbonate concentration in the lake waters. The communities of other lakes seem to distinguish themselves in correlation with the variation of other chemical parameters, such as pH or Ca^{2+} concentration (Figure 4.5).

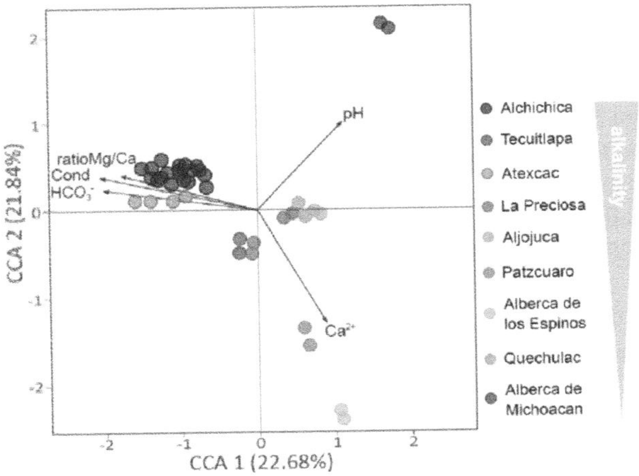

Figure 4.5. *Canonical correspondence analysis showing the distribution of microbial communities (Bray–Curtis distances) as a function of different environmental parameters. The percentage of variance explained by each axis is shown in parentheses. For a color version of this figure, see: www.iste.co.uk/benzerara/geosphere.zip*

Beyond the presence of these major lineages, are there microbial species typically associated with microbialites that play a key role in carbonate precipitation? In an attempt to answer this question, a recent study compared the fine OTU composition of microbial communities in microbialites from nine lakes of varying chemical compositions and increasing alkalinity. A few dozen prokaryotic and eukaryotic OTUs were shared by all microbialites from different lakes. Interestingly, in lakes with more massive microbialites, this shared core of OTUs, including some cyanobacteria, occupied up to 40% of the total dominant community, that of prokaryotes. As for the shared eukaryotic core, it corresponded to the majority of the eukaryotic fraction; this core was dominated by OTUs of green algae and diatoms (Figure 4.6). Interestingly, this microbial core is also found in young microbialites in formation. Thus, during colonization experiments of initially bare substrates that were exposed for 28 months in Lake Alchichica, the microbialites up to 2 mm thick that formed already had microbial communities similar to those of large microbialites on site, including this core of species (Iniesto et al. 2021). This suggests that there may be microbial species typically associated with microbialites. It remains to be seen whether they are found in microbialites other than those from Mexico and to determine what role(s) they could have in carbonate precipitation.

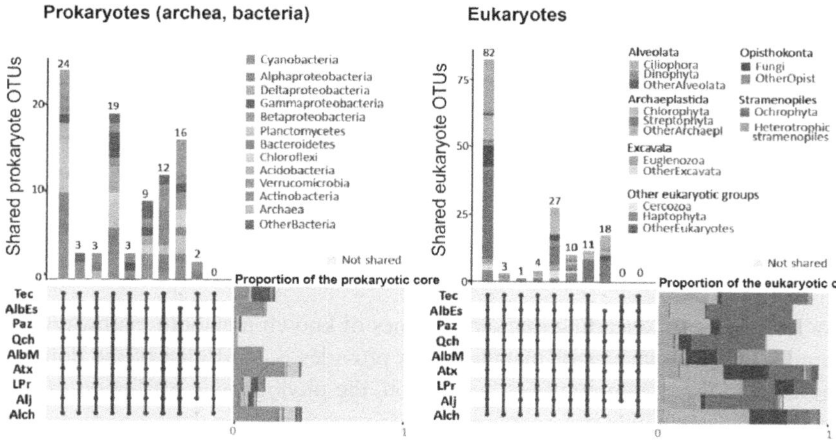

Figure 4.6. *Core of prokaryotic and eukaryotic microbial species shared by microbialites from nine lakes of the Mexican Transvolcanic Belt. Vertical black lines with dots indicate the presence of OTUs in the respective lakes (Tec, Tecuitlapa; AlbEs, Alberca de los Espinos; Paz, Pátzcuaro; Qch, Quechulac; ALbM, Alberca de Michoacán; Atx, Atexcac; LPr, La Preciosa; Alj, Aljojuca; Alch, Alchichica). Upper histograms indicate the number of shared OTUs and their phylogenetic affiliation. Histograms to the right of the lake bands indicate the fraction of total community diversity occupied by the core (colored sections) relative to the rest of the community (gray area). For a color version of this figure, see: www.iste.co.uk/benzerara/geosphere.zip*

4.3. Functions of microbial communities associated with microbialites

Microbial activity can promote the precipitation of carbonates (i) by alkalinizing the medium, thereby increasing the saturation index of the solution relative to the carbonate mineral phases, (ii) by locally increasing the concentration of Ca^{2+} or Mg^{2+} cations and/or (iii) by providing nucleation centers (see Chapter 2). The EPS secreted in abundance by certain microorganisms, notably cyanobacteria, sometimes promote nucleation (Decho et al. 2005; Benzerara et al. 2006; Obst et al. 2009). This may be partly because they release Ca^{2+} or Mg^{2+} when they are degraded by other bacteria, thus leading to a local increase in the saturation index of the solution with respect to Ca and/or Mg carbonate phases. Several microbial metabolisms can increase the pH of the medium (Dupraz et al. 2009). For example, oxygenic and anoxygenic photosynthesis, sulfate reduction or anaerobic oxidation of methane coupled with sulfate reduction. Conversely, microbial metabolisms such as aerobic respiration, sulfide oxidation (in some cases) or fermentation tend, in some cases, to acidify the medium and promote the dissolution of carbonates (Dupraz and Visscher 2005; Dupraz et al. 2009). Consequently, the balance between these different metabolisms is decisive in whether the local precipitation of carbonates occurs.

4.3.1. *Metagenomics*

Analysis of genes encoding marker enzymes of known metabolic pathways from community DNA sequences or metagenomes provides a good idea of the dominant metabolisms in these communities. In addition, the phylogenetic affiliation of these sequences indicates which organisms carry these genes and are therefore responsible for these activities (Figure 4.7). Metagenomic studies of microbial communities associated with microbialites have been conducted in a number of systems. This is the case for marine stromatolites from the Bahamas (Mobberley et al. 2015; Casaburi et al. 2016), and also for lacustrine microbialites in saline or hypersaline contexts, such as Cuatro Ciénegas (Breitbart et al. 2009; Bonilla-Rosso et al. 2012), Lake Clifton in Australia (Warden et al. 2016) or the salt lakes in Utah in the United States (Kanik et al. 2020). This is also the case for microbialites from some extreme and arsenic-rich systems in the Andes (Kurth et al. 2017), or from alkaline lakes such as Lake Alchichica in Mexico (Saghaï et al. 2016) or Lake Pavilion (White III et al. 2016) and other systems (White III et al. 2015) in Canada. In general, the diversity inferred from single-copy genes present in metagenomes is congruent with that inferred by metabarcoding analyses (rRNA 16S).

Among the metabolisms identified in these metagenomes that can promote carbonatogenesis, photosynthesis dominates. However, beyond oxygenic photosynthesis attributable to cyanobacteria and eukaryotic algae, there is a diversity of types of anoxygenic photosynthesis. These are carried out by microorganisms belonging mainly to the *Alphaproteobacteria* and *Chloroflexi* (Saghaï et al. 2016, 2020). Molecular studies combined with microscopic observations and Raman spectroscopy show a preponderant role of alphaproteobacteria in the precipitation of carbonates from microbialites of Lake Dziani Dzaha (Mayotte, Indian Ocean) (Gérard et al. 2018). This seems to confirm the idea that various functional groups, including that of anoxygenic photosynthesis, contribute to the carbonatogenic potential of these systems (Saghaï et al. 2015). Recently, the ability to hydrolyze urea has also been highlighted as another metabolic activity promoting carbonate precipitation (Medina Ferrer et al. 2021), reinforcing previous observations (White III et al. 2016).

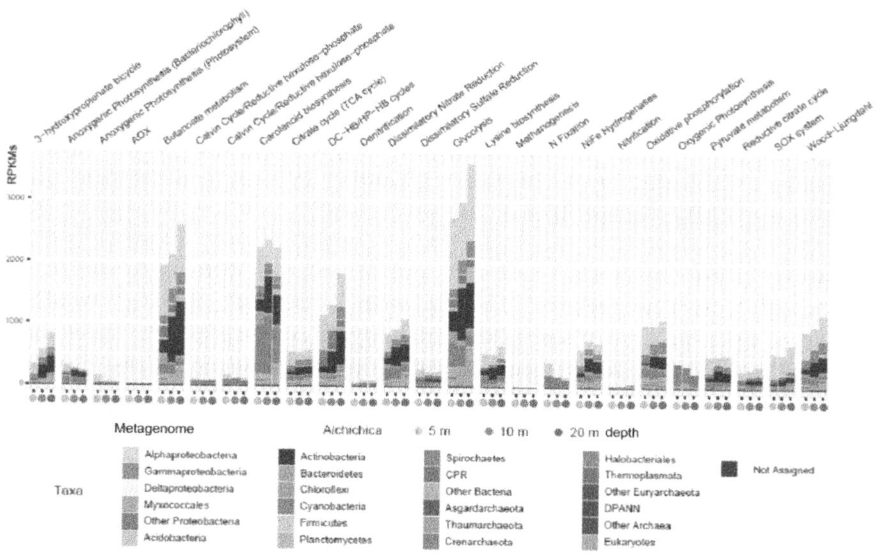

Figure 4.7. *Normalized abundance of diagnostic genes of different metabolic pathways in microbialite metagenomes from increasing depth from Lake Alchichica. Relative abundance is given in Reads Per Kilobase and per Million, RPKMs. For a color version of this figure, see: www.iste.co.uk/benzerara/geosphere.zip*

Analysis of viral sequences in metagenomes has identified an abundant presence of these obligate molecular parasites in various microbialites (Desnues et al. 2008), including Shark Bay stromatolites (White III et al. 2018).

It has been suggested that viruses may contribute directly or indirectly to carbonate precipitation by inducing cell lysis that could catalyze carbonate precipitation, and by controlling bacterial populations, possibly disrupting the "carbonatogenic equilibrium" mentioned above (White III et al. 2021).

4.3.2. *Metatranscriptomics and other "omics" methods*

Metatranscriptomic analysis, via the sequencing of reverse-transcribed RNA molecules[9] into cDNA, informs us about gene expression at a given time. Few metatranscriptomes are already available for microbialites. This is partly due to the difficulties in purifying mRNA in sufficient quantities for sequencing. Indeed, the mRNA molecule is easy to degrade and tends to adsorb onto carbonates. In general, these studies confirm the expression of metabolic genes typically associated with microbial groups composing local communities (Campbell et al. 2020). But more interestingly, they can show the change in gene expression spatially and temporally. Thus, gene expression can vary according to the depth within the biofilm forming a microbialite (Mobberley et al. 2015), or according to daily and seasonal cycles (Louyakis et al. 2018; Campbell et al. 2020).

However, these analyses are still very limited, and it is difficult to confirm the influence of local heterogeneity. The inclusion of several replicates would be necessary to limit this type of stochastic variability. In some cases, the expression of urease and carbonic anhydrase genes observed in the metagenome also correlates with measurements of their respective enzymatic activities (Medina Ferrer et al. 2021). Ideally, all of these observations should be integrated with metaproteomic and (meta)metabolomic studies in parallel to obtain a better overview of the biological functioning of a microbialite. But this type of integrative study remains a relatively distant prospect.

4.4. Reconstruction of evolutionary history and inference of ancient traits

Analysis of molecular data from contemporary organisms and communities can also provide information about evolutionary history and allow inferences about ancestral traits. It is not possible to address these issues exhaustively in this chapter, but concrete examples of information that can be inferred from studies of organisms and communities of microbial mats, both calcifying and non-calcifying, will be provided.

---

9. Reverse transcription is the conversion of a copy of mRNA into so-called complementary DNA (abbreviated cDNA). This reaction is catalyzed by an enzyme called reverse transcriptase. It occurs naturally, particularly in certain viruses, and can be used in molecular biology, as here for transcriptomics.

4.4.1. *Taxonomic sampling, new lineages, tree of life*

Mass molecular methods (metabarcoding, metagenomics) provide access to total microbial diversity, including that of groups for which we do not yet have representatives cultured in the laboratory. The inclusion of lineages distant from known taxa in the phylogenetic tree of life generally makes it possible to improve the resolution of regions of the tree that were previously sparsely populated and thus to answer evolutionary questions. A concrete example corresponds to the discovery of a new lineage of cyanobacteria, the *Gloeomargaritales* (see Chapter 2). Analyses of 16S rRNA gene diversity in Lake Alchichica had revealed several sequences that branched deeply into the cyanobacteria lineage (Couradeau et al. 2011). A little later, a species of cyanobacterium with a 16S rRNA sequence identical to one of these basal lineages was isolated from the microbialites maintained in culture in the laboratory, *Gloeomargarita lithophora*. This species of cyanobacterium produced Ca, Sr and Ba carbonates inside the cell (Couradeau et al. 2012), a first since no cyanobacteria were yet known to produce intracellular carbonates (Benzerara et al. 2014). Beyond its biomineralizing capacity, the interest of this cyanobacterium was its basal phylogenetic position compared to many other known lineages of cyanobacteria (Couradeau et al. 2012; Moreira et al. 2017). Including *G. lithophora* in phylogenetic trees using genetic markers common to cyanobacteria and chloroplasts showed its phylogenetic proximity to plastids[10] of eukaryotic photosynthetic cells, suggesting that they derive from a cyanobacterium related to the Gloeomargaritales lineage (Ponce-Toledo et al. 2017). Furthermore, since Gloeomargaritales are consistently associated with freshwater environments and never marine ones (Ragon et al. 2014), the first endosymbiosis that gave rise to the ancestor of primary eukaryotic photosynthetic organisms (the Archaeplastida, including glaucophyte, red, green algae and land plants) likely took place in a continental environment and not in a marine environment as was often assumed (Ponce-Toledo et al. 2017; Sánchez-Baracaldo et al. 2017).

The study of Gloeomargaritales can therefore provide information on the nature of the ancestor of the eukaryotic chloroplast. We now know that this lineage of benthic cyanobacteria is diverse but relatively rare (Ragon et al. 2014) and that, in addition to being present in karst or alkaline locations, it is typically associated with thermophilic biofilms and photosynthetic mats (Ragon et al. 2014). A new thermophilic species isolated from a biofilm of a hot spring in western Canada, *Gloeomargarita ahousahtiae*, has just been described (Bacchetta et al. 2023) (Figure 4.8).

---

10. Plastids are organelles observed within plant cells. They can have different functions, for example, being the site of oxygenic photosynthesis for chloroplasts.

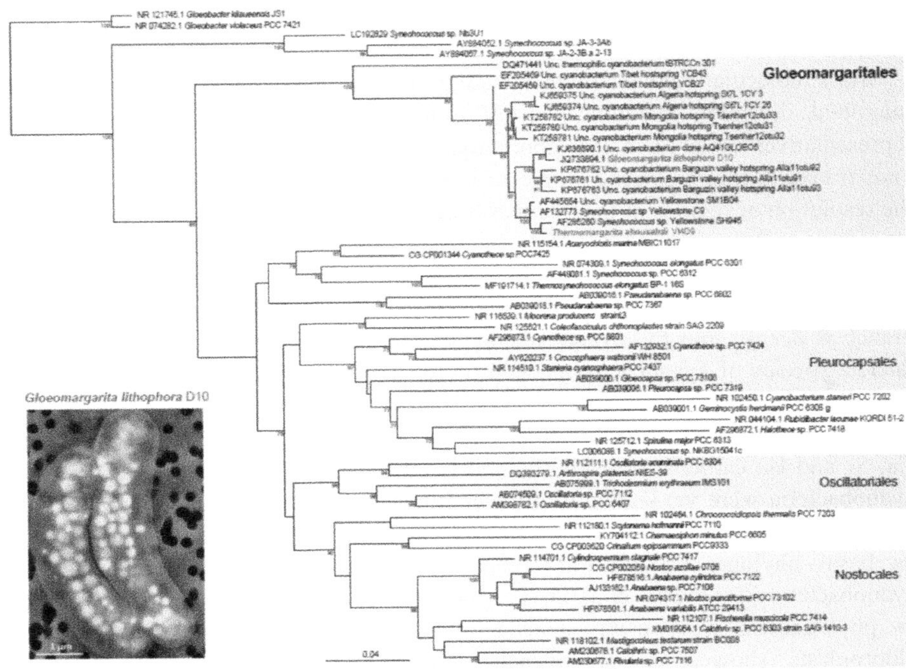

Figure 4.8. *Phylogenetic tree of 16S rRNA genes showing the position of the new order Gloeomargaritales within cyanobacteria. The tree was reconstructed by maximum likelihood using IQ-TREE with the GTR+F+R5 sequence evolution model on 1,438 conserved positions. A scanning electron microscopy image of Gloeomargarita lithophora, isolated from the microbialites of Lake Alchichica and capable of precipitating carbonates intracellularly, is shown. Thermomargarita ahousahtiae is a synonym of Gloeomargarita ahousahtiae. For a color version of this figure, see: www.iste.co.uk/benzerara/geosphere.zip*

4.4.2. *Reconstructing ancestral functions*

Ancestral functions can be reconstructed by studying the current phylogenetic distribution of genes coding for a function. Phylogenetic analyses combined with parsimony or likelihood methods then allow us to infer whether these genes were ancestral and whether they were transmitted vertically to descendants and/or horizontally to other phylogenetically distant organisms. The study of genes specific to Gloeomargaritales and other cyanobacteria that precipitate carbonates can also provide information on the evolution of intracellular carbonatogenesis mechanisms. Advanced comparative genomics using sequence homology identification tools based on hydrophobic clusters[11] and molecular phylogeny have allowed the identification of a new gene family encoding a protein, calcyanin, whose presence in a genome strongly correlates with intracellular carbonate precipitation (Benzerara et al. 2022). Likely involved in Ca homeostasis, calcyanin is an ancient protein in cyanobacteria that has undergone a complex history of loss in multiple lineages and horizontal transfers.

We can also be interested in the evolution of functions in a type of ecosystem by freeing ourselves from the organisms that carry them. We can thus infer functions in ancient ecosystems and/or help to better interpret the fossil record. For example, 2-methyl-hopanoids are biomarkers[12] well preserved in modern and ancient sediments and are classically interpreted as signaling the presence of cyanobacteria and, therefore, oxygenic photosynthesis (Rasmussen et al. 2008). However, current genomic and metagenomic analyses show that many other bacteria produce 2-methyl-hopanoids and that their abundance is higher in high-cell density, oxygen-depleted environments such as stromatolites and other microbial mats. Therefore, the presence of these biomarkers may reflect this type of ecosystem in the fossil record rather than the specific presence of cyanobacteria (Ricci et al. 2014).

Microbial mats, including microbialites, are often used as analogues of past communities. This analogy has a stronger justification at the level of central metabolic functions than at the level of the organisms that carry them. Indeed, it is known that metabolic functions in microbial ecosystems are more conserved than specific microbial diversity (Louca et al. 2016a, 2016b). At the same time, environmental selection is very strong in microbial ecology according to the often verified axiom of the Delft School of Microbiology, "everything is everywhere, but the environment selects" (de Wit and Bouvier 2006). Thus, we can imagine that, under the same environmental constraints, we find the same major types of metabolisms. If we apply this idea to the analysis of metagenomes of microbial mats located along a redox gradient that mimics the environmental transition that occurred during the great oxidation of the atmosphere approximately 2.4 Ga ago, we could, in principle, follow the evolution of central metabolisms during this distant period (Gutierrez-Preciado et al. 2018). The variation of functions in space (redox gradient) would be equivalent to that undergone in time. This approach suggests that anoxygenic photosynthesis was present but was not predominant in the Precambrian and that it diversified and expanded in parallel with oxygenic photosynthesis and

11. Hydrophobic clusters are groupings of amino acids with hydrophobic properties within the protein structure that locally determine folding patterns.

12. A biomarker is an organic molecule, often derived from a lipid compound, preserved in sedimentary archives and continuing to carry, despite alterations linked, for example, to diagenesis, signatures of its biological origin.

aerobic respiration. These studies also suggest that the Wood–Ljungdahl carbon fixation pathway dominated this type of environment in the past (Gutierrez-Preciado et al. 2018).

These are the processes that allow the conversion of inorganic carbon into organic carbon, the prerogative of organisms known as autotrophs for carbon. If we usually think of the Calvin–Benson–Bassham cycle, involved in photosynthesis, there are in fact eight different metabolic pathways (this number varies over time and depending on the authors). Among them, we can distinguish, for example, the **Calvin–Beson–Bassham cycle**: this is the first C fixation pathway to be elucidated. CO_2 binds to ribulose-1,5-bisphosphate (RuBP), a reaction catalyzed by Rubisco. RuBP then decomposes into two molecules of 3-phosphoglycerate. There is also the **Wood–Ljungdahl pathway**: non-cyclic, this pathway is used by some bacteria and some archaea. CO_2 is reduced thanks to the electrons of dihydrogen and is fixed in acetyl-CoA. There is also the **reverse Krebs cycle**: this cyclic pathway, which repeats the Krebs cycle in reverse, is used by certain bacteria that fix CO_2 in the form of acetyl-CoA using the electrons of dihydrogen or sulfide or thiosulfate ions ($S_2O_3^{2-}$). The **3-hydroxypropionate cycle** has also been identified; this pathway is used by certain bacteria of the genus *Chloroflexus* and certain archaea. It consists of two cycles sharing three reactions in common that this time fix bicarbonate ions on acetyl-CoA. There are other carbon fixation pathways with their own enzymes and their own phylogenetic distribution, conferring autotrophic properties on the microorganisms that carry them.

Box 4.1. *Autotrophic pathways of carbon fixation*

4.5. Conclusions and perspectives

Microbialites are complex microbial mats where mineral precipitation, particularly of carbonates, is favored. In addition to abiotic factors related to hydrochemistry, the microbial communities associated with these systems play a driving role in the formation of microbialites by locally promoting biomineralization. Massive molecular tools for characterizing microbial diversity, either through the analysis of amplified marker genes, typically 16S/18S rRNA genes (*metabarcoding*), or through metagenomic analyses (ideally combined with other "omics" methods), reveal a very broad diversity of microbial lineages and functions. Some of these data help us understand the evolutionary history of the organisms that populate these ecosystems and the present and past formation of these geobiological systems. Still at a very descriptive stage, the analysis of all of these molecular data in combination with physicochemical data and the spatial identification of organisms associated with particular mineral phases should allow a better understanding of these systems and the main actors in their formation.

4.6. References

Allwood, A.C., Walter, M.R., Kamber, B.S., Marshall, C.P., Burch, I.W. (2006). Stromatolite reef from the Early Archaean era of Australia. *Nature*, 441, 714–718.

Altermann, W., Kazmierczak, J., Oren, A., Wright, D.T. (2006). Cyanobacterial calcification and its rock-building potential during 3.5 billion years of Earth history. *Geobiology*, 4, 147–166.

Awramik, S.M. (1971). Precambrian stromatolite diversity: Reflection on metazoan appearance. *Science*, 174, 825–827.

Azam, F. and Malfatti, F. (2007). Microbial structuring of marine ecosystems. *Nat Rev Microbiol*, 5, 782–791.

Bacchetta, T., López-García, P., Gutiérrez-Preciado, A., Mehta, N., Skouri-Panet, F., Benzerara, K. et al. (2023). Description of *Gloeomargarita ahousahtiae* sp. nov. (Gloeomargaritales), a thermophilic cyanobacterium with intracellular carbonate inclusions. *Eur J Phycol*, 59, 11–20.

Bailey, J.V., Orphan, V.J., Joye, S.B., Corsetti, F.A. (2009). Chemotrophic microbial mats and their potential for preservation in the rock record. *Astrobiology*, 9, 843–859.

Benzerara, K., Menguy, N., Lopez-Garcia, P., Yoon, T.H., Kazmierczak, J., Tyliszczak, T. et al. (2006). Nanoscale detection of organic signatures in carbonate microbialites. *Proc Natl Acad Sci USA*, 103, 9440–9445.

Benzerara, K., Skouri-Panet, F., Li, J., Ferard, C., Gugger, M., Laurent, T. et al. (2014). Intracellular Ca-carbonate biomineralization is widespread in cyanobacteria. *Proc Natl Acad Sci USA*, 111, 10933–10938.

Benzerara, K., Duprat, E., Bitard-Feildel, T., Caumes, G., Cassier-Chauvat, C., Chauvat, F., Dezi, M., Diop, S.I., Gaschignard, G., Görgen, S. et al. (2022). A new gene family diagnostic for intracellular biomineralization of amorphous Ca carbonates by cyanobacteria. *Genome Biology and Evolution*, 14, evac026.

Bonilla-Rosso, G., Peimbert, M., Alcaraz, L.D., Hernandez, I., Eguiarte, L.E., Olmedo-Alvarez, G., Souza, V. (2012). Comparative metagenomics of two microbial mats at Cuatro Cienegas Basin II: Community structure and composition in oligotrophic environments. *Astrobiology*, 12, 659–673.

Brady, A.L., Slater, G., Laval, B., Lim, D.S. (2009). Constraining carbon sources and growth rates of freshwater microbialites in Pavilion Lake using (14)C analysis. *Geobiology*, 7, 544–555.

Braissant, O., Decho, A.W., Dupraz, C., Glunk, C., Przekop, K.M., Visscher, P.T. (2007). Exopolymeric substances of sulfate-reducing bacteria: Interactions with calcium at alkaline pH and implication for formation of carbonate minerals. *Geobiology*, 5, 401–411.

Bray, J.R. and Curtis, J.T. (1957). An ordination of the upland forest communities of Southern Wisconsin. *Ecol Monogr*, 27, 325–349.

Breitbart, M., Hoare, A., Nitti, A., Siefert, J., Haynes, M., Dinsdale, E. et al. (2009). Metagenomic and stable isotopic analyses of modern freshwater microbialites in Cuatro Cienegas, Mexico. *Environ Microbiol*, 11, 16–34.

Brown, C.T., Hug, L.A., Thomas, B.C., Sharon, I., Castelle, C.J., Singh, A. et al. (2015). Unusual biology across a group comprising more than 15% of domain Bacteria. *Nature*, 523, 208–211.

Burns, B.P., Goh, F., Allen, M., and Neilan, B.A. (2004). Microbial diversity of extant stromatolites in the hypersaline marine environment of Shark Bay, Australia. *Environ Microbiol*, 6, 1096–1101.

Callahan, B.J., McMurdie, P.J., Rosen, M.J., Han, A.W., Johnson, A.J.A., Holmes, S.P. (2016). DADA2: High-resolution sample inference from Illumina amplicon data. *Nat Methods*, 13, 581–583.

Campbell, M.A., Grice, K., Visscher, P.T., Morris, T., Wong, H.L., White III, R.A. et al. (2020). Functional gene expression in Shark Bay hypersaline microbial mats: Adaptive responses. *Front Microbiol*, 11, 560336.

Caporaso, J.G., Kuczynski, J., Stombaugh, J., Bittinger, K., Bushman, F.D., Costello, E.K. et al. (2010). QIIME allows analysis of high-throughput community sequencing data. *Nat Methods*, 7, 335–336.

Casaburi, G., Duscher, A.A., Reid, R.P., Foster, J.S. (2016). Characterization of the stromatolite microbiome from Little Darby Island, The Bahamas using predictive and whole shotgun metagenomic analysis. *Environ Microbiol*, 18, 1452–1469.

Caumartin, J., Benzerara, K., Havas, R., Thomazo, C., Lopez-Garcia, P., Duprat, E. (2023). The chemical conditions necessary for the formation of microbialites. *Geochem Persp Let*, 25, 30–35.

Couradeau, E., Benzerara, K., Moreira, D., Gerard, E., Kazmierczak, J., Tavera, R., Lopez-Garcia, P. (2011). Prokaryotic and eukaryotic community structure in field and cultured microbialites from the alkaline Lake Alchichica (Mexico). *PLoS One*, 6, e28767.

Couradeau, E., Benzerara, K., Gerard, E., Moreira, D., Bernard, S., Brown, G.E. Jr, Lopez-Garcia, P. (2012). An early-branching microbialite cyanobacterium forms intracellular carbonates. *Science*, 336, 459–462.

Darwin, C. (1859). *The Origin of Species by Means of Natural Selection*. J Murray, London.

Decho, A.W. (2010). Overview of biopolymer-induced mineralization: What goes on in biofilms? *Ecol Eng*, 36, 137–144.

Decho, A.W., Visscher, P.T., Reid, R.P. (2005). Production and cycling of natural microbial exopolymers (EPS) within a marine stromatolite. In *Geobiology: Objectives, Concepts, Perspectives*, Noffke, N. (ed). Elsevier, Amsterdam, 71–86.

DeLong, E.F. (1992). Archaea in coastal marine environments. *Proc Natl Acad Sci USA*, 89, 5685–5689.

Des Marais, D.J. (1990). Microbial mats and the early evolution of life. *Trends Ecol Evol*, 5, 140–144.

Desnues, C., Rodriguez-Brito, B., Rayhawk, S., Kelley, S., Tran, T., Haynes, M. et al. (2008). Biodiversity and biogeography of phages in modern stromatolites and thrombolites. *Nature*, 452, 340–343.

D'Hondt, S., Pockalny, R., Fulfer, V.M., Spivack, A.J. (2019). Subseafloor life and its biogeochemical impacts. *Nat Commun*, 10, 3519.

Doemel, W.N. and Brock, T.D. (1974). Bacterial stromatolites: Origin of laminations. *Science*, 184, 1083–1085.

Dravis, J.J. (1983). Hardened subtidal stromatolites, Bahamas. *Science*, 219, 385–386.

Dupraz, C. and Visscher, P.T. (2005). Microbial lithification in marine stromatolites and hypersaline mats. *Trends Microbiol*, 13, 429–438.

Dupraz, C., Reid, R.P., Braissant, O., Decho, A.W., Norman, R.S., Visscher, P.T. (2009). Processes of carbonate precipitation in modern microbial mats. *Earth-Sci Rev*, 96, 141–162.

Eloe-Fadrosh, E.A., Ivanova, N.N., Woyke, T., Kyrpides, N.C. (2016). Metagenomics uncovers gaps in amplicon-based detection of microbial diversity. *Nat Microbiol*, 1, 15032.

Eren, A.M., Esen, O.C., Quince, C., Vineis, J.H., Morrison, H.G., Sogin, M.L., Delmont, T.O. (2015). Anvi'o: An advanced analysis and visualization platform for 'omics data. *PeerJ*, 3, e1319.

Estaki, M., Jiang, L., Bokulich, N.A., McDonald, D., González, A., Kosciolek, T. et al. (2020). QIIME 2 enables comprehensive end-to-end analysis of diverse microbiome data and comparative studies with publicly available data. *Curr Protoc Bioinformatics*, 70, e100.

Farias, M.E., Rascovan, N., Toneatti, D.M., Albarracin, V.H., Flores, M.R., Poire, D.G. et al. (2013). The discovery of stromatolites developing at 3570 m above sea level in a high-altitude volcanic lake Socompa, Argentinean Andes. *PLoS One*, 8, e53497.

Franzosa, E.A., Hsu, T., Sirota-Madi, A., Shafquat, A., Abu-Ali, G., Morgan, X.C., Huttenhower, C. (2015). Sequencing and beyond: Integrating molecular 'omics' for microbial community profiling. *Nat Rev Microbiol*, 13, 360–372.

Fuhrman, J.A., McCallum, K., Davis, A.A. (1992). Novel major archaebacterial group from marine plankton. *Nature*, 356, 148–149.

Gérard, E., De Goeyse, S., Hugoni, M., Agogué, H., Richard, L., Milesi, V. et al. (2018). Key role of alphaproteobacteria and cyanobacteria in the formation of stromatolites of Lake Dziani Dzaha (Mayotte, Western Indian Ocean). *Front Microbiol*, 9, 796.

Giovannoni, S.J., Britschgi, T.B., Moyer, C.L., Field, K.G. (1990). Genetic diversity in Sargasso Sea bacterioplankton. *Nature*, 345, 60–63.

Gutierrez-Preciado, A., Saghai, A., Moreira, D., Zivanovic, Y., Deschamps, P., Lopez-Garcia, P. (2018). Functional shifts in microbial mats recapitulate early Earth metabolic transitions. *Nat Ecol Evol*, 2, 1700–1708.

Haeckel, E. (1866). *Generelle Morphologie der Organismen: Allgemeine Grundzüge der organischen Formen-Wissenschaft, mechanisch begründet durch die von Charles Darwin reformirte Descendenz-Theorie*. Georg Reimer, Berlin.

He, C., Keren, R., Whittaker, M.L., Farag, I.F., Doudna, J.A., Cate, J.H.D., Banfield, J.F. (2021). Genome-resolved metagenomics reveals site-specific diversity of episymbiotic CPR bacteria and DPANN archaea in groundwater ecosystems. *Nat Microbiol*, 6, 354–365.

Hug, L.A., Baker, B.J., Anantharaman, K., Brown, C.T., Probst, A.J., Castelle, C.J. et al. (2016). A new view of the tree of life. *Nat Microbiol*, 1, 16048.

Iniesto, M., Moreira, D., Reboul, G., Deschamps, P., Benzerara, K., Bertolino, P. et al. (2020). Core microbial communities of lacustrine microbialites sampled along an alkalinity gradient. *Environ Microbiol*, 23, 51–68.

Iniesto, M., Moreira, D., Benzerara, K., Muller, E., Bertolino, P., Tavera, R., López-García, P. (2021). Rapid formation of mature microbialites in Lake Alchichica, Mexico. *Environ Microbiol Rep*, 13, 600–605.

Kanik, M., Munro-Ehrlich, M., Fernandes-Martins, M.C., Payne, D., Gianoulias, K., Keller, L. et al. (2020). Unexpected abundance and diversity of phototrophs in mats from morphologically variable microbialites in Great Salt Lake, Utah. *Appl Environ Microbiol*, 86, e00165-20.

Kazmierczak, J. and Kempe, S. (2006). Genuine modern analogues of Precambrian stromatolites from caldera lakes of Niuafo'ou Island, Tonga. *Naturwissenschaften*, 93, 119–126.

Kazmierczak, J., Kempe, S., Kremer, B., López-García, P., Moreira, D., Tavera, R. (2011). Hydrochemistry and microbialites of the alkaline crater lake Alchichica, Mexico. *Facies*, 57, 543–570.

Kempe, S., Kazmierczak, J., Landmann, G., Konuk, T., Reimer, A., Lipp, A. (1991). Largest known microbialites discovered in Lake Van, Turkey. *Nature*, 349, 605–608.

Kurth, D., Amadio, A., Ordonez, O.F., Albarracin, V.H., Gartner, W., Farias, M.E. (2017). Arsenic metabolism in high altitude modern stromatolites revealed by metagenomic analysis. *Sci Rep*, 7, 1024.

Last, F.M., Last, W.M., Halden, N.M. (2012). Modern and late Holocene dolomite formation: Manito Lake, Saskatchewan, Canada. *Sediment Geol*, 281, 222–237.

Laval, B., Cady, S.L., Pollack, J.C., McKay, C.P., Bird, J.S., Grotzinger, J.P. et al. (2000). Modern freshwater microbialite analogues for ancient dendritic reef structures. *Nature*, 407, 626–629.

Logan, B.W. (1961). *Cryptozoon* and associated stromatolites from the recent, Shark Bay, Western Australia. *J Geol*, 69, 517–533.

López-García, P., Rodríguez-Valera, F., Pedrós-Alió, C., Moreira, D. (2001). Unexpected diversity of small eukaryotes in deep-sea Antarctic plankton. *Nature*, 409, 603–607.

López-García, P., Kazmierczak, J., Benzerara, K., Kempe, S., Guyot, F., Moreira, D. (2005). Bacterial diversity and carbonate precipitation in the giant microbialites from the highly alkaline Lake Van, Turkey. *Extremophiles*, 9, 263–274.

Louca, S., Parfrey, L.W., Doebeli, M. (2016a). Decoupling function and taxonomy in the global ocean microbiome. *Science*, 353, 1272–1277.

Louca, S., Jacques, S.M.S., Pires, A.P.F., Leal, J.S., Srivastava, D.S., Parfrey, L.W. et al. (2016b). High taxonomic variability despite stable functional structure across microbial communities. *Nat Ecol Evol*, 1, 15.

Louca, S., Hawley, A.K., Katsev, S., Torres-Beltran, M., Bhatia, M.P., Kheirandish, S. et al. (2016c). Integrating biogeochemistry with multiomic sequence information in a model oxygen minimum zone. *Proc Natl Acad Sci USA*, 113, E5925–E5933.

Louyakis, A.S., Gourle, H., Casaburi, G., Bonjawo, R.M.E., Duscher, A.A., Foster, J.S. et al. (2018). A year in the life of a thrombolite: Comparative metatranscriptomics reveals dynamic metabolic changes over diel and seasonal cycles. *Environ Microbiol*, 20, 2670.

Madigan, M.T., Martinko, J.M., Bender, K.S., Buckley, D.H., Stahl, D.A., Brock, T. (eds) (2014). *Brock Biology of Microorganisms*, 14th edition. Benjamin Cummings, San Francisco, CA.

Medina Ferrer, F., Rosen, M.R., Feyhl-Buska, J., Russell, V.V., Sønderholm, F., Loyd, S. et al. (2021). Potential role for microbial ureolysis in the rapid formation of carbonate tufa mounds. *Geobiology*, 20, 79–97.

Mobberley, J.M., Khodadad, C.L., Foster, J.S. (2013). Metabolic potential of lithifying cyanobacteria-dominated thrombolitic mats. *Photosynth Res*, 118, 125–140.

Mobberley, J.M., Khodadad, C.L., Visscher, P.T., Reid, R.P., Hagan, P., Foster, J.S. (2015). Inner workings of thrombolites: Spatial gradients of metabolic activity as revealed by metatranscriptome profiling. *Sci Rep*, 5, 12601.

Moon-van der Staay, S.Y., De Wachter, R., Vaulot, D. (2001). Oceanic 18S rDNA sequences from picoplankton reveal unsuspected eukaryotic diversity. *Nature*, 409, 607–610.

Moreira, D. and López-García, P. (2002). Molecular ecology of microbial eukaryotes unveils a hidden world. *Trends Microbiol*, 10, 31–38.

Moreira, D., Tavera, R., Benzerara, K., Skouri-Panet, F., Couradeau, E., Gerard, E. et al. (2017). Description of *Gloeomargarita lithophora* gen. nov., sp. nov., a thylakoid-bearing, basal-branching cyanobacterium with intracellular carbonates, and proposal for *Gloeomargaritales* ord. nov. *Int J Syst Evol Microbiol*, 67, 653–658.

Neilan, B.A., Burns, B.P., Relman, D.A., Lowe, D.R. (2002). Molecular identification of cyanobacteria associated with stromatolites from distinct geographical locations. *Astrobiology*, 2, 271–280.

Obst, M., Dynes, J.J., Lawrence, J.R., Swerhone, G.D.W., Benzerara, K., Karunakaran, C. et al. (2009). Precipitation of amorphous CaCO3 (aragonite-like) by cyanobacteria: A STXM study of the influence of EPS on the nucleation process. *Geochim Cosmochim Acta*, 73, 4180–4198.

Orsi, W.D., Edgcomb, V.P., Christman, G.D., Biddle, J.F. (2013). Gene expression in the deep biosphere. *Nature*, 499, 205–208.

Paerl, H.W., Steppe, T.F., Reid, R.P. (2001). Bacterially mediated precipitation in marine stromatolites. *Environ Microbiol*, 3, 123–130.

Parks, D.H., Rinke, C., Chuvochina, M., Chaumeil, P.-A., Woodcroft, B.J., Evans, P.N. et al. (2017). Recovery of nearly 8,000 metagenome-assembled genomes substantially expands the tree of life. *Nat Microbiol*, 2, 1533–1542.

Perkins, R.G., Mouget, J.L., Kromkamp, J.C., Stolz, J., Pamela Reid, R. (2012). Modern stromatolite phototrophic communities: A comparative study of procaryote and eucaryote phototrophs using variable chlorophyll fluorescence. *FEMS Microbiol Ecol*, 82, 584–596.

Ponce-Toledo, R.I., Deschamps, P., Lopez-Garcia, P., Zivanovic, Y., Benzerara, K., Moreira, D. (2017). An early-branching freshwater cyanobacterium at the origin of plastids. *Curr Biol*, 27, 386–391.

Quast, C., Pruesse, E., Yilmaz, P., Gerken, J., Schweer, T., Yarza, P. et al. (2013). The SILVA ribosomal RNA gene database project: Improved data processing and web-based tools. *Nucleic Acids Res*, 41, D590–596.

Ragon, M., Benzerara, K., Moreira, D., Tavera, R., Lopez-Garcia, P. (2014). 16S rDNA-based analysis reveals cosmopolitan occurrence but limited diversity of two cyanobacterial lineages with contrasted patterns of intracellular carbonate mineralization. *Front Microbiol*, 5, 331.

Rasmussen, B., Fletcher, I.R., Brocks, J.J., Kilburn, M.R. (2008). Reassessing the first appearance of eukaryotes and cyanobacteria. *Nature*, 455, 1101–1104.

Reid, R.P. and Browne, K.M. (1991). Intertidal stromatolites in a fringing Holocene reef complex in the Bahamas. *Geology*, 19, 15–18.

Reid, R.P., Visscher, P.T., Decho, A.W., Stolz, J.F., Bebout, B.M., Dupraz, C. et al. (2000). The role of microbes in accretion, lamination and early lithification of modern marine stromatolites. *Nature*, 406, 989–992.

Reid, R.P., James, N.P., Macintyre, I.G., Dupraz, C.P., Burne, R.V. (2003). Shark Bay stromatolites: Microfabrics and reinterpretation of origins. *Facies*, 49, 45–53.

Ricci, J.N., Coleman, M.L., Welander, P.V., Sessions, A.L., Summons, R.E., Spear, J.R., Newman, D.K. (2014). Diverse capacity for 2-methylhopanoid production correlates with a specific ecological niche. *ISME J*, 8, 675–684.

Riding, R. (2000). Microbial carbonates: The geological record of calcified bacterial-algal mats and biofilms. *Sedimentology*, 47, 179–214.

Rinke, C., Chuvochina, M., Mussig, A.J., Chaumeil, P.-A., Davín, A.A., Waite, D.W. et al. (2021). A standardized archaeal taxonomy for the Genome Taxonomy Database. *Nat Microbiol*, 6, 946–959.

Ruvindy, R., White III, R.A., Neilan, B.A., Burns, B.P. (2016). Unravelling core microbial metabolisms in the hypersaline microbial mats of Shark Bay using high-throughput metagenomics. *ISME J*, 10(1), 183–196.

Saghaï, A., Zivanovic, Y., Zeyen, N., Moreira, D., Benzerara, K., Deschamps, P. et al. (2015). Metagenome-based diversity analyses suggest a significant contribution of non-cyanobacterial lineages to carbonate precipitation in modern microbialites. *Front Microbiol*, 6, 797.

Saghaï, A., Zivanovic, Y., Moreira, D., Benzerara, K., Bertolino, P., Ragon, M. et al. (2016). Comparative metagenomics unveils functions and genome features of microbialite-associated communities along a depth gradient. *Environ Microbiol*, 18, 4990–5004.

Saghaï, A., Zivanovic, Y., Moreira, D., Tavera, R., and López-García, P. (2020). A novel microbialite-associated phototrophic Chloroflexi lineage exhibiting a quasi-clonal pattern along depth. *Genome Biol Evol*, 12, 1207–1216.

Sánchez-Baracaldo, P., Raven, J.A., Pisani, D., Knoll, A.H. (2017). Early photosynthetic eukaryotes inhabited low-salinity habitats. *Proc Natl Acad Sci USA*, 114, E7737-E7745.

Santos, F., Pena, A., Nogales, B., Soria-Soria, E., Del Cura, M.A., Gonzalez-Martin, J.A., Anton, J. (2010). Bacterial diversity in dry modern freshwater stromatolites from Ruidera Pools Natural Park, Spain. *Syst Appl Microbiol*, 33, 209–221.

Shi, Y., Tyson, G.W., DeLong, E.F. (2009). Metatranscriptomics reveals unique microbial small RNAs in the ocean's water column. *Nature*, 459, 266–269.

Souza, V., Espinosa-Asuar, L., Escalante, A.E., Eguiarte, L.E., Farmer, J., Forney, L. et al. (2006). An endangered oasis of aquatic microbial biodiversity in the Chihuahuan desert. *Proc Natl Acad Sci USA*, 103, 6565–6570.

Stanier, R.Y., Doudoroff, M., Adelberg, E.A. (1970). *The Microbial World*. Prenctice-Hall, Inc, Englewood Cliffs, N.J..

Suarez-Gonzalez, P., Benito, M.I., Quijada, I.E., Mas, R., Campos-Soto, S. (2019). 'Trapping and binding': A review of the factors controlling the development of fossil agglutinated microbialites and their distribution in space and time. *Earth-Science Reviews*, 194, 182–215.

Tice, M.M. and Lowe, D.R. (2004). Photosynthetic microbial mats in the 3,416-Myr-old ocean. *Nature*, 431, 549–552.

Venter, J.C., Remington, K., Heidelberg, J.F., Halpern, A.L., Rusch, D., Eisen, J.A. et al. (2004). Environmental genome shotgun sequencing of the Sargasso Sea. *Science*, 304, 66–74.

Vignale, F.A., Lencina, A.I., Stepanenko, T.M., Soria, M.N., Saona, L.A., Kurth, D. et al. (2021). Lithifying and non-lithifying microbial ecosystems in the wetlands and salt flats of the Central Andes. *Microb Ecol*, 83, 1–17.

Warden, J.G., Casaburi, G., Omelon, C.R., Bennett, P.C., Breecker, D.O., Foster, J.S. (2016). Characterization of microbial mat microbiomes in the modern thrombolite ecosystem of Lake Clifton, Western Australia using shotgun metagenomics. *Front Microbiol*, 7, 1064.

White III, R.A., Power, I.M., Dipple, G.M., Southam, G., Suttle, C.A. (2015). Metagenomic analysis reveals that modern microbialites and polar microbial mats have similar taxonomic and functional potential. *Front Microbiol*, 6, 966.

White III, R.A., Chan, A.M., Gavelis, G.S., Leander, B.S., Brady, A.L., Slater, G.F. et al. (2016). Metagenomic analysis suggests modern freshwater microbialites harbor a distinct core microbial community. *Front Microbiol*, 6, 1531.

White III, R.A., Wong, H.L., Ruvindy, R., Neilan, B.A., Burns, B.P. (2018). Viral communities of Shark Bay modern stromatolites. *Front Microbiol*, 9, 1223.

White III, R.A., Visscher, P.T., Burns, B.P. (2021). Between a rock and a soft place: The role of viruses in lithification of modern microbial mats. *Trends Microbiol*, 29, 204–213.

Whittaker, R.H. (1959). On the broad classification of organisms. *The Quarterly Review of Biology*, 34, 210–226.

de Wit, R. and Bouvier, T. (2006). 'Everything is everywhere, but, the environment selects'; What did Baas Becking and Beijerinck really say? *Environ Microbiol*, 8, 755–758.

Woese, C.R. and Fox, G.E. (1977). Phylogenetic structure of the prokaryotic domain: The primary kingdoms. *Proc Natl Acad Sci USA*, 74, 5088–5090.

Woese, C.R., Kandler, O., Wheelis, M.L. (1990). Towards a natural system of organisms: Proposal for the domains Archaea, Bacteria, and Eucarya. *Proc Natl Acad Sci USA*, 87, 4576–4579.

Yilmaz, P., Parfrey, L.W., Yarza, P., Gerken, J., Pruesse, E., Quast, C. et al. (2014). The SILVA and "All-species Living Tree Project (LTP)" taxonomic frameworks. *Nucleic Acids Res*, 42, D643–648.

Yooseph, S., Sutton, G., Rusch, D.B., Halpern, A.L., Williamson, S.J., Remington, K. et al. (2007). The Sorcerer II Global Ocean sampling expedition: Expanding the universe of protein families. *PLoS Biol*, 5, e16.

Yu, H. and Leadbetter, J.R. (2020). Bacterial chemolithoautotrophy via manganese oxidation. *Nature*, 583, 453–458.

Zeyen, N., Benzerara, K., Beyssac, O., Daval, D., Muller, E., Thomazo, C. et al. (2021). Integrative analysis of the mineralogical and chemical composition of modern microbialites from ten Mexican lakes: What do we learn about their formation? *Geochim Cosmochim Acta*, 305, 148–184.

Zuckerkandl, E. and Pauling, L. (1965). Molecules as documents of evolutionary history. *J Theor Biol*, 8, 357–366.

5

Oxygen: A Major Geobiological Player

Christophe THOMAZO
Laboratoire Biogéosciences, University of Burgundy, Dijon, France

5.1. Introduction

Oxygen is the eighth chemical element in the periodic table and is the third most abundant element in the universe, after hydrogen and helium.

It was discovered in 1772 by the Swedish chemist Carl Wilhelm Scheele and was described in 1777 by the Frenchman Antoine Lavoisier in *Sur la combustion en général*, following a series of experiments on air. In this contribution, Antoine Lavoisier demonstrates that air is a mixture of two gases: “vital air”, which is essential for the respiration of living organisms (in particular, all metazoans) and nitrogen (from the Greek *ἄζωτον*, “deprived of life”), which is “useless”. Lavoisier renamed “vital air” oxygen from the Greek *rootóξύς* (oxys) (acid) and *γενής* (genēs) (which generates) because it suggests that oxygen is a constituent of all acids and that oxidation and acidification are closely linked (it is in fact hydrogen and in particular the proton that forms the basis of acids).

In geochemistry, oxygen was classified by the Norwegian chemist Victor Moritz Goldschmidt as a lithophile element (literally “with an affinity for stones”) because of its particular affinity for mineral oxides (silicates and aluminosilicates). Oxygen is distributed, in different molecular forms, in all the major terrestrial reservoirs and is the most abundant chemical element in terms of mass in the biosphere, water and terrestrial rocks. Oxygen thus constitutes approximately 49% of the mass of the

Interactions between the Geosphere and the Biosphere,
coordinated by Karim BENZERARA and Christophe THOMAZO.

Earth's crust and is the main constituent of our oceans in the form of H_2O (about 89% by mass). Oxygen (O_2) is the second main component of the current Earth's atmosphere, representing 20.8% of its volume and 23.1% of its mass. The Earth, due to the high concentration of oxygen in its atmosphere, is an exception among the planets in the solar system. This is the reason for the unique evolution of our planet, as we will discuss in this chapter.

Dioxygen, as previously noted by Antoine Lavoisier, participates in oxidation reactions (including combustion). The O_2/H_2O pair forms the basis of many biological reactions including oxygenic photosynthesis (which allows energy to be stored in the form of reduced carbon compounds: sugars) and respiration (which oxidizes these carbon compounds to release energy). The importance of oxygen is also central to the history and functioning of the geosphere, whether in the spatial and temporal distribution of oxides precipitating in the oceans or in the geochemical distribution of elements in the internal reservoirs (crust and mantle) of the Earth (carbon, for example, becoming a siderophile, i.e. having an affinity for iron, in the absence of oxygen).

Oxygen, due to its particular chemical properties and its abundance on Earth in many molecular species and phases (liquid, gas, solid), is at the heart of the functioning of many biological and geological processes. However, on primitive Earth, like on Mars and Venus, free oxygen (in the form of O_2) was absent. Oxygen, although abundant, was then linked to water and silicates, and the first microorganisms evolved in an anoxic environment for several billion years. Many chemical elements (especially metallic) were then in reduced forms, often more soluble, in surface reservoirs such as oceans. The rise of free oxygen in the oceans and then in the atmosphere is undoubtedly the greatest biogeochemical change that the Earth has experienced since its formation. In this chapter, we will address the causes and consequences of this oxygen revolution on the Earth system using examples and relying on methodological and analytical tools. Particular attention will be paid to the kinetics of this change, an important scientific question, which has fueled debates in the scientific community studying the oxygenation on Earth for several decades.

5.2. Oxygen: origin and properties

5.2.1. *The cosmochemical origin of oxygen*

Oxygen originates from nucleosynthesis reactions within stars. At the beginning of a star's life, there is a cloud of gas (mainly hydrogen, synthesized during the Big Bang), which contracts by gravitational collapse. This contraction brings the protons closer together and increases their probability of collisions. When the temperature exceeds 10 million kelvins, it becomes sufficient for hydrogen nuclei to fuse into helium (proton–proton chain). Hydrogen is the major fuel of stars, and its fusion is the first step in the nucleosynthesis chain.

The carbon–nitrogen–oxygen cycle (or CNO cycle), also known as the Bethe–Weizsäcker cycle, occurs at higher temperatures and corresponds to the second type of nuclear fusion reactions by which stars convert hydrogen into helium. This cycle is also the main source of nitrogen and oxygen production by stars. As shown in Figure 5.1, this cycle is broken down into four subcycles, each of which will produce different isotopes that will serve as the basis for the next subcycle.

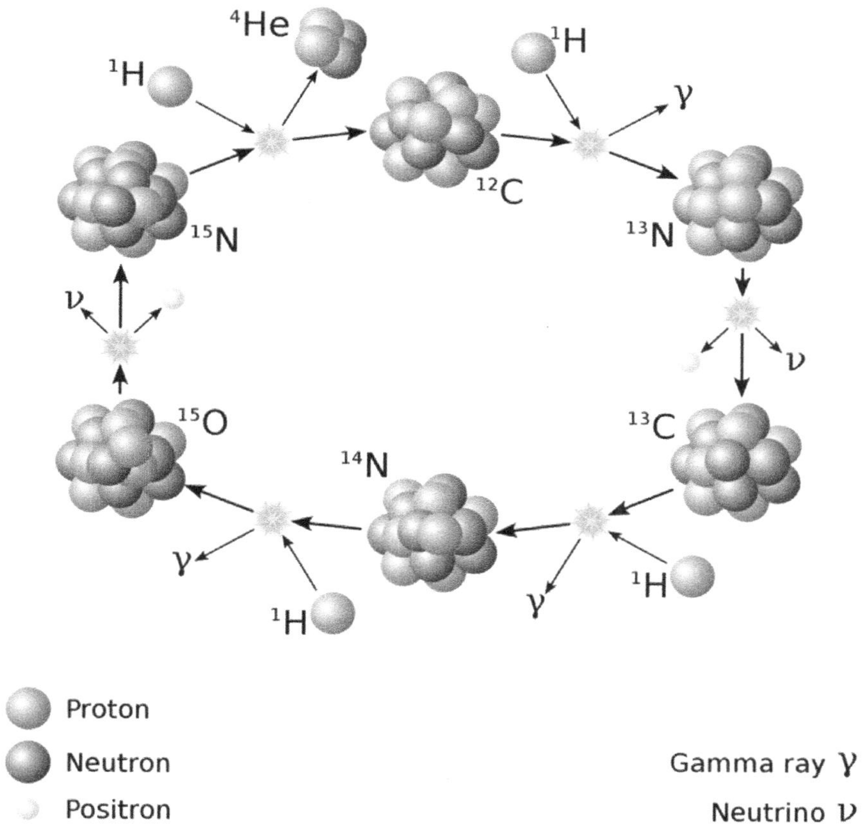

Figure 5.1. *The carbon–nitrogen–oxygen cycle (or CNO cycle) of nuclear fusion in stars. This is a catalytic nuclear fusion cycle that uses carbon, nitrogen and oxygen nuclei as intermediates and ultimately produces a helium nucleus. During a complete CNO cycle, 25 MeV of energy is released. For a color version of this figure, see www.iste.co.uk/benzerara/geosphere.zip*

Oxygen has 17 isotopes with masses ranging from 12 to 28. Naturally occurring oxygen is composed of three stable isotopes: oxygen-16 (^{16}O), oxygen-17 (^{17}O) and oxygen-18 (^{18}O). Oxygen is assigned a standard atomic mass of 15.999 $g.mol^{-1}$. This is because oxygen-16 is by far the most abundant, with a natural abundance of 99.762%.

Most oxygen-16 is synthesized at the end of the helium fusion process in massive stars, but some is also produced during neon fusion reactions. Oxygen-17 is mainly produced by the fusion of hydrogen into helium during the CNO cycle. It is therefore a common isotope in the hydrogen-burning regions of stars. Most oxygen-18 is produced when nitrogen ^{14}N, made abundant by the CNO cycle, captures a helium nucleus ^4He. Oxygen-18 is therefore commonly present in helium-rich regions of massive stars.

5.2.2. *The remarkable properties of oxygen*

5.2.2.1. *Physical properties and redox reactions*

Dioxygen is more soluble in water than the nitrogen molecule. Water in equilibrium with air contains approximately one molecule of dissolved oxygen for every two molecules of nitrogen, whereas this ratio is approximately one molecule of dioxygen for every four molecules of nitrogen in the atmosphere. The solubility of oxygen in water depends on temperature and salinity. About twice as much (14.6 mg L^{-1}) oxygen dissolves at 0°C than at 20°C (7.6 mg L^{-1}). At a constant temperature and pressure of 25°C and one atmosphere, fresh water contains about 6.04 mL of oxygen per liter, while seawater contains about 4.95 mL per liter. At 5°C, the solubility increases to 9.0 mL per liter of fresh water, 50% more than at 25°C and to 7.2 mL per liter of seawater, 45% more.

Oxygen condenses (into liquid) at 90.20 K (−182.95°C) and solidifies at 54.36 K (−218.79°C). Both the liquid and solid phases of oxygen are transparent with a slight coloration reminiscent of the blue color of the sky caused by absorption in the red.

A redox reaction is a chemical reaction during which electron transfer occurs. The chemical species that captures the electrons is called the "oxidant" and the one that gives them up is called the "reducer". Redox reactions comprise many chemical reactions, since they are involved in combustion, metal corrosion, electrochemistry and cellular respiration. These reactions play a fundamental role in biology in particular, since many metabolic processes, in particular energy generation, are based on these redox reactions. Reduction allows a molecule to gain electrons by reducing its degree of oxidation and conversely oxidation increases the degree of oxidation of a molecule by electron loss. Thus, redox reactions result in an electron transfer between two reactants, one of which is oxidized and the other reduced. This electron exchange process is described by the difference in redox potential between two redox couples (ΔE° in volts). The more negative the redox potential of a couple, the greater the reducing power. Electrons then move from a redox couple with the lowest potentials to the least weak or even positive potentials. Some examples of biological importance are given in Figure 5.2. The redox pair O_2/H_2O has a positive redox potential of +0.815 Volt. It is therefore a strong oxidizing agent!

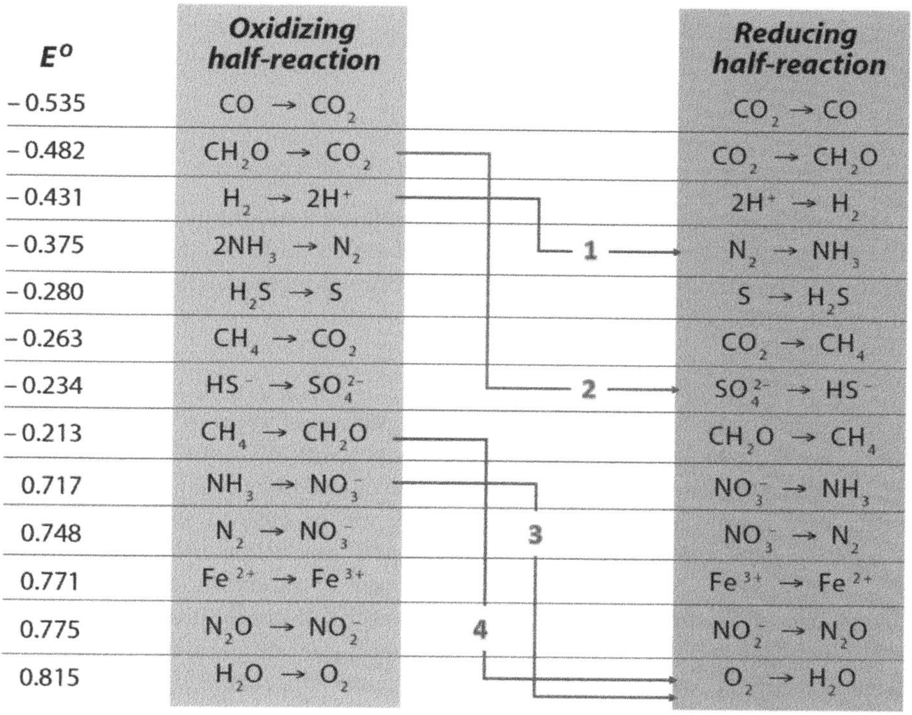

Figure 5.2. *Redox scale illustrating the main reactions between two redox couples used by living organisms. The half reactions (oxidation on the left and reduction on the right) are expressed as a function of their potential (in volts) for a pH = 7. In this representation, the reactions are represented by arrows going from left to right; the amount of energy released depends on the length of the arrows (or the difference in redox potential). The reactions illustrated are as follows: (1) reduction of dinitrogen (in biology, nitrogen fixation); (2) sulfate reduction; (3) aerobic oxidation of ammonium; (4) aerobic oxidation of methane. For a color version of this figure, see www.iste.co.uk/benzerara/geosphere.zip*

Oxygen plays a central role in biology by allowing energy to be stored and released. The two most commonly described reactions involving oxygen are (i) oxygenic photosynthesis (equation [5.1]) which allows the reduction of carbon dioxide to carbohydrates by the oxidation of water to oxygen in the presence of light energy; and (ii) respiration, which oxidizes carbohydrates and releases carbon dioxide (equation [5.2]). Oxygen is not, however, the only oxidation agent, and many so-called anaerobic metabolic pathways use alternative redox couples such as nitrate respiration during denitrification, for example, mainly when oxygen is absent (Figure 5.2).

$$CO_2 + H_2O \rightarrow CH_2O + O_2 \qquad [5.1]$$

$$CH_2O + O_2 \rightarrow CO_2 + H_2O \qquad [5.2]$$

5.2.2.2. *Molecules at the center of biogeochemical processes*

Oxygen is part of many molecules that have played a major role in the evolution of life on Earth and the establishment of biogeochemical cycles. This section presents a non-exhaustive list of these oxygen-bearing molecules that play a major role in the current geobiosphere.

5.2.2.2.1. Water

In total, 70% of water (H_2O) on the Earth's surface is found in the oceans, and although marine biomass represents only a few percent (in Gt of C) of the current total biomass, this environment was probably the evolutionary origin of early life on Earth. Living organisms themselves are made up of 60% to 95% water. The remarkable properties of water are notably linked to its electronic structure. Indeed, this structure (Figure 5.3) allows the establishment of an electric dipole, with the consequence that water molecules attract each other and can form hydrogen bonds. These hydrogen bonds, whose lifetime is very short (10^{-11}s), allow the formation of dynamic "clusters" whose size depends mainly on the temperature (250 molecules at 0°C; 60 at 25°C). It is this "clustering" property that explains the viscosity of water and its decrease with increasing temperature.

Water thus helps preserve the 3D structure of proteins up to a temperature of approximately 50°C, beyond which the reduced "clustering" effect reduces stability. Since water is a dipole, it also helps limit interactions between biomolecules by minimizing electrostatic interactions. The effects of interactions between water molecules are also behind the large stability range of liquid water (between 0 and 100°C at 1 atm), associated with a high specific heat capacity (4.25 $kJ.kg^{-1}.K^{-1}$), which has thus allowed the existence of liquid water on Earth for several billion years, despite significant variations in surface temperature (see section 5.3.1.2.2).

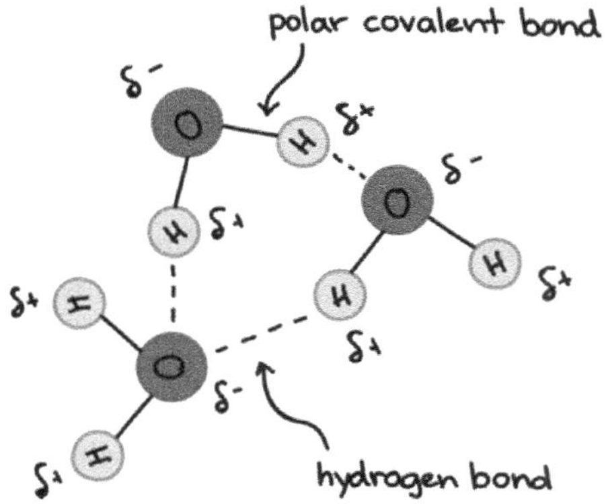

Figure 5.3. *Electronic structure of water (image credit: khanacademy.org). For a color version of this figure, see www.iste.co.uk/benzerara/geosphere.zip*

Hydrolysis is one of the important properties of water in both biology and geology. Hydrolysis (from the Greek hydro: water and lysis: to break) is a chemical and enzymatic reaction in which a covalent bond is broken by the action of a water molecule. In biology, this type of reaction is at the heart of cell energy processes, in particular by allowing the restitution of energy stored as ATP per reaction [5.3]. In geology, hydrolysis is one of the main mechanisms in silicate weathering and clays production (e.g. hydrolysis reaction [5.4] of a sodium feldspar: albite into kaolinite).

$$ATP + H_2O \rightarrow ADP + H_3PO_4 \quad [5.3]$$

$$2Na_2AlSi_3O_8\,\text{(albite)} + 2CO_2 + 11H_20 \rightarrow Al_2Si_2O_5(OH)_4\,\text{(kaolinite)} + 2Na^+ + 2HCO_3^- + 4H_4SiO_4 \quad [5.4]$$

Finally, the degree of dissociation of water into protons and hydroxyl radicals defines the pH (equation [5.5]). The higher the pH, the lower the degree of dissociation. This property of water greatly depends on temperature; the higher the temperature, the lower the pH.

$$pH = -\log [H_3O^+] \quad [5.5]$$

5.2.2.2.2. Carbon dioxide

Carbon dioxide has also played a major role in the biogeochemical evolution of the Earth system, the development of life and the climate. Carbon dioxide is the product of the complete oxidation of carbon compounds and is a very stable molecule with covalent bonds between oxygen and carbon. Carbon dioxide is a major compound in the early atmospheres of terrestrial planets and is the primary carbon source for autotrophic organisms. The level of CO_2 in the atmosphere (today approximately 420 ppm) has varied widely over the course of geological history, contributing to remarkable and drastic climate changes (see Box 5.1). In fact, the carbon dioxide molecule, by absorbing the infrared radiation re-emitted by the Earth, contributes to the greenhouse effect and, together with water and ozone, is a strong thermostat for the Earth's surface temperature.

Carbon dioxide dissolves rapidly in water, and the ions thus produced are described by the carbonate equilibrium reaction [5.6], which depends mainly on pH (95% of CO_2 dissolved is in the form of hydrogen carbonate ion HCO_3^- at pH $\approx$ 8 seawater). Thus, this equation participates in the regulation of pH both in the ocean and in living organisms (e.g. in blood). In the presence of divalent cations (in particular Ca^{2+}), hydrogen carbonate ions participate in the precipitation of carbonates throughout the living kingdom from the simplest microbial mats (see Chapter 2) to metazoans (equation [5.7]).

$$CO_2 + H_2O \leftrightarrow H_2CO_3 \leftrightarrow HCO_3^- + H^+ \leftrightarrow CO_3^{2-} + 2H^+ \quad [5.6]$$

$$2HCO_3^- + Ca^{2+} \leftrightarrow CaCO_3 + CO_2 + H_2O \quad [5.7]$$

In 4.56 billion years, Earth has seen its surface covered almost entirely by ice three times, radically disrupting and transforming the chemistry and biodiversity on the planet's surface. Beyond their extreme intensity suggested by the numerous deposits of glacial sediments at low latitudes, these glaciations are also extreme in their duration, which can reach several tens of millions of years. These three glacial episodes, known as "Snowball Earth", are explained by a major process: a positive feedback of the albedo[1] on the drop in global temperatures. Indeed, past a certain threshold of glaciation, the Earth's albedo is such that it plunges the climate system into a metastable state, giving rise to a possible total freezing of the terrestrial globe. The ice pack then extended to the lowest latitudes with an average temperature of approximately −60°C (Hoffman et al. 1998). The widespread polar temperatures would have induced the formation of a thick layer of ice several hundred meters thick, partially isolating the ocean from the atmosphere and inhibiting all photosynthetic activity. The oldest of these is the Huronian glaciation. It is dated to approximately 2.4 billion years ago and correlates with the great oxygenation of the atmosphere, probably due to intense photosynthetic activity. Subsequently, the planet went through a long period of nearly 1.5 billion years, showing a total absence of ice in the sedimentary record. It then entered what was probably the coldest period in the history

1. Albedo is the proportion of luminous energy flux reflected by the Earth's surface compared to the incident luminous energy flux received. It therefore quantifies the reflective power of a surface.

of life: the Cryogenian. The Cryogenian is divided into two major Snowball-type glaciations of unequal durations: the Sturtian glaciation (760 to 700 Ma), which lasted 60 million years and the Marinoan glaciation (650 to 635 Ma), which lasted about 15 million years. Sedimentary evidence of a glaciation of the Snowball Earth type is ubiquitous. Marinoan glacial diamictites[2] have been recorded in more than 48 countries. The paleolatitudes where these sediments were deposited, deduced from paleomagnetic data, are relatively low, and for the most part, the glacial deposits are within the tropics. Even more surprisingly, the glacial sediments are covered with thick levels of carbonates (called cap-carbonates) containing stromatolitic dolomites at their base, suggesting a rapid transition from an extremely cold environment to a warm environment (allowing the formation of cap-carbonates) by the progressive accumulation of volcanic CO_2 in the atmosphere up to a threshold of rapid deglaciation. Such climatic events necessarily redistributed life on the surface of the planet. The first glacial period correlates with the evolutionary radiation of oxygenic photoautotrophs, and the second shortly precedes the emergence of the animal world (radiation of metazoans). However, the cause–effect links between glaciations and the evolution of life remain to be clarified.

Box 5.1. *Snowball Earth*

5.2.2.2.3. Oxygen and ozone

Currently, the Earth's atmosphere is one-fifth of oxygen by volume, making it one of the Earth's original chemical signatures. The history of its evolution is discussed in the rest of this chapter.

Ozone (O_3) is formed when oxygen is excited at high energy, particularly through ultraviolet (UV) rays or electrical discharges. The UV rays responsible for the formation of ozone are those whose wavelength is less than 250 nm. At these wavelengths, the oxygen molecule dissociates into two oxygen atoms, the latter being able to react with the neighboring oxygen molecules to form the ozone molecule. This reaction occurs at an altitude of approximately 20 km in the stratosphere, where a concentration of 10^5 to 10^6 ozone molecules per cubic centimeter is measured. At lower altitudes, UV penetration is not very effective due to the absorption of these wavelengths by oxygen, the concentration of which increases with decreasing altitude (Figure 5.4). Conversely, above 20 km altitude, the concentration of oxygen becomes too low to produce ozone. The ozone continuously produced in the atmosphere is also destroyed by a UV photolysis reaction at a wavelength of 255 nm. These ozone production/destruction cycles, currently in a steady state, filter a large part of the UV radiation (below 300 nm) and

2. Glacial diamictites are poorly sorted detrital sedimentary rocks deposited during the melting of glaciers.

thus protect the current biosphere from the harmful effects (notably mutagenic). As we will see later in this chapter, the appearance of ozone in the atmosphere is sometimes recorded in sediments; it then indirectly informs us about the evolution of atmospheric oxygen and the evolution of the terrestrial biosphere.

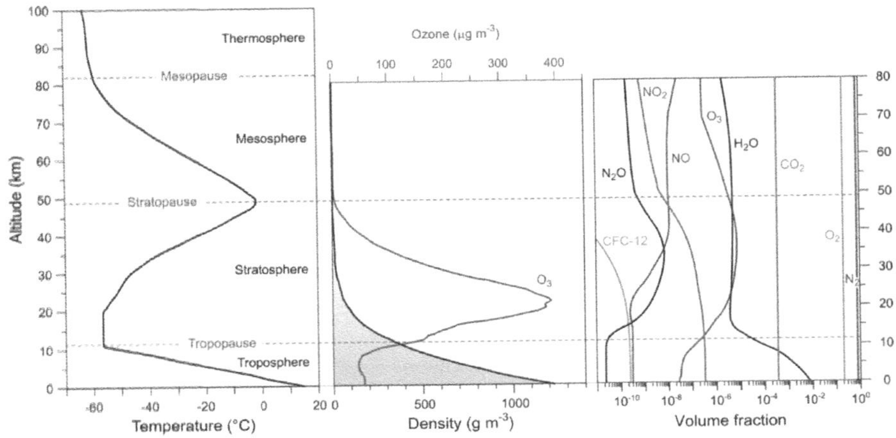

Figure 5.4. *Temperature, density, ozone and atmospheric gas concentration profiles of the Earth's atmosphere (Eni Generalic n.d.). For a color version of this figure, see www.iste.co.uk/benzerara/geosphere.zip*

5.3. The geobiological history of oxygen on Earth

Since the appearance of life approximately four billion years ago, the evolution of the biosphere has profoundly shaped the current environment. The geochemical cycles of carbon or sulfur, for example, have been largely influenced in particular by (i) the emergence of atmospheric CO_2 fixation and the production of oxygen by photosynthetic autotrophic organisms or (ii) the evolution of sulfate reduction. Since the Phanerozoic and on a scale of hundreds of millions of years, the Earth and biogeochemical cycles have appeared as a steady state system, where the physical and biological worlds self-regulate through feedback loops that are still poorly understood.

How and when did the Earth system, and in particular the biogeochemical cycles, evolve toward their current types? What are the thermodynamic and kinetic parameters that link the progressive oxygenation of the ocean and the atmosphere to the evolution of these cycles? In order to answer these questions, we will first focus on the environment of the primitive Earth.

5.3.1. *The environment of primitive Earth*

5.3.1.1. *The geological record*

The history of the Earth is subdivided into four eons: the Hadean, the Archean, the Proterozoic and the Phanerozoic, and grouped into two supereons: the Precambrian and the Phanerozoic (Figure 5.5). The Precambrian extends from the formation of the Earth 4.567 Ga ago (Patterson 1953) to about 541 Ma and corresponds to the so-called "primitive" Earth, before the diversification of metazoans. The Precambrian is thus the largest geological period in Earth's history.

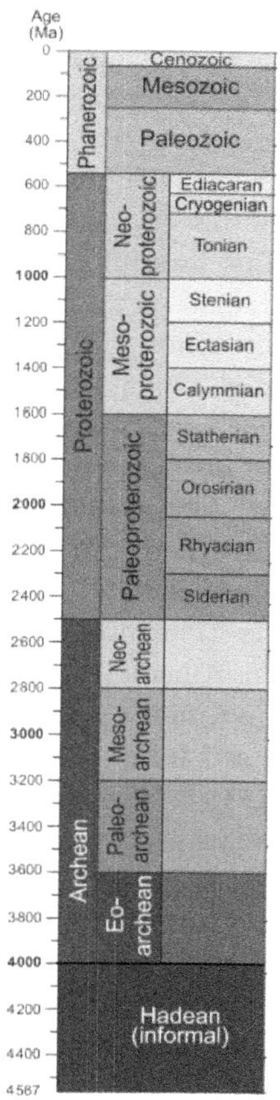

Figure 5.5. *Geological eons, eras and periods (shown here only for the Proterozoic) as defined by the International Commission on Stratigraphy (Ogg et al. 2016). For a color version of this figure, see www.iste.co.uk/benzerara/geosphere.zip*

The Hadean (Figure 5.5) is the least well-constrained period in time and the least documented because the absence of geological records does not allow it to be directly studied. The Hadean corresponds to the formation by accretion and differentiation of the Earth and the solar system in general (Kleine et al. 2002). This period is characterized by a massive bombardment of meteorites on the surface of the Earth and the surface of the Moon, the latter not having undergone any resurfacing processes (tectonics and alteration), unlike Earth (Chyba 1993; Frei and Rosing 2005; Gomes et al. 2005). Although this period cannot be directly studied, several major events occurred during the Hadean: (i) an early differentiation of the different internal envelopes of the Earth, which allowed the core and the mantle to be formed; (ii) the formation of a proto-atmosphere linked to the release of volatile elements from the primitive mantle (degassing of the primitive mantle); and (iii) the formation of a proto-hydrosphere, by condensation of water vapor from the degassing of the mantle, and present in the primitive atmosphere following a significant drop in temperature. The boundary between the Hadean and the Archean is generally set at 4 Ga, although this date is subject to debate and some authors propose instead the date of the first form of life (but this is also widely debated, ranging from 3.7 to 3.5 Ga, depending on the authors, e.g. Allwood et al. (2007); Nutman et al. (2016)) or the oldest terrestrial mineral (i.e. the Jack Hills zircon at 4.4 Ga; Halliday (2001); Valley et al. (2005)). The Archean is a period that extends from 4 Ga to 2.5 Ga. This is divided into three parts: the Lower Archean (4 Ga to 3.2 Ga; sometimes subdivided into Eo- and Paleo-Archean; Figure 5.5), the Middle Archean (3.2 Ga to 2.8 Ga) and the Upper Archean (2.8 Ga to 2.5 Ga). In general, few Archean terrains have escaped tectonic processes, and only a few cratons allow this period of geological time to be studied (Figure 5.6). The most studied Archean cratons are located in Australia (Pilbara), South Africa (Kaapvaal), Canada (Superior) and Greenland (North Atlantic). The oldest geological archives are observed from the Lower Archean, with the gneissic formations of Acasta (Canada; dated between 4 Ga and 3.9 Ga) and Itsaq (Greenland; dated between 3.9 Ga and 3.6 Ga) (Nutman et al. (2016)). It is also during the Lower Archean that the proto-continents and the first sediments formed. Carbonate bioconstructions (see Chapter 3), the oldest known traces of fossil life, appear in particular in the sedimentary formations of Isua (3.7 Ga, Greenland; Nutman et al. (2016)), Fig Tree Group (3.5 Ga, South Africa; Byerly et al. (1986)) and Strelley Pool Chert (3.4 Ga, Australia; Allwood et al. (2006, 2007)). The Middle Archean is recorded in Steep Rock (3 Ga, Ontario, Canada; Nisbet (1987)) and Pangola (2.9 Ga, Kaapvaal Craton, South Africa; Beukes and Lowe (1989)) formations, both showing the presence of stromatolites. The Upper Archean is characterized by multiple sedimentary formations with varied lithologies, including BIF deposits (Banded Iron Formation).

Figure 5.6. *World geological map showing the Precambrian cratons (in pink and purple) most studied for their sedimentary records. The geological terrains in orange, yellow, green and blue are of Phanerozoic age (Thomazo and Papineau 2013). For a color version of this figure, see www.iste.co.uk/benzerara/geosphere.zip*

The scarcity of available sedimentary records as well as secondary transformation processes (diagenesis, metamorphism) is the main constraints to the study of this period of geological time.

The Proterozoic, which extends from 2.5 Ga to 541 Ma, is the period with the largest number of sedimentary records. This period presents numerous poorly metamorphosed sedimentary series deposited in epicontinental seas and is marked by the presence of numerous stromatolites (Peters et al. 2017). Fossil traces of life are abundant in the Proterozoic, and this period marks the expansion of eukaryotic organisms (Butterfield 2014; Knoll et al. 2016).

5.3.1.2. *Fluid envelopes*

5.3.1.2.1. The atmosphere

The atmosphere, both in its chemical composition and its physical properties, evolved considerably during the Precambrian. Major events include the transition between a proto-atmosphere and the secondary atmosphere, as well as the appearance of oxygen in the "biological" atmosphere.

The proto-atmosphere, or primitive atmosphere, formed during the accretion of the Earth and must originally have had a composition close to that of solar nebulae. The study of noble gases in the current atmosphere of Earth and Mars, in comparison with solar nebulae, has made it possible to provide details of the origin of the current atmosphere, as illustrated in Figure 5.7. These results allow us to rule out a primordial origin of the current atmosphere and seem to agree with a secondary origin by intense degassing of a chondritic-type mantle (i.e. type of undifferentiated meteorite, representative of the overall chemical composition of Earth; Figure 5.7).

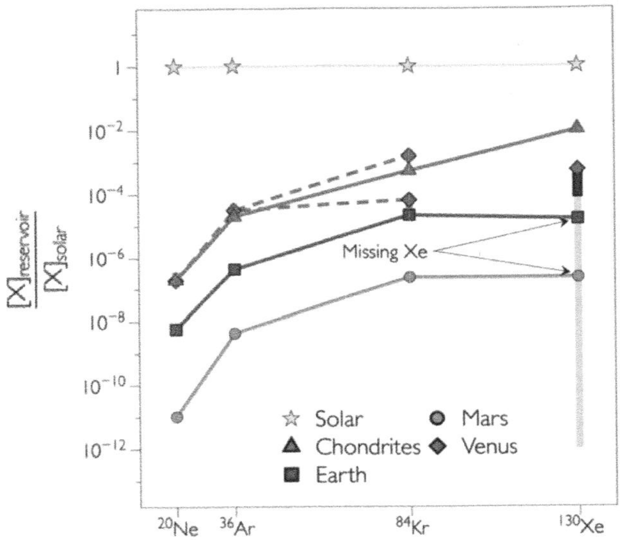

Figure 5.7. *Noble gas abundances measured for chondrites, Earth, Mars and Venus normalized to the abundance of silicium and to the solar abundances (=1). For Venus, uncertainties on the abundances of Kr and Xe appear with a light purple range and the dotted purple line depicts the expected abundances of Xe for an Earth-like/Mars-like Xe/Kr ratio. Figure from Avice et al. 2022. See also references therein. For a color version of this figure, see www.iste.co.uk/benzerara/geosphere.zip*

The first major event affecting the primitive atmosphere was therefore the transition to a secondary atmosphere, which occurred at the end of the Hadean. This is the result of the intense degassing of the upper mantle as well as the addition of a "late veneer" of extraterrestrial volatile elements for a few hundred million years after the formation of the Earth (Allègre et al. 1987; Javoy 1997). This secondary atmosphere is probably less reducing than the primitive atmosphere and was mainly composed of molecules of H_2O, CO_2, CO, N_2, and H_2 (main gases released at volcanic sources and mid-ocean ridges; Kasting 1993) and reduced molecules including CH_4, H_2S and NH_3 to a lesser extent. The atmospheres of the planets Venus and Mars have atmospheres similar to this secondary atmosphere except for the water molecule, largely lost during the geological evolution of these two planets. At the end of the Hadean and throughout the Archean, the Earth's atmosphere did not contain any oxygen, and the only process allowing its production, the photolysis of water contained in the atmosphere by UV, was not sufficient for it to accumulate due to the very reducing nature of atmospheric chemistry. Thus, methane or ammonia effectively buffers the photochemical production of oxygen by oxidizing it in the form of carbon dioxide and nitrogen.

According to the standard solar model, the luminosity of the Sun was much lower in the Precambrian due to the progressive ignition of the Sun's nuclear fusion reactions by the contraction of its core. Thus, the solar luminosity was approximately 70% of its current intensity, and the terrestrial radiation budget in the Archean would have been one-fourth to one-third lower than at present (Sagan and Chyba 1997). Water on Earth would have likely been in solid form (ice) when considering current atmospheric compositions and a greenhouse effect. However, the existence of sedimentary records since at least 3.7 Ga implies the existence of liquid water very early in the history of the Earth. It is therefore necessary to explain how to maintain surface temperatures consistent with the existence of liquid water, estimated at approximately 60°C for the Archean ocean, despite lower solar irradiation (see section 5.3.1.2.2). This paradox is commonly called the faint young sun paradox, and its resolution involves a significant greenhouse effect. The two greenhouse gases selected to resolve the paradox are CO_2 and CH_4. However, the relative importance of these two gases and their impacts on the climate at that time remain subject to debate (Kasting 2005). Indeed, high atmospheric CO_2 concentrations imply a CO_2 rich ocean which, by interaction with oceanic basalts, form sedimentary carbonates and thus tend to reduce the greenhouse effect. Different climate models therefore attempt to explain the maintenance of a significant greenhouse effect combined with the geological sequestration of CO_2, invoking in particular compensation by the contribution of CO_2 linked to volcanism or by another greenhouse gas such as methane. The latter is in fact a much more effective greenhouse gas than CO_2 (its potential as a greenhouse gas is 25 times greater than the CO_2). Some clues, such as the absence of siderite (iron carbonate) in paleosols between 2.8 Ga and 2.2 Ga, suggest that the concentration of atmospheric CO_2 in the Archean was not sufficient to compensate for the faint young sun paradox (Rye et al. 1995). Thus, a first model suggests that methane played a key role in maintaining the Archean greenhouse effect (Kasting 2005). In this case, a strong greenhouse effect would have been maintained thanks to methane until the appearance of oxygen in the atmosphere. Indeed, the presence of oxygen would likely lead to a significant decrease in CH_4 concentrations in the atmosphere through its oxidation into CO_2 (the half life of methane in the current atmosphere is around 10 years). The first major Snowball-type glaciations could thus reflect this process. A second model proposes significant CO_2

concentrations between 3.5 Ga and 3 Ga (Lowe and Tice 2004). This model is based on the presence of nahcolite ($NaHCO_3$), an evaporite mineral that can only form under conditions of high CO_2 partial pressure. The authors therefore propose that the slowdown in CO_2 sequestration would be consistent with a chemically stratified ocean and the rapid covering of the oceanic crust by impermeable chert (quartzite) deposits. These two models therefore invoke different greenhouse effect mechanisms and propose highly variable CH_4 concentrations in the atmosphere.

Box 5.2. *The faint young sun paradox*

5.3.1.2.2. The Precambrian ocean

Oceans have likely been present on Earth since the beginning of the Archean period, when a large part of them may have been formed after accretion from water vapor, which constituted a large proportion of the proto-atmosphere. This hypothesis is based on the isotopic composition of oxygen in detrital zircons from Archean granites dated between 4.4 and 2.7 Ga. This composition, on average 5.6‰, is close to that of the Earth's mantle (5.3‰; Valley et al. 2005). These isotopic signatures suggest that these zircons formed in a granitic magma. This hypothesis is confirmed by the presence of potassium feldspar and muscovite, two minerals found exclusively in granitic magmas. Since granites are hydrated magmas, formed in the presence of liquid water, this supports the idea of the existence of very early oceans.

The occurrences of BIFs from 3.8 Ga (Greenland), which are iron-rich sedimentary rocks deposited in an oceanic environment, or of stromatolitic bioconstructions (Pilbara Craton; Australia; 3.5 Ga), support these observations by suggesting the presence of early oceans. Considering this early origin of the oceans on Earth, many studies have tried to constrain the physicochemical properties of these primitive oceans to understand their functioning. Several studies have used geological paleothermometers in order to constrain the temperature of the ocean during the Precambrian and thus test the possibility of an early development of life in the Archean. The most widely used paleothermometer for the Archean period is that of oxygen isotopes, linking the temperature to the oxygen isotopic composition of cherts and carbonates (Marin-Carbonne et al. 2014). This is possible because, in the case of stable isotopes, the isotopic fractionation of an element between a mineral and the fluid in which it precipitates depends to the first order on the temperature. The isotopic compositions of minerals precipitating in the ocean can therefore be used to determine the temperature at which they precipitated in the ocean. From natural samples, several studies have attempted to experimentally determine the relationship between temperature and the oxygen isotopic compositions of minerals and the water in which they precipitate (quartz-water; Knauth and Epstein 1976. Calcite-water; O'Neil et al. 1969). The use of this paleothermometer, however, requires considering that the isotopic composition of oxygen in seawater has not varied over geological time (Herwartz et al. 2021). Taking this into account, many studies have attempted to estimate temperatures over geological time (Knauth and Lowe 2003; Robert and Chaussidon 2006; Marin-Carbonne et al. 2014; Lowe et al. 2020). These different studies have obtained a range of generally warm temperatures ranging from 30 to 70°C for the Archean oceans. However, caution should be exercised in interpreting these isotopic results because it could also reflect metamorphic or hydrothermal weathering of the surrounding sediments after their deposition (e.g. de Wit and Furnes 2016). Furthermore, the presence of gypsum in the Warrawoona sedimentary formations (3.5 Ga, Pilbara Craton, Australia), a mineral that transforms into anhydrite when temperatures exceed 57°C, suggests that Archean ocean temperatures are closer to the low range of temperatures obtained from oxygen isotopes of cherts and carbonates. Studies based on silicon isotopes of cherts are also consistent with a moderately warm Archean ocean, with temperatures close to 60°C (Tartèse et al. 2017).

Salinity is also an important parameter which has been studied over geological time and that may have influenced the solubility of oxygen. To reconstruct the evolution of ocean salinity, several methods have been used. The first, indirectly, is to list the salt deposits known in sedimentary archives to estimate the overall salinity of the Archean oceans, before the formation of these deposits on the first continents. However, the punctual formation of large quantities of evaporites on continents or in restricted oceanic environments, as well as their remobilization by erosion, must have led to significant variations in salinity over geological time, which are difficult to constrain with this method (Knauth 1998). Nevertheless, by taking into account the Phanerozoic evaporite deposits and the brines trapped in continental cratons, the initial salinity of the primitive ocean has been calculated and estimated to be up to twice that of the present ocean (Knauth 1998, 2005). The second method involves determining the ratios and elemental concentrations of fluids trapped in fluid inclusions present in sedimentary or hydrothermal rocks. The analysis of these inclusions trapped in quartz and carbonates of some Archean cratons suggests a salinity three to four times higher than that of present-day seawater (Foriel et al. 2004). Despite the differences between these two estimated salinity ranges, these two methods support the idea of an early hypersaline ocean (i.e. with a salinity higher than that of present-day seawater).

5.3.1.3. *The development of life on Earth*

Analysis of meteorite impact craters on the Moon suggests that impacts incompatible with the development of life on the Earth's surface occurred up to 3.8 Ga (i.e. the Late Heavy Bombardment hypothesis; see Koike et al. (2020), for example, for a recent challenge), setting an upper time limit for the origin of life. However, our interpretation of the role of impacts is ambiguous; indeed, two contradictory effects can be envisaged: on the one hand, the sterilization of the Earth's surface by vaporization of the ocean; on the other hand, the "seeding" of organic molecules (Chyba 1993). Recent discoveries of extremophile organisms (discoveries in the 1970s of hyperthermophilic and barophilic archaea and eubacteria in the deep sea) that can withstand conditions of temperature, pressure, and osmolarity, well above the physiological extrema of most prokaryotes known until then, seem to indicate to us that life could have emerged rapidly, before 4 Ga, in a wide range of environmental conditions. The origin of life takes place, for most authors, in an environment where the fluxes of matter and energy establish a strong gradient of physicochemical properties (e.g. fumaroles, mid-ocean ridges, ocean–atmosphere interface).

5.3.1.3.1. Primitive life without oxygen

At 4 Ga ago, when life emerged, the oceans and the Earth's atmosphere did not contain oxygen, and the Earth's atmosphere was, by analogy with the other terrestrial planets in the solar system, mainly composed of CO_2. It is thus widely accepted that the first metabolisms were anaerobic (Figure 5.8), since oxygen could not be the final electron acceptor (the oxidant). Alternative electron acceptors were then used by the first microorganisms living in this anoxic environment. This is the case, for example, of sulfate-reducing bacteria and archaea that use as an electron acceptor sulfate (SO_4^{2-}), sulfite (SO_3^{2-}), dithionite ($S_2O_4^{2-}$), thiosulfate ($S_2O_3^{2-}$), trithionate ($S_3O_6^{2-}$), tetrathionate ($S_4O_6^{2-}$), elementary sulfur (S_8) or even polysulfides (Sn^{2-}), which they reduce to sulfides. With the element sulfur being in the same column (but the row below) as oxygen in Mendeleev's periodic table, these elements have similar properties, and the reduction of sulfur to sulfide, which can give hydrogen sulfide (H_2S), is analogous to the reduction of oxygen to water, except that the redox potential ($\Delta E°$) associated with this reaction is less energetically advantageous than that of the redox couple O_2/H_2O (Figure 5.2).

Oxidized species of nitrogen, nitrates and nitrites may also have been used very early in the Archean as electron acceptors. Indeed, like sulfur, a biogeochemical cycle of nitrogen involving oxidized species seems to have emerged as early as the Middle Archean (e.g. Thomazo et al. 2009; Pellerin et al. 2024). The most abundant electron acceptor in the primitive atmosphere, CO_2, was also able to benefit very early on from methanogenic archaea (reducing carbon dioxide to methane) that are found today in large quantities in anoxic sediments rich in organic matter such as estuarine sediments, marshes, or near black smokers of mid-ocean ridges. Once again, isotopic data, particularly of carbon and hydrogen, from fluid inclusions rich in methane preserved in Archean sediments from Australia (Pilbara Craton), suggest that this type of metabolism was present very early in the history of the Earth from 3.5 Ga (Ueno et al. 2006). These microbial processes of methanogenesis, probably very effective in the primitive anoxic environment of the Archean Earth, could have notably influenced the climate by inducing organic haze such as those currently observed on Titan, one of Saturn's satellites (Catling and Zahnle 2020).

5.3.1.3.2. Oxygenic photosynthesis

Oxygenic photosynthesis, which is common to all contemporary plants and algae, and to some bacteria (cyanobacteria), uses the energy of sunlight to fix carbon dioxide into carbohydrates via the reaction [E0]. In this simplified reaction $-CH_2O-$ refers to many different types of carbohydrates, which will serve as a carbon source for heterotrophic secondary productivity. As its name suggests, oxygenic photosynthesis releases oxygen by oxidation of water molecules. This photosynthesis is certainly not representative of the first photosynthesis, because the use of water as a reducing agent requires very complex cellular and enzymatic machinery that seems to have been acquired late (Soo et al. 2017), compared to the "simpler" use of other reducing agents such as H_2S associated with anoxygenic photosynthesis carried out, for example, by green sulfur bacteria (equation [5.8]).

$$CO_2 + 2H_2S \rightarrow CH_2O + H_2O + 2S \qquad [5.8]$$

Despite their obvious advantages over non-photosynthetic anaerobic bacteria, the exact way in which the first phototrophic microorganisms arose is unknown. Microfossils have been used to trace their evolutionary history (Schopf 1993). However, their records and interpretation remain inconclusive (Brasier et al. 2002), and associated molecular biomarkers are also considered unreliable in Archean rocks (French et al. 2015). The occurrence of stromatolites in the fossil record indirectly suggests that anoxygenic photosynthesis was already present by ~3.5 Ga (Tice and Lowe 2004, 2006 ; Allwood et al. 2006, 2007). The advent of oxygenic photosynthesis is associated with the appearance of a phylum of bacteria called cyanobacteria (Fischer et al. 2016). Although the oldest cyanobacterial microfossil detection dates back to 1.9 Ga, on the Belcher Islands, Canada (Hofmann 1976), the oxygen released by this metabolism suggests that oxygenic photosynthesis participated in the oxygenation of the Earth's atmosphere (Figure 5.8; see section 5.3.2.1), probably as early as 2.9–2.7 Ga. Indeed, numerous isotopic and elemental data suggest that there were O_2 oases from the end of the Middle Archean (e.g. Anbar et al. 2007; Frei et al. 2009; Crowe et al. 2013) that can be supported by a terrestrial and coastal biosphere of benthic cyanobacteria with little effect on the chemical composition of the atmospheric reservoir (Lalonde and Konhauser 2015). These oxygenation events, localized in time and space, are described in the literature as "whiffs" of oxygen (Figure 5.8) and generate, locally, new geochemical and biogeochemical cycles due to changes in the redox speciation of elements (e.g. nitrate respiration, Figure 5.2; Thomazo et al. 2011).

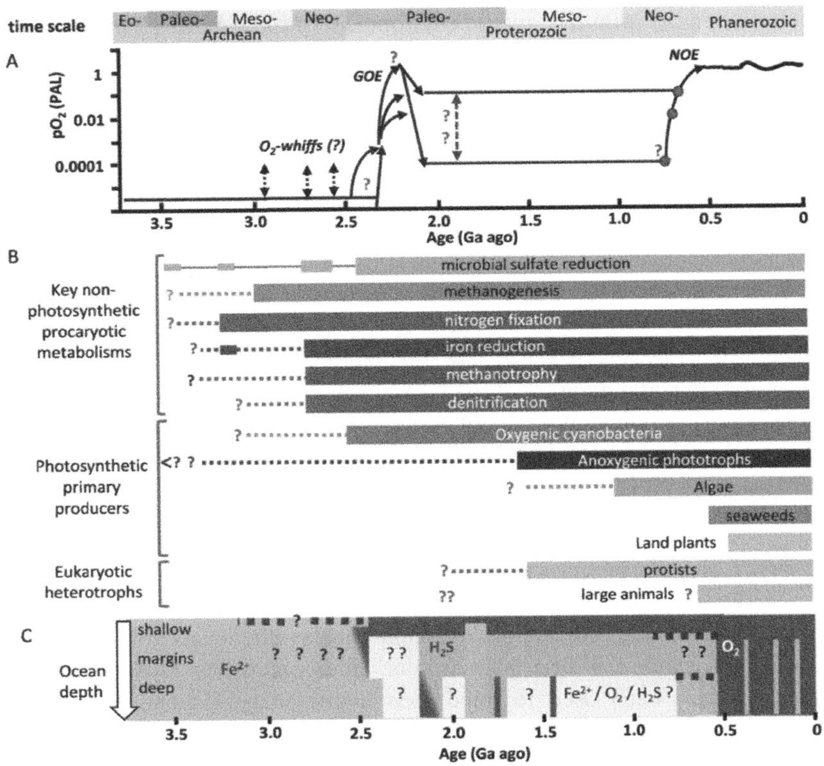

Figure 5.8. *Co-evolution of living organisms and environments (Lepot 2020). (A) Evolution of partial pressure of atmospheric O_2 (pO_2) relative to the current atmospheric level (PAL). This model includes short-lived bursts of O_2 release in the atmosphere, the Great Oxidation Event (GOE), uncertainties (question marks and multiple arrows) regarding the magnitude of the increase or decrease in oxygen levels. A range consistent with geochemical proxies is given for Proterozoic atmospheric oxygen levels. The Neoproterozoic Oxygenation Event (NOE) is also shown. (B) Model of early evolution of life. Dashed lines: uncertainties. (C) Attempt to reconstruct the evolution of seawater chemistry. Current models imply a ferruginous ocean (i.e. anoxic with Fe^{2+}, green in C) during almost the entire Archean. Surface waters gradually became oxygenated during the "whiffs" of O_2 (blue dashes in C) and during and after the GOE. Euxinic conditions (i.e. anoxic-sulfidic, orange in C) formed at the ocean margins from the bacterial reduction of sulfate formed by oxidative alteration of sulfide minerals. The deep ocean remained ferruginous throughout most of the Proterozoic until the Neoproterozoic Oxygenation Event (NOE). Highly uncertain water chemistries at various intervals are shown as question marks and pink boxes. Figure courtesy of Kevin Lepot. For a color version of this figure, see www.iste.co.uk/benzerara/geosphere.zip*

5.3.2. *Oxygenation events: tempo and consequences*

Over geological time, the chemical compositions of the atmosphere and oceans have strongly influenced the evolution of the biosphere, and conversely, the biosphere has induced major changes in the environment, such as the mass release of CH_4 in the Archean atmosphere associated with bacterial methanogenesis (Figure 5.8; Ueno et al. 2006; Thomazo et al. 2009; Zerkle et al. 2012), or the production of oxygen (O_2) and the trapping of CO_2 in the form of carbonates and organic matter via oxygenic photosynthesis (Canfield 2005). The appearance of O_2 in the ocean–atmosphere system via oxygenic photosynthesis is probably the major forcing of the early biogeochemical evolution of the Earth system and led to drastic changes in the environment, allowing the development of the biosphere through the diversification of aerobic metabolisms and the progressive colonization of continental surfaces (Anbar and Knoll 2002; Simpson et al. 2013).

5.3.2.1. *Kinetic parameters of the oxygen revolution*

The kinetic parameters of the evolution of ocean oxygenation are much less well constrained than those of the atmosphere (see section 5.3.1.3.2), but these two geological systems are closely linked. The main features of the evolution of the partial pressure of atmospheric oxygen[3], pO_2 (Figure 5.8), could be reconstructed by a certain number of mineralogical, chemical and isotopic tracers (Holland 1984; Canfield 2005; Sreenivas and Murakami 2005; Lyons et al. 2014; Knoll et al. 2016). Most authors agree that the partial pressure of oxygen in the atmosphere of the Archean Earth, before 2.3 Ga, was very low ($<10^{-5}$ PAL[4]). The exact time of crossing this 10^{-5} PAL threshold remains, however, strongly debated in the scientific community and constitutes one of the "hot spots" of current research (e.g. Phillipot et al. 2021). The evidence for a primitive Earth devoid of free oxygen is numerous. We can cite here the presence of detrital minerals containing reduced species (unstable under an oxidizing atmosphere), such as uraninite (uranium dioxide of formula UO_2, uranium being in a reduced form U^{4+} in this mineral) or pyrite (iron sulfide of formula FeS_2) in conglomerates and fluvial sediments (Rasmussen and Buick 1999; Hofmann et al. 2009). Iron depletion of paleosols before 2.25 Ga, suggesting mobilization under reducing conditions of Fe^{2+} (ferrous iron) by weathering in the continental domain, constitutes another evidence of primitive anoxia of the Earth system (Rye and Holland 1998). The contents of certain trace elements sensitive to redox reactions, such as Mo or Re, in Precambrian oceanic

3. The partial pressure of a molecule in a gas mixture corresponds to the pressure that this gas would exert if it was alone. Concretely, this corresponds to the total pressure of the gas mixture multiplied by the content of the gas in the molecule of interest.

4. Present atmospheric level of oxygen.

sedimentary rocks also confirm this scenario. Indeed, these elements are mobilized in fluids by alteration processes in oxidizing conditions. The appearance of oxygen in the atmosphere would therefore have allowed a significant transfer of these elements to rivers, then to the oceans, followed by enrichment in oceanic sedimentary rocks (Reinhard et al. 2009).

A major constraint on the evolution of the oxygen content of the atmosphere was provided in the 2000s by Farquhar et al. (2000) using the multi-isotopic compositions of sulfur in sedimentary sulfides and sulfates. Archean sediments (> 2.3 Ga) in fact present fractionations independent of the mass of the sulfur isotopes (i.e. $\Delta^{33}S$ and $\Delta^{36}S \neq 0$), known as MIF (Mass-Independent Fractionation) and are mathematically defined as follows:

$$\Delta^{33}S = \delta^{33}S - 1{,}000 \times \left(\left(1 + \frac{\delta^{34}S}{1000}\right)^{0.515} - 1\right) \quad [5.9]$$

$$\Delta^{36}S = \delta^{36}S - 1{,}000 \times \left(\left(1 + \frac{\delta^{34}S}{1{,}000}\right)^{1.90} - 1\right) \quad [5.10]$$

Using:

$$\delta^{3i}S = \left(\frac{\left(\frac{S^{3i}}{S^{32}}\right)_{sample}}{\left(\frac{S^{3i}}{S^{32}}\right)_{VCDT}} - 1\right) \times 1{,}000 \quad [5.11]$$

with i = 3, 4 or 6 (sulfur having four naturally occurring stable isotopes ^{32}S, ^{33}S, ^{34}S and ^{36}S).

Geochemists measure the isotope ratios of natural samples relative to an international reference standard and express them using δ (Craig 1961; Coplen 1996) (equation [5.12]). R_{ech} and R_{std} are the isotopic ratios of the sample and the standard. By convention, the heavy isotope is the numerator and the light isotope is the denominator. The ratios will therefore be of the type: $^{15}N/^{14}N$ for nitrogen, $^{13}C/^{12}C$ for carbon or even $^{33}S/^{32}S$, $^{34}S/^{32}S$, $^{36}S/^{32}S$ for sulfur. The various international standards are: (1) for nitrogen, atmospheric nitrogen; (2) for hydrogen and oxygen, the SMOW (Standard Mean Ocean Water), which represents average seawater; (3) for carbon, the PDB (Pee Dee Belemnite), which corresponds to the belemnites of the Cretaceous Peedee Formation, in South Carolina; (4) for sulfur, the Canyon Diablo troilite (CDT) was chosen as the first reference, then as an internationally accepted standard: it is the FeS phase of an iron meteorite collected near the Meteor crater, in Arizona.

Box 5.3. *Definition of isotopic delta*

$$\delta = \left(\frac{R_{ech}}{R_{std}} - 1\right) \times 1{,}000 \qquad [5.12]$$

These sulfur MIFs have been interpreted as reflecting the absence of ozone, and by extension, oxygen in the atmosphere for two complementary and independent reasons. First, the production of sulfur MIFs is generated by the photo-dissociation of SO_2 molecules, of volcanic origin, via high-energy UV radiation. To transfer this production in the sedimentary record, these radiations must penetrate into the lower layers of the atmosphere, which is not possible in the presence of stratospheric ozone (Farquhar et al. 2000; Baroni et al. 2007). Secondly, for MIFs to be preserved in the sedimentary record, the byproducts of SO_2 photodissociation must not be efficiently mixed by atmospheric redox chemical reactions. This mixing and hence the disappearance of MIFs occurs when the amount of atmospheric oxygen is greater than 10^{-5} PAL (Pavlov and Kasting 2002). The disappearance of sulfur MIFs in sedimentary rocks younger than 2.3 Ga thus relates to the first major stage of atmospheric oxygenation, also called GOE (Great Oxidation Event; Figure 5.8; Holland 2002; Bekker et al. 2004). According to recent compilations of trace element concentrations in Proterozoic sediments (Mo, U, Cr), it seems that atmospheric oxygen levels increased significantly between 2.3 and 2 Ga during the GOE before decreasing and stabilizing toward a moderate value between 2.0 and 0.8 Ga (Figure 5.9; Lyons et al. 2014; Knoll et al. 2016). Finally, a second important oxygenation stage seems to have taken place in the Neoproterozoic, essentially between 0.8 and 0.55 Ga. This stage, known as NOE (for Neoproterozoic Oxidation Event), would have allowed the appearance of metazoans and the explosion of Cambrian life (Butterfield 2009; Och and Shields-Zhou 2012).

The chemical evolution of the oceans is closely linked to that of the atmosphere, these two reservoirs being in constant exchange with each other. The redox evolution of the oceans has historically been subdivided into two main periods: an anoxic period persisting until ~2.0 Ga, followed by an oxidized period essentially comparable to present-day oceans (Holland 2002). Data based on the temporal evolution of the sulfur isotopic composition of sedimentary sulfides and sulfates, however, have suggested the existence of an intermediate "stratified" ocean, oxic at the surface and anoxic at depth, which would have persisted for more than a billion years from ~ 2.4 Ga (Canfield 1998; Anbar and Knoll 2002). Recent studies now seem to converge toward a global redox evolution of the oceans that can be summarized in three main periods (Figure 5.8; Knoll et al. 2016):

1. Completely anoxic primitive oceans were dominated by the iron cycle until about 2.4 Ga, followed by limited oxygenation at the ocean surface (linked to a production of oxygen by photosynthesis in the photic zones), with anoxic deep oceans still dominated by the iron cycle (we speak of ferruginous conditions), and

probably oxidation processes at the oxic–anoxic interface and reduction in the deepest zones. This period is marked by the presence of BIF (Banded Iron Formation, iron-rich sediments) in the sedimentary record and persists until about 1.8 Ga.

2. The oxygenation of the atmosphere causes an oxidation of continental sulfides into sulfates, which due to their high solubility, are mass transported by rivers to the oceans. In the still anoxic deep oceans, the reduction of these sulfates into sulfides by sulfate-reducing bacteria would have made it possible to trap iron in the form of sulfides (e.g. pyrite) in the sediments. The deep ocean thus gradually passes from a state dominated by the iron cycle (ferruginous) to a state dominated by the sulfur cycle (sulfidic or euxinic). This stage would have lasted from ~1.8 Ga (date of the disappearance of the BIF) to ~700 Ma. The occurrences of Neoproterozoic Iron Formation (NIF) during the Cryogenian (720 to 635 Ma) mark several episodes of the return of the oceans to a ferruginous state in connection with snowball episodes.

3. Oxygenation of the oceans, similar to what we know today, since ~600 Ma.

5.3.2.2. *Some biological and geological consequences of the oxygen revolution*

The progressive accumulation of oxygen in the Earth's atmosphere drastically and irreversibly reorganized the functioning of the Earth system. Making an exhaustive list of these changes is a real challenge and has been one of the research topics of the Archaean community for several decades. Indeed, all chemical elements (with the exception of noble gases) have a biogeochemical behavior that depends directly (or indirectly) on the degree of oxidation of the environment and flows between reservoirs, speciation and interactions – it is the entire system that must be reconsidered to properly understand the changes induced by the oxygen revolution.

Among these changes, some have been the subject of significant research effort in recent years and are developed below.

The increase in atmospheric oxygen concentration during the GOE and then the NOE contributed significantly to the oxidation of methane to carbon dioxide and water. The resulting decreases in greenhouse gases caused global cooling, triggering a series of ice ages known as snowball events (Figure 5.9) (Tajika and Harada 2019), between 2.3 and 2.2 Ga (Huronian glaciation), 720 and 663 Ma (Strutian glaciation) and 639 and 635 Ma (Marinoan glaciation).

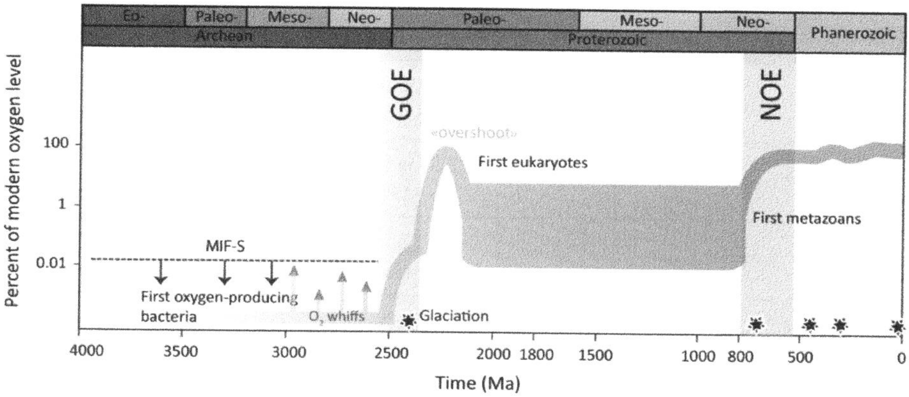

Figure 5.9. *The history of O_2 in the Earth's atmosphere. Atmospheric levels of O_2 (in percent of modern oxygen level) are thought to have increased mainly during two geological periods in Earth history: the Great Oxidation Event (GOE) at 2.4–2.0 Ga and the Neoproterozoic Oxygenation Event (NOE) at 0.8–0.6 Ga. An O_2 overshoot occurred at 2.2–2.1 Ga and O_2 bursts occurred before the GOE. Snowball Earth glaciations (blue stars) – coincided with increases in O_2 levels during the GOE and NOE. For a color version of this figure, see www.iste.co.uk/benzerara/geosphere.zip*

The Great Oxygenation Event also triggered a rapid diversification of terrestrial minerals. The GOE is estimated to be directly responsible for about half of the minerals found on Earth today (Table 5.1) (Hazen 2010).

Era	Geological age	Cumulative number of mineral species
Presolar minerals	>4.6 Ga	12
Planetary accretion (>4.55 Ga)		
Primordial meteorites and achondrites	>4.56 Ga	60
Convective crust and mantle (4.55 to 2.5 Ga)		
Evolution of igneous rocks	4.55 to 4.0 Ga	350 – 500
Granitoids and pegmatite	4.0 to 3.5 Ga	>1,000
Plate tectonics	>3.0 Ga	1,500

The living influences the mineral world (>2.5 Ga to present)		
Anoxic world	3.9 Ga to 2.5 Ga	1,500
Great Oxidation Event (GOE)	2.5 Ga to 1.9 Ga	>4,000
Stratified ocean	1.9 Ga to 1.0 Ga	>4,000
Glaciations Snowball Earth	1.0 Ga to 542 Ma	>4,000
Evolution of biomineralization in the Phanerozoic	542 Ma to present	>5,100+

Table 5.1. *Evolution of terrestrial minerals (per Hazen and Ferry 2010)*

From a biological point of view, the increase in oxygen concentrations could have had many, sometimes opposing, consequences. Indeed, the appearance of a new electron acceptor, energetically very favorable, could have supported rapid biological diversification, in particular heterotrophic metabolisms using oxygen respiration, such as methanotrophy, which carries out the oxidation of methane into carbon dioxide (e.g. Thomazo et al. 2009); it is also suggested that the increase in molecular oxygen levels created the conditions for a major biological crisis, in particular for microorganisms with strictly anaerobic metabolisms, largely predominant before the GOE. Hence, the GOE is also described by biologists as the oxygen catastrophe or the oxygen crisis. Oxidative stress involving the production of reactive oxygen species (ROS) may have acted in synergy with other environmental stresses (such as UV radiation and/or desiccation) to induce the early selection of the first eukaryotes (Gross and Bhattacharya 2010). The adverse effects of internal ROS (produced by endosymbiont proto-mitochondria) may have also promoted the evolution of meiotic sex and the selective pressure for efficient DNA repair of oxidative damage may have led to the evolution of eukaryotic characteristics such as cell–cell fusions, cytoskeleton-mediated chromosome movements and the emergence of the nuclear membrane (Hörandl and Speijer 2018).

Recently, a phylogenetic analysis of arsenic detoxification enzyme systems found a direct link between the appearance of oxidized mineral forms of arsenic, genetic evolution and the GOE (Chen et al. 2020). This example perfectly illustrates the importance of the selective pressure of the GOE on the early history of the biosphere.

5.3.2.3. *Feedback and "homeostasis"...*

After the GOE and NOE events, during the Phanerozoic, the Earth's atmosphere remained oxidizing with an oxygen concentration of between about 15% and 35% (Berner and Canfield 1989; Lenton 2001). It is the ocean reservoir that regulated the atmospheric concentration of oxygen through a deep coupling between the biogeochemical cycles of carbon and oxygen. Indeed, the production of oxygen by photosynthetic biomass is used in return by heterotrophic organisms to oxidize organic matter (via respiration processes) and, to a lesser extent, during the oxidative alteration of minerals (oxidation of Fe^{2+} during laterization processes[5] in soils in tropical climates, for example). However, only part of the organic matter is oxidized (or remineralized), the other part being incorporated into sedimentary rocks (generating future deposits of fossil fuels depending on the geological conditions of maturation of these rocks). To a large extent, it is therefore the rate of sedimentary burial of fossil organic matter (and to a lesser extent, volcanism) which controls the degree of oxidation of our planet. The variations observed in the Phanerozoic and in particular the maximum observed in the Carboniferous–Permian (about 300 Ma ago) with atmospheric concentrations of dioxygen between 25% and 35% reflect the combination of biological phenomena (the poor degradation of lignin in terrestrial plants by the fungi of the time; corresponding to the main coal deposits exploited in the world) and geological phenomena (the high rate of sedimentation and therefore burial of organic matter linked to the dismantling of the Hercynian chain). Although terrestrial vegetation may have led to a rapid increase in the oxygen content of the atmosphere during the Carboniferous period, there are, however, feedback mechanisms in the coupled biogeochemical cycle of carbon and oxygen that have contributed to the stability of the latter over the last 550 Ma. Indeed, the increase in atmospheric oxygen reduces the energy required for combustion (thus promoting the ignition of a fire), inhibits the photosynthesis reaction and increases the production of toxic oxygen species (internal ROS) (see section 5.3.2.2), thereby in turn reducing biomass. These feedbacks thus have the potential to stabilize atmospheric oxygen content by decreasing organic carbon burial (Lenton 2001). Conversely, the decline in O_2 concentration (approximately 15%) across the Permian–Triassic boundary (about 260 to 245 Ma ago) and the relative absence of coal deposition during the last five million years of this period may reflect a substantial reduction in the geographic extent of terrestrial photosynthetic biomass (Berner et al. 2007) (see Chapter 8).

5. Laterization is a pedological process affecting tropical soils and characterized by a strong alteration of primary minerals, leading to soils rich in iron and aluminum hydroxides and kaolinite, called laterites.

5.4. Conclusion

The oxygen revolution, the GOE, or the oxygen catastrophe, undoubtedly designates one of the major events in the geobiological history of the Earth. The causes and consequences of this shift from an anoxic planet such as Mars or Venus, to an oxygenated planet, thus allowing the development of complex life, remain largely unconstrained, and a significant research effort by a vast scientific community including exobiologists, planetologists, geologists and biologists is at work. Recently, it has been suggested that the Moon, by gradually slowing down the speed of rotation of the Earth by induced tidal friction, was an important player in the oxygenation of the atmosphere by modulating primary productivity and its remineralization (Klatt et al. 2021).

The biosphere is the origin of O_2, and its atmospheric abundance, unique in the solar system, is widely used, in parallel with the detection of ozone (O_3), by exobiologists as potential traces of extraterrestrial life for exoplanets located in the habitable zone. If the Earth seems close to a stationary state since the beginning of the Phanerozoic, maintaining an oxygenated atmosphere and a coupled biogeochemical cycle of carbon and oxygen in equilibrium, recent models suggest that the increase in solar luminosity should induce a cascade of feedbacks on the carbon cycle (increase in the geological sequestration of CO_2 associated with the alteration of silicates) and then on the biosphere (the reduction of atmospheric CO_2 limiting the photosynthesis reaction), which will likely lead to a return to an oxygen-poor atmosphere, heading to a new geobiological era in the evolution of our planet by about 1 Ga (Ozaki and Reinhard 2021).

5.5. References

Allègre, C., Staudacher, T., Sarda, P. (1987). Rare gas systematics: Formation of the atmosphere, evolution and structure of the Earth's mantle. *Earth and Planetary Science Letters*, 81, 127–150.

Allwood, A.C., Walter, M.R., Kamber, B.S., Marshall, C.P., Burch, I.W. (2006). Stromatolite reef from the Early Archaean era of Australia. *Nature*, 441, 714–718.

Allwood, A.C., Walter, M.R., Burch, I.W., Kamber, B.S. (2007). 3.43 billion-year-old stromatolite reef from the Pilbara Craton of Western Australia: Ecosystem-scale insights to early life on Earth. *Precambrian Research*, 158(3–4), 198–227.

Anbar, A.D. and Knoll, A.H. (2002). Proterozoic Ocean chemistry and evolution: A bioinorganic bridge? *Science*, 297, 1137–1142.

Anbar, A.D., Duan, Y., Lyons, T.W., Arnold, G.L., Kendall, B., Creaser, R.A., Kaufman, A.J., Gordon, G.W., Scott, C., Garvin, J. et al. (2007). A whiff of oxygen before the great oxidation event? *Science*, 317(5846), 1903–1906.

Baroni, M., Thiemens, M.H., Delmas, R.J., Savarino, J. (2007). Mass-independent sulfur isotopic compositions in stratospheric volcanic eruptions. *Science*, 315, 84–87.

Bekker, A., Holland, H.D., Wang, P.L., Rumble, D., Stein, H.J., Hannah, J.L., Coetzee, L.L., Beukes, N.J. (2004). Dating the rise of atmospheric oxygen. *Nature*, 427, 117–120.

Berner, R.A. and Canfield, D.E. (1989). A new model for atmospheric oxygen over Phanerozoic time. *American Journal of Science*, 289(4), 333–361.

Berner, R.A., VandenBrooks, J.M., Ward, P.D. (2007). Oxygen and evolution. *Science*, 316(5824), 557–558.

Beukes, N.J. and Lowe, D.R. (1989). Environmental control on diverse stromatolite morphologies in the 3000 Myr Pangola Supergroup, South Africa. *Sedimentology*, 36, 383–397.

Brasier, M.D., Green, O.R., Jephcoat, A.P., Kleppe, A.K., Van Kranendonk, M.J., Lindsay, J.F., Steele, A., Grassineau, N.V. (2002). Questioning the evidence for Earth's oldest fossils. *Nature*, 416(6876), 76–81.

Butterfield, N.J. (2009). Modes of pre-Ediacaran multicellularity. *Precambrian Research*, 173(1–4), 201–211.

Butterfield, N.J. (2014). Early evolution of the Eukaryota. *Palaeontology*, 58, 5–17.

Byerly, G.R., Lower, D.R., Walsh, M.M. (1986). Stromatolites from the 3,300–3,500-Myr Swaziland Supergroup, Barberton Mountain Land, South Africa. *Nature*, 319, 489–491.

Canfield, D.E. (1998). A new model for Proterozoic ocean chemistry. *Nature*, 396(6710), 450–453.

Canfield D.E. (2005). The early history of atmospheric oxygen: Homage to Robert M. Garrels. *Annual Review of Earth and Planetary Sciences*, 33, 1–36.

Catling, D.C. and Zahnle, K.J. (2020). The archean atmosphere. *Science Advances*, 6(9), eaax1420.

Catling, D.C., Zahnle, K.J., McKay, C. (2001). Biogenic methane, hydrogen escape, and the irreversible oxidation of Early Earth. *Science*, 293, 839–843.

Chen, S.C., Sun, G.X., Yan, Y., Konstantinidis, K.T., Zhang, S.Y., Deng, Y., Zhu, Y.G. (2020). The Great Oxidation Event expanded the genetic repertoire of arsenic metabolism and cycling. *Proceedings of the National Academy of Sciences*, 117(19), 10414–10421.

Chyba, C.F. (1993). The violent environment of the origin of life: Progress and uncertainties. *Geochimica et Cosmochimica Acta*, 57, 3351–3358.

Coplen, T.B. (1996). New guidelines for reporting stable hydrogen, carbon, and oxygen isotope-ratio data. *Geochimica et Cosmochimica Acta*, 60, 3359–3360.

Craig, H. (1961). Standard for reporting concentrations of deuterium and Oxygen-18 in natural waters. *Science*, 133, 1833–1834.

Crowe, S.A., Døssing, L.N., Beukes, N.J., Bau, M., Kruger, S.J., Frei, R., Canfield, D.E. (2013). Atmospheric oxygenation three billion years ago. *Nature*, 501(7468), 535–538.

Eni Generalic (n.d.). "Atmosphere". Croatian-English Chemistry Dictionary & Glossary [Online]. Available at: https://glossary.periodni.com/glossary.php?en=atmosphere [Accessed 20 October 2018].

Farquhar, J., Bao, H., Thiemens, M. (2000). Atmospheric influence of Earth's earliest sulfur cycle. *Science*, 289, 756–758.

Fischer, W.W., Hemp, J., Johnson, J.E. (2016). Evolution of oxygenic photosynthesis. *Annual Review of Earth and Planetary Sciences*, 44, 647–683.

Foriel, J., Philippot, P., Rey, P., Somogyi, A., Banks, D., Ménez, B. (2004). Biological control of Cl/Br and low sulfate concentration in a 3.5-Gyr-old seawater from North Pole, Western Australia. *Earth and Planetary Science Letters*, 228, 451–463.

Frei, R. and Rosing, M.T. (2005). Search for traces of the late heavy bombardment on Earth–Results from high precision chromium isotopes. *Earth and Planetary Science Letters*, 236, 28–40.

Frei, R., Gaucher, C., Poulton, S.W., Canfield, D.E. (2009). Fluctuations in Precambrian atmospheric oxygenation recorded by chromium isotopes. *Nature*, 461(7261), 250–253.

French, K.L., Hallmann, C., Hope, J.M., Schoon, P.L., Zumberge, J.A., Hoshino, Y., Peters, C.A., George, S.C., Love, G.D., Brocks, J.J. et al. (2015). Reappraisal of hydrocarbon biomarkers in Archean rocks. *Proceedings of the National Academy of Sciences*, 112(19), 5915–5920.

Gomes, R., Levison, H.F., Tsiganis, K., Morbidelli, A. (2005). Origin of the cataclysmic Late Heavy Bombardment period of the terrestrial planets. *Nature*, 435, 466–469.

Gross, J. and Bhattacharya, D. (2010). Uniting sex and eukaryote origins in an emerging oxygenic world. *Biology Direct*, 5(1), 1–20.

Halliday, A.N. (2001). In the beginning. *Nature*, 409, 144–145.

Hazen, R.M. and Ferry, J.M. (2010). Mineral evolution: Mineralogy in the fourth dimension. *Elements*, 6(1), 9–12.

Herwartz, D., Pack, A., Nagel, T.J. (2021). A CO2 greenhouse efficiently warmed the early Earth and decreased seawater 18O/16O before the onset of plate tectonics. *Proceedings of the National Academy of Sciences*, 118(23), e2023617118.

Hofmann, H.J. (1976). Precambrian microflora, Belcher Islands, Canada: Significance and systematics. *Journal of Paleontology*, 1040–1073.

Hoffman, P.F., Kaufman, A.J., Halverson, G.P., Schrag, D.P. (1998). A neoproterozoic snowball earth. *Science*, 281(5381), 1342–1346.

Hofmann, A., Bekker, A., Rouxel, O., Rumble, D., Master, S. (2009). Multiple sulphur and iron isotope composition of detrital pyrite in Archaean sedimentary rocks: A new tool for provenance analysis. *Earth and Planetary Science Letters*, 286(3–4), 436–445.

Holland, H.D. (1984). *The Chemical Evolution of the Atmosphere and Oceans*. Princeton University Press, Princeton.

Holland, H.D. (2002). Volcanic gases, black smokers, and the Great Oxidation Event. *Geochimica et Cosmochimica Acta*, 66(21), 3811–3826.

Hörandl, E. and Speijer, D. (2018). How oxygen gave rise to eukaryotic sex. *Proceedings of the Royal Society B: Biological Sciences*, 285(1872), 20172706.

Javoy, M. (1997). The major volatile elements of the Earth: Their origin, behavior, and fate. *Geophysical Research Letters*, 24(2), 177–180.

Kasting, J.F. (1993). Earth's early atmosphere. *Science*, 259, 920–926.

Kasting, J.F. (2005). Methane and climate during the Precambrian era. *Precambrian Research*, 137, 119–129.

Klatt, J.M., Chennu, A., Arbic, B.K., Biddanda, B.A., Dick, G.J. (2021). Possible link between Earth's rotation rate and oxygenation. *Nature Geoscience*, 14(8), 564–570.

Kleine, T., Münker, C., Mezger, K., Palme, H. (2002). Rapid accretion and early core formation on asteroids and the terrestrial planets from Hf–W chronometry. *Nature*, 418(6901), 952–955.

Knauth, L.P. (1998). Salinity history of the Earth's early ocean. *Nature*, 395, 554–555.

Knauth, L.P. (2005). Temperature and salinity history of the Precambrian ocean: Implications for the course of microbial evolution. *Palaeogeography, Palaeoclimatology, Palaeoecology*, 219, 53–69.

Knauth, L.P. and Epstein, S. (1976). Hydrogen and oxygen isotope ratios in nodular and bedded cherts. *Geochimica et Cosmochimica Acta*, 40, 1095–1108.

Knauth, L.P. and Lowe, D.R. (2003). High Archean climatic temperature inferred from oxygen isotope geochemistry of cherts in the 3.5 Ga Swaziland Supergroup, South Africa. *GSA Bulletin*, 115, 566–580.

Knoll, A.H., Bergmann, K.D., Strauss, J.V. (2016). Life: The first two billion years. *Philosophical Transactions of the Royal Society B: Biological Sciences*, 371, 20150493.

Koike, M., Sano, Y., Takahata, N., Iizuka, T., Ono, H., Mikouchi, T. (2020). Evidence for early asteroidal collisions prior to 4.15 Ga from basaltic eucrite phosphate U–Pb chronology. *Earth and Planetary Science Letters*, 549, 116497.

Lalonde, S.V. and Konhauser, K.O. (2015). Benthic perspective on Earth's oldest evidence for oxygenic photosynthesis. *Proceedings of the National Academy of Sciences*, 112(4), 995–1000.

Lenton, T.M. (2001). The role of land plants, phosphorus weathering and fire in the rise and regulation of atmospheric oxygen. *Global Change Biology*, 7(6), 613–629.

Lepot, K. (2020). Signatures of early microbial life from the Archean (4 to 2.5 Ga) eon. *Earth-Science Reviews*, 209, 103296.

Lowe, D.R. and Tice, M.M. (2004). Geologic evidence for Archean atmospheric and climatic evolution: Fluctuating levels of CO_2, CH_4, and O_2 with an overriding tectonic control. *Geology*, 32(6), 493–496.

Lowe, D.R., Ibarra, D.E., Drabon, N., Chamberlain, C.P. (2020). Constraints on surface temperature 3.4 billion years ago based on triple oxygen isotopes of cherts from the Barberton Greenstone Belt, South Africa, and the problem of sample selection. *American Journal of Science*, 320(9), 790–814.

Lyons, T.W., Reinhard, C.T., Planavsky, N.J. (2014). The rise of oxygen in Earth's early ocean and atmosphere. *Nature*, 506(7488), 307–315.

Marin-Carbonne, J., Robert, F., Chaussidon, M. (2014). The silicon and oxygen isotope compositions of Precambrian cherts: A record of oceanic paleo-temperatures? *Precambrian Research*, 247, 223–234.

Nisbet, E.G. (1987). *The Young Earth: An Introduction to Archaean Geology*. Cambridge University Press, Cambridge.

Nutman, A.P., McGregor, V.R., Friend, C.R.L., Bennett, V.C., Kinny, P.D. (1996). The Itsaq Gneiss Complex of southern West Greenland; the world's most extensive record of early crustal evolution (3900–3600 Ma). *Precambrian Research*, 78, 1–40.

Nutman, A.P., Bennett, V.C., Friend, C.R.L., Van Kranendonk, M.J., Chivas, A.R. (2016). Rapid emergence of life shown by discovery of 3,700-million-year-old microbial structures. *Nature*, 537, 535–538.

Och, L.M. and Shields-Zhou, G.A. (2012). The Neoproterozoic oxygenation event: Environmental perturbations and biogeochemical cycling. *Earth-Science Reviews*, 110, 26–57.

Ogg, J.G., Ogg, G.M., Gradstein, F.M. (2016). *A Concise Geologic Time Scale: 2016*. Elsevier, Amsterdam.

O'Neil, J.R., Clayton, R.N., Mayeda, T.K. (1969). Oxygen isotope fractionation in divalent metal carbonates. *The Journal of Chemical Physics*, 51, 5547–5558.

Ozaki, K. and Reinhard, C.T. (2021). The future lifespan of Earth's oxygenated atmosphere. *Nature Geoscience*, 14(3), 138–142.

Patterson, C.C. (1953). The isotopic composition of meteoritic, basaltic and oceanic leads, and the age of the Earth. Report, Subcommittee on Nuclear Processes in Geological Settings, National Research Council, National Academy of Sciences, Washington, D.C., 36–40.

Pavlov, A.A. and Kasting, J.F. (2002). Mass-independent fractionation of sulfur isotopes in Archean sediments: Strong evidence for an anoxic Archean atmosphere. *Astrobiology*, 2, 27–41.

Pellerin, A., Thomazo, C., Ader, M., Rossignol, C., Rego, E.S., Busigny, V., Philippot, P. (2024). Neoarchaean oxygen-based nitrogen cycle en route to the Great Oxidation Event. *Nature*, 1–6.

Peters, S.E., Husson, J.M., Wilcots, J. (2017). The rise and fall of stromatolites in shallow marine environments. *Geology*, 45, 487–490.

Philippot, P., Killingsworth, B.A., Paquette, J.L., Tessalina, S., Cartigny, P., Lalonde, S.V., Thomazo, C., Ávila, J.N., Busigny, V. (2021). Comment on "Correlation of the stratigraphic cover of the Pilbara and Kaapvaal cratons recording the lead up to Paleoproterozoic Icehouse and the GOE" by Andrey Bekker, Bryan Krapež, and Juha A. Karhu, 2020, Earth Science Reviews, https://doi.org/10.1016/j.earscirev.2020.103389. *Earth Science Reviews*, 218, 103594.

Rasmussen, B. and Buick, R. (1999). Redox state of the Archean atmosphere: Evidence from detrital heavy minerals in ca. 3250-2750 Ma sandstones from the Pilbara Craton, Australia. *Geology*, 27, 115–118.

Reinhard C., Raiswell R., Scott C., Anbar A.D., Lyons T.W. (2009). A late Archean sulfidic sea stimulated by early oxidative weathering of the continents. *Science*, 326, 713–716.

Robert, F. and Chaussidon, M. (2006). A palaeotemperature curve for the Precambrian oceans based on silicon isotopes in cherts. *Nature*, 443, 969–972.

Rye R. and Holland H.D. (1998). Paleosols and the evolution of atmospheric oxygen: Critical review. *American Journal of Science*, 298, 621–672.

Rye, R., Kuo, P.H., Holland, H.D. (1995). Atmospheric carbon dioxide concentrations before 2.2 billion years ago. *Nature*, 378, 603–605.

Sagan, C. and Chyba, C. (1997). The early faint sun paradox: Organic shielding of ultraviolet-labile greenhouse gases. *Science*, 276, 1217–1221.

Schopf, J.W. (1993). Microfossils of the Early Archean Apex chert: New evidence of the antiquity of life. *Science*, 640–646.

Simpson, E.L., Heness, E., Bumby, A., Eriksson, P.G., Eriksson, K.A., Hilbert-Wolf, H.L., Sarah Linnevelt, S., Malenda, H.F., Modungwa, T., Okafor, O.J. et al. (2013). Evidence for 2.0 Ga continental microbial mats in a paleodesert setting. *Precambrian Research*, 237, 36–50.

Soo, R.M., Hemp, J., Parks, D.H., Fischer, W.W., Hugenholtz, P. (2017). On the origins of oxygenic photosynthesis and aerobic respiration in Cyanobacteria. *Science*, 355(6332), 1436–1440.

Sreenivas B. and Mukarami T. (2005). Emerging views on the evolution of atmospheric oxygen during the Precambrian. *Journal of Mineralogical and Petrological Sciences*, 100, 184–201.

Tajika, E. and Harada, M. (2019). Great oxidation event and snowball Earth. *Astrobiology*, 261–271.

Tartèse, R., Chaussidon, M., Gurenko, A., Delarue, F., Robert, F. (2017). Warm Archaean oceans reconstructed from oxygen isotope composition of early-life remnants. *Geochemical Perspectives Letters*, 3(1), 55–65.

Thomazo, C. and Papineau, D. (2013). Biogeochemical cycling of nitrogen on the early Earth. *Elements*, 9, 345–351.

Thomazo C., Ader M., Farquhar J., Philippot P. (2009). Methanotrophs regulated atmospheric sulfur isotope anomalies during the Mesoarchean (Tumbiana Formation, Western Australia). *Earth and Planetary Science Letters*, 279, 65–75.

Thomazo, C., Ader, M., Philippot, P. (2011). Extreme 15N-enrichments in 2.72-Gyr-old sediments: Evidence for a turning point in the nitrogen cycle. *Geobiology*, 9(2), 107–120.

Tice, M.M. and Lowe, D.R. (2004). Photosynthetic microbial mats in the 3,416-Myr-old ocean. *Nature*, 431(7008), 549–552.

Tice, M.M. and Lowe, D.R. (2006). Hydrogen-based carbon fixation in the earliest known photosynthetic organisms. *Geology*, 34(1), 37–40.

Ueno, Y., Yamada, K., Yoshida, N., Maruyama, S., Isozaki, Y. (2006). Evidence from fluid inclusions for microbial methanogenesis in the early Archaean era. *Nature*, 440, 516–519.

Valley, J.W., Lackey, J.S., Cavosie, A.J., Clechenko, C.C., Spicuzza, M.J., Basei, M.A.S., Bindeman, I.N., Ferreira, V.P., Sial, A.N., King, E.M. et al. (2005). 4.4 billion years of crustal maturation: Oxygen isotope ratios of magmatic zircon. *Contributions to Mineralogy and Petrology*, 150, 561–580.

de Wit, M.J. and Furnes, H. (2016). 3.5-Ga hydrothermal fields and diamictites in the Barberton Greenstone Belt – Paleoarchean crust in cold environments. *Science Advances*, 2(2), e1500368.

Zerkle A.L., Claire, M.W., Domagal-Goldman S.D., Farquhar J., Poulton S. (2012). A bistable organic-rich atmosphere on the Neoarchean Earth. *Nature Geoscience*, 5, 359–363.

6

The Importance of Living Organisms in the Carbon and Nitrogen Cycles

Alice PELLERIN[1] and Magali ADER[2]

[1] Laboratoire Biogéosciences, University of Burgundy, Dijon, France

[2] Institut de Physique du Globe de Paris, Université de Paris Cité, France

6.1. Biogeochemical cycles

To represent the behavior of an element at the scale of the Earth and its history, geochemists developed a conceptual tool: the geochemical cycle of the element of interest. This cycle is made up of reservoirs that contain the element considered, some of which are linked together by fluxes representing the processes that transfer the element from one reservoir to another (Figure 6.1).

Biogeochemical cycles are a subset of geochemical cycles, for which living things can be a reservoir of the element considered and also an operator for some of the fluxes. When we look at cycles, we quickly note that almost all element cycles are in fact biogeochemical cycles, which, in other words, means that living organisms are, and have been, an integral part of the chemical functioning of the Earth and that we cannot consider the terrestrial environment and its evolution over time without taking them into account. The biogeochemical cycles of carbon and nitrogen are key examples, on the one hand, because carbon and nitrogen are the main constituents of life, and on the other hand, because living organisms function directly or influence, in an indirect but significant way, many carbon and nitrogen fluxes.

Interactions between the Geosphere and the Biosphere,
coordinated by Karim BENZERARA and Christophe THOMAZO.

6.2. The carbon biogeochemical cycle

6.2.1. *Why is the carbon biogeochemical cycle of interest?*

The carbon biogeochemical cycle is particularly important for understanding how the Earth functions. Not only do the levels of CO_2 and CH_4 in the atmosphere (two greenhouse gases) play a crucial role in regulating the climate, the pH of the ocean and the weathering of continental rocks (see Chapters 2 and 8), but the flux of carbon in the form of organic matter has also largely contributed to regulating the concentration of oxygen in the atmosphere and oceans over geological time (Des Marais 1997; Kasting 2013) (see Chapters 6 and 8). In this chapter, we will focus more specifically on this link between the evolution of the carbon cycle and the oxygenation of the Earth's surface.

6.2.2. *The main carbon reservoirs and fluxes*

Carbon is, and has been in the past, present in all terrestrial compartments. In the atmosphere, it is mainly present in the form of CO_2 and CH_4. In the hydrosphere, it is in the form of dissolved inorganic carbon (DIC), composed of $CO_{2(aqueous)}$, H_2CO_3, HCO_3^- and dissolved CO_3^{2-}, HCO_3^- being the dominant form in the current ocean, whose average pH is approximately 8. Finally, in soils and sediments, it is present in the form of carbonates (C_{carb}) and organic matter (C_{org}). In all of these surface reservoirs, it is also present in the form of organic carbon, mainly formed by living organisms. Because of the essential role and efficiency of the biosphere in transferring carbon from one surface reservoir to another, all living organisms are grouped together into a reservoir, often called "biomass", to facilitate the conceptualization and representation of carbon exchanges controlled by living organisms. At the scale of the whole cycle, most of the carbon is found in sedimentary, and more broadly, crustal rocks, mainly in the form of C_{carb} and C_{org}, and in the mantle, in various forms including graphite, diamond and carbonates, and other less well-known forms. It is likely that the Earth's core also contains carbon, carbon being siderophile, i.e. with a strong affinity for iron, under the physicochemical conditions of the core. We are now beginning to quantify, for recent geological times, the amount of carbon stored in these reservoirs as well as those exchanged between them (Figure 6.1). However, this is not the case for early eras, since, beyond modeling (see Chapter 8), there are very few ways to directly trace past changes in the carbon cycle. The main records of these changes are:

– the study of the carbon content of Precambrian igneous, mantle and sedimentary rocks, which provides partial information on the evolution over time of speciation and carbon stocks in the crust and mantle;

– the study of isotopic compositions of sedimentary carbonates ($\delta^{13}C_{carb}$), which provides information on carbon fluxes entering and leaving the ocean;

– the study of isotopic compositions of sedimentary organic matter ($\delta^{13}C_{org}$), which provides information on the metabolisms at the origin of the genesis of organic matter.

We will focus on these last two points in this chapter.

– Isotopic composition and notation δ

Geochemists measure the isotope ratios of natural samples relative to an international reference standard and express them using δ (Craig 1961), developed in equations [6.1] and [6.2]. The isotopic ratios of the sample and the standard are noted $(^{13}C/^{12}C)_{sample}$ and $(^{13}C/^{12}C)_{std}$ for carbon and $(^{15}N/^{14}N)_{sample}$ and $(^{15}N/^{14}N)_{std}$ for nitrogen. By convention, the heavy isotope is the numerator in isotope ratio and the light isotope is the denominator.

For carbon, the notation δ is written as follows:

$$\delta^{13}C = ((^{13}C/^{12}C)_{sample} /(^{13}C/^{12}C)_{std} - 1) \times 1{,}000 \quad [6.1]$$

For nitrogen, the δ notation is written as follows:

$$\delta^{15}N = ((^{15}N/^{14}N)_{sample} /(^{15}N/^{14}N)_{std} - 1) \times 1{,}000 \quad [6.2]$$

The isotopic composition of a sample is therefore expressed in ‰ as a deviation of the isotopic ratio of the sample from the standard. For carbon, the international standard is the PDB (Pee Dee Belemnite) which corresponds to belemnites from the Cretaceous Pee Dee Formation in South Carolina. The higher a sample's value, the lower the isotopic composition. The higher the value of $\delta^{13}C$ is above 0, the more ^{13}C it contains relative to the standard, and the lower its value, the less ^{13}C it contains (or the more ^{12}C it contains). For nitrogen, the international standard is atmospheric nitrogen, which by convention has a value of 0‰, and is expressed as follows: $\delta^{15}N_{N2} = 0$‰ (vs. air).

– Isotopic fractionation and Δ notation

The difference in mass between the two isotopes ^{13}C and ^{12}C or ^{15}N and ^{14}N leads to differences in certain thermodynamic properties of the molecules that contain these isotopes: molar volume, melting temperature, viscosity, reaction rate and equilibrium constant. These differences in properties can cause differences in behavior and therefore in distribution of isotopes during chemical reactions, which lead to isotopic fractionation. In other words, isotopic fractionation is when a reaction involving a mixture of isotopes of the same element preferentially takes place with one isotope.

Isotopic fractionation created during a reaction (A → B), denoted Δ or ε, can be estimated by the isotopic composition difference between A and B.

For example, for carbon with the notation Δ:

$$\Delta^{13}C_{A\text{-}B} = \delta^{13}C_A - \delta^{13}C_B$$

For nitrogen with the notation ε:

$$\varepsilon \approx \delta^{15}N_A - \delta^{15}N_B$$

There are two types of isotopic fractionation: thermodynamic equilibrium and kinetic isotopic fractionation.

Isotopic fractionation at thermodynamic equilibrium characterizes isotopic exchange reactions and is governed by the laws of thermodynamics. Isotopic exchange reactions accompany reversible reactions that occur at chemical thermodynamic equilibrium. There is then partitioning of isotopes of the same element between two compounds or two phases with different isotopic ratios. This is the case of the equilibrium between atmospheric CO_2 and CO_2 dissolved in water, of the equilibria between CID species and the precipitation/dissolution of carbonates.

Isotopic fractionation can also be associated with an irreversible unidirectional reaction, during which there is no possible isotopic exchange reaction. This is called kinetic isotopic fractionation. In this case, the bonds established by the light isotope will react more easily and more quickly than those involving the heavy isotope. There is thus an enrichment in light isotopes of the product compared to the initial substrate. Kinetic isotopic fractionations cannot be predicted by the laws of thermodynamics. Most often, when they are known, it is because they have been determined empirically or experimentally. This is the case for photosynthesis.

Box 6.1. *General information on stable isotopes*

6.2.3. *Isotopic systematics of the carbon cycle*

The isotopic composition of the fluxes of CO_2 that enter the atmosphere and/or the ocean (i.e. volcanic, metamorphic and weathering fluxes) is close to −5‰. The $\delta^{13}C$ value of atmospheric CO_2 is currently −8.5‰, that of CID from the ocean is approximately +1‰, and that of sedimentary carbonates ($CaCO_3$) is 0‰. The difference between the current $\delta^{13}C$ values of −8.5‰ for atmospheric CO_2 and +1‰ for ocean CID results from all the equilibrium fractionations between atmospheric CO_2 and the different species of inorganic carbon dissolved in the ocean.

The $\delta^{13}C_{org}$ value of reservoirs containing organic carbon (biomass, soils, and crustal organic matter) is close to −25‰. The isotopic composition of reservoirs containing inorganic carbon is therefore very different from reservoirs containing organic matter. This difference is due to the isotopic fractionation associated with the photosynthesis reaction, which favors the incorporation of ^{12}C during atmospheric CO_2 fixation into organic carbon.

As for the other fluxes between reservoirs, the stable isotopes of carbon do not fractionate. The fluxes that leave the ocean, such as the sedimentation of carbonates and organic matter, preserve the isotopic composition of the carbonates and organic matter at the time they are formed in the ocean upon burial. The similarity between the $\delta^{13}C_{org}$ value of sedimentary organic matter and of biomass indicates that respiration does not fractionate carbon isotopes. Similarly, the small difference between the $\delta^{13}C$ value of CID and that of crustal carbonates indicates that precipitation of carbonates from the CID hardly fractionate carbon isotopes.

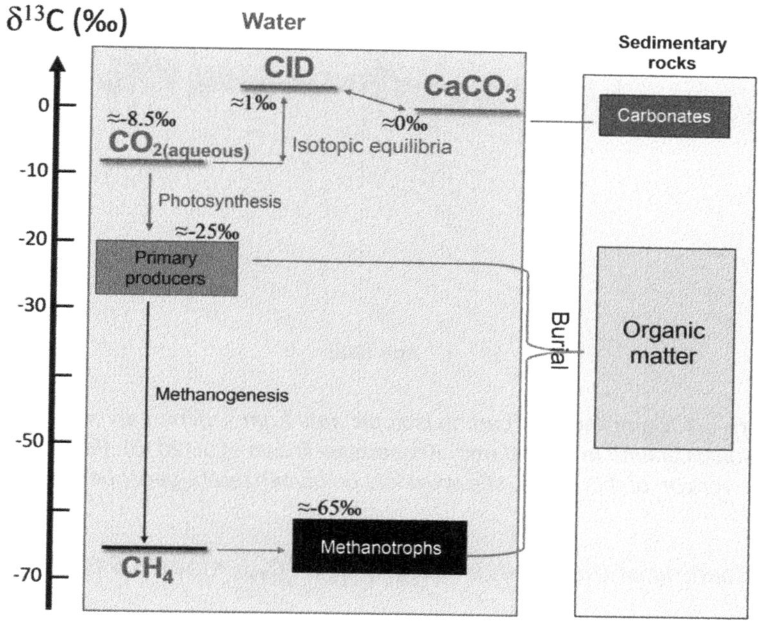

Figure 6.1. *Schematic of isotopic relationships between dissolved CO_2, DIC, primary producers, methanotrophs, and sedimentary carbonates and organic matter. Single arrows correspond to metabolism-related fractionations. Double arrows to fractionations at isotopic equilibrium and the lines without arrows to burial. Adapted from Des Marais (1997) and Hayes et al. (1999). For a color version of this figure, see www.iste.co.uk/benzerara/geosphere.zip*

6.2.4. $\delta^{13}C_{carb}$ in sedimentary rock records oceanic $\delta^{13}C_{CID}$ record

$\delta^{13}C_{carb}$ faithfully reflects the composition of DIC in the water from which the carbonate precipitates (Figure 6.1). Thus, measuring the $\delta^{13}C_{carb}$ of primary carbonates, i.e. having precipitated from the water of the depositional environment (and not during diagenesis processes from the sediment pore water), gives direct access to the $\delta^{13}C_{CID}$ of oceans, inland seas or lakes where sediments have been deposited.

Many measurements of $\delta^{13}C_{carb}$ have been done, especially in recent decades (Figure 6.2, according to Krissansen-Totton et al. 2015). They reveal a constant mean value close to 0‰ since 3.8 Ga, but a significant dispersion over time, with two periods of maximum variability between 2.3 and 2.0 Ga and between 750 and 540 Ma.

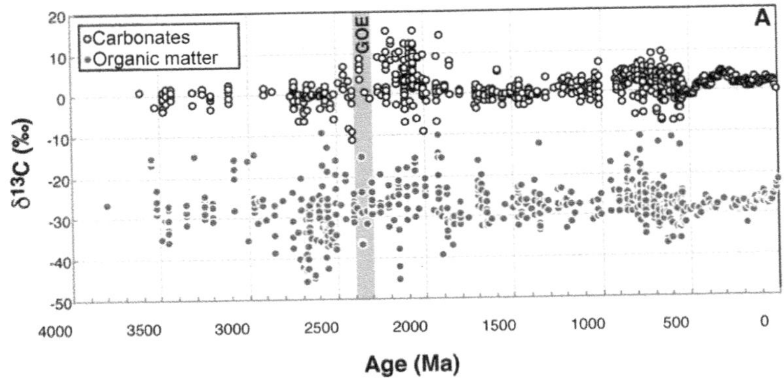

Figure 6.2. *Compilation of carbon isotopic data from sedimentary records over geological time (modified from Krissansen-Totton et al. 2015). For a color version of this figure, see www.iste.co.uk/benzerara/geosphere.zip*

6.2.5. Meaning of the relative stability of $\delta^{13}C_{carb}$ since 3.5 Ga

Over very long time scales of several Ga, the steady mean $\delta^{13}C_{carb}$ value of sedimentary rocks indicates that the ocean $\delta^{13}C_{CID}$ has varied little over time (Figure 6.2). It is therefore likely that the relative fluxes of carbon into and out of the ocean have not drastically changed over geological time either (Schidlowski 2001). We will describe the implications below.

6.2.5.1. *Quantification of relative organic matter burial fluxes by mass and isotopic balance*

We can use the average value of $\delta^{13}C_{carb}$ over geological time to obtain elements for quantifying the carbon fluxes entering and leaving the ocean. To do this, it is necessary to simplify the carbon cycle as much as possible (Figure 6.3). Here, we ignore the Earth's core, which has probably not exchanged carbon with the rest of the terrestrial reservoirs since the beginning of the Archean, and we group the ocean, the atmosphere and the biomass into a single reservoir (the ocean–atmosphere system), because on these large time scales, the fluxes between these reservoirs are in equilibrium.

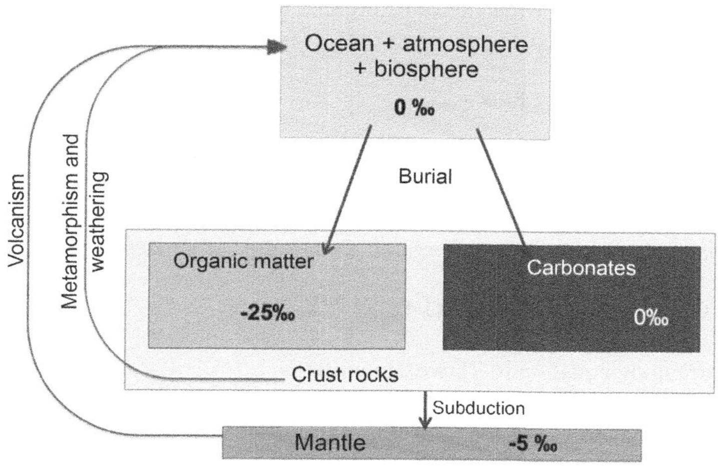

Figure 6.3. *Simplified box model representation of the biogeochemical carbon cycle. The black arrows correspond to carbon fluxes leaving the ocean–atmosphere system and the blue arrows to incoming fluxes. For a color version of this figure, see www.iste.co.uk/benzerara/geosphere.zip*

To continue to simplify the system, we assume the conservation of (i) the mass of carbon in the ocean–atmosphere–biosphere reservoir (the amount of carbon in this reservoir has not changed over time) and also (ii) that of its two isotopes (the $\delta^{13}C$ isotopic composition in this reservoir has not changed over time), known as the steady-state hypothesis, which implies that the incoming fluxes into this reservoir are equivalent to the outgoing fluxes.

This allows us to write two mass conservation equations:

– that of the mass of carbon:

$$\text{Flux}_{\text{C incoming}} = \text{Flux}_{\text{Corg buried}} + \text{Flux}_{\text{Ccarb buried}} \quad [6.3]$$

– that of the conservation of its isotopic composition:

$$\text{Flux}_{\text{C incoming}} \times \delta^{13}\text{C}_{\text{input}} = \text{Flux}_{\text{Corg buried}} \times \delta^{13}\text{C}_{\text{org}} + \text{Flux}_{\text{Ccarb buried}} \times \delta^{13}\text{C}_{\text{carb}} \quad [6.4]$$

Finally, to reduce the number of unknowns as much as possible, we can define the relative proportions of the fluxes of organic matter and carbonate in relation to the incoming carbon flux:

$$f_{\text{org}} = \text{Flux}_{\text{Corg buried}} / \text{Flux}_{\text{C incoming}} \quad [6.5]$$

$$f_{\text{carb}} = 1\text{-}f_{\text{org}} = \text{Flux}_{\text{Carb buried}} / \text{Flux}_{\text{C incoming}} \quad [6.6]$$

which allows us to obtain an equation with two unknowns, the $\delta^{13}C_{incoming}$ and f_{org}, since the isotopic compositions of organic carbon and carbonates can be measured.

$$\delta^{13}\text{C}_{\text{incoming}} = f_{\text{org}} \times \delta^{13}\text{C}_{\text{org}} + (1\text{-}f_{\text{org}}) \times \delta^{13}\text{C}_{\text{carb}} \quad [6.7]$$

By rearranging equation [6.7], we can write:

$$f_{\text{org}} = (\delta^{13}\text{C}_{\text{incoming}} - \delta^{13}\text{C}_{\text{carb}})/(\delta^{13}\text{C}_{\text{org}} - \delta^{13}\text{C}_{\text{carb}}) \quad [6.8]$$

which allows us to calculate, from the values of $\delta^{13}C_{carb}$ and $\delta^{13}C_{org}$ at each moment in the history of the Earth, the relative proportion of buried organic matter compared to buried carbonates. To calculate this, we make a final assumption by considering volcanic CO_2 as the main incoming flux and setting its $\delta^{13}C_{incoming}$ value to −5‰ (Cartigny et al. 1998). For an average $\delta^{13}C_{carb}$ value of 0‰, we find that $f_{org} = 0.2$ and $f_{carb} = 0.8$, meaning that 20% of the carbon entering the ocean–atmosphere system are buried in the form of organic matter and 80% are in the form of carbonates.

6.2.5.2. *Consequence of buried organic matter: atmospheric and ocean oxidation*

Coupling photosynthesis, respiration and the burial of organic matter closely links the carbon and oxygen cycles. Indeed, for each mole of organic matter produced by photosynthesis, one mole of O_2 is produced, but will, most of the time, be re-consumed by respiration. In the absence of oxygen, respiration is carried out using alternative electron acceptors, mainly sulfates. Thus, for each mole of organic matter removed from respiration by sediment burial, one mole of oxidant accumulates on the Earth's surface (Des Marais 1997; Kasting 2013). The oxygenation of the Earth's atmosphere (see Chapter 6) therefore involved the burial of organic matter.

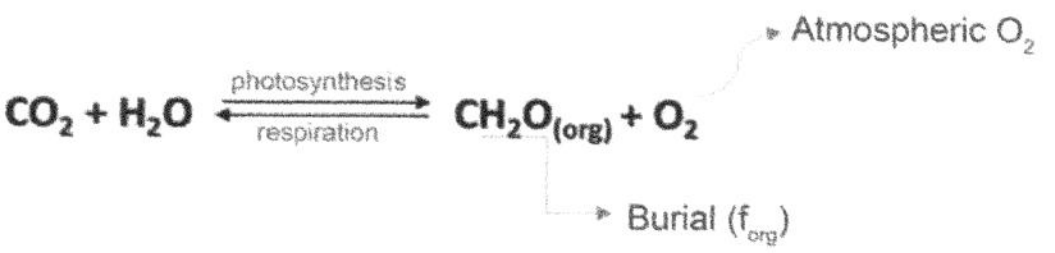

6.2.6. *Reason for the $\delta^{13}C_{carb}$ variation between 2.3 and 2.0 Ga and between 750 and 540 Ma*

The periods of greatest dispersion of $\delta^{13}C_{carb}$ values (between 2.3 and 2.0 Ga and between 750 and 540 Ma), indicate:

– Either the alteration of original features by diagenesis, which tends to lower $\delta^{13}C_{carb}$ values. Indeed, secondary carbonates can incorporate carbon from the degradation of organic matter rich in ^{12}C. This could explain most of the negative values (Grotzinger et al. 2011; Swart and Kennedy 2012).

– Or, for more positive $\delta^{13}C_{carb}$ values, significant changes in the carbon cycle. To date, there are two hypotheses to explain these values: (i) that of regional variations and (ii) global variations in ocean $\delta^{13}C_{carb}$.

6.2.6.1. *Hypothesis 1: regional disturbances of the carbon cycle*

Recent studies suggest that this dispersion may reflect sedimentary environments that were neither in equilibrium with the atmosphere nor well mixed with the rest of the oceans at the time of their deposition (Prave et al. 2022). According to this hypothesis, the strong variations between 2.3 and 2.0 Ga and between 750 and 540 Ma could be due to regional perturbations of the carbon cycle in these systems isolated from the ocean, either completely (e.g. epicontinental seas) or partially (e.g. lagoons). The two main mechanisms likely generating more positive $\delta^{13}C_{carb}$ values are evaporation and methanogenesis (Frimmel 2010; Cadeau et al. 2020; Prave et al. 2022). The mechanism of methanogenesis would be compatible with the idea that the oceans were then largely anoxic (i.e. devoid of oxygen) and low in sulfates, leaving methanogenesis as the main mechanism for the degradation of organic matter. Evaporation would be compatible with the hypothesis of a warmer climate, which could be validated by analyzing another carbonate isotope: oxygen.

6.2.6.2. *Hypothesis 2: global disruptions to the carbon cycle*

Although some of the dispersion may be related to regional effects, it is possible that the open ocean $\delta^{13}C_{CID}$ also showed global variations. To determine this, it would be necessary to obtain data from rocks deposited in an open ocean environment that were not subsequently modified by diagenetic processes. This is relatively easy to achieve for the recent times up to the Jurassic, the age of the oldest current ocean floors, because there is no doubt that the sediments deposited there are a record of the open ocean $\delta^{13}C_{CID}$. But this becomes increasingly complex as we go further back in time because sedimentary rocks often underwent subduction and deformations. For the Precambrian, systematic work on characterizing depositional environments is beginning to emerge (Prave et al. 2022), but we are not yet able to know the curve of global temporal fluctuations, around the $\delta^{13}C$ average value of 0‰ for the ocean–atmosphere system.

Producing this curve is fundamental because it will allow us to document variations over time in the global carbon cycle and thus also allow us to better understand the subtleties of the history of atmospheric and ocean oxygenation (see Chapter 6). For example, if periods of high variations in $\delta^{13}C_{carb}$ values with very positive values are associated with an overall increase in ocean $\delta^{13}C_{CID}$, this increase would indicate an increase in the burial rate of organic matter, itself responsible for oxygenation (Karhu and Holland 1996; Des Marais 1997; Schidlowski 2001; Kasting 2013). On the contrary, a decrease in the $\delta^{13}C_{CID}$ of the ocean–atmosphere system towards negative values, as may have been the case during global glaciations such as Snowball Earth episodes (714 and 630 Ma) (Halverson et al. 2005; Grotzinger et al. 2011; Och and Shields-Zhou 2012), would mark a sharp decrease in primary productivity. Organic matter burial fluxes would then fall, leaving the ocean–atmosphere system to create an equilibrium around the $\delta^{13}C$ value of incoming CO_2 fluxes, i.e. approximately −5‰. The corresponding decrease in the release of oxygen into the environment could also explain the return of anoxic conditions in the oceans during these episodes, which are also marked by the presence of iron-rich formations.

6.2.7. $\delta^{13}C_{org}$ *in sedimentary rocks records autotrophic metabolism*

Figure 6.2 shows a compilation of $\delta^{13}C_{org}$ measurements carried out over the past few decades. We can see that the average value of $\delta^{13}C_{org}$ has been approximately −25‰ since 3.8 Ga, with a variation around this average value for the Precambrian ranging from −10 to −45‰, greater than for $\delta^{13}C_{carb}$ values.

It is reasonable to assume that the $\delta^{13}C_{org}$ of ocean sediments reflects the $\delta^{13}C$ of CO_2 assimilated by marine autotrophic organisms, strongly modified by the isotopic fractionation associated with photosynthesis (Des Marais 1997; Hayes et al. 1999).

Since atmospheric CO_2 is in equilibrium with CO_2 dissolved in seawater, which is itself in isotopic equilibrium with the other species of the DIC (Figure 6.1), the $\delta^{13}C_{org}$ (like $\delta^{13}C_{carb}$) therefore also provides indirect information on the $\delta^{13}C_{CID}$ of oceans. With the average value of $\delta^{13}C_{org}$ varying little over geological time, like that of $\delta^{13}C_{carb}$, it suggests that the $\delta^{13}C_{CID}$ oceans have remained stable, and therefore, the functioning of the carbon cycle has probably not changed significantly either.

The $\delta^{13}C_{org}$ provides, from its difference from $\delta^{13}C_{carb}$, information on isotopic fractionation associated with organic matter production (Des Marais 1997). We see that, overall, this fractionation has not changed significantly over geological time, which implies that photosynthesis has been the main mechanism to produce organic matter at least since 3.5 Ga (age of the oldest sedimentary rocks with little metamorphism) and that its isotopic fractionation would subsequently have not or only slightly evolved during the biological and geological evolution of the Earth system. However, we note a clear variation in $\delta^{13}C_{org}$ values during the Precambrian–Cambrian transition, with a decrease in dispersion likely due to the disappearance of lower $\delta^{13}C_{org}$ values. This dispersion is currently interpreted as post-depositional modifications, linked to metamorphism, or the spatial and temporal variability of organic matter genesis processes (Des Marais 1997).

The highest values can be interpreted as post-depositional modifications due to metamorphism, but the lowest values observed in Precambrian sediments can be explained neither in this way nor by photosynthesis as we know it today. They imply significant metabolic activity from organic matter synthesis, much rarer in the Phanerozoic. For example, metabolisms such as methanogenesis and methanotrophy have been proposed to explain these low values, by isotopic analogy with what is known of the isotopic signature of these metabolisms today (Des Marais 1997; Shidlowski 2001) (Figure 6.1). However, we cannot exclude another type of metabolism present and active in the Precambrian that is either unknown or rare in current environments.

6.2.8. *Conclusions about the biogeochemical carbon cycle*

In summary, the carbon isotope records ($\delta^{13}C_{carb}$ and $\delta^{13}C_{org}$) indicate a quite stable relative rate of organic carbon burial of approximately 20% since at least 3.5 Ga. This burial has contributed to the progressive oxidation of the Earth's surface, leading to the oxygenation of the atmosphere and oceans. Additional oxygenation mechanisms may also have contributed, such as the burial of sedimentary pyrite, the transition from underwater volcanic activity to aerial activity (Gaillard et al. 2011) and/or atmospheric release of hydrogen by photodissociation of biological methane (Catling et al. 2001). It is also likely that fluctuations in the burial rate of organic carbon were responsible for episodes of increased oxygenation or, on the contrary, a return to more anoxic conditions at certain periods in the history of the Earth. This point will likely be clarified soon. Variations towards more positive $\delta^{13}C_{carb}$ values and more negative $\delta^{13}C_{org}$ values indicate a different functioning of the biosphere in the Precambrian compared to the Phanerozoic, with significant anaerobic metabolisms, possibly associated with the methane cycle.

6.3. The biogeochemical cycle of nitrogen

6.3.1. *Why be interested in the nitrogen biogeochemical cycle?*

Nitrogen is a chemical element present in all of Earth's geological reservoirs (core, mantle, crust), and N_2 is the dominant gas in the Earth's atmosphere. The evolution of nitrogen biogeochemistry is therefore linked to that of terrestrial environments. More specifically, nitrogen is a fundamental element of life, since it is an integral part of the main molecules of life, such as amino acids or nucleic acids, the building blocks of proteins and DNA. Furthermore, if nitrogen supplies to organisms are too low, they can limit primary productivity, since marine organic matter contains an average of 106 carbon atoms for 16 nitrogen atoms and one phosphorus atom (Redfield ratio). Nitrogen is therefore an important nutrient, which, with phosphorus and iron, controls biological activity.

Finally, different nitrogen molecules have a specific redox state, and most pathways in the nitrogen biogeochemical cycle are controlled by the presence or absence of oxygen in the environment. This makes nitrogen an excellent marker of the redox state of ecosystems. In this chapter, we will explore in more detail how studying the evolution of the nitrogen biogeochemical cycle over geological time allows us to know the oxygenation of past environments, such as during the Great Oxygenation Event of the Earth's atmosphere around the Archean–Proterozoic transition ($\approx$ 2.4 Ga).

6.3.2. *Current major nitrogen reservoirs and fluxes*

On present-day Earth, and since at least the beginning of the Phanerozoic, nitrogen has been present in the atmospheric reservoir in the form of N_2, the most abundant gas in the atmosphere. In the ocean reservoir, it is present in the form of dissolved nitrogen and bioavailable molecules such as ammonium (NH_4^+), nitrite (NO_2^-) and nitrate (NO_3^-), as well as in dissolved and particulate organic forms (DON and PON for dissolved organic nitrogen and particulate organic nitrogen). A fraction of the nitrogen in the water column can be transferred and preserved in the sediment, either as organic nitrogen or as ammonium in clays. All of these forms are interconnected by biogeochemical processes (Figure 6.4).

The biogeochemical nitrogen cycle involves large, relatively inert reservoirs, such as the atmosphere and the Earth's crust, as well as small dynamic and temporary reservoirs on the geological time scale, almost all of which are biological. Thus, the biological assimilation of nitrogen via the fixation of atmospheric N_2 into ammonium NH_4^+ (Figure 6.4), followed by the production of organic nitrogen compounds, supports biological primary production in the long term. Therefore, the biogeochemical cycle of nitrogen in the modern ocean (Figures 6.4 and 6.5C) mainly reflects the fate of nitrogen products in the ocean reservoir and their recycling in interaction with the biosphere, the atmosphere and the geosphere.

The main nitrogen reservoir at the Earth's surface is the atmospheric N_2 reservoir. Biological fixation of N_2 (Figure 6.4) requires hydrolysis of the covalent N≡N bond. This very endergonic reaction (i.e. very thermodynamically unfavorable) can only be carried out by certain prokaryotes called "diazotrophs", possessing the nitrogenase enzyme complex[1]. The biological fixation of N_2 is mainly limited by the availability of phosphate, which the organisms themselves need to multiply. Other elements such as iron or molybdenum can also be biolimiting due to their use as enzymatic cofactors of nitrogenase. Due to its high energy cost for diazotrophic organisms (16 ATP required for the hydrolysis of each N≡N bond), the biological fixation of N_2 is only advantageous when the availability of fixed nitrogen (NH_4^+, NO_3^-) in the environment becomes strongly limiting.

Once fixed (i.e. bioavailable), nitrogen can take part in different biogeochemical processes depending on the oxygen levels in the system. The mineralization of organic nitrogen following the decomposition of phytoplankton biomass releases nitrogen in the form of ammonium (NH_4^+), which can (i) be re-assimilated into the biomass; (ii) be oxidized during nitrification under aerobic conditions by nitrifying bacteria to nitrite (NO_2^-) and then into nitrate (NO_3^-). Nitrification is the source of nitrate in the present-day ocean and provides nitrogen to many heterotrophic organisms. Finally, oceanic organic nitrogen may (iii) fall to the bottom of the water column and be preserved in sedimentary organic matter or possibly as ammonium in clays (Figure 6.4).

The return of nitrogen from the ocean to the atmosphere occurs in the form of N_2. Conversion of nitrate and ammonium into N_2 is permitted by two metabolic pathways, which are: (i) denitrification and (ii) anaerobic oxidation of ammonium (anammox). These two reactions occur under suboxic or anoxic conditions (Figure 6.4). These

1. Nitrogenase is an enzyme complex specific to certain prokaryotic organisms, called diazotrophs. It catalyzes the reduction of N_2 into NH_3, resulting in biological N fixation. Iron, molybdenum, and/or vanadium are metal cofactors. Since nitrogenase is inhibited by the presence of dioxygen, diazotrophs have developed evolutionary strategies to protect it, such as cellular compartmentalization.

processes are placed in a biogeochemical cycle of nitrogen, represented in Figure 6.4, which also shows the value of isotopic fractionations, noted using the symbol ε.

Nitrification reaction:

$$\mathbf{NH_4^+ + 3/2\ O_2 \rightarrow NO_2^- + 2\ H^+ + H_2O}\ \textit{then}\ \mathbf{NO_2^- + 1/2\ O_2 \rightarrow NO_3^-}$$

Denitrification reaction:

$$\mathbf{2\ NO_3^- + 10\ e^- + 12\ H^+ \rightarrow N_2 + 6\ H_2O}$$

Anaerobic ammonium oxidation reaction (anammox):

$$\mathbf{NH_4^+ + NO_2^- \rightarrow N_2 + 2\ H_2O}$$

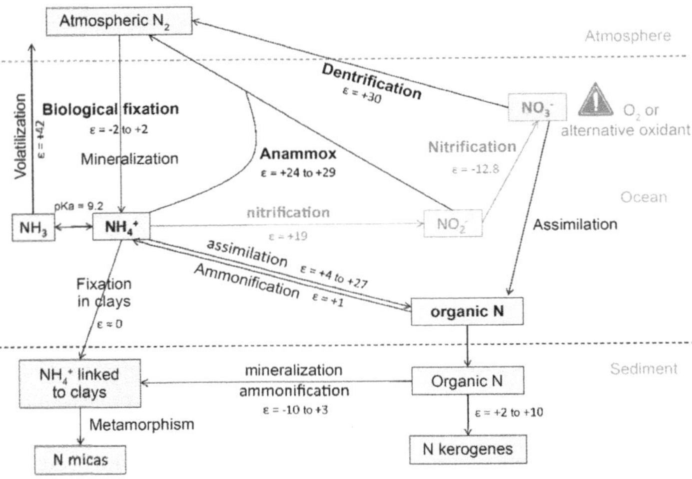

Figure 6.4. *Simplified model of the biogeochemical cycle of nitrogen in modern oceans (modified from Thomazo et al. 2011). Solid arrows represent metabolic pathways. Isotopic fractionations are noted as* $\varepsilon = \delta^{15}N_{reagent} - \delta^{15}N_{product}$. *For a color version of this figure, see www.iste.co.uk/benzerara/geosphere.zip*

6.3.3. *Isotopic systematics of the nitrogen cycle*

The biological fixation of atmospheric N_2 ($\delta^{15}N_{N2}$ = 0‰) by diazotrophs (Figure 6.4), an almost exclusive source of nitrogen for the biosphere, does not cause significant isotopic fractionation between the atmosphere and organic nitrogen (the fractionation being between -2 and +2‰, it is generally considered equal to 0‰). Similarly, the release of ammonium during the mineralization of organic matter in the water column (ammonification) (Figure 6.4) does not significantly fractionate the nitrogen isotopes ($\varepsilon = +1‰$). The ammonium released is a preferential nutrient for organisms. It is therefore rapidly assimilated into the biomass. Even though this reaction preferentially incorporates ^{14}N, it is generally quantitative, which means that the entire ammonium reservoir is consumed. As a result, the fractionation is not expressed: indeed, the isotopic composition of the product is equal to that of the reagent since it has been completely transformed. Under oxic conditions, ammonium can be nitrified into nitrite and then into nitrate by two successive nitrification reactions (Figure 6.4). The fractionations of these two reactions compensate each other ($\varepsilon = +19‰$ and $-12.8‰$, respectively). Subsequently, nitrite and nitrate can be re-assimilated by photosynthetic organisms or reduced by denitrification or anammox under dysoxic and anoxic conditions (Figure 6.4). Denitrification and anammox preferentially use ^{14}N, and, when they are not quantitative, they, respectively, leave the nitrate and ammonium reservoirs highly enriched in ^{15}N. The fractionation induced by these reactions can go as far as $\varepsilon = +30‰$.

Thus, the isotopic composition of the primary producers of an ecosystem depends on the isotopic composition of the assimilated nitrogen source(s) (NH_4^+, NO_3^-, N_2 and dissolved organic nitrogen DON), which depend on the isotopic fractionation associated with each metabolic pathway producing or consuming them (fixation, ammonification, nitrification, denitrification, anammox, etc.).

In today's oceans, sedimentary $\delta^{15}N$ values of approximately +5‰ result from the balance between biological fixation (input) and denitrification/anammox (output) (Figure 6.5C).

6.3.4. *Ancient geological nitrogen records: preservation, reservoirs and fluxes*

In sedimentary rocks, nitrogen is preserved mainly as organic nitrogen in fossil organic matter, and also as ammonium NH_4^+ which, released from decomposing organic matter during diagenesis, replaces potassium (K^+) and enters the crystal lattice of phyllosilicates (clays) such as illite or smectite (Figure 6.4). After metamorphism, this "mineral" ammonium can be found in micas. These nitrogen forms preserved in rocks over the geological time scale are, except for a few fluid inclusions, the only tools available to indirectly trace the nitrogen cycle on the primitive Earth.

Nevertheless, it is necessary to keep in mind that for the isotopic signature of organic nitrogen preserved in sedimentary rocks to be used as a tracer of the isotopic composition of primary producers in the water column at a given time in Earth history, some parameters must be respected. First, the isotopic signature must not have been modified by post-depositional processes such as metamorphism, surface diagenesis in the sediment or diagenesis in the water column. Furthermore, nitrogen must be incorporated into organic matter at isotopic equilibrium, i.e. without fractionation. Finally, the metabolic pathways of the biogeochemical nitrogen cycle and their isotopic effects must be conserved at the evolutionary scale, which allows for the application of the principle of actualism.

The analysis of N_2 contained in fluid inclusions dating back to 3.5 Ga (Nishizawa et al. 2007; Marty et al. 2013) shows isotopic values similar to current values ($\delta^{15}N_{N2} \approx 0‰$) (see Box 6.1). This suggests a geological steady nitrogen cycle since at least 3.5 Ga. If the isotopic composition of the atmospheric nitrogen reservoir has indeed remained stable since the Paleoarchean (3.6–3.2 Ga), then the evolution of metabolisms can be studied using current isotopic fractionation analyses (see section 6.3.4). Since atmospheric oxygen levels have changed dramatically since the Archean (Canfield 2005), and since biological reactions in the nitrogen cycle are strongly dependent on redox speciation in the water column, the evolution of the biogeochemical nitrogen cycle is expected to be recorded in the geological record. Therefore, if the evolution of the nitrogen cycle can be traced using nitrogen remains preserved in rocks, then we have an indirect tracer of changes in ocean redox, as detailed below.

6.3.5. *$\delta^{15}N$ in Precambrian sedimentary rocks: a record of ocean oxygenation*

Beyond the identification of past metabolisms (fixation, nitrification, denitrification), the isotopic composition of nitrogen is especially widely used as a marker of oxidation of paleoenvironments. Indeed, the isotopic composition of nitrogen in biological organic matter is dependent on the redox conditions within the water column, since the biogeochemical reactions of the nitrogen cycle occur at different redox states. Nitrification requires locally oxidizing conditions, while denitrification and anaerobic oxidation of ammonium (anammox) occur under suboxic or anoxic conditions (Figures 6.4 and 6.5). If a relative increase in ^{15}N is detected in the nitrogen of sedimentary organic matter, it is deduced that the phytoplankton biomass contains assimilated nitrates highly enriched in ^{15}N. For this to be the case, a residual nitrate reservoir (i.e. not assimilated within biomass) must be preserved despite denitrification or anammox, and therefore, the initial reservoir must be large enough that it cannot be completely reduced. This only occurs when the ocean water column is sufficiently oxygenated (Figure 6.5). Therefore, sedimentary organic matter with $\delta^{15}N > 5‰$ generally indicates oxygenated ocean conditions, at least in the upper part of the water column. However, caution should be exercised, and such an interpretation should be considered in conjunction with other indicators of oxidation (see Chapter 6).

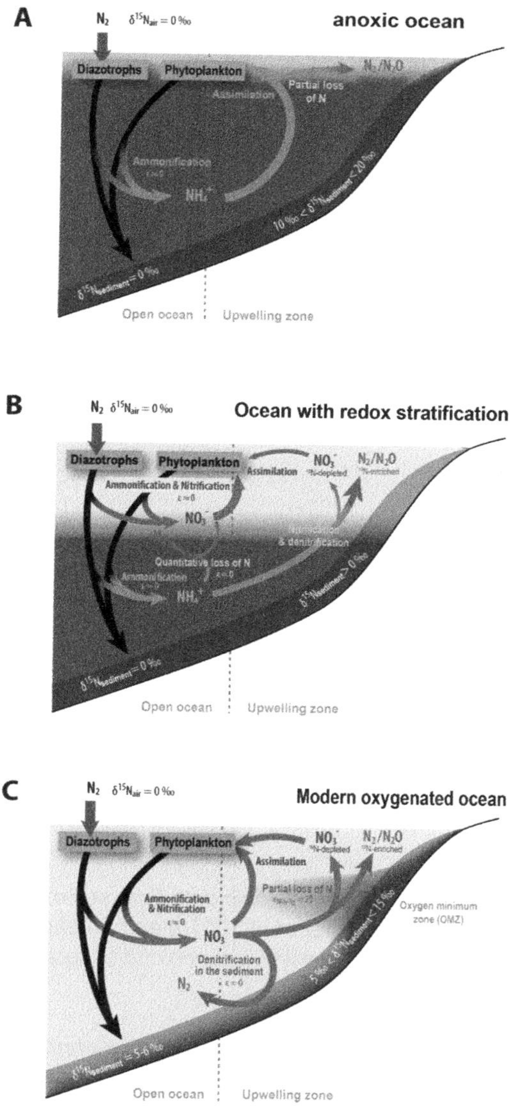

Figure 6.5. *Simplified representation of the redox evolution of the biogeochemical cycle of nitrogen in the oceans from the Precambrian to the present (A then B then C) and the associated isotopic signature of sedimentary nitrogen (modified after Ader et al. 2016). Anoxic zones are shown in red, and oxygenated zones in blue. Isotopic fractionations are indicated in notation ε. For a color version of this figure, see www.iste.co.uk/benzerara/geosphere.zip*

Thus, before the accumulation of significant amounts of oxygen or an alternative oxidant in the Precambrian ocean, the values of $\delta^{15}N$ in sedimentary rocks remain approximately 0‰ (Figure 6.6), reflecting a primitive biogeochemical cycle of nitrogen dominated by the fixation of N_2, ammonification and the assimilation of NH_4^+. The increase in dioxygen contents allowing the initiation of nitrification/denitrification coupling probably took place during the Neoarchean, where positive $\delta^{15}N$ values were measured in different geological formations (Figure 6.6) (Garvin et al. 2009; Godfrey and Falkowski 2009; Thomazo et al. 2011; Stüeken et al. 2015).

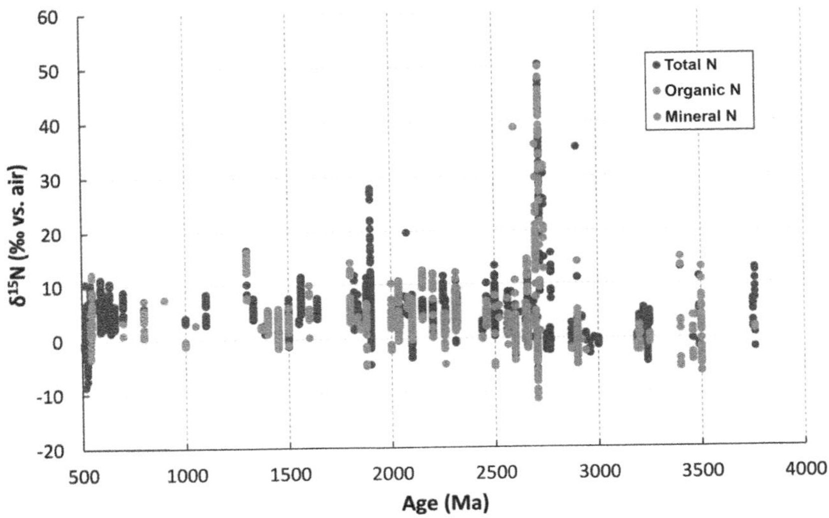

Figure 6.6. *Compilation of nitrogen isotopic data from sedimentary archives over geological time (modified from Ader et al. (2016) and Stüeken et al. (2016)). For a color version of this figure, see www.iste.co.uk/benzerara/geosphere.zip*

Currently, the small number of nitrogen isotope measurements on Archean rocks does not allow us to precisely determine the temporality of the accumulation of oxygen in the oceans, nor to know if certain localities played a key role in forming "oxygen oases", i.e. spatially limited areas where oxygen contents were higher. Increasing the number of isotope data and coupling with other redox tracers should allow us to deepen our understanding of ocean oxygenation.

6.3.6. *Distinguishing local effects from global changes*

As mentioned for carbon isotopes, one of the major difficulties in interpreting geochemical signals recorded in sedimentary rocks is to transpose them to the scale of an entire water column, a sedimentary basin or even a global ocean. In other words, it is difficult to determine whether the environmental conditions determined from the study of isotopic fractionations can be generalized on a large scale.

For example, we may wonder whether disturbances in the biogeochemical nitrogen cycle occurred on a global scale at 2.7 Ga ago. Indeed, sedimentary rocks with a strong positive nitrogen anomaly (values of $\delta^{15}N$ up to +50‰) have been found within the geological formation of Tumbiana (2.72 Ga, Pilbara Craton, Australia) (Thomazo et al. 2011; Stüeken et al. 2015). This extreme isotopic anomaly seems to correspond to a primary signature, because the rocks of the Tumbiana formation are only slightly metamorphosed. Two hypotheses have been formulated to explain it.

– the beginning of nitrification, which would correspond to the beginning of the accumulation of oxygen in the oceans several hundred million years before the GOE (see Chapter 4);

– an ammonium enrichment in ^{15}N following the volatilization of ammonia (NH_3) at a high pH, in the particular alkaline lake context where those rocks may have formed (Figure 6.1) (Stüeken et al. 2015).

The first hypothesis argues for a redox change in the oceans at approximately 2.7 Ga, therefore on a global scale, while the second argues for an alkaline lake, therefore on a regional and non-global scale. Although these two scenarios are not incompatible, this example shows how difficult it is to disentangle local effects from global changes.

The best strategy remains to couple several available indicators, for example, independent tracers sensitive to the redox degree (such as iron, manganese, molybdenum, etc.), on the same series of rock samples, then to generalize this practice to different sedimentary basins of the same age in varied geological contexts.

6.4. General conclusions – from a geochemical cycle to a biogeochemical cycle: how to detect the appearance of the first biological fluxes of nitrogen and carbon?

Several abiotic sources and fluxes of nitrogen have been identified. The most important are photochemical reduction and hydrothermal reduction of N_2, which produce ammonia (NH_3) and ammonium ions (NH_4^+), meteorite impacts and lightning which produce nitrogen oxides (NO_x, x can be 1, 2 or 3), and volcanism which produces nitric acid (HNO_3). However, modeling tends to show that these abiotic nitrogen fluxes on Earth were extremely low. Indeed, they are all estimated to have been less than 10^{12} moles N/year, while biological fixation is 10^{13} moles N/year (Stüeken et al. 2016). These fluxes therefore seem incompatible with the biomass estimated from the quantities of organic carbon (TOC for total organic carbon) from the Paleoarchean. In addition, the $\delta^{13}C_{org}$ of organic matter shows values compatible with biological metabolisms (photosynthesis, methanogenesis, methanotrophy) since at least 3.5 Ga (Schidllowski 2001). Nevertheless, it is important to emphasize that the quantities of mineral and organic nitrogen preserved in sedimentary rocks are not always representative of the quantities of nitrogen initially present in the water column. Indeed, a large part of the nitrogen in the water column is not necessarily consumed or preserved in the sediment and can also be lost by devolatilization during metamorphism.

The search for couplings with other isotopic systems at local and global scales, such as iron or sulfur, is an avenue to explore the appearance of biological mechanisms and their impact on biogeochemical cycles during the history of the Earth.

6.5. References

Ader, M., Thomazo, C., Sansjofre, P., Busigny, V., Papineau, D., Laffont, R., Cartigny, P., Halverson, G.P. (2016). Interpretation of the nitrogen isotopic composition of Precambrian sedimentary rocks: Assumptions and perspectives. *Chemical Geology*, 429, 93–110.

Cadeau, P., Jézéquel, D., Leboulanger, C., Fouilland, E., Floc'h, L., Chaduteau, C., Milesi, V., Guélard, J., Sarazin, G., Katz, A. et al. (2020). Carbon isotope evidence for large methane emissions to the Proterozoic atmosphere. *Scientific Reports*, 10(1), 1–13.

Canfield, D.E. (2005). The early history of atmospheric oxygen: Homage to Robert M. Garrels. *Annual Review of Earth and Planetary Sciences*, 33, 1–36.

Cartigny, P., Harris, J.W., Javoy, M. (1998). Eclogitic diamond formation at Jwaneng: No room for a recycled component. *Science*, 280(5368), 1421–1424.

Catling, D.C., Zahnle, K.J., McKay, C.P. (2001). Biogenic methane, hydrogen escape, and the irreversible oxidation of early Earth. *Science*, 293(5531), 839–843.

Craig, H. (1961). Standard for reporting concentrations of deuterium and oxygen-18 in natural waters. *Science*, 133(3467), 1833–1834.

Des Marais, D.J. (1997). Isotopic evolution of the biogeochemical carbon cycle during the Proterozoic Eon. *Organic Geochemistry*, 27(5–6), 185–193.

Frimmel, H.E. (2010). On the reliability of stable carbon isotopes for Neoproterozoic chemostratigraphic correlation. *Precambrian Research*, 182(4), 239–253.

Gaillard, F., Scaillet, B., Arndt, N.T. (2011). Atmospheric oxygenation caused by a change in volcanic degassing pressure. *Nature*, 478(7368), 229–232.

Garvin, J., Buick, R., Anbar, A.D., Arnold, G.L., Kaufman, A.J. (2009). Isotopic Evidence for an aerobic nitrogen cycle in the Latest Archean. *Science*, 323, 1045–1048.

Godfrey, L.V. and Falkowski, P.G. (2009). The cycling and redox state of nitrogen in the Archaean ocean. *Nature Geoscience*, 2, 725–729.

Grotzinger, J.P., Fike, D.A., Fischer, W.W. (2011). Enigmatic origin of the largest-known carbon isotope excursion in Earth's history. *Nature Geoscience*, 4(5), 285–292.

Halverson, G.P., Hoffman, P.F., Schrag, D.P., Maloof, A.C., Rice, A.H.N. (2005). Toward a Neoproterozoic composite carbon-isotope record. *GSA Bulletin*, 117(9–10), 1181–1207.

Hayes, J.M., Strauss, H., Kaufman, A.J. (1999). The abundance of ^{13}C in marine organic matter and isotopic fractionation in the global biogeochemical cycle of carbon during the past 800 Ma. *Chemical Geology*, 161(1–3), 103–125.

Karhu, J.A. and Holland, H.D. (1996). Carbon isotopes and the rise of atmospheric oxygen. *Geology*, 24(10), 867–870.

Kasting, J.F. (2013). What caused the rise of atmospheric O_2? *Chemical Geology*, 362, 13–25.

Krissansen-Totton, J., Buick, R., Catling, D.C. (2015). A statistical analysis of the carbon isotope record from the Archean to Phanerozoic and implications for the rise of oxygen. *American Journal of Science*, 315(4), 275–316.

Marty, B., Zimmermann, L., Pujol, M., Burgess, R., Philippot, P. (2013). Nitrogen isotopic composition and density of the Archean atmosphere. *Science*, 342, 101–104.

Nishizawa, M., Sano, Y., Ueno, Y., Maruyama, S. (2007). Speciation and isotope ratios of nitrogen in fluid inclusions from seafloor hydrothermal deposits at ~ 3.5 Ga. *Earth and Planetary Science Letters*, 254, 332–344.

Och, L.M. and Shields-Zhou, G.A. (2012). The Neoproterozoic oxygenation event: Environmental perturbations and biogeochemical cycling. *Earth-Science Reviews*, 110(1–4), 26–57.

Prave, A.R., Kirsimäe, K., Lepland, A., Fallick, A.E., Kreitsmann, T., Deines, Y.E., Romashkin, A.E., Rychanchik, D.V., Medvedev, P.V., Moussavou, M. et al. (2022). The grandest of them all: The Lomagundi–Jatuli Event and Earth's oxygenation. *Journal of the Geological Society*, 179(1).

Schidlowski, M. (2001). Carbon isotopes as biogeochemical recorders of life over 3.8 Ga of Earth history: Evolution of a concept. *Precambrian Research*, 106, 117–134.

Stüeken, E.E., Buick, R., Schauer, A.J. (2015). Nitrogen isotope evidence for alkaline lakes on late Archean continents. *Earth and Planetary Science Letters*, 411, 1–10.

Stüeken, E.E., Kipp, M.A., Koehler, M.C., Buick, R. (2016). The evolution of Earth's biogeochemical nitrogen cycle. *Earth-Science Reviews*, 160, 220–239.

Swart, P.K. and Kennedy, M.J. (2012). Does the global stratigraphic reproducibility of $\delta^{13}C$ in Neoproterozoic carbonates require a marine origin? A Pliocene–Pleistocene comparison. *Geology*, 40(1), 87–90.

Thomazo, C., Ader, M., Philippot, P. (2011). Extreme 15N-enrichments in 2.72-Gyr-old sediments: Evidence for a turning point in the nitrogen cycle. *Geobiology*, 9, 107–120.

7

Modeling the Biosphere and Its Interactions with the Geosphere

Guillaume LE HIR
Institut de Physique du Globe de Paris, Université de Paris Cité, France

7.1. Introduction

The physicochemical evolutions of the atmosphere and oceans are strongly influenced by interactions with the lithosphere and the biosphere (see Chapter 5). The oceans probably appeared around 4.4 Ga ago, as indicated by oxygen isotopic analyses carried out on zircons from Jack Hills (Valley et al. 2005). Exchanges with the biosphere were established later, between 4 and 3.45 Ga (i.e. after life appeared). These reciprocal interactions, closely linked to the presence of water, explain the coevolution of the Earth's outer envelopes.

Understanding the processes behind these interactions has very early on aroused interest in the scientific community. The relationships between living organisms and their environment were first explored from a zoology perspective. At the beginning of the 19th century, Georges Cuvier, based on the principles of comparative anatomy, established the existence of major paleontological disasters. These biodiversity crises, which we now call mass extinctions, were, for Cuvier, the "revolutions of the surface of the globe". To understand the recurrence of these "revolutions", Cuvier was interested in the glacial theory that Swiss geologists (Venetz, Perraudin, Charpentier, Agassiz) had just proposed. As a supporter of

Interactions between the Geosphere and the Biosphere,
coordinated by Karim BENZERARA and Christophe THOMAZO.

catastrophism, he attributed the changes in fossil faunas to a succession of catastrophes due to major climatic events. This idea of a co-evolution of geological and biological events marked the beginning of the modern study of the history of life and the Earth.

The development of isotopic dating during the 20th century made it possible to establish temporal correlations between traces of ancient life and the evolution of the Earth's environment. It was thus established that major mass extinctions were contemporaneous with exceptional geological phenomena, such as meteorite impacts, or major volcanic eruptions (Bond and Grasby 2017) (see Chapter 8). This confirmed Cuvier's intuition regarding the effect of major environmental disturbances on living things.

Today, the study of interactions between living organisms and their environment is carried out on much smaller scales. Remote sensing makes it possible to study the spatio-temporal variability of biological activity with its environment. Since 2009, the Tara-Ocean campaign has aimed to characterize the response of phytoplankton to anthropogenic disturbance, including changes in the genetic expression of the taxa present (see: https://oceans.taraexpeditions.org/). It makes it possible to obtain a combined image of the phytoplankton biodiversity and the abiotic factors of the environment such as temperature, salinity or the concentration of nutrients in the water, for example (Bork et al. 2015; Sunagawa et al. 2015).

From Cuvier's work to the Tara-Ocean mission, the interactions of living organisms with the geosphere appear infinitely complex to us today. To decipher the mechanisms involved, we can rely on numerical modeling. In the rest of this chapter, we will see how models (see Box 7.1) integrate the main biosphere–geosphere interactions through three examples: 1) anthropogenic disturbance and ocean biomass; 2) the effects of the colonization of continents by plants on the climate; and finally 3) mass extinctions.

Although computing power is improving, the extreme complexity of the interactions of living organisms with their environment requires us to make simplifications to be able to model this system. Two main paths have been taken to model the biosphere:

1) A simpler approach where the biosphere is only represented on a global scale by its biomass, independently of biodiversity (Figure 7.1). This is the approach used in box models. Box models are models where each large reservoir (ocean, atmosphere, lithosphere, etc.) is represented by a "box", of finite volume, whose physicochemical composition evolves according to the flows with the other boxes. This is the same

principle as for the geochemical cycles already presented in several chapters of this book. Thus, the biosphere (we consider it as a box) interacts with the Earth's fluid envelopes (the atmosphere and the ocean) and the surface of the lithosphere. These flows can be described in a complex way, varying according to one or more parameters (e.g. the biological pump) or simply fixed (like the water flows between the boxes). This type of model does not have spatial dimensions (longitude, latitude, altitude/depth). Box models are dedicated to the study of interactions between the different boxes and biogeochemical cycles over long periods of time (> 1 Ma). In addition, the objective is to represent the global effects on the chemical composition of the fluid envelopes. The best known of these models is the GEOCARB model (Berner 2004) and its renowned predecessor, the BLAG model (Berner et al. 1983), which we will detail later.

2) A second, more recent approach involves representing the biosphere by its biomass and biodiversity. These models explicitly describe the functioning of the main components of the Earth system (atmosphere, hydrosphere, cryosphere and biosphere). These models, developed from general circulation models ("GCM") since the middle of the 20th century, are used in so-called Earth System models (Figure 7.2). They integrate a 3D-climate model that calculates the physics and dynamics of the ocean and the atmosphere (AOGCM for Atmospheric Ocean General Circulation Model). They also include a model of marine biogeochemical cycles that simulates biogeochemical cycles (e.g. the carbon cycle) by integrating the lower trophic levels of marine ecosystems (plankton), the chemistry of carbonates as well as the biogeochemical cycles of oxygen (O) and the main nutrients: phosphorus (P), nitrogen (N), iron (Fe), silicon (Si). The Earth System models also integrate a continental surface model that simulates the hydrological cycle, vegetation and carbon cycle on the continents. It allows for the calculation of energy, water and carbon exchanges between the atmosphere and the continental biosphere by explicitly integrating the processes of photosynthesis and evapotranspiration at the soil and vegetation level. Even though they are very complex, these Earth System models simplify the diversity of the biosphere and are based on the definition of large functional groups[1] (e.g. the group "phytoplankton", "the boreal forest") and not on the specific diversity, which is far too complex. Since photosynthesis ensures 95% of global primary production, other forms of metabolism (e.g. chemosynthesis) are not included here. Similarly, among photosynthetic organisms, primary producers are grouped according to "functional" sets (e.g. phytoplankton, diatoms, zooplankton for the ocean and functional types of plants for continental surfaces). This type of model is now used for modeling exercises by the Intergovernmental Panel on Climate Change (IPCC).

Box 7.1. *Two approaches, two levels of model complexity*

1. A functional group is a grouping of species that share a common set of attributes and play a particular role in ecosystem processes.

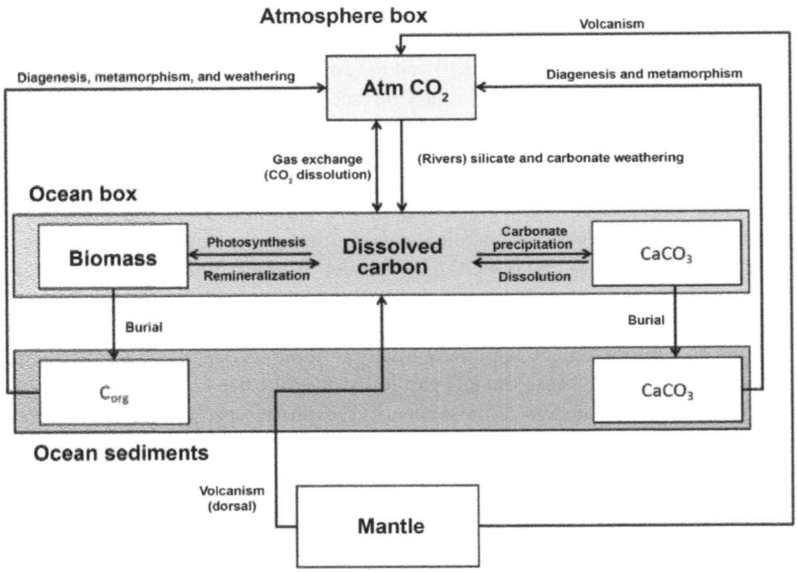

Figure 7.1. *Example of a box model of the carbon cycle. The processes generating the fluxes between the boxes are shown. For a color version of this figure, see: www.iste.co.uk/benzerara/geosphere.zip*

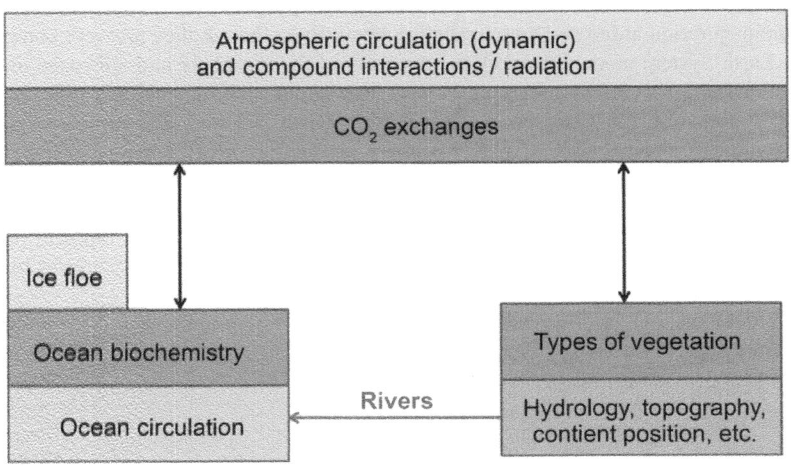

Figure 7.2. *Simplified example of an Earth System model. For a color version of this figure, see: www.iste.co.uk/benzerara/geosphere.zip*

7.2. Response of the biosphere to current global changes

7.2.1. *Anthropogenic disturbance: the fragility of the atmosphere and the ocean*

Since the industrial revolution in the 19th century, humans have been disrupting the carbon cycle (Ciais et al 2013; see: https://gml.noaa.gov/aggi/aggi.html). This disturbance may seem small compared to natural flows (approximately 7–9 $GtC.year^{-1}$ of anthropogenic emissions over the 2000–2010 decade and nearly 10 $GtC.year^{-1}$ in 2019 compared to about 120 $GtC.year^{-1}$ of CO_2 emitted by cellular respiration, for example[2]). But, unlike natural flows (including respiration), anthropogenic CO_2 emissions are not offset by new natural or anthropogenic sinks. At this rate, the increase in atmospheric CO_2 content is expected to reach 3–4 ppmv/year[3]. However, it was only approxiamtely 2 ppmv/year in the decade 2000–2010. This means that half of the CO_2 emitted is absorbed. The ocean plays a major role in this absorption (~ 25%), the second sink being the continental biosphere with a comparable action (see section 7.2.2). In parallel with this destabilization of the carbon cycle, we observe a drop in the dissolved oxygen content (O_{2d}) in the surface ocean (between 0 and 100 meters). The warming of the waters limits the dissolution of atmospheric O_2 in the surface ocean and increases its stratification (vertical mixing is reduced). These factors favor the extension of areas with low O_{2d} content, which are described as dysoxic (the O_{2d} content is less than 30% of the O_2 saturation of water) or anoxic (zero O_{2d} content). These two observations illustrate the fragility of the fluid envelopes, the atmosphere and the hydrosphere, with respect to the current anthropogenic disturbance. The atmosphere is very sensitive to variations in CO_2, while the ocean is more sensitive to those of O_2. These different responses are due to the solubility of these two gases in the ocean. The solubility of CO_2 is very high, while that of O_2 is very low (respectively, 3.3 and 0.014 g/L with water at a temperature of 0°C). The ocean therefore represents the main reservoir of carbon, while the atmosphere is the main reservoir of O_2. CO_2 is a minor gas in the atmosphere (pCO_2 ~ 420 ppmv) compared to N_2, O_2 and argon (Ar). Its concentration in the atmospheric reservoir can therefore easily vary (also modifying the intensity of the greenhouse effect) if the carbon cycle is unbalanced. Conversely, and by the same reasoning, the O_2 concentration of ocean surface waters can easily vary, and these waters can locally become too poor in O_{2d}

2. $GtC.year^{-1}$ or gigatons of carbon per year is equivalent to a flow of 10^9 tons of carbon per year. It is also equivalent to $Petagram.year^{-1}$ (10^{15} g). This is the unit usually used for quantifying carbon fluxes in the carbon cycle.

3. The unit ppmv stands for parts per million by volume, that is, a volume fraction of one-millionth.

to ensure the survival of aerobic organisms. This problem particularly concerns coastal areas subject to eutrophication.

Paradoxically, despite this fragility of the fluid envelopes, measurements of CO_2 and O_2 from ice show remarkably stable contents over the last million years. This reflects the existence of regulatory processes in the past, which are now undermined by the rate and intensity of the current anthropogenic disturbance. We will see, in the rest of this chapter, how living organisms participate in this regulation and respond to modern disturbances.

7.2.2. *The divergence of response between the continental biosphere and the oceanic biosphere*

The continental biosphere is actively responding to the increase in $CO_{2,atm}$. In fact, the increase in $CO_{2,atm}$ increases the intensity of oxygenic photosynthesis: this is the fertilization effect (equation [7.1]). This mechanism is explained by the carboxylation reaction ensured by the enzyme Rubisco, an enzyme that allows the fixation of inorganic carbon by chlorophyll organisms and ensures the autotrophy of plants with respect to carbon. CO_2 is the source of inorganic carbon necessary for the formation of organic matter (denoted CH_2O or C_{org} in the following).

$$CO_{2atm} + H_2O \rightarrow (CH_2O) + O_{2atm} \qquad [7.1]$$

Ultimately, the fertilization effect activates primary production (primary production corresponding to the synthesis of C_{org} from C inorganic from the atmosphere/ocean). Currently, the continental biosphere takes 120 $GtC.year^{-1}$ to the atmospheric carbon stock (which represents 750 GtC). The relative importance of this flow compared to the stock (15%) partly explains the limiting effect of pCO_2. In addition to this biochemical effect, photosynthesis increases as temperature increases (lengthening of plant growth periods, etc.), but remains limited by precipitation. This limit is explained by the regulation of H_2O losses (evapotranspiration), hence the absence of primary production in hot deserts (Friedlingstein et al. 1992). These three factors: temperature, precipitation and pCO_2, control continental photosynthetic activity.

Thus, the increase in CO_{2atm}, and temperature between the Last Glacial Maximum (~ 18,000 years ago) and the Holocene (~ 10,000 years ago) led to an increase in C_{org} stored in plants (biomass) of ~ 10% (Friedlingstein et al. 1992). As shown in the data (Khatiwala et al. 2009), these mechanisms adjust very rapidly to environmental variations. Since the 1980s, the continental biosphere has absorbed an increasing share of the $CO_{2,atm}$ emitted. Today, it is estimated that 25% of anthropogenic emissions of $CO_{2,atm}$ are absorbed by plants (-2 $GtC.year^{-1}$ of the 8 $GtC.year^{-1}$ emitted on average in the 2000–2010 decade). It is therefore a carbon sink. However, how this sink will evolve remains uncertain, particularly due to deforestation, artificialization of soils, fires and the increase in water stress induced by climate change.

We may expect a similar trend for the ocean biosphere. However, the latter does not seem to change as pCO_2 increases. To understand this apparent paradox, let us look at how the $CO_{2\ anthropogenic}$ is transferred into the ocean.

7.2.3. *Ocean–atmosphere exchanges*

Anthropogenic carbon emissions are initially released into the atmosphere. It is therefore at the atmosphere–ocean interface that the ocean absorbs the anthropogenic CO_2. The intensity of the total C (anthropogenic and non-anthropogenic) flow between the atmosphere and the ocean is approximately 100 $GtC.year^{-1}$. This flow is controlled by physical exchanges of CO_2, dependent on the action of wind and temperature. Henry's law allows the calculation of the content of dissolved CO_2 (CO_{2d}) in the surface ocean at equilibrium from the atmospheric partial pressure of $CO_{2,atm}$:

$$CO_{2d} = k_H\ CO_{2,atm} \qquad [7.2]$$

where k_H is Henry's constant which depends on temperature (and secondly salinity). Its value is 0.037 $mol.kg^{-1}.atm^{-1}$ at 15°C and only 0.032 $mol.kg^{-1}.atm^{-1}$ at 20°C. So, if $CO_{2,atm}$ = 300 ppmv (~ 0.3 10^{-3} atm), the direct effect of the warming of surface waters by 15 to 20°C is an ~ 15 % decrease in CO_{2d} (11.3 to 9.7 10^{-6} $mol.kg^{-1}$).

The exchange flow of CO_2 between the ocean and the atmosphere (FCO_2) is a function of the difference in CO_2 concentration between the surface ocean and the atmosphere (Etcheto et al. 1991) according to the following relationship:

$$FCO_2 = \alpha * (pCO_{2,\ atm} - pCO_{2,\ ocean}) * \text{surface ocean} \qquad [7.3]$$

where α is the diffusion coefficient, a factor dependent on temperature and wind speed.

This flow is negative (~ -2 $GtC.year^{-1}$), i.e. the ocean is a carbon sink. The ocean absorbs the $CO_{2,atm}$, mainly in the Antarctic Ocean because of its cold waters. Therefore, even without the action of living organisms, this relationship shows that the ocean passively efficiently absorbs the $CO_{2,atm}$. We are talking about a physical carbon pump (or solubility pump). In the ocean, dissolved CO_2 (CO_{2d}) reacts with water and quickly transforms into hydrogen carbonate ions (HCO_3^-), a much more stable form (~ 90% of oceanic carbon is in the form of HCO_3^-) given the basic pH of the ocean (~ 8.2). So, there is very little CO_{2d}, which makes the physical pump very efficient. Unfortunately, the dissolution of CO_2 acidifies the oceans (-0.1 pH unit over a century), which increases the concentration of dissolved CO_2 and reduces the efficiency of this carbon sink (see equation [7.2]).

7.2.4. *How the marine biosphere uses carbon*

Is the marine biosphere a carbon sink? Note that photosynthesis is not limited by the availability of water, nor by that of inorganic carbon, which is abundant in the oceans (section 7.2.1). Thus, only a small part of the inorganic carbon dissolved in the ocean is consumed by the biosphere to 1) synthesize organic matter and, in some cases, 2) to produce carbonate shells. Counterintuitively, the formation of calcite by marine organisms tends to increase dissolved CO_2 (CO_{2d}) as shown by the following reaction:

$$2HCO_3^- + Ca^{2+} \rightarrow CaCO_3 + CO_{2d} + H_2O \qquad [7.4]$$

This biocalcification (equation [7.4]) occurs mainly in the first 100 meters of the ocean (called the photic zone), leading to a slight increase in the concentration of CO_{2d}, which reduces the ocean/atmosphere transfer of CO_2 (equation [7.3]). However, this reaction is compensated by the formation of organic matter (CH_2O):

$$CO_{2d} + H_2O \rightarrow (CH_2O) + O_{2d} \qquad [7.5]$$

By consuming the CO_{2d}, reaction (equation [7.5]) activates the ocean/atmosphere transfer reaction of CO_2 (equation [7.3]), which allows an ~ 10% increase in carbon in the ocean (DeVries 2022). In addition, this organic carbon formed descends into the oceanic column, a mechanism known as a biological pump (Ducklow and Harris 1993).

Below we will discuss the representation of the biological pump in models to understand how it is affected when the pCO_2 is modified.

7.2.4.1. *A matter of speed*

To model the biological pump, it is necessary to first assess the current situation. Although the marine organic carbon stock (3 GtC) is 200 times smaller than the continental stock (600 GtC), the primary production of marine phytoplankton is 50 $GtC.year^{-1}$ (Field et al. 1998) against 120 $GtC.year^{-1}$ for the continental biosphere as mentioned before. The difference between the total stock and primary productivity is explained by the rapid proliferation of phytoplankton and its significant consumption by heterotrophic organisms. All marine ecosystems that constitute the marine biosphere therefore depend on phytoplankton, the basic link in trophic networks.

By taking dissolved carbon from the surface ocean and transforming it into C_{org} (equation [7.5]), then transferring this C_{org} towards the seabed, the biological pump promotes the transfer of inorganic carbon (CO_2) from the atmosphere to the ocean. Without a biological pump, the ocean's dissolved carbon content would be 10% lower than today, and the $pCO_{2,atm}$ at equilibrium with this ocean would be twice as high (DeVries 2022). An increase in the biological pump can therefore increase the stock of dissolved carbon in the ocean and lower the $pCO_{2,atm}$. However, if the activity of the biological pump weakens, this sequestration will cease because the ocean circulation mixes the surface layers with the deep layers on a millennial scale.

Of the 50 $GtC.year^{-1}$ produced, the biological pump exports 10 $GtC.year^{-1}$ to the deep ocean (Intergovernmental Panel on Climate Change (IPCC) 2014). This means that the 40 GtC not exported are remineralized before reaching the ocean floor. Remineralization is a conversion of the C_{org} into CO_{2d} (opposite of reaction [7.5] if the environment is oxygenated) carried out by heterotrophic organisms living in the water column (i.e. feeding on organic matter, they carry out aerobic respiration). However, there is no accumulation of C_{org} in the deep ocean, only a small portion of the C_{org} exported to the ocean floor is effectively buried in the sediment and preserved from oxidation (0.2 $GtC.year^{-1}$). The sequestration rate of the C_{org} in sediments depends on the sedimentation rate (~ 1 $cm.kyear^{-1}$). This is therefore a mechanism that does not depend on the biosphere. Only this very low flow (0.2 $GtC.year^{-1}$) is a carbon sink. Its impact is 10 times slower than the C_{org} sink generated by continental biomass (2 $GtC.year^{-1}$), and therefore very low compared to the speed of human disturbance. Paradoxically, it is this low flow that generated the large oil reserves that we consume today.

On the continent, the storage of C_{org} in sedimentary basins is similar. This storage can produce coal, such as during the Carboniferous in France. However, these episodes of coal formation are rare. It is considered that sedimentary formations are regularly eroded and altered. Consequently, the net balance of continental organic carbon storage is close to zero.

To summarize, the oceanic biosphere participates in carbon storage via the biological pump, by sequestering C_{org} in sediments. This is a very weak flux and its effect is only perceptible on long time scales (10^4 years). In the short term

(< 10^3 years), when the $pCO_{2,atm}$ increases, the carbon stock contained in the oceanic biomass does not increase, whereas the amount of carbon stored in the continental biomass increases. However, in the long term, the continental biosphere does not act as a carbon sink, because all of the buried C_{org} is oxidized during erosion and weathering processes. These different behaviors explain two points: 1) the preservation of C_{org} is different for the ocean and the continent and 2) the increase in oceanic biomass is not only dependent on the carbon content (this question will be studied in the following section).

In terms of modeling, the existence of short- and long-term effects has direct implications. To study anthropogenic disturbances, it is necessary to consider the continental biosphere, the biological pump for its effect on the dissolution of atmospheric carbon, and therefore ocean dynamics. On the other hand, the effect of C_{org} sequestration is anecdotal. Conversely, over long periods (millions of years), only C_{org} sequestration is important if we seek to understand the effects of the biosphere on pCO_2 (see section 7.3.1). In the remainder of this chapter, only factors acting in the short term will be discussed.

7.2.4.2. *Limiting factors of oceanic primary production*

Why does ocean biomass not increase when the pCO_2 levels rise? Primary production in the surface ocean is extremely variable spatially (Figure 7.3) and suggests that CO_2, temperature and light are not the only factors limiting primary production. Thus, we see that areas of high productivity are associated with upwellings, present at the eastern edge of oceans in subtropical zones. These upwellings of deep, cold, nutrient-rich waters are particularly rich in phosphate and explain this variation in productivity. Indeed, phosphate is biolimiting: it plays a major role in the synthesis of organic molecules including ATP and nucleic acids DNA and RNA. The primary production reaction can be written as follows:

$$106CO_2 + 16HNO_3 + H_3PO_4 + 78H_2O \rightarrow C_{106}H_{175}O_{42}N_{16}P + 150O_2 \qquad [7.6]$$

The stoichiometric formula obtained for the organic matter thus formed is often called the Redfield ratio after its discoverer (Redfield et al. 1963). The C/P ratio in the oceanic organic matter produced is approximately 106 C to 1 P (Anderson 1995). From this ratio, the potential primary production of the ocean can be calculated based on the available P concentration.

$$\text{Primary Production} = [PO_4^{3-}] * Vol_{ocean,surf} * C/P * M_C \qquad [7.7]$$

The assumption is that in one year, all of the phosphorus available in the surface ocean (site of primary productivity) is used to synthesize biomass. Considering the average concentration of phosphate in the ocean (denoted $[PO_4^{3-}]$ is ~ 2,000 μmol/m³), the volume of the surface ocean (denoted $Vol_{ocean,surf}$ is ~$34*10^{15}$ m³) and the molar mass of carbon (M_C = 12 g/mol), it is possible to estimate primary production at 87 GtC/year (equation [7.5]). This simple calculation gives a satisfactory order of magnitude of the value of primary production (to be compared to the ~ 50 GtC/year measured). The phosphate concentration of the surface ocean is never zero, primary production is essentially dependent on the phosphate associated with upwellings.

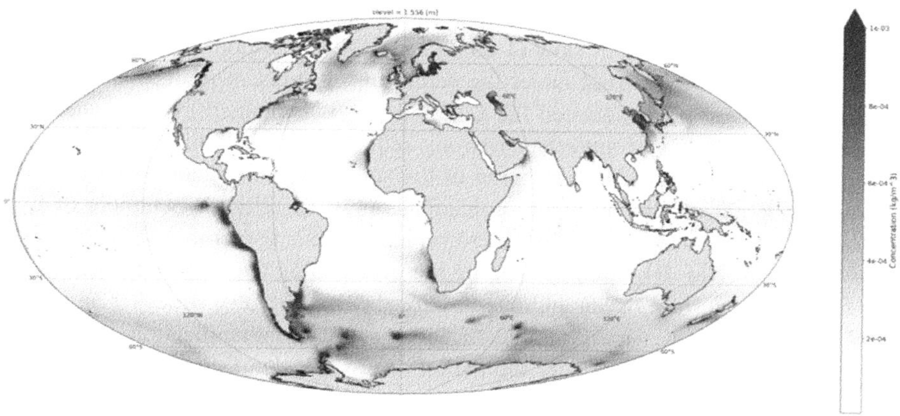

Figure 7.3. *Average chlorophyll concentration in the surface ocean simulated by the Institut Pierre Simon Laplace model for preindustrial conditions (courtesy of F. Fluteau). For a color version of this figure, see: www.iste.co.uk/benzerara/geosphere.zip*

7.2.4.3. *Modeling the biological pump*

How do we quantify the transfer or export of organic matter produced at the surface of the oceans to the ocean floor? The descent of organic matter particles into the water column is a gravitational process described by Stokes' law. This descent is slow (~ 10 m/day for a particle with a diameter of ~ 100 μm) because of the small density difference between the organic matter (ρ_{org} = 1,067 kg/m³) and water (ρ_{ocean} = 1,027 kg/m³) (Logan and Hunt 1987). The smaller the particles (diameter ≤ 100 μm), the slower their transfer. Since the biological pump depends on nutrients, we can use phosphorus, which is soluble, to simplify the problem. From then on, it becomes possible to calculate the export of organic carbon from phosphorus by considering only the vertical mixing which integrates all the vertical movements of water between the surface and deep ocean (diving zones, upwellings, etc.).

$$PO_4^{3-} \text{ export} = M\,([PO_4^{3-}]_{deep} - [PO_4^{3-}]_{surface}) \qquad [7.8]$$

where $[PO_4^{3-}]_{deep} \sim 2{,}000$ µmol/m³, $[PO_4^{3-}]_{surface} \sim 0$ µmol/m³ (here, it is assumed that all of the PO_4^{3-} is consumed at the surface and even if the PO_4^{3-} concentration is not zero in absolute terms, it is neglected), and M is the flow of water exchanged between the surface ocean and the deep ocean. This flow is close to ~ 30 Sv (1 Sv = 10^6 m³/s). This gives an export of PO_4^{3-} of approximately 0.14 Gt/year, equivalent to 1.9 GtC.year^{-1}. As mentioned earlier, there is a significant gap between the C_{org} flux reaching the ocean floor (~ 2 GtC.year^{-1}) and the C_{org} buried (~ 0.2 GtC.year^{-1}). In fact, the C_{org} is buried passively with a speed that depends on the sediment flow (1 cm.kyear^{-1}). At the bottom of the oceans, the C_{org} is therefore remineralized under the action of $O_{2,d}$ present in deep water. This biogeochemical coupling between the C_{org} and $O_{2,d}$ is explained by their chemical properties: the CO_2/C_{org} couple has a strong reducing power, while O_2/H_2O has a strong oxidizing power. The calculation of the standard free enthalpy (ΔG^0) shows that the oxidation of C_{org} by O_2 is spontaneous (420 kJ released per mole of C_{org} oxidized)[4]. This energy is used by heterotrophic organisms (aerobic respiration) to ensure their survival. By simply modeling the ocean using two superimposed boxes (one box for the surface ocean and one box for the deep ocean), Broecker and Peng (1982) showed that the main source of PO_4^{3-} is the remineralization of organic matter in the water column under the action of $O_{2,d}$. Without this remineralization and without mixing between the surface and deep ocean (including upwellings), the concentration of PO_4^{3-} of the surface ocean would rapidly tend towards 0. This means that the concentrations of phosphorus, organic carbon and other compounds present in the ocean depend as much on biological processes, through remineralization, as on its dynamics.

However, in the long term (i.e. several thousand years), this simplification also has its limits. Indeed, in theory, we should see a decrease in oceanic phosphate due to its sequestration (~ 0.77 Mt/year). This phosphate loss is compensated by continental inputs (Meybeck 1982). Transiently, the sequestration of carbon and phosphate in sediments can exceed inputs by rivers, but this situation cannot last, otherwise the ocean phosphate content would get close to 0 (equation [7.9]). Ultimately, it is therefore continental inputs that control the phosphate content of the ocean and consequently primary productivity in the oceans.

This defines a steady state where gains and losses balance out:

4. $*\Delta G^0 = - n * F * \Delta E^0$, where $\Delta E^0 = E^0$ acceptor - E^0 donor. Here, $\Delta E^0 = E^0_{O2/H2O} - E^0_{CO2/Corg}$, where $E^0_{O2/H2O} = 0.8$ V, $E^0_{CO2/Corg} = -0.29$V, n = 4 (number of electrons exchanged) and F is the Faraday constant (96500 C/mol). This chemical reaction depends on the concentration of the reactants but also on the temperature.

$$dM_P/dt = (d[PO_4^{3-}]_{surface} * Vol_{ocean\ surf})/dt = 0 \qquad [7.9]$$

where M_P is the amount of phosphorus (in moles) in the surface ocean and dM_P/dt is the variation in this quantity over time. This example illustrates the fragility of biogeochemical cycles, their balance depending on exchanges between the ocean, the atmosphere, the continents and living organisms.

7.2.5. *The biological pump and anthropogenic disturbance*

Future projections of the efficiency of the biological pump are complex and suggest its increase at high latitudes and its decrease in temperate and tropical zones (Bopp et al. 2001). This implies that no significant effect will occur on the reduction of the anthropogenic pCO_2. In detail, if surface waters become warmer, then the vertical density gradient of the water column will increase and reduce vertical mixing. This phenomenon is called "stratification" of the water column. This stratification primarily affects low latitudes where surface waters are significantly warmer than deep waters. In these regions of the ocean where nutrient availability is the limiting factor, the decrease in vertical mixing will further reduce the availability of nutrients (such as phosphate) from remineralization, and therefore potentially the biological pump. Conversely, in regions where nutrients are abundant, a slightly stronger carbon export is expected due to the increase in primary productivity, balanced by more intense remineralization. At the same time, acidification will reduce the capacity of the oceans to absorb CO_2 (see section 7.2.3). In the longer term, other factors must be considered. These mechanisms are not yet included in models and future projections. Until now, the evolution of the quantity of phosphate from continental flows for the next century is poorly constrained. Indeed, if chemical alteration is favored in a warm climate (Chapter 1), changes in the hydrological cycle are still poorly constrained. Similarly, if the temperature of surface waters increases by 2°C, the repetition of heat waves may exceed the resilience capacity of organisms. It is therefore more the environmental sensitivity of organisms that will play a role. This mechanism is still poorly understood, and it is the purpose of Tara-Ocean missions to understand how organisms respond to rapid changes in their environment.

Ultimately, the biosphere's responses can be summarized as follows: the growth of the continental biosphere is limited by CO_2[5]; the growth of the oceanic biosphere is, however, very limited by the availability of phosphorus, itself constrained by the

5. Phosphate is also a limiting factor for the continental biosphere, hence the use of phosphorus-rich fertilizers. However, the high abundance of phosphate within the continental crust makes its effect less notable.

phenomena of stratification of the water column and remineralization of organic matter at depth. In addition, this deep organic matter has a significant impact on the oxygenation of water as we detail it below.

7.2.6. *The problem of regulating ocean oxygen*

Compared to primary productivity provided by phytoplankton (~ 50 $GtC.year^{-1}$), carbon sequestration in the sediment remains extremely low (0.2 $GtC.year^{-1}$) due to the remineralization of most of the organic carbon by ocean O_{2d} via aerobic respiration. This reaction takes place as long as the dissolved oxygen concentration is sufficient (dissolved threshold O_2 > 1 $mmol/m^3$). Remineralization enriches the deep ocean with carbon, but in return it reduces the O_{2d} content in the water column: the greater the quantity of C_{org} formed at the surface, the more O_2 is consumed at depth.

As shown by Sarmiento et al. (1988), the biological pump should eventually cause anoxia of the deep ocean. The remineralization equation is the reverse reaction of photosynthesis (Anderson 1995) and in stoichiometric terms, for one mole of PO_4^{3-} released, 150 moles of O_2 are consumed (equation [7.4]). As the amount of O_{2d} in the ocean is quite low for solubility reasons (see section 7.2.1), the remineralization of one mole of organic carbon leads to an apparently critical situation for $[O_{2d}]_{deep\ ocean}$:

$$[O_{2d}]_{deep} - [O_{2d}]_{surface} = -150\ ([PO_4^{3-}]_{deep} - [PO_4^{3-}]_{surface})$$

Therefore,

$$[O_{2d}]_{deep} = [O_{2d}]_{surface} - 150\ ([PO_4^{3-}]_{deep} - [PO_4^{3-}]_{surface}) \qquad [7.10]$$

In fact, if we use the average values according to which $[PO_4^{3-}]_{deep}$ = 2,000 $\mu mol/m^3$, $[PO_4^{3-}]_{surface}$ = 0 $\mu mol/m^3$ and $[O_{2d}]_{surface}$ = 170 $mmol/m^3$), therefore $[O_{2d}]_{deep} < 0$.

Obtaining a negative value (impossible in reality) comes from the model having too low a complexity. Box models tend to simulate generalized anoxia (Sarmiento and Orr 1991). If we consider the spatial heterogeneities of the ocean (impossible to represent in box models), we see that the formation zones of deep waters are at the poles, where the surface waters are cold (and therefore richer in O_{2d}, $[O_{2d}]_{surface}$ = 330 $mmol/m^3$) and primary productivity is limited by temperature and light and not by nutrients ($[PO_4^{3-}]_{surface}$ = 1,000 $\mu mol/m^3$).

In the context of anthropogenic disturbance, Earth System models show that anoxic conditions in the deep ocean remain limited to a few regions. However, the surface ocean at mid- and low latitudes seems much more sensitive to anthropogenic disturbance because of the decrease in O_2 solubility and its stratification resulting from the warming of surface waters. Paradoxically, even if the atmospheric O_2 content remains high, there is still a risk of large suboxic zones in the Indian, Pacific and Atlantic Oceans in the future. Consequences of the development of such suboxic zones on the biosphere are very likely, but these are yet to be quantified.

The biological pump effect (equation [7.10]) is often used to explain the ocean's low O_{2d} water content of the Proterozoic (Canfield 1998) or the anoxic events of the Phanerozoic (Ordovician, Jurassic and Cretaceous), times when the Earth was warmer (warmer polar waters and therefore less oxygenated). It was long thought that this mechanism did not work in the long term because a deep ocean without O_{2d} should theoretically increase carbon sequestration in sediments (because remineralization without O_2 is less efficient than remineralization in the presence of O_2). In the long term, the preservation of organic matter in sediments reduces the consumption of O_{2d} and therefore promotes higher O_{2d} contents. This creates a negative feedback loop. However, when the ocean becomes low in oxygen, there is a significant increase in the C/P ratio in marine organic sediments (> 1,000). This means that phosphorus is recycled more efficiently than carbon, which mitigates its limiting effect in the water column.

7.2.7. *Limitations and advantages of the models*

In the short term, the biological pump could have a larger influence on the pO_2 of the ocean than on the pCO_{2atm}. As we have mentioned, its regulation involves the major biogeochemical cycles (C, O_2 and P cycles). It is important to note that the representation of marine biomass and its effects are significantly more complex in Earth System models compared to box models (for more details, see Box 7.1). On the one hand, ocean dynamics can modify the spatial distribution of chemical species (e.g. presence of upwelling on the coasts to the east of the oceans, subject to trade winds). On the other hand, Earth System models explicitly represent diurnal and seasonal cycles, which makes it possible to calculate primary production based on local conditions, with photosynthesis being limited by the level of light (zero under the ice floe, for example). Recent developments in these models also allow the integration of bio-limiting nutrients other than phosphorus. While phosphorus appears to be the ultimate limiting factor for primary production, its residence time in the ocean is approximately 50,000 years. Over shorter periods (seasons, decades, etc.), it is therefore possible that other bio-limiting factors become predominant, such as iron (provided by wind).

Given the developments of Earth System models, why use box models? Earth System models calculate the terrestrial climate state and the oceanic biogeochemical state with a high spatial resolution. However, this has a significant computational cost. Indeed, the numerical calculation cost of physical, dynamic or biogeochemical processes increases exponentially with spatial resolution. This cost is even greater since the explicit representation of atmospheric phenomena (radiation-atmospheric chemical compound interactions) requires very frequent calculations (~ more than 10 times per simulated day) because atmospheric conditions change during the day. As a result, given the current capacities of computing centers, it is not possible to extend the duration of simulations beyond a few thousand years. This type of model is therefore suitable for exploring the effects of anthropogenic disturbance over the next century, or even the Holocene, i.e. the last 12,000 years of the Quaternary. On the other hand, it is not suitable for disturbances at the geological time scale (duration > 1 Ma). However, the biosphere and its environment evolve over long periods of time. We will see in the following section how these long-term changes are modeled using another example: that of the colonization of continents by plants.

7.3. Geosphere–biosphere interaction during the colonization of continents by plants

The colonization of continents by plants during the Paleozoic has been known since the late 1950s (Andrews 1959). Currently, it is estimated that this colonization began in the Ordovician, 470–460 Ma ago, on the Gondwana supercontinent (Rubinstein and Vajda 2019), even if molecular data predict an even older origin in the Cambrian. Although the spatial distribution of the first continental organisms (bryophytes) remains unknown, it has been suggested that these organisms could have been responsible for the cooling recorded during the Ordovician (Lenton et al. 2012). This theory, linking the emergence of terrestrial plants and cooling, had been put forward at the end of the 1980s by Volk (1989). Berner (1991) also studied this link using the GEOCARB box model. This is the model that we will detail below.

In addition, it is important to note that this box model was developed and used in a context of limited computing power compared to current capabilities. This limitation led to the creation of numerous approximations that we will discuss later.

7.3.1. *How do plants cool the climate?*

As a first approximation, the Earth can be modeled using a black body[6] with a radiative equilibrium temperature of ~15°C. This temperature is obtained by considering the emissivity of the atmosphere (~ 0.65), which depends on (i) the concentration of greenhouse gases and (ii) the planetary albedo (~ 0.3). This equilibrium temperature therefore corresponds to the difference between the energy gains and losses of the Earth system, here simplified to only radiation (visible and infrared). The presence of life since at least 3.45 Ga implies that there has been a mechanism regulating the surface temperature to keep the Earth habitable and allow the presence of liquid water. The process regulating the Earth's temperature is a relationship that stabilizes the $pCO_{2,atm}$ over long time scales (> 0.1 Ma), a relationship formalized by Walker et al. (1981). The $pCO_{2,atm}$ is stable if CO_2 released from the solid Earth by volcanism (F_{vol}) is consumed by continental silicate weathering (F_{sw}):

$$F_{vol} = F_{sw}\,(T,R) \qquad [7.11]$$

The carbon source (F_{vol}) does not depend on the climate. On the other hand, the consumption of atmospheric CO_2 by continental silicate weathering (F_{sw}) is a function of two climatic parameters: surface temperature T and continental runoff R, which roughly quantifies precipitation (Walker et al. 1981). Chemical measurements of rivers (Martin and Meybeck 1979; Rotaru et al. 2006) have made it possible to establish a quantitative relationship linking climate and weathering. From this quantitative relationship (Walker et al. 1981), Robert Berner developed a box geochemical model, GEOCARB, with the aim of reconstructing the pCO_2 during the Phanerozoic (542-0 Ma). For this, the climate is assumed to be controlled by the partial pressure of atmospheric CO_2 and therefore by the carbon cycle. The GEOCARB model is therefore based on equation [7.11] where the dependence of silicate weathering on the pCO_2 is parameterized such that we obtain the following equation:

$$F_{vol} = \exp\,[-0.09*W_s(t)] * (pCO_2)^{0.09\Gamma} * [1 + 0.038*\Gamma*\ln(pCO_2) - 0.038*W_s(t)]^{0.65} \qquad [7.12]$$

where Ws(t) represents the evolution of insolation[7] over time and Γ is a constant that represents the evolution of the emerged continental surface (including the effects of crustal growth and sea level) over time. Although we do not describe the steps that

6. A black body is an object that absorbs all of the energy it receives in the form of electromagnetic radiation (here sunlight). This energy is converted into heat and increases the temperature of this body, which then reemits thermal radiation (here infrared radiation).
7. Insolation corresponds to the solar energy received per unit area on the Earth's surface.

led to the development of this equation, the consumption of atmospheric CO_2 by continental silicate weathering depends on climatic parameters (temperature and runoff) and has been explained and ultimately related to a dependence on the pCO_2. The relationships used to obtain this equation are based on the results of simulations carried out with 3D climate models in the early 1990s (Berner 1994). Ultimately, what we see in this equation is that only two unknowns remain: the release of CO_2 by the Earth (F_{vol}) and the atmospheric content of CO_2 (pCO_2). Other parameters (Γ, Ws(t)) are imported from other models. Assuming gas release (F_{vol}) is proportional to the accretion rate of oceanic ridges[8] (or eustatic variations if the accretion rate is not known), it becomes possible to determine the pCO_2 and therefore the climatic history of the Earth. The main advantage of the GEOCARB model is its simplicity, which allows for the integration of many processes influencing the carbon cycle. The main drawback is the extreme simplification of the processes represented in this model, most often in the form of multiplicative correction factors.

Berner then introduces additional terms to equation [7.12] to consider the major stages in the colonization of continents by plants. While the first remains of vascular plants are dated to the Ordovician, fossil remains prior to the Devonian (410–360 Ma) are very scarce. Thus, the Lower Paleozoic is mainly dominated by bryophytes, which are organisms without a root system. Based on these observations, plants did not colonize continents on a large scale until the end of the lower Paleozoic.

In the absence of vascular plants, Berner considers that the quantity of CO_2 in contact with rock minerals depends directly on CO_{2atm} (here, $pCO_2^{0.5}$). At the same time, the weathering of the bedrock is assumed to be much lower in the absence of the mechanical and chemical action of plants. To represent this effect, Berner applies a corrective factor "fe" (alteration factor), which he sets at 0.15 to represent an 85% decrease in the weathering effect. We then obtain the relationship [7.13] below:

$$F_{vol} = fe * [\exp[-0.09*W_s(t)] * (pCO_2)^{0.09\Gamma} * [1 + 0.038*\Gamma*\ln pCO_2 - 0.038*W_s(t)]^{0.65} * pCO_2^{0.5} \quad [7.13]$$

With the arrival of the first vascular plants, this balance is modified (equation [7.14]). First, Berner introduces in GEOCARB the effect of fertilization by the CO_2 (see section 7.2.2). The expression of this corrective factor is therefore modified

8. The ridge accretion rate is the volume of magma deposited per year at the axis of the oceanic ridges, which are the main volcanoes on Earth and therefore the main sources of CO_2 release from the mantle. The bathymetric profile of the ocean floor and consequently eustatism cycles (transgression/regression) depend on this rate.

$([2*pCO_2/(1+pCO_2)]^{0.4}$, where $^{0.4}$ represents the fertilization effect (this parameter is 0 in the absence of plants). Secondly, GEOCARB integrates the weathering effect, which results from the effects of roots. Indeed, if a plant ensures photosynthesis in its aerial part, its underground part (roots) breathes and therefore releases CO_2 into the soil, thereby increasing the amount of CO_2 in contact with minerals compared to the situation without plants. Thus, the development of the root system is assumed to directly affect weathering. For this reason, "fe" varies with time. It is given a value of 0.15 before the Devonian (> 420 Ma) and the appearance of vascular plants, then fe = 0.75 when the dominant plants are pteridophytes and "archaic" gymnosperms and finally fe = 1.0 (current case) from the extension of angiosperms in the Mesozoic, about 150 Ma ago.

$$F_{vol} = fe * [\exp[-0.09*W_s(t)] * (pCO_2)^{0.09\Gamma} * [1 + 0.038*\Gamma*\ln pCO_2 - 0.038*W_s(t)]^{0.65} * [2*pCO_2/(1+pCO_2)]^{0.4} \qquad [7.14]$$

In addition to these surface effects, GEOCARB also includes the effect of organic matter burial, as this process is a carbon sink (see section 7.2.4.1). Unlike the processes represented in Earth System models, GEOCARB calculates the percentage of organic matter buried over time based on the $\delta^{13}C$ measured in marine carbonates ($\delta^{13}C_{carbonates}$). To do this, it relies on an isotopic mass balance according to which:

$$\delta^{13}C_{volc} = \delta^{13}C_{carbonates}\,(1\text{-}f) + \delta^{13}C_{org}\,(f) \qquad [7.15]$$

where the parameter f is the proportion of carbon bound to organic carbon buried in sediments and (1-f) is therefore the remainder of the carbon, i.e. the carbon associated with carbonates. Assuming that the only carbon source in the system is volcanism ($\delta^{13}C_{volc}$ = -5‰ - value of the mantle), which is true over large time scales, and that organic matter $\delta^{13}C_{org}$ = -25‰ (value deduced from measurements on current and fossil organic matter) (see Chapter 6) then the sign reversal of $\delta^{13}C_{carbonates}$ by equation [7.15] provides the value of f. This reversal is done by measuring the $\delta^{13}C$ oceanic carbonates (values measured on carbonate tests of marine organisms (Veizer et al. 1999)). It is then possible to know the ratio of carbon consumed by the burial of the C_{org} (denoted f) to the total carbon consumed. This approach (equation [7.15]), based on the carbon isotopic mass balance, assumes that the carbon cycle is stationary (i.e. that all of the carbon emitted by volcanoes is consumed and consequently that the pCO_2 does not change over time). If this state is verified, then for a standard value of 0 ‰ for $\delta^{13}C_{carbonates}$, f is equal to 0.2 (i.e. 20% of the carbon emitted by volcanoes is buried in the form of C_{org}). Therefore, this means that 80% of the carbon emitted by volcanoes is consumed by silicate weathering (carbon stored in the long term in the form of carbonates such as $CaCO_3$), and 20% by the burial of organic matter. The consequence would be that any increase in $\delta^{13}C_{carbonates}$ ($\delta^{13}C_{carbonates} > 0‰$) is associated with an increase in the burial of organic matter.

Steady State Hypothesis

To simplify the operation of the system, we assume the conservation of the mass of carbon in the ocean and that of its two isotopes, a so-called steady-state hypothesis according to which the inflows into a reservoir are equivalent to the outflows.

Mass and isotopic balance

This allows us to write two mass conservation equations:

- that of the mass of elementary carbon

$$\text{Flux}_{\text{C input}} = \text{Flux}_{\text{Corg buried}} + \text{Flux}_{\text{Ccarb buried}};$$

- that of the conservation of its isotopic composition

$$\text{Flux}_{\text{C input}} \times \delta^{13}C_{output} = \text{Flux}_{\text{Corg buried}} \times \delta^{13}C_{org} + \text{Flux}_{\text{Ccarb buried}} \times \delta^{13}C_{carb};$$

combining the two equations, we obtain:

$$\delta^{13}C_{input} = \text{Flux}_{\text{Corg buried}}/\text{Flux}_{\text{C input}} \times \delta^{13}C_{org} + \text{Flux}_{\text{Ccarb buried}}/\text{Flux}_{\text{C input}} \times \delta^{13}C_{carb}.$$

Finally, to reduce the number of unknowns as much as possible, we can define the relative proportions of the flows of organic matter and carbonate in relation to the carbon input:

- $f_{org} = \text{Flux}_{\text{Corg buried}}/\text{Flux}_{\text{C input}};$

- $f_{carb} = 1 - f_{org} = \text{Flux}_{\text{Carb buried}}/\text{Flux}_{\text{C input}});$

which allows us to obtain an equation with two unknowns, $\delta^{13}C_{input}$ and f_{org}, since the isotopic compositions of organic carbon and carbonates can be measured.

$$\delta^{13}C_{input} = f_{org} \times \delta^{13}C_{Corg} + (1-f_{org}) \times \delta^{13}C_{carb}$$

Calculation of relative proportions of organic carbon burial

By rearranging this equation, we can write:

$$f_{org} = (\delta^{13}C_{input} - \delta^{13}C_{carb})/(\delta^{13}C_{Corg} - \delta^{13}C_{carb})$$

It is possible to calculate, using the values of $\delta^{13}C_{carb}$ and $\delta^{13}C_{Corg}$ at every moment in Earth's history, the relative proportion of organic matter burial compared to carbonate burial. To calculate this, we make a final assumption by fixing the $\delta^{13}C_{input}$ to the value of volcanic CO_2, i.e. -5‰ (Cartigny 2005).

Box 7.2. *Isotopic perspectives on global carbon cycling*

In reality, for the GEOCARB model, the increase in the burial of organic matter (and therefore of the parameter f) is not instantly compensated by a decrease in the formation of carbonates (1-f as suggested by the isotopic mass balance), which itself would be the consequence of a decrease in silicate weathering. This difference is explained by the dependence of the alteration on the climate: only a cooling (and therefore a decrease in pCO_2) reduces silicate weathering ($CaSiO_3$). By reducing the weathering, we directly reduce the transfer of HCO_3^- to the ocean and therefore the formation of carbonates ($CaCO_3$) according to the equation:

$$2\,CO_2 + H_2O + CaSiO_3 \rightarrow Ca^{2+} + 2HCO_3^- + SiO_2 \rightarrow CaCO_3 + CO_2 + H_2O + SiO_2 \qquad [7.16]$$

Finally, the results of the GEOCARB model, based on the representation mentioned above, show that the colonization of the continents by plants induces a drop in CO_2: a cooling at the Lower/Upper Paleozoic transition 300–400 Ma ago (Figure 7.4(a)). The smaller the fe values, the greater the drop (inefficient weathering). In the case where fe is set to 1.00, GEOCARB calculates a very long-term progressive reduction in the pCO_2 (4 PAL[9] at 542 Ma to 1 PAL at 0 Ma) in response to the increase in the solar constant. On the other hand, by fixing the fe factor at 0.15 (value before the emergence of vascular plants inducing low weathering and therefore low CO_2 sequestration), GEOCARB calculates a very high lower Paleozoic pCO_2 value (nearly 4,500 ppmv, i.e. 16 PAL) and a drastic decrease at the lower/upper Paleozoic transition.

In detail, however, we see that this decrease, between 350 and 300 Ma, is first controlled by significant organic carbon burial (Figure 7.4(b)), deduced from a positive $\delta^{13}C_{carbonates}$ value. This result is further corroborated by estimates of the amount of coal found at this time (hence the name of the period, the Carboniferous). This phase of organic matter burial would have been long enough to increase the pO_{2atm} (see reaction [7.5]).

9. PAL means preindustrial atmospheric level. This refers to the atmospheric CO_2 content before the industrial revolution in the late 19th century. The CO_2 content was around 280 ppm.

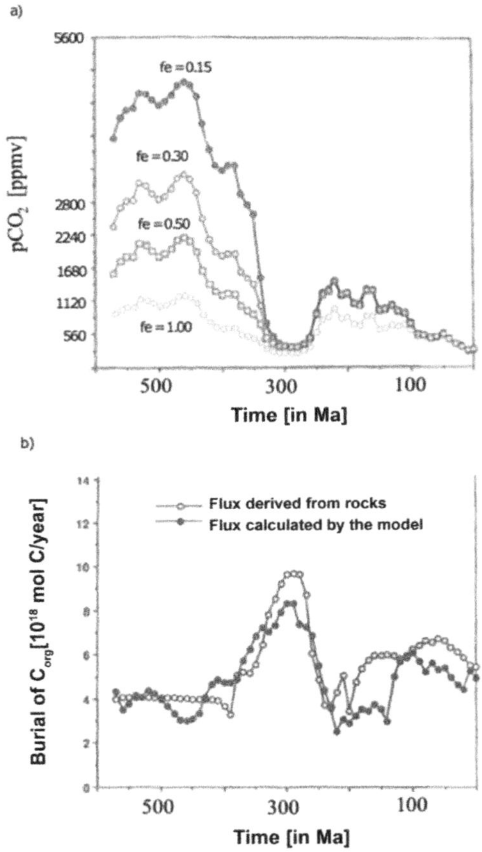

Figure 7.4. *a) pCO_2 evolution curves (in ppmv) during the Phanerozoic according to the GEOCARB model, as a function of different values of the weathering factor fe by plants. b) Organic carbon burial flux during the Phanerozoic (10^{18} mol of C year year) deduced from coal stocks and the carbon dating of carbonates (modified from Berner (1994))*

After 300 Ma, the pCO_2 rises due to the increase in volcanic degassing combined with a return to "normal" burial of organic matter ($\delta^{13}C_{carbonates} \sim 0‰$).

Thus, according to the GEOCARB model, the Paleozoic climate is essentially controlled by its sinks and therefore influenced by the development of plants. Conversely, the climate of the Mesozoic and Cenozoic is rather controlled by volcanic degassing and therefore abiotic factors. These conclusions, although still widely used by the scientific community, are now called into question, particularly because of the possible variation induced by paleogeographic effects, which significantly influence the signal (Donnadieu et al. 2006). Lenton et al. (2012) used an approach like that by Berner but summarily spatialized the problem. In addition to considering the increase in weatherability, i.e. the ease with which continents are weathered, by the appearance of different plant groups (fe factor), this study also assumed, based on paleobotanical elements, that the colonization of the continents by plants had been progressive. By fixing variable percentages of "vegetated" land, this study showed that the colonization of plants could have cooled the planet by more than 5°C.

7.3.2. *More complex modeling of the effects of plant colonization on climate*

The development of increasingly powerful supercomputers makes it possible to study ancient climates with more complex climate models. These are not Earth System models because very often these models do not systematically integrate a dynamic ocean, but only a mixed layer. This mixed layer represents only the surface ocean and its temperature changes according to the Earth's radiation balance. In addition, this mixed layer simulates warmer surface waters at the equator than at the poles. Finally, excess heat is redistributed to high latitudes by diffusion and not by advection of surface waters, as in a general ocean circulation model like an Earth System model. Although these models are simpler than Earth System models, their main interest is to integrate the surface conditions of the continents (continent–ocean distribution, relief, etc.). It then becomes possible to represent the effects of the presence of the first terrestrial plants and therefore to test the weatherability of the continents, for example, in the Devonian (416–359 Ma).

From the paleobotanical records of this period, Le Hir et al. (2011) established four eras in the colonization of continents by plants. The first era corresponds to a quasi-desert landscape, with sparse flora, which was replaced by a landscape sheltering the first "forests" of the Devonian (416–359 Ma). During this period, three fossil floras appear successively: in the Lower Devonian, it is the community of low spore plants that required high humidity for their reproduction. Then, in the Middle Devonian, Cladoxylales forests developed, with a similar appearance to tree ferns. Finally, in the Upper Devonian, progymnosperm forests appeared, architecturally similar to modern conifers. By integrating these fossil communities with their specific biophysical characteristics (albedo, evapotranspiration capacity, roughness, humidity dependence) into a vegetation model coupled with a 3D climate model, Le Hir et al. (2011) showed that during the Devonian, plant colonization was linked to the progressive emancipation of plants from water and the increase in precipitation on the continents following geographical changes that reduced the effects of continentality. Newly vegetated continental surfaces absorbed more solar radiation than formerly desert continental surfaces, which induced an increase in surface temperature and an acceleration of the water cycle. These temperature and hydrological changes caused by the colonization of continents by plants increase the alterability of continental surfaces (even without considering the effect of roots mentioned above). The combination of these complex mechanisms would have led to a paradoxical situation in which the continents would have warmed while the pCO_2 would have decreased by half (4,000 to 2,000 ppmv), a decrease likely to be underestimated considering new data (Foster et al. 2017). The calculated CO_2 values remain estimates, very dependent on the albedo values of the soils colonized by these first plants (Brugger et al. 2019). However, these results illustrate the complexity of the mechanisms involved in the interactions between the colonization of continents by plants and the climate.

Another study, quite similar in approach (a vegetation model coupled with a climate model), and focused on the expansion of Angiosperms in the Cretaceous (145-66 Ma), leads to quite similar results. Indeed, to explain the reasons for the expansion of Angiosperms and their diversification at the beginning of the Cretaceous (120 Ma), Chaboureau et al. (2014) integrated the effects of different plant groups (forests, grasslands) from different latitudes (tropical, temperate, boreal) in the calculation of water and radiation balances of continental surfaces. Unlike Le Hir et al. (2011), the characteristics of the plants used in this study are much more detailed but remain defined only on functional criteria (in other words independently of species diversity): what is known as plant functional types (PFT) to simply describe the different types of plants based on their physiology, morphology and requirements for climatic variables (Sitch et al. 2003). By considering the geographic changes during the Cretaceous such as the final breakup of Pangea, and the changes in surface properties (albedo, evapotranspiration, roughness, vegetation height) induced by the main plant groups, climate-vegetation simulations predict a strong reduction in aridity, with desert belts becoming discontinuous. This reduction in aridity, initiated by geographic effects, allowed the dispersal of Angiosperms from low to mid-latitudes. By dispersing, plants induced positive feedback on the water cycle through more efficient evapotranspiration, which also contributed to the reduction of aridity. Overall, the two studies mentioned, conducted on two main evolutionary stages of terrestrial flora, suggest that the interactions between the hydrological cycle and weathering are essential. These effects have been confirmed by recent studies (Ibarra et al. 2019; White et al. 2020), which show that the response of the water cycle to the presence of the first plants is probably not always the same and is not linear. In the coming years, a new generation of models will make it possible to couple surface properties with root effects, a step that will require linking chemical weathering with physical soil erosion. This step will also shed light on the validity of the parametric approaches carried out to date.

7.4. How to model biosphere during mass extinctions?

The transition from the 18th to the 19th century marked a turning point in the history of natural sciences. The birth of meticulous scientific collection on a global scale through famous explorations (by Von Humbolt, d'Orbigny, Wallace, Darwin) allowed, in a few decades, for the development of key scientific theories, including the theory of evolution. Among the great scientists involved, Alcide d'Orbigny (1802–1857), a student of Georges Cuvier (1769–1832), instigated the study of the history of the Earth through the history of living organisms. A great naturalist, d'Orbigny gave rise to biostratigraphy. With his exceptional knowledge of comparative anatomy and influenced by the theory of catastrophism, d'Orbigny delimited each geological period (or stage defined by a stratotype) based on the coexistence of species (or fossil fauna, most often mollusks), each period beginning with the disappearance of the preceding fauna during a catastrophe.

Following this approach, Sepkovski (1978) characterized, using marine invertebrate fossils, the largest disruptions to diversity, known as the "Big Five": Late Ordovician crisis (443 Ma); Frasnian-Famennian (372 Ma); Permo-Triassic (252 Ma); Triassic-Jurassic (200 Ma) and Cretaceous-Paleogene (66 Ma). Paradoxically, while our knowledge of past faunas has since increased considerably (see: https://paleobiodb.org/), our understanding of the interactions between past biodiversity and its environment remains very rudimentary. Thus, often, when we study the paleontological record, the link between environmental disturbance and the disappearance of fauna and flora is considered via direct temporal correlations where the biosphere responds "passively" to disturbances. However, this approach, which dates back almost two centuries, is today being revisited in a more complex manner due to new numerical tools and methods that we will discuss below.

7.4.1. *Mass extinctions, biomass crises seen by box models*

Through systematic measurements, it has been found that marine carbonates very often record negative $\delta^{13}C_{carbonates}$ excursions during major mass extinctions. An interesting example concerns the ocean of the Cretaceous-Paleogene (K-Pg) boundary (see Chapter 8), also called Cretaceous-Tertiary, ~66 Ma ago, known as the "Strangelove Ocean" (Hsü and Mckenzie 1985). At this time, isotopic compositions of inorganic carbon contained in foraminifera tests from the surface (pelagic) and deep (benthic) zones show identical values. This absence of a gradient of the $\delta^{13}C_{carbonates}$, according to the depth in the water column is an exceptional occurrence. Typically, the biological pump is supposed to increase ^{13}C in HCO_3^- from surface waters because photosynthetic organisms "prefer" ^{12}C to ^{13}C, and the marine organic matter they form thus has a negative $\delta^{13}C_{org}$, between -20‰ and -25‰. According to the mass balance, this therefore enriches the residual inorganic carbon of the waters in ^{13}C. The carbonate tests formed in surface waters are therefore enriched in ^{13}C. Conversely, due to the remineralization of organic matter in the lower part of the water column, the HCO_3^- ions of deep waters become enriched in ^{12}C. In a standard ocean, there is therefore a vertical isotopic gradient maintained by primary production on the surface and its export to the seabed.

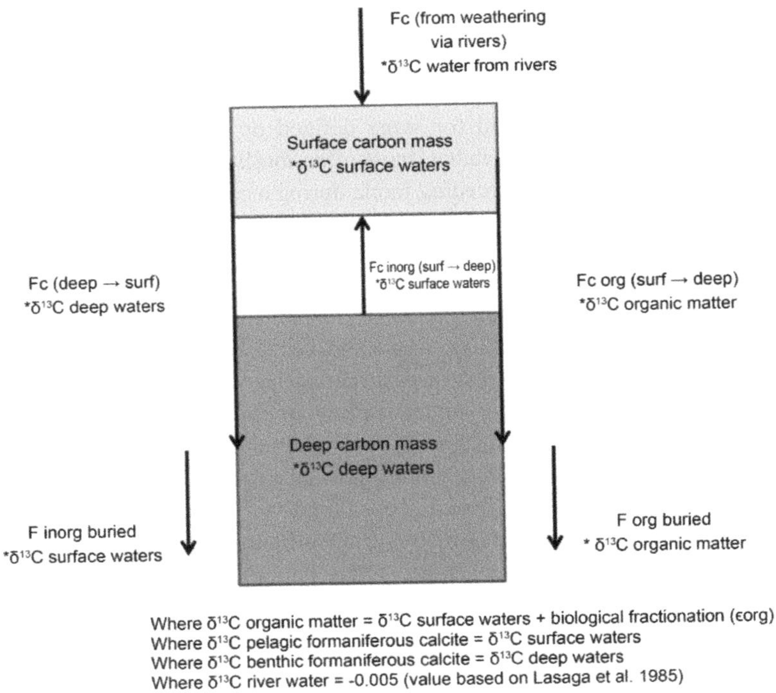

Figure 7.5. *The Peng-Broecker model only considers the ocean. It distinguishes the surface ocean and the deep ocean with an exchange between the two. The surface ocean is fed by a carbon flux from the continents, via rivers. In addition, organic and inorganic carbon fluxes from the surface ocean and the deep ocean to the sediments are represented. Strictly speaking, the carbon flux (Fc) from the ridges should be integrated into the "deep ocean" reservoir. However, ridge Fc is an order of magnitude smaller than river Fc, which explains this simplification. For a color version of this figure, see: www.iste.co.uk/benzerara/geosphere.zip*

The isotopic homogenization of the Strangelove Ocean around 66 Ma would therefore possibly be linked to a quasi-zero primary production at the surface. Even stranger, this homogenization of the $\delta^{13}C_{carb}$ lasted about 0.5 Ma, meaning that the recovery of primary productivity following the K-Pg boundary extinction took some time. To understand the Strangelove Ocean, a two-box model can be used to describe the ocean by incorporating the effect of ocean biomass (the amount of C_{org} contained in living organisms) and the carbon stored in carbonate shells ($CaCO_3$) (Figure 7.5).

The focus here will be on the deep ocean (100–3,800 m), a carbon reservoir that is much larger in size than the surface ocean (0–100 m). The amount of carbon in the deep ocean (M_{deep}) is calculated at each time step (t) based on the incoming/outgoing flows of the reservoir:

$$M_{deep} = M_{deep}(t-1) + dM_{deep}/dt \quad [7.17]$$

where $dM_{deep}/dt = Fc_{inorg\ (surf \rightarrow deep)} + Fc_{org\ (surf \rightarrow deep)} - Fc_{\ (deep \rightarrow surf)}$

where dM_{deep}/dt is the time derivative of the amount of carbon in the deep ocean (i.e. the variation of this quantity over a period dt). $Fc_{inorg\ (surf \rightarrow deep)}$ is the export of inorganic carbon from the surface ocean to the deep ocean, $Fc_{org\ (surf \rightarrow deep)}$ is the export of organic carbon from the surface ocean to the deep ocean and $Fc_{\ (deep \rightarrow surf)}$ is a carbon flux from the deep ocean to the surface ocean. It is possible to know the relative importance between these three fluxes by adding an isotopic balance.

$$d(M_{deep}\delta^{13}C)/dt = Fc_{inorg\ (surf \rightarrow deep)} * \delta^{13}C_{surf} + Fc_{org\ (surf \rightarrow deep)} * (\delta^{13}C_{surf} + \varepsilon_{bio}) - Fc_{\ (deep \rightarrow surf)} * \delta^{13}C_{deep} \quad [7.18]$$

where ε_{bio} represents the isotopic fractionation linked to photosynthesis (considered constant at -25‰), which is added to the isotopic composition of surface inorganic carbon ($\delta^{13}C_{surf}$) to obtain the isotopic composition of surface organic carbon. Thus, by carrying out a similar assessment on the surface ocean, we can deduce that the gradient of $\delta^{13}C_{carb}$ between the surface and deep reservoir (noted grad($\delta^{13}C_{carb}$) = $\delta^{13}C_{surf} - \delta^{13}C_{deep}$) is expressed as follows:

$$grad(\delta^{13}C_{carb}) = -\varepsilon_{bio} * [Fc_{org\ (surf \rightarrow deep)}/(Fc_{org\ (surf \rightarrow deep)} + Fc_{inorg\ (surf \rightarrow deep)})] \quad [7.19]$$

If $Fc_{org\ (surf \rightarrow deep)} \sim 0$ (no organic carbon is exported from the surface to the bottom) following the mass extinction of the K-Pg boundary, the gradient grad ($\delta^{13}C_{carb}$) then becomes 0. Thus, by solving equation [7.18] and as shown in Figure 7.6, the value of $\delta^{13}C_{surf}$ becomes equal to the value of the $\delta^{13}C_{deep}$ in ~ 100,000 years, because the deep ocean is the main carbon reservoir (conversely a resumption of primary productivity would induce the return of the isotopic gradient in ~ 100,000 years).

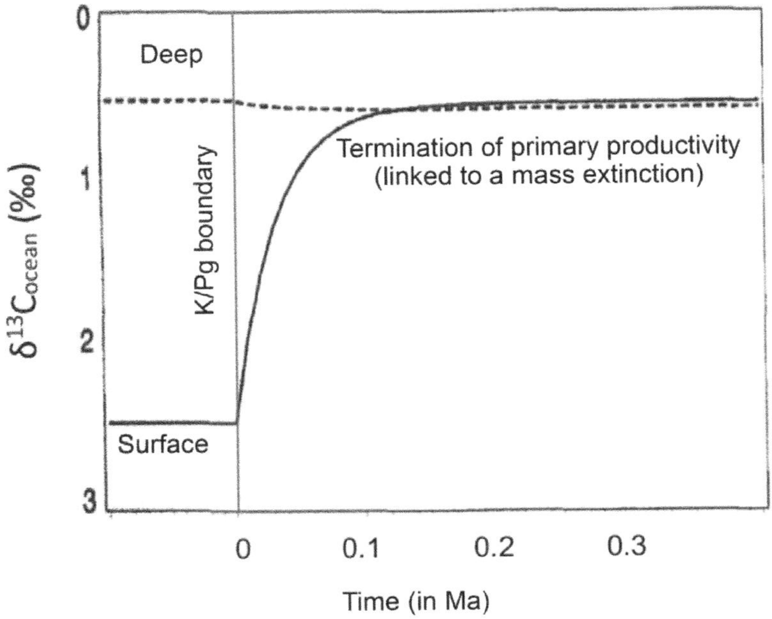

Figure 7.6. *Temporal dynamics of carbon isotopic compositions of surface ocean (dotted line) and deep ocean (solid line) carbonates. During a disruption of the carbon cycle (here biological crisis), the isotopic composition gradient becomes zero in about 0.1 million years. For a color version of this figure, see: www.iste.co.uk/benzerara/geosphere.zip*

The very strong correlation between the $\delta^{13}C_{carb}$ modeled and measured suggests that, from a geochemical point of view, reducing the biosphere to its biomass (without considering biodiversity) seems correct. This approach is the one favored in the GEOCARB model and its derivatives (Bergman et al. 2004; Berner 2004; Li and Elderfield 2013). Conceptually, this approach implies that the $\delta^{13}C_{carbonates}$ depends on a burial rate of C_{org}, which varies but without knowing the processes responsible for it. To correct this limitation, current biogeochemical models calculate the isotopic composition of carbonates based on a $\delta^{13}C_{org}$ (which remains fixed because it comes mainly from photosynthesis) and C_{org}. However, the latter depends explicitly on primary productivity and the dissolved O_2 content. Any discrepancy between the modeling and the measured $\delta^{13}C_{carbonates}$ is now attributed to an oversimplification of the processes considered, such as a poor representation of the phosphorus limitation of the ocean, both spatially and temporally, or an oversimplified diagenesis. However, this formalism is also biased because the calculation of the mass balance assumes that the biosphere only depends on nutrient inputs. This suggests that environmental conditions only influence the biosphere transiently at best by reducing the amount of nutrients available. In other words, it is assumed that the biosphere has had the same general characteristics since its appearance and that major crises do not modify its properties.

7.4.2. *Considering ecological niches in modeling the impact of an environmental disturbance on the biosphere: example of the Late-Ordovician extinction*

Mass extinctions are above all biodiversity crises described based on fossil species, most of the time marine fauna of "invertebrates". This simple observation shows that an approach based solely on biomass (and not biodiversity), such as that presented previously, does not allow us to describe in detail the nature of the mechanisms involved. It is with this in mind that recent studies have integrated the concept of ecological niche into simulations carried out with 3D climate models. For example, Saupe et al. (2020) were interested in the impact of rapid changes in temperature and sea level on the extinction of marine organisms on the continental shelf. Virtual living species were differentiated in the models according to their ability to survive strong variations in temperature (eurythermal species are those able to withstand large temperature differences and stenothermal species describe the others) as well as their ability to disperse. The authors then tested the effect of climatic cooling that occurred at the end of the Ordovician (~ 445 Ma, first Phanerozoic mass extinction) by integrating the effects of paleogeography. Using these models, Saupe et al. (2020) first suggest that the exceptional cooling of nearly 10°C at the end of the Ordovician led to the disappearance of a significant proportion of habitats in coastal tropical areas and to a more intense extinction. On the other hand, they show that the Ordovician marine organisms saw their dispersal towards refuge areas disadvantaged by the geographical configuration. Indeed, at this time, the position of the supercontinent Gondwana in the Southern Hemisphere and the existence of large islands, generated a lack of geographical continuity between the islands, which reduced the possibilities of longitudinal movements along the isotherms (i.e. lines on which the temperature is constant) leading to the extinction of stenothermic species. Ultimately, this approach, even if it remains simple, reveals that the same disturbance can be amplified by a different geographical context. The geographical context of Ordovician coastal areas seemed to negatively affect the resilience of tropical populations during this climatic cooling.

7.4.3. *Modeling theoretical habitat areas for a comparison of the effect of volcanism and an asteroid impact on the biosphere: example of the K-Pg extinction*

The role of environmental factors in the distribution of current living species is often analyzed to better understand how current organisms respond to environmental disturbances. To do this, theoretical habitat areas of species are modeled (SHM for Species Habitat Modeling) from a cross-study between the presence of individuals of a species and the associated environmental factors (topography, climate, soil, vegetation, etc.) to delimit risk areas that must be protected. This same approach has been transposed to model the past biosphere. Unfortunately, the sensitivity of fossil species to environmental factors is impossible to determine directly. So how can we overcome this difficulty? Chiarenza et al. (2020) chose to study the evolution of theoretical habitats of non-avian dinosaurs at the K-Pg boundary (66 Ma). Starting from the sites of dinosaur taxa, they established theoretical habitat maps. To know the environmental conditions for the dinosaur distribution, these authors used simulations with 3D climate models, and they selected the most relevant continental environmental factors such as annual temperature and precipitation, as well as the hottest/wetter and coldest/drier months to integrate seasonality. Once these maps were obtained, they quantified the reduction of areas likely to shelter dinosaurs when an environmental disturbance occurs. The two disturbances often discussed as possible causes of the mass extinction at the K-Pg boundary were studied: 1) the asteroid impact that formed the Chicxulub crater in the Yucatan Peninsula and 2) the intense volcanic eruptions associated with the Deccan Traps in India. Indeed, there is a temporal link between the large Deccan magmatic province dated to about 66 Ma and the mass extinction of the K-Pg boundary. This same temporal link is also established for the Chicxulub impact. These two geological events of different nature are of exceptional intensity and lead to similar effects. Both emitted significant quantities of CO_2 as well as SO_2, with the Chicxulub impact having taken place on a carbonate surface rich in gypsum ($CaSO_4.2H_2O$). If CO_2 warms the atmosphere through greenhouse effect, the sulfur gases after their conversion into sulfate aerosols cause a cooling because these aerosols become large enough to effectively intercept the incident radiation from the Sun. The main difference between the two events (asteroid vs volcanism) is the time of the disturbance: very intense but very short for the meteorite impact (100 years for the direct and indirect effects). On the other hand, the effects of volcanism are spread over a longer period (700 ka) punctuated by more intense peaks (Schoene et al. 2019). By testing these two scenarios with their model, Chiarenza et al. (2020) find that the volcanic emissions of the Deccan are too weak to induce a sufficient reduction of the theoretical habitat areas of the dinosaurs. Conversely, the intensity of the cooling induced by the meteorite impact (supposed to represent the effects of dust and sulfur gases transforming into aerosols) drastically reduces the habitat areas of terrestrial dinosaurs. This result suggests the quantitative importance of a meteorite impact to explain the extinction at the K-Pg boundary. However, it is difficult to exclude the absence of an effect of the Deccan Traps and volcanism in general (Courtillot and Renne 2003). Indeed, the effects of volcanism occur over longer periods of time (~ 700,000 years) (Schoene et al. 2019). Each eruption is of lower amplitude than the meteorite, but the cumulative effect of successive eruptions is a factor that cannot be neglected. Since the study by Chiarenza et al. (2020) does not include the long-term effect, it is therefore not possible to rule out the effect of the traps on the climate and the biosphere/or ecosystems.

7.4.4. *Ongoing developments for more sophisticated modeling of interactions between the biosphere and environmental disturbances*

The studies presented above show that the representation of the biosphere within climate models is increasingly sophisticated. These developments integrate the response of the biosphere to disturbances and show that it is not always linear. However, the fossil record shows an even more complex trend. Indeed, if the mass extinction of the Permo-Triassic boundary (252 Ma, ~ 60% extinction) seems associated with an exceptional volcanic event (i.e. Siberian Traps), how can we understand that the exceptional volcanism of the Karoo 183 Ma ago, of a volume close to the Siberian Traps with nearly $2*10^6$ km^3 of lava released, is associated with only a minor extinction (Moulin et al. 2017). Similarly, the extinction of the K-Pg boundary (66 Ma) caused by the addition of two incomparable geological events (Deccan Traps and Chicxulub impact) has an extinction rate not exceeding 35% (Ganino and Arndt 2009), the lowest extinction rate of the five major extinctions in the Phanerozoic. Ganino and Arndt (2009) showed that the effect of the nature of the substratum can partly explain the absence of proportionality between the intensity of volcanism and the induced disturbance: the degassing associated with the metamorphism of certain geological substrata emits more volatiles than others, in particular when evaporites are concerned, halogens such as chlorine and bromine, which destroy the ozone layer and induce toxicity for the biosphere via increased UV radiation.

The reaction chains explaining mass extinctions (or their absence) are probably more complex than the way they are modeled. It therefore appears necessary to explicitly model the cause-effect links between a geological event (meteorite impact, volcanism, sea level variations, etc.), the evolution of the environment and ultimately the consequences on the biosphere. This implies a coupling of the atmosphere–ocean–biosphere components by integrating both short- and long-term processes. It is with this in mind that hybrid models are developed, Earth System models of intermediate complexity, such as EcoGEnIE or ECO-Geoclim. These models can integrate short processes over very long periods (> 1 Ma) but to the detriment of the spatial resolution, which is degraded. Thus, EcoGEnIE has a dynamic ocean but a rudimentary atmosphere while Eco-Geoclim has an ocean discretized in boxes but a better resolved atmosphere because it comes from a coupling with a 3D climate model. In both cases, these models represent the complex biogeochemical mechanisms (the couplings between the major carbon, oxygen and sulfur cycles) and have recently integrated a simple ecological module (Ward et al. 2018; Le Hir et al. 2020). Schematically, marine biomass is discretized into subcategories. These subcategories of functional groups represent, for example, small phytoplankton and these functional groups can be primary producers or predators subject to a prey–predator relationship. Unlike the approach of Chiarenza et al. (2020), the spatial distribution of functional groups is not imposed from fossil groups but determined by characteristics internal to each group (sensitivity to temperature, etc.) and external characteristics (nutrient limitation, prey, etc.). This approach is in its infancy, but it could undoubtedly enlighten us soon on the behavior of the biosphere during a disturbance. Does it respond passively to a disturbance, or can it also amplify-limit this disturbance?

7.5. Conclusion

The biosphere can be described by two components: biodiversity and biomass. These two components are closely linked, but as this chapter has shown, these two components are very often studied separately, biodiversity being simplified to functional diversity. This separation of the two components of the biosphere comes from the difficulty of integrating these two aspects, and even today the links between biomass and biodiversity remain poorly understood. This separation also comes from the scientific community and its disciplinary compartmentalization. Thus, today the IPCC (Intergovernmental Panel on Climate Change) and the IPBED (Intergovernmental Science-Policy Platform on Biodiversity and Ecosystem Services) are both interested in the biosphere in the context of the Anthropocene but in very different ways. Modeling the interactions between living organisms and the environment makes it possible to estimate a broad set of effects and feedback (see: https://www.ipcc.ch/report/ar6/wg1/chapter/chapter-5/). However, the infinite complexity of life does not allow us to understand all its aspects. Thus, at present, the question of the existence of biological self-regulation of the Earth system, the existence of a set of negative feedback loops catalyzed by life and allowing for the stabilization of the system as proposed by the Gaia theory (Margulis and Lovelock 1974) remains open.

7.6. References

Anderson, L.A. (1995). On the hydrogen and oxygen content of marine phytoplankton. *Deep Sea Research Part I: Oceanographic Research Papers*, 42, 1675–1680.

Andrews, H.N. (1959). Evolutionary trends in early vascular plants. *Cold Spring Harbor Symposia on Quantitative Biology*, 24, 217–234.

Bergman, N.M., Lenton, T.M., Watson, A.J. (2004). COPSE: A new model of biogeochemical cycling over Phanerozoic time. *American Journal of Science*, 304, 397–437.

Berner, R.A. (1991). A model for atmospheric CO_2 over Phanerozoic time. *American Journal of Science*, 291, 339–376.

Berner, R.A. (1994). GEOCARB II. A revised model of atmospheric CO_2 over Phanerozoic time. *American Journal of Science*, 294, 56–91.

Berner, R.A. (2004). *The Phanerozoic Carbon Cycle: CO_2 and O_2*. Oxford University Press, Oxford.

Berner, R.A., Lasaga, A.C., Garrels, R.M. (1983). The carbonate-silicate geochemical cycle and its effect on atmospheric carbon dioxide over the past 100 million years. *American Journal of Science*, 283, 641–683.

Bond, D.P.G. and Grasby, S.E. (2017). On the causes of mass extinctions. *Palaeogeography, Palaeoclimatology, Palaeoecology*, 478, 3–29.

Bopp, L., Monfray, P., Aumont, O., Dufresne, J.-L., Le Treut, H., Madec, G., Terray, L., Orr, J.C. (2001). Potential impact of climate change on marine export production. *Global Biogeochemical Cycles*, 15, 81–99.

Bork, P., Bowler, C., de Vargas, C., Gorsky, G., Karsenti, E., Wincker, P. (2015). Tara Oceans studies plankton at planetary scale. *Science*, 348, 873–873.

Broecker, W.S. and Peng, T.H. (1982). Tracers in the sea. *Radiocarbon*, 24, b1–b2.

Brugger, J., Hofmann, M., Petri, S., Feulner, G. (2019). On the sensitivity of the Devonian climate to continental configuration, vegetation cover, orbital configuration, CO_2 concentration, and insolation. *Paleoceanography and Paleoclimatology*, 34, 1375–1398.

Canfield, D.E. (1998). A new model for Proterozoic ocean chemistry. *Nature*, 396, 450–453.

Cartigny, P. (2005). Stable isotopes and the origin of diamond. *Elements*, 1, 79–84.

Chaboureau, A.-C., Sepulchre, P., Donnadieu, Y., Franc, A. (2014). Tectonic-driven climate change and the diversification of angiosperms. *Proceedings of the National Academy of Sciences*, 111, 14066–14070.

Chiarenza, A.A., Farnsworth, A., Mannion, P.D., Lunt, D.J., Valdes, P.J., Morgan, J.V., Allison, P.A. (2020). Asteroid impact, not volcanism, caused the end-Cretaceous dinosaur extinction. *Proceedings of the National Academy of Sciences*, 117, 17084–17093.

Ciais, P., Sabine, C., Bala, G., Bopp, L., Brovkin, V., Canadell, J., Chhabra, A., DeFries, R., Galloway, J., Heimann, M. et al. (2013). Carbon and other biogeochemical cycles. In *Climate Change 2013: The Physical Science Basis. Contribution of Working Group I to the Fifth Assessment Report of the Intergovernmental Panel on Climate Change*, Stocker, T.F., Qin, D., Plattner, G.-K. et al. (eds). Cambridge University Press, Cambridge and New York.

Courtillot, V.E. and Renne, P.R. (2003). On the ages of flood basalt events. *Comptes Rendus Geoscience*, 335, 113–140.

DeVries, T. (2022). The Ocean Carbon Cycle. *Annual Review of Environment and Resources*, 47, 317–341.

Donnadieu, Y., Goddéris, Y., Pierrehumbert, R., Dromart, G., Fluteau, F., Jacob, R. (2006). A GEOCLIM simulation of climatic and biogeochemical consequences of Pangea breakup. *Geochemistry, Geophysics, Geosystems*, 7(11). doi: 10.1029/2006GC001278.

Ducklow, H.W. and Harris, R.P. (1993). Introduction to the JGOFS North Atlantic bloom experiment. *Deep Sea Research Part II: Topical Studies in Oceanography*, 40, 1–8.

Etcheto, J., Boutin, J., Merlivat, L. (1991). Seasonal variation of the CO_2 exchange coefficient over the global ocean using satellite wind speed measurements. *Tellus*, 438, 247–255.

Field, C.B., Behrenfeld, M.J., Randerson, J.T., Falkowski, P. (1998). Primary production of the biosphere: Integrating terrestrial and oceanic components. *Science*, 281, 237–240.

Foster, G.L., Royer, D.L., Lunt, D.J. (2017). Future climate forcing potentially without precedent in the last 420 million years. *Nature Communications*, 8, 14845.

Friedlingstein, P., Delire, C., Müller, J.F., Gérard, J.C. (1992). The climate induced variation of the continental biosphere: A model simulation of the Last Glacial Maximum. *Geophysical Research Letters*, 19(9), 897–900.

Ganino, C. and Arndt, N.T. (2009). Climate changes caused by degassing of sediments during the emplacement of large igneous provinces. *Geology*, 37, 323–326.

Hsü, K.J. and Mckenzie, J.A. (1985). A "Strangelove" ocean in the earliest Tertiary. In *The Carbon Cycle and Atmospheric CO_2: Natural variations Archean to Present*, Sundquist, E.T. and Broecker, W.S. (eds). American Geophysical Union, Washington, D.C.

Ibarra, D.E., Rugenstein, J.K.C., Bachan, A., Baresch, A., Lau, K.V., Thomas, D.L., Lee, J.-E., Boyce, C.K., Chamberlain, C.P. (2019). Modeling the consequences of land plant evolution on silicate weathering. *American Journal of Science*, 319, 1–43.

Intergovernmental Panel on Climate Change (IPCC) (ed.) (2014). Carbon and other biogeochemical cycles. In *Climate Change 2013 – The Physical Science Basis: Working Group I Contribution to the Fifth Assessment Report of the Intergovernmental Panel on Climate Change*. Cambridge University Press, Cambridge.

Khatiwala, S., Primeau, F., Hall, T. (2009). Reconstruction of the history of anthropogenic CO_2 concentrations in the ocean. *Nature*, 462, 346–349.

Le Hir, G., Donnadieu, Y., Goddéris, Y., Meyer-Berthaud, B., Ramstein, G., Blakey, R.C. (2011). The climate change caused by the land plant invasion in the Devonian. *Earth and Planetary Science Letters*, 310, 203–212.

Le Hir, G., Fluteau, F., Suchéras-Marx, B., Goddéris, Y. (2020). Amplifying factors leading to the collapse of primary producers during the Chicxulub impact and Deccan Traps eruptions. In *Mass Extinctions, Volcanism, and Impacts: New Developments*, Adatte, T., Bond, D.P.G., Keller, G. (eds). Geological Society of America, Boulder.

Lenton, T.M., Crouch, M., Johnson, M., Pires, N., Dolan, L. (2012). First plants cooled the Ordovician. *Nature Geoscience*, 5, 86–89.

Li, G. and Elderfield, H. (2013). Evolution of carbon cycle over the past 100 million years. *Geochimica et Cosmochimica Acta*, 103, 11–25.

Logan, B.E. and Hunt, J.R. (1987). Advantages to microbes of growth in permeable aggregates in marine systems. *Limnology and Oceanography*, 32, 1034–1048.

Margulis, L. and Lovelock, J.E. (1974). Biological modulation of the Earth's atmosphere. *Icarus*, 21, 471–489.

Martin, J.M. and Meybeck, M. (1979). Elemental mass-balance of material carried by major world rivers. *Marine Chemistry*, 7, 173–206.

Meybeck, M. (1982). Carbon, nitrogen, and phosphorus transport by world rivers. *American Journal of Science*, 282, 401–450.

Moulin, M., Fluteau, F., Courtillot, V., Marsh, J., Delpech, G., Quidelleur, X., Gérard, M. (2017). Eruptive history of the Karoo lava flows and their impact on early Jurassic environmental change. *Journal of Geophysical Research: Solid Earth*, 122, 738–772.

Redfield, A.C., Ketchum, B.H., Richards, F.A. (1963). The influence of organisms on the composition of sea-water. In *The Composition of Sea Water: Comparative and Descriptive Oceanography*, volume 2, Hill, M.N. (ed.). Harvard University Press, Harvard.

Rotaru, M., Gaillardet, J., Steinberg, M., Trichet, J. (2006). *Les climats passés de la Terre*. Vuibert, Paris.

Rubinstein, C.V. and Vajda, V. (2019). Baltica cradle of early land plants? Oldest record of trilete spores and diverse cryptospore assemblages. Evidence from Ordovician successions of Sweden. *GFF*, 141, 181–190.

Sarmiento, J.L. and Orr, J.C. (1991). Three-dimensional simulations of the impact of Southern Ocean nutrient depletion on atmospheric CO_2 and ocean chemistry. *Limnology and Oceanography*, 36, 1928–1950.

Sarmiento, J.L., Herbert, T., Toggweiler, J.R. (1988). Mediterranean nutrient balance and episodes of anoxia. *Global Biogeochemical Cycles*, 2, 427–444.

Saupe, E.E., Qiao, H., Donnadieu, Y., Farnsworth, A., Kennedy-Asser, A.T., Ladant, J.-B., Lunt, D.J., Pohl, A., Valdes, P., Finnegan, S. (2020). Extinction intensity during Ordovician and Cenozoic glaciations explained by cooling and palaeogeography. *Nature Geoscience*, 13, 65–70.

Schoene, B., Eddy, M.P., Samperton, K.M., Keller, C.B., Keller, G., Adatte, T., Khadri, S.F.R. (2019). U-Pb constraints on pulsed eruption of the Deccan Traps across the end-Cretaceous mass extinction. *Science*, 363, 862–866.

Sepkoski, J.J. (1978). A kinetic model of Phanerozoic taxonomic diversity. I. Analysis of marine orders. *Paleobiology*, 4, 223–251.

Sitch, S., Smith, B., Prentice, I.C., Arneth, A., Bondeau, A., Cramer, W., Kaplan, J.O., Levis, S., Lucht, W., Sykes, M.T. et al. (2003). Evaluation of ecosystem dynamics, plant geography and terrestrial carbon cycling in the LPJ dynamic global vegetation model. *Global Change Biology*, 9, 161–185.

Sunagawa, S., Karsenti, E., Bowler, C., Bork, P. (2015). Computational eco-systems biology in Tara Oceans: Translating data into knowledge. *Molecular Systems Biology*, 11, 809.

Valley, J.W., Lackey, J.S., Cavosie, A.J., Clechenko, C.C., Spicuzza, M.J., Basei, M.A.S., Bindeman, I.N., Ferreira, V.P., Sial, A.N., King, E.M. et al. (2005). 4.4 billion years of crustal maturation: Oxygen isotope ratios of magmatic zircon. *Contributions to Mineralogy and Petrology*, 150, 561–580.

Veizer, J., Ala, D., Azmy, K., Bruckschen, P., Buhl, D., Bruhn, F., Carden, G.A.F., Diener, A., Ebneth, S., Godderis, Y. et al. (1999). $^{87}Sr/^{86}Sr$, $\delta^{13}C$ and $\delta^{18}O$ evolution of Phanerozoic seawater. *Chemical Geology*, 161, 59–88.

Volk, T. (1989). Rise of angiosperms as a factor in long-term climatic cooling. *Geology*, 17, 107–110.

Walker, J.C.G., Hays, P.B., Kasting, J.F. (1981). A negative feedback mechanism for the long-term stabilization of Earth's surface temperature. *Journal of Geophysical Research: Oceans*, 86, 9776–9782.

Ward, B.A., Wilson, J.D., Death, R.M., Monteiro, F.M., Yool, A., Ridgwell, A. (2018). EcoGEnIE 1.0: Plankton ecology in the cGEnIE Earth system model. *Geoscientific Model Development*, 11, 4241–4267.

White, J.D., Montañez, I.P., Wilson, J.P., Poulsen, C.J., McElwain, J.C., DiMichele, W.A., Hren, M.T., Macarewich, S., Richey, J.D., Matthaeus, W.J. (2020). A process-based ecosystem model (Paleo-BGC) to simulate the dynamic response of Late Carboniferous plants to elevated O_2 and aridification. *American Journal of Science*, 320, 547–598.

8

Fluctuations in Biodiversity Over Geological Time: An Illustration of the Earth/Life Connection

Arnaud BRAYARD
Laboratoire Biogéosciences, University of Burgundy, Dijon, France

8.1. Introduction

For ~3.8 billion years, the history of the Earth and Life have been intimately linked and intertwined in a complex and chaotic way like a fluctuating puzzle. This puzzle is multi-layered and multi-compartmentalized between exo-, litho-, atmo-, cryo-, hydro- and bio-spheres. The interactions existing between these different pieces of the puzzle are therefore extremely numerous and often remain unknown.

However, they are essential to the Earth's machinery and to the Earth–Life connection, the latter ultimately being the result of the superposition of all these interactions. Contingent events can also be added to this (the chance of a meteorite falling in the right or wrong – depending on your point of view – place at the right angle and at the right time, etc.), and can cause unexpected and sudden changes in these interactions.

Interactions between the Geosphere and the Biosphere,
coordinated by Karim BENZERARA and Christophe THOMAZO.

Some interactions between the pieces of the puzzle are understood with ever increasing precision by a large community of scientists working together, from paleontologists to astronomers, geochemists and biologists. The influences of astronomical factors (orbital parameters, meteorite impact, etc.) or geological factors (tectonics, climate, water chemistry, etc.) on biological evolution are often relatively well considered and have been for a long time. For example, the conditions for the appearance of Life on our planet is one of the most intriguing multidisciplinary questionings. This case highlights the unique nature of Life, which is linked to the very particular environments of the beginning of the history of the Earth, its tectonics, its internal dynamics, as well as its position in the solar system. Another well-known example, where dinosaurs (excluding birds) on the continents and ammonites in the oceans disappear at the Cretaceous–Tertiary boundary (~65 million years ago), shows the joint influence of geological factors (massive eruptions of the Deccan Traps) and astronomical factors (Chicxulub meteorite impact) drastically diverting the course of the history of Life in an unexpected way.

On the other hand, knowledge of the influences of biological phenomena on our planet, such as on the major geochemical and climatic cycles, is relatively more recent and sometimes still incomplete. Some important examples lie in the biological engineering systems that have been able to completely modify the appearance of our planet. For example, photosynthesis by some of the first microbial organisms to modern plants has increased the oxygen content in our atmosphere and has allowed the development of new organisms and ecosystems.

Consequently, the latter have themselves been able to modulate the landscapes, climates and chemistry of the continents and oceans, allowing us to be on Earth today. Without Life, the atmospheric CO_2 level would be very different, preventing the establishment of ice caps, or modifying rock weathering and therefore the landscape. In addition, various organisms have allowed the synthesis of a myriad of minerals, otherwise impossible by inorganic processes (see Chapter 2).

Our planet therefore seems to have been strongly shaped by the complex history of Life. The fossil record in the last ~540 million years confirms this. This interval, the Phanerozoic, which extends to today, sees the establishment and consequent increase in the number of macroscopic organisms, leaving varied traces as fossils. Many events of increases and decreases in diversity or evolutionary innovations have marked the history of Life, and consequently, that of the Earth.

8.2. History of Life – how to measure it in time and space?

To understand the history of Life on Earth, it is common to assess the biodiversity represented in each geological time period. The term "biodiversity" is commonly interpreted as representing the "variability" of living organisms, i.e. all the forms that species and their ecological interactions can take. It thus includes very distinct and sometimes subjective facets. The easiest to imagine is taxonomic richness (e.g. the number of species, genera, etc.) present at a specific time and in a geographical area. Instinctively, when the species have been identified (which is often tricky, especially in the fossil record), it is enough to count. However, biodiversity is not just a number. It can also be represented in the form of morphological diversity (the "variability of forms"), functional diversity (the "variability of ecosystems" or links between species) and genetic diversity (the "variability of genes" within a taxon, a facet inaccessible in very deep time). We can be just as interested in the relative numbers of endemic or abundant species, iconic species, or even rare ecosystems.

Although several of these facets can be obtained from the fossil record, counting the number of species is the simplest and most intuitive because it allows us to quickly account for macroevolutionary trends (evolution at or above the species level, in comparison with the microevolution within a species) followed by biodiversity and possibly compare them with geological events.

8.2.1. *The pioneers*

One of the first notable attempts to highlight a differential temporal evolution of diversity between certain organisms was made by Bronn (1848). He represented the temporal distribution of the organisms studied in the form of bar diagrams whose length and thickness represented their lifespan and their intra-group diversity, respectively (Figure 8.1). Other works (such as Agassiz (1848)) have also used quite similar representations. However, one of the first to propose a diversity curve for the Phanerozoic was Phillips (1860), using count data from the English fossil record (Figure 8.2(A)). His curve had several effects: it highlighted that the fossil record was richer than often assumed, it confirmed that distinct life forms and faunas succeeded one another and it showed that these different faunas were delimited by two marked events at the end of the Paleozoic and the end of the Mesozoic that considerably restricted the existing diversity, almost to the point of extinction. Mass extinction and re-diversification events were thus highlighted. He also noted a general trend towards increasing diversity over time, a point that is still debated.

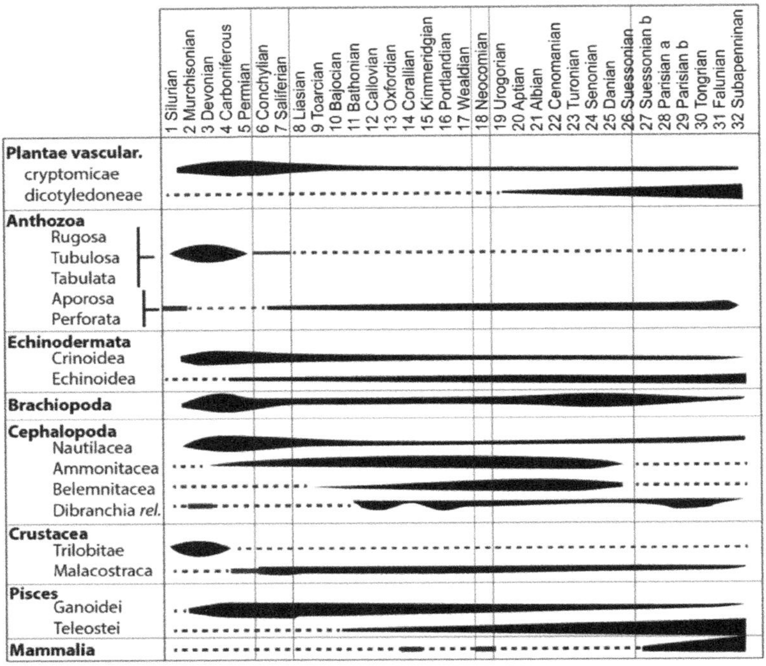

Figure 8.1. *Representation of the evolution of diversity over geological time, as proposed by Bronn (1848)*

8.2.2. *The advent of computing and big data sets*

For over a century, there have been many intense debates about the veracity of Phillips' conclusions and their potential underlying causes. However, these debates have never fundamentally changed Phillips' conclusions, because new studies have most often been based on still relatively small, compiled data or sometimes too simply estimated (Newell 1952; Valentine 1969). It was not until the 1970s and 1980s that new paleontologists researched this. The first of them was Raup (1972). Raup highlighted and confirmed the significant importance of various potential biases in the shape of the diversity curve obtained (see below). He also used statistical modeling and computer programming (in its infancy at the time) for the first time, as well as new compiled data sets to support his arguments. His main conclusion was that the post-Mesozoic increase in diversity was artifactual and that future studies on this topic should correct for, or quantify, the various known biases. This is what he set about doing, for example, in 1975, by using various statistical approaches to estimate the taxonomic diversity of a sample site.

The second contemporary figure was Sepkoski (1978, 1981), who inventoried the distributions of ~3,500 families of marine organisms throughout the Phanerozoic after several years of compilation (Figure 8.2(B)). From this, he created a global database of fossils over two decades that he used to produce new diversity curves for the Phanerozoic. Overall, the trends highlighted by Phillips were confirmed but considerably refined. This research highlighted the existence of five mass extinctions and numerous secondary extinctions, as well as different episodes of diversification. It saw a consensus since certain results were published in collaboration with Raup, even if he did not totally agree with all the conclusions presented (Sepkoski and Raup 1982).

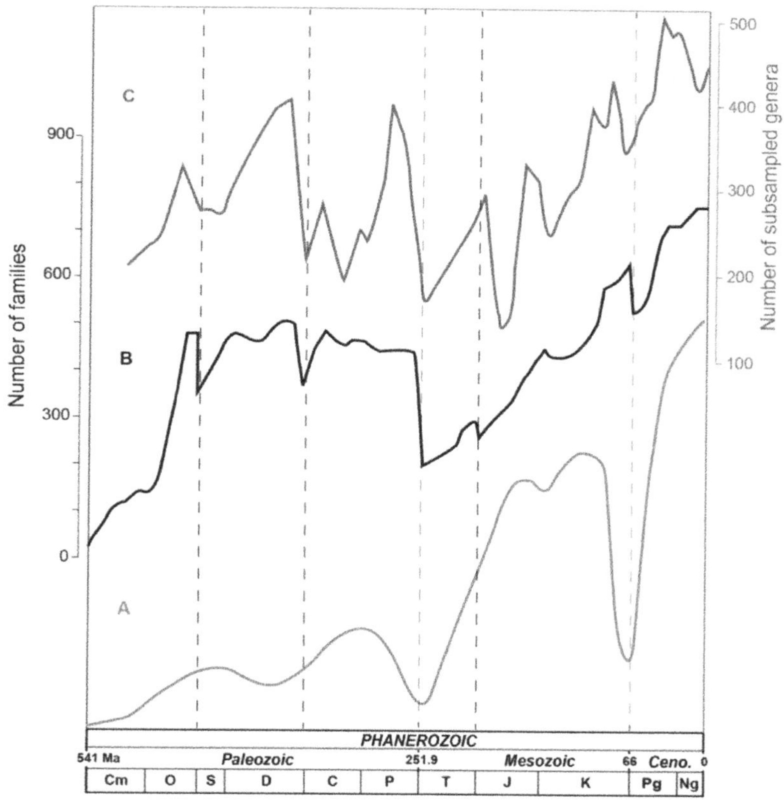

Figure 8.2. *Diversity curves over the Phanerozoic proposed by: (A) Phillips (1860), (B) Sepkoski (1981) and (C) Alroy et al. (2008). Cm: Cambrian; O: Ordovician; S: Silurian; D: Devonian; C: Carboniferous; P: Permian; T: Triassic; J: Jurassic; K: Cretaceous; Pg: Paleogene; Ng: Neogene. For a color version of this figure, see www.iste.co.uk/benzerara/geosphere.zip*

8.2.3. *Biases in the fossil record*

Raup and Sepkoski's research and conclusions have provided the basis for a myriad of other studies. However, as many authors have stated, the very nature of the fossil record makes estimating diversity over geological time much more complex than what can be achieved by simply counting. Indeed, the fossil record is inherently incomplete and distorted by heterogeneous sampling in time and space. Similarly, some organisms with mineralized tissues (bones, teeth, shells for example) will potentially leave more fossils than others with softer tissues. Added to this are many other geological and anthropogenic biases (Raup 1972, 1976; Peters and Foote 2001; Smith 2001; Peters 2005; Smith and McGowan 2011): taphonomic and diagenetic (certain environments allow for better fossilization or less loss of the initial signal), erosive (sedimentary records may be lost), tectono-eustatic (variations in sea level better preserve certain groups of organisms, fossiliferous strata or environments), historical (certain geographical areas such as Europe or North America have been more studied or have been more accessible), systematic (certain groups of organisms have been more studied than others), taxonomic (erroneous identifications) or even conservation in collections. These possible biases are thus varied and must therefore be understood as best as possible to assess whether the observed diversity signals are interpretable. For example, the existence of a correlation has often been proposed between the sampling effort and the level of diversity observed. According to this hypothesis, the increase in diversity observed during the Phanerozoic could be the consequence of the better potential preservation and the greater number of sedimentary outcrops over time, as well as of a more marked and facilitated sampling effort for the most recent geological intervals.

8.2.4. *How can this be taken into account?*

Understanding these biases in the geological record is therefore of prime importance to know whether a diversity curve is a true representation. To do this, various quantitative methods have been developed to evaluate and compensate for these biases, or even attempt to eliminate them (e.g. Foote and Sepkoski 1999; Alroy et al. 2008; Silvestro et al. 2014) (Figure 8.2(C)). Among the most used or recent approaches, those based on re- or sub-sampling are the most effective, particularly on the richest databases in terms of occurrences. These methods most often standardize contemporary samples of unequal richness before carrying out a diversity study and comparing them. Among them, we can cite the classic rarefaction method, which standardizes the samples to the same size (number of specimens or sites; on this methodological point, readers can refer to Box 8.1 and to the various explanatory syntheses by Gotelli and Colwell (2001, 2011); Gotelli and Chao (2013)). The largest samples (number of sites or individuals sampled) are generally reduced to the size of the smallest to compare these estimates of rarefied richness.

A rarefaction curve should not be confused with an accumulation curve, which represents the cumulative number of new species discovered as a function of the sampling effort. On an accumulation curve, the greater the sampling effort (number of sites or individuals), the higher the diversity (number of species, for example) by simply adding new taxa (see Figure 8.3). The shape of an accumulation curve also depends on the order of the sampled sites or individuals studied. There may therefore be different accumulation curves for the same data set. A rarefaction curve is based on a resampling within all the individuals or sites studied for a given number of individuals and for which a theoretical diversity is recalculated. In a simplified manner, the samples are reduced to the same size (e.g. the same number of individuals collected). We thus obtain for all numbers (individuals or sites) a theoretical diversity and therefore a smoothed curve which tends towards an asymptote. The rarefaction curve thus represents in a certain way an "average" of all the possible accumulation curves for the same data set. Comparing different rarefaction curves from different contexts (e.g. environmental) therefore makes it possible to graphically assess their relative diversity and partially consider possible sampling biases. A disadvantage of this method is often the obligation to compare assemblages by taking the least rich as a reference (hence its name). However, new statistical approaches now make it possible to extrapolate the "shortest" rarefaction curves so as to not lose too much information. Care must also be taken to only compare rarefaction curves corresponding to similar assemblages containing the same taxonomic groups. Similarly, we must avoid interpreting rarefaction curves that intersect.

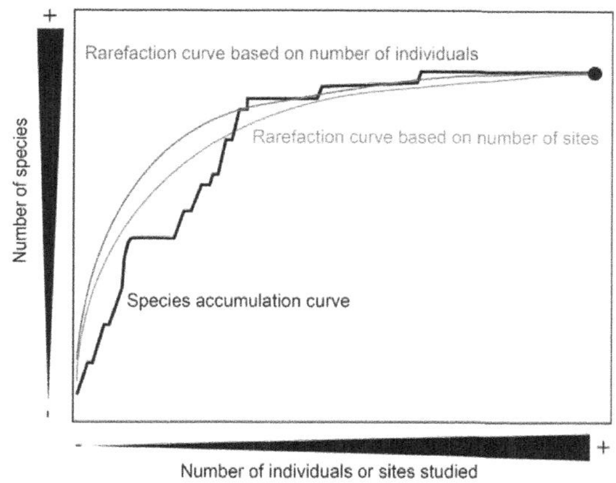

Figure 8.3. *Comparison of accumulation and rarefaction curves obtained on the same sample of individuals or sites (simplified according to Gotelli and Colwell (2011)). For a color version of this figure, see www.iste.co.uk/benzerara/geosphere.zip*

Box 8.1. *The graphical method of rarefaction curves*

Other statistical methods, called "estimators" (e.g. Chao 1984, 1987; Chao and Jost 2012), also allow partial correction of the bias on the sampling effort and even allow evaluation of the supposed diversity of the sites studied by extrapolation, i.e. the diversity sampled plus that not yet sampled. These estimators are often used in current ecology and increasingly in paleontology. In this context, however, they must be considered more as indicators of the quality of global sampling and reliable spatiotemporal comparisons than as true absolute values of diversity. However, some of these statistical approaches can have drawbacks, in particular rarefaction, which can partly underestimate the richness of certain samples that are very rich in nature (e.g. by comparing tropical sites to boreal sites). Recent estimators thus propose evaluating the completeness of the samples while keeping the real differences in diversity between the samples. From these estimators, an extrapolation of the theoretical value of diversity in the case of an increased sampling effort can even be proposed. Ultimately, this type of approach makes it possible to determine whether the sampling effort at the sites studied was sufficient and whether the observed diversity is a genuine signal.

8.2.5. *Big data*

With the combined establishment of ever larger databases, the use of sophisticated quantitative approaches, and access to ever more powerful computing resources, paleontology and fossil biodiversity estimates have also advanced. For this reason, some hypotheses regarding the real magnitude of certain extinctions or levels of diversity of certain intervals have been re-evaluated (Stanley 2016). This is the case for the supposed increase in diversity during the Cenozoic, which appears to be much less pronounced than previously considered (Alroy et al. 2008). New events or diversity patterns that were relatively hidden until now have also been highlighted, such as the existence of latitudinal diversity gradients from the early Paleozoic (Zacaï et al. 2021), or the primordial influence of temperature compared to tectonics on the establishment and increase in the provinciality of marine organisms since the Mesozoic (Kocsis et al. 2021).

Knowledge of the fluctuations in biodiversity, i.e. the duration and how these changes occur, has also been considerably refined. This has been made possible using integrated chronostratigraphies combining different approaches such as radiochronology, chemo-, magneto- or cyclo-stratigraphy, and the use of new quantitative biostratigraphy methods (e.g. the Constrained Optimization (CONOP) or Unitary Associations; Guex et al. 2016). This has resulted in a substantial improvement in the temporal precision of biozonations and their correlations at large geographic scales. It is now possible to follow diversity curves at different spatial scales with temporal resolutions of a few tens of thousands of years, which is extremely precise on the geological time scale (Brühwiler et al. 2010; Monnet et al. 2011; Ware et al. 2015; Fan et al. 2020).

The amount of available paleontological data is increasing considerably and the multiple ways of processing the data are also constantly improving. However, the inclusion of these data generally requires the active participation of paleontologists, who often must compile them one by one. Some colleagues are therefore considering soon replacing humans with artificial intelligence that would search alone in the existing bibliography for the information necessary to build these databases on fossil biodiversity (Peters et al. 2014; Kopperud et al. 2019; Hoyal Cuthill et al. 2020; Rojas et al. 2021). However, it must be admitted that the use of such approaches is far from flawless, particularly regarding the verification of source data. Such advances allow us to take a new look at the evolution of diversity over geological time. However, one constant remains: the evolution of biodiversity is closely linked to the evolution of the geosphere.

8.3. Extinctions and mass extinctions

8.3.1. *List of major Phanerozoic extinctions*

To define a mass extinction, several elements must be combined: it must be a global phenomenon, impacting many organisms (if possible both marine and continental), and in a relatively short period of time on the geological time scale. Five mass extinctions are thus documented during the Phanerozoic, during the last ~540 million years (Figure 8.2):

– the first at the end of the Ordovician (~440 Ma);

– the second at the end of the Devonian (~380 Ma);

– the third at the Permian–Triassic boundary (~252 Ma): this is the most severe with the disappearance of more than 85-90% of marine species;

– the fourth at the Triassic–Jurassic boundary (~201 Ma);

– the last one at the Cretaceous–Tertiary boundary (~66 Ma), the most famous, but not necessarily the deadliest, for example, with the disappearance of dinosaurs on the continents and of many other groups such as ammonites in the oceans.

Many other, smaller extinctions exist, for example, at the end of the Capitanian (Middle Permian), the Smithian (Early Triassic) or the beginning of the Toarcian (Early Jurassic). They often serve as a boundary between stages and substages of the geological time scale. However, these extinctions did not reach the magnitude or overall scale of mass extinctions. The assessment of extinction rates and the ecological impact of such events remains a subject of debate today, given the different biases of the fossil record or the metrics used (McGhee et al. 2013; Stanley 2016; Muscente et al. 2018). However, the five mass extinctions initially identified by Raup and Sepkoski are often at the top of the various rankings, and the assessment of their ecological impact has been considerably refined (Table 8.1).

	A) Sepkoski (1996)		B) McGhee et al. (2013)		C) Stanley (2016)		D) Ecological impact ranking (McGhee et al. 2013)
PT	58%	PT	83%	PT	62 %	**PT**	1
End Ord.	49%	TJ	73%	End Ord.	46%	**KT**	2
Capitanian	47%	End Ord.	52%	**KT**	39%	**TJ**	3
TJ	40%	End Dev.	50%	**Capitanian**	34%	**Frasnian-Famenian**	4
KT	39%	KT	40%	**End Dev.**	18%	**Capitanian**	5

Table 8.1. *(A-C) Extinction rate as a percentage of the number of genera, assessed for a few extinction events. Each study uses a different metric and dataset, leading to a slightly variable ranking of the top five extinctions. The magnitude of each extinction also sometimes appears disconnected from their ecological impact. Late Ord.: Late Ordovician; Late Dev.: Late Devonian; PT: Permian–Triassic boundary; TJ: Triassic–Jurassic boundary; KT: Cretaceous–Tertiary boundary*

8.3.2. *Causes of extinctions*

Considerable efforts have been devoted to deciphering the causes of mass extinctions, which are still hotly debated. The search for a single trigger common to all these crises remains partly illusory, as they result from combined and complex actions between different environmental parameters (Figure 8.4), ecological parameters and selectivity specific to the organisms present at the time. The most catastrophic causes most often involve massive volcanic eruptions, such as for the extinctions at the Permian/Triassic or Triassic/Jurassic boundaries, and/or a meteorite impact, such as during the Cretaceous/Tertiary crisis. The major consequence of these two phenomena is a profound destabilization of the climate by generating short coolings and/or marked warmings (Joachimski et al. 2012; Baresel et al. 2017; Bond and Grasby 2017; Capriolo et al. 2020; Chiarenza et al. 2020). In addition to climatic fluctuations, these disturbances are accompanied by the massive release or volatilization of various gases, such as CO_2, SO_2, HF or HCl. This generates numerous secondary phenomena of acidification in the oceans and on the continents, as well as hypercapnia (CO_2 poisoning) in the ocean water column. This can cause significant physiological stress for organisms. Some gases such as methane (CH_4) or hydrogen sulfide (H_2S) may have also contributed to a partial destruction of the ozone layer, allowing more UV-B radiation to reach the Earth's surface, potentially increasing mutation rates in the organisms present (Benca et al. 2018; Marshall et al. 2020). An increasingly studied potential effect of massive volcanism also lies in the significant release of mercury and other metals such as zinc, lead or arsenic, which are highly toxic elements that potentially poisoned the environment (Grasby et al. 2016, 2020; Lindström et al. 2019). The harmful effects of intense degassing of greenhouse gases and halocarbons[1] directly into the atmosphere by mass volcanism could also have been multiplied by the weathering of evaporites and sediments rich in organic matter, such as the magma rose (e.g. Svensen et al. 2009). The subsequent marked warming could in turn have destabilized large quantities of stored methane hydrate that had been stable for a long time under relatively constrained temperature and pressure conditions at the bottom of the oceans. Due to the strong greenhouse effect associated with the methane released into the atmosphere, the consequence would be positive feedback on warming, which would become catastrophic quickly.

Many other potential lethal mechanisms can be listed that have resulted from massive eruptions or meteorite impacts. All these phenomena could also have synergized or occurred in series or in the form of positive or negative feedback loops. Among these are the anoxia (very low oxygen levels) and euxinia (anoxia in addition to high hydrogen sulfide levels), prolonged or intermittent, of the ocean water column, and on a more or less large spatial scale (Wignall and Twitchett 1996; Schobben et al. 2020). We can also include a possible influence of tectonics or sea level, as well as more localized phenomena, or simply proposed ones, such as falls in primary productivity, marked increases in terrestrial sediment flows towards the oceans, large-scale fires, earthquakes and tsunamis, or even inversions of the Earth's magnetic field. Finally, some authors have suggested more distant potential causes, because they are extraterrestrial, such as the cycles of eccentricity of our planet around the Sun (the Milankovitch cycles), and sometimes less easily verifiable ones, such as bursts of cosmic rays reaching the Earth during relatively nearby supernova explosions (Fields et al. 2020).

1. Halocarbons or halogenated hydrocarbons are organic molecules with one or more covalent bonds between a carbon atom and a halogen atom such as fluorine, chlorine, iodine or bromine.

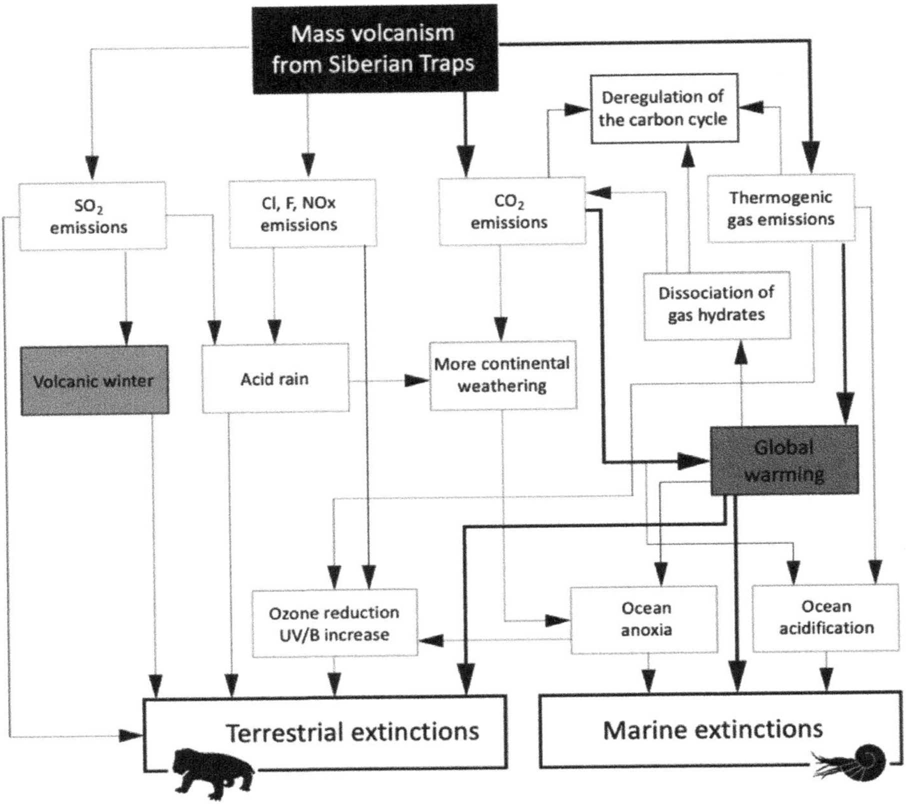

Figure 8.4. *Scenario and proposed links between environmental modifications to explain the Permian/Triassic mass extinction (simplified flowchart from Bond and Wignall (2014)). For a color version of this figure, see www.iste.co.uk/benzerara/geosphere.zip*

All these intertwined geological and astronomical events should not make us forget the possible implications of many biological parameters in extinctions, or even suggest some of them as possible triggering factors. For example, the mass extinction at the end of the Ordovician is most often associated with a marked cooling whose origin remains debated (e.g. Nardin et al. 2011; Ghienne et al. 2014). Recently, some studies have suggested as a causal hypothesis the action of the first terrestrial plants, whose expansion during this interval would have allowed the mass absorption of greenhouse gases and accelerated chemical weather of silicates (see below), all leading to a cooling (Lenton et al. 2012). Other research has also suggested an associated change in phytoplankton communities and cell size that could have increased the efficiency of the biological pump (i.e. CO_2 absorption) and thus participated in generating or reinforcing cooling (e.g. Shen et al. 2018). In fact, if confirmed, these causal hypotheses on the events of the end of the Ordovician could be a good example of the intervention of biological control factors on geological parameters (see Chapters 5 and 7). The same would potentially be true for the end of the Devonian.

Various other biological parameters have been proposed as contributing to or causing mass extinctions or secondary extinctions. These include poisoning by toxins or drops in oceanic O_2 levels generated by massive bacterial or phytoplankton blooms (e.g. during the Permian–Triassic extinction event) (Rothman et al. 2014; Schobben et al. 2015).

To summarize, the causes of extinctions are still the subject of much multidisciplinary research. In all cases, the most likely hypothetical scenarios involve multiple interactions between different geological, and sometimes astronomical, factors, and show a relatively important biological component that is sometimes difficult to grasp directly from the data documented in the fossil record. Some main causes seem to be found frequently, such as mass volcanism and associated climate changes. However, they have not been identified for all extinction events, each keeping its own causal cascade of phenomena.

8.4. (Re)diversifications: some examples of interactions between the biosphere and the geosphere

A major effect of extinctions is to destabilize ecosystems so profoundly that surviving organisms can take advantage of vacant ecological spaces or new environmental conditions to proliferate briefly (a common case among opportunistic or generalist organisms) or to diversify sustainably. This was the case, for example, with ammonoids after the Permian–Triassic mass extinction (Brayard et al. 2009). These cephalopods with an external shell show a literally explosive re-diversification, reaching in just 1 to 2 million years during the Early Triassic, levels of diversity higher than those that existed during the Permian (Figure 8.5). This example is very spectacular, but not all the surviving groups recovered after this event, and not all of them in a homogeneous way in time and space, leaving many open questions about the physiology and ecological niches occupied by these groups, as well as about the functioning of the Early Triassic ecosystems (Brayard et al. 2017).

However, an extinction is not necessary for a group to diversify at its own pace. Diversifications (or radiations) are generally the norm between two marked extinctions.

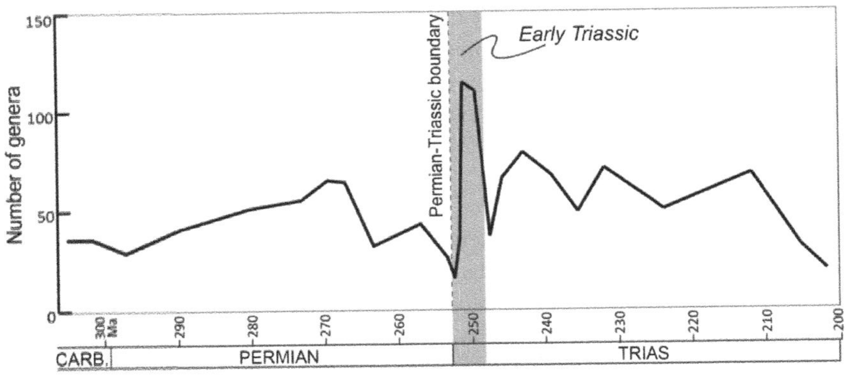

Figure 8.5. *Evolution of ammonoid diversity around the Permian/Triassic boundary. Their rapid re-diversification during the Early Triassic (gray inset) is spectacular (modified from Brayard et al. (2009))*

8.4.1. The more you dig...

One of the most spectacular radiations documented in the fossil record occurred at the beginning of the Phanerozoic during the Cambrian and part of the Ordovician. It is often referred to as the "Cambrian Explosion" because it represents a sudden increase in the diversity and morphological disparity of marine organisms in the fossil record, so much so that many of the creatures from this period could be worthy of a science fiction movie (see, for example, Gould (1989)). While many of these organisms with strange organizational structures disappeared quickly, most of the organisms that came later also originated from Cambrian fauna.

Of course, the actual history is more complex than a single instantaneous event and is also part of a complex succession of biological and geological phenomena, all interdependent (Figure 8.6) (Smith and Harper 2013; Wood et al. 2019).

This radiation could be linked to a progressive oxygenation of the superficial and deep oceans at the same time (Sperling et al. 2013). The latter would have counted as one of the chemical factors that allowed large-scale metabolic changes, by facilitating the appearance of more mobile organisms with increasingly imposing and complex biomineralized skeletons (see Chapter 2). This oxygenation and all the associated changes in geochemical cycles would therefore have promoted changes in the functioning of ecosystems and ultimately reinforced an overall increase in diversity.

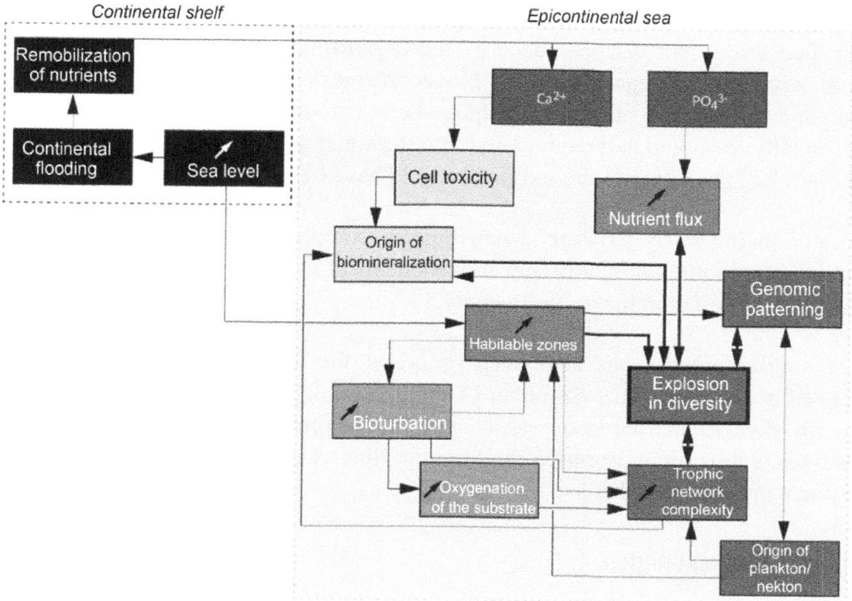

Figure 8.6. *Scenario and proposed links between environmental and biotic changes to explain the "Cambrian Explosion" (flowchart simplified and modified from Smith and Harper (2013)). Note the positive interactions involving bioturbation. For a color version of this figure, see www.iste.co.uk/benzerara/geosphere.zip*

This period also saw the establishment of an increasingly intense bioturbation in the superficial marine sediments, leading to a "substrate revolution" (Figure 8.6) (see, for example, Bottjer et al. (2000)). This biological phenomenon would have directly controlled the oxygenation of oceanic sediments by increasing it, as well as on the different biogeochemical cycles in the sediment and in the water column. Such fluctuations dependent on the intensity of bioturbation, also recorded later during the Phanerozoic, would have notably caused marked changes in the global geochemical cycles of C, P, N and S, the latter being able to generate different anoxia or oxygenation events, or even climate change (Boyle et al. 2014, 2018; van de Velde et al. 2018; Buatois et al. 2020; Tarhan et al. 2021) (see Chapter 7). The burrowing or exploration behaviors of benthic organisms, as well as their persistence or fluctuations in diversity and abundance, could therefore directly influence the geosphere. Such a mechanism has been hypothesized for the example of the

Permian–Triassic mass extinction (Hofmann et al. 2015; Cribb and Bottjer 2020). In simplified terms, the disappearance of the organisms responsible for bioturbation would have had a clear impact on biogeochemical cycles (Figure 8.7) because: (i) organic matter and nutrients reaching the sea floor would no longer have been significantly reworked and recirculated into the water column, and (ii) redox profiles and microbial processes in the sediment would have been transformed (Figure 8.8).

Later in the Early Triassic, when burrow complexity and depth increased as benthic communities reestablished, biogeochemical cycles were able to return to a new steady state favorable to biodiversity.

A similar process has also been proposed for the secondary extinction that followed at the end of the Smithian (Thomazo et al. 2019). A positive correlation between diverse marine ecosystems and the oxygenation/bioturbation of ocean substrates is thus often proposed, highlighting the reciprocal influences between the biosphere and the geosphere.

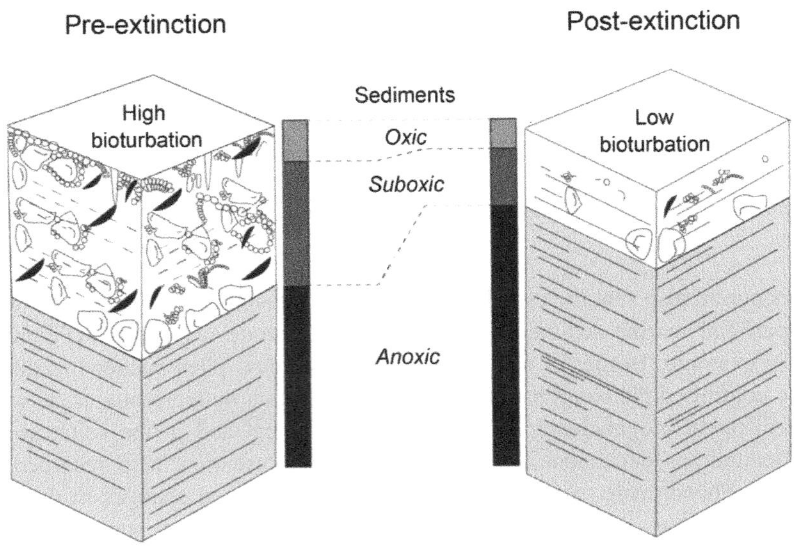

Figure 8.7. *Schematic diagrams representing a sediment column influenced by high or low bioturbation. The extent of oxic, suboxic and anoxic zones can be controlled by bioturbation at depth, promoting, or not, an active transport of solutes between the sediments and the overlying water column. For a color version of this figure, see www.iste.co.uk/benzerara/geosphere.zip*

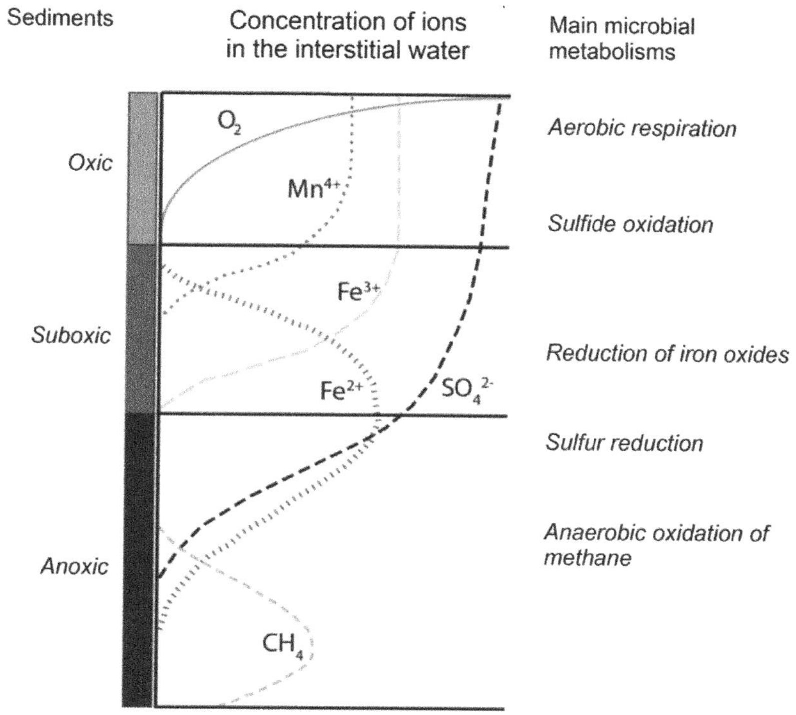

Figure 8.8. *Conceptual model of the availability of ions primarily used by the different microbial metabolisms in a sedimentary column with a parallel of the main microbial metabolisms taking place there. Any evolution of bioturbation will result in a modification of these profiles and the arrangement in depth of the associated microbial metabolisms. For a color version of this figure, see www.iste.co.uk/benzerara/geosphere.zip*

8.4.2. *The more they swim or float...*

Just as the movement of organisms within the sediment is geochemically important, their movement within the water column should also be considered, even if this effect may at first seem relatively insignificant from a quantitative point of view. It is sometimes postulated that the latter could promote a mixing of water masses (in depth and spatially), at least locally, and would notably modify the nutrient fluxes and the temperature gradient from the surface to the ocean floor (e.g. see Katija (2012) and Butterfield (2018), as well as Kunze (2019)). The metabolism of certain organisms, their behavior within the water column, as well as the fate of their carcasses could also be a factor in controlling biogeochemical cycles and gradients. Alongside plankton and fish, one of the remarkable current examples is represented by whales which, if present in large numbers, would ensure efficient recycling of nitrogen and therefore high productivity (Roman and McCarthy 2010). As the water column became increasingly occupied by active and varied animals during the Phanerozoic (e.g. Klug et al. 2009), such biological mechanisms potentially played a role in the modulation of certain biogeochemical cycles by superimposing themselves on classical physicochemical processes.

Let us cite another example of radiations, which very likely considerably influenced the geochemical cycles in the oceans and climate: the appearance at the end of the Triassic of new calcifying planktonic organisms, including coccolithophore algae and some planktonic foraminifera, and then their evolution during the Mesozoic (Figure 8.9) (Loeblisch and Tappan 1988; Gardin et al. 2012; Demangel et al. 2020). These are most often smaller than a millimeter and can mostly form, respectively, coccoliths (organomineral construction in the form of crowns and plates) or tests, both in calcium carbonate (see Chapter 2). To carry out these biomineralizations, these organisms, which are extremely abundant today, use the bicarbonate ions present in the water column. They are also extremely sensitive to climate fluctuations and ocean acidification (Erba 2006; Iglesias-Rodriguez et al. 2008; Suchéras-Marx et al. 2019). In return, they can serve as a considerable buffer when their organic and carbonate remains reach the ocean floor and become part of the sediments (Eichenseer et al. 2019). They become a carbon sink that can lessen the effects of large differences between the amount of dissolved and atmospheric CO_2 (e.g. during a mass release of volcanic CO_2). Their variable presence and abundance could therefore play an important role in the regulation of ocean–atmosphere exchanges, water column chemistry and post-Triassic climates (De Vargas et al. 2007). On this last point, the proliferation of coccolithophores could even impact the penetration of light into the water column and therefore heat transfer (Tyrell et al. 1999). Similarly, a direct action of the chemical compounds released by certain current coccolithophores is suggested to have promoted the formation of clouds, therefore modulating the albedo effect (Charlson et al. 1987). Similar hypotheses concerning the appearance and diversification of other groups of organisms with organic thecae or siliceous tests, such as dinoflagellates and diatoms, respectively, have been proposed. Due to their great oceanic abundance, the accumulation of their organic matter on the sea floor would also have served as a regulator of the major geochemical cycles in the water column, and therefore of the climate. Thus, the absence or lower abundance of these marine groups (few are very well documented in the Paleozoic fossil record), particularly during the pre-Jurassic extinctions, would have implied a lesser buffering effect (on CO_2), and therefore allowed much more prominent effects of concomitant climate and pH changes.

However, these scenarios remain relatively simplified, and the couplings remain much more numerous and complex in reality.

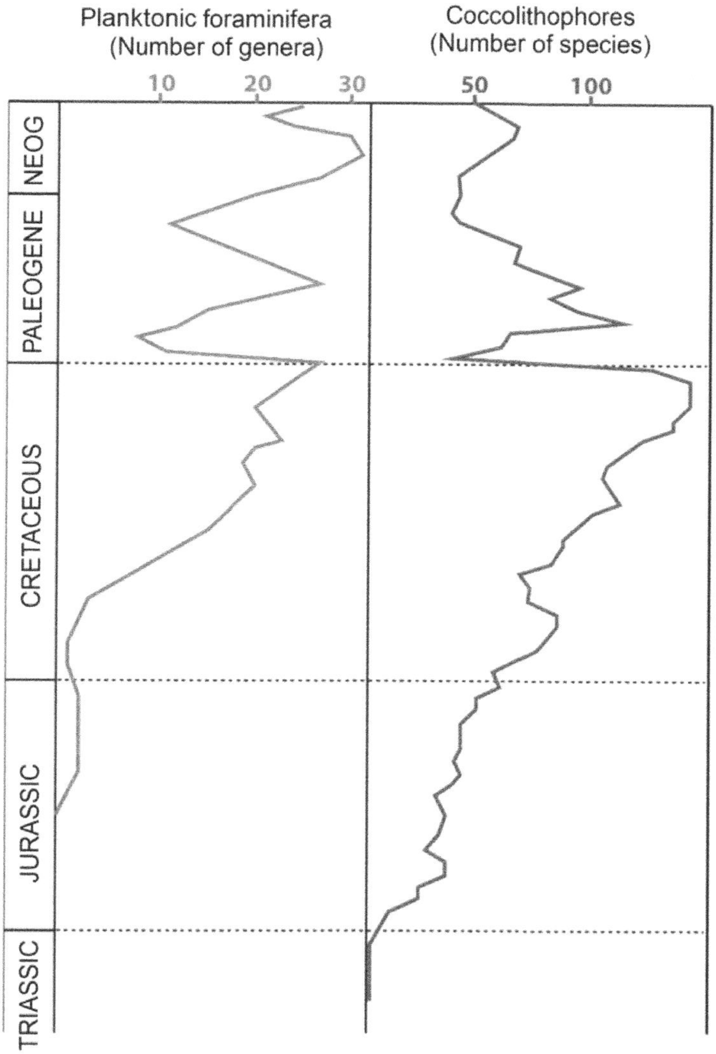

Figure 8.9. *Post-Triassic diversity of two calcifying planktonic organisms (modified from Bown et al. (2004)). Neog: Neogene. For a color version of this figure, see www.iste.co.uk/benzerara/geosphere.zip*

8.4.3. *And on the continents?*

Briefly, two remarkable examples of diversifications on the continents have very likely had major impacts on geochemical and climatic cycles. These are (i) the colonization of the continents in the Devonian by the first terrestrial vascular plants, and (ii) the development of angiosperms (flowering plants) mainly in the Late Cretaceous (Le Hir et al. 2011; Ibarra et al. 2019). These two steps are crucial and have very likely had significant repercussions, particularly on silicate weathering ($CaSiO_3 + 2H_2O + 2CO_2 \rightarrow Ca^{2+} + 2HCO_3^- + SiO_2 + H_2O$) in the continental domain. The latter represents an essential mechanism in the regulation of climates, by playing the role of an atmospheric CO_2 sink. By participating in soil formation, facilitating the diffusion of solutes within soils and locally increasing humidity in the air, terrestrial vascular plants would have facilitated and intensified continental silicate weathering, and thus catalyzed this geochemical (or here biogeochemical) process, regulating the climate over geological time (see Chapter 7). Their proliferation would therefore have made it possible to lower temperatures during the Phanerozoic. In another way, the proliferation of herbaceous plants in the Neogene is sometimes proposed as having increased the terrestrial albedo[2] (e.g. Chamberlain et al. 2014; Ibarra et al. 2019) and could thus contribute to climate changes by modulating the radiation balance of continental surfaces.

8.5. Conclusion

Even if our knowledge of the fossil record over the Phanerozoic remains incomplete, many examples illustrate a biosphere–geosphere link over this interval. All clearly indicate that these interactions are extremely complex, with sometimes cascading and feedback effects, both positive and negative. All also emphasize the influence of the biosphere, which is sometimes neglected, on the Earth system. It also appears that without its biodiversity (all aspects combined), the Earth would probably have a completely different nature in terms of climate and geochemical characteristics from the one we know today. In the end, part of the Earth's "habitability", studied by exobiologists and astronomers who are looking for a potential sister planet of Earth elsewhere in the universe, also appears to be "self-controlled" by Life and its diversity: living organisms, by flourishing, ensure the relative "stabilization" of the host planet. However, these equilibria on Earth are fragile, often shifting, and they can very quickly develop into a new state under the action of geological, extraterrestrial or biological phenomena. These intricacies highlight the uniqueness of our planet within the universe and the need to urgently

2. Albedo is the reflective power of a surface, i.e. the ratio of the reflected light energy flux to the incident light energy flux.

preserve its current biodiversity to avoid irreversible changes in its overall functioning and a total disaster.

8.6. References

Agassiz, L. and Gould, A.A. (1848). *Principles of Zoology*. Freeman and Booles, Boston.

Algeo, T.J. and Twitchett, R.J. (2010). Anomalous Early Triassic sediment fluxes due to elevated weathering rates and their biological consequences. *Geology*, 38, 1023–1026.

Alroy, J., Aberhan, M., Bottjer, D.J., Foote, M., Fürsich, F.T., Harries, P.J., Hendy, A.J.W., Holland, S.M., Ivany, L.C., Kiessling, W. et al. (2008). Phanerozoic trends in the global diversity of marine invertebrates. *Science*, 321, 97–100.

Baresel, B., Bucher, H., Bagherpour, B., Brosse, M., Guodun, K., Schaltegger, U. (2017). Timing of global regression and microbial bloom linked with the Permian-Triassic boundary mass extinction: Implications for driving mechanisms. *Sci. Rep.*, 7, 43630.

Benca, J.P., Duijnstee, I.A.P., Looy, C.V. (2018). UV-B-induced forest sterility: Implications of ozone shield failure in Earth's largest extinction. *Sci. Adv.*, 4, e1700618.

Bond, D.P.G. and Grasby, S.E. (2017). On the causes of mass extinctions. *Palaeogeogr., Palaeoclim., Palaeoecol.*, 478, 3–29.

Bond, D.P.G. and Wignall, P.B. (2014). Large igneous provinces and mass extinctions: An update. In *Volcanism, Impacts, and Mass Extinctions: Causes and Effects*, Keller, G. and Kerr, A.C. (eds). Geological Society of America, Boulder, Colorado, 29–55.

Bottjer, D.J., Hagadorn, J.W., Dornbos, S.Q. (2000). The Cambrian substrate revolution. *GSA Today*, 10, 1–7.

Bown, P.R., Lees, J.A., Young, J.R. (2004). Calcareous nannoplankton evolution and diversity through time. In *Coccolithophores: From Molecular Processes to Global Impact*, Thierstein, H.R. and Young, J.R. (eds). Springer, Berlin, Heidelberg, 481–508.

Boyle, R.A., Dahl, T.W., Dale, A.W., Shields-Zhou, G.A., Zhu, M., Brasier, M.D., Canfield, D.E., Lenton, T.M. (2014). Stabilization of the coupled oxygen and phosphorus cycles by the evolution of bioturbation. *Nat. Geosci.*, 7, 671–676.

Boyle, R.A., Dahl, T.W., Bjerrum, C.J., Canfield, D.E. (2018). Bioturbation and directionality in Earth's carbon isotope record across the Neoproterozoic–Cambrian transition. *Geobiology*, 16, 252–278.

Brayard, A., Escarguel, G., Bucher, H., Monnet, C., Bruhwiler, T., Goudemand, N., Galfetti, T., Guex, J. (2009). Good genes and good luck: Ammonoid diversity and the end-Permian mass extinction. *Science*, 325, 1118–1121.

Brayard, A., Krumenacker, L.J., Botting, J.P., Jenks, J.F., Bylund, K.G., Fara, E., Vennin, E., Olivier, N., Goudemand, N., Saucède, T. et al. (2017). Unexpected Early Triassic marine ecosystem and the rise of the Modern evolutionary fauna. *Sci. Adv.*, 3, e1602159.

Bronn, H.G. (1848). *Index Palaeontologicus, Oder, Übersicht Der Bis Jetzt Bekannten Fossilen Organismen.* E. Schweizerbart, Stuttgart.

Brühwiler, T., Bucher, H., Brayard, A., Goudemand, N. (2010). High-resolution biochronology and diversity dynamics of the Early Triassic ammonoid recovery: The Smithian faunas of the Northern Indian Margin. *Palaeogeogr., Palaeoclimatol., Palaeoecol.*, 297, 491–501.

Buatois, L.A., Mángano, M.G., Minter, N.J., Zhou, K., Wisshak, M., Wilson, M.A., Olea, R.A. (2020). Quantifying ecospace utilization and ecosystem engineering during the early Phanerozoic—The role of bioturbation and bioerosion. *Science Adv.*, 6, eabb0618.

Butterfield, N.J. (2018). Oxygen, animals and aquatic bioturbation: An updated account. *Geobiology*, 16, 3–16.

Capriolo, M., Marzoli, A., Aradi, L.E., Callegaro, S., Dal Corso, J., Newton, R.J., Mills, B.J.W., Wignall, P.B., Bartoli, O., Baker, D.R. et al. (2020). Deep CO2 in the end-Triassic Central Atlantic Magmatic Province. *Nat. Commun.*, 11, 1670.

Chamberlain, C.P., Winnick, M., Mix, H.T., Chamberlain, S.D., Maher, K. (2014). The impact of neogene grassland expansion and aridification on the isotopic composition of continental precipitation. *Glob. Biogeochem. Cycles*, 28, 922–1004.

Chao, A. (1984). Nonparametric estimation of the number of classes in a population. *Scand. J. Stat.*, 11, 265–270.

Chao, A. (1987). Estimating the population size for capture-recapture data with unequal catchability. *Biometrics*, 43, 783–91.

Chao, A. and Jost, L. (2012). Coverage-based rarefaction and extrapolation: Standardizing samples by completeness rather than size. *Ecology*, 93, 2533–2547.

Charlson, R.J., Lovelock, J.E., Andreae, M.O., Warren, S.G. (1987). Oceanic phytoplankton, atmospheric sulphur, cloud albedo and climate. *Nature*, 326, 655–661.

Chiarenza, A.A., Farnsworth, A., Mannion, P.D., Lunt, D.J., Valdes, P.J., Morgan, J.V., Allison, P.A. (2020). Asteroid impact, not volcanism, caused the end-Cretaceous dinosaur extinction. *Proc. Natl Acad. Sci.*, 117, 17084–17093.

Cribb, A.T. and Bottjer, D.J. (2020). Complex marine bioturbation ecosystem engineering behaviors persisted in the wake of the end-Permian mass extinction. *Sci. Rep.*, 10, 203.

De Vargas, C., Aubry, M.-P., Probert, I.A.N., Young, J. (2007). Origin and evolution of coccolithophores: From coastal hunters to oceanic farmers. In *Evolution of Primary Producers in the Sea*, Falkowski, P.G. and Knoll, A.H. (eds). Academic Press, Burlington, 251–285.

Demangel, I., Kovács, Z., Richoz, S., Gardin, S., Krystyn, L., Baldermann, A., Piller, W.E. (2020). Development of early calcareous nannoplankton in the Late Triassic (Northern Calcareous Alps, Austria). *Glob. Planet. Change*, 193, 103254.

Eichenseer, K., Balthasar, U., Smart, C.W., Stander, J., Haaga, K.A., Kiessling, W. (2019). Jurassic shift from abiotic to biotic control on marine ecological success. *Nature Geosci.*, 12, 638–642.

Erba, E. (2006). The first 150 million years history of calcareous nannoplankton: Biosphere–geosphere interactions. *Palaeogeogr., Palaeoclimatol., Palaeoecol.*, 232, 237–250.

Fan, J.-X., Shen, S.-Z., Erwin, D.H., Sadler, P.M., MacLeod, N., Cheng, Q.-M., Hou, X.-D., Yang, J., Wang, X.-D., Wang, Y. et al. (2020). A high-resolution summary of Cambrian to Early Triassic marine invertebrate biodiversity. *Science*, 367, 272–277.

Fields, B.D., Melott, A.L., Ellis, J., Ertel, A.F., Fry, B.J., Lieberman, B.S., Liu, Z., Miller, J.A., Thomas, B.C. (2020). Supernova triggers for end-Devonian extinctions. *Proc. Natl Acad. Sci.*, 117, 21008–21010.

Foote, M. and Sepkoski, J.J. (1999). Absolute measures of the completeness of the fossil record. *Nature*, 398, 415–417.

Gardin, S., Krystyn, L., Richoz, S., Bartolini, A., Galbrun, B. (2012). Where and when the earliest coccolithophores? *Lethaia*, 45, 507–523.

Ghienne, J.-F., Desrochers, A., Vandenbroucke, T.R.A., Achab, A., Asselin, E., Dabard, M.-P., Farley, C., Loi, A., Paris, F., Wickson, S. et al. (2014). A Cenozoic-style scenario for the end-Ordovician glaciation. *Nat. Commun.*, 5, 4485.

Gotelli, N.J. and Chao A. (2013). Measuring and estimating species richness, species diversity, and biotic similarity from sampling data. In *Encyclopedia of Biodiversity*, 2nd edition, Levin, S.A. (ed.). Academic Press, Waltham, MA, 95–211.

Gotelli, N.J. and Colwell, R.K. (2001). Quantifying biodiversity: Procedures and pittfalls in the measurement and comparison of species richness. *Ecol. Lett.*, 4, 379–391.

Gotelli, N.J. and Colwell, R.K. (2011). Estimating species richness. In *Biological Diversity: Frontiers in Measurement and Assessment*, Magurran, A.E. and McGill, B.J. (eds). Oxford University Press, Oxford, 39–54.

Gould, S.J. (1989). *Wonderful Life. The Burgess Shale and the Nature of History*. W.W. Norton and Company, New York.

Grasby, S.E., Beauchamp, B., Bond, D.P.G., Wignall, P.B., Sanei, H. (2016). Mercury anomalies associated with three extinction events (Capitanian Crisis, Latest Permian Extinction and the Smithian/Spathian Extinction) in NW Pangea. *Geol. Mag.*, 153, 285–297.

Grasby, S.E., Liu, X., Yin, R., Ernst, R.E., Chen, Z. (2020). Toxic mercury pulses into Late Permian terrestrial and marine environments. *Geology*, 48, 830–833.

Guex, J., Galster, F., Hammer, Ø (2016). *Discrete Biochronological Time Scales*. Springer, Cham.

Hofmann, R., Buatois, L.A., MacNaughton, R.B., Mángano, M.G. (2015). Loss of the sedimentary mixed layer as a result of the end-Permian extinction. *Palaeogeogr., Palaeoclimatol., Palaeoecol.*, 428, 1–11.

Houghton, I.A., Koseff, J.R., Monismith, S.G., Dabiri, J.O. (2018). Vertically migrating swimmers generate aggregation-scale eddies in a stratified column. *Nature*, 556, 497–500.

Hoyal Cuthill, J.F., Guttenberg, N., Budd, G.E. (2020). Impacts of speciation and extinction measured by an evolutionary decay clock. *Nature*, 588, 636–641.

Ibarra, D.E., Rugenstein, J.K.C., Bachan, A., Baresch, A., Lau, K.V., Thomas, D.L., Lee, J.-E., Boyce, C.K., Chamberlain, C.P. (2019). Modeling the consequences of land plant evolution on silicate weathering. *Am. J. Sci.*, 319, 1–43.

Iglesias-Rodriguez, M.D., Halloran, P.R., Rickaby, R.E.M., Hall, I.R., Colmenero-Hidalgo, E., Gittins, J.R., Green, D.R.H., Tyrrell, T., Gibbs, S.J., von Dassow, P. et al. (2008). Phytoplankton calcification in a high-CO_2 world. *Science*, 320, 336–340.

Joachimski, M.M., Lai, X., Shen, S., Jiang, H., Luo, G., Chen, B., Chen, J., Sun, Y. (2012). Climate warming in the latest Permian and the Permian–Triassic mass extinction. *Geology*, 40, 195–198.

Katija, K. (2012). Biogenic inputs to ocean mixing. *J. Exp. Biol.*, 215, 1040–1049.

Klug, C., Kröger, B., Kiessling, W., Mullins, G.L., Servais, T., Fryda, J., Korn, D., Turner, S. (2009). The Devonian nekton revolution. *Lethaia*, 43, 465–477.

Kocsis, Á.T., Reddin, C.J., Scotese, C.R., Valdes, P.J., Kiessling, W. (2021). Increase in marine provinciality over the last 250 million years governed more by climate change than plate tectonics. *Proc. Roy. Soc. B*, 288, 20211342.

Kopperud, B.T., Lidgard, S., Liow, L.H. (2019). Text-mined fossil biodiversity dynamics using machine learning. *Proc. Roy. Soc. B*, 286, 20190022.

Kunze, E. (2019). Biologically generated mixing in the ocean. *Annu. Rev. Mar. Sci.*, 11, 215–226.

Le Hir, G., Donnadieu, Y., Goddéris, Y., Meyer-Berthaud, B., Ramstein, G., Blakey, R.C. (2011). The climate change caused by the land plant invasion in the Devonian. *Earth Planet. Sci. Lett.*, 310, 203–212.

Lenton, T.M., Crouch, M., Johnson, M., Pires, N., Dolan, L. (2012). First plants cooled the Ordovician. *Nat. Geosci.*, 5, 86–89.

Lindström, S., Sanei, H., van de Schootbrugge, B., Pedersen, G.K., Lesher, C.E., Tegner, C., Heunisch, C., Dybkjær, K., Outridge, P.M. (2019). Volcanic mercury and mutagenesis in land plants during the end-Triassic mass extinction. *Sci. Adv.*, 5, eaaw4018.

Loeblich Jr, A.R. and Tappan, H. (1988). *Foraminiferal Genera and Their Classification*. Van Nostrand Reinhold Company, New York.

Marshall, J.E.A., Lakin, J., Troth, I., Wallace-Johnson, S.M. (2020). UV-B radiation was the Devonian-Carboniferous boundary terrestrial extinction kill mechanism. *Sci. Adv.*, 6, eaba0768.

McGhee Jr, G.R., Clapham, M.E., Sheehan, P.M., Bottjer, D.J., Droser, M.L. (2013). A new ecological-severity ranking of major Phanerozoic biodiversity crises. *Palaeogeogr., Palaeoclim., Palaeoecol.*, 370, 260–270.

Monnet, C., Klug, C., Goudemand, N., De Baets, K., Bucher, H. (2011). Quantitative biochronology of Devonian ammonoids from Morocco and proposals for a refined unitary association method. *Lethaia*, 44, 469–489.

Muscente, A.D., Prabhu, A., Zhong, H., Eleish, A., Meyer, M.B., Fox, P., Hazen, R.M., Knoll, A.H. (2018). Quantifying ecological impacts of mass extinctions with network analysis of fossil communities. *Proc. Natl Acad. Sci.*, 115, 5217–5222.

Nardin, E., Goddéris, Y., Donnadieu, Y., Le Hir, G., Blakey, R.C., Pucéat, E., Aretz, M. (2011). Modeling the early Paleozoic long-term climatic trend. *GSA Bull.*, 123, 1181–1192.

Newell, N.D. (1952). Periodicity in invertebrate evolution. *J. Paleontol.*, 26, 371–385.

Peters, S.E. (2005). Geological constraints on the macroevolutionary history of marine animals. *Proc. Natl Acad. Sci.*, 102, 12326–12331.

Peters, S.E. and Foote, M. (2001). Biodiversity in the Phanerozoic: A reinterpretation. *Paleobiology*, 27, 583–601.

Peters, S.E., Zhang, C., Livny, M., Ré, C. (2014). A machine reading system for assembling synthetic paleontological databases. *Plos One*, 9, e113523.

Phillips, J. (1860). *Life on the Earth: Its Origin and Succession*. Macmillan, Cambridge.

Raup, D.M. (1972). Taxonomic diversity during the Phanerozoic. *Science*, 177, 1065–1071.

Raup, D.M. (1975). Taxonomic diversity estimation using rarefaction. *Paleobiology*, 1, 333–342.

Raup, D.M. (1976). Species diversity in the Phanerozoic: A tabulation. *Paleobiology*, 2, 279–288.

Raup, D.M. and Sepkoski, J.J. (1982). Mass extinctions in the marine fossil record. *Science*, 215, 1501–1503.

Rojas, A., Calatayud, J., Kowalewski, M., Neuman, M., Rosvall, M. (2021). A multiscale view of the Phanerozoic fossil record reveals the three major biotic transitions. *Commun. Biol.*, 4, 309–309.

Roman, J. and McCarthy, J.J. (2010). The whale pump: Marine mammals enhance primary productivity in a coastal basin. *Plos One*, 5, e13255.

Rothman, D.H., Fournier, G.P., French, K.L., Alm, E.J., Boyle, E.A., Cao, C., Summons, R.E. (2014). Methanogenic burst in the end-Permian carbon cycle. *Proc. Natl Acad. Sci.*, 111, 5462–5467.

Schobben, M., Stebbins, A., Ghaderi, A., Strauss, H., Korn, D., Korte, C. (2015). Flourishing ocean drives the end-Permian marine mass extinction. *Proc. Natl Acad. Sci.*, 112, 10298–10303.

Schobben, M., Foster, W.J., Sleveland, A.R.N., Zuchuat, V., Svensen, H.H., Planke, S., Bond, D.P.G., Marcelis, F., Newton, R.J., Wignall, P.B. et al. (2020). A nutrient control on marine anoxia during the end-Permian mass extinction. *Nat. Geosci.*, 13, 640–646.

Sepkoski, J.J. (1978). A kinetic model of Phanerozoic taxonomic diversity I. Analysis of marine orders. *Paleobiology*, 4, 223–251.

Sepkoski, J.J. (1981). A factor analytic description of the Phanerozoic marine fossil record. *Paleobiology*, 7, 36–53.

Sepkoski, J.J. (1996). Patterns of Phanerozoic extinction: A perspective from global data bases. In *Global Events and Event Stratigraphy in the Phanerozoic*, Walliser, O.H. (ed.). Springer, Berlin, Heidelberg.

Shen, J., Pearson, A., Henkes, G.A., Zhang, Y.G., Chen, K., Li, D., Wankel, S.D., Finney, S.C., Shen, Y. (2018). Improved efficiency of the biological pump as a trigger for the Late Ordovician glaciation. *Nat. Geosci.*, 11, 510–514.

Silvestro, D., Schnitzler, J., Liow, L.H., Antonelli, A., Salamin, N. (2014). Bayesian estimation of speciation and extinction from incomplete fossil occurrence data. *Syst. Biol.*, 63, 349–367

Smith, A.B. (2001). Large-scale heterogeneity of the fossil record: Implications for Phanerozoic biodiversity studies. *Phil. Trans. Roy. Soc. London B*, 356, 351–367.

Smith, A.B. (2007). Marine diversity through the Phanerozoic: Problems and prospects. *J. Geol. Soc. London*, 164, 731–745.

Smith, M.P. and Harper, D.A.T. (2013). Causes of the Cambrian explosion. *Science*, 341, 1355–1356.

Smith, A.B. and McGowan, A.J. (2011). The ties linking rock and fossil records and why they are important for palaeobiodiversity studies. *Spec. Pub. Geol. Soc. London*, 358, 1–7.

Sperling, E.A., Frieder, C.A., Raman, A.V., Girguis, P.R., Levin, L.A., Knoll, A.H. (2013). Oxygen, ecology, and the Cambrian radiation of animals. *Proc. Natl Acad. Sci.*, 110, 13446–13451.

Stanley, S.M. (2016). Estimates of the magnitudes of major marine mass extinctions in earth history. *Proc. Natl Acad. Sci.*, 113, E6325–E6334.

Suchéras-Marx, B., Mattioli, E., Allemand, P., Giraud, F., Pittet, B., Plancq, J., Escarguel, G. (2019). The colonization of the oceans by calcifying pelagic algae. *Biogeosciences*, 16, 2501–2510.

Svensen, H., Planke, S., Polozov, A.G., Schmidbauer, N., Corfu, F., Podladchikov, Y.Y., Jamtveit, B. (2009). Siberian gas venting and the end-Permian environmental crisis. *Earth Planet. Sci. Lett.*, 277, 490–500.

Tarhan, L.G., Zhao, M., Planavsky, N.J. (2021). Bioturbation feedbacks on the phosphorus cycle. *Earth Planet. Sci. Lett.*, 566, 116961.

Thomazo, C., Brayard, A., Elmeknassi, S., Vennin, E., Olivier, N., Caravaca, G., Escarguel, G., Fara, E., Bylund, K.G., Jenks, J.F. et al. (2019). Multiple sulfur isotope signals associated with the late Smithian event and the Smithian/Spathian boundary. *Earth-Sci. Rev.*, 195, 96–113.

Tyrrell, T., Holligan, P.M., Mobley, C.D. (1999). Optical impacts of oceanic coccolithophore blooms. *J. Geophy. Res. Oceans*, 104, 3223–3241.

Valentine, J.W. (1969). Patterns of taxonomic and ecological structure of the shelf benthos during Phanerozoic time. *Palaeontology*, 12, 684–709.

van de Velde, S., Mills, B.J.W., Meysman, F.J.R., Lenton, T.M., Poulton, S.W. (2018). Early Palaeozoic ocean anoxia and global warming driven by the evolution of shallow burrowing. *Nat. Commun.*, 9, 2554.

Ware, D., Bucher, H., Brayard, A., Schneebeli-Hermann, E., Brühwiler, T. (2015). High-resolution biochronology and diversity dynamics of the Early Triassic ammonoid recovery: The Dienerian faunas of the Northern Indian Margin. *Palaeogeogr., Palaeoclimatol., Palaeoecol.*, 440, 363–373.

Wignall, P.B. and Twitchett, R.J. (1996). Oceanic anoxia and the end Permian mass extinction. *Science*, 272, 1155–1158.

Wood, R., Liu, A.G., Bowyer, F., Wilby, P.R., Dunn, F.S., Kenchington, C.G., Cuthill, J.F.H., Mitchell, E.G., Penny, A. (2019). Integrated records of environmental change and evolution challenge the Cambrian Explosion. *Nat. Ecol. Evol.*, 3, 528–538.

Zacaï, A., Monnet, C., Pohl, A., Beaugrand, G., Mullins, G., Kroeck, D.M., Servais, T. (2021). Truncated bimodal latitudinal diversity gradient in Early Paleozoic phytoplankton. *Sci. Adv.*, 7, eabd6709.

Conclusions

Christophe THOMAZO[1] and Karim BENZERARA[2]
[1] *Laboratoire Biogéosciences, University of Burgundy, Dijon, France*
[2] *IMPMC, UMR 7590, CNRS, Sorbonne Université, Paris, France*

In conclusion, all of the chapters in this book illustrate the fact that the Earth is a living planet, where the biosphere and the geosphere interact closely. These interactions are essential to the formation and maintenance of habitable conditions on our planet.

Thus, we first saw how the role of living organisms is particularly significant in what is called the critical zone, this thin outer envelope of the continental crust, which extends from the top of the canopy to the lower limit of surface aquifers and where almost the entire biosphere is confined. In the critical zone, the dissolution of minerals appears to be a particularly important process since it releases the nutrients essential to the development of the biosphere and at the same time participates in trapping atmospheric CO_2, with a long-term impact on the Earth's climate. A challenge of current research is to understand and quantify the factors controlling the dissolution rates of minerals. Living organisms seem to be among the accelerating factors, even if the quantification of this implication is still under research. Ultimately, a first example of a feedback loop between the biosphere and the geosphere illustrates how living organisms influence the mineral weathering, which in turn impacts vegetation and microbial communities in the environment.

A mirror process of mineral dissolution is mineral precipitation. For example, by secreting organic acids, plants promote the dissolution of rocks on continents, releasing silica in the form of an anion, orthosilicic acid and cations such as Ca^{2+}. These are then transported by rivers to the oceans where they precipitate in the form

Interactions between the Geosphere and the Biosphere,
coordinated by Karim BENZERARA and Christophe THOMAZO.

of silicates and carbonates. Here again, we have seen that these precipitation processes are strongly influenced by living organisms. Various minerals precipitate in connection with a great diversity of living organisms. This is what is known as biomineralization. For example, carbonates, a family of minerals very widespread on the surface of the Earth, are currently formed primarily by living organisms. Thus, a great biological diversity of cnidarians (corals), mollusks or foraminifera, to name just a few of them, produce calcium carbonate, which is deposited in the form of shells, tests and skeletons, sometimes leading to the formation of rocks. This action of living organisms involves, in some cases, specific genetic control. Here again, biomineralization has transformed the chemical functioning of the geosphere on the one hand, as well as played a significant role in the evolution of the biosphere on the other. Microbialites, such as stromatolites, are a characteristic example of biomineralization and interactions between the geosphere and the biosphere that have been taking place for billions of years. These rocks can contain a record of the presence of ancient traces of life on Earth and have been sought on ancient terrains of other planets such as Mars. We have seen that the study of the complex microbial communities that form them involves an interdisciplinary approach, requiring the use of cutting-edge molecular tools ("omics"), allowing for the characterization of the taxonomic and functional diversity of these ecosystems. In addition to helping us to understand the formation mechanisms of these rocks, it allows for a better understanding of the evolutionary history of the organisms populating these ecosystems.

The study of interactions between the geosphere and the biosphere does not simply consist of understanding the individuals and mechanisms involved but also comprises the description of their coupled histories. Indeed, each of these spheres has changed (evolved) over geological time and these changes have influenced each other. For example, we have described how the appearance of oxygenic photosynthesis, a biological innovation that appeared more than two billion years ago, participated in the global oxygenation of the Earth's atmosphere. This led to a major geochemical disturbance in the geosphere, with, for example, an increase in the availability of certain chemical elements essential for living organisms, such as phosphorus, and conversely a decrease in the availability of other elements, notably certain metals. In return, this irremediably changed the course of the history of life and its diversification, later allowing the development of eukaryotic life, and subsequently the appearance of plants and animals.

We have seen that the biosphere also plays a major role in the geochemical cycles of many chemical elements. Thus, living organisms are in themselves an important reservoir, on a global scale, of several chemical elements, including carbon and nitrogen. However, living organisms also influence the flux of chemical elements between the different reservoirs in the Earth system. For example, certain cyanobacteria participate in the fixation of atmospheric nitrogen in a form that can be assimilated by other organisms, which is essential for ecosystems. Sulfate-reducing bacteria are responsible for the formation of sulfide deposits, which play an important role in the sulfur cycle, the remineralization of organic matter, and by extension, the oxygen concentration of oceans and sediments. The isotopic tools provide a global and quantified vision of the cycles of these chemical elements. This highlights the importance of interactions between the biosphere and the geosphere on today's Earth, as well as outlines what these cycles may have looked like in the past.

Finally, as mentioned above, the Earth system and the biosphere have a history, the sequence of which has been determined by the laws of Darwinian evolution and those of physics as well as by more contingent events such as the impact of asteroids or intense episodes of volcanism on the surface of the Earth. We have seen that if we want to model the Earth system in the past, in the present or predict its evolution in the future, we must improve our understanding of the global functioning of the biosphere by better integrating its biodiversity and biomass into the models. Deciphering the parametric equations of these interactions is rapidly developing, but it is probably still in its early stages. In any case, these studies show that the loss of biodiversity leads to irreversible changes in the functioning of the planet. The interactions between the geosphere and the biosphere are extremely complex with cascading and runaway effects, both positive and negative. For example, the disappearance of corals could lead to a decrease in primary production and calcium carbonate production in the oceans, which could have significant consequences on the climate by reducing one of the atmospheric CO_2 sinks. These feedback loops between the geosphere and the biosphere are key to the evolution of our planet that remains largely to be explored.

Throughout the book, we have discussed multiple examples of interactions between the biosphere and the geosphere by exploring diverse spatial scales, from the scale of the atom and the cell to that of the planet. We have also discussed the equally diverse temporal scales from the fraction of a second to a billion years. We have further illustrated the diversity of disciplinary approaches needed to address this inherently interdisciplinary subject, notably combining mineralogy, geochemistry, paleontology, microbiology and evolutionary biology. Finally, and in connection with this range of disciplines involved, we have noted that while all approaches aim to assess the importance of interactions between the geosphere and the biosphere and their implications, some tend to decipher the molecular mechanisms involved, while others measure the relative importance of the different biogeochemical processes. Some precisely identify the individuals involved and try to trace their history over geological time, while others aim to model all known reactions with a necessary simplification of diversity. Of course, all approaches aim to converge towards the same objective of defining the players and processes involved in the interactions between the geosphere and the biosphere.

Several topics related to the interactions between the biosphere and the geosphere have not been addressed here, but there is no doubt that knowledge about them will continue to emerge and will be the subject of future chapters and books. For instance, the date of the first interactions between living organisms and minerals remains uncertain but may date back to the appearance of life itself, since several theories propose that the very first metabolisms could have been catalyzed by minerals.

We have outlined how the meticulous description of the conditions and feedback of interactions between the geosphere and the biosphere allows us to better define Earth's habitability conditions. This can complement strategies in the search for life on other planets, since to date Earth remains the only known example of a planet where life has developed. This book reminds us that this reflection must integrate the fact that the history of life on Earth has had its own historical contingencies that can limit our ability to predict other possibilities. Furthermore, in this context of the definition of habitability, the study of microbial life deep in the Earth, sometimes up to several kilometers deep (deep biosphere), is attracting growing interest from microbiologists and geologists, opening the prospect of a biosphere even more massive and widespread than what was imagined only a few years ago. There is no doubt that the interactions between the geosphere and the deep biosphere are particularly strong. This deep life is becoming increasingly targeted to better understand past life on our planet or for the search for life in other planetary systems.

In this book, we have only occasionally illustrated the diversity of analytical methods for identifying and quantifying interactions between the geosphere and the biosphere. These methods are constantly improving, moving towards ever finer spatial resolutions, ever greater precision, and an ever-greater number of measurable physical and chemical parameters. For example, new imaging techniques using synchrotron radiation as a light source have opened up a vast field of research aimed at understanding the modalities and spatial organization of the fine interactions that exist between mineral surfaces and microorganisms.

Finally, among the cross-cutting topics in this book, we can note that the study of interactions between living organisms and minerals generate, sometimes unexpectedly, new ideas to improve the efficiency of anthropogenic processes used, for example, for environmental decontamination, construction or even health. Human beings thus mimic living organisms by developing biomimetic processes. For example, certain applications in medicine, such as the development of therapies against cancers, use the unique characteristics of biominerals such as bacterial magnetites.

Future directions for biogeochemistry research will likely continue to encompass a wide range of interdisciplinary opportunities, including modeling the Earth system with discretized geological and biological compartments, space exploration, the study of microbial life in diverse extreme environments and the search for the origins of life on Earth. They will continue to question what is emerging as a paradigm: life, by flourishing on Earth in the past, was able to ensure a relative "stabilization" of its host planet, a vision involving the progressive modification of terrestrial environments by the biosphere according to a concept resembling in some respects that of terraforming in science fiction. At the same time, research in biogeochemistry will also seek to understand how the degradation of current biodiversity and disturbances to the Earth system could lead to irreversible changes that could damage the habitability of our planet.

List of Authors

Magali ADER
Institut de Physique du Globe de Paris
Université de Paris Cité
France

Thomas BACCHETTA
Laboratoire MAP
UMR 5240, CNRS
Université Claude Bernard Lyon 1
Villeurbanne
France

Karim BENZERARA
IMPMC
UMR 7590, CNRS
Sorbonne Université
Paris
France

Pierre BOUSSAGOL
Laboratoire Biogéosciences
University of Burgundy
Dijon
France

Anthony BOUTON
University Bourgogne Franche-Comté
Besançon
France

Arnaud BRAYARD
Laboratoire Biogéosciences
University of Burgundy
Dijon
France

Damien DAVAL
ISTerre, CNRS
Université Grenoble Alpes
Gières
France

Ana GUTIÉRREZ-PRECIADO
CNRS
Université Paris-Saclay
France

Miguel INIESTO
CNRS
Université Paris-Saclay
France

Guillaume LE HIR
Institut de Physique du Globe de Paris
Université de Paris Cité
France

Purificación LÓPEZ-GARCÍA
CNRS
Université Paris-Saclay
France

David MOREIRA
CNRS
Université Paris-Saclay
France

Alice PELLERIN
Laboratoire Biogéosciences
University of Burgundy
Dijon
France

Christophe THOMAZO
Laboratoire Biogéosciences
University of Burgundy
Dijon
France

Emmanuelle VENNIN
Laboratoire Biogéosciences
University of Burgundy
Dijon
France

Pieter T. VISSCHER
University of Connecticut
Storrs
USA

Bastien WILD
Princeton University
USA

Index

E, F

G, I

K, L

M

N, O

P, R

S, T

V, W

Printed and bound by CPI Group (UK) Ltd, Croydon, CR0 4YY
13/09/2026
14961072-0007